CACHE Level 3 Award/Certificate/Diploma in
Child Care and Education

CACHE Level 3 Award/Certificate/Diploma in

Child Care and Education

Tina Bruce
Carolyn Meggitt

Hodder Arnold

A MEMBER OF THE HODDER HEADLINE GROUP

Dedication

For the quiet but solid support, the feeling of belonging to people who help and empower, and the team spirit between us – thank you to Ian, Hannah and Tom from Tina.

This book is dedicated with love and thanks to Dave, Jonathan, Leo and Laura from Carolyn.

Orders: please contact Bookpoint Ltd, 130 Milton Park, Abingdon, Oxon OX14 4SB. Telephone: (44) 01235 827720. Fax: (44) 01235 400454. Lines are open from 9.00 – 5.00, Monday to Saturday, with a 24 hour message answering service. You can also order through our website www.hoddereducation.co.uk.

British Library Cataloguing in Publication Data
A catalogue record for this title is available from the British Library

ISBN: 978 0 340 94660 2

First Published 2007
Impression number   10 9 8 7 6 5 4 3 2
Year   2012 2011 2010 2009 2008 2007

Copyright © 2007 by Carolyn Meggitt and Tina Bruce; Jessica Walker for Chapter 8

Cover photo © Cheryl Maeder/Taxi/Getty Images
Typeset by Servis Filmsetting Ltd, Manchester.
Printed in Italy for Hodder Arnold, an imprint of Hodder Education,
a member of the Hodder Headline Group, an Hachette Livre UK Company, 338 Euston Road, London NW1 3BH

Contents

The Optional Units 11, 12, 14, 16, 18 and 20 can be found on the enclosed CD-ROM at the back of the book.

Acknowledgements

We gratefully acknowledge the help of Jessica Walker, author and teacher, for writing the chapter on Observation and Assessment.

We would also like to thank the following people for their contributions: Chris Rice (Clydebank College) for her section on operant conditioning; Ruth Forbes and the parents for the case studies of babies; Martin and Alayne Levy for the biography of their daughter, Hannah, in Unit 14; Laura Meggitt for her valuable insights and contributions to case studies in early years settings; Kirsty Smith for information on reflective practice and problem solving in Chapter 11.

The authors and publishers would like to thank the following people for the specially commissioned photographs in this book:

David Meggitt for his photography; all the staff, children and their parents at Bushy Park Nursery; Gabriel and his parents, Augusta and her parents and Liz Allen for photos of Jack.

Tom Bruce for his photography; Anne-Louise de Buriane and the staff and families of Langford Extended Primary School; Julian Grenier and the staff and families at Kate Greenaway Maintained Nursery School/Children's Centre; Elizabeth Buck and the staff and families at Newark Playgroup; Miles and his parents, Hope and her parents and Julie for the home based photographs.

Other photographs: © Tom Galliher/Corbis: p. 696; FASaware UK: p. 691; Save the Children: p. 363; Foundation for the Study of Infant Death: p. 367; Organic Picture Lib/Rex Features: p. 609 (bottom left); Adrienne Hart-Davis/Science Photo Library: p. 609 (top); Tony Robins/ABPL/Photo Library: p. 609 (bottom right); Tracy Hebden/Quaysidegraphics.com: p. 610. Illustrations: Tony Jones Art Construction, Surrey, UK: p. 460–462, 603.

The authors would like to thank the editorial team at Hodder Arnold for their help and support.

Every effort has been made to acknowledge ownership of copyright. The publishers will be pleased to make suitable arrangements with copyright holders whom it has not been possible to contact.

Introduction

The broad aim of this book is to equip readers with a basic knowledge of all aspects of child care and education up to the age of 16 years. Children, like adults, cannot be rushed in their learning. They need to reflect on what they learn practically, and they do this in their play, talk and representations of all kinds (drawings, models, dances, songs etc.). Adults reflect on and consolidate their learning by reading and writing about their new thinking and knowledge; and as they do this, they organise their ideas, share them and put them into practice.

You will find that this book is unique because whilst it introduces you to different ideas and ways of working with children and their families, it also has a logical shape. This means that it puts principles of inclusivity and equality first. It looks at children and young people in a holistic way, but never separate from the child's parents or carers, who are placed centrally in the book.

Throughout the book, you will find both *he* and *she* used in a balanced way. This is because both boys and girls need broad roles and relationships, as children and as they become adults. Activities and case studies can be found within the text and at the end of the chapters; there is also a comprehensive glossary at the end of the book.

This book is particularly recommended for students following the new **CACHE Award/ Certificate/Diploma in Child Care and Education**. Chapters 1 to 14 cover the **Mandatory Units** of this course.

The **CD-ROM** includes:

- **SIX** of the most popular **Optional Units** for you to choose from; these are presented in the same format as the Chapters in this book, with illustrations, case studies and activities to help students match theory to their practice

- a variety of **exercises** matched to each Unit

- blank charts to use when making **observations** of children, and

- a list of useful **websites** and suggestions for **further reading**.

CHAPTER 1

An Introduction to Working with Children

This chapter covers **Unit 1** and is divided into five sections:

Section 1:   The range of provision for children

Section 2:   Promoting the rights of children

Section 3:   Professional practice

Section 4:   The values and principles underpinning work with children

Section 5:   Study skills

SECTION 1: THE RANGE OF PROVISION FOR CHILDREN

• The role of the statutory, voluntary and independent services in relation to children and families • Integrated care and education of children • The UK voluntary sector • The UK private sector • What gives children a quality childhood?

THE ROLE OF THE STATUTORY, VOLUNTARY AND INDEPENDENT SERVICES IN RELATION TO CHILDREN AND FAMILIES

Statutory Services

A statutory service is one that is provided by the state. Some statutory services are provided by **central government** and funded from central taxation – e.g. the National Health Service (NHS). Others are provided by **local government** and funded by a combination of local and central taxation – e.g. education and social service departments.

The statutory sector
This sector comprises:

* central government departments in which policy is devised by a Secretary of State (who is an MP), helped by Ministers of State (also MPs) and managed by the Permanent Secretary (a civil servant);

* executive agencies (e.g. the Benefits Agency which issues social security payments) contracted by central government departments to deliver services;

* local government departments chaired by an elected member of the local council and administered by a paid officer, e.g. the Director of Children's Services;

* local health authorities and trusts, led by a chairperson and managed by a chief executive.

Statutory services are provided by the government. The services that are provided are set by laws passed in Parliament.

Health Services for Children and their Families

The government's Department of Health is responsible for providing health care through the **National Health Service (NHS)**, which was set up in 1948 to provide free health care to the entire population. Since then there have been many changes and some services are no longer free – for example, dental care, prescriptions and ophthalmic services. However, there are exemptions to these charges, so that certain groups of people are not disadvantaged by being on low incomes. The following groups are exempt:

* children under 16 or in full-time education;

* pregnant women or with a baby under 1 year;

* families receiving income support or family credit;

* people over 60 years.

The National Health Service Framework for Children, Young People and Maternity Services

This Framework is one part of the government's overall strategy to tackle child poverty. It was set up by the Department of

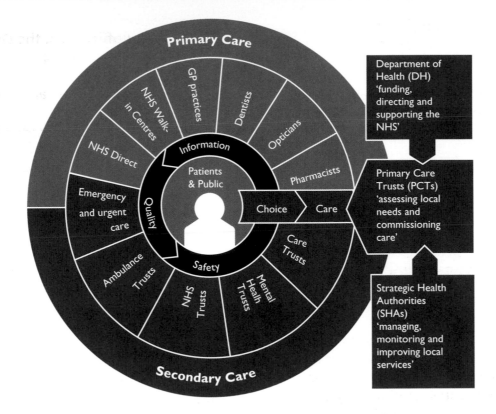

Fig 1.1 How the NHS works (in England)

Health in 2004 and divides the services it covers into three types:

* **universal services** – used by all children, young people and their families, and those who are about to become parents;

* **targeted services** – services designed to encourage their use by people who usually do not use them; and

* **specialist services** – for children and young people with difficulties or medical conditions which are identified as needing specialist care, treatment or support.

In **Part 1** of the Framework, there are five **standards** which cover services for *all* children, young people and parents or carers:

* Standard 1: Promoting health and wellbeing, identifying needs and intervening early. (This includes the Child Health Promotion Programme, covered in Chapter 12.)

* Standard 2: Supporting parenting.

* Standard 3: Child, young person and family-centred services.

* Standard 4: Growing up into adulthood.

* Standard 5: Safeguarding and promoting the welfare of children and young people.

In **Part 2**, there are five standards which cover services for children and young people who need specialist care, treatment or support:

* Standard 6: Children and young people who are ill.

* Standard 7: Children in hospital.

* Standard 8: Disabled children and young people and those with complex health needs.

* Standard 9: The mental health and psychological wellbeing of children and young people.
* Standard 10: Medicines for children and young people.

Part 3 sets out the standard for women expecting a baby and their partners and families, and for new parents:

* Standard 11: Maternity services.

This National Health Service Framework promotion strategy must link to programmes to reduce the effect of **poverty** and the **environment** on children's health and wellbeing, in particular to:

* help parents find and stay in learning or work, including having **high-quality, affordable child care** for both pre-school and school-age children) and child-friendly working practices;
* ensure that families are made aware of the **Healthy Start Scheme**, and encouraged to apply for it if they qualify. Healthy Start will provide low-income pregnant women and young families with advice on diet and nutrition, local support to eat healthily, and vouchers to buy healthy food;
* ensure families with low incomes are supported to claim all **benefits** to which they are entitled;
* **provide support** for groups especially likely to be living in poverty, for example teenage parents and families with disabled children and those who are homeless;
* ensure as far as possible that **local authority accommodation** for families with children is not damp or cold (in line with the cross-government fuel poverty strategy), has adequate space for play and privacy, and at least one working smoke alarm and a carbon monoxide detector, where appropriate; and

* minimise **environmental pollution**, in residential areas and around nurseries and schools.

Statutory Social Care Services

Children's Social Services

Until recently, children's social services have generally been provided jointly with services for adults, via social services departments within local authorities. However, structural changes in response to the **Children Act 2004** mean that, from April 2006, **education and social care services** for children were brought together under a **director of children's services** in each local authority.

Social services provide a range of care and support for children and families, including:

* families where children are assessed as being **in need** (including disabled children);
* children who may be suffering **'significant harm'**;
* children who require **looking after** by the local authority (through fostering or residential care); and
* children who are placed for **adoption**.

Social workers with responsibilities for children and families may work in the following areas:

* **Safeguarding and promoting the welfare of children:** in the great majority of cases, children are safeguarded while remaining at home by social services working with their parents, family members and other significant adults in the child's life to make the child safe, and to promote his or her development within the family setting. For a small minority of children, where it is agreed at a child protection conference that a child is at continuing

risk of significant harm, the child's name will be placed on a **child protection register**. Social services are then responsible for coordinating an inter-agency plan to safeguard the child, which sets out and draws upon the contribution of family members, professionals and other agencies. In a few cases, social services, in consultation with other agencies and professionals, may judge that a child's welfare cannot be adequately safeguarded if he or she remains at home. In these circumstances, they may apply to the court for a **care order**, which commits the child to the care of the local authority. Where the child is thought to be in immediate danger, social services may apply to the court for an **emergency protection order**, which enables the child to be placed under the protection of the local authority for a maximum of 8 days.

✳ **Supporting disabled children:** social workers must provide a range of services to families with disabled children to minimise the impact of any disabilities and enable them to live as normal a life as possible. Typically, they provide short-term breaks in foster families or residential units, support services in the home and, increasingly, assistance for disabled children to participate in out-of-school and leisure activities in the community alongside their non-disabled peers.

✳ **Supporting looked-after children:** where the local authority looks after a child following the imposition of a care order, or accommodates a child with the agreement of their parents, it is the role of the social worker to ensure that adequate arrangements are made for the child's care and that a plan is made, in partnership with the child, their parents

and other agencies, so that the child's future is secure. Children are generally looked after in foster care. A minority will be cared for in children's homes and some by prospective adoptive parents. *All* looked-after children will have a social worker and carers (e.g. foster carers, residential care staff) responsible for their day-to-day care, who should be involved in making plans or decisions about the young person.

Care Matters

The government **Green Paper**, *Transforming the Lives of Children and Young People in Care* (2006), has **seven priorities** for children and young people in care. These are:

1 More help for families who are having problems.

2 A consistent adult throughout their lives (this may be a social worker or carer).

3 A good, settled placement that is right for each child.

4 A place at a good school that is helping each child to do their best.

5 More out-of-school support for children in care.

6 Giving young people a say about when they want to move on from care and the support they need to do so safely.

7 Making care work for children by giving children and young people in care the right to be listened to.

INTEGRATED CARE AND EDUCATION FOR CHILDREN

Recent legislation has led to a number of reforms in the delivery of care and education to children. The school system now provides some fully extended primary schools, and the statutory services for children from **birth to 5 years old** are becoming increasingly **integrated**. This involves a new structure for the delivery of an integrated service, to include:

* children's trusts;
* the Early Years Foundation Stage;
* Sure Start programmes;
* children's centres;
* fully extended primary schools.

The Role of Local Authorities

Local authorities must:

* improve the outcomes of all children under 5 years and close the gaps between those with the poorest outcomes and the rest, by ensuring that early childhood services are integrated, proactive and accessible;
* take the **lead role** in facilitating the child-care market to ensure it meets the needs of **working parents**, in particular those on low incomes and with disabled children;
* ensure that people have access to the full range of **information** they may need as a parent;
* introduce the **Early Years Foundation Stage** – to support the delivery of quality integrated education and care for children from **birth to age 5** (see below);
* work within a reformed, simplified, child care and early years regulation **framework** to reduce bureaucracy and focus on raising quality.

The 'Birth to Five' Outcomes Duty

Local authorities (LAs) in England have a statutory duty to improve the **Every Child Matters outcomes** for *all* children under 5 years and to reduce inequalities in achievements, through helping them to access integrated, proactive early childhood services. In discharging these duties, LAs and

their partners in the **NHS** and **Jobcentre Plus** work together and have regard to statutory guidance which will indicate how services will be delivered through **children's centres**. Local authorities must improve the wellbeing of young children and reduce inequalities in relation to the five outcomes laid out in *Every Child Matters*:

* **Be healthy – physical and mental health and emotional wellbeing:** sexually healthy; healthy lifestyles; choose not to take illegal drugs.

Parents, carers and families promote healthy choices.

* **Stay safe – protection from harm and neglect:** safe from maltreatment, neglect, violence and sexual exploitation; safe from accidental injury and death; safe from bullying and discrimination; safe from crime and antisocial behaviour in and out of school; have security, stability and are cared for.

Parents, carers and families provide safe homes and stability.

* **Enjoy and achieve – education, training and recreation:** ready for school; attend and enjoy school; achieve stretching national educational standards at primary school; achieve personal and social development and enjoy recreation; achieve stretching national educational standards at secondary school.

Parents, carers and families support learning.

* **Make a positive contribution to society – support for the vulnerable and positive outlooks:** engage in decision-making and support the community and environment; engage in law-abiding and positive behaviour in and out of school; develop positive relationships and choose not to bully and discriminate; develop self-confidence and

successfully deal with significant life changes and challenges; develop enterprising behaviour.

Parents, carers and families promote positive behaviour.

* **Social and economic wellbeing – parents in employment:** engage in further education, employment or training on leaving school: ready for employment; live in decent homes and sustainable communities; access to transport and material goods; live in households free from low income.

Parents, carers and families are supported to be economically active.

Children's Trusts

Children's trusts are new organisations which bring together health, education and social services for children, young people and families. Some take on responsibility for *all* children's services, from child protection to speech therapy, while others will focus on particularly vulnerable children, such as those with disabilities. At first, most trusts will commission *local* children's services. The trusts will employ a range of professionals – for example:

* social workers;
* family support workers;
* health visitors;
* school nurses;
* educational psychologists;
* speech and language therapists;
* child and adolescent mental health professionals;
* head teachers and heads of integrated children's centres.

Children's trusts are underpinned by the **Children Act 2004** duty to cooperate and

to focus on improving outcomes for all children and young people. Trusts can also include **Sure Start** local programmes. Other local partners may include: housing, leisure services, the police, youth justice, independent-sector organisations such as voluntary organisations, and community-sector organisations such as churches. They will be led by local **'children's champions'** whose role is to **advocate** the interests of children across different services.

> ### Integrated childhood services
> Integrated early childhood services **must include:**
> * early years provision **(integrated child care and early education);**
> * social services;
> * relevant health services, **e.g. health visitors, ante-natal, post-natal care;**
> * services provided by Jobcentre Plus **to assist parents to obtain work;**
> * information services.

The Early Years Foundation Stage (EYFS)

This is the new single quality framework for children from birth to 5 years. All settings which offer provision for children from **birth** until the point when they begin **Key Stage 1** (subject to certain exceptions) will be required to deliver **integrated care and education** in line with the **EYFS**. The government has adopted the term **'early years provision'** to refer to integrated care and education. The free entitlement to nursery education will be recast as an entitlement to early years provision.

Sure Start

Sure Start is an extensive government programme launched in the late 1990s as a cornerstone of the government's drive to eradicate child poverty in 20 years, and to halve it within a decade. The first Sure Start local programmes were established in 1999, with the aim of improving the health and wellbeing of families and children from before birth to 4 years, so that they can flourish at home and when they begin school. They started in the most disadvantaged areas in the UK. Sure Start local programmes are delivered by local **partnerships** and work with parents-to-be, parents and children to promote the physical, intellectual and social development of babies and young children. All Sure Start local programmes are now called **Sure Start Children's Centres**.

Sure Start Children's Centres have these four key objectives:

1   **Improving social and emotional development:** in particular by supporting early bonding between parents and their children, helping families function and enabling early identification and support of children with emotional and behavioural difficulties.

2   **Improving health:** in particular by supporting parents in caring for their children to promote healthy development before and after birth.

3   **Improving children's ability to learn:** in particular by providing high-quality environments and child care that promote early learning and provide stimulating and enjoyable play, improve language skills and ensure early identification of children with special needs.

4   **Strengthening families and communities:** in particular by involving families in building the community's capacity to sustain the programme and create pathways out of **social exclusion**.

The emphasis is on prevention in order to reduce social exclusion later on, and to improve the chances of younger children through early access to education, health services, family support and advice on nurturing. These projects include support for:

*   special educational needs;
*   outreach services and home visiting;
*   families and parents;
*   good-quality play, learning and child care;
*   primary and community health care;
*   advice about child health and development;
*   advice about parent health.

Children's Centres

The majority of children's centres will be developed from Sure Start local programmes, Neighbourhood Nurseries and Early Excellence Centres. The government is committed to delivering a Sure Start Children's Centre for *every* community by 2010. Sure Start Children's Centres are places where children under 5 years old and their families can receive seamless holistic integrated services and information, and where they can access help from multidisciplinary teams of professionals. They offer the following services:

*   good-quality **early learning** combined with full day-care provision for children (minimum 10 hours a day, 5 days a week, 48 weeks a year);
*   good-quality **teacher input** to lead the development of learning within the centre;
*   **child and family health services**, including ante-natal services;
*   **parental outreach**;
*   **family support** services;

* a base for a **childminder network**;

* support for children and parents with **special needs**;

* effective links with **Jobcentre Plus** to support parents/carers who wish to consider training or employment.

In more advantaged areas, although local authorities will have flexibility in which services they provide to meet local need, all Sure Start Children's Centres will have to provide a "core offer" of services including:

* appropriate support and outreach services to parents/carers and children who have been identified as in need of them;

* information and advice to parents/carers on a range of subjects, including: local child care, looking after babies and young children, local early years provision (child care and early learning) education services for 3- and 4-year-olds;

* support to childminders;

* drop-in sessions and other activities for children and carers at the centre;

* links to Jobcentre Plus services.

Maintained Nursery Schools

These are part of the provision made by some local education authorities. Maintained nursery schools, nursery classes and nursery units are all expected to become part of the Sure Start Children's Centres programme.

Maintained nursery schools offer either full-time or part-time places for children of 3 years to the equivalent of the end of the Reception Year. Increasingly, children may start at 2 years, but only if there is a recommendation and joint decision by the education, health and social services departments/level 3 staff.

There is a head teacher who has specialist training in the age group, and graduate trained teachers working with qualified nursery nurses.

Adult-to-child ratios are 1:10 in England and Wales, but 1:13 in Scotland.

Nursery Classes and Nursery Units

* Nursery classes are attached to primary schools. The head teacher of the primary school may or may not be an expert in early years education.

* The class teacher will be a trained nursery teacher who will work alongside a fully qualified nursery nurse/level 3 member of staff.

* Nursery units are usually in a separate building with a separate coordinator. They are larger than a nursery class but will have the same adult-to-child ratio as the nursery class – which is 1 to 15. There are also foundation units where the nursery and reception classes are integrated. All these provisions come under the management of the head teacher, who again may or may not be trained to work with this age group.

Extended Services for Children and Young People

In 2005 the government launched *Extended schools: Access to opportunities and services for all*, a prospectus outlining the vision of extended schools. This vision is for all children to be able to access through schools by 2010:

* high-quality **'wraparound'** child care provided by the schools site or through other local providers, available 8 a.m. to 6 p.m. all year round;

* a varied **menu of activities** to be on offer, such as homework clubs and study support, sport, music tuition, special interest clubs and volunteering;

* **parenting support** including information sessions for parents at key

transition points, parenting programmes and family learning sessions;

* swift and easy referral to a wide range of **specialist support** services such as speech and language therapy, family support services and behaviour support;

* providing wider community access to **ICT, sports and arts facilities,** including adult learning.

THE UK VOLUNTARY SECTOR

The voluntary sector

* This sector is made up of voluntary organisations. These tend to operate with a mixture of paid and volunteer workers.

* Voluntary organisations are usually administered by a core of paid staff. Volunteers are then trained by the core staff to help the organisation in a variety of ways.

* There are both national voluntary organisations (e.g. Early Education, formerly called BAECE) and local voluntary organisations. The local branches of an organisation are not necessarily closely linked with the national or head office branch of the organisation – local groups of the Pre-School Learning Alliance are examples.

* Voluntary organisations often arise because:

 1 there is a gap in services (e.g. the Salvation Army provides hostels for homeless people);

 2 there is a need for a campaign both to alert the public to an issue and to push for action to be taken (e.g. Shelter, a

pressure group for the homeless).

* Some charities receive government grants, but not all. In addition to donations many have fee income from services they provide.

Community Nurseries

* These are often funded by voluntary organisations, such as Barnardos, and function in similar ways to family centres.

* They sometimes offer full-time care, but more usually part-time care.

* Some charitable trusts offer integrated provision to children and their families, for instance Barnardos, the Royal National Institute for the Blind (RNIB), SENSE and SCOPE.

* These might be home-based or parent/toddler groups, community nurseries, day schools or residential special schools, or groups supporting children in mainstream education.

* The Pre-school Learning Alliance was set up in 1961 at a time when there was concern from parents at the lack of nursery education available. Parents ran these playgroups, and the education and development of both parent and child were emphasised. (However, not all playgroups, e.g. Playgroup Network, are affiliated to the Pre-school Learning Alliance.)

* Preschools and playgroups: they are usually part time, and offer perhaps two or three half-day sessions a week, often in a church hall. This type of provision is often the only one available in rural areas.

THE UK PRIVATE SECTOR

> **The private sector**
> This sector comprises businesses that make profits.
> * In education, this includes private nurseries.
> * In social services, the private sector includes old people's homes run by big chains and by individuals. In health, there are private hospitals.
> * Private nurseries, hospitals and schools are legally required to be registered and inspected, and to follow guidelines laid down in laws and by local authorities.

Private nursery schools and private day nurseries are still available for those parents who can afford them, although some financial support is available through government schemes. In addition, there are workplace nurseries which subsidise places in order that staff and students in institutions can take up this form of care.

Private Day Nurseries, Private Nursery Schools, Preparatory Schools and Kindergartens

* These are required to meet current **National Daycare Standards** to be replaced from September 2008 with the integrated Early Years Foundation Stage (EYFS) statutory requirements (statutory framework for the Early Years Foundation Stage).
* The government is concerned that child care should be affordable for families, and has introduced a family tax credit to support the New Deal (an employment scheme).

Childminders, Nannies and Grandparents

* Children are looked after in their own homes by grandparents or nannies, or in the childminder's home (HLE = Home Learning Environment).
* Childminders are offered training through the National Childminding Association, CACHE and childminding networks in local authorities.
* Nannies sometimes live with a family, but not always. Sometimes, they look after children from several different families (e.g. Norland Nurses).

(For more information on the roles of childminders and nannies, see Chapter 14.)

WHAT GIVES CHILDREN A QUALITY CHILDHOOD?

Multidisciplinary Work

Children gain when parents, midwives, health visitors, nurses, doctors, nursery teachers, social workers, play therapists, educational psychologists, hospital teachers, experts in special educational needs and members of voluntary organisations all work together. Mutual respect within the team is important: on a course for nursery nurses in Enfield, 24 out of 28 said they felt deeply valued by the teachers and head teachers they worked with. However, they also said that other teaching staff in their primary and secondary schools did not always understand the depth of training they had received. Early childhood practitioners make an invaluable contribution because they work across the widest range of settings. Being a good networker will enable you to bring people together in the common cause of getting the best for young children and their families.

ACTIVITY: WHAT KIND OF PROVISION?

1 Research the early years provision made by your local authority. What proportion of 4-year-olds are in reception classes? What kind of provision are most birth to 3-year-olds and their families offered?

2 What kind of provision is available in your area for children between the ages of 8 and 12 and 12 and 16 years? Use the reference section in your library and the internet to investigate statutory provision, such as after-school and breakfast clubs, and voluntary and independent initiatives such as sports or drama clubs and voluntary work schemes.

SECTION 2: PROMOTING THE RIGHTS OF CHILDREN

• The rights of children and their families • Knowing the law relating to early years education and care • Diversity, inclusiveness and differentiation • Valuing and respecting the child's culture and family background

THE RIGHTS OF CHILDREN AND THEIR FAMILIES

What are Children's Rights?

Children are entitled to basic human rights such as food, health care, a safe home and protection from abuse. However, children are a special case because they cannot always stand up for themselves. They need a *special* set of rights which take account of their vulnerability and which ensure that adults take responsibility for their protection and development.

The UN Convention on the Rights of the Child

This is an international treaty that applies to all children and young people under the age of 18 years. It spells out the basic human rights of children everywhere. All children – without discrimination – have the right to:

* survive;

* develop to their fullest potential;

* be protected from harmful influences, abuse and exploitation;

* participate fully in family, cultural and social life;

* express and have their views taken into account on all matters that affect them;

* play, rest and enjoy leisure.

This important treaty has been signed by almost every country in the world.

The Balance of Rights and Responsibilities

Children and young people have **responsibilities** as well as rights. Many have jobs, some care for relatives, a large proportion are school or college students, and they all must respect other people's rights and act within the law. However, these responsibilities do not detract from their human rights, which everybody has from the moment they are born.

A parent is responsible for the care and upbringing of their child. The **Children and Young Persons Act 1933** imposes criminal liability for abandonment, neglect or ill treatment upon any person over the age of 16 years who is responsible for a child under 16 years. Because parental responsibility cannot be surrendered or transferred, parents are liable for neglecting their child if they choose an inadequate babysitter.

The rights embodied by the UN Convention which particularly relate to child care and education are these:

* Children have the right to be with their family or with those who will care best for them.

* Children have the right to enough food and clean water for their needs.

* Children have the right to an adequate standard of living.

* Children have the right to health care.

* Children have the right to play.

* Children have the right to be kept safe and not hurt or neglected.

* Disabled children have the right to special care and training.

* Children must not be used as cheap workers or as soldiers.

ACTIVITY: EXPLORING CHILDREN'S RIGHTS

'In the UK it is still both legal and socially acceptable for parents to smack their children.'

After considering the case of a boy who had been beaten regularly by his step-father with a 3-foot garden cane between the ages of 5 and 8, the European Court of Human Rights ruled that the British law on corporal punishment in the home failed to protect children's rights. The stepfather had been acquitted – or found innocent – by a British court of causing actual bodily harm. The stepfather had argued that the beating was *reasonable chastisement*; this means that parents could use a degree of force in order to discipline their children. Recent changes to the law have removed this defence, which dates back to 1860. In an amend-ment to the Children Bill agreed by peers in 2005, smacking is now outlawed in England and Wales 'if it causes harm such as bruising or mental harm'.

Task 1

Individually, find out all you can about:

* the arguments *against* smacking children – in particular, investigate the work of the Children are Unbeatable! Alliance whose aims are (a) to seek legal reform to give children the same protection under the law on assault as adults and (b) to promote positive, non-violent discipline (www.childrenareunbeatable.org.uk);

* the arguments *for* parents' right to smack their own children, for example, look into the Parents Have Rights campaign which is against any legislation that interferes with a parent's right to punish their children as they see fit (www.families-first.org.uk).

Task 2

In two groups, organise a debate on the issue of smacking children.

* Group A will argue that 'The law should be changed so that physical punishment of children is never permitted'.

* Group B will argue that 'Parents have the right to use whatever method of discipline works best for their children'.

Task 3

Prepare a fact file on the debate on smacking for the use of future students. Include a list of useful addresses and websites. Ensure that you find out about any recent changes to these laws in Scotland and elsewhere in the UK.

Fig 1.2 Children have the right to play

* Children have the right to free education.

KNOWING THE LAW RELATING TO EARLY YEARS EDUCATION AND CARE

It is important for early childhood practitioners to be aware of those laws which relate to their work, both in the UK and internationally. It is, of course, illegal not to obey the law. It is also important to understand the spirit and thinking that went into making the law. You won't be expected to know these laws in detail – but you should make sure you know about the principles enshrined in the main legislation relating to children and young people

(**NB** The laws relating to health and safety and equal opportunities and discrimination are described in Chapter 9.)

The Children Act 1989: a New Approach to Parenthood

* The Children Act introduced the phrase **'parental responsibility'**.

As well as rights, parents now have responsibilities.

* Sometimes, people who are not the natural parents can be given parental responsibility.

* Parenthood is seen as 'an enduring commitment'. Parents are encouraged to stay involved in bringing up their children, even if the children are not living with them.

* Parental responsibility can be shared, for example between two divorced parents, or between both parents and foster parents.

* The Children Act aimed to strengthen the relationships within the many different kinds of family that exist.

Statutory Services under the Children Act

The spirit behind the Children Act is that families should be respected and given help in bringing up their children. At the same time, the Act promotes the care and health of the child as **paramount**. Under the Children Act, statutory services for children are based on five linked principles.

1 **Children in need:** services may be provided for all children, but they must be provided for all 'children in need'. Parents, in addition, must be helped to demonstrate 'parental responsibility'. Children in need are:

   * children with a disability;

   * children whose health or development is likely to be significantly impaired, likely to be further impaired or unlikely to be maintained;

   * children without the provision of services.

Disability, in this context, is defined as being blind, deaf or dumb, having a mental disorder, or being handicapped by illness, injury, congenital deformity or any other disease or disorder as may be prescribed. It is important to appreciate the difference between 'children in need' as defined above and 'children with special educational needs' (see Unit 14 on CD-ROM). Children in need are given a degree of support that goes beyond that given by the education service.

2   **Partnership with parents:** services must emphasise partnership by actively seeking participation, offering real choices and involving parents in decisions. For example, it should be usual for parents to join case conferences. Whenever possible, help should be given by the local authority on a voluntary basis (it should not be imposed or enforced). For example, the parent should be encouraged by the authority to decide when it is best for a child to go into a foster home.

3   **Race, culture, religion and language:** services must link with children's experiences in relation to these areas. In work settings, staff should not discriminate, and the whole setting should reflect a multicultural atmosphere (see Chapter 11). Foster parents, childminders and other service providers are required to show their support for this principle.

4   **The coordination of services:** services are required to coordinate with each other in order to support a family. The idea is that families should not be passed from agency to agency. Instead, one agency (e.g. the local education authority) should request the help of another department.

5   **Meeting the identified needs of an individual family:** services must be geared to meet the identified needs of a particular family. Local authorities are therefore required to gather information and to plan services which are based on local needs. The aim is to produce a needs-led service – i.e. to make the service fit the people, rather than making people fit the service.

Children (Scotland) Act 1995

This Act has three fundamental child-centred principles which are similar to those of the Children Act 1989:

1   **The welfare of the child is paramount:** the child's interests are always the most important factor, and will always be the deciding factor in any legal decision.

2   **The views of the child must be taken into account:** courts dealing with any matters relating to children's welfare must take account of the child's views. This includes the child's right to attend their own hearing.

3   **'No order' principle:** courts and children's hearings need to be convinced that making an order is better than not making one.

Children (Northern Ireland) Order 1995

This Order came into force in October 1996 and is closely modelled on the Children Act 1989, but contains certain differences:

*   Those who provide day care and childminding for children under 12 years are required to register.

*   The Order does not provide for fees to be imposed on those providing childminding and day-care services.

* All children's homes are required to be registered, irrespective of the number of children being accommodated.
* The Order removes most of the legal disadvantages of illegitimacy (in England and Wales these had been removed by the Family Law Reform Act 1987).

Adoption and Children Act 2002

This Act aligns adoption law with the Children Act 1989 to make the child's welfare the paramount consideration in all decisions to do with adoption. It includes:

* provisions to encourage more people to adopt **looked-after children** by helping to ensure that the support they need is available;
* a new, clear duty on local authorities to provide an **adoption support service** and a new right for people affected by adoption to request and receive an assessment of their needs for adoption support services;
* provisions to enable **unmarried couples** to apply to adopt jointly, thereby widening the pool of potential adoptive parents;
* stronger safeguards for adoption by improving the legal controls on inter-country adoption, arranging adoptions and advertising children for adoption;
* a new 'special guardianship' order to provide security and permanence for children who cannot return to their birth families, but for whom adoption is not the most suitable option;
* a duty on local authorities to arrange advocacy services for looked-after children and young people leaving care in the context of complaints.

Children Act 2004

This Act does not replace or even amend much of the Children Act 1989. Instead, it sets out the process for integrating services to children so that every child can achieve the five outcomes laid out in the *Every Child Matters* legislation (see pages 6–7 in this chapter).

Childcare Act 2006

Key features of this Act include:

* **local authorities** must improve the outcomes of all children under 5 years and close the gaps between those with the poorest outcomes and the rest, by ensuring early childhood services are integrated, proactive and accessible;
* local authorities must take the lead role in facilitating the child-care market to ensure that it meets the needs of **working parents**, in particular those on low incomes and with disabled children;
* people must be enabled to have access to the full range of **information** they may need as a parent;
* the **Early Years Foundation Stage:** introduced to support the delivery of quality integrated education and care for children from **birth to age 5**;
* a reformed, simplified, child care and early years regulation **framework** to reduce bureaucracy and focus on raising quality.

DIVERSITY, INCLUSIVENESS AND DIFFERENTIATION

Planning the General Learning Environment

Planning begins with the **observation** of the child as a unique, valued and respected individual, with their own interests and needs. We could say this is all about getting to know the child. But further general planning is also necessary, because there is only so much that children can learn on their own. They need an environment that has been carefully thought through, along with the right help in using that environment. This aspect of planning ensures that the learning environment indoors and outdoors is balanced in what it offers, so that it helps all children in general, but also caters for individual children.

The 4 principles of the EYFS are:

* A Unique Child;
* Positive Relationships;
* Enabling Environments;
* Development and Learning.

Each principle is supported by 4 commitments which emphasise **inclusive practice** (children's entitlements, early support, equality and diversity).

A Curriculum which Includes All Children

Most children learn in a rather uneven way. They have bursts of learning and then they have plateaux when their learning does not seem to move forward (but really they are consolidating their learning during this time). This is why careful **observation** and **assessment for learning** of individual children plus a general knowledge of child development are all very important. In the EYFS, observation, inclusion, assessment and record-keeping will be supported by DfES guidance (Enabling Environments, EYFS). Catching the right point for a particular bit of learning during development is a skill. So is recognising the child's pace of learning. Children have their own personalities and

moods. They are affected by the weather, the time of day, whether they need food, sleep or the lavatory, the experiences they have, their sense of wellbeing and their social relationships with children and adults.

Gifted and Talented Children

People who are talented in music, dance and mathematics tend to show promise early in their lives. The most important thing is that adults provide a rich and stimulating learning environment, indoors and outdoors, which encourages children to develop and extend their thinking, understand and talk about their feelings, and understand themselves and others. It is frustrating for gifted children when they are constrained and held back in their learning.

It is also important to remember that however gifted or talented a child may be in a particular respect, he or she is still a child. They need all the things that any child needs, and should not be put under pressure to behave and learn in advance of their general development.

Children with Special Educational Needs (SEN) and Disabilities

Some children will be challenged in their learning, and those working with children with special educational needs and disabilities will need to be particularly resourceful, imaginative and determined in helping them to learn. Many children with SEN and disabilities are underestimated by the adults working with them. For example, most 6-year-old children can run confidently across a field. In general, visually impaired children in mainstream settings are not expected to try to do this, and so they don't. No one suggests it to them or offers them help to do it. With the right help, the child might manage it, becoming physically more confident and mobile as a result. The experience of running across a field depends on the child's development, personality and mood. Walking hand-in-hand first might be important. Talking as you go helps. The child may need tips about picking up their feet, and eventually perhaps running towards your voice. If the child tumbles he will need reassurance, and not an anxious adult. Saying 'Can I help you up?' is more helpful than rushing over and asking 'Are you hurt?'

VALUING AND RESPECTING THE CHILD'S CULTURE AND FAMILY BACKGROUND

Every child needs to be **included** and to have full access to the curriculum, regardless of their ethnic background, culture, language, gender or economic background. No child should be held back in their learning due to restricted access to learning opportunities.

In order to plan, it is important to work closely in partnership with the child's parents/carers. Practitioners sometimes talk about 'my children', but children are unique individuals. When parents and practitioners work well together, respecting what they each bring to the partnership, in a spirit of respect and trust, with a genuine exchange of information and knowledge, the child gains and so do the parents and staff (EYFS Positive Relationships; Parents as Partners).

SECTION 3: PROFESSIONAL PRACTICE

• What is meant by professional practice? • What makes a good early childhood practitioner?
• Your role – boundaries and limits • Developing appropriate relationships with colleagues and children • Developing professional standards
• Communication skills

WHAT IS MEANT BY PROFESSIONAL PRACTICE?

All those working with children and young people are bound by the law to respect the rights of children, young people and their families. In addition to the legal aspects, being a professional means that you must ensure that all children feel included, secure and valued; this is the cornerstone of a positive, integrated environment. As a professional, your practice should adhere to the CACHE values (see Chapter 11) and also to any **policies** and **codes of practice** in your work setting. Professional practice should include:

* developing **positive relationships** with **parents** in order to work effectively with them and their children;

* understanding the extent of your **responsibilities** and being answerable to others for your work;

* working effectively as part of a **team**;

* knowing the **lines of reporting** and how to get clarification about your role and duties;

* understanding what is meant by **confidentiality** and your role in the preserving of secret or privileged information that parents or others share with you about their children or themselves.

WHAT QUALITIES MAKE A GOOD EARLY CHILDHOOD PRACTITIONER?

Above all else, an early childhood practitioner needs to like children and enjoy being with them. Caring as a quality is largely invisible, difficult to quantify and more noticeable when absent than when present. The main individual characteristics required are shown in the box below.

Guidelines for important personal qualities in an early childhood practitioner

∗ Listening: attentive listening is a vital part of the caring relationship. Sometimes a child's real needs are communicated more by what is left unsaid than by what is actually said. Facial expressions, posture and other forms of body language all give clues to a child's feelings. A good carer will be aware of these forms of non-verbal communication. (EYFS Positive Relationships – Listening to Children.)

∗ Comforting: this has a physical side and an emotional side. Physical comfort may be provided in the form of a cuddle at a time of anxiety, or by providing a reassuring safe environment to a distressed child. Touching, listening and talking can all provide emotional comfort as well. (EYFS Positive Relationships – Key Person.)

∗ Empathy: this should not be confused with sympathy. Some people find it easy to appreciate how someone else is feeling by imagining themselves in that person's position. A good way of imagining how a strange environment appears to a young child is to kneel on the floor and try to view it from the child's perspective.

∗ Sensitivity: this is the ability to be aware of and responsive to the feelings and needs of another person. Being sensitive to others' needs requires the carer to anticipate their feelings, e.g. those of a child whose mother has been admitted to hospital, or whose pet dog has just died.

∗ Patience: this involves being patient and tolerant of other people's methods of dealing with problems, even when you feel that your own way is better.

∗ Respect: a carer should have an awareness of a child's personal rights, dignity and privacy, and must show this at all times. Every child is unique, and so your approach will need to be tailored to each individual's needs.

∗ Interpersonal skills: a caring relationship is a two-way process. You do not have to like the child you are caring for, but warmth and friendliness help to create a positive atmosphere and to break down barriers. Acceptance is important: you should always look beyond the disability or disruptive behaviour to recognise and accept the person.

∗ Self-awareness: a carer is more effective if they are able to perceive what effect their behaviour has on other people. Being part of a team enables us to discover how others perceive us and to modify our behaviour in the caring relationship accordingly.

∗ Coping with stress: caring for others effectively in a full-time capacity requires energy, and it is important to be aware of the possibility of professional burn-out. In order to help others, we must first help ourselves: the carer who never relaxes or develops any outside interests is more likely to suffer 'burn-out' than the carer who finds his or her own time and space.

Fig 1.3 Empathising: the child's-eye view of the world

YOUR ROLE – BOUNDARIES AND LIMITS

The skills required by the professional early childhood practitioner need to be practised with regard to certain responsibilities. (These aspects are covered more fully in Chapter 11.)

Responsibilities and Professionalism

Guidelines for your responsibilities as a professional early childhood practitioner worker

* Respect the principles of confidentiality: confidentiality is the preservation of secret (or privileged) information concerning children and their families which is disclosed in the professional relationship. It is a complex issue which has at its core the principle of trust. The giving or receiving of sensitive information should be subject to a careful consideration of the needs of the children and their families; for example, a child who is in need of protection has overriding needs which require that all relevant information be given to all the appropriate agencies, such as social workers, doctors etc. Within the child-care and education setting, it might be appropriate to discuss sensitive issues, but such information must never be disclosed to anyone outside the setting.

* Commitment to meeting the needs of the children: the needs and rights of all children should be paramount, and the early childhood practitioner must seek to meet these needs within the boundaries of the work role. Any personal preferences and prejudices must be put aside; all children should be treated with respect and dignity, irrespective of their ethnic origin, socio-economic group, religion or disability. The equal opportunities code of practice involved will give detailed guidelines together with EYFS.

* Responsibility and accountability in the workplace: the supervisor, line manager, teacher or parent will have certain expectations about your role, and your responsibilities should be detailed in the job contract. As a professional, you need to carry out all your duties willingly and to be answerable to others for your work. It is vital that all workers know the lines of reporting and how to obtain clarification of their own role and responsibility. If you do not feel confident in carrying out a particular task, either because you do not fully understand it or because you have not been adequately trained, then you have a responsibility to state

your concerns and ask for guidance.

* **Respect for parents and other adults:** the training you have received will have emphasised the richness and variety of child-rearing practices in the UK. It is an important part of your professional role that you respect the wishes and views of parents and other carers, even when you may disagree with them. You should also recognise that parents are usually the people who know their children best; and in all your dealings with parents and other adults, you must show that you respect their cultural values and religious beliefs. (EYFS Positive Relationships – Parents as Partners.)

* **Communicate effectively with team members and other professionals:** the training you have received will have emphasised the importance of effective communication in the workplace. You will also be aware of the need to plan in advance for your work with young children: a knowledge of children's needs in all developmental areas will enable you to fulfil these within your own structured role. (EYFS Enabling Environments – The Wider Context.)

DEVELOPING APPROPRIATE RELATIONSHIPS WITH COLLEAGUES AND CHILDREN

It is important to establish appropriate and effective relationships with all the people you encounter in your work. Relationships begin before a baby is born. They begin with the care and attention that babies receive while they are in the womb. **Bonding** is the term that is commonly used to describe the strong

Fig 1.4 Working together as a team

attachment between a baby and the important people in the baby's life. It used to be thought that babies really only bonded with their mothers but research shows that babies can bond with a number of important or significant people.

Children become confident, independent and most resilient where they are secure in the relationships around them. Relationships take time to become established, because they are based on a growing understanding of one another.

Developing Appropriate Relationships with Children

In line with the **CACHE values**, you need to ensure that the child or young person is at the centre of your practice – that their needs are **paramount**.

1   **Treat children and young people with respect.** This means you:
   * give only essential directions and **allow children to make choices**;
   * set **appropriate directions** which are realistic and consistent;

Babies can form an attachment with a variety of others, including:

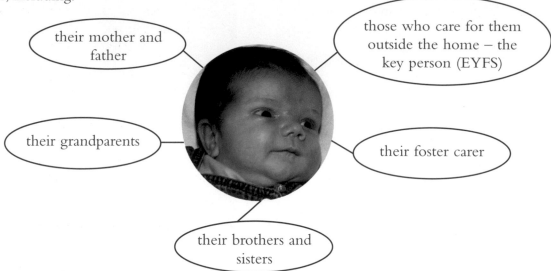

- their mother and father
- those who care for them outside the home – the key person (EYFS)
- their grandparents
- their foster carer
- their brothers and sisters

- * ask **open-ended questions** to encourage language development;
- * **avoid labelling** children;
- * are **warm** and **positive** in a way which affirms children.

2 **Keep children and young people safe.** This means you:
- * ensure they are **supervised** at all times;
- * ensure children are **safe** at all times: make sure that all potentially dangerous materials and objects are kept out of their reach and that consideration is made of a child's stage and individual ability in the use of scissors, knives etc.

3 **Value and respect children and young people.** This means you:
- * **listen** to them;
- * **do not impose your own agendas** on them;
- * **do not single out** any one child for special attention;
- * ensure that children **maintain control over their own play**;

- * are friendly, courteous and **sensitive to their needs**;
- * praise and **motivate** them; display their work;
- * **speak to** the child not **at** the child; with young children, this means getting down to their level; with young people you should ensure that you maintain eye contact;
- * respect their **individuality**;
- * develop a sense of **trust and caring** with each child and young person.

Child-care practitioners are often concerned, or feel that parents are anxious, about young children becoming 'too attached' to staff. However, babies and young children **need** to form close attachments with significant adults in their lives, and they cannot become too closely attached. Some young children spend many hours in group settings outside the home – they need and ought to develop attachments to their **key person** (EYFS, Positive Relationships; key person – secure attachment; shared care; independence). Parents who work long hours may experience a conflict of emotions. They want their child to be happy and secure in nursery care, but they don't want to feel forgotten or pushed out; parents often feel a real anxiety when their child shows affection for their key person.

Physical Contact with Babies, Children and Young People

Babies and very young children need physical contact – they need to be held and cuddled in order to develop emotionally. Hugging a baby, comforting a child when they're upset, putting a plaster on them, changing their wet pants – all these are everyday ways in which adults care for young children. However, there's a growing concern among child care professionals about *touching* children in their care. Researchers say that there is anxiety and uncertainty about what is acceptable and what is not when it comes to innocent physical contact with children. If teachers and other child-care professionals are no longer allowed to offer comforting hugs – or sometimes even to put on a plaster or sun cream – their relationship with the children they look after will certainly suffer. Your setting should have a code of conduct which will give clear guidelines on appropriate physical contact with the children or young people in your care. What is appropriate physical contact with a baby or toddler – such as hugging them when upset or sitting them on your lap to explain something – will not be seen as appropriate with an older child (EYFS gives guidance).

Maintaining a Professional Attitude

It is important to remember that your relationship with the children in your care is a professional one. You should always be friendly and approachable but not try to take the place of the child's parents. Similarly, you should communicate with each child at a level which is appropriate to their stage of development and their holistic needs – you should not act as a child would yourself when interacting with them.

Developing Appropriate Relationships with Colleagues

Most early years practitioners work with colleagues within a team. There are certain benefits for each individual from working in a team (**KEEP** – see CD-ROM; EYFS). These include:

* the sharing of responsibility – as well as knowledge;
* a sense of belonging and a sharing of problems, difficulties and successes;
* individual staff weaknesses being balanced by other people's strengths;
* children and young people benefit from seeing people working well together.

There will always be areas in your work where you experience conflict or stress – these are discussed in Chapter 11.

DEVELOPING PROFESSIONAL STANDARDS

Working in the field of child care and education can be physically and emotionally exhausting, and professionals will need to consolidate their skills and to develop the ability to be **reflective** in their practice. (See Chapter 11 for information on reflective practice.) It is important to keep abreast of all the changes in child-care practices by reading the relevant journals such as *Nursery World*, *Early Years Educator* and *Infant Education*, and by being willing to attend in-service courses.

The need for qualified early childhood workers is increasing, and more courses are being developed. National Vocational Qualifications (NVQs) in Child Care and Education are offered at some colleges, and these enable child carers to achieve competencies in the workplace. Other courses which offer professional development after achieving this Level 3 CACHE Diploma are:

* NVQ Level 4 in Early Years Care and Education;

* BTEC Professional Diploma in Specialised Play for Sick Children and Young People;

* Early Childhood Curriculum 2.5–6 yrs (Montessori Centre International Examination Board);

* BTEC Advanced Practice in Work with Children and Families;

* BTEC Advanced Practice in Work with Children and Families;

* Montessori Primary Teaching Diploma;

* Certificate in Managing Quality Standards in Children's Services;

* Level 4 Certificate in Early Years Practice (OU);

* Froebel Certificate (HE1) and Froebel Graduate Certificate (HE3);

* Norland Diploma;

* Foundation Degree in Steiner Waldorf Early Years Education;

* Specialist Teacher Assistant (STA) course;

* Advanced Diploma in Child Care and Education;

* BTEC Advanced Practice in Work with Children and Families;

* Certificate in Social Work (CSS);

* Certificate for Qualified Social Workers (CQSW);

* Hospital Play Specialist Examination Board;

* Advanced Certificate in Playgroup Practice;

* Advanced Certificate in Playwork;

* BTEC Higher National Certificate in Early Childhood Studies;

* BTEC Higher National Diploma in Early Childhood Studies;

* BTEC Professional Diploma in Specialised Play for Sick Children and Young People;

* Units of learning.

NB As these courses are constantly being revised and updated, visit the dfes.gov.uk website for further information.

Early Years Professional Status

Evidence from the **Effective Provision of Pre-School Education (EPPE)** study shows that improving the quality of the early years experience is directly related to better outcomes for children. Key factors contributing to the quality of this experience are well-qualified leaders, trained teachers working alongside and supporting less-qualified staff and staff with a good understanding of child development and learning. In particular, the response identified the benefits of developing the role of Early Years Professional (EYP) and confirmed the government's aim to have EYPs in all children's centres offering early years provision by 2010 and in every full day-care setting by 2015.

Early Years Professionals will:

* lead practice across the Early Years Foundation Stage;

* support and mentor other practitioners, and

* model the skills and behaviours that safeguard and promote good outcomes for children.

More information on this new status can be found on the government website: www.dfes.gov.uk.

COMMUNICATION SKILLS

Although your main job is to care for and educate young children, you will also need to develop positive relationships with adults. These adults will, for the most part, be your colleagues and parents of the children. However, you may also need to interact or communicate with other family members and other professionals involved with the children.

Communication has many different forms: verbal, non-verbal (including signing), written and pictorial.

For verbal communication to be effective, consideration needs to be given to:

* tone of voice: this can be as important as the words actually spoken;

* pace of speech: some parts of the message may be missed if you talk too quickly;

* clear pronunciation: words that are mumbled may not be heard easily;

* volume of speech: speaking too softly or too loudly;

* language used;

* accent or dialect.

When talking on the telephone, even though the other person cannot see you, he or she will usually be able to sense when you are not giving your full attention to the conversation.

Non-verbal Aspects of Communication

Non-verbal communication is widely used by everyone, often without any words being spoken. Waving hello or goodbye, beckoning someone, a smile or 'thumbs up' sign all, in themselves, convey messages. Used in conjunction with speech they aid understanding.

* **Eye contact:** perhaps the most important aspect of non-verbal communication is eye contact. It is extremely difficult to hold a conversation or communicate in any way without it.

* **Body language:** refers to the way we stand or sit (upright, slouched, tense, relaxed); the way we hold ourselves; or our posture;

* **Gestures:** most of us use gestures when we speak: shrugging, shaking the head or perhaps to point to something. Indeed, some people cannot communicate without using their hands and arms!

* **Touch:** sometimes it may be appropriate to use touch as a gesture of sympathy, reassurance or guidance or particularly when communicating with a person who is visually impaired.

* **Facial expressions:** our facial expressions are important in conveying what we mean and how we feel. We judge whether another person has understood what we are saying and how they feel about it by watching facial expressions.

Failure to make eye contact and a 'closed' body stance (arms folded or held across body, hunched body) can make effective communication very difficult. Similarly, an adult with a tense, possibly aggressive, body stance also poses difficulties in communicating effectively. When faced with either of these examples it is important to interact and respond in a way that reassures him/her.

Barriers to Communication

There can be many barriers to communication:

* a visual or hearing impairment;

* a different first or 'preferred' language;

* strong accent or dialect;

* technical or specialist language not being understood;

* too much background noise or poor acoustics;

ACTIVITY: ACTIVE LISTENING

* Working in threes, with one observer, one sender (parent, in this case) and one receiver (practitioner), carry out a conversation in which the parent talks about his/her difficulty sleeping and his/her tiredness.

* In the first instance, the receiver should not give any eye contact or indication that he or she is listening – no nodding, grunting or murmuring.

* How long can the sender try to make conversation? Discuss how the sender feels.

* Then change to active listening: the receiver should try to adopt an 'open' posture, maintain eye contact (without staring), indicate that he or she is listening and, at an appropriate point in the conversation, reflect back what he or she has been told.

* Change roles so that everyone tries each one.

* poor lighting so that facial expressions cannot be seen clearly.

Active Listening

Developing good listening skills is very important. Active listening involves, most importantly, **eye contact** (or, for visually impaired people, a light touch on the hand or arm to show your presence), an open body position, an interested facial expression and some murmurs of encouragement or nodding to reassure the speaker or sender that attention is being paid. To be an effective listener, you need to concentrate on the sender and understand the message that is being sent. This is different from an ordinary conversation in which you may exchange information about similar experiences and compare them. To ensure that you have understood the message you should '*reflect back*' the main points or concerns using some of the same words and checking before the sender continues.

In the following example, the early years practitioner immediately recalls her own experiences rather than focusing on, and responding to, the parent.

Parent: I slept very badly last night, I just couldn't get comfortable.

Practitioner: I'm really tired too. My little boy kept crying and I couldn't get him off to sleep till 3 o'clock this morning.

See Chapters 11 and 14 for more on communication skills.

SECTION 4: THE VALUES AND PRINCIPLES UNDERPINNING WORK WITH CHILDREN

• The welfare of the child and young person is paramount • The Children and Young People's Plan

All people working with children and young people must work within a framework that embodies sound values and principles. See also Chapter 11.

THE WELFARE OF THE CHILD AND YOUNG PERSON IS PARAMOUNT

Put children and young people first by treating their opinions and concerns seriously. Show compassion and sensitivity. Be aware that your body language can give away what you're really feeling. On no account must you slap, smack, shake or humiliate a child or young person. Besides going against the principles of child care, this is also **abuse**. As the responsible adult, it is your job to remain in control of every situation while respecting the child.

THE CHILDREN AND YOUNG PEOPLE'S PLAN

The Children Act 2004, *Every Child Matters*, Change for Children and the EYFS set out an expectation for services to improve the way they work together to give all children and young people the best possible opportunity to grow up:

* being healthy;
* staying safe;
* enjoying and achieving;
* making a positive contribution;
* achieving economic wellbeing.

Being Healthy

This involves promoting a healthy lifestyle so that children and young people are able to enjoy good health. The Plan aims to:

* provide parents and carers with access to advice, information and support to promote healthy choices;
* provide a range of services to promote children and young people's physical health – e.g. sports sessions, healthy eating classes;
* develop integrated services to promote the mental health of children and young people;
* reduce alcohol consumption and smoking among young people, e.g. by running peer support programmes on drug misuse;
* identify and respond to additional health needs of children and young people experiencing health inequalities because of long-term parental health difficulties

or because they are looked after in public care;

* develop services to ensure that children and young people with disabilities or long-term health needs receive integrated assessment and responses to their health and development needs.

Staying Safe

This involves ensuring that children and young people are being protected from harm and neglect and are growing up able to look after themselves. The Plan aims to:

* support parents and carers to provide safe homes and stability as their children grow;
* help children and young people make choices, build their confidence and avoid harm e.g. by running anti-bullying projects, safe cycling groups, after-school clubs and self-defence groups;
* identify people and circumstances that represent a serious risk to children and young people and respond to such threats quickly and effectively;
* assist children and families experiencing violence or discrimination (in the home, at school or in the community) to bring about change;
* identify and safeguard children and young people who are looked after in public or private care settings;
* encourage communities to create a supportive and stimulating environment in which children and young people can play safely while developing protective skills.

Enjoying and Achieving

This involves helping children and young people to maximise their potential and develop skills for adulthood. The Plan aims to:

* support children and young people, their families and communities to have high aspirations and expectations;

* raise achievement for all;

* raise the achievement of vulnerable and underachieving groups, including the lowest-attaining 20 per cent of children and young people;

* improve outcomes for looked-after children;

* increase attendance in schools and enjoyment in learning;

* improve access to enjoyable, challenging and enriching opportunities for children and young people, with particular focus on those with special and additional needs and those in disadvantaged and isolated communities, for example with theatre arts groups, self-advocacy skills programmes, and cultural dance and music projects.

Making a Positive Contribution

This involves enabling children and young people to use their skills and abilities in ways that enhance their own lives and the lives of their community The Plan aims to:

* support parents, carers, families, schools and communities to promote positive behaviour;

* encourage children and young people to participate in a wide range of service planning and development activities, for example conservation schemes, recycling programmes and mentoring projects;

* provide young people with access to a range of safe spaces and facilities in which they can meet and engage in positive activities;

* provide young people with increased opportunities to take up volunteering and community involvement;

* provide children and young people who are at risk of school or social exclusion with access to preventative services that will help them stay out of trouble.

Achieving Economic Wellbeing

This involves helping children and young people to overcome income barriers and achieve their full potential in life. The Plan aims to:

* support families who are dependent on benefits or low incomes to improve their wellbeing and be economically active;

* ensure children are offered the best start in life through children's centres and high-quality early years and play provision;

* improve transport accessibility and promote sustainable transport solutions for young people in rural areas;

* work with local schools, colleges and employers to create opportunities for all 14- to 19-year-olds to pursue a course of study where they will learn in a style that suits them and in subject areas which motivate them;

* ensure that impartial, comprehensive and high-quality information, advice, guidance and support are available to all young people, in proportion to need, to assist them in making successful transitions to further learning and work, for example by preparation for work and training and financial literacy classes for young people;

* support homeless and vulnerable young people or families with dependent children to sustain safe, secure and stable accommodation and engage in employment, education or training.

ACTIVITY: PLANNING YOUR TIME

Draw up a table or print one out from a calendar program on a computer, showing the seven days of the week as headings and hourly blocks of time down the left-hand side. (For example 8–9 a.m., 9–10 a.m. through to 9–10 p.m.)

Now mark on:

* Your college or school timetabled commitments, i.e. your lectures and lessons.

* Any paid work, housework or child-care/family commitments.

* Travel times.

* Times you normally spend with friends/sports activities/other leisure pursuits.

* Any 'unmissable' TV programmes (not too many!).

* What 'chunks' of time have you left for studying?

* In the day?

* In the evening?

* At weekends?

Don't forget that the half-term or end-of-term holidays can be a good time to catch up on assignments and revision. Remember to include these in your long-term calculations. However, having completed your planner, will you need to readjust any commitments to give you enough time to complete course work? How important will it be for you to spend some time studying in the day as well as in the evening?

SECTION 5: STUDY SKILLS

• Organising and planning your time • Motivation during study periods • Compiling a portfolio
• Reading, note-taking and using a library • Writing assignments, observations and reports • Planning and prioritising tasks • Monitoring and revising your work
• Writing a bibliography • When you need to take a test

ORGANISING AND PLANNING YOUR TIME

Any activity can seem preferable to working on an assignment or settling down to revision: tidying your room, staring at the wall, fetching just *one more* small snack or even doing the washing up!

However, when work is postponed regularly, deadlines and examination dates can increase feelings of disorganisation and panic and can trigger a 'flight' response. It can become tempting to produce the minimum work possible or even to abandon assignments completely. Excuses have to be invented, deadlines renegotiated, further assignments become due before the last ones are completed and before long the course begins to feel overwhelming and unmanageable. Of course, people can have very good reasons for finding their workload difficult to manage: child care or other family responsibilities, the need to earn money through part-time work, and unexpected traumas or illnesses can all increase the pressure on students. However, if you are generally enjoying your course and finding the work stimulating and interesting, you are likely to want to find a way of organising your time so that you can keep a balance between your work, your social life and your other interests and commitments.

Planning Time

There are only so many hours in a week. Although keeping rigidly to a 'weekly planner' or timetable will not always be easy or desirable, it should help you to focus on what free time you have in a week and which 'chunks' of it can be used for course work and revision.

MOTIVATION DURING STUDY PERIODS

It is important to find a place where you can work without interruptions and distractions. Even if you have the luxury of a room and a desk of your own at home, you will probably need to consider using your school, college or public library for some study periods. Settling down to a period of study is easier if you:

* Remove all distractions of hunger, noise, cold and sociable friends!

* Try not to study if you are feeling angry or upset.

* Keep a pad of paper or a jotter next to you as you work. When ideas or other things occur to you, you can note them down before you forget them.

* Give yourself realistic targets and decide for how long you will study before you start. Try not to work for more than an hour without a short break. Reward yourself for completing what you planned to do.

* Try to give yourself a variety of activities to work on.

* Have the phone number of someone else from your class or group handy in case you need to check what you need to do or want to discuss the best way to go about a task.

COMPILING A PORTFOLIO

A portfolio is a collection of the different types of evidence which can be used to show successful completion of the course. Examples of evidence include:

* **Completed assignments, projects or case studies, including action plans and evaluations:** these can be in written form or word-processed, although work in the form of video recordings, audio-tape recordings, photographs, logbooks or diaries may also be acceptable where they contain evidence of the practical demonstration of skills. Check with your teacher or tutor.

* **Past records of achievement, qualifications, work-experience or other evidence of 'prior learning'.**

* Samples of relevant **class or lecture notes, lists, personal reading records or copies of letters written** (perhaps regarding work experience, to request information or advice, or related to job or higher education applications).

Equipment and Materials

As soon as you know how many mandatory and optional units you will be taking for the course, it will be worthwhile taking advantage of any cheap stationery offers at high street stores and equipping yourself with:

* At least four large A4 lever arch files and sets of extra wide file dividers (or large A4 box files). One of these files will become your portfolio; the others can be used for organising and storing notes for each mandatory or optional unit and for a 'college and course administration' file.

* A hole punch.

* File paper, plain and lined.

* Plastic pockets or report files. These are not essential but you may feel better if finished assignments are presented neatly in a binder or pocket of some sort.

However, do not enclose each individual sheet of an assignment within a plastic pocket. This is expensive, ecologically unsound and drives your teachers and assessors crazy when they have to remove sheets to make comments on your work!

✳ Post-it index stickers can be useful to help 'flag up' important pieces of work in your completed portfolio.

✳ Small exercise books or notebooks, to act as logbooks or diaries.

✳ If you are dyslexic or have another disability which prevents or makes it difficult for you to take notes in lectures, you might consider acquiring a small tape-recorder and supply of tape cassettes, to enable you to record lectures and play them back at another time.

READING, NOTE-TAKING AND USING A LIBRARY

Textbooks such as this can offer you a basic framework for the ideas and information you need for the different subject areas covered in the course: *CACHE Level 3 Child Care and Education*. Your lectures and classes will supply you with additional material. However, you will need to carry out your own reading and research, making your own notes and updating information in areas where there is constant change (such as child-care legislation). It will be useful for you to find out how the national organisation of care and education services works in the area and in the community in which you live.

You cannot do this successfully without making full use of libraries (including their computers), newspapers and journals, television and film, and information produced by a range of national, local and voluntary organisations. If you have personal access to the internet, you may find such research decidedly easier and this book contains many references to websites worth exploring. Make sure that you are shown how to use all the relevant facilities of your library, whether school, college or public.

Using the Internet

Think before reaching for the mouse. Using the internet can be highly productive but it can also take up a lot of your time. Before you start, work out:

✳ what you need to know;

✳ how much you need to know;

✳ when you need the information by;

✳ whether you have a sensible search strategy. Do you have a list of recommended sites or know the best way to use a 'search engine' such as Google or Yahoo?;

✳ whether you could find the information you need more easily in books or a journal.

Strategies for Reading and Note-taking

We have all had the experience of reading a sentence, paragraph, or even a whole page, without being able to remember what we have just read. To be of most use to you, reading will often need to be combined with note-taking.

Taking notes is time-consuming and requires *active* concentration. Students often:

✳ worry if they are spending too much time taking endless, detailed notes without really understanding what they will be used for;

✳ give up note-taking because they cannot seem to work out what to write down and what not. This can be a particular problem when taking notes in lessons and lectures.

Essentially, note-taking is a strategy for helping you.

Think, Understand and Remember

There are many situations in life when it is important to focus on the **key issues** or points being communicated.

Example: You may have to know exactly what to do if a child in your care has an asthma attack or needs adrenaline for a peanut allergy. You may have to explain these things quickly to another person, summarising essential information.

Deciding what to write down when you take notes is easier if you think about *why* you are taking notes. You may need to take different types of notes for different reasons. You will get better at working out methods of note-taking which suit you, the more you try out different approaches. It also helps to think about ways to store your notes so that they are easily accessible to you when you need them. If they are written or designed in such a way that you can make use of them again, you will be more likely to come back to them.

Everyone develops a personal style of note-taking which is best suited to their personality.

Mind-mapping

If you work better visually or spatially rather than in writing, you can make graphic 'notes': flow charts, block designs, family trees, spider plans or other forms of **mind map**. It can be used for generating ideas and planning your work as well as, later on, note-taking and revising.

* In the centre of your page, draw a picture of, or name in words, your main topic or theme.

* Draw branches from this main topic in thick lines (use different colours or patterns). Label your branches with key words and/or images.

* Draw sub-branches from the main branches to represent sub-topics or to elaborate and extend your ideas. Again, use key words, phrases, images, pictures and colour. Use italics, underlining and capitals to highlight your work.

* Let your ideas flow and develop. Add more detail to your mind map as ideas occur to you. However, the mind map is not meant to be an art-form, more a

ACTIVITY: WHICH METHOD OF NOTE-TAKING SUITS ME BEST?

Three different methods for taking notes are summarised below. Working individually or as a small group, experiment with *each* of these methods for:

1 taking notes from this textbook;
2 taking notes from a lecture;
3 taking notes from a relevant television documentary.

Discuss and compare the results of your experiments with each method. Which method did you feel most comfortable with? Did you find yourself writing too little or too much? How much time did the exercises take? Would you find the notes useful to read again? What would you use the notes for?

way to focus your attention on the essential components of a piece of work, topic or report.

Underlining and Highlighting

If you own the book or article you are taking notes from, highlighting, underlining and marking the margin with asterisks or other symbols can be a quick and effective method of skim-reading a text, focusing your attention on it and getting to grips with the material as a whole. Again, the most important part of this activity is that you are concentrating on what you are doing.

WRITING ASSIGNMENTS, OBSERVATIONS AND REPORTS

Approximately two-thirds of the CACHE course **Child Care and Education** is assessed through course work and the completion of **practical evidence records** (PERs). Most of this written course work is set in the form of assignments and projects – although some is assessed through multiple choice question papers (MCQs). There are five main reasons for this emphasis on course work:

1   to allow you to make your own contribution to – or put your own stamp on – each subject or topic-related assignment;

2   to support you while encouraging you to use your own initiative in solving problems, answering questions and completing tasks set;

3   to enable you to use each assignment to acquire a deeper knowledge and understanding of the area you are studying and to reflect critically on the ways in which you learn;

4   to provide opportunities to work with others and gain confidence in

approaching your teachers, tutors, lecturers, friends, and others working in child care and education for help, extra information, the exchange of views, work experience and the acquisition of practical skills;

5   ultimately, to put you in charge of your own learning. To enable you to work out, after you have finished a piece of work, what you have learnt and what you still need to know, what was easy and what was more difficult and how you would improve it given another chance. To give you the ability to know when your work is good or good enough without over-relying on the approval and assessments of others. Finally, to allow you to transfer the appropriate skills and knowledge to any future study or work. When you can do this you will have well-developed **meta-cognitive** skills, i.e. you can 'think about thinking' and reflect upon your own learning style and strategies, choosing those most appropriate to a task.

PLANNING AND PRIORITISING TASKS

If you use a planner regularly (see page 29) it is easier to break up assignments, plans and observations into a series of smaller tasks, each of which you could aim to complete within a manageable time such as an hour or two. Sub-dividing your course work in this way also allows you to **prioritise** the tasks. In what order are they best done? Which really need to be done straight away? Make a list of small tasks in order of priority with the time you estimate they will take and target dates for completion. Leave room on your action plan to amend these dates when and if your plan is modified.

MONITORING AND REVISING YOUR WORK

There are likely to be many points during the completion of a piece of course work when you will change direction or modify your original plan in some way. On your action plan, keep a note of:

* the reasons for changing your plans;
* what new plans you have for the work.

WRITING A BIBLIOGRAPHY

You will be expected to write a bibliography (a list of books, articles, and other resources used) for each assignment or observation you submit. To do this properly, you need to make a note of your materials and references as you study. There is nothing worse than finishing an assignment and then spending valuable time hunting down the name of a book you read in the library but did not note the details of. As a general rule, you need to note:

* the title of the book or article (or website address);
* the author(s);
* the publisher;
* the date of publication;
* the place of publication.

Examples:

* **Book:** Bruce, T. (2005). *Early Childhood Education*. 3rd ed. London: Hodder and Stoughton.

ACTIVITY: USING YOUR KNOWLEDGE

Parminda is an early years worker at a day nursery for children under 5 years. Parents usually pick up the children by 6 p.m. On Friday, Richard, Lorna's father, turns up 15 minutes early, clearly drunk, and demanding to take his daughter home immediately. Richard does not live with Lorna's mother and there is an agreement that he picks up Lorna on Mondays and Tuesdays, and Pat, Lorna's mother, picks her up on the other three weekdays.

Parminda has answered the door to Richard, who is now shouting at her in the reception area of the nursery building. He is swearing and threatening to push Parminda out of the way if she does not let him into the room where the children are playing.

Though feeling nervous, Parminda has fortunately remembered three key pieces of advice given her at a training course on facing aggression in the workplace:

1 Stay calm and use positive, not negative, words and phrases to help change the emotion of the aggressor.

2 Show that you value and appreciate good behaviour.

3 Firmly and gently explain how the aggressor's behaviour is affecting you.

Parminda suggests to Richard that she can help him if he stops shouting. She says that she will talk to her supervisor to see what she can do to help, adding that his shouting is making her feel nervous, although she is sure that a solution to the problem could be found. Although still tense and red-faced, Richard calms down enough to listen to the nursery manager, who has now arrived at the scene. He agrees to wait to talk to Lorna's mother and, in the intervening 10 minutes, reveals that there have been problems between Pat and himself over access to Lorna.

✱ **Article:** Bruner, J., Wood, D. and Ross, G. 1976: The role of tutoring in problem-solving. *Journal of Child Psychology and Psychiatry* 17, 89–100.

The **Harvard system of referencing** is most often used. The **references** within your text use the author's name and the date of publication. Then the full details of the book or article are listed – alphabetically – in the bibliography and/or reference list at the end of the assignment.

Other sources of information or references in your work may come from the internet (give the website address), workplace (acknowledge the source), television programmes, video or film (give the title and date) or friends, family and teachers (attribute information as accurately as you can).

There are many situations like this in working life where, under pressure, it will have been important or even crucial (for example, where first-aid knowledge has had to be applied) to have memorised key information or ideas.

In more routine working situations, it will, of course, be possible, if necessary, to check one's understanding or memory by consulting reference manuals, books or colleagues. The ability to use a skill will also become more automatic with practice. In any case, being required to memorise something is good rehearsal for real-life pressures and crises.

WHEN YOU NEED TO TAKE A TEST

When the day of a test arrives, give yourself plenty of time to check equipment; have breakfast; and arrive on time but not too early. Try not to talk about the test with friends before you start. Have a last look at any brief notes or summaries you have made. As soon as you are allowed to,

✱ read the questions;
✱ make sure you understand the test instructions;
✱ ask for help if necessary;
✱ take your time;
✱ highlight key words and note down any key facts you know you will have to use at some point but may forget as the test proceeds.

UNIT 2
Development from Conception to Age 16 Years

Unit 2 is divided into the following seven chapters:

Chapter 2:   Studying Child Development

Chapter 3:   Cognitive Development

Chapter 4:   Communication, Including Language Development

Chapter 5:   Physical Development

Chapter 6:   Emotional and Social Development

Chapter 7:   Understanding the Behaviour of Children

Chapter 8:   Observation and Assessment

CHAPTER 2

Studying Child Development

Contents

• What is child development? • Why study child development? • Approaches to studying children's development • Measuring development • Critical periods, or optimal, sensitive and best times for development • The difference between development and learning • What is a theory of child development? • Theories of child development and learning • The nature–nurture debate • Adults' learning • EPPE (The Effective Provision of Pre-School Education)

WHAT IS CHILD DEVELOPMENT?

It is important to keep in mind that even a tiny baby is a person. People develop physically, but they are whole human beings from the very start.

If different aspects of a child's development are seen as separated strands, each isolated from the other, the child comes to be seen as a collection of bits and pieces instead of a whole person. On the other hand, it can be useful to look closely at a particular area of a child's development, whether to check that all is well, to celebrate progress, to see how to help the child with the next step of development and learning, or to give special help where needed. Even when focusing on one aspect of development it is important, however, not to forget that we are looking at a whole person. A person has a physical body, ideas, feelings and relationships – all developing and functioning at the same time. When we think of the complete child in this way, we are taking a holistic approach.

Child development is a fairly new subject. It is a multidisciplinary subject. This means that it draws on various academic fields, including psychology, neuroscience, sociology, paediatrics, biology and genetics.

Recently, researchers in child development have begun to think about how children develop in different cultures and in different sorts of society and how children are brought up in different parts of the world. It is very important to find out what different people in different cultures do that is the same when they bring up children. It is also very important to learn about the different ways that children are brought up and yet still turn into stable and successful adults. So, researchers are now asking two questions:

1 What is the same about all children?
2 What is different across cultures in the way that children are brought up?

WHY STUDY CHILD DEVELOPMENT?

Child development is an essential subject of study for everyone who works with young children. Looking after other people's children gives you different responsibilities compared to having your own children. So people who work with other people's children need to be trained properly and carefully. They need to be informed about how children develop and learn.

'People who work with young children must themselves continue to learn. If they do not continue to read, discuss and to think and keep up to date with current issues, with theory and practice, they show a disrespect for the people they work with, the children and the parents.' (Cathy Nutbrown in *Children's Rights and Early Education*)

The key to understanding child development is 'wholeness'. Studying holistic child development is a way of seeing children in the round, as whole people.

Parents are constantly looking for support and help as they bring up their children. Wanting to know more is part of being a parent. They find it very helpful to watch television and listen to radio programmes. They also read magazines and talk to trained and knowledgeable staff in nurseries as they try to understand their children.

APPROACHES TO STUDYING CHILDREN'S DEVELOPMENT

Integrated Development

The whole child may be looked at under six headings. You can remember these as together they make up the acronym PILESS.

PILESS

* **P**hysical development;
* **I**ntellectual development;
* **L**anguage development;
* **E**motional development;
* **S**ocial development;
* **S**piritual development.

Advantages of PILESS

The advantages of using PILESS in the study of child development are that the approach:

* recognises the important contributions of different disciplines – human biology,

psychology, linguistics, sociology, neuroscience, and so on;

* provides a useful framework for students to organise their studies;

* provides a focus for the study of children, for example in the use of observation techniques, case studies and the planning of activities for work with children.

Disadvantages of PILESS

The disadvantages of using PILESS in the study of child development are that:

* it may be difficult to view the child as a whole person;

* it may be more difficult to contextualise the child if the categories are rigidly prescribed (the contextualised child is discussed below).

The Contextualised Child

Researchers in the field of child development now realise that when children quarrel, for example, it is almost impossible to say which aspect of their behaviour is:

* emotional (anger);

* physical (stamping with rage);

* intellectual or language (what they say or do).

Researchers now know that, in order to understand what is going on, it is also very important to identify who or what made a particular child angry, starting the quarrel. This is the context of the behaviour. So, it is important to contextualise the child when studying child development. By looking at child development in context we recognise that the biological part of development (physical development and genetic factors) is integrated with the cultural part of development (social, cultural, intellectual and linguistic factors).

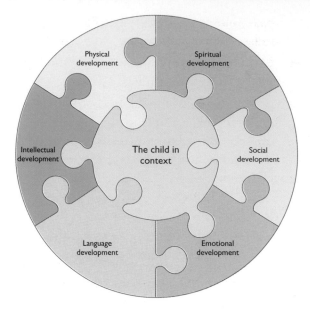

Fig 2.1 We can think of studying integrated development as being like looking at the pieces of a jigsaw

We now prefer to talk about the contextualised child because:

* development is deeply influenced by the child's cultural environment and the people she meets;

* the ideas, language, communication, feelings, relationships and other cultural elements which the child experiences have a profound influence on development.

MEASURING DEVELOPMENT

Normative Development

A traditional approach to child development study has been to emphasise normative measurement. This is concerned with 'milestones' or stages in a child's development. These show what *most* children can do at a particular age. In reality, there is a wide range of normal development, and this will be influenced by genetic, social and cultural factors. Children have been labelled as 'backward' or 'forward' in relation to the so-called 'normal' child, which is not always helpful.

So, it is important to be aware that normative measurements can only indicate general *trends* in development in children across the world. They may vary quite a bit according to the culture in which a child lives.

When children do things earlier than the milestones suggest is normal, it does not necessarily mean that they will be outstanding or gifted in any way. Parents sometimes think that because their child speaks early, is potty-trained early or walks early, he or she is gifted in some way. You should handle these situations carefully, as the child may not be gifted at all.

CASE STUDY

* Mark moved around by bottom-shuffling and did not walk until he was 2 years old. He went on to run, hop and skip at the normal times. Walking late was not a cause for concern, and he did not suffer from any developmental delay.

* African children living in rural villages estimate volume and capacity earlier than European children who live in towns. This is because they practise measuring out cups of rice into baskets from an early age as part of their daily lives. Learning about volume and capacity early does not mean that children will necessarily go on to become talented mathematicians. Children who learn these concepts later might also become good mathematicians.

Sequences in a Child's Development

Children across the world seem to pass through similar sequences of development, but in different ways and at different rates according to their culture. The work of Mary Sheridan on developmental sequences has been invaluable, but she suggests that children move through rigidly prescribed stages that are linked to the child's age: the child sits, then crawls, then stands, then walks. In fact, this is not the case. Not all children *do* crawl. Blind children often do not. Some children (like Mark in the case study below) 'bottom-shuffle', moving along in a sitting position.

Children with special educational needs often seem to 'dance the development ladder': they move through sequences in unusual and very uneven ways. For example, they might walk at the normal age, but they may not talk at the usual age.

As researchers learn more about child development, it is becoming more useful to think of a child's development as a network which becomes increasingly complex as the child matures and becomes more experienced in their culture. So, instead of thinking of child development and learning as a ladder, it is probably more useful to think of it as a web.

Tables 2.1 to 2.5 summarise normative development in each of the following areas: Physical; Communication and Language; Intellectual/Cognitive; Emotional and Social (and Behavioural); and aspects of moral and spiritual development.

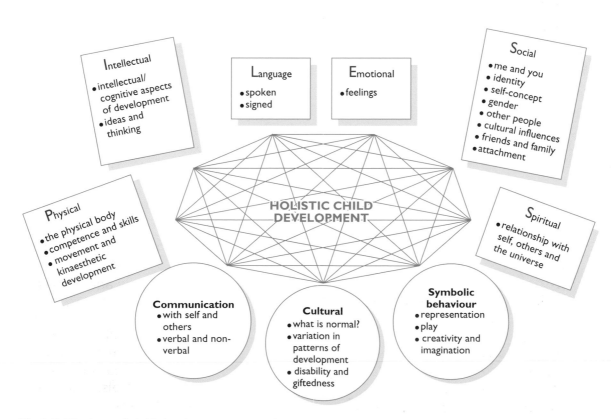

Fig 2.2 Thinking of child development as a web

Table 2.1 Normative physical development: from birth to 16 years

Age	Gross motor skills	Fine motor skills (& sensory development)
Birth to 4 weeks	Babies: ✱ lie **supine** (on their backs) with head to one side ✱ when placed on their front (the **prone position**), lie with the head turned to one side and their knees tucked under the abdomen ✱ if pulled to sitting position, the head will lag, the back curves over and the head falls forward.	Babies: ✱ usually hold their hands tightly closed ✱ often hold their thumbs tucked in under their fingers ✱ react to loud sounds, but by one month may be soothed by particular music ✱ turn their head towards the light and stare at bright, shiny objects ✱ are fascinated by human faces and gaze attentively at carer's face when fed or held.
4 to 8 weeks	✱ can now turn from side to back ✱ can lift their head briefly from prone position ✱ arm and leg movements are jerky and uncontrolled ✱ have head lag when pulled to sitting position.	✱ will open their hands to grasp an adult's finger ✱ turn their heads towards the light and stare at bright, shiny objects ✱ will show interest and excitement by facial expression and will gaze attentively at carer's face whilst being fed.
8 to 12 weeks	✱ keep their head in a central position when lying supine ✱ can now lift head and chest off bed in prone position, supported on forearms ✱ have almost no head lag in sitting position ✱ can kick their legs vigorously, both separately and together ✱ can wave their arms and bring their hands together over the body.	✱ move their head to follow adult movements ✱ watch their hands and play with their fingers ✱ can hold a rattle for a brief time before dropping it.
4 to 5 months	✱ are starting to use a **palmar grasp** and can transfer objects from hand to hand ✱ are very interested in all activity ✱ take everything to their mouth ✱ move their head around to follow people and objects.	✱ now have good head control and are beginning to sit with support ✱ roll over from back to side and are beginning to reach for objects ✱ when supine, play with their own feet ✱ hold the head up when pulled to sitting position.
6 to 9 months	✱ can roll from front to back ✱ may attempt to crawl but will often end up sliding backwards ✱ may grasp feet and place in own mouth ✱ can sit without support for longer periods of time ✱ may 'cruise' around furniture and may even stand or walk alone.	✱ are very alert to people and objects ✱ are beginning to use a **pincer grasp** with thumb and index finger to transfer toys from one hand to the other and look for fallen objects ✱ explore objects by putting them in their mouth.
9 to 12 months	✱ will now be mobile – may be crawling, bear-walking, bottom-shuffling or even walking ✱ can sit up on their own and lean forward to pick things up ✱ may crawl upstairs and onto low items of furniture ✱ may bounce in rhythm to music.	✱ have a well developed **pincer grasp** and can pick things up and pull towards themselves ✱ can poke with one finger and will point to desired objects ✱ can clasp hands and imitate adults' actions ✱ can throw toys deliberately ✱ can manage spoons and finger foods well.
15 months	✱ probably walk alone, with feet wide apart and arms raised to maintain balance ✱ are likely to fall over and sit down suddenly a lot ✱ can probably manage stairs and steps, but will need supervision	✱ can build with a few bricks and arrange toys on the floor ✱ hold crayon in **palmar grasp** and turn several pages of a book at once ✱ can point to desired objects

Table 2.1 (continued)

Age	Gross motor skills	Fine motor skills (& Sensory development)
	✳ can get to standing without help from furniture or people and kneel without support.	✳ show a preference for one hand, but use either.
18 months	Children: ✳ walk confidently and are able to stop without falling ✳ can kneel, squat, climb and carry things around with them ✳ can climb onto an adult chair forwards and then turn round to sit ✳ can come downstairs, usually by creeping backwards on their tummy.	Children: ✳ can thread large beads ✳ use pincer grasp to pick up small objects ✳ can build a tower of several cubes. ✳ can scribble to and fro on paper.
2 years	✳ are very mobile – can run safely ✳ can climb up onto the furniture ✳ can walk up and down stairs, usually two feet to a step ✳ try to kick a ball with some success – cannot yet catch ball.	✳ can draw circles, lines and dots, using preferred hand ✳ can pick up tiny objects using a fine pincer grasp ✳ can build tower of six or more blocks (bricks) with longer concentration span ✳ enjoy picture books and turn pages singly.
3 years	✳ can jump from a low step ✳ can walk backwards and sideways ✳ can stand and walk on tiptoe and stand on one foot ✳ have good spatial awareness ✳ ride tricycle using pedals ✳ can climb stairs with one foot on each step – downwards with two feet per step.	✳ can build tall towers of bricks or blocks ✳ can control a pencil using thumb and first two fingers – the **dynamic tripod grasp** ✳ enjoy painting with large brush ✳ can use scissors to cut paper ✳ can copy shapes, such as a circle.
4 years	✳ are developing a sense of balance – may be able to walk along a line ✳ can catch, kick, throw and bounce a ball ✳ can bend at the waist to pick up objects from the floor ✳ enjoy climbing trees and frames ✳ can run up and down stairs, one foot per step.	✳ can build a tower of bricks and other constructions too ✳ can draw a recognizable person on request, showing head, legs and trunk ✳ can thread small beads on a lace.
5 years	✳ can use a variety of play equipment – slides, swings, climbing frames ✳ can play ball games ✳ can hop and run lightly on toes – can move rhythmically to music ✳ have a well developed sense of balance ✳ can skip.	✳ may be able to thread a large-eyed needle and sew large stitches ✳ can draw a person with head, trunk, legs, nose, mouth and eyes ✳ have good control over pencils and paintbrushes ✳ copy shapes, such as a square.
6 and 7 years	✳ have increased agility, muscle co-ordination and balance ✳ develop competence in riding a two-wheeled bicycle ✳ hop easily, with good balance ✳ can jump off apparatus at school.	✳ can build a tall, straight tower with blocks and other constructions too ✳ can draw a person with detail, e.g. clothes and eyebrows ✳ can write letters of alphabet with similar writing grip to an adult ✳ can catch a ball thrown from one metre with one hand.
8 and 9 years	✳ can ride a bicycle easily ✳ have increased strength and co-ordination	✳ can control their small muscles well; improved writing and drawing skills

Table 2.1 (continued)

Age	Gross motor skills	Fine motor skills (& Sensory development)
	* play energetic games and sports.	* draw people with details of clothing and facial features * are starting to join letters together in handwriting.
10 and 11 years	* differ in physical maturity; because girls experience **puberty** earlier they are often as much as 2 years ahead of boys * have body proportions becoming more similar to adults.	* tackle more detailed tasks such as woodwork or needlework * are usually writing with an established style – using joined-up letters.

From 12–16 years

Physical development during adolescence is known as **puberty**. The age at which puberty starts varies from person to person but on average it begins between 9–13 in girls and 10–15 in boys.

Many physical changes occur during puberty:

⇨ **Growth** accelerates rapidly – often called a **growth spurt**. This usually happens in a particular order from outer to inner:

    – The head, feet and hands grow to adult size first; then

    – The arms and legs grow in length and strength; finally

    – The trunk: the main part of the body from shoulder to hip grows to full adult size and shape

  This sequence of growth means that for a brief period, adolescents may feel gawky and clumsy, as they appear to be 'out of proportion'. The average boy grows fastest between 14 and 15. Girls start earlier, growing fastest when 12 and 13. Girls also finish their growth spurt earlier at 18, while boys need another two years before they finish growing aged 20.

⇨ **Secondary sex characteristics** develop; these are external traits which distinguish the two sexes, but which are *not* directly part of the **reproductive system**; for example, the growth of pubic hair in both sexes, facial hair and deepened voice for males, and breasts and widened hips for females.

⇨ **Primary sex characteristics** develop: these are the penis and sperm in males and the vagina and ovaries in females. During puberty hormonal changes cause a boy's penis and testicles to grow and the body to produce sperm. Girls start to menstruate or have their monthly period. Both these events signal **sexual maturity** – the ability to reproduce.

The main features of physical development in puberty

In girls	In boys
The first *external* sign of puberty in most girls is usually breast development – often accompanied by a growth spurt. **Breasts develop**: At first, the nipples start to stick out from the chest. (often called 'budding'). Behind the nipple, milk ducts begin to grow. Next, the flat circular part of the nipple, the areola, rises and starts to expand. Glands that make sweat and scent develop beneath it. The breast begins to fill out, as fat is deposited around the nipple. Some girls feel a tingling sensation or have tender breasts. Initially the breasts stick out in a conical shape. As growth continues they gradually round off into an adult shape. **Body size and shape**: Grows taller. Hips widen as the pelvic bones grow. Fat develops on the hips, thighs and buttocks and the ratio of fat to muscle increases. The waist gets smaller and the body develops a more curved shape. **Menstruation**: Menstruation – having periods – is part of the female reproductive cycle that starts when girls become sexually mature during puberty. During a menstrual period, a woman bleeds from her uterus (womb) via the vagina. This lasts anything from three to seven days. Each period begins approximately every 28 days if the woman does not become pregnant during a given cycle. The onset of	The first *external* sign of puberty in most boys is an increase in the size of the testicles and then the penis. This is followed by the growth of pubic and underarm hair. At the same time, the voice deepens and muscles develop. Lastly, boys grow facial hair. **Voice breaking**: Testosterone causes the voice box – or larynx – to enlarge and the vocal cords to become longer. Sometimes as the voice changes to become deeper, it may change pitch abruptly or 'break' at times; the voice box tilts and often protrudes at the neck – as an 'Adam's apple'. (Many boys start to develop breasts in their teenage years, but this disappears as the testosterone levels increase.) **Body size and shape**: Grows taller. Body takes on a new, more muscular shape as the shoulders and chest become broader and the neck becomes more muscular **Chest hair** may appear during puberty – or some years later. **Penile erections**: These occur spontaneously even from infancy, but during puberty they become more frequent. Erections can occur with or without any physical or sexual stimulation and can cause acute embarrassment. **Sperm**: Once the testicles begin to grow they also develop their adult function – producing sperm. Mature sperm is

Table 2.1 (continued)

In girls	In boys
menstruation is called the menarche; it can occur at any time between the ages of 9 and 16, most commonly around the age of 12–13. It means that the body is capable of **reproduction**.	present in the male body towards the end of puberty (most commonly between the ages of 13 and 15) and means that the body is capable of **reproduction**.

In both girls and boys
Pubic hair starts to grow around the genitals and becomes coarse, dark and curly. In girls, pubic hair forms an upside-down triangle shape; in boys, the hair grows between the legs and extends up from the penis to the abdomen Hair grows in the armpits and on the legs **Sweat**: A different kind of sweat is now produced in response to stress, emotion and sexual excitement. It is produced by the apocrine glands and only occurs in the armpits, the belly button, the groin area, the ears and the nipples. As bacteria break down the sweat it starts to smell strongly – known as B.O. (Body Odour) **Oil glands**: oil-secreting glands in the skin can become over-active – this can cause skin to become greasier and can also cause acne

Table 2.2 Normative communication and language development: from birth to 16 years

	During the first three months: Babies need to share language experiences and co-operate with others from birth onwards. From the start babies need other people. Babies listen to people's voices. Babies 'call out' for company. When adults close to them talk to them in **motherese** (a high pitched tone referring to what is around and going on) babies dance, listen, and reply in babble and coo. Babies cry with anger to show they are tired, hungry, and to say they need to be changed. A hearing-impaired baby babbles and cries too. Babies are comforted by the voices of those who are close to them and they will turn especially to the voices of their family.
From birth to 4 weeks	Babies: ✱ respond to sounds, especially familiar voices ✱ quieten when picked up ✱ make eye contact ✱ cry to indicate need ✱ may move the eyes towards the direction of sound.
4 to 8 weeks	✱ recognise carer and familiar objects ✱ make non-crying noises such as cooing and gurgling ✱ become more expressive in their cries ✱ look for sounds.
8 to 12 weeks	✱ are still distressed by sudden loud noises ✱ often suck or lick lips when they hear sound of food preparation ✱ show excitement at sound of approaching footsteps or voices.
3 to 6 months	✱ become more aware of others so they communicate more and more. As they listen, they imitate sounds they can hear, and they react to the tone of someone's voice. For example, they might become upset by an angry tone, or cheered by a happy tone ✱ begin to use vowels, consonants and syllable sounds, e.g. 'ah', 'ee aw' ✱ begin to laugh and squeal with pleasure ✱ continue to do everything they did in the first three months.
6 to 9 months	✱ babble becomes tuneful like the lilt of the language they can hear (except in hearing-impaired babies) ✱ begin to understand words like 'up' and 'down' raising their arms to be lifted up, using appropriate gestures ✱ repeat sounds. Babies continue to do everything they did in the first six months.

Table 2.2 (continued)

9 to 12 months	* cooperation develops further from the early proto-conversations of early **motherese**. For example, when adults wave bye bye, or say 'show me your shoes' the babies enjoy pointing and waving. * can follow simple instructions, e.g. kiss teddy. * word approximations appear, e.g. hee haw = donkey or more typically mumma and dadda and bye-bye in English-speaking contexts. * the tuneful babble develops into 'jargon' and babies make their voices go up and down just as people do when they talk to each other. Really? Do you? No! The babble is very expressive. Children are already experienced and capable communicators by this time; they are using **emergent language**/protolanguage. It is nothing short of amazing that all this happens within one year. They know about: ⇨ facial expressions ⇨ combined sounds (hee-haw) ⇨ gestures ⇨ shared meanings ⇨ persuading, negotiating, co-operating, turn taking ⇨ interest in others, their ideas, their feelings, what they do. They know that words stand for people, objects, what they do and what happens. They are taking part in the language of their culture.
From 1 to 2 years	Children begin to talk with words or sign language. They add more and more layers to everything they know about language and communication in the first year.
By 18 months	* They enjoy trying to sing as well as to listen to songs and rhymes. Action songs (for example pat-a-cake) are much loved. * Books with pictures are of great interest. They point at and often name parts of their body, objects, people and pictures in books. * They echo the last part of what others say (echolalia). One word or sign can have several meanings (**holophrases**). For example, C-A-T = all animals, not just cats. This is sometimes called 'extension'. * They begin waving their arms up and down which might mean 'start again', or 'I like it', or 'more'. * Gestures develop alongside words. Gesture is used in some cultures more than in others.
By 2 years	Researchers used to say that children are using a vocabulary of 50 or so words but they understand more. Modern researchers do not use vocabulary counts so much and they simply stress that children are rapidly becoming competent speakers of the languages they experience. * They over extend the use of a word, e.g. all animals are called 'doggie'. * They talk about an absent object when reminded of it, e.g. seeing an empty plate, they say 'biscuit'. * They use phrases, (telegraphese) doggie-gone, they call themselves by their name, for example, Tom. * They spend a great deal of energy naming things and what they do. For example, chair, and as they go up a step they might say 'up'. * They can follow a simple instruction or request, for example, 'Could you bring me the spoon'. They are wanting to share songs, dance, conversations, finger rhymes, etc. more and more.
From 2 to 3 years	During this period, language and the ability to communicate develop so rapidly that it almost seems to explode. The development is stunning. Children begin to: * use plurals, pronouns, adjectives, possessives, time words, tenses and sentences * make what are called virtuous errors in the way that they pronounce (articulate) things. It is also true of the way they use grammar (syntax). They might say 'two times' instead of 'twice'. They might say 'I goed there' instead of 'I went there' * love to converse and chat and ask questions (what, where and who) * enjoy much more complicated stories and ask about their favourite ones over and again. It is not unusual for children to stutter because they are trying so hard to tell adults things and to talk. Their thinking goes faster than the pace at which they can say what they want to say. They can quickly become frustrated.

Table 2.2 (continued)

From 3 to 4 years	During this time children: * ask why, when and how questions as they become more and more fascinated with the reasons for things and how things work (cause and effect) * wonder what will happen 'if' (problem solving and hypothesis making) * can think back and they can think forward much more easily than before * can also think about things from somebody else's point of view, but only fleetingly. Past, present and future tenses are used more often * can be taught to say their name, address and age. As they become more accurate in the way they pronounce words, and begin to use grammar, they delight in nonsense words which they make up, and jokes using words. This is called metalinguistics. They swear if they hear swearing.
From 4 to 8 years	Children: * try to understand the meaning of words. They use adverbs and prepositions. They talk confidently and with more and more fluency. As they become more and more part of their culture they become aware of the roles of the language(s) they speak. They use language creatively * add vocabulary all the time. Their articulation becomes conventional. They are explorers and communicators * begin to be able to define objects by their function, e.g. 'What is a ball?' 'You bounce it.' Young children do not learn anything in isolation from other children and adults * begin to share as they learn. Sharing sharpens and broadens their thinking. This helps them to learn better, e.g. they begin to understand book language, and that stories have characters and a plot (the narrative) * begin to realise that different situations require different ways of talking. They establish a sense of audience (who they are talking to).
From 8 to 9 years	Children: * use and understand complex sentences * are increasingly verbal; they enjoy making up stories and telling jokes * use reference books with increasing skill.
From 10 to 11 years	Children: * can write fairly lengthy essays * write stories which show imagination and are increasingly legible and grammatically correct.
From 12 to 16 years	During this period, young people become increasingly independent and spend much of their days outside the home - at school or at after-school activities and with peers. Young people: * have a fast, legible style of handwriting * communicate in an adult manner, with increasing maturity. * comprehend abstract language, such as idioms, figurative language and metaphors * are able to process texts and abstract meaning, relate word meanings and contexts, understand punctuation, and form complex syntactic structures.

Table 2.3 Normative intellectual/cognitive and symbolic development: from birth to 16 years

From birth to 4 weeks	Concepts (ideas) are beginning to develop already. Concepts are based in the senses and in what is perceived (i.e. the baby is aware of a sensation). Babies explore through their senses and through their own activity and movement. ❏ **Touch and movement (Kinaesthetic)** From the beginning babies feel pain. Their faces, abdomens, hands and the soles of their feet are also very sensitive to touch. They perceive the movements that they themselves make, and the way that other people move them about through their senses. For example, they give a 'startle' response if they are moved suddenly. This is called the **Moro** response.

Table 2.3 (continued)

	❑ **Sound** Even a newborn baby will turn to a sound. Babies might become still and listen to a low sound, or quicken their movements when they hear a high sound. A baby often stops crying and listens to a human voice by two weeks of age ❑ **Taste** Babies like sweet tastes, for example breast milk. ❑ **Smell** Babies turn to the smell of the breast. ❑ **Sight** Babies can focus on objects 20 cm (a few inches) away. They are sensitive to light. Babies like to look at human faces – eye contact. They can track the movements of people and objects. They will scan the edges of objects. They will imitate facial expressions (for example, they will put out their tongue if you do). If you know any new-born or very young babies, try it and see! Psychologists think that babies may not see in colour during the early stages of development.
From 4 to 16 weeks	They recognise (have a concept of) differing speech sounds. By three months they can even imitate low or high pitched sounds. By four months they link objects they know with the sound, for example, mother's voice and her face. They know the smell of their mother from that of other mothers.
4 to 5 months	By 4 months babies reach for objects, which suggests they recognise and judge the distance in relation to the size of the object. This is called **depth perception**, but it also suggests that the baby is linking the immediate perception with previous ones and predicting the future, which is an early concept of dimensional objects.
5 to 6 months	Babies prefer complicated things to look at from 5 to 6 months. They enjoy bright colours. They know that they have one mother. Babies are disturbed if they are shown several images of their mother at the same time. They realise that *people* are **permanent** before they realise that *objects* are. Babies can co-ordinate more, e.g. they can see a rattle, grasp the rattle, put the rattle in their mouths (they co-ordinate tracking, reaching, grasping and sucking). They can develop favourite tastes in food and recognise differences by 5 months.
6 to 9 months	The baby understands **signs**, e.g. the bib means that food is coming. Soon this understanding of signs will lead into **symbolic** behaviour. From eight to nine months babies show they know objects exist when they have gone out of sight, even under test conditions. This is called the concept of object constancy, or the **object permanence test** (as described by **Piaget**). They are also fascinated by the way in which objects move They understand that two objects can occupy space. One toy can be covered by a cloth.
9 months to 1 year	Babies are beginning to develop images. **Memory** develops. They can remember the past. They can anticipate the future. This gives them some understanding of routine daily sequences, e.g. after a feed, changing, and a sleep with teddy. They imitate actions, sounds, gestures and moods after an event is finished, e.g. imitate a temper tantrum they saw a friend have the previous day, wave bye-bye remembering Grandma has gone to the shops. They catch the moods and feelings of other people – e.g. sadness or joy. This **emotional contagion** is the beginning of sympathy for others.
From 1 to 4 years	Children develop **symbolic behaviour**. This means that they: ❑ talk. ❑ **pretend play** – often talking to themselves as they do so. ❑ take part in simple non-competitive games. ❑ represent events in drawings, models, etc.

Table 2.3 (continued)

	Personal images dominate, rather than conventions used in the culture, e.g. writing is 'pretend' writing. Children tend to focus on one aspect of a situation. It is difficult for them to see things from different points of view. The way people react to what they do helps them to work out what hurts and what helps other people. This is an important time for **moral development**. They often enjoy music and playing sturdy instruments and join in groups singing and dancing.
From 4 to 8 years	Children begin to move into deeper and deeper layers of symbolic behaviour. Language is well established, and opens the way into **literacy** (talking, listening, writing and reading). Personal symbols still dominate until 6 or 7 years of age. Cultural conventions in writing, drawing, etc begin to influence children increasingly. Where there is a balance in the way children use personal and conventional symbols, children are described as creative. Thinking becomes increasingly co-coordinated as children are able to hold in mind more than one point of view at a time. **Concepts** - of matter, length, measurement, distance, area, time, volume, capacity and weight – develop steadily. They enjoy chanting and counting (beginning to understand number). They can use their voice in different ways to play different characters in their pretend play. They develop play narratives (stories) which they return to over time. They help younger children into the play. They are interested in their own development – from babies to now. They are beginning to establish differences between what is real and unreal/fantasy. This is not yet always stable, and so they can easily be frightened by supernatural characters. They begin to try and work out right and wrong – e.g. hurting people physically or their own feelings as language develops and deeper discussion of issues becomes more possible. But remember that even adults have difficulty knowing what is right in some situations.
From 8 to 9 years	Children: <ul><li>have an increased ability to remember and pay attention, and to speak and express their ideas</li><li>are learning to plan ahead and evaluate what they do</li><li>have an increased ability to think and to reason</li><li>can deal with abstract ideas</li><li>enjoy different types of activities – such as joining clubs, playing games with rules, and collecting things</li><li>enjoy projects which are task-oriented, such as sewing and woodwork.</li></ul>
From 10 to 11 years	Children: <ul><li>begin to understand the motives behind the actions of another</li><li>can concentrate on tasks for increasing periods</li><li>begin to devise memory strategies</li><li>may be curious about drugs, alcohol, and tobacco</li><li>may develop special talents, showing particular skills in writing, maths, art, music or woodwork.</li></ul>
From 12 to 16 years	Around this time, young people experience a major shift in thinking from **concrete** to **abstract** – an adult way of thinking: Piaget described this as the **formal operational stage** of cognitive development. This involves: <ul><li>*thinking about possibilities*: younger children rely heavily on their senses to apply reasoning, whereas adolescents think about possibilities which are not directly observable.</li><li>*thinking ahead*: young people start to plan ahead, often in a systematic way; for example, younger children may look forward to a holiday, but they are unlikely to focus on the preparation involved.</li><li>*thinking through hypotheses*: this gives them the ability to make and test hypotheses and to think about situations which are contrary to fact.</li><li>*thinking about their own thought processes*: this is known as **metacognition**. A subcategory of metacognition is **metamemory**, which is having knowledge about your memory processes – being able to explain what strategies you use when trying to remember things – e.g. for an exam.</li><li>*thinking beyond conventional limits*: thinking about issues which generally preoccupy human beings in adulthood, such as morality, religion and politics.</li></ul> They approach a problem in a systematic fashion and also use their imagination when solving problems.

Table 2.4 Normative emotional and social development: from birth to 16 years

From birth to 4 weeks	Babies: ✱ first smile in definite response to carer is usually around 5–6 weeks ✱ often imitates certain facial expressions ✱ use total body movements to express pleasure at bath time or when being fed ✱ enjoy feeding and cuddling ✱ are learning where they begin and end, e.g. a hand is part of *them* but mother's hand is not.
From 4 to 8 weeks	Babies: ✱ will smile in response to adult ✱ enjoy sucking ✱ turn to regard nearby speaker's face ✱ turn to preferred person's voice ✱ recognise face and hands of preferred adult ✱ may stop crying when they hear, see or feel their own carer.
From 8 to 12 weeks	Babies: ✱ show enjoyment at caring routines such as bath time ✱ respond with obvious pleasure to loving attention and cuddles ✱ Fix the eyes unblinkingly on the carer's face when feeding ✱ stay awake for longer periods of time.
4 to 5 months	Babies: ✱ enjoy attention and being with others ✱ show trust and security ✱ have recognisable sleep patterns. By 5 months babies have learnt that they only have one mother. They are disturbed when shown several images of their mother at the same time.
6 to 9 months	Babies: ✱ manage to feed self with fingers ✱ are now more wary of strangers, showing **stranger fear** ✱ offer toys to others ✱ show distress when the mother leaves ✱ begin to crawl and this means they can do more for themselves, reach for objects and get to places and people ✱ are now more aware of other people's feelings. They cry if a sibling cries, for example. They love an audience to laugh with them. They cry and laugh with others. This is called recognition of an emotion. It does not mean they are really laughing or crying, though.
9 to 12 months	Babies: ✱ enjoy songs and action rhymes ✱ still like to be near to a familiar adult ✱ can drink from a cup with help ✱ will play alone for long periods ✱ have and show definite likes and dislikes at meal and bedtimes ✱ thoroughly enjoy peek-a-boo games ✱ like to look at themselves in a mirror (plastic safety mirror) ✱ imitate other people, e.g. clapping hands, waving bye bye, but there is often a time lapse so that they wave after the person has gone.
1 to 2 years	Children: ✱ co-operate when being dressed ✱ begin to have a longer memory ✱ develop a **sense of identity** (I am me) ✱ express their needs in words and gestures ✱ enjoy being able to walk, and are eager to try to get dressed – 'me do it!' ✱ are aware when others are fearful or anxious for them as they climb on and off chairs, etc.

Table 2.4 (continued)

2 to 3 years	Children: ✱ begin to be able to say how they are feeling ✱ can dress self and go to the lavatory independently, but need sensitive support in order to feel success rather than frustration. **Pretend play** develops rapidly when adults foster it.
3 to 4 years	Children: ✱ are beginning to develop a gender role as they become aware of being male or female ✱ make friends and are interested in having friends ✱ learn to negotiate, give-and-take through experimenting with feeling powerful, having a sense of control, and through quarrels with other children ✱ are easily afraid, for example, of the dark, as they become capable of pretending. They imagine all sorts of things. Pretend play helps children to **decentre**. (This means they begin to be able to understand how someone else might feel.)
4 to 8 years	Children: ✱ have developed a stable self concept ✱ have internalised the rules of their culture ✱ can hide their feelings once they can begin to control their feelings ✱ can think of the feelings of others ✱ can take responsibility, e.g. in helping younger children.
8 to 12 years	*At 8 or 9 years old*, children: ✱ may become discouraged easily ✱ take pride in their competence ✱ can be argumentative and bossy, but can equally be generous and responsive ✱ are beginning to see things from another child's point of view, but still have trouble understanding the feelings and needs of other people. *At 11 or 12 years old*, children: ✱ may be experiencing sudden, dramatic, emotional changes associated with puberty (especially girls who experience puberty earlier than boys) ✱ tend to be particularly sensitive to criticism ✱ prefer to spend leisure time with friends and continue to participate in small groups of same sex, but are acutely aware of the opposite sex ✱ succumb to peer pressure more readily and want to talk, dress, and act just like friends.
12 to 16 years	Young people: ✱ may become self-conscious or worried about the physical changes (too short, too tall, too fat, too thin etc) ✱ develop a sexual identity; self-labelling as gay or lesbian tends to occur around the age of 15 for boys and 15½ for girls, although first disclosure does not normally take place until after the age of 16½ years for both sexes ✱ often feel misunderstood ✱ can experience wide emotional swings; e.g. fluctuate between emotional peaks of excitement and depths of moodiness ✱ want to become accepted and liked ✱ tend to identify more with friends and begin to separate from parents; they are less dependent on family for affection and emotional support.

Table 2.5 Normative moral and spiritual aspects of development: from birth to 16 years

Birth to 1 year	Even a tiny baby experiences a sense of awe and wonder, and values people who are loved by them. Worship is about a sense of worthship. People, and loved teddy bears, a daisy on the grass grasped, looked at (put in the mouth!) all help to build the child's spiritual experiences. These have nothing to do with worship of a god or gods. Spirituality is about the developing sense of relating to others ethically, morally and humanely.
1 to 3 years	Judy Dunn's work suggests that during this period children already have a strongly developed moral sense. They know what hurts and upsets their family (adults and children). They know what delights them and brings warm, pleased responses. Through their pretend play, and the conversations in the family about how people behave, hurt and help each other, they learn how other people feel. They learn to think beyond themselves.
3 to 8 years	With the help and support of their family, early childhood workers and the wider community, children develop further concepts like being helpful, forgiving, and fairness. By the age of 7 years, they have a clear sense of right and wrong – for example, they realise that it is wrong to hurt other people physically.
8 to 12 years	By 8 or 9 years, children continue to think that rules are permanent and unchangeable because they are made up by adults who must be obeyed and respected. They have a clear idea of the difference between reality and fantasy, and are highly concerned about fairness. By 10 and 11 years, children understand that certain rules can be changed by mutual negotiation; often, they do not accept rules that they did not help make. They may begin to experience conflict between parents' values and those of their peers.
12 to 16 years	Young people are able to think beyond themselves more and to understand the perspective of another. They are developing their own ideas and values which often challenge those of home; they may deliberately flout rules or only keep to them if there is otherwise a risk of being caught.

Assessing the Development of Children with Disabilities

Lilli Neilsen, a Danish specialist working with children who have multiple disabilities (complex needs), stressed the importance of carefully assessing the development of the whole child. For example, she observed a child with cerebral palsy. He was lying on his stomach on a mat, with toys around him. He looked at a toy but each time he reached for it, his shoulder jerked involuntarily and he pushed the toy away. She gently weighted down his shoulder. He reached for the toy, and was able to grab it. He smiled and made a contented sound.

It would have been easy to check his physical development, and say '**cannot reach and grasp**'. Instead, we have a picture of a boy who:

* **had an idea** (to reach for the toy);
* **knew what to do** (but his body could not manage it);
* **was given the right help**, based on Nielsen's careful observation;
* **experienced success and pleasure**;
* **developed the motivation to have another go**.

Intellectual, physical, emotional and social aspects all merge together.

CRITICAL PERIODS, OR OPTIMAL, SENSITIVE AND BEST TIMES FOR DEVELOPMENT

Are there Critical Times for Development?

Until recently it was thought that there were **critical times** when children learned to talk and walk, for example. If a child missed out on bonding with people by being able to crawl – perhaps through having an operation on the feet or being kept confined in a cot without objects for play – it was believed that the damage was irreparable.

However, recent research suggests that it is **not always too late to catch up**. This is a much more positive way of thinking about a child's development. As neuroscience develops we are seeing that catching up is only possible if the physical mechanisms are present. They may have become latent, buried or weakened through being restrained.

A visually impaired woman, who had been blind throughout her life, had an operation on her eyes. She was delighted to find that every oak tree looked completely different. She had learnt that there were things called oak trees but had not realised how completely different every oak tree's shape is. She was able to catch up once her sight had been restored. In the same way, a child who learns to walk after an operation at 3 years of age can 'catch up' on learning about walking and what it involves.

Optimal, Sensitive and Best Times

Rather than critical periods, it seems much more likely that there are **optimal** times, **best** times or **sensitive** times in the child's development for learning to talk, walk, ride a bike, draw, sort out right from wrong, and so on.

Children who for any reason are held back from development during these sensitive or best times for learning have more difficulty becoming skilled in these areas later on. However, this does not always mean that they cannot catch up after the best time has passed.

These optimal times usually last for a number of months, except in the case of the critical time for the baby's development *in utero* (in the womb). Once born, it is as if nature has designed children so that there is plenty of time to learn things at every stage of their development. This is why it is so important not to rush children in their learning.

While it is never too late to catch up, bear in mind that it does seem to get harder and harder once the sensitive period is missed. It is easier for babies to learn about holding rattles and toys in their hands than it is for a 3- or 4-year-old. You should understand that it will take more time to introduce such skills to the older child.

Early is not Always Best

The existence of 'optimum periods' does not mean that 'early is best' for young children. In fact, neuroscientists think that a window of opportunity for a particular area of development is also a period of great *vulnerability* for the child's development in that area. Those working with children need to develop the skill of observing children in enough detail to support them at the optimal or best moment for development, whenever this should come. This means not pushing children to do things too early, and it also means not waiting for maximum signs of 'readiness' until it is rather late for children to attempt things – the window may have passed.

✳ Children who are pushed on in advance of optimal times of development usually survive, but can also 'burn out' by 8 or 9 years of age. When children are being pushed to do academic work (reading, writing and number work) too early and too fast, they can be put off school. This pushing of children is sometimes called **intellectual abuse** (see Chapter 9).

* Children who are held back during optimal times of development through lack of stimulation also usually survive, but often suffer low self-esteem because they cannot do things. They lack the competence and skill which they know they need. In an extreme form, this lack of stimulation is sometimes called **intellectual neglect** (see Chapter 9).

* Children who are helped appropriately, at their optimal or best times of development, in a stimulating environment by people who are sensitive and observant of what an individual child can manage (regardless of norms and average ages for doing things) usually do better than survive. They burgeon and flourish in their own unique way. Malaguzzi, the Italian who pioneered the **Reggio Emilia Approach**, calls these 'rich' children.

Adults working with young children need to know about child development so that they are informed enough to use their observations of children to encourage them into appropriate activity at the appropriate point of development: not too early, not too late, but just right. Because development is uneven and each child is a unique person, different from everyone else in the world, each child will need what is 'just right' *for them*. What helps one child will not necessarily help another. Different children need different sorts of help in learning.

CASE STUDY

Tom and Hannah

Tom and Hannah, both from the same family, needed completely different help. At 6 years of age, Tom, the second child in the family, liked his parents and older sister to read stories to him at bedtime. He enjoyed quite different stories from his sister, especially *The Tales of Narnia* by C.S. Lewis. He showed no interest in looking at the book. He preferred to lie down and listen before he settled down to sleep. Tom did enjoy looking at non-fiction books about beetles and bugs. He would willingly look up pictures of spiders, ladybirds and ants to identify the creatures he found in the garden. He would read the short sentences describing them – this was his way in to reading, rather than being read to.

Hannah, when she was 6 years of age, liked to find books that she could read easily. She would read these aloud to her parents at bedtime. She also liked to read them to her younger brother, Tom, who was then 4 years old. She read books like *Spot*. Then she wanted her parents to take a turn at reading, asking them to read books that were too difficult for her to read on her own. She liked to sit and follow the text as a parent read to her. In this way, Hannah began to fill in bits of reading and even to take over from the adult when she could manage it. She felt in control when tackling more difficult texts and did not lose the flow of the story because the adult took over as soon as she stopped reading.

Guidelines for thinking about child development

1 Children are whole people. It can be useful to focus on one area of development (e.g. communication and language), but it is not useful to isolate thinking about one aspect from thinking about the whole child's development.

2 Children seem to go through the same sequences of development but will vary in the exact way that they do.

3 Milestones can be very misleading for the reason outlined in point 2 above. Children with disabilities or gifted/talented children (children with a great talent or intellectual gift, for example in dance, music or mathematics) may not be 'normal' in the way they go through a sequence.

4 Cultural differences mean that norms vary across the world in terms of what young children are expected to do at different points. For example, in some cultures children are expected to speak only one language, while in others they are expected to speak several languages from the moment they can form words.

5 Normative development tends to make us compare children with each other. It is also important to compare the child with his or her own previous development. We mustn't forget to ask 'Is this good progress for this particular child?'

ACTIVITY: ASPECTS OF DEVELOPMENT

When you have looked at these milestones of normative development, turn to Figure 2.2.

1 Now draw seven circles with the same diameter.

2 Cut them out.

3 Write in the aspects of development.

4 Thread the circles on a string.

5 Bunch them together to remind yourself that these are seven parts of a whole.

6 Spread them out to focus on one aspect of the child, but return them to the whole at the end.

ACTIVITY: REMEMBERING OUR LEARNING

Think back to your own schooldays. Were any of the lessons based on a transmission model of learning? Evaluate your learning experience.

ACTIVITY: A SCALE OF NORMATIVE DEVELOPMENT

Make your own scale of normative development, trying to make it as holistic as possible. Apply it in each of the four following ways. In each case, ask yourself this question: 'Do I know this child better than I did before, and in what ways?'

1 Observe a baby girl and then, in a different family, a baby boy. Both children should be 6–9 months in age. Use the circles activity above and the holistic child development chart (Figure 2.2) in this chapter to find out everything you can about the children under those headings.

2 Observe a boy toddler of 15–20 months in age. Again, use the circles activity and the holistic child development chart.

3 Observe two 3- to 4-year-olds and repeat exercise 1. Choose children from different cultural backgrounds, with different language backgrounds, or observe one child with a disability and one without. Remember, it is not useful to do this just to see if children are behind or ahead of 'norms'. Instead, you are using guidelines to help you to build up a complete picture of each child. Then you can see where help is needed, and how to facilitate and extend each child's development and learning.

4 Observe two 5–7-year-olds in the same spirit.

THE DIFFERENCE BETWEEN DEVELOPMENT AND LEARNING

It is important to be clear about the difference between development and learning.

✳ **Development** is about the general way in which a child *functions* biologically.

Example: Matthew (2 years old) can run and jump. He cannot hop or skip yet. He runs across spaces. He jumps to music. Matthew's development is spontaneous, and depends on his physical progress, his ability to think about a concept of 'hop' or 'skip', his mood, and whether he has seen someone else hop or skip.

✳ **Learning** is *provoked*. Learning occurs in a specific situation, at a specific moment, or when a specific problem needs to be tackled. People help children to learn by creating environments and atmospheres which promote learning and bring about development.

Example: Matthew is taken to the fair, where he learns to jump in a new way – on an inflatable castle. Most of the learning children do happens while they are developing. We don't even notice that they are learning. It is one of nature's safety mechanisms. It is actually difficult to stop children learning as long as they are with people who encourage their general development – for example, if the adult knows and understands that 2-year-olds need to run and jump.

Children are held back in their learning if they are not allowed to develop. There have been tragic instances of this in the orphanages of Romania, where children who have been left sitting in a cot all day have been held back intellectually because their general development has not been allowed to move forward. This example shows that an unstimulating environment can hold back development.

It is important to take care that children with disabilities are not held back in their learning just because their general development is constrained in some way. For example, the child with a hearing impairment needs to communicate, otherwise learning about relating to other people will be held back. Use of facial expression, gestures, sign language and finger spelling, as well as a hearing aid and help with lip-reading, will all help the child's general development. The child can then, in particular situations, communicate, and learn to think and socialise.

WHAT IS A THEORY OF CHILD DEVELOPMENT?

A theory of child development is someone's idea about how a child might develop. Theories help people to predict, for example, that before children talk, they usually babble. Theories about how children develop are products of research and so are influenced by the culture in which they are thought out. Research by human beings provides all the evidence for and against various theories of child development. It is very important to remember this, because humans are not objective, they agree and disagree. You must realise that there is no such thing as 'the truth' about child development. We always need to stop and ask: who is doing the research? Who is formulating the theory?

Two examples illustrate this point:

1   The child psychologist **Vygotsky** (1896–1935) grew up in the Soviet Union, where Marxist and Communist ideas dominated. He came from a large family. Is it coincidence that his theory emphasises social relationships and the community?

2   The psychologist **Piaget** (1896–1980) grew up in Europe. He was an only child. Is it coincidence that his theory emphasises the child as an individual and as an active learner trying to experiment and solve problems?

Using Theories in your Work

You need to have an open mind and to look at various different theories, bringing together those ideas that are useful from each so that you can use them in your work. Some theories will help you to make predictions about a child's learning. You need to see where theories like those of Vygotsky and Piaget are the same and where they are different.

Sometimes the differences between theories are so big that it is not possible to use them together. But, as with Piaget's and Vygotsky's work, they are often very similar. This means they can be blended into a useful template for our work with children. Both theories help us to look at how children learn.

THEORIES OF CHILD DEVELOPMENT AND LEARNING

Two Groups of Theories

Historically, theories of child development have tended to fall into one of two groups. Some theories take the view that learning is closely linked with development. Examples of this type of theory are '**leave it to nature**' theories and **social constructivist** theories. The other group of theories dismisses the importance of a child's development as the basis of learning. These theories follow the transmission model which says that children learn what they are shown by adults.

When describing how children learn, therefore, it is important to say which theory is being used. In the following section, we will look first at transmission theories, and then at 'leave it to nature' and social constructivist theories.

Transmission Models of Learning

In the seventeenth century the British philosopher John Locke thought that children were like lumps of clay, which adults could mould into the shape they wanted. At the beginning of the twentieth century in the USA a psychologist, Watson, and the Russian psychologist **Pavlov** were developing similar theories about how people learn. In the past, these theories have had a strong influence on thinking about development.

Classical Conditioning

Ivan Petrovich **Pavlov** (1849–1936) experimented with conditioned responses in dogs. He liked to be described as a

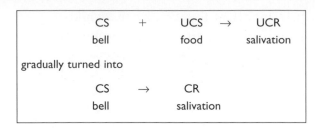

Fig 2.3 A summary of Pavlov's experiment

physiologist, rather than as a psychologist, because he believed that psychological states (such as conditioning) are identical to physiological states and processes in the brain. He thought this approach was useful and scientific. In his experiments, there was a neutral **conditioned stimulus** (CS) which was a church bell ringing. This was paired with food which was an **unconditioned stimulus** (UCS). The dogs were fed when the church bells rang. This produced an **unconditioned response** (UCR), which was saliva flowing in the dog's mouth when the food appeared. Gradually, the sound of any bell would

Table 2.6 The advantages and disadvantages of transmission models of learning

Advantages	Disadvantages
✳ Adults feel secure. They feel that they know what to teach children about different subjects, behaviour, etc. ✳ They can make up ways of testing children in order to check what they have learned. ✳ They can see if children are doing things properly (i.e. are doing what adults think children should do). ✳ This approach produces quick success, which makes adults feel they are good teachers. ✳ It makes children who succeed in performing adults' tasks feel that they are good learners, who can perform as adults require them to do.	✳ Adults think they know what they have taught children. In fact the child might have learned something quite different. Example: the child might stop hitting a younger child in front of the adult; but they may have learned that they can still hit the younger child – but not when an adult can see them doing it. ✳ This approach encourages children to be passive receivers of the learning that adults think is important for them; but they are not likely to want to attempt something new and also less likely to take risks in case they make mistakes. ✳ Children will only want to do things if they think they can do it successfully and get it right. ✳ The child's learning is controlled by the adult. This quickly leads to a narrow approach to the curriculum. ✳ Children are likely to be labelled as poor learners, or even as failures, if they do not complete adult tasks and tests in the way the adult wants. ✳ The approach undermines creativity and imagination.

Fig 2.4 Pavlov's dog: an illustrated summary of the experiment

CASE STUDY

An example of learning through classical conditioning

Year-2 children (aged 6 and 7) in a primary school were working in groups. One group was painting. Another was writing. Another was involved in a maths game. Another was cooking. The school bell rang. Immediately, the children stopped what they were doing and started to tidy up quickly and go out to play. The children were conditioned to expect playtime when the bell sounded, so they tidied up in readiness. They would have tidied up even if they had not been allowed subsequently to go out to play.

bell (conditioned stimulus) + playtime (unconditioned stimulus) = tidy up (unconditioned response)

bell (conditioned stimulus) = tidy up (conditioned response)

produce a conditioned response in the dogs, which would produce saliva ready for the food that usually accompanied the ringing of the bell.

Classical conditioning is the way in which responses come under the control of a new stimulus. In this case, food normally produces salivation. Classical conditioning changes the stimulus, so that the sound of a bell produces salivation. Pavlov would have fed the dogs whether or not they salivated at the sound of the bell.

Operant Conditioning

Burrhus Frederic **Skinner** (1905–1990) was a behavioural psychologist who worked in the USA. He did not believe it was useful to theorise about mental states that could not be observed. He thought this was unscientific.

Whereas Pavlov fed his dogs when the bell rang whether or not they salivated, Skinner only fed his rats or pigeons if they did as he required. For example, he gave rats a reward of food if they pressed a lever. This was positive reinforcement: the desired behaviour was rewarded. Conversely, undesired behaviour could be negatively reinforced. For example, the rats might receive an electric shock each time they went near one area of a maze. They would then begin to avoid that area. The undesired behaviour was extinguished and the desired behaviour was encouraged.

Chris Rice is a lecturer in early childhood courses at Clydebank College in Scotland. This is how she explains positive and negative reinforcement.

Positive and Negative Reinforcement

If behaving in a certain way leads to a pleasing outcome, then the behaviour will be repeated. For example, a baby points to a toy monkey and looks at the adult. The adult hands her the toy, making appropriate monkey noises which they both find funny. The baby then repeats the behaviour with other objects in order to be similarly amused (**positive reinforcement**).

Negative reinforcement is concerned with a child behaving in a particular way in order to avoid something unpleasant, to stop pain or to prevent discomfort. For example, the baby cries because she has a wet nappy and feels uncomfortable. The adult responds by changing the nappy and the baby feels better. The next time she feels discomfort she will repeat the behaviour (that is repeat the crying) in order to stop the unpleasant feeling.

A **reinforcer** causes the behaviour to be repeated – it may be some form of reward for showing a desired behaviour or something that is linked to the avoidance of unpleasantness or pain. In the positive reinforcement example, the monkey noises are the reinforcer – the entertaining reward for asking for the toy. In the negative reinforcement example, getting a nappy change is the reinforcer – the reward for crying. In both these situations, the baby is learning that a certain behaviour will elicit a certain response from other people. As long as these responses occur, she will **repeat the behaviour**. If the adult ignores the behaviour instead of rewarding it, it will stop eventually (extinction).

Another example of negative reinforcement would be that while playing in the water tray, a toddler may try to take a jug from another child. Neither child will let go and both will look to the nearest adult, with cries of distress to get attention. If, in the past, this has led to a satisfactory conclusion – the adult finding a bottle which one child accepts as a substitute – the children will repeat the behaviour in the future.

Bribery and Behaviour Shaping

Bribery is quite different to **behaviour shaping** or **behaviour modification**. We might want a child to put away the floor puzzle that she has been working on and which is spread all over the floor. If we tell her she can have a sweet if she tidies it up, this *is* bribery. The child, understandably, feels she is being given a choice and weighs up the behaviour against the reward. Is it worth it? She may decide it is not – and she will be baffled if the adult is displeased with her choice. (Older children may see this as an opportunity to negotiate, asking for two sweets!) With bribery, the child learns that the point of the behaviour is to please the adult and gain the reward, in this case a sweet – not to ensure that all the pieces of the puzzle are stored safely for another time.

In behaviour shaping or modification, there is no 'if' and no mention of reward. The reinforcer comes only *after* the behaviour has appeared, usually in a way that is linked to the behaviour. 'Well done,' the adult might say, 'you have tidied that up quickly'.

The only time, when using behaviour shaping, that there is any mention of future outcome is in terms of what will be happening next, for example, 'When everyone is sitting quietly, then we can start the story'.

Punishment

Just as positive reinforcement must not be confused with bribery, negative reinforcement must not be confused with punishment. Ignoring undesirable behaviour (leading to extinction), together with clear and consistent reinforcement of desired behaviour, is more effective than punishment.

Problems with Behaviourist Techniques

It is important that adults are very clear about their purpose if they use these techniques:

* What behaviour is to be extinguished?
* What behaviour does the adult want to increase?

The adult must make sure that what they intend is what actually happens, and that the child does not pick up an entirely different message. For example, a child may learn that, if he says sorry within an adult's hearing and quickly enough after hitting another child, he may avoid punishment irrespective of whether or not he has any feelings of remorse.

Often, adults ignore children when they are behaving appropriately, only giving them attention when they are disruptive. However, children need to realise the advantages (enjoyment and satisfaction) of cooperating with others in different situations, so that enjoyment and satisfaction become the reinforcers. Other kinds of reward are not then necessary.

Leave it to Nature: a Laissez-faire Model

In the eighteenth century the French philosopher Jean Jacques Rousseau thought that children learned naturally, and that they were biologically programmed to learn particular things at a particular time. He thought that just as a flower unfolds through the bud, so a child's learning unfolds – for example, babbling leads into language and then on into reading and writing, and kicking the arms and legs leads to crawling and walking.

In this approach, adults help children to learn by making sure that the environment supports the child's learning as it unfolds. For example, children learn the language that

Table 2.7 Operant conditioning

Subject	Behaviour	Reinforcer	Outcome
child	has tantrum in supermarket	GETS sweets	POSITIVE REINFORCEMENT –
salesperson	meets sales target	GETS bonus	
teenager	pushes over old woman in street	GETS money from handbag	
dog	sits up and begs	GETS food	BEHAVIOUR WILL BE REPEATED
baby	points to toy	GETS toy handed to her	
holidaymaker	puts on suntan oil	AVOIDS sunburn	
tutor with headache	takes aspirin	STOPS headache	
driver	slows down before speed camera	AVOIDS speeding ticket	NEGATIVE REINFORCEMENT –
student	hands medical certificate in	AVOIDS losing bursary	
baby with wet nappy	cries	STOPS discomfort (adult changes nappy)	BEHAVIOUR WILL BE REPEATED
neighbour	complains about loud music next door	STOPS noise	

(With permission from Chris Rice, Clydebank College)

they hear spoken as they grow up. If children hear Chinese, they learn to speak Chinese. If they hear English, they learn to speak English. If children hear more than one language, they are able to learn more than one language and become bilingual or multilingual. This model of learning suggests that children are naturally programmed to learn languages.

This view of learning suggests that children naturally do as they need in order to develop and learn. It sees children as active in their own learning. Children may be helped by other people or may learn on their own. Because adults need not act, according to this theory, it is sometimes referred to as a laissez-faire view of how children learn.

Arnold Gesell

In the 1930s Arnold Gesell mapped out some norms of development (normative measurement was discussed earlier in this chapter). These were used to chart milestones in the child's development as it unfolded. Gesell believed that normal development progressed according to a set sequence. His milestones could be used to check that the pattern of development was 'normal'. Gesell's developmental scales looked at motor, adaptive, language and personal-social areas. If children reached particular milestones, such as walking, within the 'normal' age range, then their development was said to be making 'normal' progress. This approach is depressing if used with children with special educational needs as they are constantly labelled 'abnormal'.

Sigmund Freud, Anna Freud and Melanie Klein

Sigmund Freud (1856–1939) did not concentrate very much on the development of the youngest children. However, his daughter Anna Freud did, and so did Melanie Klein who was working at the same time as Anna Freud. **Anna Freud** and **Melanie Klein** were both nativists.

Sigmund Freud and later psychoanalysts – such as Anna, her student Erikson and Klein – argued that development in children unfolds quite naturally. They also thought that when children suffer trauma, they can be helped to find self-healing forces by being given as normal a childhood as possible and by experiencing loving relationships. They believed in the power of love, security, play and interesting experiences, as well as in being valued. A few children may need additional help through therapy.

Anna Freud did her work with children in Nazi Germany but had to escape to England with her father. Later on, in Hampstead, she cared for children who had survived concentration camps in Nazi Germany. There is now a museum in Hampstead which honours her work with children, and the Anna Freud Centre which works with children and their families.

Sigmund Freud emphasised the unconscious mind (unlike Pavlov and Skinner, who both emphasised observable behaviour). Freud believed that:

* our unconscious minds influence the way we behave;
* our early experiences cause later adult behaviour;
* symbolic behaviour is important, and he tried to interpret dreams.

Freud linked thinking, feeling, and sexual and social relationships with early physical behaviour, such as breastfeeding, toilet training and separation from parents.

The Social Constructivist/ Interactionist Approach

In the eighteenth century the German philosopher Immanuel Kant believed that a

CASE STUDY

An example of learning through a 'leave it to nature' approach

Because most children of around 3 to 4 years of age begin to enjoy drawing and painting, the rooms in a nursery school were set up to support this. Great care was taken in the way that a variety of colours were put out in pots, with a choice of thick and thin paint brushes. Children could choose paper of different sizes. A drying rack was close

to the area and children could choose to paint at a table or on an easel.

Adults would be on hand to help if needed, but would be careful not to talk to children while they were painting, in case they cut across the children's thinking. Adults would not 'make' children paint, because not all children would be ready to do so. Readiness is important in this approach to learning.

child's learning was an interaction between the developing child and the environment. He said that children constructed their own understanding and knowledge about things. The approach is called a **social constructivist** view of how children learn. This model:

* is the approach currently most favoured by early years workers;

* has the best support from research into child development in the Western world;

* draws on both the transmission model and the laissez-faire (leave it to nature) model of a child's learning, rearranging elements of both into something that is helpful to those working with children.

Piaget, Vygotsky and Bruner all used a social constructivist/interactionist approach and their work is discussed below.

Jean Piaget (1896–1980)

The important elements of Piaget's theory of how children learn are that:

* children go through stages and sequences in their learning;

* children are active learners;

* children use first-hand experiences and prior experiences in order to learn;

* children imitate and transform what they learn into symbolic behaviour.

Piaget did not explicitly emphasise the importance of social and emotional aspects of learning and he did not dwell on social relationships as much as the other social constructivists. This means he took social and emotional development for granted and he did not write about it in detail. Instead, his writing emphasises intellectual/cognitive development and learning. Piaget's theory is called **constructivist** (rather than social constructivist) for this reason.

Lev Vygotsky (1896–1935)

Vygotsky stressed the importance for development of someone who knows more than the child and who can help the child to learn something that would be too difficult for the child to do on his or her own. Vygotsky described:

* the **zone of potential development**, sometimes called the zone of proximal development. It means that the child can do with help *now* what it will be

Table 2.8 Advantages and disadvantages of the 'leave it to nature' view of development and learning

Advantages	Disadvantages
* Adults can learn about how to offer the right physical resources, activities and equipment for each stage of development. * Children can actively make choices, select, be responsible, explore, try things out and make errors without incurring reproach or a feeling of failure. * Adults value observing children and act in the light of their observations. This might mean adding more materials, and having conversations with children to help them learn more. * Adults are able to follow the child's lead and be sensitive to the child.	* Adults may hold back too much because they are nervous of damaging the child's natural development: for example, by not talking to a child while she is drawing or by holding back from playing with children. * Adults only support children in their learning, rather than extending the learning children do. * Children might be understimulated because adults are waiting for signs of readiness in the child. The signs might never come! Adults wait too long before intervening. * Children might not be shown how to do things in case it is not the right moment developmentally to teach them, which leaves them without skills. * Children with special educational needs or from different cultures might be labelled 'abnormal' or 'unready'. In fact, they might reach a milestone earlier or later, but still within the normal sequence. They might develop unevenly but in ways which make 'normal' life possible. Milestones in one culture might be different in another culture.

possible for him or her to do alone with no help *later in life*;

* the **importance of play** for children under 7 years. Play allows children to do things beyond what they can manage in actual life (such as pretend to drive a car). It is another way through which children reach their zone of potential development;

* the **zone of actual development**. This is what the child can manage without help from anyone.

Vygotsky believed **social relationships** are at the heart of a child's learning, So his theory is called a social constructivist theory. Barbara Rogoff (1997) has extended Vygotsky's work and writes about the way adults and toddlers co-construct their learning; they each learn from each other.

Jerome Bruner (b. 1915)

The essence of Bruner's theory is that children learn through:

* **doing** (the **enactive** mode of learning);

* **imaging** things that they have done (the **iconic** mode of learning);

* making what they know into **symbolic codes**, e.g. talking, writing or drawing (the **symbolic** mode of learning).

Adults can tutor children and help them to learn. They do this by 'scaffolding' what the child is learning in order to make it manageable for the child. This means that children can learn any subject at any age. They simply need to be given the right kind of help. For example, when a baby drops a biscuit over the side of the high chair, the baby can learn about gravity if the adult 'scaffolds' the experience by saying something like: 'It dropped straight down on to the floor, didn't it? Let's both drop a biscuit and see if they get to the floor together.' Bruner's theory is also called a social constructivist theory, as social relationships are central to 'scaffolding'.

THE NATURE–NURTURE DEBATE

The nature–nurture debate is concerned with the extent to which development and learning are primarily to do with the child's

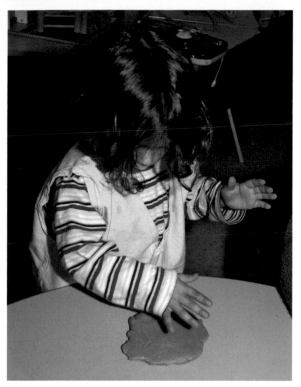

Fig 2.5 Using dough to express feelings

natural maturing processes, and the extent to which development and learning progress as a result of experience.

The debate has been very fierce, and it is not over yet. Modern psychologists such as Sir Michael Rutter believe that the child's learning is probably about 60 per cent nature and 40 per cent nurture. Neuroscientists, such as Colin Blakemore, stress the importance of relationships (nurture), and how these actually cause the brain to change and be altered physically. What do you think, now that you have read this chapter?

We can think about the developmental theories in terms of nature and nurture:

* The transmission approach stresses experience and nurture.

* The 'leave it to nature' approach stresses maturation and nature.

CASE STUDY

An example of a social constructivist/interactionist view of development and learning

Using a team approach to record-keeping in an early years setting, staff had built up observations of children. They noted that Damian (5 years) kept punching; he punched other children, furniture and other objects. It seemed to be his main way of exploring.

The staff decided to introduce activities which allowed punching:

* They put huge lumps of clay on the table.

* They made bread and encouraged energetic kneading.

* They sang songs like 'Clap your hands and stamp your feet' and 'Hands, knees and bumps-a-daisy'.

* They encouraged vigorous hand printing and finger painting.

* They helped children to choreograph dance fights when acting out a story.

* Damian told the group about 'baddies' from another planet.

* He helped to 'beat' the carpet with a beater as part of spring cleaning.

* He spent a long time at the wood-work bench hammering nails into his model. He soon stopped hitting other children, and began to talk about what he was doing in the activities with adults and other children.

Observation enabled adults to support Damian's learning in educationally worthwhile ways. Adults were also able to extend his learning so that hitting people stopped and became learning to hit in a rich variety of ways that didn't hurt anyone.

* The social constructivist approach to learning stresses both nature and nurture. A modern way of describing this is to say that both the biological and sociocultural paths of development are important for learning.

(The nature–nurture debate is discussed in more detail in Chapter 6.)

ADULTS' LEARNING

Remember, theories about learning are not just about how children learn; they are about how adults learn too. Adults who enjoy learning and being with children are much more likely to provide a high-quality early childhood setting for children and their families. When a setting is described as demonstrating good practice, or high-quality practice, it is usually seen that adults and children are *both* active in their learning.

Chomsky: Language Acquisition Device

Noam Chomsky's theory is described as nativist. It supposes that humans are born with a special biological brain mechanism, called a **Language Acquisition Device** (LAD) although Chomsky now refers to it as *universal grammar*. Chomsky believed that:

* the ability to learn language is inborn (or innate);

* **nature** is more important than **nurture**; and

* experience using language is only necessary in order to activate the LAD.

Chomsky argues that language is not learned – rather, that this innate knowledge about the basic principles of language allows the child to 'decode' the stream of sounds coming from others – turning that stream into a set of rules for a specific language.

Table 2.9 Advantages and disadvantages of the social constructivist/interactionist view of learning

Advantages	Disadvantages
* This approach is very rewarding and satisfying because adults and children can enjoy working together, struggling at times, concentrating hard, stretching their thinking and ideas, celebrating their learning, and sharing the learning together. * Trusting each other to help when necessary creates a positive relationship between children, parents and staff. It means taking pride in the way that indoor and outdoor areas of the room are set up, organised, maintained and cared for. * It means teamwork by the adults, which is the way to bring out everyone's strengths in a multiprofessional group of teachers and early years workers. * It means sharing with parents and children all the learning that is going on. * It means adults need to go on learning about children's development. When adults continue to develop as people and professionals, learning alongside children, they have more to offer the children. * Adults and children respect and value each other's needs and rights, and help each other to learn. * Although it takes time, training and experience for adults to build up skills for working in this way, it is very effective in helping children to learn during their early years.	* It is very hard work compared with the other two approaches to learning that we have looked at in this chapter. This is because there is much more for adults to know about, more to think about, more to organise and do. * It is much more difficult for those who are not trained to understand how to work in this way. * In Sweden there are now local plazzas where early years workers explain the way they work to parents, those working with older children, governing bodies and politicians.

Guidelines for using the different approaches to development and learning

1   Figure 2.6 shows that in a 'leave it to nature' approach to learning, children make a very high contribution to the learning they do, but adults hold back and take a very small part.

2   This is very different from the transmission model. In this approach the adult has a very high input into the child's learning and takes a high level of control. The child's contribution is quite low.

3   The 'by-the-book' approach to learning is not valuable and has not been covered in this chapter. Here, both the adults and the children have a very low level of participation. It is not really an approach to learning; it is just a way of keeping children occupied. Worksheets, colouring in, tracing, templates, filling in gaps, joining the dots all fall under this heading.

4   In the social constructivist (sometimes called 'interactionist') approach to learning both the adult and the children put an enormous amount of energy into active learning.

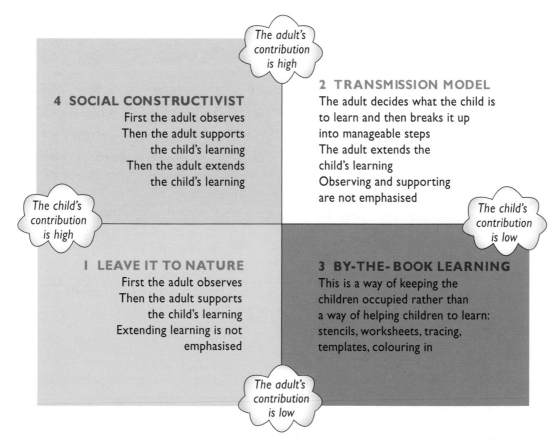

Fig 2.6 The four approaches to development and learning

The main contribution of Chomsky's work has been to show that children's language development is much more complex than the behaviourist theory, which supposed that children learn language merely by being rewarded for imitating. This theory has been criticised as not taking enough account of the influence that thought (cognition) and language have on each other's development.

Margaret Donaldson

Margaret Donaldson, a child psychologist, undertook groundbreaking research which made us look at Piaget's research in a completely new way. She showed that when children are involved in everyday situations which have meaning for them because they are in a familiar context, they can function at higher levels of thinking than when they are in a laboratory or test situation. Her work concentrates on 2- to 7-year-olds, yet her ideas about child development have practical implications for all age groups. She says that learning must make human sense if thinking is to be at the highest level a child can manage.

Donaldson introduced the term '**disembedded thought**', which is equivalent to formal, abstract thinking. She particularly emphasises the ability of a child to place a task in a socially meaningful context. If a situation is disembedded from a natural environment it will be more difficult to solve by children. The children will understand things much better if they are presented in a natural and familiar setting.

EPPE (THE EFFECTIVE PROVISION OF PRE-SCHOOL EDUCATION)

This project, chaired by Kathy Sylva, Professor of Educational Psychology at the University of Oxford, set out to investigate:

* What is the impact of pre-school on young children's intellectual and social/behavioural development?

* Are some pre-schools more effective than others?

* What is the impact of home and child-care history (before age 3) on children's development?

* Can pre-school experience reduce social inequalities?

The key findings of the report, published in 2003, were:

Impact of Attending an Early Years Setting

* Pre-school experience, compared to none, enhances children's development.

* The duration of attendance is important with an earlier start being related to better intellectual development and improved independence, concentration and sociability.

* Full-time attendance led to no better gains for children than part-time provision.

* Disadvantaged children in particular can benefit significantly from good-quality pre-school experiences, especially if they attend centres that cater for a mixture of children from different social backgrounds.

The Quality of Practices in Early Childhood Settings

* The quality of pre-school centres is directly related to better intellectual/cognitive and social/behavioural development in children.

* Good quality can be found across all types of early years settings. However quality was higher overall in integrated settings, nursery schools and nursery classes.

✳ Settings which have staff with higher qualifications, especially with a good proportion of trained teachers on the staff, show higher quality and their children make more progress.

✳ Where settings view educational and social development as complementary and equal in importance, children make better all-round progress.

Effective **pedagogy** includes interaction traditionally associated with the term 'teaching', the provision of instructive learning environments and 'sustained shared thinking' to extend children's learning.

Type of Early Childhood Setting

✳ There are significant differences between individual pre-school settings in their impact on children. Some settings are more effective than other in promoting positive child outcomes.

✳ Children tend to make better intellectual progress in fully integrated centres and nursery schools.

The Importance of Home Learning

The quality of the learning environment of the home (where parents are actively engaged in activities with children) promoted intellectual and social development in all children. Although parents' social class and levels of education were related to child outcomes the quality of the **home learning environment** was more important. The home learning environment is only moderately associated with social class. What parents do is more important than who they are.

ACTIVITY: MODELS OF LEARNING

Make a chart with these three headings:

✳ Transmission model of learning;

✳ Laissez-faire or 'leave it to nature' model of learning;

✳ Social constructivist or interactionist model of learning.

Which sentences go under which heading?

1 Adults should mould children's learning. After all, adults know more than children.

2 Children know what they need in order to learn.

3 Do you want to have a story first, or tidy up first?

4 We need to tidy up, we'll have the story after.

5 Children are full of ideas if they are encouraged to have them.

6 Do it because I say so.

7 That child has been 'off task' all morning.

8 Children are born with everything they need in order to learn.

9 Children enjoy conversations with adults.

10 Children must be free to try things out.

11 Children will learn when they are ready and not before.

12 That child performed the task successfully today.

13 Nature knows best.

14 Adults know best.

15 Children must be free to try things out and to learn from the mistakes they make.

Compare your answers with those of a working partner. Discuss your answers together.

CHAPTER 3
Cognitive Development

Contents

STAGES AND SEQUENCE OF COGNITIVE DEVELOPMENT FROM BIRTH TO 16 YEARS

In recent years there has been strong criticism of the view that children develop in stages which are narrowly defined according to their age. This means that the frequently used phrase, that children develop according to age and stage, is now out of date. But children do develop sequentially. They sit before they walk, and they walk before they jump. They jump before they hop, and they hop before they skip. Some children do not crawl, but, interestingly, research shows that they might be more likely to experience difficulties later in learning to read and write. The ages at which children do these things varies enormously, depending on where they grow up in the world, heredity, whether they are given opportunities which encourage their development, and whether they have special educational needs or disabilities. Although the sequence of sitting, then walking, then jumping, hopping and skipping is common to most humans, the way we walk, and so on, is completely unique – just like our fingerprints. (see Learning and Development, **EYFS**, and also A Unique Child - Child Development.)

IDEAS AND THINKING

Intellectual or cognitive development (the development of thinking and ideas) cannot be separated from all the other areas of development. The ideas children have are emotional, physically experienced and can be shared with other people. Thinking is social, emotional, physical and cultural, and it involves the moral and spiritual aspects of development too. It is deeply linked with communication and language, and with the way symbolic behaviours of all kinds develop, for example art, music, mathematics and dance.

CONCENTRATION AND ATTENTION

Children concentrate best when they find something interesting. Even children who have an attention deficit (a problem concentrating) will concentrate much more when they have:

* a choice of activities;

* an adult who helps them to do things that interest them – children can manage to do things which they could not do alone if an adult is supporting them;

* enjoyment in what they do – laughter and play, according to experts, help to

develop the brain's ability to work well (one expert even believes that play and laughter fertilise the brain!).

Measuring Concentration and the Child's Involvement

The Effective Early Learning Project (EEL), directed by Christine Pascal and Tony Bertram, uses two observation scales which help staff working with young children to find out how deeply the children are concentrating.

1   The **Leuven Involvement Scale**: this helps adults to discover whether children are involved in what they are doing in a creative and deep way, whether they are only superficially involved and can be easily distracted, or whether they are not involved at all.

2   The **Adult–Child Engagement Scale**: this helps adults to look at what they are providing for the children and to see whether they are being helpful to children by being sensitive to their needs or by helping them to be autonomous, independent, self-motivated and self-disciplined in what they are doing.

Concentration Problems

If a child does not concentrate or become involved in anything at any point in the day, there may be a reason. The child may:

* be under stress;
* be unwell;
* have learning difficulties or disabilities;
* be tired;
* be poorly nourished;
* have nothing that is interesting to them.

If there is cause for concern, the team will have to observe the child at different times of day, and to note, monitor and assess the child's progress. It may be necessary to seek advice from the child's parents or from other professionals. An action plan to support and help the child's concentration and involvement in their learning will be needed. Often, only minor changes in the way activities are set out, in the way the room is arranged, in the amount of choice given to children or in how much freedom there is to be outdoors can bring about changes in the child's behaviour. Too many adult-led activities and too little freedom of movement are bad for a child's concentration span. See EYFS and 'Creating the Picture' DfES (1. Assessment and Record-Keeping; 2. Including All Children).

INTELLIGENCE – IS IT FIXED OR CAN IT GROW?

Are children born intelligent or not? This is one part of the nature–nurture debate. This has provoked fierce argument. The nature–nurture debate continues and has become a political issue. There are those who believe that people are born intelligent (or not). There are others who feel equally strongly that children's life experiences and the people they meet have a huge influence on how their intelligence develops. The idea that children are born with a fixed amount of intelligence, and that this can be given a score which is measured and which does not change throughout their lives, was not seriously challenged until the 1960s.

Intelligence Can Grow

During the 1960s, Piaget's work made researchers think again about what intelligence is. His theory suggested that intelligence is not fixed and unchangeable – it is not something people are born with or without. His theory suggested that intelligence is plastic. This means it can stretch, grow and increase. The idea that intelligence is plastic has been supported by recent studies in neuroscience. We now think that children can increase their intelligence if they:

* mix with adults and other children who help them to develop their intelligence;

* experience a stimulating environment which encourages thinking and ideas, and emotional intelligence.

IQ TESTS AND COMPENSATORY EDUCATION

Children were often tested in the past to find their IQ (intelligence quotient) using scales such as the Standford–Binet or Merrill–Palmer intelligence tests. Because these tests were developed by white, male psychologists with middle-class ways of looking at life, they favoured white, middle-class, male children, who thus scored higher than other groups of children. It became obvious after the 1944 Education Act that mainly white, middle-class children went to grammar schools, and there were more places in grammar schools for boys than for girls. Children from other groups went to secondary modern schools and technical schools. This began to worry some researchers, who found that IQ tests:

* favour children from the culture from which the tests emerged – this means the tests are not as objective as they were first thought to be;

* measure particular kinds of intelligence, such as memory span and ability with numbers – this means that they only look at intelligence in a narrow way; they do not help us to look at outstanding ability in dancing, music or interpersonal sensitivity, for example.

Multiple Intelligence

The psychologist Howard Gardner says that there are seven kinds of intelligence. He calls this multiple intelligence. The different domains of intelligence proposed by Gardner are:

1 linguistic intelligence;

2 logico-mathematical intelligence;

3 bodily kinaesthetic intelligence;

4 social intelligence;

5 musical intelligence;

6 spatial intelligence;

7 personal intelligence (access to personal feelings and relationships with others).

Howard Gardner believes these seven aspects of intelligence are partly genetic, but are also open to cultural influences, and so can be helped through education. According to Gardner, IQ tests:

* measure only a small part of intelligence;

* often give children labels which are likely to stick, such as 'bright or 'average ability' or 'low ability';

* do not encourage teachers to have high enough expectations of children – a teacher might say 'After all, she's only got an IQ of 80'.

Intelligence tests can be useful as part of a whole barrage of different ways of making an assessment of a child's needs (especially for children with special educational needs). They are not useful, however, when used in isolation from other forms of assessment. A child's motivation (will) to learn is very important. Two children might have the same IQ, but the one with the greater will to learn might do better simply because of this disposition.

CASE STUDY

Fountain Hospital and the Brook Experiment

A group of children with severe learning difficulties were taken from the wards of the Fountain Hospital during the 1960s. They were placed in a stimulating environment of people and first-hand interesting experiences. Their intelligence was found to develop rapidly. This research project was called the Brook Experiment. Research like this led, in 1971, to children with special needs in hospitals and day centres being given, by law, education as well as hospital-type care. Until then, such children, and young people with IQs below 50 on the IQ scale, had been considered ineducable.

Compensatory Education

During the 1960s and 1970s, programmes of compensatory education developed in the USA and the UK. In the USA, these were called the Head Start Programmes, and in the UK a series of research projects was set up under the direction of Albert Halsey, a sociologist. Researchers were beginning to realise that intelligence can grow, and so children who were thought to be growing up in non-stimulating environments were placed on these education programmes. The idea was that a good education would compensate for the poverty and social disadvantage of their lives. However, this view rejected and ignored some important influences on a child's developing intelligence, thinking and understanding:

* It did not put enough emphasis on the language and cultural background of children.

* It did not emphasise the importance of the child's parents and family life.

By contrast, the Froebel Nursery Research Project, directed by Chris Athey in 1972–77, worked in close partnership with parents. The home language of children was respected and valued, and they were offered interesting, real experiences through a quality curriculum. This included:

* cooking;
* play;
* stories and books;
* outdoor play;
* a home area;
* a workshop area with clay, paint, junk modelling and woodwork;
* a graphics area.

The IQs of the children rose, especially the IQs of the younger children who joined the project when they were babies. This project had a long-lasting effect on children's development because it:

* worked in close partnership with parents;
* offered children a stimulating, well-planned environment (i.e. a quality curriculum);
* valued the children's language and culture.

IMAGINATION AND DEVELOPMENT

Intelligence tests favour people who are convergent thinkers – these are people who can give 'correct' answers and who are able to solve questions that are set by the testers. However, intellectual development is also about having imaginative and creative ideas.

What is the Imagination?

Having imagination is about being able to rearrange your past experiences and to put them together to make new ideas. Imaginative people have all sorts of ideas in art (drawing, painting, sculpture), architecture, music, dance, drama, scientific research and mathematics. These people are divergent or creative thinkers. This means they can gather together many different ideas and organise them into a single interesting idea. Imagination is about having new and fascinating ideas.

What is Creativity?

Creative people – children or adults – take an imaginative idea they have had (which is a rearrangement of past experience in new and fascinating ways) and turn it into an act of creation (which is made up of the process of gathering an idea unconsciously, incubating it, becoming aware that something is developing and hatching it into a creation). They might make a dance, devise a recipe for a cake, compose a poem or develop a new scientific theory. (For more detail of what is involved in creativity, see Bruce, *Cultivating Creativity: Babies, Toddlers and Young Children*, 2004.) Marian Whitehead, an expert on the teaching of reading and writing, believes that creativity and the imagination are basic in learning to read and write. Imaginative children read and write with more pleasure and interest. They have imaginative ideas and make (create) stories. (See EYFS, Learning and Development - Creativity and Critical Thinking.)

Barriers to Creativity

Activities which discourage imagination and creativity use:

* templates;
* colouring in;
* tracing;
* the screwed-up-tissue-paper syndrome of filling in a pre-cut outline, colouring in or using stencils.

These activities are all pre-structured by adults and allow almost no opportunity for the children's own ideas and thinking to develop. Such activities are sometimes referred to as 'busy work', but they are low-level ways of keeping children occupied. Children might enjoy doing them, but then they enjoy all sorts of things which are not good for them, such as eating sweets. Templates are not helpful to a child who is becoming creative by developing their own thinking and ideas. In the long term, they can even undermine a child's self-esteem by making them believe that they cannot draw or make things without a template or an outline. Children can become very preoccupied with the 'right' or 'correct' ways of doing things, and they often end up by learning other people's formulas for drawing. This destroys creativity. Children should be encouraged to develop their own style in their drawings and paintings, models, dances and stories. A child who has learnt to become creative might be rather frustrated and even miserable if their creativity is undermined by pre-structured activities.

Guidelines for encouraging imagination and creativity

Young children need support and help if their creativity is to develop well. Imagination and creativity do not arise naturally, although it is true that some children learn about being creative much more easily than others.

* Children need a wide range of material provisions and to be encouraged to use them in lots of different ways.

* Children need plenty of opportunities to represent their ideas. Having an idea of your own and making it come alive is creative.
* Children need plenty of time for their play. They must not be over-organised by adult-led tasks. Play helps them to have imaginative ideas and to turn these into creative pretend play.
* Children learn about becoming creative thinkers through the people they meet and the materials they are encouraged to use.

Being Creative Means Taking Risks

A child who has never 'had a go', taken risks or experimented with different ways of doing things will not become a confident active thinker. Instead, such children only know how to carry out adult instructions or ideas. They do not become imaginative or creative.

CASE STUDY

The importance of play for thinking actively

Dale, 2 years, saw a fireman's hat in the dressing-up clothes. He carried it upside down like a shopping bag, and put his pretend shopping in it. He had never seen a fireman in his uniform, but he knows about shopping. He used the hat to fit the play scenario he had selected to use. He concentrated deeply as he did his 'shopping' and he made flexible (imaginative) use of the helmet, using it as a pretend bag instead of a hat. Play is good for active thinking. (See EYFS Creativity and Critical Thinking – Making Connections.)

THE IMPORTANCE OF PLAY

The strength of play lies in the way it helps children to be agents of their own learning. Children who play are good at choosing and selecting, concentrating with deep focus on what they choose; they are flexible thinkers, who are highly motivated to learn (see Chapter 13).

PROBLEM SOLVING – MAKING HYPOTHESES AND PREDICTIONS

There is a saying: 'Happiness is not the absence of problems. It is being able to solve them.' Children are natural problem solvers from the moment they are born. It used to be thought that there is a rigid developmental sequence by which children learn to solve problems. It was thought that, at first, children tried to solve problems through trial and error, and that only later could they develop a theory or hypothesis. However, more recently researchers have found that even newborn babies can make a hypothesis.

Making a hypothesis means having a theory which can be tested to see if it is right. It is amazing to think that babies can do this. But researchers have found that they do not behave in a trial-and-error way. They do not try random solutions until, by luck, they solve the problem. (See EYFS Creativity and Critical Thinking – Transforming Understanding, Sustained Shared Thinking.)

Making a False Hypothesis

Children aged 2 years and onwards will often make a 'false' or incorrect hypothesis. They can be very obstinate about an idea they have! Experts think that finding out that a hypothesis is wrong is a very important part of learning to solve problems. In order to learn about problem solving, children need to test out their false or wrong hypotheses, as well as correct and true ones.

CASE STUDY

Jo

Jo was given a card with the outline of a butterfly on it. She was asked to fill in the outline with pieces of screwed-up coloured tissue paper. She cried. She found a piece of paper and made her own picture. She made a path through a wood. This was an imaginative idea and a creative piece of work. The butterfly would only have been a low-level piece of 'busy work'. The butterfly cards were going to be given to mothers as Mother's Day cards. The family worker explained to Jo's mother why Jo's card was different. Mum was pleased that her daughter had been so creative and did not mind the fact that Jo's card did not look so good. The imaginative thinking that went into the card and the creative result were far more important than how it looked. (See EYFS Creativity and Critical Thinking – Making Connections.)

CASE STUDY

Baby makes a hypothesis

Every time a newborn baby heard a buzzer and turned towards it, the baby would find a honeyed dummy to suck on. Every time a bell rang, the baby would turn towards it, but would not find a honeyed dummy (this experiment took place in the 1970s; as evidence now shows that honey is dangerous to babies under 1 year old, it would need consideration if undertaken now). Soon the baby only turned for the buzzer. Once the baby had made the hypothesis that the buzzer signified honey and the bell did not, the baby felt the problem had been solved. The hypothesis the baby had made was correct. Soon it became boring to keep solving the same old problem repeatedly, and so the baby would not do it over and over again. The baby's interest was to solve the problem rather than to get the honey. Once the hypothesis was found to be correct and the problem was solved, there was no reason to carry on with this activity.

Newborn babies can hypothesise and make theories to solve such problems even when they are only a few hours old. (See EYFS Creativity and Critical Thinking – Transforming Understanding.)

CASE STUDY

Segun's hypothesis

Segun (4 years) saw some paint which glowed in the dark. His mother told him (wrongly) that it was called fluorescent paint. He asked his mother for some fluorescent paint. Having painted the stone owl from the garden, Segun put it in his bed so that it would glow in the dark. It did not glow in the dark! He then painted all sorts of stones from the garden. He put these in his bed each night. They did not glow in the dark either! Next he painted sticks from the garden and put them on his bed each night. They did not glow in the dark!

Segun's uncle visited him and told him that what he needed was iridescent paint. Segun, however, carried on with his idea of making objects glow in the dark using fluorescent paint. Then he saw a pot that glowed in the dark. He asked the owner what sort of paint they had used. The answer was 'iridescent'. Segun finally agreed to try the new sort of paint. His owl glowed in the dark. So did his stones. So did his sticks.

Segun had worked out, by thoroughly exploring his mistaken hypothesis, that fluorescent paint does not make things glow in the dark. Segun will now know this for the rest of his life. And he also knows that iridescent paint does make things glow in the dark. This is real learning which no one can take away from him. It shows he is making predictions and a hypothesis, concentrating and problem solving actively. (See EYFS Creativity and Critical Thinking – Transforming Understanding.)

Guidelines for encouraging children with problem solving

* Encourage children to make a hypothesis by asking 'What do you think is going to happen?'

* Help children to use their prior experience – what they already know. You could ask 'What happened when you did . . .?'

* Let children try out their ideas. If something does not work, do not argue or dismiss it as wrong. Just point out the bits that did not work as if you are interested in 'why', and leave it at that.

* Try to set up situations which help children to go on testing their hypothesis and talking about it. Ask 'Does that give you any ideas for trying again?' (See EYFS Creativity and Critical Thinking.)

MEMORY

Imitation and memory are closely linked. If you poke out your tongue at a newborn baby, the baby will imitate you, after a time. You can see the baby concentrating hard and then managing to imitate the adult. Gradually, as babies become toddlers, they begin to remember things and to imitate them after a time delay. One famous example is Piaget's daughter Jacqueline. She saw a friend have a temper tantrum when she was about 18 months old. She was very impressed by this dramatic event! The next day she tried it out herself – she imitated the temper tantrum.

The Influence of Having a Longer Memory

Between 2 and 3 years, children are able to remember more. This means that, when they are in unfamiliar situations, they tend to be able to plan things. They do not immediately rush to try new things. Instead they pause until they have an idea about what they would like to do. In this way, they organise their thinking. They remember what they have done before with similar or different objects and people, and they use this memory to help them plan ideas for this new situation. This is called 'inhibition to the unfamiliar', and it means the children can 'think before they do'.

Different Kinds of Memory

Neuroscientists now think that our feelings, sensory perceptions and memories are bound together as a seamless whole. In other words, the feelings children have are of central importance in the way their thinking develops, and the way they remember what they learn and feel as they learn. There are different kinds of memory:

* **Procedural memory**: for example, how to ride a bike. Remembering how to do this is a deeply ingrained habit.

* **Fear memory**: for example, flashbacks and phobias.

* **Semantic memory**: facts we remember.

* **Episodic memory**: such memories are clothed in personal experiences which are emotional, such as the day you dropped your ice cream and a dog rushed over and ate it, and you cried! This kind of memory develops rapidly as children begin to walk, talk and pretend.

BECOMING AWARE: FROM SENSATION TO PERCEPTION

When we say someone is a very perceptive person, we mean that they are very aware of things. Children and adults perceive and understand the world through their senses. The senses and what they tell us about the movements of our body give us immediate feedback about how we are moving and what is happening to us.

If you sit awkwardly and your leg goes to sleep, it is very difficult to walk. There is not enough sensory feedback from your leg to enable you to walk! You cannot perceive your leg! Perceiving something means constructing an idea of that thing which is based on information you have received through your senses. The senses make it possible for us to perceive and experience life. For some children with severe learning difficulties it can be difficult to be sure whether they have awareness. Are they receiving messages through their senses which tell them they are having an experience? Observing children is always important, but it is particularly important in

this situation. For most babies, the senses help them to perceive experiences, even in the first months of their life. Remember, all the senses are important – touch, smell, taste, hearing and sight, along with movement or kinaesthesia (see Unit 18 on CD-ROM for how the senses develop in babies). Most people are very aware that babies need love and care, and need to feel secure. However, it is also very important to give interesting and new experiences to newborn babies:

* We need to choose the right moment to introduce a baby to a new experience.

* The feedback from their senses (perceptions) helps babies to develop ideas (concepts). Researchers are beginning to realise that concepts develop much earlier than had been thought previously.

* Research is also showing that **proprioception**, being aware of how different bits of your body work together and a sense of embodiment (feeling comfortable inside your own body), helps children to develop a sense of self.

Embodiment and a Sense of Self

Knowing yourself is important for learning. Can you climb that high? Will you trip on the rug? Can you reach that far without toppling over? All this is important as children begin to know themselves and develop a sense of self and identity. Our feelings, thoughts and physical selves all work together as we learn.

EARLY CONCEPTS

Researchers have shown that concepts develop early in babies, as follows:

* Very early on, babies think beyond their immediate perceptions (that is, they have an awareness beyond their immediate

sensory feedback about things). They begin to link present feedback with their past perceptions.

* Then babies use these links to predict the future – what will happen next.

* When babies think back to prior experience and forward to the future, they begin to develop early concepts, which become stable thoughts in their mind.

So, early concepts link past, present and future around a particular idea. This means that children can predict and plan ahead. They get better at this as their memory develops. These factors are important for thinking, and for creativity to develop. Concepts enable children to:

* organise their thinking;

* organise previous experience and perception – Piaget calls this **assimilation**;

* predict things about the future;

* have ideas;

* take in new knowledge and understand it – Piaget calls this **accommodation**.

CASE STUDY

Bill

Bill is 10 months old. He stands at a coffee table and bangs a biscuit on it. His mother comes in. He perceives his mother by using his sense of sight (i.e. he is aware that she has come into the room). Bill then links the prior experience he has of his mother with this present one. He has a concept that she will come and talk to him – she has always done this in the past.

CASE STUDY

Concepts of food

A baby of 5 months is beginning to take solids on a spoon and is often offered mashed banana. This is a taste that is known. It fits the baby's previous experience (assimilation). If the baby is given apple purée, which is a new taste, this will mean taking in a new experience (accommodation). The baby might spit the apple out.

Balancing Assimilation and Accommodation

Piaget would say that we are never quite balanced, but that we are always trying to keep balanced! This is what Piaget calls the process of **equilibration**. The balancing act between assimilation (taking in what is known) and accommodation (adjusting to what is new) helps children and adults to organise past experiences into concepts (ideas). This is an active process, so Piaget refers to **active learners**.

Stranger Fear and Children's Concepts

The phenomenon of stranger fear is very interesting in relation to children's concepts. The child (usually at about 6–9 months) is exploring and getting to know about faces. A face that looks different is frightening because it does not fit with what they know. Babies might cry with fear when they see someone with glasses, a bald head, a different skin colour or a beard if they have not seen this before. A reassuring adult helps babies to broaden their experience and make the unfamiliar more familiar. The case study of Hannah (below) also shows how closely linked the child's ideas are with their feelings and their relationships with people.

CASE STUDY

Hannah

One baby, Hannah, cried when her Uncle Dan, who was bald, came to the house. She had never seen a bald person before. She cried. This happened every time Hannah saw her Uncle Dan for a month or so.

Hannah had to accommodate her new knowledge that some people do not have hair on the tops of their heads. At first Uncle Dan was very upset, but he was reassured when this was explained.

Cognitive, emotional, physical and social development are all combined in this story.

Schemas

Even babies as young as 1 month are organising their perceptions and linking them with previous experiences of people and events. They are using these concepts to work out what will happen next. Piaget calls these ready concepts **schemas**. Recent researchers have developed this part of his work. Schemas are patterns of linked behaviours which the child can generalise and use in a whole variety of different situations. For example, children are often fascinated by things that **rotate**. We see this in toddlers particularly, but in older children too. For example, a 4-year-old might:

* be fascinated by the way the water rotates as it swirls down the plughole;
* try to touch the steering wheel in the car (a dangerous interest);
* want to watch an adult mixing food round and round in a bowl;
* be interested in the wheels going round on a toy car;

* do a roly-poly down a grass slope;
* join in with a movement song such as 'Round and round the garden, like a teddy bear'.

Every time the child meets a situation which involves rotation, either the situation will fit the experience of what is already known and the child will assimilate it, or the child will have to change their concept to accommodate the situation. Rotating as in the song 'Round and round the garden' means taking turns and not rotating all the time. And it means standing up straight as you rotate. This is very different from the kind of rotation involved in doing a roly-poly down a grass slope, which means rotating on your side.

The Different Levels of Schema

'Up' and 'down' are important schemas that children often explore at the same time. Their exploration will be at a different level, depending on their stage of development and on their existing concepts of up and down.

1   **Senses and actions level of schemas.** At first, schemas occur when babies and toddlers use their senses and movements to link past and present perceptions. For example, a baby might move their arms up and down when shaking a rattle. The baby already knew how to move her arms in this way and applied it to a new situation.

2   **Symbolic level of schemas.** Typically during the second year, the child begins to use schemas in a new way. As well as using feedback from actions and senses, the child begins to experiment with symbolic behaviour. For example, a 2-year-old child might be painting at the table, making a line that goes up and down on the paper. The child might then say 'Daddy'. The line on paper

stands for Daddy, and the drawing of the line is, therefore, an example of symbolic behaviour.

3   **Cause and effect level of schemas.** A 3-year-old child makes a thin line go up and down on the paper with the paintbrush. Then with a different paintbrush makes a wide line, saying 'Big one, little one'. The child is interested in the causes and effects of using different paintbrushes.

The 'up' and 'down' schemas have thus been used in three different ways:

*   The **sensori-motor** level was used by the child with the rattle.

*   The **symbolic behaviour** level was used by the child who painted Daddy.

*   The **cause and effect** level was used by the child who was interested in the thick and thin painted lines.

Operational Concepts

Between the ages of 2 and 7 years, children become able to combine early concepts or schemas in a logical way. They start to link the different aspects of their experiences, developing what Piaget calls operational thinking. Most children become proficient in operational thinking from middle childhood onwards (from 7 years), but during early childhood (2–7 years) they are already moving towards this, although they still find it difficult to think about more than one aspect at a time. Young children cannot easily go forwards and backwards through their ideas in quick succession, because every event is a bit like a separate photograph. They need to focus on one thing at a time.

Piaget calls this **centration**: they centre on something. It is a very good way of making sense of things. This period when children 'centrate' is often called the start of

pre-operations. However, most early years workers do not like the idea that children are 'pre' anything, because it undervalues what children can do. Indeed, it concentrates too much on what children cannot do, conveying a negative image of the young child. It is much more useful to think in terms of developing operations, of the development into operational thinking or of the move from early childhood to middle childhood. As children start to develop operational concepts during early childhood, they begin to use the following ways of thinking:

*   **Sequencing:** a sequence has a beginning, a middle and an end. Understanding how sequences work helps children to learn about cause and effect. For example, if I roll the clay, it will change its shape from a lump to a sausage.

*   **Seriating:** this is seeing the differences between things. Think of a xylophone. It has many keys that are lines, but they are all of different lengths.

*   **Classifying:** this is seeing the similarities between things. For example, pigs, dogs, cats and cows are all animals.

*   **Transformation:** children begin to ask if a process can be reversed. For example, water freezes into ice, but you can melt it back to water again. However, if you break an egg you cannot put it back together again; if you burn the wood from a tree, you cannot get the wood back again; after cooking a cake, you cannot get the original ingredients back. Reversibility is an important concept.

Class Inclusion

As children develop they gradually begin to link their previous experiences together much more easily: the experiences become more like a video film than a sequence of still photographs. As well as the operational concepts outlined above, children also form concepts about the shapes, sizes, colours and classes of objects and animals. The class of animals might be divided into pets and farm animals, while the class of cutlery might be divided into knives, forks and spoons. This is called class inclusion.

CONCRETE OPERATIONS AND CONSERVATION

As concept formation elaborates, children begin to understand that things are not always as they seem to be. This typically occurs as children (aged 7–12 years) begin to go to junior school, according to Piaget. Children can now hold in mind several things at once when they are thinking and they can run backwards and forwards through their thoughts. Piaget says the child's thinking gradually becomes more mobile. Children's concepts develop to include concrete operation, such as the conservation of mass and number.

Conservation of Mass

Give children two balls of clay, play dough or plasticine. Check that the child agrees that there is the same amount in each ball. Roll one into a sausage shape while the child is watching. Then ask if there is the same amount of clay in both pieces as before. Children under 7 years usually do not conserve mass in a formal test situation like this. This means that they all think that either the sausage shape or the ball shape has more clay in it. This is because these children cannot hold in mind several ideas at once (the balls were the same), but can only concentrate on one aspect (the sausage versus the ball).

Conservation of Number

Show the child two rows of similar buttons. Check that the child agrees that the rows have the same number. Spread one row out to make it longer. Ask the child which row has the most buttons. Children under 7 usually do not conserve number in a formal test situation like this. This means they are likely to think that the spread-out row has more buttons. Again, young children usually cannot yet hold in mind more than one thing at a time.

JEAN PIAGET

Piaget is often talked of as the elder statesman of child development study. He has left us a very rich description of how children develop in their thinking, and he has given us detailed observations which are very sensitively made. He deserves great respect for this. His contribution has also helped others to extend, modify and add to his findings. His work has helped people who study child development to move forward in their understanding of how young children think. The following section – which brings together many of the elements discussed above – outlines the four stages that occur in a child's thinking and ideas, according to Piaget. The exact ages vary, but the sequences are still thought to be useful.

Piaget's Stages of Cognitive Development

1 Sensori-motor stage (0–18 months);
2 Developing operations (18 months–7 years);
3 Concrete operations (7–12 years);
4 Formal operations (12 years–adulthood).

Recent research actually questions whether all children go through these stages in the

Table 3.1 Schema focus sheet

Name of schema	Description
Transporting	A child may move objects or collections of objects from one place to another, perhaps using a bag, pram or truck.
Positioning	A child may be interested in placing objects in particular positions, for example on top of something, around the edge, behind. Paintings and drawings also often show evidence of this.
Orientation	This schema is shown by interest in a different viewpoint, as when a child hangs upside down or turns objects upside down.
Dab	A graphic schema used in paintings, randomly or systematically, to form patterns or to represent, for example, eyes, flowers or buttons.
Dynamic vertical (and horizontal)	A child may show evidence of particular interest by actions such as climbing, stepping up and down, or lying flat. These schemas may also be seen in constructions, collages or graphically. After schemas of horizontality and verticality have been explored separately, the two are often used in conjunction to form crosses or grids. These are very often systematically explored on paper and interest is shown in everyday objects such as a cake-cooling tray, grills or nets.
The family of trajectories	(a) VERTICAL (up) and HORIZONTAL (down) A fascination with things moving or flying through the air – balls, aeroplanes, rockets, catapults, frisbees – and indeed, anything that can be thrown. When expressed through child's own body movements, this often becomes large arm and leg movements, kicking, or punching, for example. (b) DIAGONALITY Usually explored later than the previous schemas, this one emerges via the construction of ramps, slides and sloping walls. Drawings begin to contain diagonal lines forming roofs, hands, triangles, zig-zags.
Containment	Putting things inside and outside containers, baskets, buckets, bags, carts, boxes, etc.
Enclosure	A child may build enclosures with blocks, Lego or large crates, perhaps naming them as boats, ponds, beds. The enclosure is sometimes left empty, sometimes carefully filled in. An enclosing line often surrounds paintings and drawings while a child is exploring this schema. The child might draw circles, squares and triangles, heads, bodies, eyes, wheels, flowers, etc.
Enveloping	This is often an extension of enclosure. Objects, space or the child herself are completely covered. She may wrap things in paper, enclose them in pots or boxes with covers or lids, wrap herself in a blanket or creep under a rug. Paintings are sometimes covered over with a wash of colour or scrap collages glued over with layers of paper or fabric.
Circles and lines radiating from the circle	(a) SEMI-CIRCULARITY Semi-circles are used graphically as features, parts of bodies and other objects. Smiles, eyebrows, ears, rainbows and umbrellas are a few of the representational uses for this schema, as well as parts of letters of the alphabet. (b) CORE and RADIALS Again common in paintings, drawings and models. Spiders, suns, fingers, eyelashes, hair and hedgehogs often appear as a series of radials.
Rotation	A child may become absorbed by things which turn – taps, wheels, cogs and keys. She may roll cylinders along, or roll herself. She may rotate her arms, or construct objects with rotating parts in wood or scrap materials.
Connection	Scrap materials may be glued, sewn and fastened into lines; pieces of wood are nailed into long connecting constructions. Strings, rope or wool are used to tie objects together, often in complex ways. Drawings and paintings sometimes show a series of linked parts. The opposite of this schema may be seen in separation, where interest is shown in disconnecting assembled or attached parts.
Ordering	A child may produce paintings and drawings with ordered lines or dabs; collages or constructions with items of scrap carefully glued in sequence. She may place blocks, vehicles or animals in lines and begin to show interest in 'largest' and 'smallest'.
It is important to remember that the sensori-motor stage of the schema is at an earlier level, and that the cause and effect, together with the symbolic levels, both emerge out of this.	

same way. It also questions whether all adults reach the stage of formal operations. Piaget did not believe it possible to 'teach' conservation, and researchers disagreeing with his point of view have not managed to prove conclusively that it is possible.

The Sensori-motor Stage: Birth to 18 Months

* Babies explore and recognise people and objects through their senses and through their own activity and movements.

* Schemas are patterns of action which the baby can generalise, and which become increasingly coordinated. For example, at 4½ months the baby can see a rattle, reach out for the rattle, grasp the rattle and put the rattle in their mouth – tracking, reaching, grasping and sucking schemas.

* Toddlers still see things mainly from their own point of view, and cannot **decentre** to look at things from somebody else's point of view. Furthermore, they tend, at any one time, to focus on only one aspect of an event (centration). Piaget says they are **intellectually egocentric**.

* By the end of their first year, most children have understood that people and objects are permanent and constant, that is, they go on existing even when they cannot be seen, for example if they are under a cloth or in another room.

Pre-operational Stage: 18 Months to 7 Years

* Action schemas – for example, rotation or trajectory (up and down) – now become **representational**. This means that children begin to use symbolic behaviour, which includes language, representational drawings and pretend play. Action schemas are internalised by

the child, and they become thinking beings. Thinking backwards and forwards with ideas (concepts) is still heavily linked, however, with perception of immediate experiences (i.e. the perception of objects, people and events).

* The development of memory – recalling past perceptions and prior experiences – is now important. In their minds, children will form images of a smell, of something they have seen, of something they have heard, of something that moved, of something they tasted or something they touched. They also now anticipate the future.

* They imitate things they remember from past experiences.

* Using past and future, as well as immediate, experiences, children now begin to develop ideas (concepts). This frees them to think more about time and space.

* Children begin to refer to things and people who are not present.

* They begin to try to share what they know, feel and think with other people.

* Because children still only look at one aspect of a situation, it influences the way that they classify or seriate things.

* At this stage, children also tend to assume that objects have consciousness (**animism**), for example they get cross with a door for slamming shut. Furthermore, they form an idea of what is right or wrong in what actually happens (**moral realism**).

Moral realism
If a cup breaks, children think the person who broke it has been naughty. They are not, at this stage, interested in how the event came about (i.e. the

---

motive). They are likely to think that a child who breaks a cup helping to wash up is naughtier than the child who takes a valuable cup from the dresser when they had been told not to, even if they did not break it.

Concrete Operations: 7–12 Years

* Children now begin to understand **class inclusion**.

* They begin to understand about the **conservation of mass**, **number**, area, quantity, volume, weight.

* They realise that things are not always as they look.

* However, they still need real situations to help them to think **conceptually**, and they have great difficulty thinking in the abstract. For example, they need practical work in understanding number or time concepts in mathematics.

* Although the children can now see things from somebody else's point of view (this means they have established **Theory of Mind**), they still tend to try to make ideas fit other ways of thinking.

* They will use symbols in writing, reading, notation in music, drawing, maths and dance if they are introduced to these.

* Children at this stage of development can also take into account several features of an object at the same time when they are classifying and seriating. This means that they no longer centrate, that is, they no longer concentrate on just one thing at a time. They realise that there might be several correct solutions to a problem or several outcomes of an event or action.

* Children also now enjoy games and understand about rules.

Formal Operations: 12 Years to Adulthood

* Children can now understand abstract concepts, such as fairness, justice or peace.

* They also understand that it is possible to create laws and rules which help them to test things out, to have a hypothesis and to solve problems.

* They think about time, space and reasons through **formal operations**, and this means they can speak in an abstract way about subjects – they do not need to do things practically to work them through.

* Some adults never reach this stage and continue to rely on concrete situations rather than being able to think in the abstract. Most adults remain concrete-operational for large parts of their lives. For example, a car mechanic might use high levels of formal thought to find out what is wrong with a car, but not do so when organising a weekly shop for the family. In fact, it is possible to live a fulfilled adult life without using formal thinking at all.

Guidelines for promoting cognitive development
Throughout cognitive intellectual development it is important to:
* see the child as an active learner;
* offer a wide range of experiences (look at Chapter 13);
* use skilled observations to inform planning of the next step in the child's learning.

FURTHER DEVELOPMENTS IN PIAGET'S WORK

Piaget concentrated on children's thinking, intellectual development and ideas. This does not mean that he did not think that social, emotional and physical development were also important – he did. It is just that he did not make these the main area of study in his theory. Some people have argued that Piaget ignored social relationships and the cultural aspects of the child's life. In fact, Piaget thought they were so important that he took these for granted.

* Social and cultural relationships with other people are now thought to be just as central to a child's development as the other kinds of experience which Piaget emphasised more, such as the way children build up an understanding of objects.

* People, first-hand experiences of materials and all sorts of provision in indoor and outdoor areas are all of great importance because they help children in the development of their ideas. Neuroscience supports this approach.

* Piaget – as already pointed out – tended to start with what children cannot do, rather than what they can do. However, we now realise that even very young children, including babies, can decentre and see things from somebody else's point of view, providing they are in a situation that holds personal meaning for them.

* Children are not isolated from other people when they learn. Piaget did not emphasise this fact, although he did know it. Recent research stresses the importance of interdependent relationships with others in order for children to learn effectively.

* Children know that people and objects are permanent much earlier than Piaget realised. His test of object permanency (see page 87) proved difficult for babies at 5 months who did not realise two objects – a cloth over a cup, for example – could occupy the same space. By the age of 9 months they have worked this out and they remove the cloth to get the object underneath. However, the multiple-mother image test demonstrates that at 5 months, babies know they only have one mother.

When children are in a situation which makes what researchers call 'human sense', they can conserve and they can understand reversibility. It is just that children find formal test situations rather difficult. This is because it is very hard for a child to understand what it is the questioner is asking.

Instead of Piaget's rather linear stages of development, researchers now tend to look at **networks** of sequences of development. These give us the basic order, rules and strategies that children develop and learn through.

Piaget worked with a Western, middle-class, white, industrialised model of society – after all, that is what he knew about – so his stages of development are culturally biased towards this kind of society. In cultures where there is a different lifestyle, children might appear to be 'backward' according to Piaget's theory. For example, the Swiss children he studied had a much better-developed understanding of the different points of view you would get from different mountaintops than, for example, a child living on the flat Norfolk Broads would have had. It is very important to remember this point when studying Piaget's work. These biases are called contextual sensitivities, and they result in variations in the way children think, depending on the different places and cultures in which they live (Moss, Pence and Dahiberg 1999).

Recent researchers are beginning to look more at the importance of context:

* Piaget's work was used to focus on intellectual processes in the child until the 1970s.

* By the 1970s and 1980s **social cognition** was emphasised. **Vygotsky's** work was influential. The context, and the people especially, moderated the way a child's thinking developed.

* In the 1980s researchers were beginning to think that both the **social** and **physical contexts**, including the physical and biological development of the child, are crucial to the development of thinking. It is important to look at the situation in which a child thinks and learns. This approach is called **situational cognition**.

Piaget has been criticised mostly for what he did not say, and he left lots of gaps which more recent researchers have been trying to fill in. It is a bit like putting more pieces into the jigsaw puzzle. Although Piaget started our thinking in this area of symbolic behaviour, other people have then developed his work.

Was Piaget right or are the modern researchers who criticise him right? They are both right! This often happens when we look at Piaget's work. Piaget is not wrong, but in one lifetime he did not have time to discover all the pieces of the jigsaw puzzle. Modern researchers are helping us to put more pieces into the puzzle so that we can have a fuller picture than the one he gave us.

Permanence of the object

Piaget used a test called 'the permanence of the object'. He would cover an object, and the baby had to sit and watch this. By 9 months of age, the baby would reach for the object by uncovering it and picking it up; younger babies did not do this. It is now thought that babies have to realise that two objects (the object and the cover) can be in one place in order to complete the test. Later researchers gave babies of 5 months of age an object which might be put in either their right hand or their left hand. When the light went out they found that the babies reached for the object as soon as it was dark. The object could not be seen, but the babies still reached out and almost always they reached out in the right direction. The babies seemed to know that the object was still there, even though they could not see it in the dark. They also know that they only have one mother and so become disturbed if they are shown multiple images of her as early as 5 months old.

LEV VYGOTSKY

Vygotsky believed that:

* Play helps children to make sense of what they learn. During play they are free from all the practical constraints of a real–life situation.

* Children can have better ideas and do better thinking when an adult or child who knows more is helping them. For example, an adult can help a child to experience a story like Spot the Dog by reading the book for the child. Later on the child will be able to read the story for themselves. Vygotsky called the

things that children can only do with help the **zone of potential development**.

* The zone of potential development is as important as the zone of actual development (what the child can do alone, without any help from anyone else). He said that the zone of actual development shows the results, the fruits of learning, while the zone of potential development shows the buds, the future of learning.

JEROME BRUNER

Bruner believed that:

* Children need to move about and be active, having real, first-hand, direct experiences. This helps their ideas to develop, and it helps them to think. He agrees with Piaget in this, and he calls the thinking involved here **enactive thinking**.

* 'Codes' are important. Languages are very important kinds of code. Codes also include drawing, painting, dancing, making stories, play, music and maths. He calls the thinking involved here **symbolic thinking**.

* Children need books and interest tables with objects displayed on them to remind them of prior experiences. He calls the thinking involved here **iconic thinking**.

* Adults can be a great help to children in their thinking, because adults can be like a piece of scaffolding on a building.

Adults scaffolding children's thinking
At first, the building needs a great deal of scaffolding (adult support of the child's learning), but gradually, as the children extend their competence and control of the situation, the scaffolding is removed until it is not needed any more. When scaffolding, the adult arranges the experience, rather than transmitting what is to be learnt. For example, a child learning to weave among the Zinacantecon in Southern Mexico goes through six steps of learning, each scaffolded by the adult. First, the child learns to set up the loom and to finish off the piece of weaving. The first time the child weaves, the child is helped most of the time.

YOUR ROLE IN PROMOTING COGNITIVE DEVELOPMENT

Guidelines for promoting cognitive development
Your role is to:

* observe children carefully and to record your observations;
* act on those observations as various points in the sequence are recognised;
* make sure that you do not underestimate children, just as it is very important not to overestimate them;
* encourage children to try new things and to express their own ideas and creativity;
* ensure that children are neither rushed along in their learning by adults, nor held back while adults wait for the correct age or stage of development to occur;
* offer appropriate activities and experiences; these should be planned to suit individual interests and the needs of each individual;

* ensure a wide range of materials is available;
* intervene when appropriate, with sensitivity;
* adapt activities and experience to suit children with special educational needs and sensory impairments. (See EYFS and 'Creating the Picture', DfES.)

LEARNING STYLES OR A MULTISENSORY ENVIRONMENT

Some researchers think that different people have different dominant learning styles (visual, tactile, auditory and kinaesthetic). Others stress the importance of offering children a multisensory environment with opportunities for freedom of movement, which is language-rich, so that all kinds of learning styles are encouraged.

CHILDREN WHO EXPERIENCE SENSORY IMPAIRMENT

A child with one or more sensory impairments is challenged in learning, but there are famous role models who have shown that cognitive development can be very deep. Helen Keller is a famous example. She was both blind and deaf. Now she would probably be described as having both a visual and a hearing impairment.

Given that learning through the senses and movement feedback is central to the learning of young children, it is important to offer children with sensory impairments the kind of support which allows them to do this as much as possible.

Hearing Impairment

For the child with a hearing impairment it is important to get the most out of a hearing aid(s). This means having expert help in finding the optimal settings for the child. This will vary with each child. For a partial loss of hearing, a loop system might help the child to pick up normal conversational voice levels while cutting out the background noise. For a child with a profound hearing loss there may be benefits in using British Sign Language (BSL) as well as organising expert help for the child to learn to lip-read. Although hearing aids can be a huge help to children with partial hearing loss, and may give considerable help to a child with a profound loss through vibrations and rhythms of language patterns, which help them to decipher what is being said, it is important to remember that a hearing aid never gives a child normal hearing. Communication and language are of great importance in learning, so great effort needs to be made to help children with a hearing loss in this respect. Hearing loss can also bring loneliness when communication is very difficult. Children appreciate people explaining things to them one-to-one when they miss what is said in a group. They are helped if they can face the adult directly at group times, and if the sun falls on the group leader's face. They are not helped if people keep holding their face and turning it to look at them, because this is invasive.

Visual Impairment

Just as a hearing aid does not give a child normal hearing, so a pair of glasses will not bring normal eyesight. The child who is partially sighted is not just a child who is, for example, short-sighted, and so wears glasses. There will be a considerable loss of sight for a child to be identified as partially sighted.

Children with a sight-challenge lose things easily. They try to stay in touch with people by chatting to them, so that they feel very connected and can work out where they are in space; or they 'still', so that they can listen carefully and work it out that way. It is helpful if things are put on trays, so that they do not fall off the edge of the table. If adults explain where things are, it helps too: 'Your lunch is straight in front of you on the table. The peas are on the side of the plate nearest to you.' It does not help if people grab a child suddenly. In fact it can frighten them if they are picked up without warning or taken by the hand, and it is difficult if they are left suddenly, because they cannot see that you have gone!

ACTIVITY: CHILDREN AT PLAY

1 Set up an area using found materials (see Chapter 13 for ideas to help you in this). Observe what children do in general. Describe how a child aged 3–7 years uses the area.

 * Did you see any imaginative ideas developing?

 * Did any of the children make anything creative?

 * Are the children used to being creative, or are they already dependent on adults giving them outlines or templates?

 * How can you help them to have more confidence in their own ideas?

2 Evaluate your observations, relating them to your target child's development.

ACTIVITY: CHILDREN PROBLEM SOLVING

1 Plan an area with a water tray or sand tray. Observe children (try to have as wide a range of ages as possible) to see if they demonstrate any examples of problem solving. Evaluate your observations. What role did you take in helping the child? If possible, repeat the observation of water play, observing a child at bath-time, in a paddling pool or in a swimming pool. How do children solve problems in these settings?

2 Try to observe children in a sandpit in a park, or using sand on the beach. Focus on the children's problem solving and how you supported them. Evaluate your observations, in whatever settings you made them.

ACTIVITY: ENCOURAGING CREATIVITY AND CONCENTRATION

1 Plan some ways to encourage creativity in the development of young children. Set up an area of the room for this purpose, making sure materials are appropriate and accessible, and that children can use them freely. Evaluate the help you have given in the way you communicated with the children and through the materials you offered.

2 Plan ways of encouraging a child's concentration and involvement. See how successful you have been by finding out about and using the Leuven Involvement Scale to observe a child in your setting who you have noticed lacks concentration (use time-sampling or event-sampling observation techniques – see Chapter 8). When does the child concentrate most? Evaluate your observations.

ACTIVITY: INTERESTS AND SCHEMAS OF THE YOUNG CHILD

1 Plan ways of finding out about what fascinates a child aged 2–5 years. Observe and note what the child does on a particular day. If possible, observe the child continuously for an hour. Write down a description of what the child does and says. You might use video and photographs to enhance your observations. Use Table 3.1 on schemas to help you identify and name the areas of interest the child has. Remember, children are interested in a variety of things, but might particularly enjoy one activity. Use your observations to add to the available materials. For example, if the child is particularly interested in rotation, add whisks and spinners or cogs. If the child is interested in covering things over, you could provide finger-painting activities, dressing-up clothes such as cloaks, or sand for burying things.

2 Evaluate your observations.

3 Look at the basic equipment in the room. How does it support the children's schemas? Either look at a book on the subject or visit a museum of childhood. Look at the toys children had, for example, in the last century. How do traditional toys encourage children to develop their schemas?

ACTIVITY: NEUROSCIENCE AND CHILDREN

1 Neuroscience is showing us that young children need to learn through movement, rhythm, sounds and their senses. Plan a learning experience for a child aged Birth–3 years or 3–5 years. Use songs with actions. Evaluate your observations.

2 Play short extracts of different kinds of music to a group of children, again aged Birth–3 or 3–5 years. How do they react? What movement or sounds do they make? Evaluate your observations.

ACTIVITY: TESTING PIAGET'S WORK

1 Plan and carry out Piaget's conservation of mass test (see page 82) with children aged 3, 5 and 7 years. Can the children conserve? Evaluate the activity.

2 Then try the conservation of number test devised by Piaget (see page 82). You can use buttons or other objects, as long as they are all the same. Do children aged 3, 5 and 7 years conserve? Evaluate your findings.

3 Carry out an experiment with a child, based on the work of Martin Hughes in the 1980s. You will need two small dolls, the size of doll's house dolls. One will be the 'parent', the other the 'child'. Keep the mother fixed to one point. Ask your target child to move the child doll around, so that sometimes the mother can see the child and sometimes not. Does the target child know when the mother doll will be able to see the child doll and when she will not? Margaret Donaldson found that when a situation made 'human sense', children were able to decentre and

see things from other people's points of view (or from the doll's point of view). However, if the task was very formal, removed from real-life experience, the children could not manage it.

4 Try also the object permanency test (see page 87). Evaluate your observations of a baby of 6 months and one of 10–18 months. Refer to the cognitive development of the baby.

5 Plan how you can promote a child's cognitive development in ways which also value the social relationships and feelings of children. Plan experiences with number, seriation and classification. You might decide to help children to choose a recipe, go with them to shop for ingredients, and then help them to cook the recipe. Evaluate your activity, commenting on the cognitive, social and emotional aspects of the child's development, as well as on the way you provided the experiences.

CHAPTER 4

Communication, Including Language Development

Contents

COMMUNICATION AND LANGUAGE

When we communicate, we connect with other people, but we also connect with ourselves. Some forms of communication are spoken/signed, but about 85 per cent of communication is non-verbal.

From the beginning, babies seem to want to communicate with other people. Remember that babies with a disability may have difficulty in this, or their carers may find it hard to 'read' the baby's communication signals. Babies love to share experiences with people, and communication is a huge part of the way in which people relate to each other. Communication in babies involves:

* **facial expressions** (a smile, frown, raised eyebrows) and eye contact;

* **gesture and body language** (hugs, beckoning, clapping hands and applause, a shrug, jumping with surprise, being stiff and ill at ease) – body language varies according to the culture;

* **verbal** or **sign language** – this can be a very limited kind of communication, through a personal language that is only understood by those who are very close to the baby; for example, 'bubba' might stand for all children and young animals;

* **intonation** (how the baby's voice sounds – angry, gentle, playful, sharp, cooing, pausing, encouraging);

* **pauses** – these are very important; often we do not give babies, toddlers or young children enough time to respond;

* moving in tune (in **synchrony**) with someone when they 'talk' together – a proto-conversation. It is like a conversation without words, and it lays the foundations for later conversations with words. Moving in tune with each other has several aspects. It can mean doing the same movement together at the same time – mirroring – or imitating;

* **'Oogly Boogly'** is for young children aged 12–18 months on the edge of spoken/signed language, who attend, eight at a time, with their parent/carer. A group of professional actors/dancers, trained in improvisation, mirror what the toddlers do and the sounds they

make. The children seem to understand quickly that they can lead the adults in a kind of dance that unfolds. Some children stay close to their important adult and watch the others, although they seem to appreciate the actors mirroring their smallest movements too. Many children have now experienced 'Oogly Boogly', and at the end of the session, which typically lasts for about 45 minutes, they and their parents/carers report that the children and they feel calm and have a sense of deep wellbeing. Perhaps this is because the children, their important adults and the actors/dancers have all connected in deep forms of non-verbal communication. (It seems to be a powerful experience for children with autism on the edge of language.)

Using language usually means talking aloud and listening to the spoken word. However, talking and listening can also be done through signs (e.g. British Sign Language, which is now an officially recognised language).

Babies, toddlers and some children with special educational needs – for example, children with complex needs – will use personal communication systems which are known and understood by those who live with and care for them. Two examples are **Objects of Reference** and **Makaton**.

Both spoken and sign languages use agreed codes which develop according to the cultures in which they arise. They suit that culture, and they are an expression of its important ideas and values. The rhythms, tone and melody of language (its musical aspects) are each of great importance as children's language develops. So are the gestures and movements, especially of the face and hands, as recent studies in neuroscience show. The brain actually develops abilities in music, movement and language at the same time. If spoken language is not possible (perhaps the child is deaf) the brain develops the movement aspects more extensively (sign language).

Fig 4.1 Elementary cross-cultural marks made by children

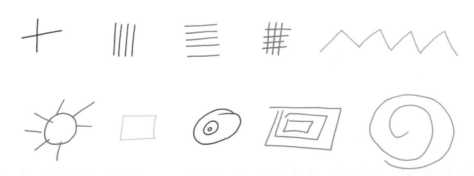

Fig 4.2 Coordinated marks

Fig 4.3 Although children's marks are personal and idiosyncratic, there are common basic features

Language:

* helps people to communicate internally: children (and adults!) often talk out loud to themselves; they begin to internalise speech more and more until they can think of the words rather than saying them out loud;

* can be spoken, signed or thought;

* helps people to move from here and now into the past or the future;

* helps people to use symbolic behaviour;

* helps people to put ideas (concepts) into words and to express imaginative thoughts;

* helps abstract thinking;

* helps people to express feelings and to think about emotions.

In order to use language effectively, we need to master its two modes:

1 listening or watching, and understanding (reception of language);

2 communicating, which involves facial expressions, gestures and verbal or sign speech (expression of language).

LANGUAGE DEVELOPMENT AS SYMBOLIC BEHAVIOUR

It is not possible to study language development without looking at the rich variety of symbols that human beings use. Before studying the development of language in young children it is important to know a little bit about symbolic behaviour.

What are Symbols?

Symbols are a way of making one thing stand for another. For example, a drawing of mum and saying the word 'Mum' are both symbols for mother. She does not have to be there. These symbols, the drawing and the word stand for her when she is not there.

Is it Only Humans Who are Symbol Users?

Whether animals use symbols has been debated for centuries. Until recently it was argued that humans were superior to other animals. Nowadays there are many people who prefer to look at similarities and differences between humans and other animals. One similarity, for example, is that animals such as chimpanzees, gorillas and orang-utans also seem to use symbolic systems. This means that all these animals can make one thing stand for another. Children make connections like Washoe the chimpanzee did as they learn to share the language of their culture. Washoe was a symbol user just like a human child (see page 97). However, it does seem that humans can go further and deeper in their ability to make one thing stand for something else. For a start, humans have a larynx – or voice box – so they can talk. In addition, humans can:

* draw and paint;

* make dances;

* make sculptures;

* write;

* make music;

* think scientifically;

* use mathematical notations, such as those for numbers, geometry and algebra.

Layers of Symbols

There is a huge variety in the kinds of symbol that human children begin to use, even very early in their development. And the symbolic layers keep on accumulating throughout life as the culture is taken in and used by the child as he or she grows up. Indeed, we never stop adding to our symbolic layers as long as we live.

Washoe the chimpanzee

There was a famous example of an animal using symbols in Washoe the chimpanzee in the 1960s. She was taught American Sign Language by her researchers, the Gardners, and she knew the signs for both water and bird. One day, she saw a duck fly over a pond. She did not know the sign for a duck, but without any prompting, she signed 'water bird'.

Pamela is dancing

Fig 4.4 Drawing

Since Piaget began his pioneering work in the 1930s, researchers have been finding deeper and deeper layers in the symbolic behaviour of people. More is now known about how children start to become symbol users. The psychologist Howard Gardner believes that we have multiple intelligences which help us to use a wide range of different kinds of symbols. Neuroscientists like Trevarthen, however, do not see the brain as having separate domains in this way. Instead they show that the brain forms connected networks which feed off and into each other, so that sound, gesture and movement are linked, but can be used for music, language, dance or other things. There is now a training project led by Penny Lancaster (Coram Family) called 'Listening to Children'. We already know that symbolic behaviour is about making one thing stand for another. It also involves thinking about the **past**, the **present** and the **future**.

Symbols help people to think at an abstract level. This means they can go beyond the here and now in their imagination, ideas, feelings and relationships.

THE GRAMMAR OF A LANGUAGE

Every language has its own kind of grammar. In some languages, such as Latin and British Sign Language, the verb is not placed the same way as it is in English. This can make languages seem ungrammatical. The grammar of a language is the rules that make it work. To set out the rules of grammar is not to specify how people ought to speak. It is simply a way of describing how a language works. For example, the grammar of the English language includes:

* **verbs** (doing words) – 'I am *going* home';
* **nouns**, which might involve either a subject – 'The *cat* is asleep in the chair' – or an object – 'The cat is asleep in the *chair*';
* **adjectives** (words which describe nouns) – 'The baby likes the *red* rattle best';

Fig 4.5 Sharing a home-made book together

* **adverbs** (words which describe verbs) –
'The baby *quickly* grabs the red rattle';

* **pronouns**, such as 'they', 'you', 'he' or
'she', as well as the personal pronouns,
'I' and 'me';

* **apostrophes** (which indicate possession) – 'The *child's* rattle' (the rattle that
belongs to the child).

COMMUNICATION DIFFICULTIES

It can be very difficult for some children –
those who may have a hearing impairment,
severe learning difficulties, moderate learning
difficulties or physical challenges such as
cerebral palsy – to talk or listen. Not being
able to talk or listen with ease can bring
frustration, loneliness and a feeling of power-
lessness. It is very important, therefore, that
every child be encouraged to find ways of
communicating with other people. Research
on the brain now suggests that when people
learn to speak they do not use rules of
grammar at all. When a sound is heard, it fires
certain neurons and impedes the firing of
others. Gradually, as the sound is heard over
and over again, a neural pathway is forged and
a language pattern forms. This fire dance, as it
is called by neuroscientists, is part of the con-
nectionist theory of how language develops.
The language involved here does not have to
be a verbal language, and a considerable
minority of children are now taught to use
sign languages or personal references.

These can be based on:

* gestures or touch;

* agreed shared signs;

* finger spelling, computers and keyboards.

A small number of children will not use
shared signs which are understood by others.
They will continue to use personal communication signs, which only those close
to them will understand. Most children, but
not all, will move gradually into the world of
shared language, and may learn to speak in a
verbal language. It is important to remember
that all children – and adults too – find it
difficult to express their feelings and
thoughts when they are:

* put under pressure to speak;

* under stress for any reason (such as a
child who has been hit by another child).

No child should be put in a position where
they feel uncomfortable about talking – for
example in a large group – or where they
are rushed by adults who do not take the
time to listen to what they are trying to say.
All children need adults to take time to listen
to them.

REPRESENTATION

Representation means keeping hold of an
experience by bringing it back to the mind
and making it into some kind of product.

(**Time to choose:** if you do not want to study the different kinds of early representation in the next section, it is not necessary for you to do so. Studying is a kind of travelling: some people like to go directly to their destination; other people like to go down country lanes, stopping off along the way to explore things. This takes longer, but they enjoy the journey. What about you? If you want to go direct, turn to page 101. If you want to explore and find out more about representation in young children, read this next section.)

Keeping Hold of Experiences – Procedural Representations

Researchers believe that babies (typically at 5 months) can:

* remember;
* anticipate;
* make images;
* conceptualise people and objects that are not present.

Babies are starting to 'keep hold' of experiences, which is what representation is about. The next step is for babies to begin to share their highly personal ways of doing this.

Declaring is Sharing – Declarative Representations

Babies (typically at around 9 months) begin to be able to share their representations of things with other people. In fact, they want to share very much. They seem to have a deep need to do things with other people. Sharing symbols is only possible with those who are close to the child because the symbols are unique to each particular child.

Gesturing, **naming** and **pointing** begin around this time. Naming is likely to be very idiosyncratic – the child might say 'hee-haw' when they see a horse. A baby of 9 months will often wave 'bye-bye' after a person has

CASE STUDY

Sharon

Sharon, 4 years, ate an ice cream on a hot day. It melted and dripped down her hand. Later she did a painting. She chose white paint and made it run all over the paper. She then said 'It's my ice cream'. Sharon was keeping hold of her experience of a dripping ice cream by representing it in a painting.

gone. When babies do this it is cause to celebrate and, perhaps, to say to the baby 'Yes, you are right, Jill has gone, hasn't she, and we said bye-bye to her'.

Gradually, other kinds of representation become possible. A child begins to be able to draw or paint a person waving bye-bye. A child might make a model of someone waving bye-bye or do a dance about waving bye-bye. A child might make music, singing 'bye-bye', or write about saying bye-bye to Jill. There are many ways in which children begin to keep hold of their experiences and to represent them.

From 1 to 8 years of age, there is amazing development in the way that children begin to represent their experiences and share symbolic behaviour with other people. They now begin adding cultural layers to what they know about symbols.

Experience and Representation

The most important thing to remember about representing experiences is that children cannot represent an experience they have not had! Some other important things to bear in mind are that children need:

* real first-hand experiences;
* to experience things, actively;

Experience and representation

A teacher of a class of 5-year-olds asked the children to paint pictures of people skiing. There was a problem: none of the children in the class had been skiing! This meant that they had no experience of skiing and so could neither think back to when they had skied nor think forward to when they would ski again. Skiing was not included in their own experience of life.

Fig 4.6 An interested adult takes time to listen and support a child's thinking

* to feel ownership of the experiences they have – it is difficult for them to think deeply if their ideas are controlled by other people all the time;

* to be encouraged to think back and to think forward about experiences they have had or are looking forward to.

Representation and the Ability to Decentre

Very young children simply have not had enough experiences of their own to be able to:

* think what it is like to experience something as if they were someone else;

* understand an experience from someone else's point of view, unless it is very like their own experience.

As we have seen, the ability to understand what it is like to be someone else is called being able to decentre, or to have **Theory of Mind**.

Before children can learn to decentre they need help in finding ways of keeping hold of their own experiences, not those of other people. This means that tracing someone

else's outline, colouring in someone else's outline with tissue paper or coloured pencils, or drawing round a template are low-level activities because they do not allow children to represent their *own* experience in their *own* way.

GRAPHIC REPRESENTATION

Watch out for the first marks that young children make: they are cross-cultural. Children use them quite naturally and without needing to be taught, although they do need to see other people drawing and mark-making. Initially children use these marks separately (as shown in Figure 4.1). Later on they will begin to use them in combination; that is, they can coordinate them (see Figure 4.2). Remember, if you ask children to copy these shapes, they will not 'own' them. They will be doing it for you as an adult-led task – this will not be their own representation of their own experience which they have chosen to do. It is easy to make children copy; it is not so easy to help children express their own ideas, feelings and relationships with others on paper. As they grow up, many children leave behind these early and personal ways

CASE STUDY

Helping children to remember a first-hand experience

Consider a walk to the shops. There is lots of chatting and you all make stops to look at things. The children might see a dog, or they might help to buy things, give the money to the shopkeeper, or carry the bags. Then they might go back to the setting and help to do cooking. Later you might set up an interest table to remind the children about the shopping and cooking they have done. Books and cooking utensils might be put on the table. You could display packaging.

Children might want to do cooking again the following day.

The children might want to represent some of their experiences. They might want to make a model of the dog. They might want to make a model of the food they cooked. They might want to act out the way somebody walked down the street. There are many different ways the children might represent the walk to the shops. There are many different aspects of the experience that they might have enjoyed and will choose to represent. (EYFS Enabling Environments.)

of representing their experiences of life. As they grow older, they only use the conventional symbols and ways of representing which are specific to their culture. When this happens, the creative side of the child disappears and learned formulas take its place. This is why it is very important to keep representation alive, at the same time as introducing children to the shared and agreed conventions of writing and other ways of representing. Creative, imaginative children keep their personal representations and symbols, but can also use the conventional symbols of their culture.

LANGUAGE AND LITERACY

Researchers believe that people are capable of using many complex symbolic layers in what they do. Language is only one kind of symbolic behaviour, and it accumulates more symbolic layers when it moves into writing and reading. Developing writing and reading is called literacy.

Writing

Writing means that the person has to put language into a **code** (encoding).

Reading

Reading means that the person has to decode what is written. Young children use pictures in books as an extra help when they try to decode what is written. Reading and writing move along together with the development of spoken language. Some psychologists think that children are rather like scientists trying to discover things: they seem to try to find out how language systems work in the culture in which they are growing up. Not being able to read or write (illiteracy) is a serious disadvantage in many cultures. However, not all cultures use the written word. Although there is a written form, the Celtic language has an oral culture. This is why Celtic stories and songs have lasted so well: they are handed down orally and use dance and song to great effect. The

Maori culture in New Zealand also has an oral tradition.

THEORIES OF LANGUAGE DEVELOPMENT

Some Terminology

In order to take part in discussions about language theory, you need to know the meanings of some words:

* **Phonology**: the sounds of the language (or the visual aspects of a sign language).

* **Grammar**, sometimes called **syntax**: the word order, and the rules which describe how a language works (but not how we ought to speak).

* **Arbitrary symbols**: these refer to the past, help speakers to learn from the past, imagine the future, make jokes, tell lies and have fantasies.

* **Articulation**: how words are spoken in order to be understood.

* **Intonation**: the mood of the language and the way sounds go up and down.

* **Vocabulary** or **lexicon**: the words.

* **Semantics**: meanings of the language.

* **Communication**: shared meaning with self and others.

* **Conversations**: these require a sense of audience (meaning a sense of who you are talking to and listening to).

There are four approaches to studying language:

1   The **normative approach**, devised by Gesell in the 1930s–1960s.

2   The **behaviourist** theory (or the nurture approach), put forward by Skinner in the 1920s–1960s.

3   The **nature** theory that language development is innate and genetically predetermined, proposed by Chomsky in the 1960s. (See Chapter 2.)

4   The **social constructivist** theory of Piaget, Vygotsky and Bruner (see Chapter 2).

Literacy Around the World

Some languages are more phonologically complex than others. (The sounds are more difficult to learn.) Some languages are less consistent than others in the way they spell words. English is difficult in both ways. With the introduction of the **EYFS** early formal teaching is discouraged because starting early does not bring better results in reading and writing attainment later.

Normative Accounts of Language Development

Until the 1960s, experts like Gessell studied the development of language in young children mainly by using vocabulary counts. They counted the number and types of words that children used. They looked at whether children used single words, phrases and different types of sentence. This approach tended to stress what children could do at particular ages, and it could be very misleading. For example, recent research suggests that babies say words like 'up' and 'gone', but this is not recognised by adults. Adults do seize on babble like 'Mum', which adults want babies to say. Research shows that in fact the first word children in different parts of the world say is usually a comment on how people or objects have 'gone'. In Korea, adults say 'It's moving in' when they give babies a drink. In Western cultures adults are more likely to say, 'Here's your cup'. Korean babies say 'moving in' before they say 'cup'. Western babies say 'cup' before they say 'moving in'. Although it is not always useful to take a normative approach, it is important that those working with young children know about the general way in which all languages develop. (The terminology explored above is useful in this respect.) It will help you to remember that there is more to language development than vocabulary building.

The Language Development Revolution of the 1960s

From the 1920s a group of theorists called the **behaviourists** thought that language had to be 'put into' children, who started out as empty vessels. An exciting revolution occurred when the behaviourist view – that children learn language entirely by imitating – was challenged in 1968. Chomsky showed that children can invent new sentences that they definitely had not heard before. He believed children are born ready to learn whatever languages they hear around them. He proposed that they did this through what he called a **language acquisition device** (LAD). Chomsky said that:

* babies are born with a predisposition to learn, talk and listen;

* children learn to talk because they are genetically equipped to do so; they learn partly through the people they meet, communicate and socialise with.

Researchers studied the mistakes or errors that children make when they talk. They found that these gave important clues about the innate language rules that children all over the world seem to be born with. This was also true for children using sign languages rather than spoken languages.

THE SOCIAL CONTEXT OF LANGUAGE DEVELOPMENT

It became apparent in the 1960s and 1970s that some children were not as developed

in language as others. At that time it was thought that children from working-class homes were disadvantaged because they used what the researcher Bernstein called a restricted language code. Their language seemed to have limited vocabulary and used less complex forms. He believed that this held them back in school. This code contrasted with children from middle-class backgrounds, who Bernstein said used an elaborated language code. He thought that this was why they achieved more in school. As a result, in both the UK and the USA, compensatory education programmes were launched which tried to enrich the school language environment of the so-called disadvantaged children.

In fact, it is much more likely that, because staff in schools often come from different cultures and backgrounds from the children they work with, they do not always understand the richness of the child's own particular language and culture. Recent research shows that children growing up in Japan who are described as lower class do badly in school compared with the children described as upper class, but if their family moved to the USA, they were simply thought of as Japanese. Whether they were lower-class or upper-class Japanese, they did well in the USA, perhaps because there is a perception among American people that Japanese children study well at school.

Early years workers can promote children's language development if they:

* value and respect the child's language and culture, and try to learn about it;

* have real, everyday conversations with children, using gestures, eye contact, props and spoken language;

* encourage children to listen to and enjoy stories, including those from their own culture;

* introduce children to what is sometimes called 'storytelling language' or 'book language', for example 'Once upon a time, far, far away. . .'. (See EYFS, the principles and commitments on equality and diversity.)

These measures help children to take a full part in school life, in ways which build on their language or culture.

The theories of Piaget, Vygotsky and Bruner help practitioners to look at the social aspects of language development. This is the sociocultural approach. It is now thought that positive relationships and communications between people who respect each other are the most important factors in language development and in the development of the child's thinking. To be part of a culture is a need human beings are born with. There is a wide variation in the way that children begin to:

* understand;

* communicate;

* represent and express things through new language.

This variation depends on the culture in which the child grows up, as much as on the child's genetic and biological development.

SUPPORTING LANGUAGE DEVELOPMENT

All children need a supportive language environment. The DfES have initiated an accredited training course for practitioners at level 2 and above, 'Communicating Matters', which is taught through the local authorities. This looks at how to support language development in all children. It gives guidance on working with children using English as an additional language, who may benefit from gestures and actions when learning (action songs, for example).

Chapter 9 gives details about ways of supporting and extending the language development of bilingual and multilingual children.

It is essential for anyone working with young children to understand the importance of the child's first or home language. See also Chapter 9 for a discussion of home language.

Appreciating language and bilingualism

Children are more likely to feel that they belong if their first language or home language is understood and encouraged in the early years setting, as well as in their family. It is also important to value dialect or regional accents.

* **Dialect** is a variant form of a language. In the Caribbean, for example, Patois is spoken. It might seem to a standard English speaker that a Patois speaker is speaking ungrammatical and poor English. However, Patois is actually a combination of French language with the local (mainly English) language, as used on the different islands. In Trinidad, it will be a combination of French and the particular way English is used on that island. The word, phrases and speed of speaking will sound a bit like English, but Patois is not English.

* **Accent** is mostly to do with the way the words are pronounced. Some accents, such as Geordie or Glaswegian, can be difficult to understand for those who are not used to hearing them spoken.

Being bilingual should never be considered a disadvantage. In fact, the opposite is true. Learning how to communicate in more than one language helps children to learn in a much broader way. Recent studies in neuroscience give evidence to support this.

So, it is very important that you value a child's first language. It has been known for children to be labelled as having 'no language' when in fact they simply speak a different language from English. (See EYFS A Unique Child, Commitment, Equality, Diversity and Inclusion.)

* **Balanced bilingualism** – this is when children speak more than one language, each with equal fluency. In fact, a child's home language is usually more fluent than English. Very few children are completely balanced across two languages. Most children are unbalanced with one language more developed than the other.

* **Transitional bilingualism** – in some early childhood settings the first language has been valued only as a bridge for learning English. This is transitional bilingualism. It is assumed that the child will no longer need to speak the first language once English begins to take over. For example, a child who speaks Punjabi at home might be expected to speak English at school and gradually to speak English rather than Punjabi at home. In fact children need to continue to use their first language to help them transfer later on to reading and writing in the second language, which is usually English. If the child's first language is not valued as well as the new language that is being learnt, the opportunities for bilingualism and the advantages that bilingualism brings will be wasted.

Guidelines for promoting balanced bilingualism

Providing comprehensible input

This phrase, used by Stephen Krashen, means enabling the child to make sense of what is being said. If an adult picks up a cup, points at the jug of orange juice and asks: 'Would you like a drink of orange juice?', the meaning is clear. If the adult just says the words without the actions and props, the meaning is not at all clear to the child. The adult could be saying anything.

Allowing for a period of silence

At first there is often a period of silence on the part of the child, while he or she listens to all the sounds of the new language, and becomes familiar with them. The adult should understand this and be patient.

Providing 'opportunities' for listening

Children need plenty of opportunity to listen to what is being said and to make sense of it before they begin to speak in the new language. The process of learning occurs in three phases:

1 First there is understanding (comprehension).
2 Then the child speaks (production).
3 Eventually they become fluent (performance).

Exposure to fluent speakers

When children first begin to speak a new language they will not be fluent. They will make approximate sounds and communicate by intonation (tone of voice), rather than use words. They are greatly helped if they can talk with people who are completely fluent and comfortable with the new language. This is why children are no longer separated and taken out of classrooms to be 'taught' English. They learn much more effectively in a real-life setting, which is relaxed and not formal, and with other children and adults who can already speak the language.

Above all, children need to feel that becoming bilingual is a benefit and not a disadvantage. This is a message that we can help to support.

Helping Children towards Balanced Bilingualism

In order for balanced bilingualism to occur, rather than just transitional bilingualism, children need to be given appropriate help. You can help in the following ways.

Some children are fortunate enough to grow up learning more than one language. This helps them to learn in a broader way. When children learn more than one language they are, at the same time, being introduced to more than one culture in a deeply meaningful way. By doing several things at once, the brain learns to think more flexibly.

* They are learning two languages.

* They are learning the culture that is linked with each language. In Gujarati, the words 'thank you' are used in special situations. In English they are used often, but usually just as a way of being polite rather than as an expression of deep gratitude. And while in English there are two separate words for 'teaching' and 'learning', in Swedish there is only one, which is translated as 'helping children to learn'.

* They can think in different ways about the same thing. For example, the Inuit language has seven words for snow. This makes it possible to think about snow in much greater detail.

* They grow up understanding different ways of thinking, and different cultural layers. This helps them to respect and value differences between people.

* They understand more easily that names are arbitrarily assigned to objects and that names for things can be changed. This helps them with concept formation.

* They find it easier to separate meanings and sounds.

* They are more sensitive to the emotional aspects of language, such as intonation, and they can interpret situations more easily.

* They can think more broadly. This is often called divergent thinking.

Practitioners need to support the language development of children who have special educational needs and disabilities. It is important to remember that some children do not use verbal ways of communicating. They will need to be introduced to British Sign Language (BSL), Makaton or Objects of Reference.

LANGUAGE DELAY

A child who has a hearing or visual impairment, has Asperger syndrome or is **autistic** may be constrained in understanding and using language (i.e. in their *reception* and *expression* of language). (A definition of the term 'autistic' can be found in Unit 14 on CD-ROM.) Speech therapists, specialist teachers and other professionals may be needed to support the language development of these children. All children need to mix with other children and adults who speak fluently so that they can hear the patterns of the language they are trying to learn.

However, if they are always in the company of other people who are also learning a new language, they will not hear the correct patterns of the language in question and may learn incorrect grammar patterns. They may have to unlearn some of the things they have picked up. Hearing other people speak fluently means experiencing what is called comprehensible output (see page 105).

Children Who Do Not Speak

* It does not help development if children are made to speak. But it does help if they are invited to speak, as long as they can turn down the invitation

without being made to feel bad or a failure.

* It is very important to check that a silent child can still see and hear.

* It is crucial to be sure that the child understands what is being said.

* It is important to monitor children who do not speak through your **observations**. Share your observations with your line manager and the rest of the team.

* Bear in mind that children under emotional stress sometimes become withdrawn.

* Other children can sometimes be a great help in explaining things meaningfully to a child.

* Stories and rhymes can be made clearer by using props and pictures.

TALKING TO BABIES – LANGUAGE AND ACTION

When adults talk to babies, they tend to talk about things that are happening all around. They speak slowly, in a high-pitched voice, and use a lot of repetition. This is called 'Motherese' or 'Fatherese'.

Adults will pause, waiting for the baby to 'reply', using babble. However, in some cultures adults do not speak in Motherese or Fatherese to babies, but instead the babies watch their mothers working and talking with other adults.

Language needs to accompany action. For instance, the adult lifts the baby and says 'Up we go. Let's put you in the pram now'. It is important that adults continue to describe what is happening when babies become young children – 'You've got to the top of the slide, haven't you? Are you going to come down now?' Actions help children to understand what is being said

Fig 4.7 Discussion that is two-way is important in developing language

to them. Actions give children clues about meaning. This is comprehensible input (see page 105).

LANGUAGE AND THOUGHT/COGNITION

Remember that all areas of a child's development are interrelated. Language and thought (or cognition) are often considered to be particularly closely linked. Can we think without words? Some psychologists have suggested that thinking is not possible without language. Language is especially important for abstract thinking. This means that it would be difficult to understand the idea, for example, of what is fair or honest unless a child has enough language. Piaget, however, emphasised that children learn to think using a variety of different ways to represent their experiences, ideas, feelings and relationships symbolically. Indeed, he thought that language is only one kind of symbolic mode that people use to do this. Piaget's work has been very positive in helping those working with children with language delay or impairment, and with all children who do not begin to use coded or shared language systems. This is because he stressed the personal and individual ways through which children can communicate, as well as their later use of the arbitrary symbols of their culture. Personal communication can include:

*   gestures;
*   props – the handbag represents mother when she goes for coffee, and the child knows she is coming back because her handbag is there;
*   evidence – the footprint in the sand tells the child someone was there;
*   links – the child has a teddy bear while the mother is away; this gives the child a link with the absent mother; the communication is personal between this particular child and this particular mother.

Thinking about Thinking, and Thinking about Language

*   **Cognition** means thinking and having ideas (concepts).
*   **Metacognition** means that children begin to think about their own thinking. They reflect on their own ideas, such as, 'That was a good idea', 'That was a bad idea.'
*   **Metalinguistics** means children beginning to think about what they say. By 4 years, children usually make jokes and 'play' with words, devising nonsense words for fun.

LANGUAGE AND FEELINGS

Children experience problems when they are not able to put their feelings into words or to express themselves in any way. This has a damaging impact on the development of their self-esteem. If children are full of anger, anxiety, frustration or fear, they need to

express this. Talking about feelings is just as important as talking about ideas. Children who cannot explain or put into words how they feel often have temper tantrums or show other kinds of challenging behaviour. In fact, it is often easier to help children to put their ideas into words than it is to help them to express their feelings or emotions in words. The next section contains some suggestions for promoting talk, including talk about feelings.

LANGUAGE AND CONVERSATION

Talking to Oneself

Children talk to themselves when they:

*   need to think through different ideas;
*   are feeling frustrated;
*   need to talk about their feelings;
*   need to organise their thinking;
*   want to regulate what they do (i.e. tell themselves what to do).

Textbooks often say that this egocentric speech fades when children begin to internalise their thinking more easily. In this context, egocentric does not mean selfish, it just means thinking from their own point of view. Young children can put themselves in someone else's shoes if that person's experience is linked with their own.

Conversations with Another Person

'Conversations' begin when tiny babies are spoken to by adults close to them in Motherese or Fatherese. Visually impaired babies respond by becoming still and listening intently. Sighted babies 'dance' in response to speech. 'Conversations' continue as toddlers babble in response to adult talking. It is quite possible to have a conversation with sounds but no words. Researchers have noticed that although toddlers often turn their backs during a conversation and say 'No!' to their mother's suggestions, they do in fact take up and imitate the ideas that are offered to them. It is as if toddlers need to have conversations with other people, even when they can still only say a few words, even if the words do not fit the situation.

Small-Group Discussions

Children also need help when taking part in group discussions. Stories, songs and dances are useful catalysts. These are best used with children aged 3–8 years, in small groups. Having to wait for a turn frustrates children. It will not help them to discuss and enjoy things. In fact, it could put them off stories, songs and dancing. Even children aged 5–8 years cannot wait too long before being allowed to have their say in a discussion or a conversation. Chapter 13 gives examples of strategies for storytelling with small groups.

Encouraging Conversations and Group Discussions

Conversations need to:

* be two-way;
* involve sharing ideas and feelings;
* involve thinking of each other;
* be a real exchange of ideas and feelings between adults and children;
* include taking turns;
* involve thinking about things of interest to each other, as well as about things of interest to oneself.

LANGUAGE AND CONTEXT

Different situations bring about different sorts of language. A **formal situation** – being

introduced to the mayor or buying a bus ticket – is different from an **informal** one, for example chatting with friends over a cup of coffee or playing in the park. It takes years for children to learn the different ways of talking which are appropriate to formal and informal situations. Understanding the difference in context is important in most cultures.

Being with Familiar Adults

Children need to be with the same adults each day, so that they learn the subtle signals about how people talk to each other in different situations. In different situations people comment, describe, give opinions, predict, give commands, use formal phrases, reminisce, and so on. Meaning changes according to context. For example, 'Go into the hall!', when said at home, might be a reference to the small area near the front door. In another setting, it might be a reference to a huge room, full of chairs, with a platform at one end.

Fig 4.8 Children learn through talking together as they engage in solving a problem

Guidelines for promoting language skills

∗ Children need to be spoken to as individuals.

∗ Be patient: young children find it hard to put their thoughts and feelings into words, so listening takes patience. It is very tempting to prompt children and say things for them. Instead, try nodding or saying 'Hmm'. This gives children time to say what they want to.

∗ It does help children when adults elaborate on what they have just said and give the correct pattern. For example, Shanaz, at 2 years, says 'I falled down'. The adult replies 'Yes, you did, didn't you? You fell down. Never mind, I will help you up'.

∗ However, research indicates that children are not helped when adults make them pronounce things properly or repeat things to get the grammar 'right'. Remember, grammar is not about how children 'ought' to speak, but about showing adults that children understand things about the language they speak.

∗ It is important that all children experience unrushed, one-to-one conversations with both adults and other children, for example when sharing a drink together at the snack table, or chatting while using the clay. (See EYFS Principles on Learning and Development, Communication, Language and Literacy Development.)

Children can tell the difference between someone who sincerely wants to talk with them and someone who is being patronising and puts on a 'talking to children' voice. They appreciate adults who take their ideas and feelings seriously and respect and value them.

Fig 4.9 A relaxed atmosphere and a shared focus of attention between adults and children help conversations to develop

Guidelines for encouraging conversations

∗ It is important to remember that anybody in a group can start or end a conversation.

∗ Two speakers can talk together, even using different languages.

∗ In good conversation, there must be comprehensible input. This means using actions and props which show *meaning*, as well as gestures and facial expressions. The lack of comprehensible input is probably one reason why many people dislike talking on the telephone, which only gives intonation (mood and sounds) clues. Communication is 85 per cent non-verbal.

∗ Children must not be rushed to speak, and they must feel relaxed.

∗ It is better to elaborate on what children say, rather than to correct their errors. This respects children's feelings and promotes their wellbeing. It gives them confidence in themselves as learners.

LANGUAGE DEVELOPMENT – A SUMMARY

From Birth to 1 Year: Emerging Language

The first year of a baby's life is sometimes called 'pre-linguistic'. This is an inaccurate, negative and misleading term. It gives us a much more helpful and positive image of a baby if we think of this stage as one of early communication before words or signs are used. Thus it is sometimes called the stage of emerging language.

From 1 to 4 Years: Symbolic Development

This is sometimes called the period of language explosion. Every aspect of language seems to move forward rapidly at this time. Language development is part of symbolic behaviour, so this is often called the period of symbolic development. It is the best time to learn other languages, or to become bilingual or multilingual.

From 4 to 8 Years: Consolidating Learning

This is the time when what has been learnt and understood about language is consolidated, so further developments are enhancements rather than being brand new. For example, children now become better at articulation, conventional grammar patterns, thinking about whom they are talking to, the context and situation, and putting ideas and feelings into words.

ACTIVITY: INVESTIGATING REPRESENTATION, COMMUNICATION AND LANGUAGE DEVELOPMENT

1 Make an audiotape of a baby of 6–12 months, or of a child of 1–3, 3–5 or 5–7 years. Write down the sounds or language that you find. Note any vowels, consonants, syllables, words, **holophrases** (single-word utterances expressing multiple thoughts, ideas or feelings) or sentences. Make a transcript. Do not use more than 5 minutes of the tape, as transcripts take a long time to make. Analyse the transcript, using the section on page 102 to help you identify the different aspects of language. Refer to the child's phonology, vocabulary, syntax, semantics, communications, arbitrary symbols, sense of audience and context, intonation and articulation. Then evaluate the language development of the child.

2 Observe a one-to-one relationship between an adult and a child at 18 months, 3½ years and 5½ years. Note the differences in language in the conversations, and the kinds of non-verbal communication involved. Evaluate the observation.

3 Observe a small group (three or four children) and then a large group (six or more children) with an adult. Note examples of turn-taking and any of the things listed on pages 93. Note the ages of the children involved. Evaluate the activity.

A summary of representation, communication and language development

1 Language development is deeply linked with the processes of representation and play, and communication.

2 Language makes it easier for us to represent (to keep hold of experiences), to communicate (to share these experiences with the self and other people) and to think in abstract ways beyond the here and now (as in play).

3 Once children can listen and talk, they are well on the way to adding more layers of symbolic behaviour. The symbolic layers in language acquisition are:

* non-verbal communication (gesture, etc.);
* listening;
* talking;
* writing;
* reading.

CHAPTER 5

Physical Development

Contents

• Common patterns in physical growth and development • Defining terms • What is physical development? • Factors affecting physical development • Normative physical development, 0–16 years • Physical development in relation to other areas of development • Physical activity and exercise • The importance of physical play • Promoting physical development in children with special needs

As we have seen, babies and young children follow standard basic patterns when acquiring physical skills, but there are wide individual variations. A child's range of physical skills or abilities has a major effect on other areas of development. For example, once the child has learned to crawl or shuffle on her bottom, she will be more independent and will be able to explore things that were previously out of reach.

The responses of other people to a child who has developed new skills will also alter. Adults will make changes to the child's environment – putting now reachable objects out of harm's way – and they will say 'no' more often.

COMMON PATTERNS IN PHYSICAL GROWTH AND DEVELOPMENT

Height

The most important factors controlling a child's growth in height are the genes and chromosomes inherited from the parents. Growth in height may be divided into four distinct phases:

✳ **Phase 1:** this is a period of very rapid growth which lasts for about two years.

The baby gains 25–30 cm in length and triples her body weight in the first year.

✳ **Phase 2:** this is a slower but steady period of growth which lasts from about 2 years of age through to adolescence. The child gains 5–8 cm in height and about 3 kg in body weight per year until adolescence.

✳ **Phase 3:** this is a period characterised by a dramatic growth spurt, when the child may add 8–16 cm per year to her height for some years. The biggest weight gain occurs between the ages of 10–14 in girls and 12–16 in boys.

✳ **Phase 4:** this is a period of slow growth with only small increases in height and weight until the final adult size is reached. The age at which the final adult size is reached is variable, but is usually between 18–20 years.

It is essential that those who work with children know how a child grows and develops. Remember that every child is unique – the 'average' or 'normal' child does not exist. Learning about child development involves studying patterns of growth and development, but these are taken only as guidelines for 'normality'. You are ideally placed to notice when a child is not progressing according to these guidelines.

DEFINING TERMS

Growth

Growth refers to an increase in physical size, and can be measured by height (length), weight and head circumference. Growth is determined by:

* heredity;
* hormones;
* nutrition;
* emotional influences.

Growth Charts

These charts are used to compare the growth pattern of an individual child with the normal range of growth patterns that are typical of a large number of children of the same sex. The charts are used to plot height (or, in young babies, length), weight and head circumference. Note that:

* The fiftieth centile (or percentile) is the **median**. It represents the middle of the range of growth patterns.

* The tenth centile is close to the bottom of the range. If the height of a child is on the tenth centile, it means that in any typical group of 100 children, 90 would measure more and 9 would measure less.

* The ninetieth centile is close to the top of the range. If the weight of a child is on the nintieth centile, then in any typical group of 100 children, 89 would weigh less and 10 would weigh more.

Body Proportions

As a child grows, the various parts of the body change in shape and proportion, as well as increasing in size. The different body parts also grow at different rates, e.g. the feet and hands of a teenager reach their final adult size before the body does. At birth, a baby's head accounts for about one-quarter of the total length of the body, whereas at 7 years old, the head will be about one-sixth of total length.

Physical Development

Development is a continuous process from conception to maturity. It depends upon the maturation of the nervous system. Variation in the rate of development is due to the interaction between the individual's genetic make-up and the environmental experiences encountered during the development process.

Development is concerned with the possession of skills. Physical development proceeds in a set order, with simple behaviours occurring before more complex skills – for example, a child will sit before he or she stands, and will walk before being able to skip or to hop.

Directions of Development

Human development follows a sequence:

* from simple to complex, e.g. a child will walk before she can skip or hop;

* from head to toe (cephalo–caudal development), e.g. head control is acquired before coordination of the spinal muscles. So a child learns to crawl by using upper body movements before he can creep, a movement involving the use of his legs;

* from inner to outer (proximo–distal development), e.g. a child can coordinate her arms to reach for an object before she has learned the fine manipulative skills necessary to pick it up;

* from general to specific, e.g. a young baby shows pleasure by a massive general response (eyes widen, legs and arms move vigorously, etc.). An older child shows pleasure by smiling or using appropriate words and gestures.

Norm

A norm is a fixed or ideal standard. Developmental norms are sometimes called 'milestones', denoting markers in the recognised pattern of physical development which it is expected that children will follow. Each child develops in a unique way – using norms helps us understand the patterns of development while acknowledging the wide variation between individuals.

Normative Measurements in Child Development

Normative measurements describe averages or norms which provide a framework for assessing development; these norms are the result of observations and research by many professionals in the field of child development (see Chapter 2). They are useful in helping parents and carers to know what to expect at a certain age, especially when planning a safe, stimulating environment.

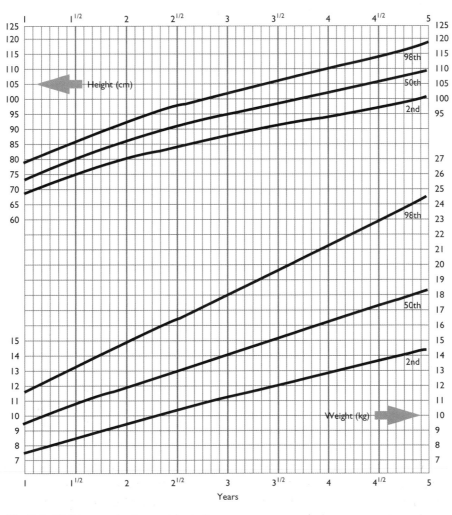

Fig 5.1 Child growth chart: girls, 1–5 years

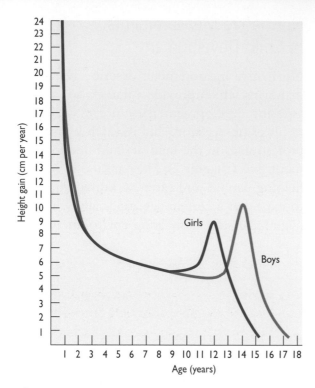

Fig 5.2 Height gain in childhood

Their use can, however, lead people to label children as 'slow' or 'bad' if they fall behind the norm. Using norms in this way is not helpful and will not enable you to promote development. Although professionals caring for children need to have a framework of the patterns of expected development to help them promote children's health and to stimulate the children's all-round development, they should be aware of the pitfalls of using norms.

The Development of Gross Motor Skills

These are sometimes called skills of **movement**. Gross motor skills use the large muscles in the body and include walking, running, climbing, and so on.

The Development of Fine Motor Skills

These use the smaller muscles and include:

* **gross manipulative skills** which involve single-limb movements, usually the arm, for example throwing, catching and sweeping arm movements;

* **fine manipulative skills** which involve precise use of the hands and fingers, for example for drawing, using a knife and fork, writing, doing up shoelaces and buttons.

The Skills of Locomotion and Balance

* **Locomotion** is the ability to move around on one's own. It is central to the pattern of development changes which occur at the end of the baby's first year, and begins with crawling or bottom-shuffling.

* **Balance** is the first of all the senses to develop. It is crucial to posture, movement and **proprioception** (see page 119).

The 8-month-old child who rolls backwards and forwards across the floor with no particular goal in sight, is preparing her balance for:

* sitting;

* standing; and

* walking.

Eye–hand Coordination

The ability to reach and grasp objects in a coordinated way requires months of practice and close attention:

* In the first months after birth, eye–hand coordination takes effort.

* By around 9 months of age, a baby can usually manage to guide their movements with a single glance to check for accuracy, e.g. when feeding themselves with a spoon.

WHAT IS PHYSICAL DEVELOPMENT?

Physical development is the way in which the body gains skills and becomes more complex in its performance. Physical development is the most visible of all the abilities shown in childhood and includes the less observable development of all the senses: hearing, vision, touch, taste and smell.

There are several aspects of physical development, which are outlined in Table 5.1.

Sensory Development

Sensation is the process by which we receive information through the senses. These include:

* vision;
* hearing;
* smell;
* touch;
* taste;
* proprioception.

Perception is making sense of what we see, hear, touch, smell and taste. Our perception is affected by previous experience and knowledge, and by our emotional state at the time. There are therefore wide variations in the way different individuals perceive the same object, situation or experience.

Visual Development

A newborn baby's eyes are barely half the size of an adult's and, although they are structurally similar, they differ in two ways:

1 A baby's focus is fixed at about 20 cm, which is the distance from the baby to her mother's face when breast-feeding. Anything nearer or farther away appears blurred. She will remain short-sighted for about 4 months.

2 The response to visual stimuli is slower in babies because the information received by the eye takes longer to reach

Table 5.1 A summary of activities related to physical skills development

Gross motor skills (locomotion or movement)	Fine motor skills (manipulation)	Balance and stabilisation
walking	throwing	bending
running	catching	stretching
skipping	picking up	twisting
jumping	kicking	turning
hopping	rolling	balancing
chasing	volleying	squatting
dodging	striking	transferring
climbing	squeezing	landing
crawling	kneading	hanging

Fig 5.3 (a) and (b) Gross motor skills (locomotion)

(c) Fine motor skills (manipulation)

the brain via the nervous pathway. A newborn baby is able only poorly to fix her eyes upon objects and follow their movement. Head and eye movement is also poorly coordinated; in the first week or two, the eyes lag behind when the baby's head is turned to one side, a feature known by paediatricians as the 'doll's eye phenomenon'.

Research has shown that babies prefer looking at:

* patterned areas rather than plain ones, especially stripes;
* edges of objects in 3D;

* anything which resembles a human face – babies will actually search out and stare at human faces during their first 2 months of life;
* brightly coloured objects.

By around 4 months a baby can focus on both near and distant objects and her ability to recognise different objects is improving steadily. By 6 months the baby will respond visually to movements across the room and will move her head to see what is happening. By 1 year her eye movements are smoother and she can follow rapidly moving objects with the eyes (a skill known as **tracking**). A squint is normal at this point.

The Development of Hearing

Newborn babies are able to hear almost as well as adults do.

* Certain rhythmic sounds – often called 'white noise' – seem to have a special soothing effect on babies. The drone of a vacuum cleaner or hairdryer is calming!
* The sound of a human voice evokes the greatest response and the rhythms of lullabies have been used for centuries in all cultures to help babies to sleep, or to comfort them.
* Babies can recognise their own mother's voice from the first week and can distinguish its tone and pitch from those of other people.
* Sudden changes in noise levels tend to disturb very young babies and make them jump.
* From about 6 months, a baby learns to recognise and distinguish between different sounds; for example, the sound of a spoon in a dish means that food is on its way.

* Babies can also discriminate between cheerful and angry voices, and will respond in kind.

The Development of Smell, Taste and Touch

The senses of smell and taste are closely linked. If our sense of smell is defective, for example because of a cold, then our sense of taste is also reduced. Babies as young as one week old who are breastfed are able to tell the difference between their own mother's smell and other women's smells. From birth babies are also able to distinguish the four basic tastes – sweet, sour, bitter and salty.

The sense of touch is also well developed in infancy, as can be demonstrated by the primitive reflexes (see Unit 18 on CD-ROM). Babies seem to be particularly sensitive to touches on the mouth, the face, the hands, the soles of the feet and the abdomen. Research has shown that babies would rather be stroked than fed.

Proprioception is the sense that tells the baby the location of the mobile parts of his body (e.g. his legs) in relation to the rest of him – in other words, where his own body begins and ends.

Sensory Deprivation

A congenitally blind baby (i.e. a baby who is born blind) will develop a more sophisticated sense of touch than a sighted baby, although they both start life with the same touch potential. As the sense of touch develops, so the area of the brain normally assigned to touch increases in size for the blind baby, and the area of the brain normally assigned to sight decreases.

Similarly, in a congenitally deaf baby, the part of the brain that normally receives auditory stimuli is taken over by the visual and movement input from sign language.

FACTORS AFFECTING PHYSICAL DEVELOPMENT

Children's physical development is influenced by their:

* growing confidence and sense of identity;
* enjoyment of physical play;
* increasing ability to control their own bodies through movement;
* physical wellbeing and strength.

As children develop, they become faster, stronger, more mobile, more sure of their balance, and they start to use these skills in a wider range of physical activities.

There are many other factors that affect children's physical development:

1 **Genetic factors** – the genes children inherit from their parents affect both growth and development (see Unit 14 on CD-ROM).

2 **Nutrition** – family income, lifestyle and culture all affect the diet a child receives. Children who are on poor diets are more susceptible to infection as their immunity is affected by the lack of adequate minerals and vitamins.

3 **Environmental factors** which include:
   * overcrowded housing;
   * air pollution (e.g. lead poisoning from traffic exhausts and adults smoking in the home);
   * lack of access to a play area or garden.

4 **Social factors** – such as:
   * love and affection;
   * stimulation;
   * opportunities to play.

Healthy growth and development can be affected when a child receives too little (or too much) stimulation.

NORMATIVE PHYSICAL DEVELOPMENT: 0–16 YEARS

From Birth to 4 Weeks

Gross Motor Skills

* Baby lies supine (on her back) with head to one side.
* When placed on her front (the prone position), she lies with head turned to one side and by 1 month can lift her head.
* If pulled to sitting position, her head will lag, her back curves over and her head falls forward.

Fine Motor Skills

* She will turn her head towards the light and stare at bright, shiny objects.
* She is fascinated by human faces and gazes attentively at her carer's face when fed or held.
* Her hands are usually tightly closed.
* She reacts to loud sounds, but by 1 month may be soothed by particular music.

Guidelines for promoting development: birth to 4 weeks

* Encourage the baby to lie on the floor to kick and experiment safely with movement.
* Provide an opportunity for her to feel the freedom of moving without a nappy or clothes on.
* Always support the baby's head when playing with her as her neck

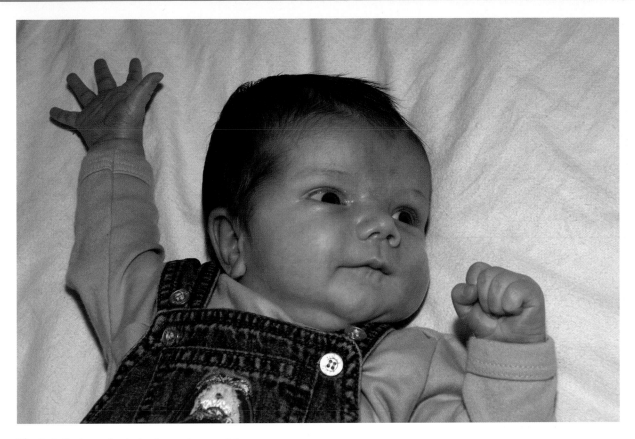

Fig 5.4 0–4 weeks: baby in supine position

muscles are not strong enough to control movement.

* Use bright colours in furnishings.
* Provide a mobile over the cot and/ or the nappy-changing area.
* Feed on demand, and talk and sing to her.
* Provide plenty of physical contact and maintain eye contact.
* Talk lovingly to her and give her the opportunity to respond.
* Introduce her to different household noises. Provide contact with other adults and children.
* Encourage bonding with main carer by enjoying the relationship.
* Expect no set routine in the first few weeks. Pick her up and talk to her face-to-face.

4–8 weeks

Gross Motor Skills

* Baby can now turn from her side to her back.
* She can lift her head briefly from the prone position.
* Her arm and leg movements are jerky and uncontrolled.
* There is head lag if she pulled to a sitting position.

Fine Motor Skills

* Baby turns her head towards the light and stares at bright, shiny objects.
* She will show interest and excitement by facial expression and will gaze attentively at her carer's face while being fed.
* She will open her hand to grasp your finger.

Fig 5.5 4–8 weeks: baby gazing at mobile

8–12 Weeks

Gross Motor Skills

* When lying supine, baby's head is in a central position.
* She can now lift her head and chest off the bed in a prone position, supported on forearms.
* There is almost no head lag in the sitting position.
* Her legs can kick vigorously, both separately and together.
* She can wave her arms and brings her hands together over her body.

Fine Motor Skills

* Baby moves her head to follow adult movements.
* She watches her hands and plays with her fingers.
* She holds a rattle for a brief time before dropping it.

Guidelines for stimulating development: 4–8 weeks

* Use a special supporting infant chair so that the baby can see adult activity.
* Let her kick freely, without nappies.
* Massage her body and limbs during or after bathing.
* Use brightly coloured mobiles and wind chimes over her cot and/or changing mat.
* Let her explore different textures.
* Light rattles and toys strung over her pram or cot will encourage focusing and coordination.
* Talk to and smile with the baby.
* Sing while feeding or bathing her – allow her time to respond.
* Learn to distinguish her cries and to respond to them differently.
* Tickling and teasing her may induce laughter.
* Talk to her and hold her close.

Guidelines for stimulating development: 8–12 weeks

* Place the baby in a supporting infant chair so that she can watch adult activity.
* Encourage her to kick without nappies.
* Massage and stroke her limbs when bathing or if using massage oil.
* Use brightly coloured mobiles and wind chimes to encourage focusing at 20 cm.
* Place a rattle in her hand and attach objects which make a noise when struck above the cot.
* Read her nursery rhymes.
* Talk sensibly to her and imitate her sounds to encourage her to repeat them.

* Holding her close and talking lovingly will strengthen the bonding process.
* Encourage contact with other adults and children.
* Respond to her needs and show enjoyment in caring for her.

From 4–5 Months

Gross Motor Skills

* Baby has good head control.
* She is beginning to sit with support and can roll over from her back to her side.
* She is beginning to reach for objects.
* When supine, she plays with her own feet.
* She holds her head up when pulled to a sitting position.

Fine Manipulative Skills

* She is beginning to use palmar grasp.
* She can transfer objects from hand to hand.
* She is very interested in all activity.
* Everything is taken to her mouth.
* She moves her head around to follow people and objects.

Guidelines for stimulating development: 4–5 months

* Practise sitting with the baby on the carer's knee.
* Play rough and tumble games on the bed. Play bouncing games on the carer's knee to songs.
* Offer rattles and soft, squashy toys to give a variety of textures.
* Homemade toys (e.g. transparent plastic containers with dried peas inside or empty cotton reels tied together) offer interest. NB Check lids are secure and always supervise play.
* Continue talking to the baby, particularly in response to her own sounds.
* Provide different toys with a range of textures and sounds.
* Sing nursery rhymes combined with finger play, e.g. This little piggy . . .
* Give her the opportunity to find out things for herself and begin to choose play activities.
* Encourage playing alone and in the company of other children.
* Waterproof books in the bath give a lot of pleasure.

6–9 Months

Gross Motor Skills

* The baby can roll from front to back.
* She may attempt to crawl but will often end up sliding backwards.
* She may grasp her feet and place them in her mouth.
* She can sit without support for longer periods of time.
* She may 'cruise' around furniture and may even stand or walk alone.

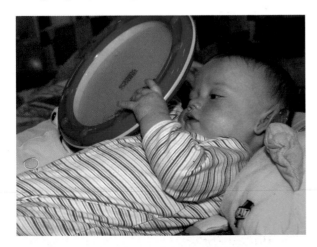

Fig 5.6 6–9 months: baby playing alone

123

Fine Manipulative Skills

* The baby is alert to people and objects.
* She is beginning to use pincer grasp with thumb and index finger.
* She transfers toys from one hand to the other.
* She looks for fallen objects.
* Everything is explored by putting it in her mouth.

Guidelines for stimulating development: 6–9 months

* Encourage confidence and balance by placing toys around the sitting baby. Make sure furniture is stable and has no sharp corners when baby is using it to pull herself up.
* Encourage mobility by placing toys just out of baby's reach.
* Encourage visual awareness by providing varied experiences.
* Small objects, which must be safe if chewed by the baby, will encourage the pincer grasp (small pieces of biscuit are ideal, but always supervise).
* Build a tower of bricks with her and watch her delight when they all fall down.
* Look at picture books together and encourage her to point at objects by naming them.
* Talk to her about everyday things.
* Widen her experiences by going on outings which include animals.
* Imitate animal sounds and encourage her to copy you.
* Allow plenty of time for play.
* Provide simple 'musical instruments', e.g. xylophone or wooden spoon and saucepan.
* Use a safety mirror for the baby to recognise herself.

9–12 Months

Gross Motor Skills

* The baby will now be mobile; she may be crawling, bear-walking, bottom-shuffling or even walking.
* She can sit up on her own and lean forwards to pick things up.
* She may crawl upstairs and onto low items of furniture.
* She may bounce in rhythm to music.

Fine Motor Skills

* Her pincer grasp is now well developed and she can pick things up and pull them towards her.
* She can poke with one finger and will point to desired objects.
* She can clap her hands and imitate adult actions.
* She throws toys deliberately.
* She manages spoons and finger foods well.

At 15 Months

Gross Motor Skills

* The baby probably walks alone with feet wide apart and arms raised to maintain balance.

Fig 5.7 9–12 months: baby crawling

Guidelines for stimulating development: 9–12 months

* Provide large-wheeled toys to push around – brick trucks serve the dual purpose of walking and stacking games.
* Ensure furniture is safe and stable for climbers.
* Go swimming, or walking in the park.
* Provide small climbing frames – closely supervised – to increase her balance and coordination.
* Offer stacking and nesting toys.
* Roll balls for her to bring back to you.
* Encourage sand and water play – always supervised.
* Offer cardboard boxes and saucepans to put things into and take things out of.
* Partake in plenty of talking to the baby which requires a response that will develop language ability.
* Encourage self-feeding – tolerate messes.
* Talk constantly to her and use rhymes and action songs.
* Offer lots of play opportunities with adult interaction – sharing, taking turns and so on.
* Encourage her to join in and help with regular chores.
* Foster a feeling of self-worth by providing her with her own equipment and utensils, e.g. she will need her own flannel, toothbrush, cup and spoon.

* She is likely to fall over and land suddenly on her bottom.
* She can probably manage stairs and steps, but will need supervision.

* She can stand without help from furniture or people.
* She kneels without support.

Fine Manipulative Skills

* The baby can build with a few bricks and arrange toys on the floor.
* She holds crayons in palmar grasp.
* She turns several pages of a book at once.
* She can point to desired objects.
* She shows a preference for one hand, but uses either.

Guidelines for stimulating development: at 15 months

* Provide stacking toys and bricks.
* Provide push-and-pull toys for children who are walking.
* Read picture books with simple rhymes.
* Offer big, empty cardboard boxes for play (very popular).
* Provide thick crayons or thick paintbrushes.

Fig 5.8 15 months: child looking at a book

> * Arrange a corner of the kitchen or garden for messy play involving the use of water or paint.
> NB This is a high-risk age for accidents – be vigilant at all times.

At 18 Months

Gross Motor Skills

* The baby walks confidently and is able to stop without falling.
* She can kneel, squat, climb and carry things around with her.
* She can climb onto an adult chair forwards and then turn round to sit.
* She comes downstairs, usually by creeping backwards on her tummy.

Fig 5.9 18 months: child bending down to pick up an object

Fine Manipulative Skills

* The baby can thread large beads.
* She uses a pincer grasp to pick up small objects.
* She builds a tower of three or more cubes.
* She scribbles to and fro on paper.

> **Guidelines for stimulating development: at 18 months**
> * Push-and-pull toys are still popular.
> * Teach the baby how to manage stairs safely.
> * Provide threading toys, and hammer and peg toys.
> * Encourage and praise early attempts at drawing.

At 2 Years

Gross Motor Skills

* The child is very mobile and can run safely.
* She can climb up onto the furniture.
* She walks up and down stairs, usually two feet to a step.
* She tries to kick a ball, with some success, but cannot yet catch a ball.

Fine Manipulative Skills

* The child can draw circles, lines and dots, using preferred hand.
* She can pick up tiny objects using a fine pincer grasp.
* She can build a tower of six or seven bricks, with a longer concentration span.
* She enjoys picture books and turns pages individually.

Fig 5.10 2 years: trying to kick a large bal

* She can stand and walk on tiptoe and stand on one foot.
* She has good spatial awareness.
* She rides a tricycle using pedals.
* She can climb stairs with one foot on each step – downwards with two feet per step.

Fine Manipulative Skills

* The child can build a tower of nine or ten bricks.
* She can control a pencil using her thumb and first two fingers – the dynamic tripod grasp.
* She enjoys painting with a large brush.
* She can copy a circle.

Guidelines for stimulating development: at 2 years

* Provide toys to ride and climb on, and space to run and play.
* Allow trips to parks and opportunities for messy play with water and paints.
* Encourage use of safe climbing frames and sandpits, always supervised.
* Provide simple models to build (e.g. Duplo®), as well as jigsaw puzzles, crayons and paper, picture books and glove puppets.

At 3 Years

Gross Motor Skills

* The child can jump from a low step.
* She walks backwards and sideways.

Fig 5.11 3 years: standing on one leg

Guidelines for stimulating development: at 3 years

* Provide a wide variety of playthings – dough for modelling, sand and safe household utensils.

* Encourage play with other children. Allow swimming, trips to the park, maybe even enjoy long walks.

* Read to the child and discuss everyday events.

* Encourage art and craft activities.

* Promote independence by teaching her how to look after and put away her own clothes and toys.

* Encourage visits to the library and story times.

Fig 5.12 4 years: building a tower of ten bricks

At 4 Years

Gross Motor Skills

* Sense of balance is developing; she may be able to walk along a line.

* She can catch, kick, throw and bounce a ball.

* She can bend at the waist to pick up objects from the floor.

* She enjoys climbing trees and on frames.

* She can run up and down stairs, one foot per step.

Fine Manipulative Skills

* The child can build a tower of ten or more bricks.

* She can draw a recognisable person on request, showing head, legs and trunk.

* She can thread small beads on a lace.

Guidelines for stimulating development: at 4 years

* Provide plenty of opportunity for exercise.

* Play party games – musical statues, and so on.

* Use rope swings and climbing frames.

* Obtain access to a bike with stabilisers.

* Provide small-piece construction toys, jigsaws and board games.

* Encourage gluing and sticking activities, as well as paint, sand, water and play dough.

* Prepare child for school by teaching her how to dress and undress for games, and to manage going to the toilet by herself.

At 5 Years

Gross Motor Skills

* The child can use a variety of play equipment – slides, swings, climbing frames.

* She can play ball games.

* She can hop and run lightly on toes, and move rhythmically to music.

* Her sense of balance is well developed.

Fine Manipulative Skills

* The child may be able to thread a large-eyed needle and sew large stitches.

* She can draw a person with head, trunk, legs, nose, mouth and eyes.

* She has good control over pencils and paintbrushes.

* She can copy a square and a triangle.

Guidelines for stimulating development: at 5 years

* Provide plenty of outdoor activities.

* Encourage non-stereotypical activities, e.g. boys using skipping ropes, girls playing football.

Fig 5.13 5 years: drawing a person

* Team sports may be provided at clubs such as Beavers, Rainbows and Woodcraft Folk.

* Encourage the use of models, jigsaws, sewing kits and craft activities, as well as drawing and painting.

* Introduce tracing and image patterns.

At 6 and 7 years

Gross Motor Skills

* The child has increased agility, muscle coordination and balance.

* She develops competence in riding a two-wheeled bicycle.

* She hops easily, with good balance.

* She can jump off apparatus at school.

Fine Manipulative Skills

* The child can build a tall, straight tower with bricks.

* She can draw a person with detail, e.g. clothes and eyebrows.

* She writes letters of the alphabet with a similar writing hold to an adult.

* She can catch a ball thrown from a metre away with one hand.

Guidelines for stimulating development: at 6 and 7 years

* Provide opportunity for vigorous exercise.

* Team sports, riding a bike and swimming can all be encouraged; give plenty of praise for new skills learnt and never force a child to participate.

* Provide books and drawing materials, board games and computer games.

* Encourage writing skills.
* Display the child's work prominently to increase self-esteem.

8–12 Years

Gross Motor Skills

* The child has increased body strength, muscle coordination and a quicker reaction time.
* She can ride a two-wheeled bicycle easily.
* She can skip freely.
* She enjoys energetic games and sports.

* Towards the end of this period, girls experience puberty and are more physically mature than boys (see Chapter 2 for information on the changes which take place in puberty).

Fine Manipulative Skills

* The child has more control over small muscles, and can therefore write and draw with greater skill and dexterity.
* She can draw a person with detail, e.g. clothes and facial features.
* Between 8 and 9 years, she is beginning to join letters together in handwriting.
* At 10 and 11 years, she tackles more detailed tasks, such as woodwork or needlework, and has an established writing style, usually with joined-up letters.

Guidelines for stimulating development: 8–12 years

* Provide opportunity for physical activities, such as dance, yoga and gymnastics.

* Encourage children to dance or skip to music.
* Make time for hopping, skipping, jumping and climbing.
* Encourage writing skills.

12–16 Years

Physical development in this period (adolescence) is generally referred to as **puberty**. Puberty is the stage of growth where a child's body turns into that of an adult. The child or young person undergoes physical, hormonal, and sexual changes and becomes capable of reproduction. They also experience a **growth spurt**, which involves rapid growth of bones and muscles. This begins in girls around the ages of 9–12 and in boys around the ages of 11–14. The development in puberty is described in Chapter 2.

Guidelines for stimulating development: 12–16 years

* Provide opportunity for plenty of physical activity. Exercise will help young people to burn off excess energy and may help to increase their self-esteem.
* Encourage them to get enough sleep, which is important to stimulate growth.
* Encourage healthy eating habits. Adolescents need more calories to fuel their rapid growth.

PHYSICAL DEVELOPMENT IN RELATION TO OTHER AREAS OF DEVELOPMENT

Physical development is linked to other areas of development – such as emotional and social development and cognitive and language development. Each affects and is affected by the other areas. For example:

* once babies have mastered crawling, they are free to explore the world on their own. They become more independent and confident when away from their familiar adults.

* the ability to reach and grasp objects (usually achieved at around 6 months) develops their understanding of the nature of objects. This often results in a surprise, for example, when they try to pick up a soap bubble or a shaft of sunlight. Babies are interested in edges, e.g. of a book on a floor. Where does one object end, and the next object begin?

PHYSICAL ACTIVITY AND EXERCISE

Exercise is essential for children's growth and development, because it:

* strengthens muscles;

* helps strengthen joints and promotes good posture;

* improves balance, coordination and flexibility;

* increases bone density, so bones are less likely to fracture;

* reduces their risk of developing heart disease in later life.

Apart from these obvious physical benefits, regular exercise develops a child's **self-esteem** by creating a strong sense of purpose and self-fulfilment; children learn how to interact and cooperate with other children by taking part in team sports and other activities.

Promoting exercise in children

Children need to learn that exercise is fun; the best way to convince them is to show by

example. Bear in mind that some team games do not provide all children with the same opportunity for exercise, as they often involve several children standing around for long periods. Some children dislike being competitive and prefer, for example, to dance. Early years workers and parents should try to find an activity that the individual child will enjoy, such as swimming or roller-skating. Older children could be encouraged to join a local sports or gym club; some areas provide 'gym and movement' or yoga classes for toddlers. It is often easier to persuade a child to take up a new activity if she knows she will meet new friends. Family outings could be arranged to include physical activity, such as swimming, walking or boating.

THE IMPORTANCE OF PHYSICAL PLAY

Through opportunities for physical play, children steadily become better at those skills requiring coordination of different parts of the body; for example:

* hands and eyes for throwing and catching;

* legs and arms for skipping with a rope.

Physical play helps children to:

* **express ideas and feelings:** children become aware that they can use their bodies to express themselves by moving in different ways as they respond to their moods and feelings, to music or to imaginative ideas;

* **explore what their bodies can do:** children become aware of their increasing abilities, agility and skill. Children's awareness of the space around them and what their bodies are capable of can be extended by climbing and balancing on large-scale apparatus, such as a climbing frame,

wooden logs and a balancing bar and by using small tricycles, bicycles and carts;

* **cooperate with others** in physical play and games: children become aware of physical play both as an individual and a social activity: in playing alone or alongside others, in playing throwing and catching with a partner, in using a see-saw or push cart, or in joining a game with a larger group;

* **develop increasing control of fine movements** of their fingers and hands (fine motor skills). For example, playing musical instruments and making sounds with the body, such as clapping or tapping, helps develop fine motor skills in the hands and fingers, while also reinforcing the link between sound and physical movement. Helping with household tasks – washing up, pouring drinks, carrying bags – also develops fine motor skills;

* **develop balance and coordination**, as well as an appreciation of distance and speed; energetic play which involves running, jumping and skipping helps children to develop these skills;

* **develop spatial awareness**, for example dancing and moving around to music develop a spatial awareness while also practising coordination and muscle control.

Providing Opportunities for Physical Play

Opportunities for physical activity should be provided both inside and out. Regular sessions of indoor physical play or visits to local sports and leisure centres are particularly important when the weather limits opportunities for outdoor play. The outdoors can provide a scale and freedom for a type of play which is difficult to replicate indoors. For example, outdoors there are opportunities for children to:

* dig a garden;
* explore woodland;
* run on the grass and roll down a grassy slope;
* pedal a car across a hard surface.

Visits to swimming pools, where these can be arranged, can help children to enjoy and gain confidence in the water at an early stage.

Problem Solving, Physical Development and Play

Any conscious movement involves making judgements or assessments. Assessment of the situation and of your ability (speed, power, etc.) will help you to make the appropriate movement. For example, a child might make an assessment of:

* how hard to throw;
* how fast to run;
* how much effort to use to jump so high;
* when to start to stop.

CASE STUDY

Petra

Petra walks towards a ball. She wants to pick it up. She leans over to touch the ball, but instead, her foot hits it and the ball slides across the floor. She walks towards it again, and this time she tries to kick the ball on purpose. She misses the ball; her foot goes past the left side of the ball. Petra tries again, and again. She kicks it and she begins to run after the ball, tries to stop in front of it, and falls forward. She stands up and kicks it to a new location and she laughs.

ACTIVITY: A LEARNING EXPERIENCE

1 How old do you think Petra is?
2 What has Petra learned during this activity? Try to list at least six things

and then compare them with the list at the end of this chapter (see page 136).

These are all examples of decision-making needed in school and social life.

PROMOTING PHYSICAL DEVELOPMENT

Physical development is the easiest aspect of development to observe and to measure. Parents are usually proud of their child's physical achievements, but children are often unfavourably compared with their peers and may also be judged by others. We should always stop and consider how both parents and their child may feel when the child is not able to perform certain physical tasks. Rather than feeling sorry for the child who has a physical disability or illness, we should aim to maximise their individual potential for development.

Children do not need lots of expensive toys and play equipment in order to grow and develop physically. The most important factors for healthy development are that you should:

1 recognise the skills a child has developed and provide plenty of opportunities for him or her to practise them;

2 ensure that children have the freedom to explore their environment in safety;

3 be there for the child, to offer reassurance, encouragement and praise;

4 provide access to a range of facilities and equipment. This need not be expensive – for example, a visit to the local park or toddlers' playgroup will provide facilities not available in a small flat.

Guidelines for promoting physical development

* Always focus on all aspects of development; the child's self-esteem and wellbeing are paramount.

* Help children to see physical activities as fun rather than as tests of competency.

* Help children to compete with themselves – 'Can I do this better than I managed last time?' – rather than comparing themselves with others.

* Provide a balance of activities, exposing children to as many experiences as possible.

* Be sensitive to insecurities. Be aware of why a child might be hesitant.

* Always acknowledge effort, rather than results.

* Never ridicule a child for being 'clumsy'.

* Use technology where possible to help in the development of skills.

* Help children to develop the ability to praise others' achievements without feeling degraded.

* Be fair to all children: encourage patience, understanding and teamwork.

* Recognise and allow differences between siblings and friends – try not to compare.

Promoting the Development of Fine Motor Skills

Children should be provided with a rich variety of opportunities to develop their skills in using different materials and a range of tools. They also need to develop the skills required to take care of their own bodies, for example in washing and dressing themselves, cleaning their teeth and becoming more independent at mealtimes.

To strengthen the hands and promote the development of **fine motor skills**, you should provide:

1 **play dough** or clay: for squeezing, rolling, squashing, making holes with fingers and tools;

2 **newspaper:** for scrunching up using one hand at a time; tearing into strips and crumpling them into balls;

3 **scissors:** when safety scissors are held correctly, and when they fit a child's hand well, simple cutting activities will exercise the same muscles that are needed to manipulate a pencil in a mature **tripod grasp**. The correct scissor position is with the thumb and middle finger in the handles of the scissors, the index finger on the outside of the handle to stabilise, with fingers four and five curled into the palm. For cutting, provide:

* junk mail or similar thick paper;

* straws;

* play dough;

4 **mark-making** opportunities with chunky pens, pencils and paintbrushes for drawing, writing, painting, tracing and so on;

5 a **peg game** promotes the development of the **pincer grasp**: give each child a cardboard plate and provide lots of brightly coloured plastic pegs. Using a sand timer or clock timer, see how many pegs the children can arrange around their plate. This activity is also good for learning their colours;

6 a **finger gym** promotes the development of fine manipulative skills, such as pinching, screwing, threading, winding and so on. Provide a basket or box in which you have collected items that need small fingers to work but that are also attractive and appealing to children, for example:

* old clocks and radios;

* spinning tops;

* squeezy toys;
* eye droppers to 'pick up' coloured water for colour mixing or to make patterns on paper;
* buttons and fasteners;
* dried pasta shapes and chopsticks for picking them up;
* wind-up toys;
* jar tops – opening and closing or other twisting toys;
* threading – cotton reels, chunky beads (and smaller ones as the children get older);
* shape sorters and 'posting' toys;
* pegs of various sizes, with boards.

Promoting Hand–eye Coordination

This involves accuracy in placement, direction, and spatial awareness:

* Throw beanbags or soft 'koosh' balls into a hoop placed flat on the floor. Gradually increase the distance.

* Play throwing and catching with a ball; start with a large ball and then work towards using a smaller ball.

* Practise hitting skittles with a ball; improvise by using weighted plastic bottles.

Promoting Physical Development in Children with Special Needs

Although the sequence of physical development may remain the same for a child with a special need, the rate at which a 'stage' is achieved may be slower. The attitudes and actions of parents and early years workers will have a great influence on the child's behaviour and self-esteem.

* All children should be appreciated and encouraged for any personal progress made, however small, and should not be compared to the normative measurements. This is because children with special needs often seem to 'dance the developmental ladder' – they move through developmental stages in unusual and very uneven ways. For example, they might sit or walk at the usual time, but not talk.

* Adults should recognise and understand that a child who is having difficulty in acquiring a skill may become frustrated and may need more individual attention or specialist help; also that the child may not yet be ready to acquire the particular skill.

* Every child must be seen as an individual first; activities and equipment should be tailored to the specific needs of that child.

* Plan activities to encourage exercise and movement of all body parts.

ACTIVITY: TOYS FOR BABIES

1   Visit a toy shop and look at the range of toys for babies under 1 year old. List the toys and activities under two headings:

* Toys that strengthen muscles and improve coordination.
* Toys which particularly stimulate the senses of touch and sight.

What safety symbols are shown on the toys?

2   If you are asked to suggest toys and activities for a baby with a visual impairment, what specific things could you suggest?

ANSWERS TO ACTIVITY: A LEARNING EXPERIENCE (PAGE 133)

1 Petra has just had her second birthday.

2 These are some of the things that Petra has learned (you may have found more):

   * That you need to watch your feet as well as your hands.

   * If you hit something with your foot, it moves.

   * You have to aim at the ball, not just swing your leg.

   * Not to give up even when it is difficult.

   * Not to run too fast when you go after a ball.

   * To slow down before trying to stop.

   * To start stopping at a certain distance ahead, depending on the speed you are moving.

   * How to assess speed, distance and force.

   * The connections between cause and effect.

   * To keep trying, because you can succeed.

   * That learning is fun.

CHAPTER 6

Emotional and Social Development

Contents

• The stages/sequences of emotional and social development from birth to 16 years • Influences on emotional and social development • The importance of play in social and emotional development • The role of the adult in promoting social and emotional development • Relating to others • Children's feelings • Children who express themselves or relate to others in particular or challenging ways • Self-image, self-esteem and well-being • Adolescence and self esteem • Moral development – theories and stages • The effects on children of attachment, separation and loss

THE STAGES/SEQUENCES OF EMOTIONAL AND SOCIAL DEVELOPMENT FROM BIRTH TO 16 YEARS

From Birth to 3 Months

Researchers do not think that babies, in their first month, know that they are separate from other people. Babies are only beginning to learn where they begin and end: a toe is part of them; a bed cover is not, neither is the mother's hand. Up to 3 months, babies start to:

* recognise people they know well – feelings and relationships develop;
* smile;
* turn to a familiar person's voice, especially that of their mother;
* know their own face and hands;
* react when they hear, see or feel their carer (they may stop crying, for example).

Babies who are visually impaired often become very still, as if listening and waiting for more information. Researchers believe that it is almost as if babies are born in order to relate to people.

From 3 to 6 Months

From the beginning, babies find faces interesting to look at. They turn to their mother's voice, in particular, and they like to be held in the arms of someone they love and know. Even very young babies prefer being held by those they are emotionally close to.

By 5 months babies have learnt that they have only one mother. They are very disturbed if several images of their mother are shown to them. They might cry or look away because they are worried.

From 6 to 12 Months

Babies begin moving about. As they crawl and begin to walk they develop more of a self-image and are able to do more things for themselves. They become more aware of other people's feelings. They realise that people and objects are separate from them.

* They love to play 'peek-a-boo'.
* They like to look at themselves in the mirror.
* They know their name and respond to it.
* They love to have an audience. They use social referencing, looking to see how other people react to what they do.

* They imitate other people, for example clapping hands or copying sounds.

* They are very affectionate when they are shown love.

* They often show fear of strangers.

* They recognise how other people feel.

* They become anxious if someone they love begins to cry. They express their own feelings too. The way they are influenced by the feelings of other people is called being **affectively tuned**.

* They understand the word 'no'.

* They can become full of rage.

* They cooperate when they are being dressed.

From 1 to 2 Years

* Babies start to show that they have a mind of their own.

* They are developing a sense of identity.

* They are developing a longer memory span.

* They are beginning to express their needs using words and gestures.

* They love to do things for themselves – this is called **autonomy**. They enjoy their developing physical skills, such as walking.

* However, when they try things which are new, they quickly sense when others fear for them, for example when they try to climb onto or off a chair at the meal table (this awareness is called **social referencing**).

* They love their efforts to be appreciated.

* It is still easy to distract children and take their attention from one thing to another.

From 2 to 3 Years

* Children imitate what other people do and begin to become engrossed in symbolic **play**. This means they pretend to be someone else, for example someone pouring out the tea or the person who delivers the post. This is called **role play** because children rehearse adult roles.

* They begin to explain how they are feeling.

* They are very anxious to try things for themselves.

* They quickly become frustrated, for example when something does not go well. They need a great deal of support from adults as they learn to go to the toilet, put their clothes on and feed themselves.

From 3 to 4 Years

* Children begin to develop a more complex **Theory of Mind** as they try out what it is like to be someone else in their imaginative role play.

* During this time, children are becoming more influenced by each other. They begin to be interested in having friends. They love to use 'silly talk' and to laugh together.

* They often have one special friend. They value companionship, but they also value being alone. This means that they need:

  1 solitary times;

  2 times to do things in parallel;

  3 times to be cooperative.

* Sometimes they follow the lead of another child; sometimes they show leadership. Children of this age love to feel power and to have control: over things and people. Sometimes they negotiate at their own level.

* Children are easily afraid at this time. For example, they might be afraid of the dark and so need a night light in their bedroom.

✳ During this time children are beginning to think about things that are right and things that are wrong. They are developing moral values. They often argue with adults in a dogmatic way, and will not shift their position.

From 4 to 8 Years

✳ During this period, the child is establishing a stable self-concept.

✳ They take in and internalise the social rules of their culture. They have begun to work out the difference between:

1 **social rules:** which vary from culture to culture (e.g. the way to greet somebody);

2 **display rules:** which govern when we hide our feelings (e.g. disappointment that a present is not what we hoped for);

3 **moral values:** which are to do with respect for other people (e.g. not hitting people).

✳ Children respond very positively to being given explanations and reasons.

✳ They are able to follow a series of events from beginning to end, and to be sensitive to the needs of other people as they do so.

✳ They are also able to take considerable responsibility, and enjoy helping other younger children. There is a terrific desire to be accepted by other children and adults. It is also important to encourage children to be people in their own right and not simply to conform to what others want. Children with a strong sense of identity learn to be strong people. They learn to be assertive without being aggressive.

From 8 to 12 Years

✳ The timing of the onset of puberty will affect the way children feel about themselves, how they get along with others and what they do. Most girls will experience puberty between the ages of 9 and 13, whereas for boys it starts between the ages of 10 and 16.

✳ Children develop a sense of self and find it important to gain social acceptance and to experience achievement.

✳ Friends become increasingly important; close friends are almost always of the same sex, although children are becoming increasingly interested in peers of the opposite sex.

✳ They begin to see parents and authority figures as fallible human beings and may defy adult authority.

From 12 to 16 Years

Adolescence involves intense physical, emotional and psychological changes, with a huge variation in what is considered 'normal'. During this time, adolescents move away from parental influence and become more independent. Peer groups tend to be mixed gender and gradually give way to one-to-one friendships and romances. There is often increasing conflict between adolescents and their parents. Young people are beginning to develop a social conscience, becoming concerned about social issues such as racism, global warming and poverty.

INFLUENCES ON SOCIAL AND EMOTIONAL DEVELOPMENT

Environmental Influences

There are many reasons why children may experience a lack of emotional and social wellbeing. In the government initiative,

Every Child Matters, the importance of being healthy, staying safe, achieving and enjoying, making a positive contribution and experiencing economic wellbeing is emphasised. A child who has poor physical and mental health will be challenged in this respect. When children experience physical, emotional or sexual abuse, or neglect over time, this has a detrimental impact on their emotional lives and their social relationships. When children do not have any sense of personal achievement, their self-esteem is low. When children do not feel any sense of belonging to a family, a community or an early childhood group, they do not have the enriching experience of feeling that they are contributing. Poverty has a damaging effect on emotional and social relationships, especially when it is of the grinding and long-term kind.

Personality and Temperament

Every person has a different **personality**. Recently, researchers have begun to realise that a child's temperament in early childhood is the beginning of their later personality. It used to be thought that personality was fixed at birth (just as it used to be thought that intelligence was fixed at birth and unchangeable thereafter). As in other areas of development, it seems that a child's temperament is partly biological, but is also influenced by other factors:

* the experiences of life;
* physical challenges;
* the people children meet.

Temperament is the style of behaviour that is natural to the child. So the child's temperament influences the personality that emerges later on, during late childhood and early adolescence. For example, some babies seem almost 'prickly' when you hold them, while others are full of smiles. Some children

are always crying and may seem unattractive to adults. Some children are accident-prone because their temperament is to be very impulsive and active. They move into less safe situations more readily than a child with a more cautious temperament.

It is very important that adults working with young children do not favour smiling children. And it is critical that they do not take against children with more difficult temperaments. Working professionally with children means being determined to uphold principles of equality of opportunity and inclusivity (see Chapter 9). The way adults help children willingly and with pleasure has a deep influence on how they develop and learn. People's reactions to a child's temperament can influence that child's self-esteem. Different temperaments can lead children to behave in different ways:

1 Emotionality and feeling.
   * Some children have more happy moods.
   * Others are sad or distressed.
   * Some children are more at ease than others in unfamiliar situations.
   * Some children can manage better than others when they are bored.
   * Some children can wait longer than others to eat when they are hungry.
   * Some children are more serious temperamentally, while others love to have a go at things.

2 Activity.
   * Some children are very vigorous and active, and always on the go.
   * Some children are able to change and modify what they do more easily.
   * Some children are very flexible.
   * Some children are impulsive, while others hold back.

3   Sociability.
*   Some children are easily comforted when they are upset and distressed, while others are not.
*   Some children positively enjoy meeting new people and going to new places, while others do not.
4   Variation in concentration.
*   Some children are easily distracted, while others are not.

The child's temperamental features will be stable across different times of the day and night, and in different places and with different people. This means that they will have their own style of doing things and of relating to people. Shy, timid children will be more cautious than communicative, sociable children.

Temperament and Personality Clashes

Sometimes people clash: adults clash with other adults; children clash with other children. Sometimes an adult can have a personality clash with a child. This is why it is so helpful to work in a team with other members of staff. It is very important that every early years worker tries their best to get on with every child, even though it is easier to do this with some children than with others. It is only natural, according to researchers, that there is sometimes a better 'goodness of fit' between some people than others, but this does not give us an excuse to show favouritism or to scapegoat children.

The interdependency between physical, emotional, intellectual and social development

It is important to remember that it is not possible to isolate emotional and social development from any other areas of development. Piaget thought that it was unfortunate that there are two separate words for thinking and feeling. He thought the two were completely inseparable: he said that it was impossible to think without feeling, or to feel without thinking. In the same way, relationships with other people (emotional and social development) cannot be separated from intellectual (cognitive) aspects of development.

Is love a feeling? The development of thoughtful feelings

We have seen that it is not possible to separate feelings (emotions) from social relationships (which involve thoughts about the people we love). Love is a feeling in yourself and it is also a social relationship with another person. People who love each other care about each other's feelings as much as they care about their own feelings. As people share their feelings they use words or a cuddle, for example. The words contain ideas and cuddles are physical demonstrations. There may be a spiritual experience too.

Knowing how the person who is loved thinks about things is an important part of loving someone. For example, to organise a surprise birthday party for someone who would hate it would not be loving. Making breakfast in bed for them, when they love to get up slowly, as a treat, would be a loving thing to do.

Cultural Influences

Different families and different cultures show or do not show their feelings in different ways. The neuroscientist Damasio says that feelings are 'preludes to emotion'. They can stay hidden, but we cannot hide our emotions so easily, because these are physical reactions. Helping children to manage their emotions so that they learn to understand their feelings and how they lead to emotional reactions is very important.

For cultural or personality reasons, some people are very private about their feelings, but it is important for mental health that they learn to understand how they feel, and to feel that they have some control over this emotionally. Bottling up feelings by trying to suppress emotion is damaging long-term, and so is expressing feelings in emotional outbursts which are socially unacceptable.

The sociocultural aspect of development and the influence of social exchanges with other people, especially those who are close to and love the child, are crucial. Babies have feelings and emotions from the moment they are born. As children become increasingly aware of themselves, they can be helped to become more aware of how other people feel. Children who feel loved and receive plenty of warm affection and cuddles will find it easier both to give love to other people and to like themselves. Neuroscientists call the first years of life the period when children develop an understanding of 'personhood'.

THE IMPORTANCE OF PLAY IN SOCIAL AND EMOTIONAL DEVELOPMENT

In the 1930s, Mildred Parten identified the following different kinds of play:

1 **Solitary play:** children sometimes want to have personal space and do things alone.

2 **Spectator play:** a child may choose to watch what others do, and not want to join in.

3 **Parallel play:** there are times when children want companionship but not much interaction; for example, two children may sit side by side and draw together, but not look at each other or talk very much about what they are doing.

4 **Associative play:** two children might both choose to be the chef in a cafe, each oblivious to what the other is doing. They are each busy with their own play agenda. If their agendas do conflict, then there will be a problem! When each child has a separate idea that is not shared by the other, there will be frequent conflicts. This is partly why young children need help and support in their social play or when sharing materials together. It is often not appropriate, however, to force sharing. Instead adults might need to bring in another saucepan for the extra chef. Separate ideas are separate, and if children are not able to share ideas, they cannot share materials! Helping children at moments like this is an important role for the early years worker

5 **Cooperative play:** this develops as the children grow older, especially when they experience help and positive treatment from adults. The 'peek-a-boo' game enjoyed by babies as young as 6 months of age is an early kind of cooperative behaviour. Gradually, children begin to share; for example, a set of wooden building blocks. They decide, together, to make a road. They negotiate and exchange ideas. If the sharing breaks down, adults can help by stating each child's ideas. For example, 'Sean, you want to build a bridge. Meg, you want to build a row of shops. You both want to use the same blocks. What can we do about this?' Children often find solutions and then return to work together again.

In Chapter 13, play is discussed in more detail. Play helps children to understand their feelings and to experiment with showing emotions. They become the cross mum, the grumpy shopkeeper, the kind aunty when a child falls over, or the angry bus driver. It also helps them to experience what someone else might feel when someone is cross, grumpy, kind or angry towards them. It is important to know the features of play (Bruce) and what play gives to children who are developing emotionally and socially.

THE ROLE OF THE ADULT IN PROMOTING EMOTIONAL AND SOCIAL DEVELOPMENT

Babies

Encourage babies to bond with their main carer by allowing time for them to enjoy the relationship. Once weaned, encourage babies to feed themselves and be tolerant of any messes. Tune in to the baby. When a baby is upset, help the baby to return to what Sue Gerhardt calls their **comfort zone**. Babies and very young children experience constantly changing emotional states. They need a huge amount of support and help in moving back to their comfort zone once it has been wobbled or disturbed. Try to enter the baby's state of emotion by mirroring the sound he or she is making, and gradually leading the way into a calmer sound by toning your voice down and taking the baby into a calmer state. Babies usually like to be held gently while you do this; some like to be rocked in time to your heart beating. Try it. It is one of the most satisfying things you will ever experience when you tune in to a baby and calm them. (See **EYFS** Principle – Positive Relationships – key person.)

Children Aged 2–3 Years

It is very important, during this time, that adults help children to experience success as they try to become more autonomous. This helps children to deal positively with problems. They need clothes which are easy to put on and take off, and easy to do up and undo – straps, laces and small buttons are not helpful, whereas elasticated waistbands and Velcro on shoes are great for children who want to dress themselves.

General advice

* It is very important that children be encouraged to learn about being cooperative, positive and caring towards each other. During the last 20 years, the work of Judy Dunn has shown how children learn through quarrels with others. They need a great deal of support from adults when learning in this way; they need to be helped to turn difficult situations into positive ones.

* They are helped if principles of inclusion and equality of opportunity are explained, so that they do not stereotype people and see them narrowly.

* It is important that children are prepared to have a go at things, to take risks and not be anxious about making errors.

* If children are smacked or hit by adults, they learn that it is acceptable behaviour for bigger people to hit smaller, less powerful people. It is illegal for early years workers in institutions to hit or smack children.

RELATING TO OTHERS

* From the start, it seems as if babies are born to relate to other people. This is called pro-social behaviour. It is important to encourage sociability by providing opportunities for babies and

young children to meet other children and adults. As early as 6 months of age, babies enjoy each other's company. When they sit together, they touch each other's faces. They look at each other and smile at each other. They enjoy 'peek-a-boo' games with adults and older children. This is cooperative social behaviour. It involves turn-taking. Babies delight in having a shared idea, and they really laugh with pleasure.

* Toddlers' behaviour also shows how very young children cooperate socially. One might pick up a toy, and the other will copy. They laugh together. There is plenty of eye contact. One drops the toy intentionally, and the other copies. They laugh with glee. They have a shared idea which they can enjoy together.

* By the age of 2 or 3 years, the widening social circle becomes important. Children need varying amounts of help and support as they have new social experiences. This might include joining an early childhood group of some kind. Settling children into a group is probably one of the most important aspects of the role of the early years worker (see later sections of this chapter).

When beginning to explore social relationships it is important that children are not frightened by aggressive and demanding behaviour from their peers. Different kinds of social behaviour can show themselves at different times of the day, in different situations and according to the child's mood, personality, physical comfort (tired, hungry or needing a nappy change/lavatory) and previous experiences of relating to people.

Getting on with Other Children

A young child, seeing a friend distressed, may make a gesture spontaneously – such as giving them a treasured teddy bear – to ease the pain and provide comfort. This means that young children are, in their own way, very giving. They are also very forgiving. Being able to give means that a young child has managed to think of someone else's need and to control their behaviour accordingly. It takes enormous effort for young children to do this. It is an ability that will come and go depending upon the situation, the people involved and how tired the children are. Children who become skilled in this way are often popular leaders, and other children want to be with them. Children tend to behave according to the way they experience life. If they are ridiculed or smacked, they are likely to laugh at and hit others, especially children younger or smaller than themselves. This is because children use adults as a model of how to behave. As already mentioned, this is called **social referencing**. Some children need a great deal of support to play well and get on with other children. Children who know how to join in get on better with other children. They have good 'access strategies':

1. First, a child will tend to circle around the edge of an activity, perhaps on a tricycle, trying to work out what is happening, or will watch what is happening from the safe viewpoint of being at the sand tray or water tray.

2. Then they will imitate what the other children are doing, for example pouring sand in and out of pots and laughing as each pot is upturned. We call this using a **side-by-side** strategy. Doing the same helps the child to join in with other children.

How You can Help a Child to Join in

You might say to the child 'Do you want to join in? Let's look at what they are doing, shall we? Don't ask if you can do the same as them, just do the same as them'. This advice is given because if children ask if they can join in, they are usually rejected. If, on the other hand, children simply do what the other children are doing, they are very likely to be accepted into the group. This is an important access strategy which adults can help children to develop. It is also a useful strategy for adults to use if they are joining a group of children.

Friendships

Early friendships are important and may last throughout life, or they may be more fleeting. As a child's interests change and they go off in a different direction, the old friendship may fade. Early friendships are like adult ones; they are based, at least in part, on people sharing the same interests. As children become more able to play imaginatively together, the possibilities grow for sharing and enjoying each other's company. This is because, in play, children can rearrange the real world to suit themselves: you can pretend anything when you play!

Sharing

Young children can only manage to socialise cooperatively for a small part of their day: it is too much to expect them to cooperate with others for large parts of the day. Indeed, children who are just settling in might not manage to share at all: instead all their energy is going into adjusting to the new social setting.

How Adults can Help Children to Relate Positively to Others

No one gets on with everyone all the time. Children are just like adults in this way. All children need:

* the **personal space** to do things on their own, without interruptions or pressure from anyone else;
* to feel **nurtured and loved** as a person in their own right;

* **to be able to choose** whom to be with and what to do for most of the day (always having to do adult-led tasks is a great pressure for young children);
* their **difficulties to be addressed with sensitivity and care** by adults;
* **individual attention** so that they feel they have enough time to talk and share without the pressure of being in a group (e.g. a child might appreciate a one-to-one story); individual attention is especially important for younger children.

Guidelines for helping children with social difficulties

* Give children the words they need: teach them to say 'I need some help'.
* Help children to understand social rules: 'If you stamp your feet and cry, I can't help you. I need to know the problem. Can you show me the problem?' 'Can you see my face? It is easier for us to listen to each other if I look at your face. You look unhappy. How can I help?'
* Help children to make sense of what you want them to do.
* Try to ensure that children see you as someone who wants to help, who does not nag, who is warm and encouraging, and who does not stop what the children are doing by saying 'no' all the time. Be positive.
* Look at what the children are doing and find things in the room and outdoors that you think make a good fit with their interests and moods. Children who are constantly frustrated in what they do become angry children. Angry children are very challenging to work with.

Every Child Needs the One-to-one Attention of an Adult

If children do not receive individual attention, they may begin to demand it. It is important to have a policy that every child and every parent should be greeted on arrival, and that goodbyes should also be said at the end of the day. This gives an important message that 'you matter to me'. In some families, bedtime stories or going to the shops give these experiences to the child. If children have access to the full attention of an adult they do not need to use attention-seeking behaviour. Every child matters, and every child needs to feel that they matter to people they love and who are important to them because they spend time with them.

Helping Children to Manage their Feelings in their Social Relationships

Learning to be Assertive

Children who bully have low self-esteem. Name-calling and shouting insults are one kind of bullying. Children pick on weaker children or children who are different. For example, they tease or make racial, gender or disability insults. Physical hitting or menacing is another kind of bullying. Teaching children to be assertive helps to prevent bullying and the creation of victims.

How You can Help to Develop Assertiveness

* Try not to use the words 'bully' or 'disruptive'. Instead, talk to children about learning to be assertive by being less timid or less aggressive. This creates a positive image of all children.

* Swearing can create similar problems to name-calling. Often it is simply the case that swearing is an everyday part

Fig 6.1 Sensitive, consistent, loving care from familiar adults gives children high wellbeing

of the child's language experience. However, it is quite a different thing when children swear in order to shock. Any child who swears needs help in:

1 learning which are the words they cannot use in the early years setting;

2 finding new words to replace the swear words (they still have to be able to express their thoughts and feelings);

3 building up their vocabulary so that they have a wider choice of words.

Formal Social Relationships and Role Behaviour

As children experience and understand the culture and society in which they are growing up, they gradually learn how to relate to people in ways which are not about friendship, companionship, family or carers in the early years setting. These formal relationships occur, for example, when you buy something in a shop, go to the post office or thank someone for giving directions in the street. Such relationships do not develop and they do not last. They demand certain kinds of behaviour. It is not until adulthood that formal behaviour becomes totally stable (if then). Each society has rules which shape formal relationships and create role behaviour. For example, MPs in Parliament have to ask questions and speak in formal ways; they take on the role of an MP. Children learn how to answer the telephone and take messages; they are assuming the role of 'message taker'. When parents ask 'Have they been good?' they are expressing a hope that their children are beginning to learn about formal social relationships. As children become more able to do this, they are described as socially skilled.

ADOLESCENCE AND SELF-ESTEEM

The development of self-esteem in adolescence depends mainly upon attractiveness and peer acceptance. Most studies confirm that young people are more self-conscious and more self-critical during early adolescence than before. During the period of adolescence most young people:

* begin the struggle for their own independence;

* want to make their own decisions and test the limits of authority;

* want to express their own individuality;

* feel the strength of peer pressure and want to conform to the peer norms in matters of fashion;

* take a greater interest in music.

Erikson viewed adolescence as a time of stress and confusion; in his theory of psychosocial development, he suggests that those who *do not* suffer an 'identity crisis' as adolescents are less mature and healthy as adults than those who *do* have a crisis and who manage to resolve it successfully.

The Focal Theory of Adolescence

John Coleman challenged the traditional view that adolescence is a time of conflict and turmoil. Coleman conducted a study of 800 young people in the UK in which girls and boys aged 11, 13, 15 and 17 completed various identical tests devised to investigate their self-image, friendships and parental relationships. Although crises *do* occur during adolescence, Coleman found that the process of adaptation is spread over the years and that problems are dealt with one at a time. He called this the **focal model** because relationship patterns and other issues come into focus at different times. In this way adolescence may be seen as not significantly different from any other period of development; the only exception is that there are more problems to be resolved within a shorter time span during adolescence. Coleman also emphasised the role of the adolescent as an active agent in shaping the course of an individual's life.

In any one day a teenager may choose to confront a parent over the breakfast table; to argue with a sibling; to accept the suggestion of a best friend; to stand up to an authoritarian teacher; to conform to peer pressure; to resist the persuasion of a girlfriend or boyfriend, and so on. Every one of these situations offers the young person a choice, and all may well have a bearing on the interpersonal issues with which the focal model is concerned. Different problems and different relationship issues come into focus and are tackled at different stages, so that the stresses resulting from the need to adapt to new modes of behaviour are rarely concentrated all at one time. It follows from this that it is precisely in those who, for whatever reason, do have more than one issue to cope with at a time that problems are likely to occur (*Coleman and Hendry, 1990*).

See Chapter 12 for details on Eating Disorders in Childhood and Adolescence.

Self-harm

Self-harm, or self-injury, is a way of dealing with very strong emotions. It is almost always a symptom of another underlying problem. While the problem can be addressed directly, through behavioural and stress-management techniques, it may also be necessary to look at and treat other problems. This could involve anything from medication to psychodynamic therapy.

Types of Self-harm

The most common forms of self-harm are:

* cutting: usually the arms, hands and legs; less commonly the face, abdomen, breasts and even genitals;

* burning or scalding;

* inflicting blows on their bodies.

Other forms of self-harm include scratching, picking, biting, scraping and occasionally inserting sharp objects under the skin or into body orifices, and swallowing sharp objects or harmful substances. There are also other forms of self-harm which often remain undetected by medical staff – such as people pulling out their own hair and eyelashes, or scrubbing themselves so hard that they break the skin.

About 10 per cent of medical admissions in the UK are as a result of self-harm. Women have higher rates of self-harm than men and are at the most risk of self-harming between the ages of 15 and 19; men typically self-harm between 20 and 24.

There are different reasons why people self-harm; these include:

* low self-esteem;

* poor physical self-image;

* painful experiences in childhood;

* neglect or abuse;

* experience of a violent or chaotic family background;

* experience of physical or emotional cruelty.

Another theory for self-cutting is that it triggers release of the body's natural opiate-like chemicals to reduce the pain. Perhaps self-cutters have become addicted to their body's heroin-like reaction to cutting, which is why they do it again and again. They may also experience withdrawal if they haven't done it for a while.

How to Help

As a professional, you can help by:

* recognising signs of distress, and finding some way of talking with the young person about how they are feeling;

* listening to their worries and problems, and taking them seriously;

* offering sympathy and understanding;

* helping with solving problems;

* being clear about the risks of self-harm – making sure they know that, with help, it

will be possible to stop once the under-lying problems have been sorted out;

* making sure that they get the right kind of help as soon as possible.

MORAL DEVELOPMENT

Moral development is concerned with how children understand ideas of right and wrong and matters of conscience. A conscience is a set of moral principles that each individual develops and tries to live by. Psychologists who have studied the development of moral reasoning in children have asked the following questions:

* How do children understand notions of right and wrong?

* Do children understand the world in the same (albeit a less developed) way, or are there qualitative differences between the thought of children and of adults?

* If there are such differences, what stages do children go through in their moral reasoning as they grow to adulthood?

THEORIES OF MORAL DEVELOPMENT

Piaget's Theory

Piaget developed his theory of moral development from the observation of a relatively small number of children. He was concerned with: (a) the child's ideas about rules; (b) how a child decides what is right and what is wrong; and (c) the child's ideas about punishment and justice. Piaget proposed that moral behaviour and moral reasoning develop in two identifiable stages:

1 The stage of **heteronomous** morality (sometimes called moral realism).

2 The stage of **autonomous** morality (or subjective realism).

The Stage of Moral Realism (Age 3–7 or 8 Years)

In this stage, characteristic of children aged 3–7 or 8 years, children believe that all rules are fixed and unchallengeable. They can see the difference between intentional and unin-tentional actions, but base their judgement on the severity of an outcome. Piaget pre-sented children with several pairs of short stories which posed a problem of moral judgement. One pair is as follows:

* A little boy who was called John was in his room. He was called to dinner. He went into the dining room. But behind the door there was a chair, and on the chair there was a tray with 15 cups on it. John couldn't have known that there was all this behind the door. He went in, the door knocked against the tray, bang go the 15 cups and they all got broken!

* Once there was a little boy called Henry. One day when his mother was out he tried to get some jam out of the cupboard. He climbed onto the chair and stretched out his arm. But the jam was too high up and he couldn't reach it and have any. But while he was trying to get it he knocked over a cup. The cup fell down and broke.

Piaget would tell a child this pair of stories and ask them to repeat each one to ensure that they remembered them. Next, he asked them to make a judgement as to which child was the naughtiest. These were their answers:

Answer from a Child Aged 6

Piaget: Are those children both naughty, or is one not so naughty as the other?

Child: Both just as naughty.

Piaget: Would you punish them the same?

Child: No. The one who broke 15 cups.

Piaget: And would you punish the other one more, or less?

Child: The first broke a lot of things, the other one fewer.

Piaget: How would you punish them?

Child: The one who broke 15 cups: two slaps. The other one: one slap.

Answer from a Child Aged 9

Child: Well, the one who broke them as he was coming in isn't naughty, 'cos he didn't know there was any cups. The other one wanted to take the jam and caught his arm on a cup.

Piaget: Which one is the naughtiest?

Child: The one who wanted to take the jam.

Piaget: How many cups did he break?

Child: One.

Piaget: And the other boy?

Child: 15.

Piaget: Which one would you punish the most?

Child: The boy who wanted to take the jam. He knew, he did it on purpose.

In the stage of moral realism, children judge by the *objective* amount of damage, and tend to view punishment as inevitable and retributive. Children are unable to understand alternative interpretations which take motives or intentions into account.

The Stage of Subjective Realism (Aged 8 Years and Over)

In this stage, characteristic of children aged 8 years and above, children begin to learn that rules can be changed by experiment and trial and error. The motive or intention is taken into account, and the punishment is viewed more as a lesson suited to the offence.

Piaget's theories of moral development correspond to his theories of cognitive development (see Chapter 3). The child in the pre-operational stage uses moral ideas which are imposed on it from the outside. The child in the operational stage is able to invent their own rules and to change their own ideas of what is right and what is wrong.

Evaluation of Piaget's Theory

Various criticisms of Piaget's theory have been put forward:

* that he presented children with poorly designed stories which tempt them to ignore motive or intention;

* that he assumed that moral development is complete by about 12 years of age, whereas subsequent research has shown that our ideas about morality continue to develop and change throughout adolescence and adulthood;

* that his theory may not be relevant to other (non-European) cultures;

* that he underestimated the nature and extent of parental influence in shaping children's moral development;

* that he had a 'romantic' view of childhood which is not supported by the opposite 'problem' view which emphasises the effects on children of negative playground behaviours such as bullying, taunting and aggression.

In spite of these criticisms, many researchers have agreed that children do pass through similar stages of moral reasoning, and some have used similar techniques to develop their own theories.

Kohlberg's Theory

Kohlberg carried out work on moral reasoning over a 12-year period in the late 1950s and 1960s. He drew substantially on Piaget's research into moral development, but extended the scope of study right through to middle adulthood. Kohlberg studied children from the USA over a period of 12 years and compared them with children from Taiwan, Mexico, Turkey and Yucatan. Unlike Piaget's, his research was both longitudinal and cross-cultural.

Kohlberg proposed a six-stage theory of moral development which was sub-divided into three levels: see Table 6.1.

The most famous moral dilemma posed by Kohlberg (adapted here) is that of Heinz and the chemist:

A Moral Dilemma

In Europe, a woman was near death from a special kind of cancer. There was one drug that the doctor thought might save her: it was a form of radium that a chemist in the same town had recently discovered. The drug was expensive to manufacture, and the chemist was charging 10 times what the drug cost him to make: £2,000 for a small dose. The sick woman's husband, Heinz, went to everyone he knew to borrow the money, but he could raise only about £1,000, which is half of what it cost. He told the chemist that his wife was dying, and asked him to sell it cheaper or to let him pay later. But the chemist said 'No, I discovered the drug and I'm going to make money from it'. So Heinz got desperate and broke into the man's store to steal the drug for his wife.

Questions: Should Heinz have done that? If so, why? Or if not, why not?

Characteristic responses from children in the different levels of morality were:

* Level 1: Heinz must not steal the medicine because he will be put in jail.

* Level 2: Heinz should steal the drug because one day he might have cancer and would want someone to steal it for him.

* Level 3: If I was Heinz, I would have stolen the drug for my wife. You can't put a price on love, no amount of gifts make love. You can't put a price on life either.

Another example from Kohlberg's research:

Why shouldn't You Steal from a Store?

Kohlberg posed the same question to the same individual when he was 10 years old, when he was 17, and again when he was 24:

To Joe, aged 10 years:

Kohlberg: Why shouldn't you steal from a store?

Joe: It's not good to steal from a store. It's against the law. Someone could see you and call the police.

To Joe, now aged 17 years:

Kohlberg: Why shouldn't you steal from a store?

Joe: It's a matter of law. It's one of our rules that we're trying to help protect everyone, protect property, not just to protect a store. It's

Table 6.1 Kohlberg's stages of moral development

Level	Age	Stage	Characteristics
1 Pre-conventional	6–13	1	**Punishment and obedience orientation** Something is wrong if it is punished or punishable. The physical consequences of an action regardless of its human meaning or value determine its goodness or badness.
		2	**Instrumental hedonism** People conform to rules and laws to gain rewards, or to have a favour they have done to somebody returned. Right is what's fair, a deal or an equal exchange.
2 Conventional	13–16	3	**Good boy–good girl orientation** Good behaviour is that which pleases or helps others and is approved by them. Behaviour is often judged by intention – 'He means well' becomes important for the first time.
		4	**Law and order orientation** What is right is doing one's duty, showing respect for authority and maintaining the given social order for its own sake. Society's laws should only be disobeyed in extreme circumstances.
3 Postconventional	16–20+	5	**Social contract orientation** Whilst laws should be upheld, they can be changed by agreement. Right action tends to be defined in terms of non-relative values and rights like life and liberty. The result is an emphasis upon the 'legal point of view'.
		6	**Universal ethical principles** Following self-chosen ethical principles. Most laws conform to these principles, but where they do not, one acts in accordance with the principle. These principles are abstract and ethical; they are universal principles of justice, equality of human rights and respect for the dignity of human beings as individual persons.

something that's needed in our society. If we didn't have these laws, people would steal, they wouldn't have to work for a living, and our whole society would get out of kilter.

To Joe, now aged 24:

Kohlberg: Why shouldn't you steal from a store?

Joe: It's violating another person's rights, in this case to property.

Kohlberg: Does the law enter in?

Joe: Well, the law in most cases is based on what is morally right so it's not a separate subject, it's a consideration.

Kohlberg: What does 'morality' or 'morally right' mean to you?

Joe: Recognising the rights of other individuals, first to life and then to do as he pleases as long as it doesn't interfere with somebody else's rights.

Evaluation of Kohlberg's Theory

Kohlberg hypothesised that in all societies, individuals would progress upwards through these three levels in sequence – neither missing out a stage nor regressing. He also thought that an individual would be attracted towards reasoning just above their own level on the scale, but would not be able to understand reasoning more than one stage above. There are various criticisms of Kohlberg's approach:

* that Kohlberg's research was biased towards males, as his original participants were all male. Carol Gilligan (1982) conducted research into the very real moral dilemma faced by women attending an abortion and pregnancy counselling service. Gilligan found that women put people before principles, rather than principles before people (the latter she believed to be a 'male' characteristic). Instead of using abstract, principled judgements which are universally applicable, the women used an alternative ethic of care and responsibility;

* that the dilemmas posed by Kohlberg were unrealistic and did not represent the actual moral debates which children engage in.

THE EFFECTS ON CHILDREN OF ATTACHMENT, SEPARATION AND LOSS

Separation of Children from Primary Carers

D. W. Winnicott (1896–1971) was involved with children at the Tavistock Clinic. His work has helped early years workers to be sensitive to how children feel when they separate from those they live with and love. Winnicott taught us to see the importance of the teddy bears and other comforters that children seem to need to carry about with them. He called these transitional objects. He believed that children need such objects to help them through the times when they begin to realise that they are a separate person. The teddy might stand for the mother when she leaves the baby in the cot; it is also a symbol of the mother who will return. It helps children through being alone or feeling sad. Naturally, the child might enjoy the teddy's company more when the mother is there. This reinforces the value of the teddy as a transitional object when the mother is absent.

Many adults still use transitional objects when they first leave home or when their partner goes away. It is not only children who have to deal with feelings of being separated from someone they love. Until recently children were not allowed to take teddy bears into hospital in case they carried germs. In some early years settings, transitional toys are still taken away from children when they arrive, in case they get lost. Adults working in early years settings need to discuss this as a team and plan a policy which takes care of the deep feelings that children have about their transitional objects. Some children have imaginary friends. These are another kind of transitional object, but they are imaginary rather than real. Children may use other early comfort behaviour, such as sucking, stroking or smelling. These do not have an imaginative dimension as in the case of a transitional object or an imaginary friend, but they are important ways in which children cope with transitions and separation. Children usually grow out of this behaviour quite naturally, and it is best to let this happen in its own time.

Bowlby's Theory of Attachment, Separation, Loss and Grief

John Bowlby (1907–1990) looked at:

* how babies become attached to the mother figure (**attachment**);

* what happens when babies are separated from the mother figure (**separation**);

* what happens when babies experience **loss** and grief when separated from the people they feel close to.

Babies and the people who care for them usually form close bonds. As the baby is fed, held and enjoyed, these emotional, loving relationships develop and deepen. Babies who find that adults respond quickly to their cries become trusting of life and are well attached in stable, warm relationships. They know that they will be fed, changed when soiled, comforted when teething, and so on. Babies and parents who, for one reason or another, do not make close emotional bonds experience general difficulty in forming stable, warm and loving relationships.

Mary Ainsworth, who worked with Bowlby, found that if adults responded quickly to a baby's cries, the child, by 3 years of age, was less demanding than those babies who had generally been left to cry. The individual temperament of a baby becomes obvious very early on and has an effect on the carers. For instance, some babies become hysterical very quickly when hungry, while others have a calmer nature. Bonding is partly about adults and babies adjusting to each other and understanding each other – learning how to read each other's signals. Bowlby thought that early attachment was very important – that the relationship between the mother figure and the baby was the most important. This was because mothers tended to be at home with their babies. He did not believe that the most important attachment figure should be the natural mother, but he did say

that babies need *one central person*, or a mother figure. It is now realised that babies can have deep relationships with several people – mother, father, brothers, sisters, carers and grandparents. Indeed, babies develop in an emotionally and socially healthy way only if they bond with several different people. In many parts of the world, and in many cultures, this is usual.

Babies might enjoy playing with one person and having meals with another. It is the quality of the time the child spends with people which determines whether or not the child becomes attached to them. Attachment can be difficult at first, especially in cases where it is hard for the adult and child to communicate. For example, if:

* the birth has caused mother and baby to be separated and the mother is depressed;
* the child is visually impaired and eye contact is absent;
* the child is hearing-impaired and does not turn to the parent's voice; eye contact is also harder to establish here because the child does not turn to the parent's face when he or she speaks;
* the child has severe learning difficulties and needs many experiences of a person before bonding can become stable.

Bowlby's work was important because it led to the introduction of key worker systems in institutions. (This will be looked at in more detail in Chapter 11.) Children no longer had a series of different nurses looking after them as each work shift changed. They were placed in smaller 'family' groups and were consistently looked after by the same team of staff. Furthermore, increasing numbers of children began to be fostered in family homes rather than placed in large institutions. This helped children to form good attachments with a limited number of people who cared for them. Children could develop warm, physical,

CASE STUDY

Tracey's imaginary dog

Tracey, 4 years, pretended that she had a dog. On holiday in the summer, she led the dog about wherever she went, feeding and stroking it. The dog helped her to get ready in her mind for starting at school after the holiday. It helped her to think about separating from her parents for a whole day, instead of just the half-day she spent at her nursery.

loving relationships, and found it easier to communicate with their carers. By 5 or 6 months, many babies are so closely attached to the people they know and love that they show separation anxiety when they are taken away from these attachment figures. When a baby is handed from the parent figure to a new carer, it is best if the new carer:

* approaches slowly;
* talks gently before taking the baby from the parent;
* holds the baby so that he or she can look at the parent during the handover.

Researchers have found that toddlers will happily explore toys and play with them if an attachment figure (usually their parent) is present. If the parent goes out of the room, however, young children quickly become anxious, and stop exploring and playing. They need the reassurance of someone they know to be able to explore, play and learn. Children who have had many separations from those with whom they have tried to bond find it very difficult to understand social situations and relationships. When young children's social signals for help and attention are ignored they:

* become frustrated;
* do not learn how to ask for help or attention or indeed how to give help in the usual ways;
* do not understand the social conventions that adults and children expect to use when they get together in a group.

Bear in mind that it is not helpful to concentrate on what children in this kind of difficulty cannot do. It is helpful to begin with what they can do. There is a famous series of films by James and Joyce Robertson which show Bowlby's theory of loss and grief in action. Children who were hospitalised and separated from their families went through various stages in their loss and grief:

1 **They protested:** they were angry, cried out and tried to resist the change.

2 **They despaired:** they acted as if they were numb to any feelings or interest in life.

3 **They became detached:** they related poorly to people, although they began to join in with their new situation.

We now know that children (and adults) move in and out of these stages, and that the stages do not occur in any strict order. Bowlby's findings have led to important work on how best to deal with the hospitalisation of children. His work has also helped early years workers to settle children into nurseries using positive strategies, and has led to the establishment of an organisation to help parents understand why their children become detached in their relationships after being sent to boarding preparatory schools at 6 or 7 years.

Examples of Separation

Sometimes separations are temporary, but sometimes they are permanent:

* A mother goes to hospital to have a new baby and the child stays with people he does not know well.
* A child is taken into care and experiences a series of caregivers.
* A family is split up in a war zone and perhaps never find each other again.
* A family become refugees and they are split up.
* One parent no longer sees the child, perhaps as a result of divorce.
* A parent is in hospital and is unable to see the child, for example after a serious accident or through clinical depression.

* A loved one is sent to prison.

* A loved one goes abroad.

* A loved one dies.

The separation process involves working through feelings of:

* disbelief and numbness;

* shock and panic;

* despair and yearning for the lost person;

* anger;

* interest in life (it takes time to reach this stage).

There are several far-reaching consequences of Bowlby's work:

* These days babies and mothers usually stay together on maternity wards. Often parents can stay in hospital with their children: there may be a bed for a parent next to the child's bed.

* Social workers are more careful about separating children and parents when families experience difficulties.

* There is more awareness of the seriousness of the situation of many asylum seekers and refugees, and understanding of the need for more positive action to be taken.

* Most early years settings now have policies on how to settle children so as to make it a positive experience.

* In the new EYFS statutory framework, every child in a group setting will have a **key person**.

ACTIVITY: INVESTIGATING EMOTIONAL AND SOCIAL ASPECTS OF DEVELOPMENT

1 Think about getting up in the morning. Choose a cultural tool – an alarm clock, telephone or a spoon – and discuss with a friend how you think it has influenced your behaviour in your culture, and how you in turn have influenced the culture you live in by using that cultural tool.

2 Plan ways to find out about the friendships young children develop. Observe a group of children aged 3–4 years playing together. Who is friends with whom? Look again a few weeks later at the same children. Are they still friends? Evaluate your observations.

3 Research the role of a key person or family worker. Make a list of pros and cons of using a key person or family worker. Discuss this with the group.

4 What are three important things about theories which support: (a) nurture, (b) nature, (c) nature and nurture?

CHAPTER 7

Understanding the Behaviour of Children

Contents

• Managing behaviour (or developing self-discipline) • Offering alternative distractions • Being a role model
• Behaviour management strategies which encourage self-discipline • Challenging behaviour in a group situation
• Setting clear boundaries • Opportunities for movement • Theories of emotional and social development • The
child's concept of death • Behaviourist theory • Socialisation theory • Social learning theory • Sociobiological
theory • Judy Dunn • Social evolution theory • Open societies and closed societies

MANAGING BEHAVIOUR (OR DEVELOPING SELF-DISCIPLINE)

There are two ways of looking at the behaviour of children:

* When we try to manage the child's behaviour, we work from the outside in. We try to control how the child behaves, using a variety of techniques. But what will happen when we are not there?

* When we give children strategies to develop their own self-discipline, we work from the inside out. We try to help the child to manage their own behaviour; this is called self-discipline. But what will happen when we are not there?

Research shows that self-discipline is the only kind of discipline worth having if we want behaviour to be lastingly good for the child, and for us as a society. When Judge Tumin, who died recently, was the Chief Inspector of Prisons, he found that the predominantly male prisoners (18–25 years) had low self-esteem and no self-discipline. They were dependent on others to manage their behaviour.

OFFERING ALTERNATIVE DISTRACTIONS TO CHILDREN

Sometimes an adult can see trouble looming and can avoid a confrontation by offering an alternative. Alternatives are better than confrontations, which often result in temper tantrums and more challenging behaviour.

BEING A ROLE MODEL

Remember that children notice and learn from your feelings, actions and reactions. You are a powerful source of learning for the child. So you should:

* give children a predictable environment (but not necessarily a rigid routine);

* try to avoid confrontations or humiliation by respecting a child's personality and mood, and knowing what the child can manage without too much struggle;

* explain that there is a real boundary if a confrontation becomes unavoidable – a boundary that a child cannot cross.

ANTI-SOCIAL BEHAVIOUR IN ADOLESCENCE

The majority of adolescents are law-abiding most of the time and have developed a strong sense of right and wrong. A small minority of young people do engage in serious anti-social conduct – such as muggings, knifings, rapes and armed robberies. This does not mean that they are incapable of the conventional moral reasoning described in Chapter 6. Research into such aggressive behaviour point to a wide range of contributory factors, including the following:

* **Genetic predisposition**
  Twin studies show that some individuals are genetically pre-disposed to have hostile touchy temperaments and to engage in aggressive behaviour.

* **Conflict between the life and death instincts**
  Psychodynamic theorists – e.g. Freud – argue that all humans are driven by two instincts: the life instincts which aim for survival, and the death instincts which are destructive forces; these destructive tendencies can be shown as aggression or may be sublimated (or displaced) into sport or some other physical activity.

* **Coercive family environments**
  Highly anti-social adolescents tend to come from families whose members are locked in power struggles, each trying to control the others by coercive tactics – e.g. threatening, shouting and hitting. In such families, parents gradually lose control over their children's behaviour, with sanctions and physical punishment having increasingly little effect.

* **The specific cultural context**
  Inner-city areas and areas where poverty is extensive are more likely to foster aggression. The USA leads all industrialised countries in the incidence of rapes and murders.

* **A response to frustration**
  Some psychologists believe that frustration always leads to aggression and that aggression is always caused by frustration. Others argue that not all frustration leads to aggression; they believe that frustration leads to aggression because it causes general arousal, but this arousal is only expressed as aggression if the appropriate environmental cues are in place.

* **Reinforcement and observation of aggressive behaviour**
  Social learning theorists (e.g. Bandura) argue that in many societies male aggression is respected. They also place great emphasis on the power of the mass media (especially television) to influence behaviour.

* **De-individuation**
  This refers to a loss of personal **identity** in which the individual surrenders his or her own independence and conscience and simple merges anonymously into the crowd. De-individuation can be liberating in its release of inhibitions, as well as encouraging anti-social behaviour.

BEHAVIOUR MANAGEMENT STRATEGIES WHICH ENCOURAGE SELF-DISCIPLINE

Young children often do not realise that they are doing something unacceptable. They need help to begin to understand when something is inappropriate.

Froebel believed that every bad act has a good intention. He thought that adults should try to find out what this intention was, and help the child by acknowledging it. Then, he believed, it is easier to put right the 'bad' that the child has done. When children do things that we do not want them to do, it is easy to feel annoyed and impatient. However, thinking positively and keeping a sense of humour enable us to remain professional with children who challenge our patience and stamina. There are four main approaches to the management of behaviour (the fourth type is most appropriate to your work and you should always use it in preference to the other strategies):

1   Using punishment as revenge;
2   Behaviour modification;
3   Time out;
4   Focusing on reform.

Using Punishment as Revenge

This *unacceptable* and *unethical* approach can be summed up in the statement 'An eye for an eye, a tooth for a tooth'. This means that what you do to me, I will do to you; if you hit me, I will hit you. In many countries, such as Sweden, it is now illegal to smack, beat or 'strap' a child. In the UK it is illegal in early years settings. Children who are smacked often hit other children, usually younger and smaller children. They are imitating the fact that big adults smack small children. Children do not understand punishment as revenge – as well as being a cruel strategy, it simply does not work.

Behaviour Modification

This strategy takes two forms:

*   **negative reinforcement** (see page 60);
*   **positive reinforcement**.

Adults can also encourage children to do what they want them to do by giving them rewards. However, the strategy only works in the short term, and the effect wears off quite quickly. The problem is that rewards do not make

children think about why they want to do things. Any motivation is short-lived.

Time Out

The adult might say to the child 'If you scribble on the books again, you will have to sit on the time-out chair for a few minutes'. This might put the child off scribbling in books, but in a different situation, for instance when staying at grandma's, it will not prevent the child scribbling on the wall of the bedroom. Children can only make the obvious connection and may not be able to extend what they have learned to a different context. Vivian Gussin-Paley has written a book about the limitations of the time-out chair; the book is 'Wally's Stories'. In a similar way, it is not helpful to punish children some time after the event. They do not connect what they did earlier with what is being done to them now.

Always remember, it is a mistake to make children do a drawing or look at a book as a

CASE STUDY

Using rewards may not be effective

Marion Dowling gives this example:

. . . in one study in a nursery school, a group of children were provided with drawing materials and told that they would receive a prize for drawing which, in due course, they did. Another group were given the same materials but with no mention of prizes. Some time after, drawing was provided as one of a range of optional activities . . . significantly, the children who chose to spend the least time on drawing were those who had been previously rewarded.

punishment because this will give the message that these are unpleasant activities.

Focusing on Reform

Research shows that from about 3 years children begin to feel guilt and shame about the things they do. However, they cannot learn about social behaviour if they cannot make sense of what is done to them. That is why a focus on reform rather than on revenge or deterrent is effective in the long term. In the section below, strategies are given which encourage reform and the development of self-discipline. Never humiliate a child. This is a damaging emotion.

Containment and Holding

It is important not to leave a child in the middle of a tantrum. Quietly holding them and being there for them provides support through this time until they begin to feel calm. Psychologists refer to this as **containment**. Containing a child's feelings with gentle and calm physical support helps the child to feel cared for. It also reassures the child that they will not be left alone to lose control. It is important that children have a good relationship with adults who hold their feelings of anger for them in this way. The adult acts as a 'container' which holds the child's anger in a safe way so that the child does not feel out of control. This helps the child to regain a sense of calm. It is no good trying to discuss what has happened with a child who is in the middle of a temper tantrum or who is being aggressive. The child needs to become calm before talking.

Preventing Aggressive Behaviour

Aggressive behaviour (hitting, shouting or spoiling another child's painting, for example) can sometimes be prevented if adults put on their running shoes! The adult must get there before the behaviour happens,

gently saying 'no' and removing the child. This can be a very useful strategy, particularly with children under 3 years.

Discussing the Situation

Eye contact is very important in your dealings with children. So are your body language and the gestures you use. These can be more important than what you say. Communication is 85 per cent non-verbal.

CHALLENGING BEHAVIOUR IN A GROUP SITUATION

Disruptive behaviour in a group is best dealt with by not giving the challenging child attention: concentrate instead on all the other children who are not being disruptive. You might say: 'I can see most of you are ready for the story. You have all found your cushions and are sitting there looking really interested. I am so looking forward to reading this story because it is one of my favourites.'

Being ignored is not what an attention seeker hopes for. Children are helped if they realise that they gain positive and warm attention from you if they are cooperative.

SETTING CLEAR BOUNDARIES

Children need clear, consistent boundaries in order to manage their own behaviour. They will test out boundaries that are not clear or consistent: they will check to see if a boundary is still there; to see if it can be moved; whether all the adults will uphold a particular boundary. This can become very tedious from the adult's point of view! It is best to have just a few boundaries, agreed to by everyone in the team – and agreed by the children, if at all possible. It helps children to feel secure when a boundary is strong, clear and comforting – 4-year-olds often say with great satisfaction 'You're not allowed!' When a child oversteps a boundary, it is important that they are not made to feel worthless or disliked for what they have done. This can be avoided if the child's actions are criticised, rather the child themselves. For example, say 'Kicking hurts. Jo is very upset because it hurt', rather than, 'Don't do that. You are very naughty, and I am cross with you'. The message needs to be: I am not rejecting you; I am rejecting what you did.

OPPORTUNITIES FOR MOVEMENT

Developmental Movement Play (DMP) shows that often children simply need opportunities for play involving extensive physical movement. This is becoming increasingly important now that more children spend time in extended provision. Children who do not spend time on the floor, spinning and tilting, and climbing and jumping often develop behaviour problems, and even a mild form of ADHD, which has been socially induced because they are required to sit and be still too much.

THEORIES OF EMOTIONAL AND SOCIAL DEVELOPMENT

The Nature–nurture Controversy

Nature and Inheritance

In the past it was thought that personalities are fixed from the moment we are born (this is the nature argument). It is probably too extreme a view, just as the view that intelligence is fixed at birth is extreme. Children who have grown up without other people do not seem to show the kind of social behaviour we think of as human; they do not make human sounds, smile, use eye contact or walk like humans. This suggests that their social behaviour is not simply fixed in their genes and inherited. Such children include:

* feral children, sometimes known as 'wolf children';
* children who are kept isolated from other people.

The nature approach includes the psycho-dynamic theories of Freud, Erikson, Winnicott and Bowlby, which concentrate on the feelings we have inside us, and on how other people can help us to **express and deal with** these. These theorists believe that our early feelings and experiences never leave us. They are always deep inside us and they affect us throughout our lives.

Social Behaviour as a Result of Nature

Nurture theories include:

* Skinner's behaviourist theory;
* socialisation theory;
* Bandura's social learning theory.

These theories, which state that social behaviour is learned, have been challenged since the 1980s.

Fig 7.1 When children are bored they behave badly. Here the adult is providing interesting experiences and supporting the baby in the choice she has made so that she does not become frustrated

CASE STUDY

Jody hits Amandip

The adult says 'Amandip is crying because that hurt. He is very upset. What happened? He took your toy? Did you take Jody's toy, Amandip?' [Amandip nods] 'Next time, Jody, try saying "It's mine". Then he will know how you feel about it.'

This approach signals to Amandip that he must not snatch Jody's toy, but it also allows him to find a way out with dignity, without humiliating him.

Furthermore, it gives Jody the words that she needs to use instead of hitting. It rejects what both children did, but it does not reject either child. It helps both children to have some ideas of how they might tackle the situation next time. This is punishment as reform, and it will help the children to think about moral matters and to develop self-discipline. It helps children to examine the results of what they do.

Guidelines for managing children's behaviour

* Can you distract the child? If a child keeps grabbing the paint pot from another child, ask the first child to help you mix more pots of paint. This distracts the child and takes you both out of a negative situation.

* Does the child need personal space? Sometimes children cannot share or be with other children for too long. They need to do their own thing. Respect this and help the child to move into a solitary activity.

* Does the child need help to express and talk about how they feel? Opportunities for role play or to bash and bang a lump of clay can be very helpful in this situation.

* Does the child need help with a side-by-side strategy?

* Should two children be left together? They may have been together too long, or perhaps their personalities are clashing and they find it hard to spend time together. When this happens it is usually best to find a way of separating the children.

* Can you help children to negotiate? (Remember, they may be too angry or upset to do this.)

* Sometimes children's feelings just erupt. They can be a danger to themselves or to other children. It is always best if children can be helped before this point is reached, but sometimes the eruption of feelings is unavoidable. Children can be very frightened by the power of their feelings and may be overwhelmed if they lose control. They need you to contain their anger and feelings for them.

* Are the children bored? Are the room and outdoor area interesting enough places? Are the children free to choose activities for themselves?

* Is the child hungry? Hunger can make us all crabby.

* Is there any physical reason for the behaviour? Does the child lack pain sensation in some aspects, and is the child clumsy?

* Is the child tired or uncomfortable? If so, try to find out why. (Maybe they have wet themselves.)

* Do they need rough-and-tumble play? Children need safe

movement spaces where they can be noisy and move about freely, both indoors and outdoors.

* Do they need to slow down? Children need calmer periods where they have personal space, perhaps making a little den for themselves, reading alone in the book area or having a story read by an adult.

* Can you redirect the situation? Sometimes you will see something building up and may be able to prevent the situation arising by moving in before it happens.

* Do you value children's efforts and express your feelings? Children are able to tidy up with adult help, but they need their efforts to be recognised and warmly appreciated.

* Do the children have enough opportunities to play? Indoors and outdoors?

* Do you know about the child's background? It is important to remember that what is positive behaviour in one culture might be interpreted differently in another. For example, owning possessions and learning to respect other people's possessions might be valued in one family culture or society more than in another.

* Are you taking a flexible view? Showing initiative and negotiating might be valued in some situations, but conformity might be more important in others, such as crossing the road.

* Remember that behaviour which is valued universally in the world has to do with helping others, having feelings for others, sharing and taking turns, and understanding somebody else's feelings and ideas.

Fig 7.2 Listening to children and respecting their ideas and feelings are important

Nature and Nurture Theories

Theories which involve both nature and nurture include:

* The **social constructivist** theories of Trevarthen, Dunn and Vygotsky. According to this approach, children and adults are constantly adjusting to each other and learning from each other.

* Dawkins's **social evolution** theory, which concentrates on the whole human race and does not look at individuals at all.

* **Brain studies**. Colin Blakemore, a neuroscientist at Oxford University, says that nurture shapes nature. The experiences we have with people and objects quite literally change the physical chemistry of our brains. For example, children who are exposed to music from an early age develop more auditory cortex than most people.

Psychodynamic Theories

Sigmund Freud (1856–1939)

Freud is the founder of psychoanalytic theory. He believed that:

* our unconscious feelings direct the way we behave; we are not aware of these feelings, and this means that we often do not know why we behave as we do in a particular situation;

* our earliest childhood experiences deeply influence what we believe and how we feel as adults;

* people go through psychosexual stages of development which he called oral, anal, phallic, latency and genital stages;

* he could help the people he psychoanalysed to understand their behaviour and feelings, and even to change.

Freud thought that people have:

* an **id:** which makes 'want' demands;

* an **ego:** which tries to resolve conflicts between the id and the superego;

* a **superego:** which conveys the demands made by parents or society about how to behave.

Erik H. Erikson (1902–1994)

Erikson took Sigmund Freud's work as the rock on which he based his own personality theory. He was also a pupil of Anna Freud, Sigmund's daughter. Erikson concentrated on the superego and on the influence of society on a child's development. He showed how, when we meet a personal crisis or have to deal with a crisis in the world (for example, living through a war), we are naturally equipped to face the difficulties and to deal with them. Erikson thought that there were eight developmental phases during a person's life (five during childhood and three during adulthood). He said that during each phase we have to face and sort out the particular kinds of problem that occur during that phase.

In the days before equal opportunities, Erikson called his developmental stages the eight phases of Man. It is important to bear in mind that theories evolving from Freud's ideas are based on white, middle-class patients in Western Europe. The theories need to be used carefully for that reason. However, they still seem to be useful in many of Erikson's eight developmental phases.

* **Phase 1: babyhood.** We have to sort out whether we feel a basic sense of trust or mistrust in life. This phase is about being a hopeful person or not.

* **Phase 2: the toddler and nursery years.** We develop either a basic sense of being able to do things ourselves (autonomy) or a basic sense of doubt in ourselves, leading to shame. This phase is about our self-identity.

* **Phase 3: the infant school years.** We either take the initiative and go for it or we feel guilty and hold back in case we upset people. This phase is about leading an active life with a sense of purpose, or not.

* **Phase 4: the junior years.** We either begin to be determined to master things or we do not try hard in case we cannot manage something. This phase is about becoming skilled.

* **Phase 5: adolescence.** We either begin to be at one with ourselves or we feel uncertain and unsure. We learn to have faith in ourselves, or not.

* **Phase 6: young adults.** We begin to have a sense of taking part in our society

and of taking responsibility in it as a shared venture, or we think only of ourselves and become isolated.

* **Phase 7: middle age.** We begin to be caring of the next generation and the future of our society, or we reject the challenge.

* **Phase 8: old age.** We return to our roots and overcome feelings of despair, disgust about new lifestyles or fear of death, or not. This is Erikson's phase of wisdom.

THE CHILD'S CONCEPT OF DEATH

People say different things when someone dies. For example, they may tell children that the person has:

* gone to heaven;

* gone to sleep;

* gone away;

* turned into earth.

Children can become very confused. They get frightened that they will be taken away to this place called heaven, or that if they go to sleep they might not wake up. Children need honest and straightforward explanations of death which make it clear that the person will not come back, and that it is not their fault that the person died.

Guidelines for helping children to grieve

* Explain things. Say that someone is terminally ill, that parents are divorcing or that a person is going to prison. Children need to be told of the reality of the situation.

* Make sure the child does not feel responsible for what has happened.

* Do not exclude the child – let them be part of the family. If someone has died, let the child go to the funeral or visit the grave and share the sadness.

* Be especially warm and loving; cuddle the child, be calm and quietly be there for them.

* Give the child reassurance that it is alright to feel grief; help the child to know that, although these feelings will last for a long time, they are normal. Tell them that the pain will ease over time.

* Find photographs and evoke memories.

* Some children are helped by play therapy, but ordinary childhood play heals most children.

Be prepared for the child to regress; do not demand too much of the child. When the child begins to show an interest in things once more, gently encourage them.

Children need to grieve, just as adults do. If they are not helped to grieve, they may experience mental ill health later on in adult life. If they are helped, however, they will experience positive relationships with other people and come to terms with their loss in a positive way.

BEHAVIOURIST THEORY

Until the mid-1980s this theory had a great influence. It suggested that adults regulated children's behaviour. Skinner thought that adults shape children's behaviour, so that children conform to the expectations and conventions of the culture in which they grow up. Skinner believed that children could be positively or negatively reinforced so as to behave in the ways adults wanted (see examples of positive and negative reinforcement on page 60). Adults often give children rewards (sweets, badges, stars, smiley faces, verbal praise) for good behaviour. 'Good' behaviour in this context means behaviour that adults want to see. 'Good' behaviour in one culture might be bad behaviour in another. For example, in some cultures it is considered rude for a child to look an adult in the eye when being reprimanded, but it is very rude not to do so in other cultures. It is important for adults working with young children to decide whether or not they believe in extrinsic rewards – for example, stars for good behaviour. Research suggests that this approach can quickly bring successful results, but that these are short-lived. It is probably more successful in the long term if children do something because they realise its benefits, for example sitting quietly ready for a story because they know they will enjoy listening to it. This is called **intrinsic motivation**, and it helps children to become self-disciplined and to manage their own behaviour.

SOCIALISATION THEORY

Socialisation is the process by which children learn the expected behaviour for their culture and society. The theory of socialisation, which developed out of behaviourist theory, found favour between the 1960s and 1980s. According to this theory, children learn the rules of the society they live in, which vary from society to society and from culture to culture. Being socialised in certain cultures can mean that children learn about things that we should consider unacceptable, for example the denying of human rights to blacks in South Africa under the regime of apartheid.

There are two levels associated with this theory:

* **Primary socialisation theory:** this is about the way the family and those close to the child help the child's social development. The child learns to behave as part of the family, adapting to its social ways.

* **Secondary socialisation theory:** the child's social circle begins to widen to include neighbours, perhaps an early childhood group and society at large. The influences on social development thus become broader.

SOCIAL LEARNING THEORY

This emphasises that young children learn about social behaviour by:

* watching other people;
* imitating other people.

Albert Bandura found that children tend to imitate people in their lives who they believe hold status, especially if those people are warm or powerful personalities. This research study did not replicate a natural situation for the children, but it does suggest that adults can be very influential on a child's behaviour. This should lead us to think about our own behaviour and the effect we have on children:

* If children are smacked by adults, they are likely to hit other children.
* If children are shouted at by adults, they are likely to shout at others.
* If children are given explanations, they will try to explain things too.
* If children are comforted when they fall, they will learn to do the same to others.

People who work with young children are very important status figures in the child's social learning.

CASE STUDY

Bandura's work

Bandura showed three groups of children a film in which an adult was hitting a Bobo doll and shouting at it. The film had a different ending for each of the three groups:

First ending: the adult was given a reward for hitting the doll.

Second ending: the adult was punished for hitting the doll.

Third ending: nothing was done to the adult for hitting the doll.

Then the children were given a Bobo doll like the one in the film. The children who saw the adult rewarded for hitting the doll tended to do the same.

Role Play as Social Learning

Children copy directly what adults do, but they also pretend to be adults (they role-play being adults) when they begin to play imaginatively. The home area is an important area for this, and so is the outdoor area, which can become all sorts of places (shops, markets, streets and building sites, for example). The problem with this approach is that it does not see role play as children experimenting with different ways of doing

CASE STUDY

Joe, 4 years

Joe pretended to be an early years worker. He told a story to a group of dolls and imitated the way in which the worker talked gently to the children, smiled and held the book.

things: it suggests that children merely copy what they see. We now know that role play is a more complex activity than the social learning theory would suggest.

SOCIO-BIOLOGICAL THEORY

Modern research has revealed that how adults and children relate to each other is a two-way process. From a very early age, babies and children:

* actively choose whom they want to be with;
* have an influence on the way their family, carers and friends behave towards them;
* are influenced by those they care about;
* develop social and emotional relationships through this two-way process.

This means that children are not passively 'shaped' or 'regulated' to do what adults want. Some adults find it hard to understand and accept that even a young baby can have preferences for particular people, and that they can 'call' adults to them and get them to do the things that they want. In fact, from the start of their lives, young children give and take, contributing to relationships just as adults do.

* Sometimes they need other adults or children.
* Sometimes they follow what other people do.
* Sometimes they negotiate with other people.

JUDY DUNN

Judy Dunn has studied family social life in the Cambridge area of the UK for a number of years. She believes that the social and moral development of children is closely linked with their family relationships. In the first year of life, babies begin to notice and be sensitive to the actions of people in their family. She calls this affective tuning; it is sometimes also called social referencing. From 1 to 3 years children show self-concern. They need to:

* get the attention of others;
* understand what other people feel and say;
* comfort someone in distress.

If they do these things they can get what they want and need for themselves. Children also begin to work out what is allowed. They begin to understand what behaviours will meet with disapproval from other people, and how other people will respond to the way they express their feelings. Young children are curious about other people, and they experiment to discover what happens when they try to:

* hurt other people;
* help other people;
* show care for other people.

The concern that children have for themselves leads them to consider the needs of other people. In order to feel that they are getting fair treatment, children have to find out if they are being treated in the same way as other children. Children learn about these things through their family relationships. Before they can talk and discuss these events, they also learn through situations. Children learn about situations which make them angry, for example. Being angry makes people react to the child; and children also learn what makes other people angry!

Through their relationships with people in their families, they also learn how to care and to be considerate, kind and helpful. These are the basic experiences needed for moral development. In contrast to the behaviourist, social learning and socialisation approaches, the sociobiological approach supposes that children learn more through experimenting in social situations than just by copying what other people do. Children experiment in social situations:

* when they do things that other people do not allow or do not approve of;
* when people share fun together;
* through having conversations and discussing things;
* when people confront or tease each other;
* when playing with other children.

Every culture in every early years setting is based on a different set of relationships. Learning how to ask for things means that children learn how things get done in their particular family, in their particular early years setting and in their particular culture. Sociobiological theory says it is the way that people interact together which is important for social development. These are important aspects of the theory:

* Social development is a two-way process.
* Children learn as much from confrontation and angry exchanges as they do from having fun with other people.
* Adults such as early years workers are very important influences in the social constructivist approach.
* The way that children are helped to believe in themselves enables them, in turn, to develop positive relationships with other people.

It is important that adults help children to negotiate with other people, rather than to manipulate them. If adults manipulate children using bribes – 'If you do the clearing up quickly, you can have the first go on the swings when we get to the park' – they damage the child's developing self-discipline and moral development. When adults **negotiate** with children it shows that they respect each other. Adults and children should try to find the best solution together, in a spirit of being partners.

When children are helped to negotiate, this enhances both their social and their emotional development, and this in turn affects their moral development.

Behaviourist, socialisation and social learning theory: a summary

The following points are true according to these theories:

1   Children are born with reflexes. They do not inherit social behaviour; it is thought to be learned.

2   Children copy what adults do and thus learn accepted behaviour in their culture.

They will experience:

*   role transition (e.g. when they go from nursery to school);

*   role loss (e.g. when an only child has a baby brother or sister born into the family);

*   role conflict (e.g. when other children want the child to do something that he or she knows adults will disapprove of);

*   the learning of a gender role (e.g. what it means to be a boy/male or a girl/female).

3   Children are influenced by other children: they want to be like their friends, perhaps wearing the same shoes. This can mean that some children are easily led because they copy others, or that they are

easily bullied because they fear losing the approval of other children.

4   Children rehearse adult life through role play. For example, they learn the correct adult roles for a mother, doctor or receptionist, and these are rehearsed in their play. Children imitate the roles of people who have high status for them.

5   Children experience positive reinforcement. They are praised and extrinsically rewarded for their good behaviour (behaviour that is wanted by adults).

6   Children may experience negative reinforcement. They will avoid an unpleasant situation (which involves behaviour not wanted by adults). Instead, they do something adults approve of.

7   Children begin to sort out how adults expect them to behave, and also how they can expect adults to behave. Children thus begin to realise that different people have different roles, and that people behave according to their own particular role.

SOCIAL EVOLUTION THEORY

The Development of Social Behaviour in Different Cultures

Throughout this book, we stress that modern researchers think about development in terms of two linked strands:

*   the biological path;
*   the sociocultural path.

Social evolution theory focuses on the interplay between the two strands over thousands of years, and we consider social development in this light. The brain, especially in the first 5 years of life, is constantly modified by experience, for example by the food eaten or by emotional and social encounters. Human beings are social animals. This means that when they work together adults can solve jointly all sorts of problems which would be much too hard for one person to manage alone. The same is true of children. For example, moving a truck that is stuck in the mud in the garden is difficult for a 4-year-old on his own, but a group of children working together may well solve the problem. Working together can be hard for children:

* They need to hold in mind others' ideas as well as their own.

* They have to be able to think in quite abstract ways to manage their own and others' ideas.

* All this takes a lot of brain power. It means thinking deeply.

* Each child has to control their feelings if the group is to work well together.

* They will work better together if they can use words or signs to communicate. New knowledge can then be handed on to other people: 'I know a good way to move a truck', shouts Lee to Jo.

Once humans began to walk about on two legs instead of four, their hands became free. They began to make and use tools. They worked together when foraging and hunting for food, and when defending themselves as a group from enemies. Social cooperation has evolved because it makes people successful in managing new and difficult situations. Over time humans developed larger brains so that social and cultural learning could be handed down to other people. This transfer of social and cultural knowledge is still important today. It helps people to deal with things that are uncertain in life and to cope with lives which are full of changes.

Negotiating with children

The adult might say to the child 'I know that you want to go to the shops, but we haven't cleared the toy cars away yet. It will leave a mess behind that won't be very nice for the other children and some of the toys might get broken. I think we need to clear up before we go. Do you want to do that while I get the coats ready, or shall we clear up together and get the coats afterwards?' Given a choice which is simple and clear, the child usually negotiates a solution that is positive.

Cultural Tools and Social Evolution

Ever since Neanderthal men and women devised practical tools, social development has involved the development of cultural tools which help shared group thinking. These tools are not necessarily physical instruments. They help the exchange of ideas and information between people and include:

* a shared number system and languages;

* the sharing of plans and ideas;

* social rules, for example about sitting down for a meal together;

* practical tools which are used in technology and science.

Richard Dawkins, the biologist, believes that social learning is a shared process, based around cultural tools. He calls this the **social evolution** approach.

The Social Evolution Approach in Practice

At first a baby uses a spoon (which is a cultural tool) in their own way. Once the baby has got used to the spoon, the adult might help by putting some food on it. The baby then tries to do this. The baby's behaviour is influenced by being given the spoon in the first place, by watching what the adult does and by experimenting in their own way.

The baby might use the spoon in a new and interesting way. For example, they might balance a pea on the upturned spoon and take it into their mouth that way. The baby is developing an idea about how to use a spoon, as well as taking ideas from the way the adult uses the spoon.

OPEN SOCIETIES AND CLOSED SOCIETIES

In some cultures new ideas are very acceptable. These societies are called open societies, rather than closed societies where new ideas are less welcome. Every culture develops particular ways of doing things. These become customs and rituals which are handed down and give a sense of continuity with the past. The laws of the society and the rules of its different institutions give an indication of the society's values and show how they are put into practice. Cultures which are rich in the expressive arts – exciting dance groups, music events, drama performances – and the sciences – with original research and novel ideas in abundance – usually value these activities and provide the cultural tools which are needed to help these things blossom. It is only humans, with their cultural tools, who have achieved such activities. People are very influenced by the culture in which they grow up and each person can also influence that culture. In the same way, each child is influenced by the people and cultural tools in the early years setting; but just as surely each child also influences the people and cultural tools that they find.

ACTIVITY: COPING WITH CHANGE

Make a book which helps a child to develop a concept of death, or which looks at the birth of a sibling. Evaluate your book.

ACTIVITY: READING

Choose one of the books from the list below. Read to a child aged 3–5 years. Observe the child, concentrating on their feelings. Evaluate your observations and the book you chose.

* Ruth Brown, *Copycat*, Andersen Press.

* Marilyn Talbot, *Shy Roland*, Andersen Press.

* Selina Young, *Whistling in the Woods*, Heinemann.

* Catherine and Laurence Anholt, *What Makes Me Happy*, Walker Books.

- Anni Axworthy, *Along Came Toto*, Walker Books.

- Sue Lewis, *Come Back Grandma*, Red Fox.

- Susan Varley, *Badger's Parting Gifts*, Collins Picture Lions.

- Catherine Robinson, *Leaving Mrs Ellis*, Bodley Head.

- Sue Cowlishaw, *When My Little Sister Died*, Merlin Books.

- Bryan Mellonie and Robert Ingpen, *Lifetimes*, Hill of Content (Australia).

- John Burningham, *Granpa*, Jonathan Cape.

CHAPTER 8

Observation and Assessment

Contents

• Observation and assessment frameworks • The role of observation and assessment in the early years settings • Limits of professional role and competence • Sharing of information • Work settings' policies, rules and procedures • Rights and involvement of parents/primary carers • What to observe • Observational and recording techniques • The impact of the observer • Observing and assessing naturally-occurring and structured activities • Using norms • Types of observation

OBSERVATION AND ASSESSMENT FRAMEWORKS

For a long time, it has been the role of health and medical professionals to carry out regular checks, measurements and assessments on children, initially as foetuses in the womb during pregnancy, through birth and into the early years.

* **Health visitors** oversee infant health, referring to paediatricians when necessary. They monitor weight, diet, general growth and development, usually until the child begins school.

* **School health services** continue sight and hearing tests, and may administer immunisations or vaccinations (e.g. in cases of hepatitis or meningitis outbreaks).

* **Child clinics, family health centres and paediatric wards** in hospitals also carry out health surveillance, which relies on observation and assessment of children.

Why Observe and Assess Children in Early Childhood Settings?

The trend towards babies and infants being cared for in settings other than their own homes has led to the need for parents and other caregivers, including early childhood practitioners, to gather information – formally and informally – and to share it for the benefit of the children. Record-keeping and assessment has always been good practice in early years settings but there is now a **legal requirement** to demonstrate the process as part of the Early Years Foundation Stage (**EYFS**) framework coming into statutory force in September, 2008. All practitioners working in HLEs (Home Learning Environments), in Childminding Networks or Nannies, schools or group care of any kind in the private, voluntary or independent sector must, by law, follow and implement the 'Statutory Framework for the Early Years Foundation Stage: Setting the Standards for Learning, Development and Care for Children from Birth to Five'. This states that all practitioners must observe children and respond appropriately, so that from birth they make progress towards the early learning goals. Providers must ensure there is training for practitioners so that they can assess capably and objectively with support. Observations must be based on what children do in their everyday experiences and activities, and acted upon, informed by observations gathered from rich learning experiences (indoors and outdoors).

All practitioners, including the **key person** and the parents, will observe. There will be dialogues and regular meetings with parents throughout the EYFS.

There is a **registration and inspection framework** for settings providing care and/or education for babies and children. Day care and early education are regulated by **Ofsted**.

Assessment during the EYFS

The 'Practice Guidance for the Early Years Foundation Stage' sets out suggestions supporting practitioners so that they make systematic observations and assessments of each child's interests, strengths and achievements, and individual ways of learning. These observations will be used to identify learning needs and priorities, building on a child's interests, and planning that is relevant and captures the dispositions to learn of individual children. This will help practitioners to use their observations in taking children on their individual journey towards the early learning goals from birth to five years. This will mean in practice:

* a **calendar or cycle** indicating opportunities to report to parents in both formal and informal ways;

* the **key person** and other staff being involved in planning and carrying out observations and assessments as a team;

* a **daily record** of the routine aspects of daily care, e.g. feeding, nappy–changing, sleeping etc.;

* **regular observations** of a 'new' child throughout the day for the first few attendances;

* **observations of every child** as part of planned and ongoing assessment (perhaps on a rotating basis);

* regular observations to check **safety aspects**;

* **records of responses** to parental concerns or requests;

* **responses to changes** noticed in children's health, attitude, etc.;

* **observations to check, plan for, and review** changes to the provision;

* **an outline of observations and assessment practice and methods of record-keeping** (the different practices and methods are covered later in this chapter).

The EYFS Profile – End-of-Stage Assessment

The Early Years Foundation Stage Profile is used as a way to sum up each child's development and learning at the end of the EYFS. It is important to note that this summative record, the Early Years Foundation Stage Profile, is based on the continually gathered observations and assessments in the six areas of Learning and Development.

These are:

* Personal Social and Emotional Development;

* Communication, Language and Literacy;

* Problem Solving, Reasoning and Numeracy;

* Knowledge and Understanding of the World;

* Physical Development;

* Creative Development.

The four principles/themes of the EYFS are important for assessing and planning for each child's needs. These are:

* A Unique Child;

* Positive Relationships;

* Enabling Environments;

* Learning and Development.

The level of each child's development must be recorded against the 13 assessment scales derived from the early learning goals. Practitioners must use their observations gathered in situations where children can choose activities and initiate as they engage spontaneously in experiences. Judgements about where the child is in relation to the 13 scales will be made according to how consistent and independent the child's development, learning and behaviour is. Local Authorities have a duty to monitor and moderate the EYFS Profile judgements to ensure consistency across settings. Providers must take part in these arrangements. Within the last term of the EYFS, all providers must give parents:

* a written summary of the child's progress against the early learning goals;

* a copy of the EYFS Profiles if the parent requests one;

* details and opportunities to discuss the Profile and its results with the practitioner.

If children move to a new provider, the Profile (in the last term of EYFS only) must be sent on. The EYFS and the assessment and record are in statutory force across all settings and provisions, including reception and nursery classes in schools. The DfES 'Continuing the Learning Journey' helps teachers and teaching assistants in Year 1 of primary school to build on the next steps in the Early Years Foundation Stage Profile, as they are required to do using the spirit of the principles in the EYFS. Observation will inform planning and assessment throughout the Foundation Stage leading to a summarised set of observations at the end of the reception year, in the Foundation Profile. In England and Northern Ireland there are **Standard Assessment Tasks** at the end of Key Stage 1, but not in Wales and Scotland.

THE ROLE OF OBSERVATION AND ASSESSMENT IN EARLY YEARS SETTINGS

The most important reason for carrying out observations and assessments is to get to know the child and what the child needs. What can we learn from observation?

Observing Children

Observations provide us with, and need to be shared with parents to give, valuable information about **individual children**:

* *where* children are in their interests, development and learning;

* supporting children with English as an additional language (EAL);

* their progress in the different areas of development and learning;

* information can be analysed to emphasise what a child can do or decide on the need for further help and support;

* aspects of their health and wellbeing;

* personality, temperament, likes and dislikes;

* including all children;

* response to different experiences;

* behaviour in a range of contexts, for example in different social and physical environments;

* closing the inequality gap;

* helps practitioners decide on next steps for the child's learning.

We can also observe **groups of children** to learn about:

* differences between individual children; their health and growth;

* their response to similar situations; their response to adults;

* the interaction between individuals;

* communication within the group;
* the way conflicts arise and children's strategies for dealing with them;
* the ways in which children learn from each other in interdependent relationships.

Observing Adults

In addition, through making observations and by generally watching what is going on around you, you can also learn a lot about the way adults make 'positive relationships' with children and as a team working together:

* the ways in which they communicate with children – using both verbal and non-verbal forms of communication;
* how they support children and deal with issues about the ways in which children develop self-discipline;
* how they interact with parents, other staff and other professionals;
* how they support and extend play.

Observing Features of the Setting

Observation can tell you a lot about the **work environment**:

* how children use and enjoy the equipment and resources provided;
* the use of space and the effectiveness of the setting's layout;
* the appropriateness of storage of, and access to, equipment;
* safety and hygiene issues;
* the effectiveness of supervision.

In addition, workers and researchers make use of observations to:

* find out more about different aspects of child development;

* identify ways in which children learn;
* reflect on what providers must do to promote development and learning and, thus, further develop good practice.

Observation and Assessment Inform Planning

Figure 8.1 shows how observation and assessment inform the planning process. The cycle is a continuous one and settings adapt their provision to suit the needs of the children and families they are working with at any one time. It is through close observation, monitoring and assessment that staff can ensure that they introduce appropriate changes in their practice to meet the specific needs of individual children, as well as the whole group. This is particularly relevant to identifying children's schemas (see Chapter 13) which can be taken into account when planning. It ensures practitioners plan next steps that take account of a child's development, interests and needs. It marks significant points in a child's learning journey and helps assessment for learning as a continual process.

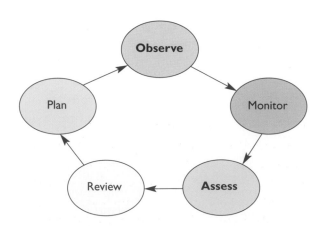

Fig 8.1 The planning cycle

LIMITS OF PROFESSIONAL ROLE AND COMPETENCE

Even the most experienced early childhood practitioners may find that, although they have observed a child and made efforts to adapt their provision, they need help from outside the setting. This is particularly true if there is a specific medical condition or developmental delay. In these cases the people who best know the child – almost always the parents or main carer – will provide the most valuable suggestions, alongside the advice and guidance of other expert or specialist professionals.

The development of an individual 'care plan' or special educational programme will take account of evidence gathered from different sources – e.g. from parents, early childhood practitioners, health visitors, doctors, social services, speech and language therapists, and so on. These provisions can only meet the child's needs when there is cooperation between all the services involved, and those who are competent to do so make accurate assessments. This is called integrated multi-agency working. For some children with additional needs, the Common Assessment Framework (CAF) is used to give a fuller picture of the child. It gives information from the child, parents and all aspects of development, including health, education and social.

SHARING OF INFORMATION

Cooperation between professionals requires sharing of information. However, in a work setting, observations and records must be kept confidentially and access given only to certain people – these may include the individual child's parents or legal guardian, supervisor, teacher or key person and other involved professionals (e.g. the health visitor). **Note that any information about a child may be shared only if the parent or legal guardian gives consent.**

Where there is a positive partnership between professionals and parents, it will be clearly understood that ongoing observation and monitoring is part of the setting's role in caring for and educating children. Indeed, parents and main carers are the people who know a child best and they have valuable information which helps us to know the 'whole' child. The Children Act 2004 seeks to provide a legal framework to underpin its programme for changes to children's services. In recognition of the uncertainty some practitioners may feel about their legal position in sharing information and gaining consent, the government offers guidance for cases when a child's welfare may be at risk. *Cross Government Guidance* addresses this issue in relation to different settings and circumstances. The case study on page 178 is based on one example concerning a child attending a playgroup.

Confidentiality

Maintaining confidentiality is an important aspect of your role but it is particularly important when carrying out observations, especially those which are written and recorded. For your own training and assessment purposes, the identity of the child and setting is not important. They must, therefore, be protected (see below). You are developing your observational and record-keeping skills as you learn more about children in general, children as individuals and the various work settings.

CASE STUDY

Josh

Josh's parents are both professionals and work full-time (sometimes longer) hours. They employ an au pair who cares for Josh, takes him to the local playgroup three times a week and carries out household tasks. The au pair does not speak much English and her understanding is only slowly developing. Josh tends to sit quietly by himself and does not socialise or play with any of the other children. He does not seek adult company or attention and rarely communicates with them at playgroup. Staff are concerned about his lack of communication and are unable to assess his level of social interaction and speech.

Apart from at Josh's initial registration, the playgroup leader has never seen or spoken to either of Josh's parents. She writes to the parents, asking them to contact her or come in to discuss how Josh has settled. There is no response and the au pair does not understand. The family uses private medical care and is not registered with a NHS doctor.

In this situation the guidance is that the playgroup leader should:

* continue attempts to make contact with the parents to express her concerns about Josh and why she needs to talk to them;

* make it clear that she would like to share information with health practitioners and to do that she would like their consent;

* also make it clear that their refusal to give consent would increase her concerns and anxieties, and then she may seek any information available from a health visitor or other agency.

Hopefully, Josh's parents would respond positively, but if they did not, then the playgroup leader should use her professional judgement to consider the risks to Josh's welfare of not sharing and seeking more information. She could consider referring Josh to 'Social Care for a Child In Need of Assessment' if she believed that, by withholding consent or giving no response, Josh's parents were neglecting his needs. If information is shared then any developmental problems may be detected at an early stage and extra treatment and support provided. Should information not be shared, any problems Josh has may go undiagnosed which would probably result in them being harder to treat at a later stage. The leader should keep accurate records of all correspondence and actions taken.

Ethical guidelines for maintaining confidentiality in your observation

* Ensure you have permission for making an observation – from your supervisor and the parent/main carer (this is confirmed by an authorising signature).

* Use codes rather than names to refer to the individuals involved – you should never use a child's first name. An initial or some other form of identification, e.g. 'Child 1', is sufficient. (You may use 'T' for 'teacher' or 'A' for 'adult'.)

* Understand and abide by policies and procedures in the setting.
* Remember that photographic and taped evidence can reveal identity and should be used only with appropriate authority.
* Take extra care when sharing observations with fellow students – they may have friends or family involved in a work setting and could easily identify individuals.
* Never discuss children or staff from your work setting in a public place, e.g. when sitting on a bus or in a café.
* Never identify individuals when talking at home about your daily experiences (e.g. they could be neighbours' children).

WORK SETTINGS' POLICIES, RULES AND PROCEDURES

As we have seen, all settings have to monitor individual children's progress and maintain records. There may not be a policy in the setting specifically called 'Observation and Assessment' but other policies, such as 'Partnership with Parents' or 'Behaviour' and 'Equal Opportunities', will contain relevant information. Such policies provide the framework for rules and procedures – these may relate to safety, hygiene, the management of behaviour and the develop-ment of self-discipline, communicating with parents, and aspects of security. You will find that some policies vary little from one setting to another as they are based on national legislation, e.g. the Children Act 1989 and EYFS, but others will reflect the setting's nature, function, location and community, and may be quite individual.

Every setting should identify the following:

* the person having overall responsibility for record-keeping (usually the nursery manager, supervisor or head teacher);
* how and where records are to be stored, and who may have access to them;
* who will be responsible for collecting and collating observational and assessment material – including information from home – for particular children or groups of children (e.g. the key person, room supervisor or teacher);
* procedures for reporting to parents;
* procedures and rules for carrying out observations and making assessments;
* when and how the policy and procedures will be reviewed.

Recording Individual Progress and Development

It is the duty of all work settings to maintain individual and confidential records of a child's progress and development. Such a profile needs to be up to date, stored carefully and be made available only to those who have authorised access. It should contain relevant information, such as:

* the full name of the child (as on the birth certificate and any other name by which the child is commonly or otherwise known);
* date and place of birth;
* medical details (e.g. problems at birth, medication, hereditary conditions);
* child's first language;
* name and home address of the parent(s)/ main carer with whom child lives;
* name and address of an absent parent (if appropriate);

* a record of any legal aspects which affect access to information;

* information as to who may, or may not, collect the child;

* observations – in a range of formats and, possibly, carried out by two or three different members of staff, including the key person – which track development, skill acquisition, growth, response to different experiences;

* information and contributions from parents/main carers and the child himself;

* regular assessments of the child's development, based on observations and any other relevant information;

* action taken (and any future plans) in response to assessments of the child's changing needs;

* records of meetings and discussions with parents/main carers.

In addition, the child's record should be presented in such a way as to be readily understood by his or her parents or main carers and other professionals. It should record positive achievements and all entries should be accurately dated with the source identified.

Observations made on Student Placements

Most settings provide clear guidance (sometimes in a booklet or sheet written especially for students) about working with children. Some settings now also have an Observations Policy – see the example below. As a student, you should also be given information which will help you understand what a particular setting is trying to achieve and how it goes about it. You will always need to gain permission to carry out an observation and your placement supervisor may well wish to read your work. This is not only to check it through, but also out of interest, to find out more about the children, activity or safety aspects that you observed. Remember that information accurately observed by you can be just as valuable to the setting as that gathered by staff.

At each new placement you will need to settle in as quickly as possible. Problems can arise when:

* you fail to communicate your needs to your supervisor;

* staff in the setting fail to communicate their needs to you.

Many experienced staff are unaware of many of the more recent changes in child care course requirements. Your study centre should outline what you are expected to achieve during your time on placement but you also need to be clear about specific tasks and observations that you must complete. Visiting tutors often discover that a student has very different perceptions of a situation from the placement supervisor, as the case study opposite shows.

A Sample Observations Policy

Observations Policy: Mayfield Nursery Unit

Staff will carefully observe children, using their observations to inform the planning. Staff will use their observations to find out about the children:

* What they know and understand.

* What learning should take place next.

* Their strengths and areas of development.

* Their learning behaviours and patterns.

* Their attitudes, opinions and interests.

* Use of language.

* If they have difficulties, to monitor progress and to identify obstacles to learning.

CASE STUDY

Student's account

'My supervisor wouldn't let me do my taped observation because she had me down to supervise children on the large apparatus. I had my tape recorder with me. All I needed was some time to get everything ready and to fix up a session with a member of staff and W.'

Supervisor's account

'I have asked G several times whether she has observations to do and she has been very vague. Last week, however, she arrived in the morning and asked if she could carry out a taped observation of one child. I had already planned for her to help supervise outdoor play because she said this was something she needed to do. Also the child she wanted to observe was involved in a structured task which had been specially planned for him and two other children.'

Had student G made thorough preparation and discussed her intention with her supervisor, she would probably have been given some helpful advice and, perhaps, a particular task or activity would have been set up for the purpose. Instead, she feels disgruntled and her supervisor is frustrated as to how best to help her.

---

* What experiences need to be enriched and repeated.

All children will be allocated a named key person. The key person is responsible for:

* keeping their key children's profiles and other record books up to date;

* liaising with other members of staff about the child's progress, and

* liaising with parents about their child's progress and development.

The following techniques will be used when observing children:

* All staff to contribute to recording observations of children, even when not their key person.

* Participating in 'focused activities' – recording children's particular skills and developing knowledge, e.g. use of scissors, mixing colours, etc.

* Time samples – particularly during the child's settling-in period.

* Narrative observations – these will be central in the EYFS as observation for learning. This type of observation will inform assessment and planning as children initiate and chose the activities and experiences they are interested in engaging in.

* The key person will co-ordinate the child's record which will be based on the four principles/themes in the EYFS. The fourth principle/theme, 'Learning and Development', includes the six areas of learning. In the final year of the EYFS, this will involve the Early Years Foundation Stage Profile. All records (Profile included) will be informed by the continuous narrative records gathered.

* A child's record of the time spent with us will be built up using samples of work, photographs, written evidence and experiences shared from home. This will be given to the child's parents when the child leaves.

Parents' permission will be sought for students to carry out observations and to share our findings with other professionals where necessary.

The Early Years Foundation Stage Profile will be passed on to the child's next provider and the parent. Year 1 teachers must build on the next steps outlined in the Profile in the spirit of the EYFS.

Practitioners, especially the key person, will liaise with the parents on a regular basis, to discuss their child's progress and share information about the child's overall development.

Other meetings may be arranged at the request of the parent/key person.

Each child's development will be closely monitored to ensure that any concerns relating to Special Educational Needs are dealt with promptly in accordance with the group's Special Needs Policy and requirements of the EYFS.

Any concerns will be discussed with the child's parents and the group's SENCO. Closing the inequality gap is a priority, and so there is great emphasis placed on diversity and inclusion.

* For children starting school in September, the profiles will be completed by July. For children starting school in January, the profiles will be completed by December.

Guidelines for maintaining positive working relationships

To help you negotiate your needs and maintain positive working relationships on placements you should:

* identify a regular, mutually convenient, time when you can discuss your progress and course

requirements with your placement supervisor;

* check with your tutor what you need to do in each setting and in each age range;

* plan your tasks at least one week ahead and agree with your supervisor and/or other staff when you will implement them (be prepared to adapt your plans at short notice if emergencies arise);

* be well prepared for each placement session;

* try to settle quickly into the setting's routine;

* ask questions about rotas and duties etc., so that your observations can be implemented with the minimum of disruption to routines;

* arrive early enough to set up your activity or observation so you do not keep groups of children waiting;

* make sure you obtain authorising signatures and show your work to your supervisor if asked;

* try to reflect on each day's experiences – some students have to keep a placement journal – and learn from them to improve your own understanding;

* share your thoughts and feelings with your supervisors when time allows and try to become part of the team.

RIGHTS AND INVOLVEMENT OF PARENTS/PRIMARY CARERS

Parents' rights and responsibilities were clearly defined in the Children Act 1989 and continue in the EYFS, which says that they have a right to be involved in decisions affecting their children's care and education. In addition, we have already seen that parents, or whoever is legally responsible for a child, have the right to see their own child's records unless there is a legal restriction which prevents it (e.g. the child is subject to a care order and someone else has 'parental responsibility'). Work settings will explain to parents that attendance at the setting means their child will be observed within the setting's confidentiality rules and may be asked if the placement supervisor can give authority for student observation of children on the parents' behalf.

Purpose of Entry Assessment

Initial information is provided by parents on a child's admission to a setting. The amount and type of further information contributed by parents will depend, probably, on the age of the child, his or her stage of development, family events, any particular needs the child may have and the type of setting. Information from other professionals usually comes via the parents unless there is a **child protection** issue, in which case it may be shared confidentially, between professionals.

Involving parents in the assessment of their child is of central importance, so they can:

* share achievements and celebrate success;
* look at observational material; and
* discuss with the setting any concerns which have arisen, perhaps to do with eating problems or behaviour towards a new sibling.

Positive partnership with parents benefits children, their families and the setting. Parents, and anyone involved with children, generally share the aim of helping children to develop healthily and to achieve their own individual potential.

Entry Assessments

To be able to track progress it is necessary to identify a 'starting point'. Therefore, settings will, in addition to collecting admission information, carry out a range of observations and assessments to plan for further development. In settings for younger children, workers will automatically want to find out:

* what individual children can do;
* what they understand and feel;
* how they respond to different experiences and learning opportunities;
* how they express themselves;
* their likes and dislikes.

Such entry assessments are used to plan and provide for individual children's needs and, as such, may highlight aspects which need monitoring, for example physical difficulties or apparent hearing difficulties. The different rates at which children normally develop mean that there is diversity and difference between the skills of children of the same age. Regular observation and monitoring identifies a developmental delay outside the usual range which may need the attention of other professionals. Similarly, outstanding giftedness and talent in any developmental area may indicate the need for specialist provision (such as music).

For children identified as having a 'special' need, the monitoring of achievements over a period of time is essential to planning and can reassure parents and staff that progress is being made, even if it is rather slow.

Good observational skills develop over a period of time and through experience, but are essential for all early childhood practitioners. It is worth **learning and practising these skills** now, as a student, so you have a good foundation for your future work with children. There is a wide range of methods to choose from and you will be given opportunities to try several, if not all. Deciding what to observe and which method best suits your purposes is, in the initial stage, a question of following whatever guidance you are given. The more methods you try for yourself, the better able you will be to make your own selection and to justify it when required.

Assessment must have a purpose. This means that it is important to remember that the EYFS requires assessment that helps practitioners to support and extend a child's learning as it is happening in everyday activities and experiences. Capturing significant, important and spontaneous movements in learning is possible when observations are ongoing.

WHAT TO OBSERVE

You may find it helpful to identify categories of things you can observe, such as shown in Table 8.1. It is clear, though, that these categories can overlap so you may be observing a small group of children playing with Lego and decide to focus on their communication or manipulative skills. The range and scope is very wide and the requirements of your course may dictate generally what you should observe. You may be required to carry out an observation which focuses on babies or toddlers using the EYFS or on Year One or Year Two of Key Stage 1 of the National Curriculum.

In consultation with your tutor and/or placement supervisor, you will not only need to choose what you are going to observe, but also need to identify an aim for your observation. You must ensure that what you observe will (or, at least, be likely to) produce the information which will enable you to achieve your identified aim. Potential difficulties with this are highlighted by the following case study.

OBSERVATIONAL AND RECORDING TECHNIQUES

As a student you will be required to produce a **portfolio** containing several observations of children using a variety of methods. Although you will learn about the planning cycle of observation and assessment shown in Figure 8.1 (page 176), carrying out regular observations in your various placement settings can be problematic and you may have few opportunities to see the relevance of individual observations in the context of the complete process.

Using a Standard Format

For the requirements of your course you will be taught to follow a commonly used structure so that each observation comprises:

1 **Standard information** (often recorded on a front sheet). This includes:
   * the aim of your observation;
   * your name;
   * date of observation;
   * start and finish times;
   * location and type of setting (e.g. outdoor play area, educational nursery);
   * number of children in observed group;
   * number of adults present and involved during the observation – do not count yourself unless you are involved in the activity;
   * age(s) of child or children (in months, e.g. 7 months, or years and months, e.g. 3 years 2 months);
   * identity code for those mentioned in observation, e.g. Child A, Child B, T = teacher;
   * the child or children's gender, if relevant;

Table 8.1 Examples of subjects for observation

Aspect of development	Social context	Aspect of behaviour	Health/growth	Aspect of daily routine
Physical skills: e.g. gross and fine motor **Intellectual:** e.g. concept development; problem solving; memory; reasoning; decision making; concentration **Communication and literacy:** e.g. speaking (incl. fluency), listening, reading and writing (incl. early stages of symbol recognition and mark making) **Emotional:** e.g. expression of feelings; self-esteem; feelings for others **Social:** e.g. relationships with other children/adults; independence; self-reliance resolving conflicts	**Individual child:** e.g. alone; with adult (familiar/unfamiliar) **Two children (familiar/unfamiliar):** e.g. same age; different ages; same/different gender; with/without adult(s) (familiar/unfamiliar) **Small group (familiar/unfamiliar/mixed):** e.g. same or mixed ages; same or mixed gender; with/without adult(s) (familiar/unfamiliar) **Large(r) group (familiar/unfamiliar/mixed):** e.g. same or mixed ages; same or mixed gender; with/ without adult(s) (familiar/unfamiliar)	**Aggression** **Being withdrawn** **Habit:** e.g. thumb-sucking, hair-pulling, head-banging	**Physical measurements:** length/height; weight; foot size **General wellbeing:** appetite and diet; sleep; exercise; energy **Record of illness/ immunisations**	**At home:** e.g. mealtime; bath-time; bedtime; getting dressed; going out **At work setting:** e.g. arrival; group or story registration (if appropriate); outdoor play; snack; meal; going home

Table 8.1 (continued)

Spontaneous	Structured situation	Special event	Aspect of play	Use of equipment/play area
A child or group of children responding to a new or unexpected experience: e.g. a rainbow, large puddles, snow, hail, bouncy castle **In response to an awareness that a child seems different from usual self:** e.g. unusually loud or withdrawn or tearful **In response to child/ren playing in an original way:** e.g. using crayons and paints cooperatively and linking all the pieces together rather than making individual creations	**A particular activity designed to promote specific learning or skill development:** e.g. water activity for floating and sinking; music activity for loud and soft sounds **A play activity structured through selection of equipment or grouping of children**	**An outing:** perhaps an annual event or one which happens more regularly e.g. to local library, park or shops **Visitor(s):** e.g. theatre company, emergency services **Seasonal festivals:** e.g. Christmas party or play, Diwali celebrations	**Outdoor/adventure:** e.g. building dens, large apparatus **Imaginative:** e.g. dressing up, small world, puppets **Exploratory:** e.g. water, sand, mud, clay, play dough, lentils **Constructional:** e.g. Lego, BRIO **Creative:** e.g. music, dance, painting, modelling, collage **See Chapters 3 and 13**	**Messy:** use of material and utensils provided e.g. hoses and tubes in water or containers with holes in sand or water **Role play:** e.g. use made of 'home' equipment, different types of dressing-up materials **Book/quiet corner:** e.g. monitoring reading behaviour, favourite books, concentration and attention **Small world/construction** ways in which resources are used e.g. for cooperative play and joint projects, monitor children's manipulative and imaginative skills **See Chapters 3 and 13**

CASE STUDY

Observation

A student had been asked to observe a group of 5- to 7-year-old children who were involved in a maths activity with a view to identifying what aspects of the maths curriculum they were addressing and to find out how the children tackled the work, i.e. what maths skills and processes (counting, reasoning, checking, etc.) they used to complete the task.

The student decided to observe a group of children involved in a 'money' activity during the daily mathematics session. It involved selecting appropriate coins to make a given amount of money, e.g. 4 × 2p coins or 1 × 5p plus 3 × 1p coins to make 8p.

On the face of it, this would seem an ideal activity to observe, as it should provide opportunities to hear and watch children adding, subtracting, counting, counting on, recognising coins and showing their understanding that one coin can represent a multiple (more than one). However, the children were completing a worksheet of written 'sums' and, rather than handling and counting out the coins, they merely filled in their answers on the worksheet. As the children did their reasoning and working out in their heads, all the student could comment on was whether or not they had answered correctly and appeared to enjoy the task.

---

* method or technique used and rationale;

* authorising signature.

2 **Introduction** to explain the context of your observation.

3 **Actual observation**, presented in an acceptable format.

4 **Evaluation** which **summarises** and **analyses** the information collected and reaches some conclusion about what has been discovered. This section also sets out any implications for the future – with regard to the child or children, the setting and your own development and learning.

5 **Reference and bibliography section** which acknowledges your sources of information. (Sections 2, 3, 4 and 5 are covered in greater detail later in this chapter.)

Planning Your Observation

You cannot carry out an observation without planning what you are going to do.

Figure 8.2 is a flow chart which outlines the steps you need to take to plan effectively.

Deciding on an Aim

Identifying an aim which is specific and focused makes it easier to plan what sort of information you will need to record. It is also helpful at this stage to think about how, or in what context, you will try to find out what you need to know.

The EYFS stresses observation of child-initiated situations, rather than an adult-led 'task'. They find out, whilst a child is exploring the natural material or in a real conversation, whether or not the child understands 'full' and 'empty' or can name colours of pegs or sort socks into pairs.

Some of the aims presented in the box on page 188 sound fine until you try to work out exactly what you need to record – in Aim 1 'physical skills' is far too broad a category and it is unlikely that you would be able to observe, on a single occasion, the full range

1 What do I want to find out?

This is the aim of your observation. Your aim might be to find out how children explore natural materials, or to see what children understand about making bread in a cookery activity.

2 What should I observe, and whom should I observe?

Is there a particular activity or routine that will give you the best chance of achieving your aim? For example, to find out how children explore natural materials, you might want to observe a free-play situation. To find out whether one child can achieve a colour-sorting task, you might observe how children use the painting area.

❑ Do you need to plan a particular experience or activity?

❑ Do you need to make sure that certain resources are available to the children?

❑ Do you need to ensure that identified children have available specific resources, e.g. for cooking bread?

3 How long should I observe for?

This depends on what you have decided in relation to step 1 and step 2. Your observation of children playing with natural materials might take 10 or 20 minutes, or it could last until the children move naturally on to another activity. You need to find out how much the child knows about water and its properties and any appropriate vocabulary.

4 How will I record what I see and hear?

You must consider what sort of detail you require to be able to achieve your aim. Do you need an exact description of every word and movement? Or can you use a pre-made chart to record what happens?

❑ Do you need to observe from outside the activity, or could you make your observation while taking part?

❑ Think about whether you need to have a conversation with the child in order to find out what the child thinks, feels and understands

Fig 8.2 Flow chart

of fine and gross motor skills. Aim 4 is not specific enough. What exactly do you want to find out? What the baby eats or drinks, how much, how quickly, who gives the feed, how often or when? All of these, some of these, something else? Your identified aim will affect what you include in your introduction and what information you record from your actual observation. For example, if you are focusing on communication skills then you will need to include all aspects of communication – speech, facial expression, body language, posture and tone of voice as well as actions. Getting your aim right will help you decide on the method of observation best suited for your purpose.

Some examples of aims for observations

1 To find out about a 3-year-old's physical skills.

2 To find out what gross motor skills a particular child uses when playing on large apparatus, and to see whether she has co-ordinated movement control and is confident.

3 To find out how a group of children communicate and cooperate with each other when involved in imaginative role play.

4 To find out about a baby feed.

5 To see how a child behaves in the setting. Does she have self-discipline?

6 To see how a child uses manipulative skills when playing with Lego.

7 To observe what children do in order to compare the heights of a large group of children – boys and girls – in relation to their ages and to consider variations in growth (Key Stage 1)

ACTIVITY: AIMS FOR OBSERVATIONS

Using the suggested Aims 1–7 in the box above, create two lists – one for aims that you think are sufficiently specific and another for those which are too general or vague.

For each aim in the first list, decide what particular skills or competencies you might look for to help you achieve your aim.

For each aim on the second list, choose two more refined aims and then decide on the activity or situation which will be best to observe.

Compare and discuss your lists and suggestions with others in your group.

Rationale for Selecting a Particular Method

This is a brief statement explaining why you have selected a particular type of observation and recording method. Table 8.2 might help you to decide on the advantages and disadvantages of different techniques.

Note that you may improve your grade if you are able to reflect upon the effectiveness of your chosen method and to consider whether any alternatives would have met your identified aims equally well or even better. You would discuss this aspect of your observation in your evaluation section, which is covered later in this chapter.

Examples of rationales for two different methods
Observing the child at regular intervals throughout the day using a time-sampling method enables me to see her/him in different situations, with different people and participating in a range of activities. I will be able to prepare a recording chart, in advance, choosing my own headings, and this will help to ensure I record significant details. It will also provide me with an overview of the child's day.

The descriptive method will allow me to record events as they happen, as well as to note small details of movement and communication. It is suitable for my purpose because I am looking at specific skills in a structured activity and am observing a single child for a short period of time. It will help me to observe effectively in assessing and recording as part of the EYFS.

Introduction

This section explains:

1 The **conditions** under which you are observing.

* Are you observing from a distance as onlooker (uninvolved)?

* Are you observing from a distance but retaining some supervisory responsibility?

* Are you observing as a participant helper/supervisor?

2 The **context** – that is, the physical and social background of the activity or routine.

* Are you in the book corner, messy area, outdoor play area or baby room?

* Who are you observing? One child playing in a group with two adult supervisors present? Or two children playing at the sand tray with no adult involved?

* Did the child choose the activity or experience?

* Are you observing a child-chosen activity which is adult directed?

* Is it an adult-led activity with little opportunity for the child to choose?

* What equipment is being used? Computer software? A book? Give a brief description of it and say what is required of the child.

3 Any **relevant information** about the individual child or group of children.

* For an observation of gross motor skills you might make reference to a child's physical build.

* For an observation about growth you may mention factual knowledge about the child's history, perhaps an

illness, medical condition or other aspect which needs to be taken into consideration when reaching your conclusion.

4 Any **particular reason** for observing this particular child/group/activity/ routine.

* Are you responding to a request from staff?

* Has there been a noticeable change in behaviour, appetite or concentration?

* Is your work part of a series of observations which will contribute to a longitudinal study?

* Have you noticed a child experiencing difficulty in a particular developmental area?

The Record of Your Observation

It is at this stage in the chapter that you need to familiarise yourself with the wide range of observation types and recording methods available. Further on in this chapter you will find a list (not exhaustive), and descriptions, of those most commonly used.

Having recorded your observation (in rough or note form) using one of these methods, you need to write it up in a presentable format. This may mean:

* copying out what you have already recorded in the same format, but neatly;

* translating your findings into another appropriate format (e.g. presenting measurements of children's heights as a bar chart);

* adapting your original record to include further significant information (for

ACTIVITY: OBSERVATIONS

Read the two brief examples below and identify where the observer has substituted a conclusion or interpretation for what was actually seen.

G stops fiddling with her hair and looks at the teacher. 'I think it will hide', she says, and laughs as she turns to N next to her . . .

Observation A

. . . G is sitting on the floor with her legs crossed and her left hand in her lap. She is twiddling her hair with her right hand and staring at a picture on the wall display behind the teacher's head. She is smiling. The teacher says 'G, what do you think will happen to the cat next?'

Observation B

. . . G is sitting cross-legged on the floor in front of the teacher. She is fiddling with her hair and looking bored. The teacher asks her a question: 'G, what do you think will happen to the cat next?' G says 'I think it will hide'. . . .

example, you might find that your original chart for the 'detailed' method has extra information in the 'other' column which can be given a more specific heading).

Remember, your observation must be clear and accessible to those who read it, while maintaining **confidentiality**.

Objectivity

When you record your observational findings you need to be as objective as possible. This means that you must record factual information – what you actually see and hear – rather than information which you have already begun to interpret.

By including plenty of detail to describe what you see, you are providing yourself (and any reader) with a lot of information for analysis. The first extract presents a much fuller picture of the situation than the second and may lead you to a different conclusion about G's interest and attention.

It is often difficult to describe facial expressions and actions accurately which is why many students produce work in the style of Observation B rather than in the style of A.

Preparing for Observations

In preparation for your observations, in pairs or small groups, try to compile a comprehensive list of suitable adjectives to describe facial expressions, actions, tones of voice and any other useful vocabulary. The more experienced you become at observing children, the more readily you will use appropriate vocabulary and enrich your work with the necessary detail.

Anti-Discriminatory and Anti-Bias Practice

You must be careful not to make assumptions about children's responses based on what you know of their home lives or their cultural backgrounds. Stereotyping must always be avoided. Read the case study below.

CASE STUDY

Child C

On an outing to a 'live' music event, a class of 28 children was seated in the front rows. They all thoroughly enjoyed the jazz-style pieces and many of them were standing up and swaying or moving in time with the music. Child C was the only mixed-race child present, being Afro-Caribbean and part English. One of the adult helpers, watching the children with pleasure, said 'I suppose it's because she's black that C has such a good sense of rhythm'.

The comment about Child C was said with admiration rather than malice or criticism, but is based on a stereotypical view. Other observers may have noticed that C was only one of many in the class who showed good rhythmical movement.

We all have biased opinions as a result of our own upbringing and experiences. Being aware of the possibility of bias will help us not to prejudge children.

CASE STUDY

Gender bias

Child R is leaning over Child M and saying 'I'm going to build a house and I need those red bricks'. R bends down, keeping eyes on M, and picks up four red bricks which M has just laid out on the floor. M pushes R and says 'No. this is my fence'. R walks off with the bricks and joins S in another part of the area. M watches and then walks to the box and gets out several more red bricks – different shapes and sizes. S comes over to M and says 'R wants some more bricks', and begins to pick up some of them. M begins to cry and approaches T who is supervising snacks.

Children – R, M, S. Teacher – T

Summary 1

Child M was playing happily and independently when R came over. She had taken some time choosing the bricks she wanted. Child R had just come in from playing outside and he rushed straight over to the construction area. R didn't ask if he could have the bricks and watched

carefully to see how M would react. M gave R a push but didn't pursue him. R took the bricks away to play elsewhere and with another boy – S. M appeared to be well motivated because she just began to choose her bricks again. S was obviously following R's instructions – he didn't ask for the bricks either. M did not seem to know how to cope with this second incident and turned to an adult for support.

Summary 2

Child M was playing on his own, which he quite often does, when R came over. R had just come in from playing outside and she rushed over to M. She was quite bossy because she just demanded the bricks and took them. She was not bothered at all by M's push. M didn't challenge R but went to the box for more bricks. When S came along and said that R needed them, M just let him take them. He did not attempt any physical retaliation but just ran off to the teacher. He is often rather clingy to his mum and she says that he is a bit of a mummy's boy.

The above case study demonstrates how gender bias can lead us to use different language to describe essentially similar behaviour by a boy and by a girl. The language used for M as a girl is different from that used for M as a boy. Think carefully about the assumptions you made when you read the observation extract for the first time and whether you showed gender bias.

When writing up an observation you need to describe how your own **anti-discriminatory and anti-bias practice**, and your understanding of **equality of opportunity**, affected what you did and what you have written.

You should also:

* check there is no cultural, gender or other bias in the vocabulary you use;

* ensure headings for charts are appropriate for use with all children and do not reflect prejudice or limited expectations;

* evaluate your findings in light of cultural differences which may affect children's responses or behaviour.

Evaluation

This is the section which usually causes students the most difficulty. If you were clear in identifying your original aim you will find this section easier to complete.

The evaluation can be broken down into sub-sections as follows:

* **Summary** – read through your observation section and summarise (recap) the main points, relating your findings back to your aim.

* **Analysis** – look again through the main pieces of information you gathered that relate to what you wanted to find out. Use them to **analyse** (consider or evaluate) what your evidence tells you about the child or children, about the situation, the environment or the equipment that you set out to study.

In your evaluation, you will need to refer to **theories** about various aspects of development and growth to put your findings into context. This means doing some **background reading**. For example, given all the information you have, does the child appear to be at the developmental point associated with what is known of developmental sequences? (Remember to take into account cultural and health aspects.) If not, what factors may be affecting development? Remember, also, that a child may be ahead of the 'expected' stage in some aspects.

Your background reading should include not only textbooks, but also journal articles, information leaflets, and websites if appropriate, as well as the EYFS. You need to get into the habit of noting sources as you use them and copying accurately brief statements or phrases (noting page numbers) that you may wish to quote. Do not write your analysis and then turn to books and articles for 'quotes' to include as an afterthought.

Using Quotes in Your Report

The box below shows an extract from a student's evaluation. The work demonstrates the correct way to embed quotes and theoretical views within the report.

In Extract A, the student has selected brief sentences or statements which relate directly to the tasks which were observed – dressing, eating, washing hands – and has identified that the child lacks confidence.

Extract A

. . . It is clear from the way GD is reluctant to try simple tasks for herself and from her need for adult support that she lacks confidence and is not developing the level of independence which might be expected for a child of her age. Carolyn Meggitt states that 4-year-olds are likely to be able to 'eat skilfully . . . wash and dry their hands . . . undress, and dress themselves' and that they 'like to be independent' (2006: 85). Bruce and Meggitt suggest there is a clear link between confidence and self-esteem, and that children need to feel good about themselves and their bodies to be able to develop self-confidence . . .

Extract B, also from an evaluation, uses a quote incorrectly. Here, the student has not selected statements which are relevant to her observations but has quoted a large section 'wholesale'. In addition, she has not checked that the text will make sense. At the beginning of the extract 'should be able to' is followed by 'can', which is clearly incorrect.

Extract B

Four-year-olds should be able to: 'can eat skilfully with a spoon and a fork, can wash and dry their hands, and brush their teeth, can undress and dress themselves, except for laces, ties and back buttons, often show a sense of humour, both in talk and in activities, like to be independent and are strongly self-willed, like to be with other children' (Meggitt, 2006: 85). GD needed help with some of these things so she is not at the right stage of development for her age.

In your evaluation you should also include:

* **Future planning ideas:** here you should show your understanding of what you have observed by indicating what the next step might be for a particular child or for the setting. What would you suggest for a child who is very dependent on a staff member? How would you encourage more boys to use the dressing–up equipment? What are your ideas for improving safety in the outdoor play area? Your suggestions should reflect what you have discovered through your observation and what you understand about children's development and learning and the work setting. Remember also to consider and explain your own learning and say how your findings from this observation will affect your future practice.

* **A review of your method or technique:** if you believe your choice of method has been successful then say so and explain why. If, on reflection, you think a different method would have been more appropriate, then say which one and give your reasons.

Reference and Bibliography Section

You need to acknowledge material that you read, see or hear in connection with your observations. You will find this easy if you develop good habits when you first begin your course. A good general rule when note-taking from a source is always to write down the 'bibliography' information – author, date of publication, full title, name of publisher, place of publication – and the page number of any quotes. There are various methods for presenting such information – the 'Harvard' method is easy to use – and your tutor will advise you which to follow, as well as guiding you about referencing other materials.

THE IMPACT OF THE OBSERVER

The term 'observer' implies an onlooker, someone who is not directly involved in what is going on. Ideally, this is what you should aim to be. However, as anyone who works with children knows, they expect any adult present to be available to help them, comfort them, appreciate and encourage as well as discipline them. So for most types of observation it is not sensible to try to observe an activity which you are supervising. This can result in the children's needs being ignored and may even risk their safety. You should negotiate with your placement supervisor when and how you may conveniently carry out an observation so that the children can be supervised by someone else. This is particularly important for some methods (see below) which require short observations at regular or irregular intervals. Similarly, if you need to observe the same child or event over a period of several days, you will need to make special arrangements.

Guidelines for minimising the impact of the observer

* You should be as unobtrusive (not noticeable) as possible because your presence can affect the way the children play and behave, especially if you are making a video, audio or photographic record!

* Try to position yourself a little away from the play area or activity so you can see and hear what goes on but are not in the middle of the children's activity.

OBSERVING AND ASSESSING NATURALLY OCCURRING AND ADULT-LED ACTIVITIES AND EXPERIENCES

Chapter 13 describes these different kinds of play in more detail. As we have seen, when planning your observations you will need to consider your **aim** carefully. If, for example, you want to find out about a child's play or social relationships, you are likely to choose to observe 'free play' without adult supervision or leadership – perhaps role play or 'small world'. However, if you want to check a child's understanding of 'loud and soft' sounds or whether a child can count up to five items accurately, you will probably find an adult-initiated activity suits your needs best, such as singing some number action songs as a group.

Remember:

* that the language used by the adult and the way the activity is planned, presented and implemented can affect children's responses;

* not to make assumptions about a child's understanding on the basis of one, single activity;

* in a group of children there can be an element of copying.

For those reasons it is usual for settings to assess a child's understanding of the same thing in a range of contexts. For example, to see if a child can count to five you could:

* observe the child laying the table for five people;

* suggest a child makes five cakes or snails or worms when playing with play dough;

* ask the child to count steps or stairs in the course of a journey;

* play at counting fingers during a nursery rhyme.

Your opportunities for observing children in free-play situations may be quite limited in such Key Stage 1 classes and may be best carried out at daily playtimes, although there is not always play equipment available. However, with the DfES 'Continuing the Learning Journey' initiative in Year 1, classrooms are becoming more in the spirit of the EYFS principles.

USING NORMS

Measurement and observation of children over many years throughout the world have led to the construction of tables and statistics which illustrate patterns of growth and development. Such measurements, most of which are age-related, provide us with **norms** – what is usual, or common, for a particular aspect of development at a particular age, for example the average height of 5-year-old boys or the likely age for reaching a milestone such as walking unaided. These 'norms' are useful for doctors, teachers, early childhood practitioners and parents but must be used with care. For example, growth patterns change over long periods of time and some tables that are still available are based on outdated statistics. There are also cultural and racial variations in some physical measurements, such as height, which you may need to consider when drawing conclusions from your data.

TYPES OF OBSERVATION

There are different types of observation.

1   **Narrative:** this is perhaps the most common type (also called descriptive observation). This attempts to record everything that happens, as it happens, with plenty of detail. Methods which fit into the narrative framework are:

* descriptive/running record;
* detailed;
* target child;
* diary description;
* anecdotal record;
* tape and transcript (may be considered to fit into this category so long as the section focused upon and used for evaluation purposes is continuous and not a series of edited extracts);
* video recording (as for tape and transcript).

2   **Time sampling:** this is specific, selected information recorded at chosen time intervals. A chart format is most often used.

3   **Event sampling:** this involves specific actions, incidents or behaviour observed whenever they occur. A chart format is most often used.

4   **Diagrammatic:** these provide a visual and accessible display of collected information or, in the case of growth charts, information plotted in the context of identified norms:

* pie charts;
* bar graphs;
* flow diagrams;
* sociograms;
* growth charts.

5   **Checklists:** this type of observation is carried out with a prepared list of skills or competencies that are being assessed and is often used for 'can-do' checks in the context of a structured activity.

6   **Longitudinal study:** usually a collection of observations and measurements taken over a period of time using a variety of recording methods.

Pre-coded Observations

What is Pre-coding?

Pre-coding means using an agreed code or abbreviation for activities, expressions, types of play or particular behaviour.

When should I Use it?

When you want to concentrate on detail and avoid writing repetitive terms or expressions (much as we tend to use PIES as shorthand for all-round development)

Why should I Use it?

Pre-coding should help in the actual process of recording information because it reduces the practical writing task. It also means that all staff in a setting are likely to understand each other's observations when carrying out assessments or writing a child's profile.

As you consider the examples of the various types and methods of observation you will see that codes and abbreviations are often used (always with a 'key'). Below are some abbreviations being used by early years settings in carrying out observations and assessments (in the EYFS framework, see the Practice Guidance: Principles into Practice cards).

Abbreviations used in early years settings

Personal, social and emotional development

DA = dispositions and attitudes
SD = social development
ED = emotional development

Communication, language and literacy

LCT = language for communication and thinking
LSL = linking sounds and letters

Problem-solving, reasoning and numeracy development

NLC – numbers as labels and for counting
C = calculating
SSM = shape, space and measures

It is important that all staff are using the same code or abbreviation to describe, or stand for, the same thing. This is where interpretation becomes so important.

 You can find sample observation sheets on the CD-ROM in the 'Resources Bank' for Unit 2.

Descriptive/Running Record Observation

For this method, sometimes called free description or narrative observation, you write down action (including movements and expression) and speech as it happens in the present tense. When you record your initial observations you will jot down what happens in note form and use abbreviations, but the finished piece must be written in continuous prose – complete sentences which are in chronological sequence.

This narrative method was developed by Susan Isaacs in the 1930s. When using it you describe, as exactly as possible, the child's actions and language and evaluate afterwards.

Example of narrative observation 1
N drops a bottle which he had picked up. Imitates S, who says 'Dropped it'. Picks up the bottle, sits down and chews it. Crawls to the left with the bottle in the right hand. Gets up, leaving the bottle, and walks 3 metres to his mother.

CASE STUDY

Coding

A university research team decided to carry out a study of children playing to find out how frequently they engaged in 'complex' play when in small groups or in pairs. In order to do this the observers needed to decide how to identify 'simple' and 'complex' play. Simple play was to refer to play activities that were routine, familiar, unoriginal, and/or repetitive while complex play was to refer to activities which were imaginative, productive and original and involved some concentration. In addition two practitioners observed the same children and activity to try to ensure results were reliable. When two practitioners observing the same children compared their findings they discovered that they had differed on their coding for play activities they had been observing and recording. One practitioner coded a little girl's play as 'simple' because during her play, even though she had fitted Lego bricks together and produced an original building, she had only been concentrating for short spells on her own activity and watching other children nearby in between. The second practitioner had coded the same activity as 'complex' because the model the child had created from Lego involved sequenced stages (e.g. a base built up into walls and a gap to allow for a door). They needed to be more specific about their coding.

Example of narrative observation 2

* Age of children: A = 4 years 2 months; B = 3 years 7 months; C = 3 years 11 months.

* Location: Sand tray in messy room of a school nursery unit.

* Aim: To find out how the children respond to, and use, the equipment provided and how they interact with each other.

* Introduction: The nursery is following a theme of 'holes' and the sand tray has been set up with a variety of equipment with holes, e.g. sieves, flour sifters, plastic bottles and containers, some with large holes punched into them. The tray is two-thirds full with dry sand. The three children playing at the tray have all chosen the activity themselves.

* Observation: Child A is bending over the edge of the tray at one end, putting his weight on his elbows and forearms while swinging his legs (bent at the knees) underneath the tray. He is watching Child B who has picked up a red flour sifter. It is empty and she is shaking it, turning it around in her hands and fiddling with the 'knob' in the middle of the base. Child A stands up and says 'Give it here, I can do it'. He gently takes the sifter from Child B in his right hand and tries to prise off the 'holed' top. He then looks at the bottom of the sifter and, using his left hand, holds the knob and twists the base to the right and the left until it moves. He shouts 'I've done it. It's easy'. He then holds the sifter upside down and starts to scoop sand into it using a large measuring spoon. Child B says excitedly, 'Look. It's comin' out there –

stop!', pointing to the 'holed' top. Child C picks up another sifter and begins to do what she has seen Child A do. She removes the base and then holds the sifter in her left hand and tips it horizontally as she fills it with sand using a spoon in her left hand. Child B says 'Yeah, that's how you do it. Give it me an' I'll do it'. She reaches for the sifter from Child A who turns away and accidentally spills sand on the floor. 'Now look what you've made me do. I'm telling.' He looks around and calls over to the nursery teacher: 'Mrs L., look what B's made me do.'

Detailed Observation

This is a very useful method for recording observations of one or more children (perhaps up to four individuals). You record and present your information in a chart which is best laid out in landscape orientation (see Figure 8.3). Headings for columns might include time, location or activity, social context, actions, language and 'other' – this last one is very useful for noting down unexpected happenings (e.g. the arrival of a visitor or a sudden interruption from outside, such as an ambulance siren). Alternatively, you could have a column for each child if you are observing a group activity, such as registration or story time. If your observation takes place in the same location and with the same people present throughout, you could dispense with the 'location/activity' and 'social context' columns, as long as you remember to include the information in your introduction.

Target Child

This method is more usually used in nursery settings to focus on one particular child and was originally devised to observe concentration. A chart with four columns – 'activity record', 'language record', 'task' and 'social context' – is needed to present the information. For this method you need to use a pre-selected code for recording regular or repeated aspects such as **RP** = role play, **A** = art activities, **SOL** = solitary, **SG** = small group, **LG** = large group.

For these observations to be shared successfully within a setting an agreed common code must be used.

For your portfolio you can devise your own code, which will also be useful for other methods that require a shorthand for speed. A key to the codes being used must always be provided in your final presentation.

Diary Description

This is usually kept to monitor learning and development of an individual child (but can also be used for a group) and provides a day-to-day account of significant events. It may include **anecdotal records** and other forms of observation. A diary is time-consuming to keep and you need to be sure that the information gathered is helpful and remains objective, rather than being mundane, repetitive and subjective. This type of observation can help to record the progress of every child in a group over time.

Anecdotal Record

This is a brief description of an incident written soon after it has occurred. This is a widely-used method of observation and is useful because it is recorded only a short time after the incident. The adult records a

Time	Location/activity	Social context	Actions	Language	Other
9.02 a.m.	Messy area at sand tray	1 adult, 4 children	G picks up blue bucket and snatches yellow spade from J. T holds out green spade to G.	G: 'I need that.' T: 'J was using that spade, G. Here you are, have this one.'	H leaves the sand tray.
9.05 a.m.		1 adult, 3 children	G and J begin to fill a large, empty tub with sand, putting in a spadeful each in turn. J pats the top with her hand when it is full.	T: 'Well done. You've filled it.' J: 'We can't get any more sand in now.'	L arrives and asks J to go for her snack.

Time	Location/activity	Social context	Child 1	Child 2	Child 3
11.30 a.m.	Book corner/ story-time	3 adults, 22 children	Sitting at front of group on bottom, legs crossed, one hand in lap, other hand fiddling with buttons on dress. Looking at storybook.	Sitting at back of group, kneeling with bottom resting on heels. Both hands on knees. Looking at T and book.	In middle of group. Sitting on bottom with knees bent and legs to one side. Holding a piece of Lego in both hands and turning it over. Looking at Lego.
11.35 a.m.			Puts up hand. 'He's under the bed.'	Puts hand up and then down again.	Looks up as children around put hands up. Looks at T and book.

Time	Activity	Language	Facial expression
9.24 a.m.	Puts on apron and sits down at collage table next to T. Picks up scissors in right hand, correct grip, opens and closes them 4 times. Points to piece of Christmas wrapping paper.	T: "Are you coming to make a picture, K?" K: 'What can I have? Can I have some of that?'	D smiles and looks at the trays containing collage materials. Looks at trays, eyes open wide at pieces of wrapping paper – turns to T with hesitant look.

Fig 8.3 Example of a detailed observation

RP = role play, SOL = solitary, SG = small group, LG = large group, TC = target child, C = child, A = adult, BC = book corner, SW = small world, W = waiting
Child initials: JG   Gender: M   Age: 3 yrs 10mths   Date/Time: 6/3/07 2.15 p.m.

ACTIVITY RECORD	LANGUAGE RECORD	TASK	SOCIAL
1 min TC on carpeted area, playing with farm animals and buildings.	TC→C My cow wants to come in your field. C→TC No. You'll have to wait till my tractor has finished.	SW	SG
2 min TC sitting at edge of carpet, looking at wall display.		W	SOL
3 min Now in dressing-up area, putting on a floppy hat and laughing.	C→TC You look funny in that. TC→C Let me see. Where's the mirror?	RP	SG
4 min Sitting in a small chair at a table, holding a knife and fork in his hands.	TC→C Where's my tea? I want my tea. Not fish fingers again!	RP	SG
5 min Standing at 'cooker' and stirring something in a pan.	A→TC What are you cooking? TC→A I'm a good cooker. It's basgetti.	RP	SG
6 min Taking off hat and tidying equipment.		RP	SOL
7 min Sitting in story corner, looking at book.		BC	LG

Fig 8.4 Example of a target child observation

significant piece of learning, perhaps a model a child has made (a photograph of the model can be useful as an addition), or an important development in relationships with other children. This method enhances the descriptive, narrative and detailed observations made. Anecdotal observations are often made in a different-coloured pen, to show that they are not 'on-the-spot' but recalled events.

Tape and Transcript

This is an ideal method for observing language and interaction. It can be used to assess speech and, to some extent, a child's understanding. It is usual to tape-record a complete conversation or task but the transcript (the written record of what has been recorded) can be a selected brief section – perhaps 2 minutes.

Several factors need to be taken into account when carrying out a taped observation:

* The children's (and possibly the adult's) awareness of the tape recorder and you, writing notes, could affect their behaviour.

* Children's familiarity with being recorded in this way will affect the extent of the impact on their behaviour.

* Background or surrounding noise can distort the recording.

* The distance of the children from the microphone can be a problem.

* The clarity and volume of the children's voices can be a problem.

* Children may talk over each other when in a group.

* Accents or dialect may make transcription of the recording difficult.

* Interruptions are disruptive.

**See Resource Bank for Unit 2 on CD-ROM for charts to help with making a taped observation.

Guidelines for achieving a successful taped observation

* Make sure your tape recorder is working properly – check the batteries or the power supply.

* Some students use smaller Dictaphones, but you need to check with your tutor that the college has a suitable machine on which to play your tape for assessment purposes.

* Check that the tape you are using is undamaged. Wind the tape through the blank 'lead-in' and record your name, PIN, observation number, date, time and setting.

* Check that your recording worked. Leave the tape ready for recording your observation. A 20-minute tape (10 minutes each side) is usually sufficient.

* In consultation with your supervisor, choose the location for your recording – preferably somewhere quiet, with soft furnishings (they absorb sound and reduce 'echo'

factor) where you are unlikely to be interrupted.

* Decide when will be the best time to make your recording – not 5 minutes before snack-time or going home.

* Depending on whether you are recording a naturally occurring event or a structured situation, you need to place yourself in a position to note other significant information (e.g. facial expression, actions).

* If you are observing interaction then it would be a good idea to draw up a chart (use the detailed method) with headings to help you add important detail.

* When transcribing, try to write down exactly what you hear rather than the word you know is being attempted, e.g. 'barf' when the child wants to say 'bath', or 'somethink' instead of 'something'. This is especially important if you are trying to identify speech difficulties. You can always write the intended word alongside in brackets.

* When you have finished the recording, read quickly through your notes to check that they make sense to you.

* Listen to the tape at least twice, reading your notes and adding any detail.

* Refer back to your aim and decide which portion of the recording will be most useful for analysis. If your machine has a counter on it then make a note of the section you will transcribe.

* Play the chosen section a little bit at a time and write down everything that is said. You may

need to do this several times, until you are satisfied that you have transcribed it correctly. This first transcription can be very rough.

* Using both the transcript and your chart information, write out the spoken language, using a new line for each speaker. Put actions and other information alongside to correspond with the speech. For example:

Child 1: *This is my best story. I like Spot.* (Opens book and points to Spot. Looks up at T, smiling.)
T: *What is he doing in this picture*? (Reaches over to point to right-hand page.)

* Check through your work as you listen to the selected section of tape. Ensure you have included all the relevant detail.

* Use your information to complete the evaluation and reference or bibliography.

Video Recording

This would seem to be a comprehensive method for recording all aspects of behaviour – actions, speech, tone of voice, facial expression, posture, interaction – as they happen and without having to do a lot of writing. This method conveys information about a child's personality and appearance that can be difficult to describe in written forms.

You need to consider:

* whether you use a hand-held or a fixed camera;

* whether the children are used to being filmed in this way;

* what you are trying to film.

Note that video presents issues of **confidentiality** as anyone filmed can be easily identified.

A fixed camera has very limited scope but can be useful for monitoring safety, access and use, or interest in one area or room. You need to consider carefully where it will be best sited and ensure children are unable to interfere with it. You may need to edit the tape if there are periods when not much is happening. In your report, clarify why any edits were made. An edited recording may not be considered to fit into the 'narrative' category.

A hand-held camera is more flexible, but more intrusive. Remember that, if you are carrying out the filming, you cannot maintain an overview and may miss interesting events. Also, filming as you are moving along can be unsatisfactory – be careful if walking backwards! Practise a bit first!

Time Sample

This involves making a series of short observations (usually up to 2 minutes each) at regular intervals over a fairly long period. The interval between observations and the overall duration is your decision, depending on exactly what you are observing and why. For example, you may choose to record at 20-minute intervals over the course of a whole day or every 15 minutes during a half-day session.

It can be a useful way of finding out how children use particular toys or resources, to monitor how a new child has settled in, or to observe the behaviour of an individual child. When observing an individual child's behaviour, time sampling can raise awareness of positive aspects which may, in the normal run of a busy day, be overlooked. Staff can then make a point of noticing and appreciating the incidents of

Child observed = HR   Teacher = T   Other children = A, B, C, D, E.
LG = large group, SG = small group, P = pair of children
Aim: To find out how well a child, newly arrived from another school, has settled in, looking particularly at interaction with other children.

Time	Setting	Language	Social group	Other
9.00	Registration – sitting on carpeted area.	None	LG	At back of class group, fiddling with shoelaces and looking around the room.
9.20	At a table, playing a language game.	HR: 'It's *not* my turn.'	SG	One parent helper and 3 other children.
9.40	On floor of cloakroom.	HR: 'You splashed me first and my jumper's all wet, look.'	P	Had been to toilet and is washing hands.
10.00	In maths area, carrying out a sorting activity using coloured cubes.	T: 'Can you find some more cubes the same colour, HR?' HR: 'There's only 2 more red ones.'	SG	Concentrating and smiling as he completes the task.
10.20	Playground – HR is standing by a wall, crying.	Sobbing sounds – won't make eye contact with or speak to T on duty.	SOL	Small group of children look on.
10.40	Music activity - playing a tambour to beat the rhythm of his name.	Says his name in 2-syllable beats.	LG	Showing enjoyment by smiling – T praises him.
11.00	Tidying away instruments with another child.	A→HR: 'We have instruments every week. It's good, isn't it?' HR→A: 'Yeh. I liked it.'	P	
11.20	Playing with construction equipment with A and B.	B→HR + A: 'I've got loads of Lego at home.' HR→B + A: 'So have I. I like the technical stuff best.' B→HR: 'What's that like?'	SG	Children working together to build a garage for toy cars.
11.40	HR fetching reading book to read to T.	Humming to himself.	SOL	
12.00	Lining up with other children to go for lunch.		LG	Nudging A, who is standing in front of him. A turns round and grins.

Fig 8.5 Example of a time sample in a Year 1 class

positive behaviour and encourage these as part of a strategy to reduce unwanted aspects.

The difficulty many students experience is managing to step away at regular intervals from whatever else they are doing to make their record. Negotiation with your supervisor and other staff is essential so that children's safety is not put at risk.

You can choose your own headings for the chart format to match the detail you need to include. Usual headings are 'time', 'setting or location', 'language' and 'social group' but you may want to include 'actions' and 'other'.

Event Sample or Frequency Count

This is similar to a time sample but, instead of recording at regular intervals, you record particular identified events, for example every time the observed child seeks adult help or every time he or she displays aggressive behaviour. This is usually done over a long period of time, depending on the child and the type of event. You may observe over the course of a week or even longer (see Figure 8.6). You might need to record each event for the duration of the incident; every time the child has a temper tantrum you would observe from the time you are first aware of it until the child has calmed down and resumed an activity. If you want to gain a clear picture of how many times a particular event occurs then you may use your record for a frequency count and note down less detail (see Figure 8.7).

Again, you can structure your chart to suit the information you require. This method is more problematic than time sampling because you have no idea when you will need to make your records. And again, it is essential that others in your work setting understand that you are carrying out this type of observation.

Pie Charts and Bar Charts

These are pictorial or diagrammatic ways of representing information which you have already recorded using different techniques. Although not appropriate for individual child observation, they are ideal for presenting your findings about groups of children, e.g. measurements such as height; foot or shoe size; food likes and dislikes; skill competence such as use of scissors or hopping. You would first gather the data and then present your results in the chosen form. This would take the place of the observation section in your report, but you will still need to complete front-sheet information, and to write an introduction, an evaluation and a reference or bibliography (see Figures 8.8 and 8.9).

Flow Diagram (or Movement Chart)

This method allows you to present information about an individual child or a group of children, activities, safety in a work setting or use of equipment. It can be very simple with very basic information (see Figure 8.10) or more detailed to highlight more than one aspect (see Figure 8.11). If you want to track one child from one area or activity to another during the course of a morning session then it might help to have a prepared plan of the room on which to map her or his movement.

From this type of observation you can see:

* which activities the child visited;
* the order in which she visited them;
* how long she spent at each one;
* which activities she visited on more than one occasion;
* which activities she did not visit at all.

The more detailed version provides the following additional information:

* which activities had adult-led tasks;
* which ones had an adult permanently supervising or helping;
* which other children were at an activity when the observed child arrived.

From this level of detail you may gain further insight into the child's movements. Repeated observations may enable you to find out if the child never visits the sand, always heads for an activity with an adult present, or always follows another child.

Child observed = KD Age: 3 years 4 months Teacher = T Other children A, B, C, D, E, etc. NN = nursery nurse
Aim: To monitor the frequency and nature of aggressive outbursts and, where possible, identify 'trigger' factors. Also to record KD's response to adults.

Time	Setting/ context	Social context	Behaviour	Adult/KD response
9.02	By coat pegs	KD and A	A standing in front of KD's peg. KD pulls A's hair. A screams and runs to T.	T explains to KD that she needs to tell A the problem, that A is upset because it hurts to have her hair pulled. KD pats A's head.
9.51	In book area	Small group	KD snatches book from B. A page is torn. B begins to cry.	NN takes book gently from KD and says she must be more careful. Puts arm around B and suggests that they both sit with her and share another story. KD on verge of crying, sits down next to NN.
10.34	Outdoor play area where bikes, prams and pushchairs are available.	Large group	KD and C both holding handle of a pram, arguing. KD pushes C away and runs off, pushing pram.	NN follows KD, telling her she may have a turn, but must then bring it back for C to have a go. Explains that she must not push anyone and that she needs to take turns, or ask an adult to find another pram. KD has a turn and the adult finds C another pram.
10.47	As above	Large group	D takes doll from KD's pram. KD chases her, snatches back doll and pinches D's arm.	T explains to D the doll is being used by KD (who is crying) and it makes her sad when the doll is taken from the pram. T helps to find a different doll and encourages D to give back the doll to KD, who returns it to the pram.
11.50	Singing activity –carpet area	Large group	E accidentally treads on KD's fingers as he walks past to sit down. KD pushes him and he falls over onto another child.	T asks NN to check nobody badly hurt. KD is looking anxious and NN takes KD away from group. Explains that E didn't mean to tread on her and that she must not hurt other children, and needs to say 'That hurt me!' to show E how KD feels.

Fig 8.6 Event sample

Sociogram

This is a diagrammatic method used to show an individual child's social relationships within a group, or to find out about friendship patterns between several children within a group (see Figure 8.12). Identifying girls and boys separately can sometimes make it immediately clear whether girls play with girls, and boys with boys, or if they play in mixed-gender groups. You should record the ages of the children involved. You may find that an older child habitually plays with a group of much younger children. You will be able to identify any child who always plays alone or who always seeks the company of an adult. There are many factors which will affect the play relationships – friendship of parents, proximity of homes, presence of

Usual information on front sheet
Child observed = LP   Teacher = T   Nursery Nurse = NN
Aim: To monitor the frequency of acts of aggression and record whether they are provoked or unprovoked

Day	No.	Duration	Provoked/ unprovoked	Comments
Monday	1	3 secs	u.p.	LP pinched mother as she left.
	2	10 secs	p.	LP sat on HJ after he had knocked down his brick tower.
Tuesday	1	4 secs	u.p.	LP pushed KP over as he ran around outdoor area.
	2	5 secs	u.p.	LP pinched GD as they were sitting down for story-time.
Wednesday	0			
Thursday	1	10 secs	u.p.	LP kicked SR several times as she walked past him to go to the toilet.
	2	4 secs	u.p.	LP bit WT's hand because he wanted the truck that WT was playing with.
	3	3 secs	u.p.	LP bit FD's hand (no apparent reason).
	4	2 secs	p.	LP pushed RA, who had drawn on his picture.
Friday		absent		

Fig 8.7 Frequency count

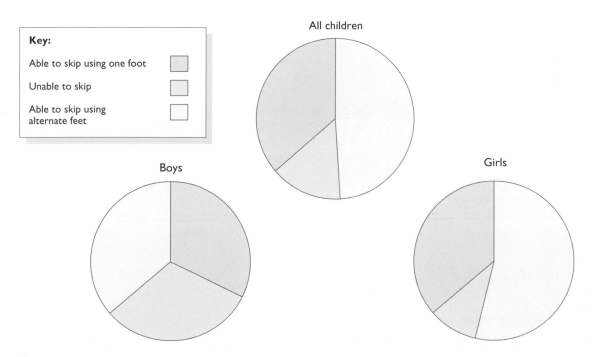

Key:

Able to skip using one foot ▨

Unable to skip ▨

Able to skip using alternate feet ☐

All children

Boys

Girls

Fig 8.8 Pie chart to show the development of skipping in boys and girls

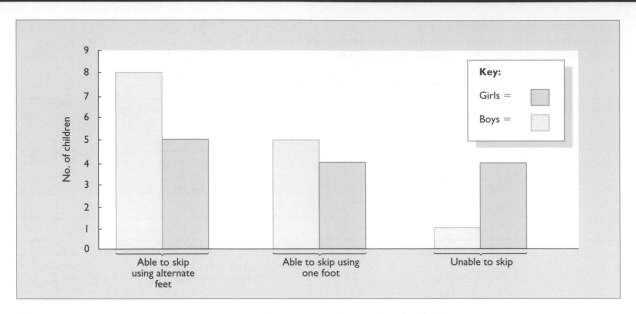

Fig 8.9 Bar chart to show the development of skipping in boys and girls of different ages

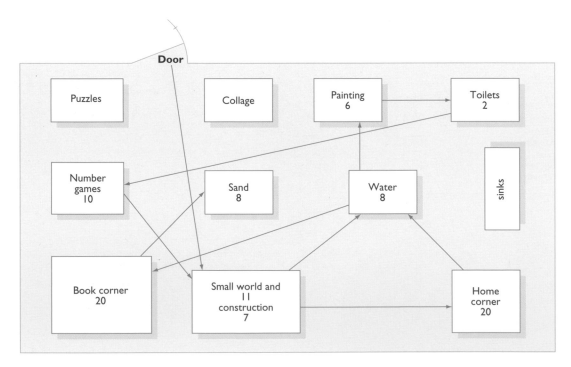

Fig 8.10 Flow chart

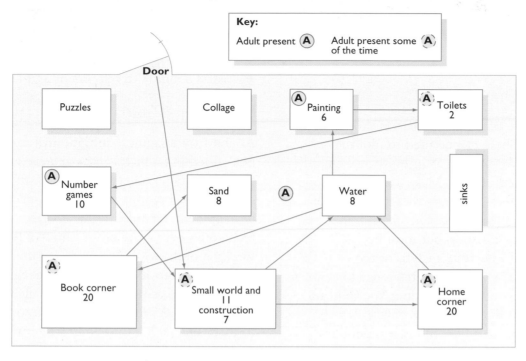

Fig 8.11 Flow chart – with extra detail

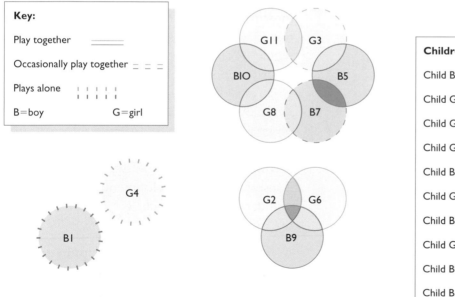

Fig 8.12 Sociogram

siblings and, not least, pattern of attendance. These factors need to be taken into account when drawing your conclusions.

Growth Charts

An example of a growth chart is shown on page 115. These can be used to plot the height and/or weight of an individual child over a period of time. Make sure you use one for the correct gender, as there are variations between boys and girls. The chart cannot be submitted in isolation but must be accompanied by your analysis of the information which makes reference to centiles and shows your understanding. You must use the chart to interpret 'your' child's information. This type of chart is good to include in a longitudinal study. Even if you are studying a child aged 2 or over, it is quite likely that the parents will have a record of length/height and weight at birth and at some intervening intervals which you can plot.

Checklists

This form of recording is very limited:

* giving no detail or supporting evidence;
* being narrow in focus;
* making practitioners feel that they have more information than they really do;
* being time-consuming to create.

It should only be used in addition to other methods, especially as from September 2008 narrative observation will be the central technique in informing assessment, record-keeping and planning in the EYFS in order to:

* monitor developmental progress, of an individual child or several children;
* assess children on a regular basis over a period of time;

* enable staff to plan for the children's changing needs;
* consider one area of development;
* assess a child's development and learning.

Longitudinal Study

As you may imagine, a longitudinal study is not something which can be achieved through a single observation. It consists of a series of observations of different aspects of development, recorded using a variety of techniques over a period of time – a few weeks, months, a year or more. It provides opportunities to look at the 'whole' child by observing and assessing progress in all areas of development. As a student you are most likely to carry out such a study on a child whom you know well or whose family you know well. In this case you may be given permission to include photographs and/or video footage. The initial part of the study will involve gathering background and factual information, followed by observations carried out at agreed intervals (not necessarily regular). You may get the chance to observe special events, e.g. outings, birthdays, clinic visits, as well as the child's time spent in a setting. When you have recorded all your observations you can collate the information. You might choose to present them in strict chronological order or in groups of observations of different developmental areas. This will depend on the focus of your study and the individual observations.

In work settings a longitudinal study can be useful in planning long-term strategies for a child with special needs.

Assessments Must Actively Engage Parents/Carers and Children

In the EYFS, practitioners, parents and children are all contributing to the assessment of development and learning.

Possible use: for monitoring reading skills
Title of book used: *The Birthday Cake* Date:

Skill	Child 1	Comment	Child 2	Comment
1. Holds book right way up	✔	Held book correctly in both hands	✔	Took book from me and turned it right way
2. Knows which is the front of a book	✔	Looked at front cover before opening book	✔	Pointed to character on cover picture
3. Follows text/pictures left to right	✔	Followed pictures as story was read	✔	Head movements showed was doing this
4. Knows text 'works' top to bottom	✔	As above	✔	As above
5. Can point to known characters in illustrations	✔	Pointed to Chip and Floppy	✔	Named characters as they appeared in illustrations
6. Can talk about illustrations	✔	Did so when prompted	✔	Pointed to things in pictures which he found funny
7. Can recap the story partway through	✗	Needed prompting and had to turn back through pages	✔	Good recall of what had happened
8. Can suggest what might happen next	✗	Could offer no ideas	✔	Good suggestions with reasons
9. Identifies some individual letters	✔	Named and pointed to 'c', 'd' and 'a'	✔	Named and pointed to 'c', 'd', 'a', 'g', 'h', 'l', 'b', 'n', 'w', 't', 's', 'r', 'y', 'p'
10. Can identify a capital (upper-case) letter	✔	Named and pointed to 'C' – own initial letter	✔	Named and pointed to 'C', 'F', 'B', 'H', 'T', 'R'
11. Can identify a full stop	✗		✗	

Fig 8.13 Example of an enhanced and expanded checklist showing reading development using the principles of the EYFS: A Unique Child; Positive Relationships; Enabling Environments; Development and Learning. This type of observation is similar to a 'running record'. It has much in common with a 'target child' or 'narrative descriptive' record.

Children are encouraged to talk about what they find enjoyable, interesting, what they are good at and what they find difficult. Babies and toddlers can show this too. Consider including a photograph of an experience they obviously enjoyed and which engaged them deeply, or something they avoid and seem to dislike.

Records often used practitioner observations and assessments with some from parents and some from children. This type of record is often treasured by children and families. Childminders and nannies in home learning environments develop these as well as practitioners working in private, voluntary, independent or maintained settings.

CHAPTER 9

Supporting Children

This chapter covers **Unit 3** and is divided into five sections:

Section 1:   The implications of relevant legislation on working practices with children

Section 2:   Safeguarding children

Section 3:   Promoting children's self-confidence and self-esteem

Section 4:   Supporting children to prepare for transfer or transition

Section 5:   The causes and effects of discrimination in society

SECTION 1: THE IMPLICATIONS OF RELEVANT LEGISLATION ON WORKING PRACTICES WITH CHILDREN

• Legislation relating to equality of opportunity
• Promoting effective equal opportunities through anti-discriminatory and anti-bias practice • Promoting a child's sense of self-worth • Avoiding stereotypes
• Inspecting our own attitudes and values • Principles of inclusivity • Legislation relating to working practices with children

LEGISLATION RELATING TO EQUALITY OF OPPORTUNITY

Our laws deal with the overt discrimination that results from prejudice, especially when combined with power. The person who shows prejudice is unwilling to change their views even when their 'facts' are clearly shown to be wrong. If the prejudiced person has power, they may discriminate against the people towards whom they are prejudiced. This might be in the form of racism or sexism, or being disablist, ageist or homophobic (afraid of and hostile to homosexual people). There are laws which try to deal with all these kinds of discrimination. However, while legal restraints on racism and sexism exist, legal protection against disablism, ageism and sexual prejudice is less well developed.

Codes and Policies in the Workplace

A code of practice is not a legal document, but it does give direction and cohesion to the organisation for which it has been designed. Codes of practice and policy documents cover areas of ethical concern and good practice, such as:

* equal opportunities;
* confidentiality;
* safety aspects;
* partnerships with parents;
* first aid responsibilities;
* staff training;
* food service;
* record-keeping;
* child protection;
* staff-to-children ratios.

All workplace policies and codes of practice must be drawn up within the framework of current legislation; and the laws which are most relevant to child care and education services are:

* the Children Act 2004;
* the Education Reform Act 1988;
* the Race Relations Act 1976;
* the Sex Discrimination Act 1975;
* the Disability Discrimination Act 1995.

Equal Opportunities Policy

An equal opportunities policy represents a commitment by an organisation to ensure that its activities do not lead to any individual receiving less favourable treatment on the grounds of:

* gender;
* race;
* ethnic or national origin;
* age;
* disability;
* marital status;
* religious belief;
* skin colour.

Having such a policy does not mean reverse discrimination in favour of black people, but *equality for all*. An effective policy will establish a fair system in relation to recruitment, training and promotion opportunities, as well as to the staff's treatment of children, parents and one another.

Table 9.1 Laws relating to discrimination

Sex Discrimination Act (1975 and 1986)	These Acts make it illegal to discriminate against someone on the grounds of their gender – when employing someone, when selling or renting a property to them, in their education or when providing them with goods and services. It also protects people from sexual harassment. The Equal Opportunities Commission was set up in 1975 to enforce the laws relating to sexual discrimination.
Equal Pay Act (1984)	This Act gave women the right to equal pay for equal work.
Education Reform Act (1988)	Local education authorities (LEAs) must provide access to the national curriculum to all children including those with special needs and must identify and assess children's needs.
The Children Act (1989)	This Act states that the needs of children are paramount (i.e. the most important). Local authorities must consider a child's race, culture, religion and languages when making decisions. Childcare services must promote self-esteem and racial identity.
Disability Discrimination Act (1995)	Disabled people are given new rights in the areas of employment, access to goods, facilities and services, and buying or renting property. A National Disability Council (NDC) advises the government on discrimination against disabled people.
The Race Relations Act (1976)	This Act makes it unlawful to discriminate against anyone on grounds of race, colour, nationality (including citizenship), or ethnic or national origins. It applies to jobs, training, housing, education and the provision of goods and services. The Commission for Racial Equality (CRE) was set up to research and investigate cases of alleged racial discrimination.
Special Educational Needs and Disability Act (2001)	The Special Educational Needs and Disability Bill was a part of the government's commitment to a 'significant extension of the rights of children'. It aimed to 'strengthen the right' of a disabled child to be educated in mainstream schools where it is appropriate, although there will still be a 'vital' role for special schools. Local Education Authorities are obliged to provide parents and children with information and advice, and a means of resolving disputes when they arise. For more details of these Acts, see Unit 14 on CD-ROM.

The Policy Statement

Each employing organisation should set out a clear policy statement that can be made available to employees and service-users. The statement should include:

* a recognition of past discrimination;
* a commitment to redressing inequalities;
* a commitment to positive action.

Training should be provided to explain to all staff the implications and practical consequences of the policy. The organisation must also provide information about the law on direct and indirect discrimination.

Any policy which attempts to promote equality is only effective if the individuals working in the organisation incorporate its principles into their individual practice.

PROMOTING EFFECTIVE EQUAL OPPORTUNITIES THROUGH ANTI-DISCRIMINATORY AND ANTI-BIAS PRACTICE

As early years workers, we are responsible for ensuring equal opportunities within our settings. There are many ways in which we can promote anti-discriminatory practice. We can do this by:

* promoting a sense of belonging;

* appreciating language and bilingualism;

* valuing cultural diversity and respecting difference;

* giving individual children individual help;

* understanding religions;

* including children with disabilities;

* having an awareness of gender roles;

* avoiding stereotypes;

* promoting a sense of belonging.

As children grow up, they need to feel that they belong to the group, whether that group is their family, their culture, the community they live in and experience, or their early years setting.

Belonging to a group is the result of either:

* being allocated to a group defined by someone else, for example being British-born;

* deciding to join a group, for example choosing to be a vegetarian, or joining a football club.

Until recently, people tended to be seen as belonging to a particular ethnic group if they shared a culture, language, physical features (e.g. skin colour) or religion. This way of grouping people is no longer thought to be useful. Increasingly, people choose the groups they want to be identified with. The early childhood setting is often the first group outside the family and its friendship network that the child joins. It is important when welcoming families to a setting that they feel a sense of belonging.

Taking a Multicultural Approach

In the UK we live in a diverse and multicultural society. This means that it is important to appreciate and understand different cultural and religious ideas, and that we respect them. The whole environment of the early childhood setting needs to reflect a multicultural and multilingual approach. For example, the home area, like every other area of the environment, should include objects which are familiar to children and link with their homes and culture. These are often called **cultural artefacts**.

Using Everyday Activities to Explore Different Cultures

It is particularly important to introduce children to different cultures through the activities of daily life, such as preparing food and cooking. This is because they can most easily relate to these events.

For example, for those children who have not met Chinese people or who have not experienced Chinese food, it might be possible to invite someone to the nursery to demonstrate and introduce the children to another culture. Remember that it is important not to stereotype your visitor. For instance, not all people of Chinese background will use chopsticks at home: some families may be using knives and forks. Sets of cultural artefacts should not be mixed up in one home area, as this confuses everyone. It also makes it difficult for the children to value the area and take pride in keeping it looking attractive.

There are opportunities for mathematical learning in sorting out chopsticks from spoons, knives and forks, and Chinese soup spoons, or in knowing which sets of utensils relate to Chinese life, which to African, Indian or Asian cooking, and which to European culture.

Encouraging Children to Use What They Know

Children gain by using their own cultural experience and knowledge in an open way. For example, the advantage of play dough, rather than pre-structured plastic food, is that children can bring their own experiences to it. They can make it into roti, pancakes, pasties or pies, depending on their own past experiences. All experiences can be valued, not just those that a toy manufacturer has set in plastic.

Introducing Cultural Artefacts

A home area needs to reflect familiar aspects of each child's home. It needs to build on all the children's prior experiences. This means that it should have crockery, cutlery and cooking utensils in the West European style. If, for example, there are children from Chinese backgrounds in the group, it would be particularly important also to have chopsticks, bowls, woks, and so on, to reflect their home culture. These would need to be available all the time.

But many children will not know about Chinese woks because they do not meet anyone who cooks with one. These children will need extra help in understanding about cultures other than their own. It is very important to include activities which introduce them to the purpose and function of, for example, Chinese ways of cooking. So, it is important not only that Chinese children see

their own culture reflected, but also that other children have the opportunity to learn about different cultures in ways which hold meaning for them and, therefore, are not **tokenist**.

A child who has never seen a wok before will need to do *real* cookery with it, and be introduced to this by an adult. **Remember, children learn through real, first-hand experiences.** It is no good simply putting a wok in the home area and hoping the children will then know about Chinese cooking. That would be tokenist.

Giving Individual Children Individual Help

There may be children with special educational needs using, for example, the home area, and they may need to have special arrangements to allow them access. A child in a wheelchair will need a lower table so that a mixing bowl can be stirred; it might be necessary to make a toy cooker of an appropriate height. This could be done quite simply, using a cardboard box. Children love to construct their own play props and allowing them to do so makes for a much more culturally diverse selection, because they can say what they need in order to make a play setting like their homes.

Sharing Books, Stories, Poems, Songs, Action Songs and Games

These are useful in linking children with their previous experiences. For example, stories are available about children with disabilities and about children from different cultures. There are stories which look at gender issues. In the last 20 years authors have been recognising the need for children's books to link with the huge range of experiences that different children have.

Understanding Religions

Children do not choose their religion. They are born into it. As they grow up they will either accept the belief structure or not. This is also true for children who are born into families who are atheist, agnostic or humanist. Atheists do not believe in a god, gods or God. Agnostics think that we cannot know whether a god, gods or God exist. Humanists believe that people can be good without believing in a god, gods or God. They think that the world can be understood through science and research.

Some children are taught **monotheist** revelatory religious beliefs (one god). Others learn **polytheistic** revelatory beliefs (more than one god). A revelatory god is a supernatural being who is believed to have created the world and who intervenes. Buddhists have beliefs which are not revelatory of a god. They believe in a god, gods or God who created the world but who does not intervene.

In order that every child feels accepted beyond their home, those working with young children and their families need to learn about belief structures other than their own. It is also important to remember that being a good person, and leading a good life, has nothing to do with belief in any god or gods. There are many people who lead good lives who are humanists, agnostics or atheists.

Some children are brought up in families which follow more than one religion. For example, there might be a Roman Catholic Christian father and a Jewish mother, or an atheist father and a Quaker Christian mother.

PROMOTING A CHILD'S SENSE OF SELF-WORTH

Children need to feel a sense of their own worth. This comes from:

* feeling that they matter to other people;
* feeling able to take an active part in things;
* feeling competent and skilled enough to do so.

Valuing Language and Culture

A feeling of belonging obviously contributes to a sense of worth, and language is of deep importance to both. In the last section, the importance of including cultural artefacts that are familiar from the child's home was stressed. The same goes for language. If a child's first language is not reflected in settings beyond the home, a large part of the child's previous experiences is being ignored or even actively rejected. Some linguistic experts argue that 'language is power': the dominant language of the culture gives those who speak it the power to discriminate against those who do not.

Ideas for Promoting a Sense of Belonging through Equality of Opportunity

* Be willing to find out about different religions and to respect them. Every religion has variety within it. For example, there are Orthodox and Reformed Jews; Roman Catholic Christians, Church of England Christians, Methodist Christians, Quaker Christians, Jehovah's Witness Christians, and Mormon Christians. Ask religious leaders and parents for information.

* Find out about different disabilities. Ask parents and voluntary organisations (e.g. SCOPE, RNIB or RNID) to help you.

* Do not be afraid to say that you don't know and that you want to find out and learn. Remember that minority groups of all kinds are as important as the majority groups and are included as part of the whole group.

* Respect and value the child's home language. Think how you can make yourself understood using body language, gestures and facial expression; by pointing; by using pictures; by using actions with your words. Try asking children if they would like a drink using one of these strategies. You could use objects as props. It is important to be warm towards children.

* Remember to smile and to show that you enjoy interacting with them. Make sure that you are giving comprehensible language input.

* Create opportunities for children to talk with other children and adults who are already fluent in English. Try to accompany a child's actions with language by describing what is happening. For example, talk with the child and describe what they are doing when they cook, or use clay.

When telling stories you could:

* use puppets and props, flannel boards, magnet boards and so on;

* invite children to act out pictures as you go through the story;

* use facial expressions, eye contact and body language to 'tell' a story and make it meaningful for the children;

* use books in different languages and tell stories in different languages. Remember that there can be problems with dual-language textbooks because, although a language like English reads from left to right, a language like Urdu reads from right to left;

* invite someone who speaks the child's language to come and tell stories. For example, ask a Hindi speaker to tell a story such as *Where's Spot?* in Hindi, using the book in that language but in a session that is for all the children in a story group. Then tell the story and use the book in English at the next session, again with all the children in the story group. Remember that grandparents are often particularly concerned that children are losing their home language as they become more fluent in English (transitional bilingualism). They may enjoy coming into the group and helping in this way.

Standard English is the usual way of communicating in English in public, educational, professional and commercial aspects of life. However, young children need to be confident in talking, reading and writing in their home language and to be supported in this early childhood setting. This actually helps children to develop fluency and literacy in English. So, it is very important that the child's own language is valued and

Fig 9.1 Making sense of what you are saying by using a 'prop'

that efforts are made to develop balanced bilingualism.

Awareness of Gender Roles

Creating an environment where girls and boys are respected and cared for equally in early childhood is the first step towards breaking cycles of discrimination and disadvantage, and to promoting a child's sense of self-worth as it relates to their gender.

It is important to remember that some children will have learnt narrow gender roles. In the traditional home situation, mothers usually do housework and fathers mend cars. Children need to see adults taking on broader gender roles, and to learn about alternative ways for men and women to behave as men and women.

Sometimes staff think there should be 'girls only' sessions on bicycles or with block play and 'boys only' sessions in the home area, when cooking, or with the dolls. This introduces children to experiences which broaden ideas of gender roles away from traditional stereotypes. It helps to dispel the idea that 'boys will be boys' or that girls are born to be mothers. However, such single-sex sessions do not help girls and boys to learn about negotiating with each other, helped and supported by adults. Many researchers and educators now think this is very important, and Dunn says that relationships between boys and girls matter as much as what boys do or what girls do.

The way that fathers and mothers work together in bringing up children is an area of great interest for researchers. Children often see their fathers at times when children and parents relax and have fun together, but spend more time with their mothers doing the chores and tasks of daily life. Research is showing that fathers and mothers want to

Fig 9.2 Boys like to play with dolls too

redefine the roles they play in the family, so that both parents are involved in daily life tasks, and both have leisure time to enjoy with their children. This is the case whether family members live apart from or with their children. In countries like Sweden, where there is paternity and maternity leave after children are born, these issues are being actively explored.

AVOIDING STEREOTYPES

Choosing How You Want to be Described

When adults fill in forms they decide whether to be described as 'Mr', 'Ms', 'Mrs' or 'Miss', and whether or not they wish to describe themselves according to different ethnic categories. An adult can choose whether to be described as 'deaf', 'hearing-impaired' or 'aurally challenged'. Children need to be given as much choice as possible about these aspects of their lives. If adults describe a child as 'the one with glasses', or comment 'what a pretty dress', or talk about 'the Afro-Caribbean child', they are stereotyping these children and seeing them narrowly rather than as whole people.

The Restricting Effect of Stereotypes

The most important thing about working with 'the child with glasses' might be the fact that he loves music. The most important thing about 'the Afro-Caribbean child' might be that she loves mathematics, and can remember all the sequences and measurements of cooking even at 3 years of age. The most important thing about the girl in 'the pretty dress' might be that she is worried about getting it dirty and so never plays with clay. Gender stereotypes are also restricting because behaviour is seen as 'what boys do' and 'what girls do'. Through encouraging boys and girls alike to be active and to explore, to be gentle and nurturing, all children are enabled to lead fuller lives with broader roles. It equips them much better for their future lives.

Adults working with children need to empower them rather than narrowly to stereotype them. To focus on one feature of the child is much too narrow. It is important not to stereotype children through labels. Children are people, and they have names, not labels!

Guidelines for helping children to have a sense of their own worth

* Provide familiar objects for every child in the different areas of the room. These artefacts of their culture might be cooking utensils, clothes or fabrics.

* Positive images of different children in different cultures are important. Remember that the important thing about a child is not how they look or the extent of their learning impairment, but that they are a person. The way you behave and talk will give messages about your mental image of each child.

* Make sure you tell stories, and make displays and interest tables with positive images of children with disabilities and children from different cultures. These stories should also be in the book area.

* Make sure that children meet adults with broad gender roles, to show them that men and women are not restricted respectively to a narrow range of activities.

* Encourage children to speak to other children and adults within the early childhood setting. Remember that children might feel powerless if they cannot speak to other people.

* Use stories from different cultures to introduce children to myths, legends and folk tales. The same themes crop up over and over again in different stories across the world. Find some of these universal themes in the stories you look at from different cultures, e.g. the wicked stepmother, the greedy rich person, good deeds being rewarded after suffering.

* Make sure the indoor and outdoor areas offer full access to activities for children with disabilities.

INSPECTING OUR OWN ATTITUDES AND VALUES

In the UK there is now legislation on race, gender and disability discrimination, which helps teams of people working together to have an impact on racism, sexism, and disablist attitudes and work practices, however unconscious these may be. In addition, it is important that each of us inspects what we do so that we become aware of our attitudes and values. Only then can we act on the unwittingly discriminatory behaviour that we will almost inevitably find. Discriminatory behaviour occurs when, usually without meaning it, we are sexist, racist or disablist. For example, an early childhood worker might ask for a strong boy to lift the chair. We need to look to see whether what we say we believe matches what we actually do. It doesn't usually! So then we have to do something about it.

Each of us has to work at this all the time, right throughout our lives. It is not useful to feel guilty and dislike yourself if you find you are discriminating against someone. It *is* useful to do something about it.

The process of inspecting our basic thinking needs to be done on three levels:

1   within the legal framework;
2   in the work setting as part of a team;
3   as individuals.

Cultural and Gender Identity, and Self Labelling

All of the following play their part in **cultural identity** and in the way children build images of themselves:

*   disability;
*   language (spoken or sign);
*   gender;
*   skin colour;
*   food and dress;
*   music and songs;
*   heritage, myths and legends;
*   culturally specific home objects (artefacts);
*   family relationships and occupations.

It is important to remember that children are people, and every person in the world is of worth. When we stereotype children, we limit them to our image of what we think they can do. This means that we hold them back in their development.

The Role of the Individual Member of Staff

Each individual worker needs to be committed and empowered to carry out the team's policy using the code of practice. In the last two sections of this chapter there are many examples of different ways in which individual staff members can play a very important part in promoting the aims and values of the team in their work. You can make a difference to the lives of the children and families you work with. You can make a difference in your work setting.

Making a Difference

One person can have a great impact. Remember, you matter and you can have an influence on combating discriminatory behaviour:

* By **challenging discriminatory behaviour**. It is important to be assertive and not aggressive. Being assertive means talking clearly and politely about how you feel. This is very different from being rude and angry.

For example, you might say: 'I felt very uncomfortable when you asked me to give a drink to the girl with a hearing aid. I felt I needed to know her name, because I am worried that I might stop seeing her as a person if I just think of her as "the girl with a hearing aid".'

* By **challenging situations**. If you see a child hurt or insult someone, explain that such behaviour is not acceptable. Criticise the behaviour rather than the child.

* By **being aware of discrimination in children's resources**. Books which are discriminatory can be discussed with other early childhood workers, removed and replaced with others (chosen as a team) containing positive images of people with disabilities, different cultures and of different genders.

* By **learning from experience**. From time to time you will make mistakes. You will say and do things you regret. For example, someone who had lived in Dorset all her life came to London and laughed at the idea of people eating goat meat. She quickly realised how insulting this was to her new friends, and apologised, explaining that it was simply a new idea to her.

* By **learning about other cultures and respecting the differences**. It is very important to try to pronounce and spell names correctly, and to try to understand the different systems that different cultures use when choosing names for people. It is also very important to learn about the different clothes people wear in different cultures and to try to learn what garments are called.

Assertiveness Training

We have seen that being assertive is important for staff, but it is also vital for children. Reference needs to be made in the team's code of practice to the promotion of children's assertiveness to combat aggression through bullying. Children need to feel protected from aggression and to be able to assert themselves sufficiently to take a full part in the activities provided. In some early childhood settings children are helped to learn to be assertive.

Both the bully *and* the victim need help to be assertive: one needs help with aggression, and the other with timidity. Visualisation techniques can help children to use positive images (seeing themselves as assertive) rather than negative images (being the bully or victim).

Aggression is not always physical. Being pushed by adults to be highly academic at the expense of taking part in childhood pursuits is also a very important issue. Moore and Klass have identified four categories of 'hurrying' children out of childhood in the USA and in the UK:

* academic 'hurrying';
* overscheduling children's lives, leaving no time for them to have personal space;
* expecting children to excel all the time;
* expecting children to assume adult responsibilities.

Guidelines to help you inspect your own feelings and attitudes

* Know the legislation on discriminatory behaviour.
* Work within the team to construct a policy on equality of opportunities.
* Use the code of practice drawn up by the staff in the work setting.
* Make sure your team reviews the code of practice together regularly.
* Be assertive (not aggressive) and try to work towards greater equality of opportunity in your work setting.
* The need for assertiveness rather than aggression or an overdominant manner in relation to early childhood workers is covered in Chapter 11.

Examining Our Attitudes to Strangers

Humans are not very good at dealing with new situations or meeting new people. They feel more comfortable with the people they know, and situations they are very familiar with. Meeting people who are in some way different can sometimes cause a reaction called 'stranger fear'. Rather than deal with our feelings we might ignore or avoid the person or situation. But this is discriminatory and we must confront our own feelings before we can help children with theirs.

It is very important that children are helped to meet a wide range of different people. Positive images help children towards positive experiences.

Valuing Cultural Diversity and Respecting Difference

Much can be gained from respecting different ways of bringing up children. For example, the Indian tradition of massaging babies is now widely used in British clinics and family centres; so is the way that African mothers traditionally carry their babies in a sling on their backs. It is important to understand and respect what the child has been taught to do at home. For example, in some cultures it is seen as disrespectful for a child to look an adult directly in the eye, whereas in others children are considered rude if they do not look at an adult directly.

Guidelines for helping children to form positive images of people

* Story-telling: asking storytellers (for example, parents) from different ethnic groups to tell stories in their own languages, as well as in English. This helps children to hear different languages, so that the idea becomes familiar that there are many languages in the world.
* Using arts, crafts and artefacts from different cultures (fabrics, interest tables, books, posters, jigsaws, etc.): this helps children to realise, for example, that not everyone uses a knife, fork or spoon when eating: they might use fingers, or chopsticks, instead. Children are helped to learn that there are different ways of eating, something which might seem strange to them at first.

* Including music and dances from different cultures: listening to them, watching them, perhaps joining in a bit. In every culture children love to stand at the edge while people perform. Children often 'echo dance'. Watch out the next time you go to a fête. If there are Morris dancers or folk dancers you are likely to see children watching them and 'echo dancing' at the sides. Being introduced to different cultures in this way helps children not to reject unfamiliar music. For example, Chinese music has a pentatonic scale; African music sometimes has five beats in a bar; European music has two, three or four beats but not usually five. A child who has never seen ballet before or a child who has never seen an Indian dance before might find these strange at first.

* Doing cookery from different cultures: you might have multi-language, picture-based cookery books that families can borrow (you might need to make these). For example, there could be a copy of a recipe for roti in English, Urdu and French, or for bread in English, Greek and Swahili; the choice of languages would depend on which were used in the early childhood setting.

* Planning the menu carefully: make sure that the menu includes food that children will enjoy and which is in some way familiar. One of the things young children worry about when they are away from home is whether they will like the food. Food and eating with others is a very emotional experience.

* Helping children to feel that they belong.

* Ensure that children who look different, because they are from different cultures or because they have a disability, feel at ease and part of the group.

Having an Impact on the Bigger Picture

There are some equal opportunities issues that seem too big for one person to tackle alone. But there are other things that are easier for each and every one of us to do something about. One individual person can have a great impact on the lives of young children and their families.

* **Action on children's rights** – working towards children's rights through international cooperation is an important way to make progress towards better-quality early childhood services. It might seem that an individual cannot do very much in this respect. However, in every country there are organisations with which you can link up. In the UK these include the **National Children's Bureau, Save the Children**, the **British Association for Early Childhood Education** (BAECE now called Early Education), **UNICEF** and the **Organisation Mondiale Education Pre-Scholaire** (OMEP). It is also important to remember that you can get in touch with your MP and your MEP via their local surgeries or by writing.

* **Action on poverty** – many children in the world live in poverty. Reports by voluntary organisations estimate that around one in three children in the UK are living in poverty. There are absolute limits to the lack of food, shelter and clothing which humans can bear. These result in starvation, disease and slow death. However, in the developed world poverty is more often relative. The reports on poverty in the UK show that, in relation to most people living in the UK, an increasing number of families are living below an acceptable minimum level. This creates stress as families struggle to make ends meet, especially when most other people appear to be financially comfortable. The 'Every Child Matters' strands (including economic well-being) and 'Change for Children' agenda as part of the 'Early Years Foundation Stage' are part of the government initiative to 'close the gap' in outcomes for children between those who are flourishing increasingly and those living in poverty and disadvantage.

In the early childhood setting it is important not to have expensive outings or activities, and to be sure to invite all parents to take part in the life of the group. No parent or child should be left out because of their economic background. This is an important equality of opportunity issue.

Guidelines to help individuals promote equality of opportunity

1   You cannot be trained to know everything. You cannot be an expert in every area, but you *can* be a good networker. This means linking people together who might be useful to each other. Get in touch with people who know about:
   * welfare rights and social services;
   * health services;
   * voluntary organisations and self-help groups.

2   Remember that you are part of a multiprofessional team, and that each member has something different to bring to early childhood work.

3   When you meet children, whether they are in a mainstream school, a special school or an early child-hood setting, make sure that your expectations of what each child can do are high enough.

4   Set children tasks which help them to make decisions and to exercise choice. It is important to let all children make choices and deci-sions so that they feel a sense of control in their lives. When people feel they have some control over what they do, they learn better. It gives them greater equality of opportunity.

5   Respect yourself and others alike. Try to think why people have different views and customs from yours. Keep thinking about what you do. Think about issues of race, gender, sexual orientation, age, economics, background, disability, assertiveness, culture and special educational needs. Keep changing what you do not like about what you do. Do this without feeling guilt or shame.

> 6 Value the things you keep learning about equality, diversity and inclusion so that you can look forward with positive images about yourself and other people.
>
> 7 Remember: equality of opportunity is about giving every child full access to the group.

1 **Plan a multicultural cooking library:** make six cookery books with simple recipes from a variety of cultures. Find or draw pictures to illustrate the books. Write the text in English, and another language if possible. If you write in Urdu or Chinese, remember you will need to make two separate books, as Urdu text runs from right to left and Chinese text goes up and down. Use the books with groups of children and run a series of cookery sessions.

Observe the way the children use and respond to the cookery books. Evaluate the aim of your plan, the reason for the activity, how the activities were carried out and what you observed in the children's cooking activities.

2 **Story-telling:** plan a story which you can tell (rather than read from a book). Choose a story you enjoy and make or find suitable props. You could make puppets out of stuffed socks, finger puppets out of gloves, stick puppets or shadow puppets; or use dolls and dressing-up clothes and various other artefacts.

Observe the children listening as you tell the story. Focus on their understanding and their language, especially children whose first language is not English. Evaluate your activity.

3 **Religious festivals:** plan how you can make the children you work with more aware of religious festivals in a variety of cultures. For example, how could you introduce the children to Diwali in a way which is not tokenist? Remember to offer children meaningful first-hand experiences.

Observe the children and assess how much they understand. Look particularly at the reactions of children who are familiar with the festival you choose, and compare their behaviour to that of children for whom this is a new experience. Evaluate your plans and observations.

4 **Inclusion:** plan how you would include a child with disabilities in your early childhood setting. Remember your plans will be different according to each child's needs. A child with a hearing impairment will need different help from a child who is a wheelchair user, for example.

Carry out and observe your plan in action. Focus on how you meet the child's individual needs through your plan. Evaluate your plan.

5 **Equality of opportunity:** read your setting's policy on equality of opportunity, and look at actual practices in the daily routine, e.g. mealtimes, books. Does what happens match the policy? Evaluate your observations.

6 **Musical development:** plan a series of activities which introduce children to the music of a variety of cultures. You will need to help children to listen to music and make music. Make musical instruments out of

cardboard boxes, elastic bands, yoghurt pots, masking tape and other materials.

7 **Booklet:** plan a booklet which introduces different religious festivals and helps parents to understand different religious perspectives in your early childhood setting. Make the booklet and use it in your early childhood setting. Evaluate it.

8 **Display:** plan and make a display using a multicultural theme. Evaluate it. How did the adults use it? How did the children react?

9 **International book:** choose one picture, book, story or poem from each of the five continents: Africa, America (North and South), Asia, Australia and Europe. Make the collection into a book which you can use with children of 3–7 years of age. Evaluate the activity.

10 **Multicultural provision:** plan an area of provision which is multicultural in approach, for example, the home area. Perhaps you can add more ideas to those suggested in this section. Implement and evaluate your plan.

LEGISLATION RELEVANT TO WORKING PRACTICES WITH CHILDREN

The main legislation you need to know about is presented in the boxes below.

Legislation relevant to working with children and young people

Health and Safety at Work Act 1974

Employers have a duty to:

* make your workplace as safe as they are able;

* display a health and safety law poster or supply employees with a leaflet with the same information. This is available from the Health and Safety Executive;

* decide how to manage health and safety. If the business has five or more employees, this must appear on a written health and safety policy.

As an employee, you have a duty to:

* work safely;

* if you are given guidance about how to use equipment, you should follow that guidance. You should not work in a way that puts other people in danger.

Fire Precautions (Workplace) Regulations 1997

Fire officers must check all childcare premises while they are in the first registration process. They will advise what is needed to make the workplace as safe as possible.

Evacuation procedures should be in place, known to all the adults, and practised regularly, using all available exits at different times, so that everyone can leave the building quickly and safely if an emergency occurs.

Some exits may be locked to prevent children wandering away or intruders entering, but adults must be able to open them quickly in the event of an emergency.

Designated fire exits must always be unlocked and kept unobstructed. Fire extinguishers should be in place and checked regularly. A fire blanket is needed in the kitchen.

Health and Safety (Young Persons) Regulations 1997

In childcare workplaces there may frequently be young people on training placements or work experience. Young people are generally less safety aware than older workers as they have far less experience. Therefore, employers must conduct special **risk assessments** for people under the age of 18. These should take into account possible exposure to physical, biological and chemical hazards and outline the amount of supervision and training a young person needs to be able to carry out a particular task.

Young people may be less strong than you think as they may still be growing. For trainees under the age of 18, you should make sure that you give clear instructions and training in tasks such as lifting, carrying and using cleaning materials.

Care Standards Act 2000

The Care Standards Act sets out 14 minimum standards that childcare workplaces must meet. Ofsted inspects these each year. It produces a booklet, which employers should read and consider thoroughly, making sure that they check and maintain the guidance given. The standards are very slightly different, depending on whether you work as a childminder, in full daycare, in sessional daycare, in out-of-school care or in crèches. They cover the following aspects of practice:

* suitable person;
* organisation;
* care, learning and play;
* physical environment;
* equipment;
* safety;
* health;
* food and drink;
* equal opportunities;
* special needs (including special education needs and disabilities);
* behaviour;
* working in partnership with parents and carers;
* child protection;
* documentation.

Control of Substances Hazardous to Health Regulations 1994 (COSHH)

Things such as bleach or dishwasher powders, some solvent glues and other materials in your setting can be hazardous. You should have a risk assessment that tells you what these things are, and what to do to minimise the risks involved. Any new person coming to the team must be made aware of what to do.

Reporting of Injuries, Diseases and Dangerous Occurrences Regulations 1995 (RIDDOR)

An accident book must be kept in which incidents that happen to staff are recorded. If an incident occurs at work that is serious enough to keep an employee off work for three or more days, employers will need to fill in the relevant paperwork and send the report to the Health and Safety Executive. It may investigate serious incidents and give advice on how to improve practice if needed.

Health and Safety (First Aid) Regulations 1981

Employers should make sure that at least one person at each session has an up-to-date first aid qualification and is the 'appointed' first aider. In childcare settings regulated by Ofsted, there is also a requirement for a staff member to be trained in 'paediatric first aid'. Methods of dealing with incidents to adults and children are not the same, particularly where resuscitation is involved. Recommendations change. For this reason, first aid qualifications must be renewed every three years.

Food Handling Regulations 1995

If you prepare or handle food, even something as basic as opening biscuits or preparing food for a snack, you need to comply with Food Handling Regulations. These cover what might be seen as common sense things:

* washing your hands before preparing food;
* making sure the surfaces and utensils you use are clean and hygienic;
* making sure food is stored safely at the correct temperature;
* disposing of waste hygienically.

But it also includes knowledge of safe practices in the use of chopping boards, having separate sinks for hand washing and preparing foods, how to lay out a kitchen and so on. There should always be people who have completed a Basic Food Hygiene certificate available to ensure that guidance is properly carried out.

Personal Protective Equipment at Work Regulations 1992

Under these regulations, employers must make sure that suitable protective equipment is provided for employees who are exposed to a risk to their health and safety while at work. This is considered a last resort, for the risk should be prevented wherever possible. In childcare the most important piece of personal protective equipment that is provided will be **gloves**, to be used when dealing with body fluids.

Employees and students should be made aware of the need to use these when changing nappies or dealing with blood spillage or vomit. Good hygiene protects both adults and children.

Data Protection Act 1998

Anyone who keeps records, whether on computers or on paper, should comply with this Act. It should be clear to service users for what purpose the data is being kept. Information about a child should also be accessible to his or her parent/carer and shared with them. It is not necessary to do this 'on demand'. A convenient time to be able to discuss the information can be arranged. Information should not be kept for longer than necessary, though accident and incident records will need to be kept in case they are needed for reference at some time in the future. Records must also be stored securely.

Children Act 1989

The Children Act brought together several sets of guidance and provided the basis for many of the standards we maintain with children. It first outlined the amount of space that should be available as well as the adult:child ratio for work with under-

8-year-olds. This is based on the age of the children being cared for. The minimum ratio is set out as follows:

Age of children	Number of adults to children (ratio)
0–1	1:3
2–3	1:4
3–8	1:8

Some places have slightly different ratios, depending on local conditions, such as the number of rooms used, or the location of the toilets if not directly off the main room. Local authority nursery classes and schools may also work on a ratio of one adult to 10 children where a trained teacher is in charge. Children in Reception classes or older do not have specified ratios, though 1:6 is recommended for outings.

The Children Act also outlined some of the principles that we now take for granted:

* the welfare of the child is most important;

* we should work in partnership with parents;

* parents should care for their children whenever possible;

* children's opinions should be taken into account when matters concern them.

Children Act 2004

This Act was introduced following high-profile inquiries into child protection (e.g. Victoria Climbié) and the introduction of the Government's Green Paper *Every Child Matters*. As this Act affects the way you should work with other professionals to benefit children and their families, it is important that you have a sound knowledge of its contents. Briefly, it states that there are five outcomes and four key themes that must be considered when working with children.

Five outcomes for children
1 Stay safe.
2 Be healthy.
3 Enjoy and achieve.
4 Achieve economic wellbeing.
5 Make a positive contribution.

Four key themes of the Children Act 2004
1 Supporting parents and carers.
2 Early intervention and effective protection.
3 Accountability and integration – locally, regionally and nationally.
4 Workforce reforms.

Childcare Act 2006

The needs of children and their parents are at the heart of this Act, with local authorities as the champions of parents and children, ensuring that their views are heard in the planning and delivery of services which reflect the real needs of families. The Act:

* requires local authorities to improve the outcomes of all children under 5 and close the gaps between those with the poorest outcomes and the rest, by ensuring early childhood services are integrated, proactive and accessible;

* places a duty giving local authorities the lead role in facilitating the childcare market to ensure it meets the needs of working parents, in particular those on low incomes and with disabled children;
* ensures people have access to the full range of information they may need as a parent;
* introduces the Early Years Foundation Stage – to support the delivery of quality integrated education and care for children from birth to age 5;
* leads to a reformed, simplified, childcare and early years regulation framework to reduce bureaucracy and focus on raising quality.

SECTION 2: SAFEGUARDING CHILDREN

• Child protection and the Children Act • Family relationships and the Children Act • Enabling children to protect themselves • Forms of abuse, and effects on child, family and workers • Child protection procedures – recording and reporting • Supporting children • Helping children and families to deal with the effects of child abuse and neglect

DEFINING TERMS

The following are accepted definitions which reflect the legislation in England, Wales and Northern Ireland.

1 **Children:** a child is anyone who has not yet reached their eighteenth birthday. 'Children' therefore means '**children and young people**' throughout. The fact that a child has become sixteen years of age, is living independently or is in further education, or is a member of the armed forces, or is in hospital, or is in prison or a young offenders institution does not change their status or their entitlement to services or protection.

2 **Children in need:** children whose vulnerability is such that they are unlikely to reach or maintain a satisfactory level of health or development, or their health and development will be significantly impaired, without the provision of services – plus those who are disabled.

3 **Significant harm:** some children are in need because they are suffering or likely to suffer significant harm. There are no absolute criteria on which to rely when judging what constitutes significant harm. Consideration of the severity of ill treatment may include the degree and the extent of physical harm, the duration and frequency of abuse and neglect, the extent of premeditation, and the presence or degree of threat, coercion, sadism, and bizarre or unusual elements.

4 **Safeguarding and promoting the welfare of children** is defined as:

* protecting children from maltreatment;
* preventing impairment of children's health or development;
* ensuring that children are growing up in circumstances consistent with the provision of safe and effective care and undertaking that role so as to enable those children to have optimum life chances and to enter adulthood successfully.

5   **Child protection** is a part of safe-guarding and promoting welfare. This refers to the activity which is undertaken to protect specific children who are suffering, or are at risk of suffering, significant harm.

CHILD PROTECTION AND THE CHILDREN ACT

The Children Act was drafted at a time when there was great public and professional concern about children who suffered abuse. It has led to a new approach, centred on the belief that children are better off when brought up and cared for in their own family. The emphasis is now on:

* **Prevention** – this means supporting and helping the family in situations which involve stress, and which expose children to harm.

* **Intervention on a voluntary basis** – when children are at risk, whenever possible it is best for a voluntary agreement to be made with the parents about how to keep their children safe.

* **Enforced intervention only if 'significant harm' for the child could result** – this might include sexual abuse, physical or emotional abuse, or neglect. Significant harm is prevented by using a child assessment order, an emergency protection order, a recovery order or a police order.

The Children Act 2004

The Children Act 2004 was prompted by the statutory inquiry into the death of Victoria Climbié in February 2000, which revealed a catalogue of errors within the agencies with which the 8-year-old came into contact. The West African girl was starved and tortured to death by her great-aunt, Marie-Therese Kouao, and the woman's boyfriend, Carl Manning. Victoria died from hypothermia; there were 128 separate injuries on her body. She died despite being known to four London boroughs, two hospitals, two police child protection teams and the National Society for the Prevention of Cruelty to Children. The government ordered a statutory public inquiry into Victoria's case. This was the first tri-partite inquiry into child protection, investigating the role of social services, the NHS and the police, under the Children Act 1989, the National Health Service Act 1977 and the Police Act 1997. The inquiry found that health, police and social services missed *12* opportunities to save the child from abuse at the hands of her great-aunt and her boyfriend.

Under the Children Act 2004, the protection of children was divided into four broad areas:

1   early intervention;
2   improving accountability and coordination of children's services;
3   improving support for parents and carers;
4   a childcare workforce strategy.

1   **Early intervention:** a nationwide database will keep track of England's 11 million children. A file will be kept on every child, with contact details of any care agency working with that child. If a child is known to more than one agency, a care worker will be assigned to coordinate that child's care. The database will enable local authorities, the NHS and other agencies to share information on suspected abuse or neglect in a family. The system hopes to identify vulnerable children more easily by also using multi-agency, community-based teams, consisting of teachers, social workers, and other child experts.

2 **Accountability and coordination:** children's trusts will be set up to combine education, social services and health. Councils must appoint a children's director who will take over from the chief education officer and the director of social services. The school watchdog Ofsted will oversee the inspection of all children's services. A children's commissioner will champion children and ensure their needs are heard.

3 **Supporting parents and carers:** parents will be given more support and advice, such as a 24-hour helpline, for looking after a family. However, those who fail to accept support may be given parenting orders which will force them to address problems within the family.

4 **Workforce strategy:** the Act will do more for childcare professionals, offering rewards and incentives to help retain and recruit staff, and offering more flexible training options. The chief nursing officer plans to assess what more health visitors, nurses, and midwives can do to protect children at risk.

Smacking and the Children Act 2004

One part of the Act that was much debated in Parliament and received much media attention was the right to smack a child. Supporters of a ban stated: 'Battery of a child cannot be justified in any proceedings on the grounds that it constituted reasonable punishment.' But they agreed smacking *could* be used to prevent danger to a child, another person, damage to property or a crime. The government managed to put through a 'compromise' that allowed mild smacking of children but barred any physical punishment that caused visible bruising or mental harm.

Procedures for State Intervention

* Under the Children Act 1989, a range of private and public law court orders is available.
* The courts decide what is to happen.
* The parents are present.
* Anyone else with parental responsibility is present.
* A **guardian *ad litem*** is appointed who will represent the child's interest in the court.
* There is a **'no delay' policy**; the court makes a timetable and sees written information beforehand, so as to avoid delays once the case comes to court.

Care Order

The court may decide that a care order is the best interests of the child. When a child is taken into care, the parents still have parental responsibility, but they now share it with the local authority. The parents must still be consulted about their child's welfare. They are encouraged to participate and keep contact with their child. However, their decisions may not be the final ones.

Children have a Voice

The wishes and feelings of children must be identified; children must be involved as active participants in decisions that are made about them. This is especially important when a situation is being reviewed.

Complaints and complaints procedures must be set up for children.

Children can be offered the choice of having a resident order, living with a relative or of going into care with a family.

Above all else, children should:

* be treated with respect;
* be listened to;
* have their ideas treated seriously;
* play a part in decisions which are made about them;
* be protected from harm;
* be loved and cared for.

Family Relationships and the Children Act

Mothers

According to the law:

* the mother is the person who gives birth to the child;
* someone can be a mother if there is a court order under the Human Fertilisation and Embryology Act 1990;
* someone can be a mother through adopting a child.

Fathers

According to the law, someone is a father if:

* they are the genetic father;
* his wife, with his agreement in law, has a child through artificial insemination by a donor.

An unmarried father can apply for **parental responsibility**.

When Parents Separate

When married parents separate and divorce, there will be:

* a divorce petition;
* a statement of arrangements for children;
* maintenance agreements.

If the parents cannot agree, the court may make a family assistance order. This will give short-term help to support parents in making a joint decision about what is best for the children. Usually, a social worker or probation officer will provide the support.

The Duties of the Local Authority to Children in Need

Children Living with Their Families

In a situation where a child is in need but is living with the family, the local authority must provide advice, information and counselling. In addition, the local authority might:

* need to provide home help, e.g. help with the laundry;
* need to provide help with travel so that the family can make use of social, cultural or recreational services;
* need to help the child have a holiday;
* require the child to attend a family centre or day care;
* need to provide for after-school care or holiday care.

Children Who are not Living with Their Families

A court order is necessary if children are not going to be living with their families.

Regulating and Registering Services

Anyone who looks after children for more than 2 hours a day, other than in the child's home, must register with their local authority. The local authority can refuse or cancel registration.

Services which must be registered are:

* day care;
* family centres;
* childminding;
* private fostering.

The number of children in a given setting is always specified. The environment is inspected indoors and outdoors to check for health and safety compliance. A record must be kept, with the names and addresses of children attending. In addition to being registered themselves, childminders must also register other people living in the house, or anyone who is likely to be working alongside them.

Everyone working with children is subject to a police check. A police check ensures that people working with children have no criminal record relating to child abuse.

Why do Children Need Protection?

You may think that at the beginning of the twenty-first century it should not be necessary to have an International Convention on the Rights of the Child, or to make UK Acts of Parliament and laws which protect children's rights. However, for many complex reasons, a minority of children are neglected or abused, which means that their rights and needs are being violated.

There are many different ways of bringing up children; the aim of UK legislation and international agreements on child protection is not to standardise the way children are brought up. However, there are certain aspects of growing up which do seem to be essential for children's wellbeing, and child protection focuses on these crucial elements: if they are missing, the child's development may suffer.

Keeping a Sense of Proportion

It is easy to imagine that child abuse and child neglect are present on a vast scale. This is because the media tend to sensationalise and focus on these cases. Also, in the past, child abuse and neglect were not so frequently recorded or reported. In comparison, nowadays, with child protection registers in every local authority and a central register kept by the NSPCC (National Society for the Prevention of Cruelty to Children), recording is much more vigorous. You should note that not all children on the child protection register are actually abused or neglected. This is because the modern emphasis is on prevention as much as it is on dealing with the aftermath of abuse or neglect. Public concern over child protection has certainly increased in recent years and the public is anxious to see local authorities become highly accountable in the child protection work they are required by law to carry out.

Why are Children Abused and Neglected?

There have been various theories about why adults abuse or neglect children. Some of these are discussed in the box below.

Theories about why people abuse children

The cycle of abuse found in some families was called the 'battered child syndrome' by Kempe and Kempe in 1962. This made it appear that abuse was something predictable, like an illness, which it is not.

* Feminist views about the sexual politics of relationships between men and women have been another approach to child protection. However, because both men and women abuse both boys and girls, this view has been criticised.

* Dysfunctional families, in which relationships break down, may lead to a child being scapegoated (blamed). This model sees therapy as the way forward, but

scapegoating does not necessarily come as a result of the family breaking down.

* The poverty cycle, and other health and social factors, are thought to predispose some families to abuse.

* However, rich, poor, healthy and unhealthy people may all abuse and neglect children – child abuse is found in *all* sections of society.

* None of the theories outlined above has been found to be correct. This is because abuse and neglect have been found across a wider range of people than any of these theories would suggest. It is always difficult to develop a convincing theory in areas which are very complex and difficult to study. Child protection is one of these areas.

* The most positive approach we can take, until theory is better developed, is to prevent abuse by looking at what helps people to be 'confident parents'.

Factors which make Child Abuse More Likely to Occur

Child abuse is more likely to occur when people (often parents):

* have little knowledge about children's needs or how children develop;

* find it hard to use the knowledge that they have about the way children develop;

* experience a great deal of stress in their lives;

* are poor decision-makers;

* find it hard to take responsibility for things that they do;

* find it difficult to relate to or communicate with other people;

* are inconsistent;

* find it hard to change their ideas, to change what they have always done, or to change what was done to them when they were children.

Children at Risk

Certain factors within the family home can mean that children are at a higher risk of being abused:

* **Drug or alcohol abuse** by parents can lead to children being put at risk, even if the parents are not actually mistreating them; such abuse is a familiar trigger for **violence** in the home and it can also lead to parents having a disordered lifestyle which can leave children in danger.

* **Mental illness:** although this does not prevent individuals from being good parents, it can sometimes move a child up the scale from being one in need to one at significant risk of harm.

Some Facts about Child Abuse

* All sections of society produce adults who abuse or neglect children. It is very dangerous to form stereotypes about the kind of people who might violate a child's rights or about the situations which could lead to child abuse or neglect.

* As evidence gathers on the subject of child protection, it is becoming apparent that the abusive or neglectful person is almost always known to the child, e.g. a parent, a family member, a friend of the family, a carer or cohabitee.

* Premature babies and children of 0–4 years of age are most likely to be abused or neglected.

* Separation of the mother and the baby for a period of time after birth can be associated with child abuse or neglect.

* Children who cry a great deal are much more likely to be abused or neglected.

* Children who do not enjoy eating are more likely to be abused or neglected.

* Stepchildren are vulnerable.

* Children with disabilities are more likely to be abused or neglected.

* Children who are boys when parents wanted girls, or vice versa, are more likely to be neglected.

ENABLING CHILDREN TO PROTECT THEMSELVES

Kidscape is a national charity committed to preventing bullying and child abuse. It has produced a pack that aims to empower children and to help to keep them safe from abuse. The Kidscape Kit covers the following areas:

* general rules about feeling and keeping safe – telling an adult if you are frightened, saying *no*;

* how to deal with bullies;

* how to recognise and deal with approaches from strangers ('stranger danger');

* strategies for what to do if you get lost;

* saying *no* when someone, even someone they know, tries to touch them in a confusing, unsafe or frightening way;

* body awareness and self-protection;

* refusing to keep secrets of any kind;

* knowing the difference between safe and unsafe secrets (for example, secrets about surprises, parties or presents are OK, but secrets about touching, hugging or kissing are not);

* 'yelling and telling' – learning to shout and run away in a frightening situation, telling an adult.

Your Role in Enabling Children to Protect Themselves

You have an important role to play in safeguarding children from abuse. You should always:

* **listen to them** and take their concerns seriously; often when a child has been bullied or abused in another way, he or she will try to put into words what has happened – they need to know that you are there to listen and, most importantly, you will believe what they tell you;

* encourage children to think about their own **personal safety**, for example never allowing them to leave the setting with anyone other than the person designated to collect them;

* create opportunities for children to **express their feelings**; they need to know that it is OK to feel sad or afraid;

* aim to **increase children's confidence** by praising them for any achievements and showing a genuine interest in what they have to say;

* **observe children:** keep regular records of children's behaviour – you are in a strong position to note any changes of behaviour or signs of insecurity which could be a result of child abuse.

FORMS OF ABUSE, AND EFFECTS ON CHILD, FAMILY AND WORKERS

What forms do child abuse and neglect take?

There are various types of child abuse and neglect:

* physical abuse;
* physical neglect;
* emotional abuse;
* emotional neglect;
* intellectual abuse;
* intellectual neglect;
* sexual abuse;
* grave concern (faltering growth or failure to thrive).

Physical Abuse

A child who has been physically abused may present various signs and symptoms.

Non-accidental Injury

Non-accidental injury (NAI) involves someone deliberately harming a child. This may take the form of:

* bruising – from being slapped, shaken, squeezed or punched;
* cuts, scratches, bite marks, a torn frenulum (the web of skin inside the upper lip);
* burns and scalds;
* fractures;
* poisoning.

It is vital that all people working in early years settings be aware of the indicators of child abuse, although it is important not to jump to conclusions. Any concerns that you may have about the nature of an injury

should be dealt with according to the procedures outlined on page 243. Any injury to a *baby* is considered suspicious, as babies have a limited capacity to move about and injure themselves. In non-accidental injury the explanation of the parent or carer as to how the injury occurred is usually inadequate, and their attitude may even seem bizarre. The parents may have delayed seeking medical help, or may have done so only when prompted by others.

Physical Indicators of Physical Neglect

* The child may be underweight and show other signs of failure to thrive (see page 242).
* Clothing may be inappropriate for the weather, and be smelly and dirty.
* The child may have poor skin tone and dull matted hair; a baby may have a persistent rash from infrequent nappy changing.
* The child may be constantly hungry, tired and listless.
* The child has frequent health problems, and is prone to accidents.

Behavioural Indicators of Physical Abuse and Neglect

Changes in behaviour may include:

* being sad, listless, preoccupied or withdrawn;
* being extra vigilant about what is going on around them (sometimes referred to as an expression of 'frozen watchfulness');
* showing signs of poor self-esteem;
* being aggressive towards other children;
* showing signs of a false independence or offering indiscriminate attention to any adult who shows an interest;
* improbable excuses or refusal to explain injuries;

* wearing clothes to cover injuries, even in hot weather – refusal to undress for gym;
* self-destructive tendencies;
* fear of physical contact – shrinking back if touched;
* admitting that they are punished, but the punishment is excessive (such as a child being beaten every night to 'make him study');
* bedwetting, bizarre behaviour or eating problems;
* lacking concentration.

Physical Neglect

1 The adult fails to give the child what they need in order to develop physically.

2 Frequently the child is left alone and unattended.

3 The children may not have adequate food, sleep, clothing, a clean environment or medical care. The child may suddenly change from thriving to not thriving.

4 The causes of child neglect are very complex, but most children who are physically neglected are often left un-supervised at home. Children who are neglected in this way are frequently injured in accidents, both in their own homes and on the roads where they play.

5 None of the behavioural indicators listed above is exclusive to abused children, nor are they exhibited by all children who suffer abuse. How children react depends upon several factors:

   * the child's personality and stage of development;
   * particular family circumstances and relationships;
   * the nature and severity of the abuse inflicted;
   * the duration of the abuse.

Emotional Abuse

In cases of emotional abuse, children are threatened by the adult. They are insulted and undermined, shouted at and constantly ridiculed. It is not known how common this form of neglect is, because it is not as easy to detect as physical abuse or neglect.

Emotional Neglect

In this case, children do not receive love and affection from the adult. They are often left alone without the support and company of someone who loves them.

Behavioural Indicators of Emotional Abuse and Neglect

Some children become withdrawn and will not play or take an active part in things. Life does not seem to be fun for them. Their self-esteem might be low, showing itself in a lack of confidence and reluctance to 'have a go' at doing things. Other children react by cons-tantly seeking attention: they seize upon any adult in an attempt to gain their attention. Tantrums might continue to a later age than usual, and speech disorders might emerge. The child might tell lies, and even steal. Emotional abuse or neglect is not easy to detect.

There may be:

* withdrawn movements, or signs of frustration;
* anger and sadness in the form of temper tantrums;
* sudden speech disorders;
* continual self-depreciation ('I'm stupid, ugly, useless', etc.);
* overreaction to mistakes;
* extreme fear of any new situation;

* inappropriate response to pain ('I deserve this');
* neurotic behaviour (rocking, hair twisting, self-mutilation).

Intellectual Abuse

Some adults may 'force' children into doing so-called 'academic' work for much of their waking lives. Children are pushed to achieve intellectually and can suffer severe stress.

Intellectual Neglect

At the opposite extreme of intellectual abuse is intellectual neglect. Children are left with little or no intellectual stimulation and cannot develop their own ideas and thinking. Sometimes, children are wrongly thought to have learning difficulties when, in fact, they are suffering from a severe lack of intellectual stimulation.

Sexual Abuse

The adult uses the child in order to gratify their sexual desires. This could involve sexual intercourse or anal intercourse; it may involve watching pornographic material with the child. Children may be forced to engage in sexually explicit behaviour or oral sex, masturbation or the fondling of sexual parts. Most sexual abusers are men; 10 per cent are women. Both boys and girls may be sexually abused. Sexual abuse can continue undetected for some years. It is in the child's interest to recognise it early so that the abuse does not escalate over time. It is difficult to know how many children are sexually abused, but it is quite likely, on the basis of existing evidence, that about one in five girls and one in 10 boys have had this experience.

Physical Indicators of Sexual Abuse

* Children may have bruises or scratches, as in an accidental injury.

* There may be itching, or even pain, in the genital area. This might make walking or sitting uncomfortable for the child.
* It might lead to bed-wetting and poor sleeping and eating patterns.
* Underclothes might be bloody or torn, and there may be discharges from the penis or vagina.

Behavioural Indicators of Sexual Abuse

The child may:

* become rather withdrawn from other children or from adults;
* seem to be lacking in self-confidence, and wanting to be 'babied';
* have poor self-esteem and feelings of being dirty or bad;
* not eat or sleep well;
* show an unusual knowledge of sexual behaviour, demonstrated by the things that they say, play with (often in the home area) or draw;
* seem fascinated by sexual behaviour and may flirt with adults, as if trying to please;
* show other extreme reactions, such as depression, self-mutilation, running away, overdoses, anorexia;
* become insecure or clinging;
* regress to younger behaviour patterns such as thumb sucking or bringing out discarded cuddly toys;
* show an inability to concentrate;
* show a lack of trust or fear of someone they know well, such as not wanting to be alone with a babysitter or child minder;
* start to wet again, day or night/nightmares;

* become worried about clothing being removed;
* try to be 'ultra-good' or perfect, overreacting to criticism.

Cause for Grave Concern (Failure to Thrive)

When a child does not develop physically, even though there may seem to be no apparent reason for this, it is a matter of grave concern which needs to be investigated by a multiprofessional team.

The Abuse of Disabled Children

Disabled children can be more vulnerable to abuse because their disability can make them dependent on parents or carers for help in everyday matters such as toileting, washing, feeding and getting dressed. Although one of the indicators that a child has been abused is a change in their behaviour, with disabled children any such change can be mistaken as being a result of their disability. Children with a physical or learning disability are especially vulnerable to all kinds of abuse; they might have communication difficulties which make it hard for them to reveal what has happened. Some children are abused by the people who care for them, while others are victims of society's view of disabled people as an 'inferior' minority group.

CHILD PROTECTION PROCEDURES

Your Role in Protecting Children from Abuse

If you are working in an early years setting other than the child's home, you should develop the good practice of keeping accurate and detailed records of children's development. These observations can be very important when assessing any changes in a child's behaviour; if you work alone – as a childminder or a nanny – you should also keep short observations of a child in order to help you build up a picture of their progress.

If you work in an early years setting you will be required to follow the **policies and procedures** of the setting; among many others, these include:

* settling in;
* safety at home times;
* safety on trips and outings; (for information on these aspects of care, see Chapter 10)
* child protection policies.

You also need to be able to:

* recognise the **signs and symptoms of abuse**;

CASE STUDY

Failure to thrive

An interesting study in Mexico in the 1960s looked at children who were failing to thrive. The children were taken to hospital, where they put on weight before returning to their families. The failure to thrive then recurred. Instead of re-admission to hospital, a team of workers visited the homes and found that the families never came together around a table to share a meal. When the families were encouraged to do this, the children gained weight and began to thrive. Eating is about the food that is eaten, but it is also about enjoying good company and conver-sations. Eating is an emotional and social activity; an opportunity to share thoughts and ideas.

* know **how to respond** to a child who tells you that he or she has been abused (**disclosure**);
* know how to **report your suspicions**;
* maintain **confidentiality** according to the guidelines in the setting's policy.

What to Do if a Child Tells You They Have Been Abused

When a child tells an adult that they have been abused, this is called a **disclosure interview**. It is very important not to be judgemental about a person who has abused a child – although it can be very hard not to, especially if you are committed to children and their rights. There are many reasons why an adult might abuse a child, and you should not try to 'second guess' someone's motivation.

The modern approach to child protection is to help the child by *preventing* further abuse or neglect. In the past, this was often done by removing the abusing person or the child from the family. However, even in cases of abuse, separating a child from their parents is not necessarily best for the child; under the Children Act this is a principle that is paramount. Separation might result in the child feeling punished for telling about what happened.

There are now programmes whereby families are supported through a family centre, a day nursery or a special therapeutic centre. These enable families to stay together, but to be supported and supervised by health visitors, educational welfare officers, psychologists, social workers and early childhood practitioners.

Guidelines for dealing with disclosure

* Reassure the child, saying that you are glad they have told you about this.
* Believe the child. Tell the child that you will do your best to protect them, but do not promise that you can keep them safe.
* Remember that the child is not to blame. It is important that you make the child understand this.
* Do a lot of listening. Don't ask questions.
* Report your conversation with the child to your senior designated manager.

Procedures for Reporting Suspicions of Abuse and Disclosures

If child abuse or neglect is suspected, it is very important that procedures be followed which are regarded as good practice and which fulfil the legal requirements. The NSPCC and, in Scotland, the RSSPCC (the Royal Scottish Society for the Prevention of Cruelty to Children) are the only voluntary organisations with **statutory** powers to apply to a court for protection orders for a child.

Recording Suspicions of Abuse and Disclosures

You should make a record of:

* the child's name;
* the child's address;
* the age of the child;
* the date and time of the observation or the disclosure;
* an objective record of the observation or disclosure;

Procedures involved in cases of child abuse

Police protection order

Specially trained police officers can remove a child who is in danger into foster care for 72 hours. This is to make sure that the child is safe. This officer is required to inform:

* the child;
* the parent or carer;
* the local authority.

Emergency protection order

A concerned adult (who may be a teacher) can apply, in an emergency, to a court or to an individual magistrate for an emergency protection order which lasts for up to eight days. (This can be extended for another seven days.) The child is then taken to a safe place, such as a foster home. After eight days, if the situation is safe, the emergency protection order can be discharged.

Child assessment order

Either the local authority or the NSPCC can apply for a child assessment order, giving seven days during which the child can be assessed. This might be used in a situation in which the parents will not cooperate but where there is not an emergency.

Child protection conference

* When it has been established that there is evidence suggesting child abuse or neglect, a child protection conference is arranged.
* Professionals involved with the child or family join together in a multi-professional discussion of written evidence.
* The early years worker may also be asked to attend.
* The chairperson decides whether it is appropriate to invite the parents to attend. In any case, the parents must be informed that the conference is taking place.
* It is a requirement that local authorities work towards parents attending at least part of, if not the whole, conference.
* An action plan called the child protection plan is made.
* The child may be placed on the child protection register.

The child protection plan

1 Assessment: the first stage in putting together a plan is to initiate an assessment. This will involve assessing both the child and the family situation.

2 Protection of the child: this would be achieved by either:
   * a care order – the child will be taken into the care of the local authority's social services department (in a foster home or community children's home);
   * a supervision order – the local authority will support and supervise the family and the child in the home setting for 1 year.

3 Regular review: the child protection plan is regularly reviewed in a review conference attended by the multiprofessional team involved with the family, and perhaps also by the parents. These conferences take place every 6 months, or more often. The child may be deregistered if the situation changes and the child no longer requires support or supervised protection.

* the exact words spoken by the child;
* the name of the person to whom the concern was reported, with date and time; and
* the names of any other person present at the time.

These records must be signed and dated and kept in a separate confidential file.

Confidentiality

As a general rule, information about a child protection issue should be shared with people only on a '**need to know**' basis. This means that only staff working directly with the child or the parents will have access to any information about a disclosure or investigation. Gossip must be avoided; names and identities must never be disclosed outside the group designated as having a 'need to know'.

Risk Assessment

A risk assessment is the name given to the detailed report, which a social worker and other professionals have to complete once a child's name has been placed on the **child protection register**. On the basis of this information, plans are discussed about what steps need to be taken to provide a parent and children with the best possible help.

Whistleblowing Procedures

What is Whistleblowing?

Whistleblowing, or public interest disclosure, is when a worker reports a concern about the improper actions or omissions of their colleagues or their employer which may cause harm to others or to the organisation. The disclosure must be made out of real concern about wrongdoing. The whistle-blower should reasonably believe the

Guidelines for reporting child abuse or neglect

1 Clarify your own thinking. Is this a situation which demands instant action, for example, if a child is injured and needs immediate medical attention? Put the child's feelings and physical care first. Be calm, reassuring and warm. This will help the child to have as high self-esteem as possible.

2 Usually, evidence about child abuse or neglect emerges in a much less sudden way. Report the indicators which have led you to suspect child abuse or neglect to your designated senior manager. You will need to supply written evidence within 24 hours, and it is particularly helpful if you make observations of the child on that day. If there is already a well-established record-keeping system in the work setting, this will be easier to manage.

3 Your line manager will help you to follow the correct procedures, but you should know them too. They will be written down in every work setting (this is legally required under the Children Act).

4 You will need to continue to keep carefully written observations. This is because you will be required to make a report, and for this you must have written evidence.

5 The police, social services and perhaps the National Society for the Prevention of Cruelty to Children (NSPCC) will be involved, and will consult each other in order to:

* be sure there is evidence;
* decide whether to issue a police protection order, an

emergency protection order or a child assessment order (see box on page 244).

information and allegation is substantially true, even if the information later turns out to have been incorrect.

A whistleblower is usually not directly or personally affected by the concern and therefore rarely has a direct personal interest in the outcome of any investigation into their concerns.

Some organisations have a **whistleblowing policy**, which details how and to whom a report should be made.

Child Protection and Schools

When a child starts or is already attending a nursery school, nursery class or primary school, social services are required to notify the head teacher if a child's name is put on the child protection register. The register states:

* whether the child is subject to a care order;
* the name of the key person on the case;
* what information may be known to the parents.

The school is required to monitor how the child, especially in terms of their development, is getting along. The school's observations should be shared with the social services department should any concern arise.

Working together under the Children Act 1989

* Every school is required to appoint a teacher who is responsible for linking with the social services department.

* Every school is required to have a written policy on child protection procedures, making clear the lines of reporting to social services and, sometimes, to the NSPCC.

* Registers of named staff taking on this role are kept by the LEA. Regular training and support are given to these teachers.

* Schools, as well as care settings, are encouraged to develop curriculum plans which help children to develop skills and practices which protect them from abuse.

SUPPORTING CHILDREN

The Use of Play Therapy

Play therapy is a mode of therapy that helps children to explore their feelings, to express themselves and to make sense of their life experiences. It is appropriate for children of all ages, but is most often used for children aged between 3 and 12 years. Play therapists generally work with individual children but many have experience of working with groups and with siblings. Play therapy is particularly effective in supporting children who have experienced abuse. Play therapy can help children by offering:

* **play** – children's natural medium to learn, communicate and to explore their worlds;
* **freedom of expression** in a safe and trusting environment;
* a space in which the feelings their experiences generate can be expressed and contained. It cannot change what has happened but it can promote resilience within each child to enable him or her to discover a more hopeful view of the world;

CASE STUDY

Child abuse

Late one Saturday night, the police are called out by neighbours to a flat where it is reported that a child is screaming and no one will answer the door. The police try to gain entrance by the front door but end up forcing their way through a window. In the main living room, a child of about 4 years is strapped to a chair, watching television; she appears not to notice her surroundings. The screams have stopped, but slight whimpering sounds are coming from the bedroom. The two police officers enter the bedroom and find a thin baby of about 10 months, in a filthy nappy, with tobacco and ash over his hands and mouth; his eyes look dull and he is moaning softly. The officers notice an open pack of cigarettes and an upturned ashtray on the chair next to the baby's cot. The children are taken to hospital and the baby is kept in overnight for observation; the duty social workers are contacted and the 4-year-old girl is taken to emergency foster parents for the night. The children's parents arrive home at 2 a.m., drunk and high on drugs, having been to a party. The father finds out from neighbours that the police have been and is furious. He demands the return of his children and claims that they had never left the children on their own before – the mother claimed that a friend had promised to stop by and look after the children at 10 p.m.

ACTIVITY

1 Divide into groups and list the indicators of neglect and abuse in the case study.

2 What do you think will happen to the children now? Discuss the alternatives.

---

* the opportunity to explore and understand these feelings. It can enable them to shift their perspective of abuse or difficulty so that they are less likely to internalise blame. The resulting empowerment and increased self esteem can be the springboard to help the child to cope with difficulties in the real world.

Consistency is also important, so play therapy sessions usually take place once a week, at the same time. This may be at the child's home, school or clinic.

Play therapists take a specialist course; it is usual for trainees to hold a first qualification in either teaching, social work, occupational therapy or another related field and to have extensive experience of working with children. Personal therapy and supervised practice are essential elements of the training. For further information on all aspects of play therapy, contact the British Association of Play Therapists at www.bapt.org.com.

Working with Voluntary Organisations to Prevent Abuse

* **Kidscape** works with schools and other early years settings to devise assertiveness training programmes which give young children protection from abuse.

* **Childline** is a voluntary organisation which operates a 24-hour free telephone line for children. They can call in to discuss with trained counsellors situations which place them under stress for one reason or another.

HELPING CHILDREN AND FAMILIES TO DEAL WITH THE EFFECTS OF CHILD ABUSE OR NEGLECT

Children are best helped when early childhood practitioners are not judgemental about the child's family and, in particular, about the person who has abused the child.

Building Self-esteem

* It is important to build the self-esteem of both the child and the family.

* Low self-esteem is associated with children who have been abused or neglected, and also with adults who abuse or neglect children.

* Improving self-esteem can be difficult when parents who are required to bring their children, under a child protection order, to a family centre, day nursery or children's centre do not appear responsive or positive to staff or to the child.

* It takes time to build self-esteem.

* Staff who give messages of warmth, who respect other people's dignity and who value people, although they may reject what they have done, are more likely to help parents in this way. Feeling valued as an individual, whatever you have done, builds self-esteem.

Guidelines for helping children deal with abuse and neglect

* Encourage children to play.

* Some children will need to be supported by trained play therapists or psychologists. Where there has been sexual abuse, anatomically correct dolls are sometimes used with the child. With help from these professionals, you might be also be able to use the dolls with the child. These can help children to play, acting out their experiences and expressing how they feel about what has happened to them.

* Be warm – just be there for the child. Don't ask questions.

* Encourage the child to try to enjoy activities with you.

* Remember that children who have been abused or neglected are often challenging. Remind yourself about ways of helping children who boundary-push and challenge (Chapter 7).

* Help parents to feel confident in their parenting.

* Don't undermine parents with remarks such as 'He doesn't do that here!' Instead, tackle problems together. Try saying to parents, 'Let's both try the same approach. When she does it next time, either at home or in the nursery, shall we both make sure we have the same reaction?'

* The aim is to get parents and children relating well to each other.

* Remember that many people who work with young children were themselves abused as children. It is important to manage feelings about this subject in a professional way.

CASE STUDY

John

One early years worker had enjoyed telling stories to John (3 years), who had been referred to the nursery under a child protection order. One day, she went to tell him a story and found that his mother had arrived early. She was in the book area with John, reading him a story. They were completely involved. The early years worker felt a pang of disappointment, but it did not last, as she knew it was more important for the parent and child to enjoy stories together than it was for her to do so. She also knew that she had helped to bring about this situation. She began to realise that working with children who have been hurt in some way can bring a different kind of satisfaction even though it was also distressing sometimes.

SECTION 3: PROMOTING CHILDREN'S SELF-CONFIDENCE AND SELF-ESTEEM

• Children's feelings • Theory of emotional intelligence
• The role of adults in promoting a positive self-image and sense of wellbeing in children

CHILDREN'S FEELINGS

Children live life to the full. This means that they have powerful feelings. They need adult help to learn to deal with the strength of their feelings. Feelings are hard to manage – even adults do not always succeed in dealing with how they feel. These strong feelings can quickly overwhelm the child. This can lead to:

* sobbing and sadness;
* temper tantrums that are full of anger and rage;
* jealousy that makes a child want to hit out;
* joy that makes a child literally jump and leap with a wildness that is unnerving to many adults.

The Fears Children Develop

The fears children have are very real to them. Some (especially babies and toddlers) are afraid that their parent or carer might leave them. Some are afraid of loud noises (such as thunder); of heights (perhaps they do not like to come down from the climbing frame); or of sudden movements (such as a dog leaping up at them). Going to a strange place, such as the clinic, might bring on feelings of fear, and many children are afraid of the dark.

Children's Body Language

Children need to express their feelings. They do so through:

* **physical actions:** such as stamping with rage, screaming with terror, hitting out, jumping with joy or seeking a cuddle;
* **facial expressions:** a pout tells the adult the child is not happy, compared with eyes that are shining with joy;
* **the position of the body:** playing alone with the doll's house or hovering on the edge of a cooking session might indicate that the child wants to join in but does not know how; playing boats right in the centre of a group of children tells an adult something quite different;
* **body movements:** children who keep twisting their fingers together are not at ease, compared with children who sit in a relaxed way.

Guidelines for dealing with children's fears

* Talking about fearful feelings and showing the child that you understand they are important.

* Later on, children can use imaginative play – for example in the home area, doll's house or toy garage – to face and deal with their fears and worries.

* Feeling jealous and anxious about the arrival of a new baby at home can be helped by allowing children to take out their aggressive feelings on a soft toy. This channels the aggression, giving the child permission to express their feelings.

* The traditional early childhood curriculum provides opportunities for children's feelings to be expressed: for example, boisterous outdoor play, bashing lumps of clay, knocking down wooden blocks or working at the woodwork bench all allow children to channel their energies.

Putting Feelings into Words

* It helps children to manage their feelings if they can put them into words. The child who can say 'Stop hitting me! That hurts! I don't like it!' has found an appropriate way to deal with an unpleasant situation.

* The cries that babies make are early attempts to 'tell' others how they feel.

* Early on, children may shout a term of abuse in a difficult situation rather than using appropriate words. Adults need to decide whether this is a step forward along the way from physical hitting (via use of unacceptable language) to an appropriate expression of feelings in words.

* It takes time, experience and adult support for young children to learn how to express their feelings in words and to negotiate in dialogue with others. It can help to give them examples of rather staccato-sounding words, such as 'Stoppit!', so that they can take control of situations. Children learn the language of feelings through real situations that hold great meaning and that engage their whole attention.

Helping Children Under Emotional Stress

When children do not experience warm, loving relationships, they react differently according to their personality. They may:

* become aggressive;
* be very quiet, watchful and tense;
* begin bedwetting or soiling themselves;
* find it difficult to eat;
* return to babyish ways – they may want a bottle again or a comforter; they might want to be held and cuddled, or carried about; they could want help with eating and dressing.

When children are under emotional stress, their behaviour can change quite quickly. It is important, therefore, that early years workers be alert to the changes listed above and that they respond sensitively, with understanding. If you suspect a problem of this kind it is important to talk with your line manager about your observations. The discussion will probably open up to the staff team and the parents. You will all look at the child's progress and agree what steps should be taken, depending on whether the situation is a temporary one for the child or one that is more likely to be long-term.

Guidelines for developing the social behaviour of children by helping them to understand their feelings and manage their emotions positively

* Children need to understand, express and deal with their feelings.

* They need to develop positive relationships with people.

* Children feel things deeply and they need a great deal of help in coming to terms with their emotions. Feelings are hard to deal with. It is important to remember that even adults do not succeed all the time in coping with how they feel.

* Helping children to express and deal with their feelings constructively and positively is probably one of the most important things an adult can do if children are to feel they matter, and are valued and respected.

Remember to work as a team to decide together on what is unacceptable behaviour and how to deal with it. Many early years settings now have behaviour policies. These should always use positive images of the child as the starting point. Negative images, for example that of a bully, can be made positive through visualisation techniques: the bully becomes a child who needs help to become assertive without being aggressive. They need to emphasise the development of self-discipline by the child, rather than adults managing the behaviour for the child.

It is important that adults working with young children be guided by each child's personality. What helps one child might not help another. Every child is different.

Remember that all children need:

* personal space;
* one-to-one attention;
* friends;
* to feel part of the group;
* to feel secure.

EMOTIONAL INTELLIGENCE

Emotional intelligence (sometimes known as **emotional literacy**) is a relatively new concept in education. It may be defined as the ability to recognise, understand, handle and appropriately express emotions. Children are encouraged to **explore their emotions** in school and learn about manners, respect and good behaviour in an attempt to raise school attendance and to improve learning.

In 2005, the Department for Education and Skills sent out guidance booklets to thousands of **primary schools**, covering 14 areas, under the titles 'New beginnings', 'Getting on with falling out' and 'Good to be me'.

Children's emotions have a huge impact on school life. Anger, in particular, has a damaging effect on the atmosphere in a classroom. Schools which seek specifically to promote emotional literacy among pupils have provided evidence that it helps to raise achievement. Teachers use various different approaches. For example, they might:

* adopt **key emotions** such as anger and happiness or fear and excitement each half-term. This encourages awareness of the impact that emotions can have on our lives;

* ask children to think about **contrasting emotions:** when they might experience

them and how they might express them differently;

* use fiction, themed displays or music to help children of any age feel more connected to their emotions.

How human beings develop emotionally is of core importance in planning effective **sex and relationship education (SRE)** in schools. In his book *Emotional Intelligence*, Daniel Goleman identifies five emotional and social competencies. Goleman argues that young people need to be able to:

* recognise and name feelings and use these confidently to guide their decisions and actions;

* manage their emotions positively and recognise that sometimes we have to wait for things;

* use their emotions positively to motivate themselves and work towards their hopes for the future;

* recognise and empathise with other people's emotions and feelings;

* develop a range of skills to manage emotions such as negotiation, conflict resolution.

Children who Express Themselves or Relate to Others in Particular or Challenging Ways

The Shy or Withdrawn Child

Although it is important for every child to have their own personal space and to be allowed opportunities to do things alone, some children have difficulty socialising with other children or with adults. These children have too much personal space. There are a number of things that you can do to help a child overcome their shyness:

* **Making introductions:** when the adults are new to the child, you can introduce them. 'Michael, this is Jane. Jane wants to do a painting. Can you help her to get started? Can you tell her how to find the colours she wants?'

* **Being welcoming:** if a child is shy with adults, it can be helpful to join the child with a warm smile, but to say nothing. You might find that a welcoming gesture, such as handing the child a lump of clay if they join the clay table, reassures them.

* **Observing children:** keeping good observations of children's social relationships is important. If a child who is normally outgoing and has the full range of social behaviour suddenly becomes quiet, withdrawn and solitary, this should be discussed with the team and parents should be included in the discussion. Outside, multiprofessional help may be required if the problem cannot be solved within the team.

The Overdemanding Child

Having too much individual adult attention can lead to children being labelled as 'spoilt' or 'overdemanding'. This negative image of the child is not helpful. Some children, for example only children, are the main focus of their family and are given one-to-one attention by adults most of the time. They have not experienced waiting for things or taking turns. Is it the child's fault if he or she seems demanding of adult attention, insecure or ill at ease with other children? This child needs sensitive help to become involved in parallel, associative and cooperative social behaviour with other children. Some children gain attention by being dominant and demanding. These are the so-called 'bossy' children. But this is another negative and unhelpful image. Such children need help in turn-taking and learning to give and take. They are usually afraid of losing control of situations; for example, in the play and home area, they may control the other children by saying what the storyline is going to be and by making the other children do as they say. These children need an adult to help them to see that the 'story' will be better if other children's ideas are allowed in. It takes a bit of courage for the child to dare to let the play 'free-flow', because no one knows quite how the story will turn out. Once children experience this kind of free-flow play, however, they usually want more of it!

Moving into Free-flow Play

Adults can help 'bossy children' into the give and take of play, as the following example shows.

Adult: Did you say you had a dog in your story?

Child: Yes. I call it to come here.

Adult: But Jack says it is a horse. You could call the horse over. See what happens.

Child: Horsey, come here!

Adult: Ah, here comes the horse. Shall we stroke it?

Sibling Jealousy

When a new baby is born, it can be hard-going for a child who is used to having a lot of attention. Sibling jealousy often results in very demanding behaviour, which may last for some time, until the family adjusts to its new social relationships. Recent research shows that the older child needs to feel that they are being treated in exactly the same way as the new baby.

Children who Own Status Possessions

Children in capitalist societies often have difficulties with possessions. From 2 years of age, they may become eager to own objects. Owning possessions helps them to gain attention and enables them to control things. Children who have not experienced secure social relationships are often especially anxious to possess fashionable objects which carry high status, for example a special toy or particular clothes and shoes. The status accorded to these usually comes through advertising. Adults can help children to see that these objects are not vital for having friends and being part of the group. Children need to learn that friends like you because of who you are, and not because you own a fashionable hat. Sometimes children are so desperate to 'have' that they will steal. If such children cannot return an object on their own because this is too difficult for them emotionally, they need to be helped to do so. Many children steal, but when a child does so regularly it is usually a sign that he or she is under stress. The child needs individual warmth, love and attention from an adult. Sometimes such children need the help of a specialist such as an educational psychologist.

Angry Children

Hitting, kicking, spitting, biting, swearing and disrupting other children's activities are behaviours that children use to demand attention. But these behaviours all lead to negative images of a naughty or disruptive child. In order to help such children, adults need to clear their heads of negative images. This can be done by using a visualisation technique:

* Try to think of the child positively.
* Try to see why the child might be angry.
* Try to create a better atmosphere for all the children in the group.

Bored and Frustrated Children

The way the indoor and outdoor areas are set up may be causing boredom and frustration in the children, leading to challenging behaviour. Thus it is important to bear in mind that children need:

* a good choice of activities, and interesting people to be with;
* interesting and exciting things to do;
* new and challenging activities;
* comfortable and familiar things to do.

Dealing with Temper Tantrums

Temper tantrums can be:

* **noisy** – the child might hurl themselves about, perhaps hurting themselves, usually in rather a public way;
* **quiet** – the child holds their breath, and might even turn blue.

Positive Images of Children are Vital

Children need positive images of themselves. Such positive messages come, in part, from the social behaviour of the staff in the early years setting. Discriminatory practice, by children or adults, that applies negative labels to children – even if these are not conveyed directly to the child – damages social and emotional development, and can result in difficult behaviour and poor development of social skills. There may be certain experiences in the child's life which are causing the anger and distress. Bad behaviour needs to be monitored carefully, reported to your supervisor and acted on by the team. Again, it may be necessary to involve outside help such as a social worker, educational psychologist, health visitor or GP.

Self-image, Self-esteem and Wellbeing

Children develop a sense of self (self-conceptual sense of identity) during the first year of life, and this becomes more stable as they develop socially. The way we feel about ourselves is called our self-image, and this is deeply influenced by how we think that others see us. If we feel loved, valued, appreciated and that we matter to people who matter to us, then our sense of wellbeing is high. Developing a positive self-image is about:

* realising you exist;
* developing self-esteem and good wellbeing;
* learning to like and respect yourself;
* knowing who you are;
* knowing and understanding yourself;
* developing skills of caring for and looking after yourself;
* feeling you are making a caring contribution to others.

Having strong attachments to people and learning about feelings helps babies to develop socially. Being loved and shown warm affection also helps babies to learn socially. It is now thought that emotions cause chemical reactions which influence the development of the brain. Upset and fear bring corrosive cortisol, while wellbeing opens up the brain to learning and positive relationships, with feel-good chemicals. Neuroscientists are suggesting, for example, that a baby who is shouted at will not develop intellectually as much as a baby who is spoken to gently and lovingly.

It used to be thought that once children turned into mature adults this was the end point of social development. This is not true: we go on developing socially throughout our lives, from birth to death. The psychologist Erikson helped us to begin thinking about this with his eight stages of social and emotional development, which go from birth to old age (see Chapter 2). It is important for each of us to know ourselves, and to be able to respect and value ourselves.

People who value and respect themselves have:

* a positive sense of self (self-concept);
* a positive self-image (feel valued and that they matter to others);
* good wellbeing (self-esteem).

From an early age, children are aware of differences between them and others. This can be a positive or negative aspect of their lives. Many things influence our self-image, including:

* ethnicity;
* gender;
* language;
* particular and special needs;
* abuse;
* economic circumstances.

Fig 9.3 Attachment is an important part of making positive relationships with people

Every child needs to know that they matter. From a loving beginning, a child can face and cope with the emotions of life.

Name-calling and harassment can damage a child's self-image. It is important to help children to be self-aware in ways which bring positive comments about difference. Because young children are very interested in differences in physical appearance, they are also very aware of differences in skin colour or clothing.

For example: Sam says to Susu, a refugee from Somalia: 'Why do you wear that hat?' The practitioner joins and says: 'Susu has come from Somalia with her family, and so her clothes are different. If you went to another country, your clothes would look different.' Sam replies: 'If I went to Somalia, what would I wear?' This positive conversation is helping Sam and Susu to gain knowledge of each other's cultural backgrounds, so that each develops positive images of different cultures and people. This makes a child feel they matter, that they belong and that they are valued.

When English is an additional language, it is important that the child's first language and home languages are valued (see section on language development).

The child who has special needs can also quickly lose a good self-image. Children who use a wheelchair, wear glasses, use a hearing aid, walk differently or think differently, such as a child with a learning difficulty, would all need to be supported so that they develop a good self-image. Other children also need support to understand how and why children are different, and what this involves. They need to understand that when everyone makes it a priority to learn how to help each other and be well informed, the whole community gains and everyone in it can then make a strong and positive contribution.

Because of the embarrassment and ignorance of many people, children with a disability have to come to terms not only with their disability, but also with the way people react to it. It is very important that children meet a wide range of people so that this kind of 'stranger fear' gradually disappears from society. This will make it easier for every child to develop a positive self-image with good wellbeing. Wellbeing does not mean being in a constant state of happiness. It brings a state of mind which is positive and forward-looking.

Every Child Matters emphasises the importance of economic background. Of course, *making poverty history* is a huge challenge for governments and needs large-scale action, but the small-scale aspects matter too. It is important not to charge for extra visits, outings and resources, and to be sensitive to the fact that families may not be able to afford to contribute.

Children who experience different kinds of abuse are very vulnerable in relation to the development of self-image. Poor self-image is associated with emotional, intellectual, physical and sexual abuse. It is especially important to show a child they are valued and appreciated as a unique person.

Boys and girls are different, and research is beginning to help our understanding of the gender aspects of brain development. Boys often prefer non-fiction books (about fish, trains or dinosaurs, for example) to fiction. They often develop spatial concepts earlier than girls. Girls tend to start enjoying reading at an earlier age than boys, which is why attention is now being paid to helping boys enjoy reading. If boys are always expected to read from storybooks and never encouraged to share books about nature or other facts with others, they lose confidence and interest in books.

Principles of equality, diversity and inclusivity help early years workers to encourage a good self-concept in young children. The same is true of very young babies and children. Very young babies, when they begin to move about, will keep looking at the adult who is caring for them. Babies need to see adults' reactions and to seek their approval. This is called **social referencing**.

Babies have individual personalities and need to settle into their particular family and its way of life. In the same way, the family learns about this new person who has come to live with them. There will be huge adjustments on all sides.

The way children feel about themselves and their bodies (how comfortable you feel in your body is part of your sense of self, and is called **embodiment**) is also linked to self-image. This develops in children as they feel unconditionally valued, respected and that they are of worth.

THE ROLE OF ADULTS IN PROMOTING A POSITIVE SELF-IMAGE AND SENSE OF WELLBEING IN CHILDREN

* Value children for who they are, not what they do or how they look.
* A child needs love, security and a feeling of trust. There is no one way to give these feelings to children. It will depend on where children live, their family and culture. There is no standard family. There is no standard institution. There is no one best way to love children and give them self-esteem.
* People who give children positive images about themselves (in terms of skin colour, language, gender, disability, features, culture and economic background) help children to develop

good self-esteem. Look at the book area and the displays on the walls in your setting. Are you giving positive messages?

* Visitors to the nursery can provide positive images. The people children meet occasionally or on a daily basis will all have a strong influence on them. If children almost never see men working in early years settings or women mending pieces of equipment, they form very narrow ideas about who they might become. Books, pictures, outings and visitors can all offer positive images which extend children's ideas of who they might be.

* Adults who are positive role models help a child's self-esteem. However, adults need to have a positive self-concept; a depressed, self-doubting adult will not be a really good role model for a child.

* Children need to feel some success in what they set out to do. This means that adults must avoid having unrealistic expectations of what children can manage, for example dressing, eating or going to the lavatory. It is important to appreciate the efforts that children make.

* They do not have to produce perfect results. The effort is more important than the result.

* Adults help children's self-esteem if they are encouraging. When children make mistakes, do not tell them they are silly or stupid. Instead say something like 'Never mind, let's pick up the pieces and sweep them into the bin. Next time, if you hold it with two hands it will be easier to work with'.

* Children need to feel they have some choices in their lives. Obviously, safety and consideration for others are important, but it is usually possible to allow children to make some decisions.

* Children need clear, consistent boundaries or they become confused. When they are confused they begin to test out the boundaries to see what is consistent about them.

* Children need consistent care from people they know. Many early years settings have now introduced a key worker or family worker system, which provides continuity.

* Children need to have a feeling of trust that their basic needs for food, rest and shelter will be met. Rigid rituals are not helpful, but days do need a shape or routine. This will give children a predictable environment. They will have the know-how to help in setting the table, for example, or washing their hands after going to the lavatory.

* Children and their families need first to be given respect in order that they can then develop self-respect. So children, parents and staff need to speak politely and respectfully to each other.

* Children have strong and deep feelings. They need help, support and care from adults.

SECTION 4: SUPPORTING CHILDREN TO PREPARE FOR TRANSFER OR TRANSITIONS

• Transition from the home environment to other settings • Strategies to enable children and families to cope with change and separation

TRANSITION FROM THE HOME ENVIRONMENT TO OTHER SETTINGS

Children and young people naturally pass through a number of stages as they grow and develop. Often, they will also be expected to cope with changes such as movement from primary to secondary school – and for children with disabilities or chronic ill health, from children's to adult services.

Such changes are commonly referred to as **transitions**.

Some children may have to face specific and personal transitions not necessarily shared or understood by all their peers. These include:

* family illness or the death of a close relative;
* issues related to sexuality;
* the process of asylum;
* parental mental health;
* divorce and family break-up;
* adoption;
* disability;
* the consequences of crime.

It is important that times of transition are as positive as possible for both the individual child and the family as a whole. Transitions can be painful, and some of the separations in the list of examples could never be happy experiences for children or those who love them and whom they love. However, it is always possible to ease the impact of difficult separations through thoughtful, sensitive support. But this needs to be well thought out and organised.

The First Meeting with the Family

This might be when the family visits the early childhood setting or it might be through a home visit. It is important that parents do not feel forced into accepting a home visit from staff. Often, families welcome home visits as an opportunity to get to know the early years worker. A home visit, or a visit to the setting before the child starts there, gives staff the chance to find out what the parents are expecting from the setting. See Unit 20 on CD-ROM for more details about working in a close partnership with parents or carers.

All this helps parents and children to make the transition from being at home to starting in a group setting. Childminders and nannies often make photograph albums with short captions in the same spirit.

Parents and children often appreciate having a booklet of their own to keep, and this can build into a record of the child's time with the setting, childminder or nanny, and often helps a child to make future transitions.

When settling a child and family, transitions are made easier if there is sensitivity about the way you use gesture and body language, such as eye contact. The photographs in the brochure can be invaluable when staff and family do not share the same language.

Settling Children into the Setting

Probably the most important thing an early years worker does is to settle a child into an early years group, in partnership with the parent(s). Many settings have a very clear policy on admissions and settling-in. This is discussed in greater detail in Unit 20 on CD-ROM.

Supporting Times of Transition

* Remember that if the parent is anxious about leaving their child, the child will be anxious about being separated from the parent. Make sure that each adult and child is welcomed. Put notices in the languages of the community as well as in English.
* A notice board with photographs of staff and their role helps people to feel part of things.
* An attractive display of some of the recent experiences children have gained

helps people to tune in to the setting's way of working.

* A notice with the menu for the week gives valuable information to parents/carers.

* Something for children to do is vital; watching fish in a fish tank or having a turn on a rocking-horse are popular examples.

Typical points of transition for children are:

* The first time parents leave their baby with a relative or friend after birth.

* If the baby/toddler/young child starts attending a group setting regularly.

* When the child begins school (in England this is at the end of the Foundation stage; in Scotland it is when entering Primary 1, and so on).

* When leaving infant school years (England – Key Stage 1) to enter the junior school years.

What Went Before?

Whenever there is a transitional point for a child and family, it is important to look at *what went before*. This is so that we can learn about and tune in to the child, and support them and make as seamless a transition as possible. There should be **continuity**, not discontinuity, of experience for the child and family.

This means that every practitioner working with children in the birth to 16 years range should know what comes before and what comes after the time the child will spend with them.

For example, an English practitioner will need to know about:

* Early Years Foundation Stage;
* Key Stage 1.

Primary School Admission

The DfES has developed a mainstream training package for the transition between the Early Years Foundation Stage and Key Stage 1, called *Continuing the Learning Journey*. Teachers create a classroom in the spirit of the reception class and build individually on the child's Early Years Foundation Stage profile identified 'next steps'.

STRATEGIES TO ENABLE CHILDREN AND FAMILIES TO COPE WITH CHANGE AND SEPARATION

Being separated from our loved ones is difficult at any age, and a kind of bereavement is experienced, similar in some ways to that when someone loved dies. In situations when children are repeatedly separated from their families, through home circumstances or war and conflict, it helps when those the child is left with understand the elements discussed in this chapter, so that vulnerable children feel a sense of belonging and wellbeing, and feelings of being valued, loved and respected.

It is also important to remember that Anna Freud, working with children who had experienced the Holocaust, found that their friendships with each other were very important, and so was having a normal childhood with opportunities for sensitively supported play. Play seemed to have a self-healing power.

The Key Person

Throughout the **EYFS**, there is a requirement that there is a key person for the child. The important thing is that there are opportunities for warm, intimate relationships between practitioners and babies and young children spending time together. For this to be possible, children need constant and stable people, and to be in very small groups. Then there are opportunities to listen to children and tune in to them. This approach respects the child as unique, with an emotional need for warm, affectionate, positive relationships and feeling valued, which forms the crucial elements, so that the child feels safe and secure.

Some families will have a lead professional working with them to ensure that there is more joined-up thinking and that different professionals link with each other. This has developed through the Children Act 2004 and the embedding of the *Every Child Matters* agenda. It will also be an important way of reducing inequality, which became a local authority duty under the Childcare Act 2006.

Supporting Parents

Parents who have experienced war and conflict are often anxious about leaving their children with those outside the family. They appreciate:

* having their youngest children in the next room while they learn English and learn about life in England;

* their older children being near them in school in the same building;

* all their children joining them at the end of the session, to try out a story they have learnt, using props (e.g. *Goldilocks and the Three Bears*);

* meeting other parents who have experienced war, conflict and trauma;

* meeting practitioners who help them and their children to develop and learn and who care for their emotional wellbeing.

Accessing Further Support

Families need information about a wide range of topics. Much information can be gained from the media – radio, television and newspapers. The internet is also a valuable source of information, but not every family has easy access to computing and internet connections. The box below shows the sources of information generally available.

Public library	Usually with internet services; local information about a wide range of services for children and families; also a reference section with books giving information on benefits and other government services.
Citizens Advice Bureau (CAB)	Most towns have a CAB; rural areas may have to access one by telephone. They offer independent legal and financial support.
Childcare Information Service	This service was set up by the government to provide information for parents about the range and costs of child care in their area. Their website (www.childcarelinks.gov.uk) has links to all local authorities. Parents without internet access could write directly to their local authority for printed information.

Benefit Agency	Most large towns have a Benefits Agency office with a wide range of leaflets – often printed in different languages – and experienced staff to explain what is available.
Local authority (LA) or council	Many local authorities have a separate department to provide support for children and families who are vulnerable or need help with everyday living. They can be accessed directly or via the internet.
Voluntary organisations	Local charities often hold meetings and host events to publicise their work and to raise money; examples include: Gingerbread (a charity for the support of lone parents), the National Council for One Parent Families, the Daycare Trust (a national childcare charity) and Families Need Fathers.

SECTION 5: THE CAUSES AND EFFECTS OF DISCRIMINATION IN SOCIETY

• What is discrimination? • The causes of discrimination in child care and education • The effects of discrimination

WHAT IS DISCRIMINATION?

* Discrimination is the denial of equality based on personal characteristics, such as race and colour. Discrimination is usually based on **prejudice** and **stereotypes**

* **Prejudice** literally means to prejudge people based on assumptions. For example, racial prejudice is the belief that physical or cultural differences (e.g. in skin colour, religious beliefs or dress) are directly linked to differences in the development of intelligence, ability, personality or goodness.

* The word **'stereotype'** comes from the process of making metal plates for printing. When applied to people, stereo-typing refers to forming an instant or fixed picture of a group of people, usually based on false or incomplete information. Stereotypes are often negative.

THE CAUSES OF DISCRIMINATION IN CHILD CARE AND EDUCATION

We need to be aware of different forms of discrimination so that we can act to promote **equality**

* **Racial discrimination:** racism is the belief that some races are superior, based on the false idea that things such as skin colour make some people better than others.

  Examples: refusing a child a nursery place because they are black; failing to address the needs of children from a minority religious or cultural group, such as children from traveller families; only acknowledging festivals from the mainstream culture, such as Christmas and Easter.

* **Institutional racism:** following the Stephen Lawrence Inquiry (1999) this has been defined as 'the collective failure of an organisation to provide

an appropriate and professional service to people because of their colour, culture or ethnic origin. It can be seen or detected in processes, attitudes and behaviour which amount to discrimination through unwitting prejudice, ignorance, thoughtlessness and racist stereotyping which disadvantage minority ethnic people'. It can be difficult to detect and combat institutional racism as it tends to be integrated into an organisation's culture and practices as a result of its past history. For this reason, it is vital that all early years settings adhere to an up-to-date **policy of equal opportunities**, and that the policy is regularly monitored.

* **Disability discrimination:** children with disabilities or impairments may be denied equality of opportunity with their non-disabled peers.

   Examples: failing to provide children with special needs with appropriate facilities and services; organising activities in a nursery setting in a way that ignores the special physical, intellectual and emotional needs of certain children.

* **Sex discrimination:** this occurs when people of one gender reinforce the stereotype that they are superior to the other.

   Examples: boys are routinely offered more opportunities for rough-and-tumble play than girls; early years workers may encourage girls to perform traditional 'female' tasks such as cooking and washing.

No law can prevent prejudiced attitudes. However, the law can prohibit discriminatory practices and behaviours that flow from prejudice.

CASE STUDY

Sade

Sade (4 years) is British-born Nigerian but she has never been to Nigeria. Both Sade's parents were born in the UK and grew up there. Sade only ever eats Nigerian food at the family gatherings that happen a few times a year when relatives visit. She finds it rather hot and spicy compared with the European food that she usually eats at home and at nursery. She does not understand her key person's question about the spices her mother cooks with at home.

THE EFFECTS OF DISCRIMINATION

Children can experience discrimination in a number of ways. Discrimination can be direct or indirect:

* **Direct discrimination** occurs when a child is treated less favourably than another child in the same or similar circumstances.

   Example: when a child is bullied, by being ignored, verbally or physically abused, or teased (see also page 238 on bullying).

* **Indirect discrimination** occurs when a condition is applied that will unfairly affect a particular group of children when compared to others; this may be either deliberate or unintended.

   Example: when children from a minority ethnic or religious group (such as Sikh, Muslim or Plymouth Brethren) are required to wear a specific school uniform which causes difficulties within their cultural code.

Childminder escapes jail for racial assault on 2-year-old

A childminder who crayoned the word 'nigger' on the forehead of a 2-year-old girl in her care narrowly escaped jail after a judge accepted pleas that she was 'ignorant rather than evil'. The 57-year-old childminder made different excuses during her trial, when a jury found her guilty of aggravated racial assault. She thought up the name-crayoning as a way of entertaining a group of children she was minding at her home. She scrawled the first names of the others, who were all white, on their foreheads, but then wrote 'nigger' on the little girl's.

She first claimed that the word was a private joke between her and the girl, but then changed her story to say that she had meant to write 'Tigger,' because the child been playing the character in a game based on AA Milne's *Winnie the Pooh*.

The insult was still visible when the child returned home, and police and social workers were called in. The childminder tried to laugh the incident off when first interviewed by officers, claiming that the girl had 'pestered' her to use the word instead of her actual name, which cannot be given for legal reasons.

The recorder told her: 'You abused this girl by demonstrating the clearest hostility to her mixed race status by writing the word "nigger" . . . You told the police you only wrote the word because she asked you to and that she often referred to herself as "the little black bastard". But where did a young girl get that phrase from? This child was brought up in a climate of neglect, hostility and racial abuse, and it is clear that on this occasion when she was in your care you simply continued the abuse.'

The childminder was not registered with Ofsted as a childminder but is likely to face a social services ban on looking after children in future.

(Adapted from a news story in *The Guardian* (2005))

ACTIVITY: THE EFFECTS OF DISCRIMINATION

Read the case study above and discuss the following questions:

1 Was the 2-year-old girl a victim of *direct* or *indirect* discrimination?
2 What are the likely consequences for the child's self-esteem?

The effects of discrimination can be very obvious, such as in the case of a child whose self-esteem is seriously damaged by others' behaviour towards them. However, there can also be more subtle, less personal effects, such as the perpetuation of general misunderstandings and stereotypes. When this happens, different groups in society tend not to treat each other with proper respect.

For example, there is a prevalent stereotype that all arranged marriages are unhappy, and that love marriages are 'better'. In fact, most arranged marriages are in the modern form whereby loving parents take great care in their choice of potential partners and encourage their daughters and sons to meet to see if they like one another before they embark on marriage. The reality is that love marriages are less likely to be sanctioned and subsequently supported by the parents of those getting married, and more than one-third of love marriages end in divorce.

ACTIVITY: EXPLORING STEREOTYPES

You could arrange to carry out this activity with a group of children in Reception class. The aim is to develop children's understanding of stereotyping.

1 Present children with a choice of two videos: one is in its own bright colourful cover; the other is a very popular film inside a plain box.

2 Ask children which video they wish to watch. After viewing the selected video for 5 minutes, show the children some of the other video.

3 Repeat with two books, one of which is covered in plain brown paper. Talk to the children about what these examples tell us (you shouldn't judge a book by its cover).

CHAPTER 10

Keeping Children Safe

This chapter covers **Unit 4** and is divided into four sections:

Section 1:   Maintaining healthy, safe and secure environments

Section 2:   The procedures for dealing with accidents, illnesses and other emergencies

Section 3:   How to plan and provide an enabling physical environment for children

Section 4:   How to develop age-appropriate routines which encourage children to care for themselves

SECTION 1: MAINTAINING HEALTHY, SAFE AND SECURE ENVIRONMENTS

• Health and safety legislation • Health and safety policy • Recording mechanisms and reporting procedures • Risks/hazards • Food hygiene/ basic hygiene

HEALTH AND SAFETY LEGISLATION

There are many regulations, laws and guidelines dealing with health and safety. You don't need to know the detail, but you *do* need to know where your responsibilities begin and end. The most relevant laws relating to health and safety in the child care setting are:

* the Health and Safety at Work Act 1974;
* the Management of Health and Safety at Work Regulations 1999;
* COSHH (Control of Substances Hazardous to Health Regulations 2002);
* RIDDOR (Reporting of Injuries, Diseases and Dangerous Occurrences Regulations 1995);
* the Electricity at Work Regulations 1989;
* the Manual Handling Operations Regulations 1992;
* the Fire Precautions (Workplace) Regulations 1997;
* the Children Act 1989.

Table 10.1 Legislation etc

Legislation relevant to working with children and young people	
Health and Safety at Work Act 1974 *Employers have a duty to:* ⇨ make your workplace as safe as they are able. ⇨ display a Health and Safety Law poster or supply employees with a leaflet with the same information. This is available from the Health and Safety Executive. ⇨ decide how to manage health and safety. If the business has five or more employees, this must appear on a written Health and Safety Policy. *As an employee, you have a duty to:* ⇨ work safely. If you are given guidance about how to use equipment, you should follow that guidance. You should not work in a way that puts other people in danger. **Fire Precautions (Workplace) Regulations 1997** Fire Officers must check all childcare premises while they are in the first registration process. They will advise what is needed to make the workplace as safe as possible. ⇨ Evacuation procedures should be in place, known to all the adults, and practised regularly using all available exits at different times, so that everyone can leave the building quickly and safely if an emergency occurs.	**Control of Substances Hazardous to Health Regulations 1994 (COSHH)** Things such as bleach or dishwasher powders, some solvent glues and other materials in your setting can be hazardous. You should have a Risk Assessment that tells you what these things are, and what to do to minimise the risks involved. Any new person coming to the team must be made aware of what to do. **Reporting of Injuries, Diseases and Dangerous Occurrences Regulations 1995 (RIDDOR)** An accident book must be kept in which incidents that happen to staff are recorded. If an incident occurs at work that is serious enough to keep an employee off work for three or more days, employers will need to fill in the relevant paperwork and send the report to the Health and Safety Executive. They may investigate serious incidents and give advice on how to improve practice if needed. **Health and Safety (First Aid) Regulations 1981** Employers should make sure that at least one person at each session has an up to date first aid qualification and is the

Table 10.1 (continued)

⇨ Some exits may be locked to prevent children wandering away or intruders entering, but adults in case of an emergency must quickly open them.

⇨ Designated fire exits must always be unlocked and kept unobstructed. Fire extinguishers should be in place and checked regularly. A fire blanket is needed in the kitchen.

Health and Safety (Young Persons) Regulations 1997

In childcare workplaces there may frequently be young people on training placements or work experience. Young people are generally less safety aware than older workers as they have far less experience. Therefore, employers must conduct special **risk assessments** for people under the age of 18. These should take into account possible exposure to physical, biological and chemical hazards and outline the amount of supervision and training a young person needs to be able to carry out a particular task.

Young people may be less strong than you think as they may still be growing. For trainees under the age of 18, you should make sure that you give clear instructions and training in tasks such as lifting, carrying and using cleaning materials.

Care Standards Act 2000

The Care Standards Act sets out 14 minimum standards that childcare workplaces must meet. OfSTED inspect these each year. They produce a booklet, which employers should read and consider thoroughly, making sure that they check and maintain the guidance given. The Standards are very slightly different depending on whether you work as a childminder, in full daycare, in sessional daycare, in out of school care or in crèches. They cover the following aspects of practice:

1 Suitable person
2 Organisation
3 Care, learning and play
4 Physical environment
5 Equipment
6 Safety
7 Health
8 Food and drink
9 Equal opportunities
10 Special needs (including special education needs and disabilities)
11 Behaviour
12 Working in partnership with parents and carers
13 Child Protection
14 Documentation

'Appointed' first aider. In childcare settings regulated by OfSTED, there is also a requirement for a staff member to be trained in 'Paediatric First Aid'. Methods of dealing with incidents to adults and children are not the same, particularly where resuscitation is involved. Recommendations change. For this reason, first aid qualifications must be renewed every three years.

Food Handling Regulations 1995

If you prepare or handle food, even something as basic as opening biscuits or preparing food for a snack, you need to comply with Food Handling regulations. These cover what might be seen as common sense things:

✳ Washing your hands before preparing food
✳ Making sure the surfaces and utensils you use are clean and hygienic
✳ Making sure food is stored safely at the correct temperature
✳ Dispose of waste hygienically

But it also includes knowledge of safe practices in the use of chopping boards, having separate sinks for hand washing and preparing foods, how to lay out a kitchen and so on. There should always be people who have completed a Basic Food Hygiene certificate available to ensure guidance is properly carried out.

Personal Protective Equipment at Work Regulations 1992

Under these regulations employers must make sure that suitable protective equipment is provided for employees who are exposed to a risk to their health and safety while at work. This is considered a last resort for the risk should be prevented wherever possible. In childcare the most important piece of personal protective equipment that is provided will be gloves, to be used when dealing with body fluids.

Employees and students should be made aware of the need to use these when changing nappies or dealing with blood spillage or vomit. Good hygiene protects both adults and children.

Data Protection Act 1998

Anyone who keeps records, whether on computers or on paper, should comply with this Act. It should be clear to service users for what purpose the data is being kept. Information about a child should also be accessible to its parent/carer and shared with them. It is not necessary to do this 'on demand'. A convenient time to be able to discuss the information can be arranged. Information should not be kept for longer than necessary, though accident and incident records will need to be kept in case they are needed for reference at some time in the future. Records must also be stored securely.

Table 10.1 (continued)

Children Act 1989

The Children Act brought together several sets of guidance and provided the basis for many of the standards we maintain with children. It first outlined the amount of space that should be available as well as the adult: child ratio for work with under eights. This is based on the age of the children being cared for. The minimum ratio is set out as follows:

Age of children	Number of adults to children (ratio)
0 – 1	1 : 3
2 – 3	1 : 4
3 – 8	1 : 8

Some places have slightly different ratios depending on local conditions, such as the number of rooms used, or the location of the toilets if not directly off the main room. Local authority nursery classes and schools may also work on a ratio of one adult to 10 children where a trained teacher is in charge. Children in Reception classes or older do not have specified ratios, though 1: 6 is recommended for outings.

The Children Act also outlined some of the principles that we now take for granted:
⇨ The welfare of the child is most important.
⇨ We should work in partnership with parents.
⇨ Parents should care for their children whenever possible.
⇨ Children's opinions should be taken into account when matters concern them.

Children Act 2004

This Act was introduced following high profile enquiries into child protection (e.g. Victoria Climbie) and the introduction of the Government's Green Paper 'Every Child Matters'. As this Act affects the way you should work with other professionals to benefit children and their families it is important that you have a sound knowledge of its contents. Briefly, it states that there are 5 outcomes and 4 key themes that must be considered when working with children.

Five outcomes for children:	**Four key themes of the Children Act 2004:**
⇨ Stay Safe	⇨ Supporting parents and carers
⇨ Be Healthy	⇨ Early intervention and effective protection
⇨ Enjoy and Achieve	⇨ Accountability and integration – locally, regionally and
⇨ Achieve Economic Well-being	nationally
⇨ Make a Positive Contribution	⇨ Workforce reforms

Childcare Act 2006

The needs of children and their parents are at the heart of this Act, with local authorities as the champions of parents and children, ensuring that their views are heard in the planning and delivery of services which reflect the real needs of families. The Act:
⇨ requires **local authorities** to improve the **outcomes** of all children under 5 and close the gaps between those with the poorest outcomes and the rest, by ensuring early childhood services are integrated, proactive and accessible
⇨ places a duty giving local authorities the lead role in facilitating the childcare market to ensure it meets the needs of **working parents**, in particular those on low incomes and with disabled children
⇨ ensures people have access to the full range of **information** they may need as a parent
⇨ introduces the **Early Years Foundation Stage** – to support the delivery of quality integrated education and care for children from **birth to age 5**
⇨ leads to a reformed, simplified, childcare and early years regulation framework to reduce bureaucracy and focus on raising quality.

YOUR ROLE AND RESPONSIBILITIES

These include:

∗ taking reasonable care for your own safety and that of others;

∗ working with your employer in respect of health and safety matters;

∗ knowing about the policies and procedures in your particular place of work – these can all be found in the setting's health and safety policy;

* not intentionally damaging any health and safety equipment or materials provided by the employer;
* immediately reporting any hazards you come across;
* apart from your legal responsibilities, knowing how to act and being alert and vigilant at all times can prevent accidents, injury, infections and even death – this could be in relation to you, your fellow workers or the children in your care.

Risk Assessment

Risk assessment is a method of preventing accidents and ill health by helping people to think about what could go wrong and devising ways to prevent problems:

* look for the hazards;
* decide who might be harmed and how;
* weigh up the risk: a risk is the likelihood that a hazard will cause harm;
* decide whether existing precautions are enough;
* if not, decide what further precautions are needed to reduce risk;
* record your findings.

Reporting Illness, Injury or Accident (RIDDOR)

You have a responsibility to report all accidents, incidents and even 'near misses' to your manager. As you may be handling food, you should also report any personal incidences of sickness or diarrhoea. Most early years settings keep two separate accident report books – one for staff and other adults, and one for children. These should always be filled in as soon as possible after the incident.

HAZARDS IN CHILD CARE SETTINGS

General Safety – Slips, Trips and Falls

You'll need to check before, during and after play sessions and remove any items that prevent children – and yourself – from getting from A to B safely. Always be aware of children with special needs – for example, those with mobility problems or a visual impairment. Whenever children are playing with or near water – even indoors at the water play area – they must be constantly supervised. Babies need to be protected from falls – again, close supervision is needed. Everyone who works with children should take a recognised 'baby and child' first-aid course and should periodically take refresher courses.

Moving and Handling

Lifting and carrying children and moving the equipment used in child care settings could lead to manual handling injuries such as sprains and strains.

If you do have to lift something or somebody from the ground, you should follow these rules:

* keep your feet apart;
* bend your knees and keep your back upright;
* use both hands to get a secure hold;
* keep your shoulders level, your back upright and slowly straighten your legs;
* to put the load down, take the weight on the legs by bending your knees.

COSHH – Control of Substances Hazardous to Health Regulations

Safe workplaces depend on the careful use and storage of cleaning materials and other potentially hazardous substances. Every workplace must have a COSHH file which lists all the hazardous substances used in the setting. The file should detail:

* where they are kept;
* how they are labelled;
* their effects;
* the maximum amount of time it is safe to be exposed to them;
* how to deal with an emergency involving one of them;
* never mix products together: they could produce toxic fumes. Some bleaches and cleaning products, for instance, have this effect.

Infection Control

Children who play closely together for long periods of time are more likely than others to develop an infection – and any infection can spread very quickly from one child to another and to adults who care for them. Your setting's health and safety policy will establish procedures to reduce the risk of transferring infectious diseases. These include:

* providing staff members and parents with information on infection control policies and procedures;
* stating the exclusion criteria that will apply when a child or a staff member is sick;
* providing training for staff members so that they understand and can use the infection control procedures;
* providing adequate supervision to make sure everyone follows the policies and procedures;

* providing adequate supplies of protective equipment;
* providing adequate facilities for hand-washing, cleaning and disposing of waste;
* providing safe work practices for high-risk activities, such as dealing with blood and body fluids, nappy changing and toileting, handling dirty linen and contaminated clothing and preparing and handling food;
* policies relating to health and safety issues.

All early years settings *must* have a written policy for dealing with health and safety issues. The guidelines below include points which are often part of the policy document.

Guidelines for addressing health and hygiene issues

* Always wear disposable gloves when dealing with blood, urine, faeces or vomit.
* Always wash your hands after dealing with spillages – even if gloves have been worn.
* Use a dilute bleach (hypochlorite) solution to mop up any spillages; (or product specified by your setting's policy).
* Make sure that paper tissues are available for children to use.
* Always cover cuts and open sores with adhesive plasters.
* Food must be stored and prepared hygienically.
* Ask parents to keep their children at home if they are feeling unwell or if they have an infection.
* Children who are sent home with vomiting or diarrhoea must

remain at home until at least 24 hours have elapsed since the last attack.

✳ Parents must provide written authorisation for child care workers to administer medications to children.

Guidelines for disposing of waste

✳ Staff should *always* wear disposable gloves when handling any bodily waste, i.e. blood, urine, vomit and faeces. Always dispose of the gloves and wash your hands after dealing with such waste, even though gloves have been worn.

✳ A dilute bleach (hypochlorite) solution should be used to mop up any spillages.

✳ Different types of waste should be kept in separate covered bins in designated areas; food waste should be kept well away from toilet waste.

✳ Soiled nappies, dressings, disposable towels and gloves should be placed in a sealed bag before being put in a plastic-lined, covered bin for incineration.

✳ Always cover any cuts and open sores with waterproof adhesive plasters.

HYGIENE AND HEALTH

Providing a healthy and hygienic environment for children is vital to their development. A balance also has to be struck where a child is allowed to get dirty when playing, but understands that they will need to wash afterwards. Developing good hygiene routines is important because:

✳ It helps to prevent infection and the spread of disease. Children who play closely together for long periods of time are more likely than others to develop an infection – and any infection can spread very quickly from one child to another.

✳ Being clean increases self-esteem and social acceptance. Nobody likes to be close to someone who appears dirty or whose clothes smell.

✳ It helps to prepare children in skills of independence and self-caring. All children benefit from regular routines in daily care. Obviously, parents and carers have their own routines and hygiene practices and these should always be respected. (For example, Muslims prefer to wash under running water and Rastafarians wear their hair braided so may not use a comb or brush.)

Being a Good Role Model

You need to set a good example by always taking care with your appearance and your own personal hygiene. Often your early years setting will provide you with a uniform – usually sweatshirt and trousers – but if not, choose your clothing carefully, bearing in mind the sort of activity you are likely to be involved in.

Guidelines: Personal hygiene: being a good role model

Personal hygiene involves regular and thorough cleaning of your skin, hair, teeth and clothes. The following are particularly important:

✳ The most important defence against the spread of infection is hand-washing; wash your hands frequently – especially before eating, and before and after touching your mouth or nose. You should not use the kitchen sink to wash your hands.

* Parents and carers must wash their hands after they blow the nose or wipe the mouth of a sick child.

* Use paper towels to dry your hands if possible; if cloth towels are used, make sure they are washed daily in hot water.

* Keep your nails clean and short as long finger nails harbour dirt. Don't wear nail varnish because flakes of varnish *could* chip off into the snack you are preparing.

* Avoid jewellery other than a simple wedding ring and a watch.

* Avoid contact with the secretions (especially on stray facial tissues) of somebody with a runny nose, sore throat or cough.

* Cover any cuts or sores on the hands with a clean, waterproof plaster. Use a new plaster each day.

* Don't share utensils or cups with somebody who has a cold, sore throat or upper respiratory tract infection.

* Wear disposable gloves when changing nappies or when dealing with blood, urine, faeces or vomit.

* Hair should be kept clean, be brushed regularly and be tied back, if long.

Providing a Safe, Hygienic Indoor Environment

Children need a clean, warm and hygienic environment in order to stay healthy. Although most large early years settings employ a cleaner, there will be many occasions when you have to take responsibility for ensuring that the environment is kept clean and safe; for example if a child has been sick or has had a toileting accident.

All early years settings should have set routines for tidying up and for cleaning the floors, walls, furniture and play equipment; details may be found in the setting's written policy for health and hygiene issues.

Guidelines for providing a safe and hygienic indoor environment

1 **Adequate ventilation** is important to disperse bacteria or viruses transmitted through sneezing or coughing. Make sure that windows are opened to let in fresh air to the nursery – but also make sure there are no draughts.

2 Cleaning routines:

* All surfaces should be damp dusted daily. Floors, surfaces and the toilet area must be checked on a regular basis for cleanliness.

* All toys and play equipment should be cleaned regularly – *at least* once a week. This includes dressing-up clothes and soft toys. Use antiseptic solutions such as Savlon to disinfect toys and play equipment regularly; toys used by babies under 1 year should be disinfected daily.

* Check that sandpits or trays are clean and that toys are removed and cleaned at the end of a play session; if the sand pit is kept outside, make sure it is kept covered when not in use. Keep sand trays clean by sieving and washing the sand regularly.

* Water trays should be emptied daily, as germs can multiply quickly in pools of water.

* The home area often contains dolls, saucepans and plastic food; these need to be included in the checking and in the regular wash.

* As well as routine cleaning, you should always clean up any spills straight away; both young children and adults often slip on wet surfaces.

4 Use paper towels and tissues, and dispose of them in covered bins.

5 Remove from the nursery any toy that has been in contact with a child who has an infectious illness.

6 Throw out any plastic toys that have cracks or splits in them, as these cracks can harbour germs.

7 Particular care should be taken to keep hats, head coverings and hairbrushes clean, in order to help prevent the spread of head lice.

8 Animals visiting the nursery or nursery pets must be free from disease, safe to be with children and must not pose a health risk. Children should *always* be supervised when handling animals, and make sure they always wash their hands after touching any pet.

9 A 'no smoking' policy must be observed by staff and visitors.

Providing a Safe and Hygienic Outdoor Environment

Children benefit from playing in the fresh air, as long as they are dressed for the weather. All early years settings should be checked regularly to make sure that a safe and hygienic environment is being provided.

Guidelines for ensuring a hygienic outdoor environment

* Check the outdoor play area daily for litter, dog excrement and hazards such as broken glass, syringes or rusty cans.

* Follow the sun safety code: provide floppy hats and use sun cream (SPF 15) to prevent sunburn (if parents give their permission).

* Check all play equipment for splinters, jagged edges, protruding nails and other hazards.

* Supervise children at all times.

* Keep sand covered and check regularly for insects, litter and other contamination.

* Keep gates locked and check that hinges are secure.

SAFETY AND SECURITY

One of the cornerstones of early childhood care and education is to offer an exciting range of experiences to children, which will stimulate them and extend their skills in all areas of development. As they grow, you need to be responsive to their changing safety needs at each stage of development.

Close supervision is the most effective way of ensuring children's safety.

Supervising Children's Safety

The most important thing to remember when caring for children is to treat each child as an individual – with individual needs. Babies' and young children's abilities will differ over time; it may be surprising when they do things for the first time but you should be able to anticipate, adapt and avoid dangerous situations in order to maintain their safety and security. In particular, babies have no awareness of danger and are therefore totally dependent on their carers for protection and survival. Appropriate levels of supervision, provided by you, are therefore essential.

Example: Babies under 1 year old are able to wriggle, grasp, suck and roll over and are naturally curious. Toddlers, too, can move very quickly, so accidents often happen in seconds. As children get older and their physical skills increase, they are better able to explore their environment, which means they are more likely to have knocks and bruises and you need to ensure that they can play in safety.

It's not just broken or damaged equipment and toys that can be a risk to children's safety. You need to make sure that the activity or plaything a child uses is suitable for them; this means that the child is at the right stage of development to be able to play safely with the toy.

Special needs: children with special needs *may* need specialised equipment and playthings in order to participate safely in the daily activities in any child care setting; more often, they just need to have very slight changes made to the environment. For example, a child with physical difficulties might benefit from having Velcro straps attached to the pedals of a bike.

Providing a safe and secure environment for children also involves:

* ensuring that the environment and equipment is checked for safety;

* knowing how to maintain the environment to ensure safety for children;

* knowing why accidents happen and how to prevent them;

* encouraging children to be aware of their own safety and the safety of others;

* knowing about safety issues when taking children out of the setting;

* checking the environment and equipment for safety.

* Doors, gates and windows should be appropriately fastened to ensure the safety of the children. Any nursery or playgroup must be secure so that children cannot just wander off without anyone realising; there should also be a policy which guards against strangers being able to wander in without reason.

* Many early years settings now have door entry phones, and staff wear name badges or identifiable uniform. Be sure to challenge, politely, anyone who is unfamiliar to you in the setting or gives you cause for suspicion as to why they are there, and keep a record of any visitors.

* Access points and fire exits must be unobstructed at all times.

* Play equipment: all equipment used for children's play should be checked routinely and any damaged items should be removed from the scene and reported to your supervisor. You will be expected to check for objects which stick out on equipment and could cut a child or cause clothing to become entangled, e.g. screws or bolts on trucks or playground equipment. Plastic toys and equipment can be checked for splits and cracks when you clean them. Check wooden equipment, such as wooden blocks or wheeled carts for splinters and rough edges.

* Sandpits: check that sandpits are covered overnight or brought indoors to prevent contamination

from animals, such as cats. You should also check that no hazardous litter is in the sand – such as sharp sticks, broken glass or insects.

* Safe storage: sharp objects, such as scissors and knives, must be stored out of children's reach – scissors used for craft work should be children's safety scissors – and remember to remove knives from tables where children might grab them.

* Water: check that buckets or bowls of water are never left where children could trip into them, as children can drown in water that is only a few inches deep. If there is open water, such as a pond, drains or a pool, at or near to the setting, make sure they are made safe and inaccessible to children, and that children are closely supervised at all times when playing with or near water.

* Electrical equipment: most early years settings have a variety of electrical equipment – including TV, video, tape recorder and a computer. You need to check that the electric sockets are covered with socket covers when not in use and that there are no trailing wires on the floor or where children could grab them.

* Outdoor safety: before outdoor play sessions, you must check that surfaces are safe to play on – for example, not icy or slippery – and that objects which could cause children harm have been removed. Also ensure that children are properly equipped for outdoor play. They should always be dressed according to the weather,

with waterproof coats and wellington boots in wet weather and warm hats and gloves on in cold weather. You also need to ensure that children are protected against strong sun – by following the Sun Safety Code. Children playing outside should be supervised at all times.

RISKS AND HAZARDS

On a day-to-day basis, you need to be alert to the changing abilities and safety needs of children and also to identify and address hazards in the child care setting. Your employer will do this on a formal basis, carrying out a health and safety risk assessment. To ensure children's safety, you need to be able to:

* **identify a hazard:** at every stage of a child's life, you must think again about the hazards that are present and what you can do to eliminate them. This could be play equipment left on the floor, obstructing an exit – or small

Fig 10.1 Sun Safety Code

items which have been left within reach of a baby;

* **be aware of the child's interaction with the environment:** this means understanding the different stages of child development – for example, babies explore objects with their mouths and run the risk of choking – and young children tend to run everywhere and could trip over toys on the floor;

* **provide adequate supervision,** according to each child's age, needs and abilities;

* **be a good role model:** ensuring that the child's environment is kept safe and that you follow the setting's health and safety guidelines;

* **know how to use the safety equipment provided,** e.g. safety gates, window locks, baby harnesses and security intercom systems;

* **teach children about safety:** encourage children to be aware of their own personal safety and the safety of others.

FOOD HYGIENE

Good food hygiene is essential for the prevention of food poisoning; young children are particularly vulnerable to the bacteria which cause gastro-enteritis or food poisoning.

How Bacteria Enter Food

Bacteria can enter food without causing the food to look, smell or even taste bad. Bacteria thrive in warm, moist foods, especially those rich in protein, such as meat and poultry (both cooked and raw), seafood, gravy, soup, cooked rice, milk, cream and egg dishes. Harmful bacteria multiply rapidly, dividing into two every 10–20 minutes, and soon build up a colony of thousands that will cause poisoning. To live and grow, bacteria must have:

* food – especially the foods mentioned above;

* **moisture:** fresh foods are more susceptible to bacterial contamination than dried foods;

* **warmth:** bacteria thrive best at body temperature (37 °C);

* **time:** bacteria reproduce rapidly in warm, moist food.

The Prevention of Food Poisoning

Guidelines for safe storage of food

* Keep food cold. The fridge should be kept as cold as it will go without actually freezing the food (1–5°C or 34–41°F). To be safe, use a fridge thermometer and open the door as few times as possible.

* Cool food quickly before placing in the fridge.

* Cover or wrap food with food wrap or microwave cling film.

* Store raw foods at the bottom so that juices cannot drip onto cooked food.

* Freezers must be at a low enough temperature (21°C or 0°F maximum).

* Never refreeze food that has begun to thaw.

* Label each item with the use-by date.

* Thaw frozen meat completely before cooking.

Guidelines for safe preparation and cooking of food

* Always wash hands using warm water and soap, and dry on a clean towel. Do this: before handling food; after using the toilet; after touching raw food; after coughing into your hands; after using a hankie; and after touching your face or hair.
* Never cough or sneeze over food.
* Always cover any cuts or boils with a waterproof dressing.
* Never smoke in any room that is used for food – apart from being unhygienic, it is illegal.
* Keep clean, and wear clean protective clothing that is solely for use in the kitchen.
* Cook food thoroughly.
* Eggs should be cooked so that both the yolk and the white are firm.
* Chicken must be tested to ensure that it is thoroughly cooked.
* Joints of meat and mince dishes must be cooked right through.
* Avoid cook–chill foods, which need very careful handling.
* Avoid eating leftovers – they are a common cause of food poisoning.
* Do not reheat food – even if it appears wasteful not to.
* Do not reheat food using a microwave oven.
* Do not use a microwave oven to heat babies' bottles.
* Always follow instructions for cooking using a microwave oven and include 'standing' time to avoid burns.
* Keep the oven clean.

Guidelines for maintaining a safe kitchen

* Keep the kitchen clean – the floor, work surfaces, sink, utensils, cloths and waste bins should be cleaned regularly.
* Clean tin-openers, graters and mixers thoroughly after use.
* Tea towels should be boiled every day, and dishcloths boiled or disinfected.
* Keep flies and other insects away – use a fine mesh over open windows.
* Keep pets away from the kitchen.
* Keep all waste bins covered, and empty them regularly.
* Stay away from the kitchen if you are suffering from diarrhoea or sickness.

Food-Poisoning Bacteria

Several types of bacteria can cause food poisoning (see Table 10.2), including the following:

* *salmonella*;
* *clostridium botulinum*;
* *staphylococcus*;
* *clostridium welchii*;
* *listeria*.

PREVENTING ACCIDENTS

Accidents are the most common cause of death in children aged between 1 and 14 years, accounting for half of all child deaths:

* Three children are killed in accidents every day.
* 10,000 children are permanently disabled each year.

Table 10.2 Food poisoning bacteria

Bacteria	Typically found in	Symptoms	To reduce risk
Salmonella	Meat, poultry, raw eggs, meat pies and pasties, left-over food, unpasteurised milk	Starts suddenly 12 to 14 hours after eating: nausea, vomiting, abdominal pain and headache	Good personal hygiene; cook eggs well; avoid cross-infection from raw to cooked foods; cook food thoroughly
Clostridium welchii	Meat, poultry, meat dishes, left-over food, gravy	Starts 8 to 18 hours after eating: diarrhoea, abdominal pain, but no fever. Lasts 12 to 24 hours	Cook food thoroughly; heat to 100°C
Listeria	Chilled foods, e.g. soft cheeses and meat pâté	Starts 5 to 30 days after eating: 1 in 4 cases fatal; miscarriage, blood poisoning, meningitis. Babies especially at risk	Avoid high-risk foods; avoid storing chilled foods for long periods; ensure proper reheating
Clostridium botulinum	Canned food not heated properly at time of canning; raw fish	Starts 12 to 36 hours after eating: often fatal; double vision, breathing difficulties	Avoid damaged or 'blown' cans; avoid keeping vacuum-packed fish in warm temperatures
Staphylococcus	Food that needs careful handling; custards and creams, cold desserts, sandwiches, unpasteurised milk	Starts 1 to 6 hours after eating: abdominal cramps, vomiting. Lasts up to 24 hours	Good personal hygiene; avoid coughing and sneezing over food; avoid cross-infection from raw to cooked food; heat to 70°C for 15 minutes

* Each year, one in six children attend accident and emergency departments.
* The pattern of accidents tends to vary with age, depending on the child's developmental progress and exposure to new hazards.

Why do Accidents Happen?

Babies are vulnerable to accidents because they have no awareness of danger and cannot control their environment; they are totally dependent on their parents or carers to make their world safe. Children are naturally curious and need to investigate their surroundings. As children get older and their memory develops, they start to realise that certain actions have certain consequences (for example, touching a hot oven door hurts), and so they begin to learn a measure of self-protection. Carers of young children need to have a sound knowledge of child development in order to anticipate when an accident is likely to happen. Carers also have a duty to make the home, car and child care setting safer places, and should know where to go for advice and equipment.

Situations When Accidents are More Likely to Happen

* **Stress:** when adults and children are worried or anxious, they are less alert and less aware of possible dangers.
* **Lack of awareness:** parents tend to react to an existing threat of danger, rather than to anticipate things that may

happen. For example, parents may report that they had not realised their child could even climb onto a stool, so had not thought to remove the dangerous object.

* **Overprotection:** a child whose parents are overprotective may become timid and will be less aware of dangers when unsupervised.

* **Poor role models:** adults who are always in a hurry may dash across the road instead of crossing in a safe place. Children will imitate their actions, and are less able to judge the speed of traffic.

* **Underprotection:** children under 7 should never be left alone in a house, not even when they are apparently safely asleep. Children who are underprotected generally have not been made aware of dangers, and their natural curiosity leads to dangerous play activities.

Guidelines for preventing accidents

1 Be a good role model – set a safe example.

2 Make the home, garden and child care setting as accident proof as possible.

3 Teach children about safety – make them aware of dangers in their environment.

4 Never leave children alone in the house.

5 Always try to buy goods displaying the appropriate safety symbol:

* The Kite Mark (see Fig 10.2(a)). This mark on any product means that the British Standards Institution (BSI) has

checked the manufacturer's claim that its product meets specific standards.

* The new safety sign (BSI Safety Mark) (see Fig 10.2(b)). The safety mark means that a product has been checked to ensure that it meets the requirements of the BSI for safety only.

* The Lion Mark (see Fig 10.2(c)). This symbol is only found on British-made toys and means that they have met the safety standards required.

* The age advice safety symbol (see Fig 10.2(d)). This symbol means 'Warning: do not give the toy to children of less than 3 years, or allow them to play with it'.

NB Toys and games bought from market stalls, and cheap foreign imports may be copies of well-known brand-name toys but may not meet the safety standards.

Preventing Accidents in the Home and in Child Care Settings

Guidelines for preventing choking and suffocation

Choking followed by suffocation is the largest cause of accidental death in babies under 1 year; and older children are also at risk when playing on their own or eating unsupervised.

* Do not leave rattles, teething rings or squeeze toys in the baby's cot; they can become wedged in the baby's mouth and cause suffocation.

* Do not use a pillow for babies under 1 year old. Baby nests must

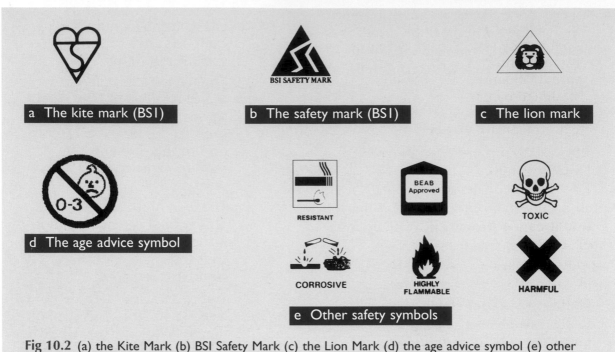

a The kite mark (BSI)　　b The safety mark (BSI)　　c The lion mark

d The age advice symbol

0-3

RESISTANT　　BEAB Approved　　TOXIC

CORROSIVE　　HIGHLY FLAMMABLE　　HARMFUL

e Other safety symbols

Fig 10.2 (a) the Kite Mark (b) BSI Safety Mark (c) the Lion Mark (d) the age advice symbol (e) other safety symbols

meet British Standard 6595 and have a flat head area. Baby nests should be used only for carrying a baby – not for leaving a sleeping baby unattended.

* Do not let a baby or young child get hold of tiny items such as coins, marbles, dried peas, buttons or Lego; small children explore with their mouths and can easily choke on small objects.

* Do not leave babies alone with finger foods such as bananas, carrots, cheese and so on. Always supervise eating and drinking.

* Do not give peanuts to children under 4 years because they can easily choke on them or inhale them into their lungs, causing infection and lung damage.

* Do not leave a baby alone propped-up with a bottle – always hold the baby while feeding.

* Do supervise a baby who is playing with paper, as she may bite off small pieces and choke on them.

* Do use a firm mattress that meets British Standard 1877. For children over 1 year old, use a pillow that meets the same standard for allowing air to pass through freely, whatever position the baby is in.

* Do check that there are no hanging cords – for example, from a window blind – which could catch around a child's neck and strangle them if they fall.

* Do keep all plastic bags away from babies and children, and teach older children never to put plastic bags on their heads.

* Do be aware that dummies on long ribbons, and cardigans with ribbons around the neck can pull tight around a baby's neck if caught on a hook or knob; a

dummy must meet safety standards with holes in the flange, in case it is drawn into the back of the throat. Older children have been strangled by tie-cords on anoraks.

* Do check that any toys given to babies and young children are safe, with no small, loose parts or jagged edges.

Guidelines for preventing burns and scalds

As children learn to crawl, climb and walk, the risk of scalds or burns increases.

* Do not leave burning cigarettes in ashtrays.

* Do not use tablecloths which young children can pull down on top of themselves.

* Do not use gas or paraffin heaters in children's bedrooms.

* Do not leave a hose lying in the sun; water in it can get hot enough to scald a baby.

* Do not leave a hot iron unattended.

* Do not iron where children are likely to run past, and try to use a coiled flex.

* Do keep the water temperature for the house set at about 60°C (140°F), to prevent scalds and burns.

* Do protect fires with a fixed, fine-mesh fireguard. Note that it is illegal to leave a child under 12 in a room with an open fire.

* Do keep matches and lighters well out of reach.

* Do choose night clothes and dressing gowns that are flame-resistant.

* Do install automatic smoke alarms.

* Do use fire doors in nurseries and schools; and check that you know the location of fire extinguishers and fire blankets.

* Do keep children away from bonfires and fireworks. Attend safe, public displays.

* Do keep a young child away from your area while you are cooking; always turn pan handles inwards; cooker guards are not a good idea, as they can get very hot.

* Do keep kettles and hot drinks well out of reach; use a coiled kettle flex, and never pass hot drinks over the heads of children.

* Do test bath water before putting a child in; always put cold water in first and then add the hot water. A special plastic-strip thermometer can be stuck to the side of the bath to check the temperature.

* Do teach children about the dangers of fire.

Guidelines for preventing falls

All children fall, but there are ways of ensuring that they do not fall too far or too hard.

* Do not use baby-walkers. Child-safety experts agree that these are dangerous and cause many accidents, as babies steer themselves into dangerous situations.

* Do not place furniture under windows where children may be tempted to climb.

* Do not leave babies unattended on a table, work surface, bed or sofa; lie them on the floor instead.

* Do use stair gates at the top and the bottom of stairs and at doors which might be left open

* Do fit vertical bars to dangerous windows (note: horizontal bars encourage climbing).

* Do fit child-proof window safety catches on all windows.

* Do use a safety harness in the highchair, pram, pushchair or supermarket trolley.

* Do teach children how to use the stairs safely; teach them to come down stairs backwards, on all fours.

* Do ensure that older children wear safety helmets when riding bikes or using skateboards or roller blades.

Guidelines for preventing poisoning

The peak age for accidents with poisons is 1–3 years old, when children are highly mobile and inquisitive.

* Do not store dangerous household chemicals – e.g. bleach, disinfectant, white spirit – in the cupboard under the sink. Use a safer, locked cupboard instead.

* Do not transfer chemicals – e.g. weed killer – into other containers such as lemonade bottles, as a child will not know the difference until it is too late.

* Do keep all medicines in a locked cupboard.

* Do use child-proof containers and ensure that they are closed properly.

* Do teach children not to eat berries or fungi in the garden or in the park.

* Do keep rubbish and kitchen waste in a tightly covered container or, better still, behind a securely locked door.

* Do make sure that if surma is used on a child's eyes it is a lead-free brand. (Surma, or kohl, is a preparation used as eye shadow in some Asian cultures.) Check with a pharmacist.

* Do store children's vitamins in a safe place. Poisoning by an overdose of vitamins is very common.

Guidelines for preventing cuts

Glass presents the biggest safety hazard to young children; every year, about 7,000 children end up in hospital after being cut by glass.

* Do use special safety glass in doors; this is relatively harmless if it does break, whereas ordinary glass breaks into sharp, jagged pieces.

* Do mark large picture windows with coloured strips to make it obvious when they are closed.

* Do use plastic drinking cups and bottles.

* Do keep all knives, scissors and razors out of reach.

* Do teach children never to run with a pencil or lolly stick in their mouth.

* Do use safety scissors when cutting paper and card

* Do teach children never to play with doors; if possible, fit a device to the top of doors to prevent them from slamming and pinching fingers.

Guidelines for preventing drowning

A baby or toddler can drown in a very shallow amount of water – even a bucket with a few inches of water in it presents a risk. If a small child's face goes underwater, they will automatically breathe in so that they can scream. This action will fill their lungs with water.

* **Do not** ever leave a child alone in the bath.
* **Do not** leave an older child looking after a baby or toddler in the bath.
* **Do** use a non-slip mat in the bath.
* **Do** always supervise water play.
* **Do** guard ponds, water butts and ditches.
* **Do** keep the toilet lid down at all times or fit a locking device; toddlers are fascinated by the swirling water action, and can fall in and drown.
* **Do** encourage children to learn to swim.

Guidelines for preventing electric shocks

Children may suffer electric shock from poking small objects into sockets or from playing with electric plugs.

* **Do** fit safety dummy plugs or socket covers to all electric sockets.
* **Do** check that plugs are correctly wired and safe.
* **Do** prevent children from pulling at electric cords, by installing a cord holder which will make the cord too short to reach over the edge of the table or work surface.

Guidelines for sun safety

* **Do not** let children run around in only a swimsuit or without any clothes on.
* **Do not** let children play in the sun between 11a.m. and 3p.m., when the sun is highest and most dangerous.
* **Do** keep babies under the age of 9 months out of the sun altogether.
* **Do** cover children in loose, baggy cotton clothes, such as an oversized T-shirt with sleeves. Some special fabrics have a sun protection factor.
* **Do** protect a child's shoulders and back of neck when playing, as these are the most common areas for sunburn: let a child wear a 'legionnaire's hat' or a floppy hat with a wide brim that shades the face and neck.
* **Do** cover exposed parts of the child's skin with a sunscreen, even on cloudy or overcast days. Use one with a minimum sun protection factor (SPF) of 15 and reapply often.
* **Do** use waterproof sun block if the child is swimming.

Guidelines for ensuring safety in the child care setting

* Children should be supervised at all times.
* Premises must be large enough, and – in early years settings – should provide a separate area for the care of babies and toddlers.
* The nursery environment, and all materials and equipment,

should be maintained in a safe condition.

* Low-level glass (e.g. in doors and cupboards) should be safety glass or must be covered with boarding or guards; sharp corners on low-level furniture should be padded.

* There must be adequate first aid facilities and staff should be trained in basic first aid.

* Routine safety checks should be made daily on the premises, both indoors and outdoors.

* Fire drills should be held twice a term in schools and nurseries and every 6 weeks in day nurseries. Fire exits must be left accessible and unlocked at all times.

* Electric sockets should be covered.

* Floor surfaces should be clean and free of splinters.

* Access should be easy for prams, pushchairs and wheelchairs.

* Kitchen facilities must be adequate in terms of hygiene, storage and safety.

* Children should only be allowed home with a parent or authorised adult.

SECTION 2: THE PROCEDURES FOR DEALING WITH ACCIDENTS, ILLNESSES AND OTHER EMERGENCIES

• Identify accidents, emergencies and signs of illness
• Following appropriate procedures • Providing appropriate comfort and reassurance • Cross infection and its prevention • Establishing healthy and safe routines • Emergency procedures e.g. fire, missing children, evacuation • Notification of illness

RECOGNISING GENERAL SIGNS OF ILLNESS IN BABIES AND CHILDREN

Small children are not always able to explain their symptoms, and may display non-specific complaints such as headache, sleeplessness, vomiting or an inability to stand up. Babies have even less certain means of communication, and may simply cry in a different way, refuse feeds or become listless and lethargic. In most infectious illnesses, there will be fever.

Signs and Symptoms

* **Signs** of illness are those that can be observed directly, for example a change in skin colour, a rash or a swelling.

* **Symptoms** of illness are those experienced by the child, for example pain, discomfort or generally feeling unwell. Detection of symptoms relies on the child being able to describe how they are feeling.

Identifying Signs of Illness in Children with Different Skin Tones

Both within and between different ethnic groups there is a wide variety of skin tones and colours affecting the way skin looks during illness. When dark-skinned children are ill they may show the following signs:

* **Skin appearance:** normal skin tone and sheen may be lost; the skin may appear dull and paler or greyer than usual. You must pay attention to those parts of the body with less pigmentation – the palms, the tongue, the nails beds and the conjunctiva (the insides of the bottom eyelids) – all of these will be paler than usual.

* **Rashes:** in children with very dark skin, raised rashes are more obvious than flat rashes.
* **Bruising:** the discoloration that is obvious in pale skin may not be easily observed in darker-skinned children. When bruised, the skin may appear darker or more purple when compared with surrounding skin.
* **Jaundice:** in a fair-skinned child, gently press your finger to his forehead, nose, or chest, and look for a yellow tinge to the skin as the pressure is released. In a darker-skinned child, check for yellowness in his gums or the whites of his eyes.

Recognising Illness in Babies

The responsibility of caring for a baby who becomes ill is enormous; it is vital that carers should know the signs and symptoms of illness and when to seek medical aid.

What You Should Do

* **Observe the baby carefully** and note any changes; record his or her temperature and take steps to reduce a high temperature.
* **Give extra fluids** if possible, and carry out routine skin care. The baby may want extra physical attention or prefer to rest in his cot.

Table 10.3 Common signs of illness in babies

Raised temperature or fever	Refusing feeds or loss of appetite
The baby may look flushed or be pale, but will feel hot to the touch (black babies and those with dark skin tones may look paler than usual and the eyes may lose sparkle). Occasionally a high temperature may trigger a seizure (fit) or febrile convulsion.	A young baby may refuse milk feeds or take very little. An older baby may only want milk feeds and refuse all solids.
Diarrhoea	**Vomiting**
Persistent loose, watery or green stools can quickly dehydrate a baby. Dehydration means that the baby is losing important body salts.	This may be persistent or projectile (i.e. so forceful that it is projected several feet from the baby) – more violent than the usual **possetting**.
Excessive and persistent crying	**Lethargy or floppiness**
If the baby cannot be comforted in the usual way or if the cry is very different from usual cries.	The baby may appear to lack energy and does not exhibit the normal muscle tone.
Dry nappies	**Persistent coughing**
If the baby's nappies are much drier than usual because he or she has not passed urine, this can indicate **dehydration**.	Coughing in spasms lasting more than a few seconds. Long spasms often end with vomiting.
Difficulty with breathing	**Discharge from the ears**
If breathing becomes difficult or noisy with a cough, the baby may have bronchitis or croup.	Ear infections may not show as a discharge, but babies may pull at their ears and may have a high temperature.
Sunken anterior fontanelle	**Seizures (also called convulsions or fits)**
A serious sign of **dehydration**, possibly after diarrhoea and vomiting. The anterior fontanelle is a diamond-shaped 'soft spot' at the front of the head just above the brow. In dehydrated babies, this area is sunken and more visible.	During a seizure the baby either goes stiff or jerks their arms or legs for a period lasting up to several minutes. The eyes may roll upwards; the skin and lips become blue; the baby may dribble and will be unresponsive to you.

Meningitis in Babies

Meningitis is an inflammation of the lining of the brain. It is a very serious illness, but if it's detected and treated early, most children make a full recovery. The early symptoms of meningitis – such as fever, irritability, restlessness, vomiting and refusing feeds – are also common with colds and 'flu. However, a baby with meningitis can become seriously ill within hours, so it is important to act quickly if meningitis is suspected.

Symptoms of Meningitis

In **babies under 12 months**:

* tense or bulging **fontanelles**;
* high temperature;
* a stiffening body with involuntary movements, or a floppy body;
* may be difficult to wake;
* blotchy or pale skin;
* may refuse to feed;
* a high-pitched, moaning cry;
* red or purple spots (anywhere on the body) that do not fade under pressure. Do the 'glass test' – see below.

In **older children**:

* headache;
* neck stiffness and joint pains; the child may arch the neck backwards because of the rigidity of the neck muscles;
* an inability to tolerate light;
* fever.

The 'Glass Test'

Press the side or bottom of a glass firmly against the rash – you will be able to see if the rash fades and loses colour under the pressure. If it *doesn't* change colour, summon medical aid immediately. If spots are appearing on the child's body, this could be septicaemia, a very serious bacterial infection described as the 'meningitis rash'.

General Signs and Symptoms of Illness in Children

When children feel generally unwell, you should ask them if they have any pain or discomfort and treat it appropriately. Take their temperature and look for other signs of illness, such as a rash or swollen glands. Often, feeling generally unwell is the first sign that the child is developing an infectious disease. Some children can also show general signs of illness if they are anxious or worried about something, either at home or at school.

Emotional and Behavioural Changes

Children react in certain characteristic ways when they are unwell. Some of the more common emotional and behavioural changes include:

1 being quieter than usual;
2 becoming more clingy to their parents or primary carer;
3 attention-seeking behaviour;
4 changed sleeping patterns; some children sleep more than usual, others less;
5 lack of energy;
6 crying: babies cry for a variety of reasons (see Unit 18 on CD-ROM). Older children who cry more than usual may be physically unwell or you may need to explore the reasons for their unhappiness;
7 regression: children who are unwell often regress in their development and behaviour. They may:

* want to be carried everywhere instead of walking independently;
* go back to nappies after being toilet-trained;
* start to wet the bed;
* play with familiar, previously outgrown toys.

Common Signs and Symptoms of Illness in Children

* **Loss of appetite:** the child may not want to eat or drink; this could be because of a sore, painful throat or a sign of a developing infection.
* **Lacking interest in play:** he may not want to join in play, without being able to explain why.
* **Abdominal pain:** the child may rub his or her tummy and say that it hurts – this could be a sign of gastro-enteritis.
* **Raised temperature (fever):** a fever (a temperature above 38 °C) is usually an indication of viral or bacterial infection, but can also result from overheating.
* **Diarrhoea and vomiting:** attacks of diarrhoea and/or vomiting are usually a sign of gastro-enteritis.
* **Lethargy or listlessness:** the child may be drowsy and prefer to sit quietly with a favourite toy or comfort blanket.
* **Irritability and fretfulness:** the child may have a change in behaviour, being easily upset and tearful.
* **Pallor:** the child will look paler than usual and may have dark shadows under the eyes; a black child may have a paler area around the lips and the conjunctiva may be pale pink instead of the normal dark pink.
* **Rash:** any rash appearing on the child's body should be investigated – it is usually a sign of an infectious disease.

High Temperature (Fever)

The normal body temperature is between 36°C and 37°C. A temperature of above 37.5°C means that the child has a fever. Common sense and using the back of your hand to feel the forehead of an ill child are almost as reliable in detecting a fever as using a thermometer.

A child with a fever may:

* look hot and flushed; the child may complain of feeling cold and might shiver. This is a natural reflex due to the increased heat loss and a temporary disabling of the usual internal temperature control of the brain;
* be either irritable or subdued;
* be unusually sleepy;
* go off their food;
* complain of thirst.

Children can develop high temperatures very quickly. You need to know how to bring their temperature down, to avoid complications such as dehydration and febrile convulsions.

How to Take a Temperature

All family first aid kits should contain a thermometer. There are three types: clinical thermometer; digital thermometer; and plastic fever strips

Clinical Thermometer

This is a glass tube with a bulb at one end containing mercury. This tube is marked with gradations of temperature in degrees Centigrade and/or Fahrenheit. When the bulb end is placed under the child's armpit, the mercury will expand, moving up the tube until the temperature of the child's body is reached.

Table 10.4 Illness in babies

Condition (and cause)	Signs and symptoms	Role of the carer
Colic	This occurs in the first 12 weeks. It causes sharp, spasmodic pain in the stomach, and is often at its worst in the late evening. Symptoms include inconsolable high-pitched crying, drawing her legs up to her chest, and growing red in the face.	Try to stay calm! Gently massage her abdomen in a clockwise direction, using the tips of your middle fingers. Sucrose solution (3 × 5 ml teaspoons of sugar in a cup of boiling water and left to cool) is said to have a mild pain-killing effect on small babies. Dribble 2 ml of this solution into the corner of the baby's mouth twice a day. If the problem persists, contact the doctor.
Diarrhoea	Frequent loose or watery stools. Can be very serious in young babies, especially when combined with vomiting, as it can lead to severe dehydration.	Give frequent small drinks of cooled, boiled water containing glucose and salt or a made-up sachet of rehydration fluid. If the baby is unable to take the fluid orally, she must be taken to hospital urgently and fed intravenously, by a 'drip'. If anal area becomes sore, treat with a barrier cream.
Gastroenteritis (virus or bacteria)	The baby may vomit and usually has diarrhoea as well; often has a raised temperature and loss of appetite. May show signs of abdominal pain, i.e. drawing up of legs to chest and crying.	Reassure baby. Observe strict hygiene rules. Watch out for signs of dehydration. Offer frequent small amounts of fluid, and possibly rehydration salts.
Neonatal cold injury – or hypothermia	The baby is cold to the touch. Face may be pale or flushed. Lethargic, with runny nose, swollen hands and feet. Pre-term infants and babies under 4 months are at particular risk.	Prevention Warm *slowly* by covering with several light layers of blankets and by cuddling. No direct heat. Offer feeds high in sugar and seek medical help urgently.
Reflux	Also known as gastro-intestinal reflux (GIR) or gastro-oesophageal reflux (GOR). The opening to the stomach is not yet efficient enough to allow a large liquid feed through. Symptoms include grizzly crying and excessive **possetting** after feeds.	Try feeding the baby in a more upright position and bring up wind by gently rubbing her back. After feeding leave the baby in a semi-sitting position. Some doctors prescribe a paediatric reflux suppressant or antacid mixture to be given before the feed.
Tonsillitis (virus or bacteria)	Very sore throat, which looks bright red. There is usually fever and the baby will show signs of distress from pain on swallowing and general aches and pains. May vomit.	Encourage plenty of fluids – older babies may have ice lollies to suck. Give pain relief, e.g. paracetamol. Seek medical aid if no improvement and if fever persists.
Cough (usually virus)	Often follows on from a cold; may be a symptom of other illness, e.g. measles.	Keep air moist. Check the baby has not inhaled an object. Give medicine if prescribed.

Table 10.4 (continued)

Condition (and cause)	Signs and symptoms	Role of the carer
Croup (virus)	Croup is an infection of the voice box or larynx, which becomes narrowed and inflamed. Barking cough (like sea lions), noisy breathing, distressed; usually occurs at night.	If severe, seek medical help. Reassure her and sit her up. Keep calm and reassure the baby. Inhaling steam may also benefit some babies. You can produce steam by boiling a kettle, running the hot taps in the bathroom, using a room humidifier or putting wet towels over the radiator. If using steam, take care to avoid scalding.
Bronchiolitis (virus)	A harsh dry cough which later becomes wet and chesty; runny nose, raised temperature, wheeze, breathing problems, poor feeding or vomiting. May develop a blue tinge around the lips and on the fingernails (known as cyanosis).	Observe closely. Seek medical help if condition worsens. Increase fluids. Give small regular feeds. Give prescribed medicine. Comfort and reassure.
Febrile convulsions (high temperature)	Convulsions caused by a high temperature (over 39° Centigrade, 102° Fahrenheit) or fever are called febrile convulsions. Baby will become rigid, then the body may twitch and jerk for one or two minutes.	Try not to panic. Move potentially harmful objects out of the way and place the baby in the recovery position. Loosen clothing. Call doctor. Give tepid sponging. Comfort and reassure.
Otitis media (virus or bacteria)	Will appear unwell; may have raised temperature. May vomit, may cry with pain. May have discharge from ear.	Take to doctor, give antibiotics and analgesics (or painkillers). Increase fluids; comfort and reassure.
Conjunctivitis (virus or bacteria)	Inflammation of the thin, delicate membrane that covers the eyeball and forms the lining of the eyelids. Symptoms include a painful red eye, with watering and sometimes sticky pus.	Take to doctor who may prescribe antibiotic eye drops or ointment. Bathe a sticky eye gently with cool boiled water and clean cotton wool swabs. Always bathe the eye from the inside corner to the outside to avoid spreading infection.
Common cold (coryza) (virus)	Runny nose, sneeze; tiny babies may have breathing problem.	Keep nose clear. Give small frequent feeds. Nasal drops if prescribed.
Meningitis (virus or bacteria)	Raised temperature, may have a blotchy rash. May refuse feeds, have a stiff neck, have a seizure. Bulging fontanelles; may have a shrill, high-pitched cry.	Seek medical help urgently. Reduce temperature. Reassure.

Digital Thermometer

This is battery operated and consists of a narrow probe with a tip sensitive to temperature. It is easy to read via a display panel and is unbreakable.

Plastic Fever Strip

This is a rectangular strip of thin plastic which contains temperature-sensitive crystals that change colour according to the temperature measured. It is not as accurate as the other thermometers but is a useful check.

Whatever the cause of a high temperature, it is important to try to reduce it. There is always the risk a fever could lead to convulsions or fits.

Using a Clinical Thermometer

✳ Explain to the child what you are going to do.

✳ Collect the thermometer; check that the silvery column of mercury is shaken down to 35°C.

✳ Sit the child on your knee and take their top layer of clothing off.

✳ Place the bulb end of the thermometer in the child's armpit, holding her arm close to her side for at least 2 minutes.

✳ Remove the thermometer and, holding it horizontally and in a good light, read off the temperature measured by the level of the mercury. Record the time and the temperature reading.

✳ After use, wash the thermometer in tepid water, and shake the column of mercury down again to 35°C. Dry carefully and replace in the case.

✳ Decide whether to contact the parents – you may need to obtain their consent to give paracetamol.

✳ A clinical thermometer should never be placed in a child's mouth, because of the danger of biting and breaking the glass.

Using a Digital Thermometer

✳ Place the narrow tip of the thermometer under the child's arm, as described above.

✳ Read the temperature when it stops rising; some models beep when this point is reached.

Using a Fever Strip

✳ Hold the plastic strip firmly against the child's forehead for about 30 seconds.

✳ Record the temperature revealed by the colour change.

Guidelines for bringing down a high temperature

✳ Offer cool drinks: encourage the child to take small, frequent sips of anything he will drink (though preferably clear fluids such as water or squash, rather than milky drinks). Do this even if the child is vomiting as, even then, some water will be absorbed.

✳ Remove clothes: keep the child as undressed as possible to allow heat to be lost.

✳ Reduce bedclothes: use a cotton sheet if the child is in bed.

✳ Sponge the child down: use tepid water (see 'Guidelines for tepid sponging' below).

✳ Give the correct dose of children's paracetamol: Make sure you have written consent from the parents to use it in case of emergency. If not, contact the parents and try to obtain consent.

✳ Cool the air in the child's room: use an electric fan or open the window.

* Reassure the child: they may be very frightened. Remain calm yourself and try to stop a baby from crying as this will tend to push the temperature higher still.

* If the temperature will not come down, call the doctor. Always consult a doctor if a high fever is accompanied by symptoms such as severe headache with stiff neck, abdominal pain or pain when passing urine.

NB Early childhood practitioners are advised that medicines should not be given unless the written permission of the parent or next-of-kin is obtained.

Guidelines for tepid sponging to reduce a temperature

* Make sure the air in the room is comfortably warm – not hot, cold or draughty.

* Lay the child on a towel on your knee or on the bed and gently remove their clothes; reassure them by talking gently.

* Sponge the child's body, limbs and face with tepid or lukewarm water – not cold; as the water evaporates from the skin, it absorbs heat from the blood and so cools the system.

* As the child cools down, pat the skin dry with a soft towel and dress only in a nappy or pants; cover them with a light cotton sheet.

* Keep checking the child's condition to make sure that he does not become cold or shivery; put more light covers over the child if he is shivering or obviously chilled.

* If the temperature rises again, repeat sponging every 10 minutes.

COMMON INFECTIOUS DISEASES OF CHILDHOOD

Everyone concerned with the care of babies and young children should be aware of the signs and symptoms of the common infectious diseases, and should know when to summon medical aid.

WHEN TO CALL A DOCTOR OR CALL FOR AN AMBULANCE

Table 10.5 When to call a doctor

If you think the child's life is in danger, dial 999 if you are in the UK, ask for an ambulance urgently and explain the situation.	
Contact the family doctor (GP) if the child has any of the following symptoms. If the doctor cannot reach you quickly, take the child to accident and emergency department of the nearest hospital:	
* Has a temperature of 38.6°C (101.4°F) which is not lowered by measures to reduce **fever**, or a temperature over 37.8°C (100°F) for more than one day.	* Has **convulsions**, or is limp and floppy.
* Has severe or persistent **vomiting** and/or **diarrhoea**, seems dehydrated or has projectile vomiting.	* **Cannot be woken**, is unusually drowsy or may be losing consciousness.
* Has symptoms of **meningitis**.	* Has **croup** symptoms.
* Is pale, listless, and **does not respond** to usual stimulation.	* **Cries or screams** inconsolably and may have severe pain.

Table 10.5 (continued)

✳ Has bulging **fontanelle** (soft spot on top of head) when not crying.	✳ Appears to have severe abdominal pain, with symptoms of **shock**.
✳ **Refuses** two successive feeds.	✳ Develops **purple-red rash** anywhere on body.
✳ Passes bowel motions (stools) containing blood.	✳ Has **jaundice**.
✳ Has a suspected **ear infection**.	✳ Has been **injured**, e.g. by a burn which blisters and covers more than 10% of the body surface.
✳ Has inhaled something, such as a peanut, into the air passages and may be **choking**.	✳ Has swallowed a **poisonous** substance, or an object, e.g. a safety pin or button.
✳ Has bright pink cheeks and swollen hands and feet (could be due to **hypothermia**).	✳ Has difficulty in **breathing**.

Disorders of the Digestive Tract

One of the most common signs that something is wrong with the digestive system is diarrhoea, when the bowel movements are abnormally runny and frequent. Other symptoms of infection or illness are vomiting and abdominal pain. Although these symptoms are often distressing – both to the child and his carer – they are rarely a serious threat to health.

Vomiting

Vomiting is the violent expulsion of the contents of the stomach through the mouth. A single episode of vomiting without other symptoms happens frequently in childhood. It could be a result of overeating or too much excitement. Vomiting has many causes, but in most cases there is little warning and after a single bout the child recovers and quickly gets back to normal. The box below details possible causes of vomiting in children over 1 year old, and what to do about it.

Possible causes of vomiting with accompanying symptoms	**What to do**
Gastro-enteritis The child also has diarrhoea	See the doctor within 24 hours Prevent **dehydration** (see page 296)
Intestinal obstruction The child's vomit is greenish–yellow	**Call an ambulance**; don't give the child anything to eat or drink
Meningitis The child has a fever, a stiff neck or flat, purplish spots that do not disappear when pressed	**Call an ambulance**
Head injury The child has recently suffered a blow to the head	**Call an ambulance**; don't give the child anything to eat or drink

Appendicitis The child has continuous abdominal pain around the navel and to the right side of the abdomen	**Call an ambulance;** don't give the child anything to eat or drink
Infection The child seems unwell, looks flushed and feels hot	**Reduce the fever;** see the doctor within 24 hours
Hepatitis The child has pale faeces and dark urine	See the doctor within 24 hours
Travel sickness When travelling, the child seems pale and quiet and complains of nausea	Give the child a travel sickness remedy before starting journey; take plenty of drinks to prevent dehydration
Migraine The child complains of a severe headache on one side of the forehead	See the doctor if accompanied by severe abdominal pain – it could be **appendicitis**
Whooping cough (pertussis) The child vomits after a bout of coughing	See the doctor within 24 hours

Helping a Child Who is Vomiting

* Reassure the child, who may be very frightened.

* Stay with the child and support their head by putting your hand on their forehead.

* Keep the child cool by wiping the face with a cool, damp cloth.

* Offer mouthwash or sips of water after vomiting.

* Give frequent small drinks of cold water with a pinch of salt and a teaspoon of glucose added – or you can buy special rehydrating powders.

* Encourage the child to rest lying down with a bowl by their side. Don't leave them until they have fallen asleep – and stay within call in case they vomit again.

Dehydration

Children can lose large amounts of body water through fever, diarrhoea, vomiting or exercise; this is called dehydration. In severe cases, they may not be able to replace this water simply by drinking and eating as usual. This is especially true if an illness stops them taking fluids by mouth or if they have a high fever.

Signs of Dehydration in Babies

* **Sunken fontanelles**: these are the areas where the bones of the skull have not yet fused together; they are covered by a tough membrane and a pulse may usually be seen beating under the anterior fontanelle in a baby without much hair.

* **Fretfulness**.

Table 10.6 Common infectious illnesses

disease and cause	spread	incubation	signs and symptoms	rash or specific sign	treatment	complications
COMMON COLD (coryza) Virus	Airborne/droplet, hand-to-hand contact	1–3 days	Sneeze, sore throat, running nose, headache, slight fever, irritable, partial deafness		Treat symptoms*. Vaseline to nostrils	Bronchitis, sinusitis, laryngitis
CHICKENPOX (varicella) Virus	Airborne/droplet, direct contact	10–14 days	Slight fever, itchy rash, mild onset, child feels ill, often with severe headache	Red spots with white centre on trunk and limbs at first; blisters and pustules	Rest, fluids, calamine to rash, cut child's nails to prevent secondary infection	Impetigo, scarring, secondary infection from scratching
DYSENTERY Bacillus or amoeba	Indirect: flies, infected food; poor hygiene	1–7 days	Vomiting, diarrhoea, blood and mucus in stool, abdominal pain, fever, headache		Replace fluids, rest, medical aid, strict hygiene measures	Dehydration from loss of body salts, shock; can be fatal
FOOD POISONING Bacteria or virus	Indirect: infected food or drink	½ hour to 36 hours	Vomiting, diarrhoea, abdominal pain		Fluids only for 24 hours; medical aid if no better	Dehydration – can be fatal
GASTROENTERITIS Bacteria or virus	Direct contact. Indirect: infected food/drink	Bacterial: 7–14 days Viral: 1 hour to 36 hours	Vomiting, diarrhoea, signs of dehydration		Replace fluids – water or Dioralyte; medical aid urgently	Dehydration, weight loss – death
MEASLES (morbilli) Virus	Airborne/droplet	7–15 days	High fever, fretful, heavy cold – running nose and discharge from eyes; *later* cough	Day 1: Koplik's spots, white inside mouth. Day 4: blotchy rash starts on face and spreads down to body	Rest, fluids, tepid sponging. Shade room if **photophobic** (disliking bright light)	Otitis media, eye infection, pneumonia, encephalitis (rare)

Table 10.6 (continued)

disease and cause	spread	incubation	signs and symptoms	rash or specific sign	treatment	complications
MENINGITIS (inflammation of meninges which cover the brain) Bacteria or virus	Airborne/droplet	Variable – usually 2–10 days	Fever, headache, drowsiness, confusion, photophobia, arching of neck	Can have small red spots or bruises	Take to hospital; antibiotics and observation	Deafness, brain damage, death
MUMPS (epidemic parotitis) Virus	Airborne/droplet	14–21 days	Pain, swelling of jaw in front of ears, fever, eating and drinking painful	Swollen face	Fluids: give via straw, hot compresses, oral hygiene	Meningitis (1 in 400), orchitis (infection of testes) in young men
PERTUSSIS (Whooping cough) Bacteria	Airborne/droplet; direct contact	7–21 days	Starts with a snuffly cold, slight cough, mild fever	Spasmodic cough with whoop sound, vomiting	Rest and assurance; feed after coughing attack; support during attack; inhalations	Convulsions, pneumonia, brain damage, hernia, debility
RUBELLA (German measles) Virus	Airborne/droplet; direct contact	14–21 days	Slight cold, sore throat, mild fever, swollen glands behind ears, pain in small joints	Slight pink rash starts behind ears and on forehead. Not itchy	Rest if necessary. Treat symptoms	Only if contracted by woman in first 3 months of pregnancy – can cause serious defects in unborn baby
SCARLET FEVER (or Scarlatina) Bacteria	Droplet	2–4 days	Sudden fever, loss of appetite, sore throat, pallor around mouth, 'strawberry' tongue	Bright red pinpoint rash over face and body – may peel	Rest, fluids, observe for complications, antibiotics	Kidney infection, otitis media, rheumatic fever (rare)
TONSILLITIS Bacteria or virus	Direct infection, droplet		Very sore throat, fever, headache, pain on swallowing, aches and pains in back and limbs		Rest, fluids, medical aid – antibiotics, iced drinks relieve pain	Quinsy (abscess on tonsils), otitis media, kidney infection, temporary deafness

* **Refusing feeds**.
* **Dry nappies** – because the amount of urine being produced is very small.

Signs of Dehydration in Children

Mild to moderate dehydration	Severe dehydration
Dry mouth	Very dry mouth
No tears when crying	Sunken eyes and dry, wrinkled skin
Refusing drinks	
At first thirsty, then irritable –	No urination for several hours
then becomes still and quiet	Sleepy and disorientated
Inactive and lethargic	Deep, rapid breathing
Increased heart rate	Fast, weak pulse
Restlessness	Cool and blotchy hands and feet

What To Do

If you think a baby or child might have dehydration, don't try to treat them at home or in the setting. Call the doctor immediately, or take the child to the nearest accident and emergency department. The doctor will prescribe oral rehydrating fluid to restore the body salts lost.

FIRST AID FOR BABIES AND CHILDREN

First aid is an important skill. By performing simple procedures and following certain guidelines, it may be possible to save lives by giving basic treatment until professional medical help arrives. Practice of first aid skills is vital; in an emergency there is no time to read instructions. If you've memorised some of the most basic procedures, these will help you to react quickly and efficiently. All those who work with children should take a recognised first aid course, such as those run by the St John's Ambulance Association or the British Red Cross Society. You should also take refresher courses periodically, so that you feel competent to deal with any medical emergency. The following pages explain the major first aid techniques for babies and children. They should not be used as a substitute for attending a first aid course with a trained instructor.

How to Get Emergency Help

* Assess the situation: stay calm and don't panic.
* Minimise any danger to yourself and to others; e.g. make sure someone takes charge of other children at the scene.
* Send for help. Notify a doctor, hospital and parents etc. as appropriate. If in any doubt, call an ambulance: dial 999.

Calling an Ambulance

Be ready to assist the emergency services by answering some simple questions.

* Give your name and the telephone number you are calling from.
* Tell the operator the location of the accident. Try to give as much information as possible, e.g. are there any familiar landmarks, such as churches or pubs nearby?
* Explain briefly what has happened: this helps the paramedics to act speedily when they arrive.
* Tell the operator what you have done so far to treat the casualty.

An ABC of resuscitation, 0–1 years

If a baby appears unconscious and gives no response:

A: Airway – open the airway.

* Place the baby on a firm surface.
* Remove any obstruction from the mouth.
* Put one hand on the forehead and one finger under the chin, and gently tilt the head backwards **very slightly** (if you tilt the head too far back, it will close the airway again).

B: Breathing – check for breathing.

* Put your ear close to the baby's mouth.
* Look to see if the chest is rising or falling.
* Listen and feel for the baby's breath on your cheek.
* Do this for 5 seconds.

If the baby is not breathing:

1 Start **mouth-to-mouth-and-nose resuscitation**:

* Seal your lips around the baby's mouth and nose.
* Blow **gently** into the lungs until the chest rises.
* Remove your mouth and allow the chest to fall.

2 Repeat 5 times at the rate of 1 breath every 3 seconds.

3 Check the pulse.

C: Circulation – check the pulse.

Lightly press your fingers towards the bone on the inside of the upper arm and hold them there for 5 seconds.

If there is no pulse, or the pulse is slower than 60 per minute, and the baby is not breathing, start **chest compressions**:

1 Find a position a finger's width below the line joining the baby's nipples, in the centre of the breastbone.

2 Place the tips of two fingers on this point and press to a depth of about 2 cm (3/4 inch) at a rate of 100 times per minute.

3 After 5 compressions, blow gently into the lungs once.

4 Continue the cycle for 1 minute.

5 Carry the baby to a phone and dial 999 for an ambulance.

6 Continue resuscitation, checking the pulse every minute until help arrives.

If the baby is not breathing, but does have a pulse:

1 Start **mouth-to-mouth-and-nose resuscitation**, at the rate of 1 breath every 3 seconds.

2 Continue for 1 minute, then carry the baby to a phone and dial 999 for an ambulance.

If the baby does have a pulse and is breathing:

1 Lay the baby on its side, supported by a cushion, pillow, rolled-up blanket or something similar.

2 Dial 999 for an ambulance.

3 Check breathing and pulse every minute, and be prepared to carry out resuscitation.

An ABC of resuscitation, 1–10 years

A: Airway – open the airway.

* Lay the child flat on their back.
* Remove clothing from around the neck.
* Remove any obstruction from the mouth.
* Lift the chin and tilt the head back slightly to open the airway.

B: Breathing – check for breathing.

* Keep the airway open and place your cheek close to the child's mouth.
* Look to see if their chest is rising and falling.
* Listen and feel for their breath against your cheek.
* Do this for 5 seconds.
* If the child is not breathing, give 5 breaths, then check the pulse.

C: Circulation – check the pulse.

* Find the carotid pulse by placing your fingers in the groove between the Adam's apple and the large muscle running down the side of the neck.
* Do this for 5 seconds.

If the child is not breathing and does not have a pulse:

1 Begin a cycle of 5 chest compressions and 1 breath. Continue for 1 minute.

2 Dial 999 for an ambulance.

3 Continue at the rate of 1 breath to 5 compressions until help arrives.

If the child is not breathing but does have a pulse:

1 Give 20 breaths in 1 minute.

2 Dial 999 for an ambulance.

3 Continue mouth-to-mouth resuscitation, rechecking the pulse and breathing after each set of 20 breaths, until help arrives or until the child starts breathing again. When breathing returns, place the child in the recovery position.

Mouth-to-mouth resuscitation

1 Open the airway by lifting the chin and tilting back the head. Check the mouth is clear of obstructions.

2 Close the child's nose by pinching the nostrils.

3 Take a deep breath and seal your mouth over the child's.

4 Blow firmly into the mouth for about 2 seconds, watching the chest rise.

5 Remove your mouth and allow the child's chest to fall.

6 Repeat until help arrives.

Chest compression

1 Make sure the child is lying on their back on a firm surface (preferably the ground).

2 Find the spot where the bottom of the ribcage joins on to the end of the breastbone, and measure a finger's width up from this point.

3 Using one hand only, press down sharply at a rate of 100 times a minute, to a depth of about 3 cm (1.25 inches). Counting aloud will help you keep at the right speed.

4 Continue until help arrives

Choking

Check inside the baby's mouth. If the obstruction is visible, try to hook it out with your finger, but do not risk pushing it further down. If this does not work, proceed as follows:

* Lay the baby face down along your forearm, with your hand supporting her head and neck, and her head lower than her bottom (an older baby or toddler may be placed face down across your knee, with head and arms hanging down).

* Give 5 brisk slaps between the shoulder blades.

* Turn the baby over, check the mouth and remove any obstruction.

* Check for breathing.

* If the baby is not breathing, give 5 breaths (see **mouth-to-mouth-and-nose resuscitation**, page 298).

* If the airway is still obstructed, give 5 chest compressions (see **chest compressions**, page 298).

* If the baby is still not breathing, repeat the cycle of back slaps, mouth-to-mouth-and-nose breathing and chest compressions.

* After 2 cycles, if the baby is not breathing, dial 999 for an ambulance.

NB Never hold a baby or young child upside down by the ankles and slap their back – you could break their neck.

Head injuries

Babies and young children are particularly prone to injury from falls. Any injury to the head must be investigated carefully. A head injury can damage the scalp, skull or brain.

Symptoms and Signs

If the head injury is mild, the only symptom may be a slight headache and this will probably result in a crying baby. More seriously, the baby may:

* lose consciousness, even if only for a few minutes;

* vomit;

* seem exceptionally drowsy;

* complain of an ache or pain in the head;

* lose blood from her nose, mouth or ears;

* lose any watery fluid from her nose or ears;

* have an injury to the scalp which might suggest a fracture to the skull bones.

Treatment

If the baby or young child has any of the above symptoms, dial 999 for an ambulance or go straight to the accident and emergency department at the nearest hospital. Meanwhile:

* if the child is unconscious, follow the ABC routine;

* stop any bleeding by applying direct pressure, but take care that you are not pressing a broken bone into the delicate tissue underneath; if in doubt, apply pressure around the edge of the wound, using dressings;

* if there is discharge from the ear, position the child so that the affected ear is lower, and cover with a clean pad; do not plug the ear.

Burns and scalds

Burns are injuries to body tissue caused by heat, chemicals or radiations. Scalds are caused by wet heat, such as steam or hot liquids.

Superficial burns involve only the outer layers of the skin, cause redness, swelling, tenderness and usually heal well. Intermediate burns form blisters, can become infected and need medical aid. Deep burns involve all layers of the skin, which may be pale and charred, may be pain-free if the nerves are damaged, and will **always** require medical attention.

Treatment for Severe Burns and Scalds

* Lay the child down and protect burnt area from ground contact.

* Check ABC of resuscitation and be ready to resuscitate if necessary.

✱ Gently remove any constricting clothing from the injured area before it begins to swell.

✱ Cover the injured area loosely with a sterile, unmedicated dressing or use a clean, non-fluffy tea towel or pillowcase.

DO NOT remove anything that is sticking to the burn.

DO NOT apply lotions, creams or fat to the injury.

DO NOT break blisters.

DO NOT use plasters.

✱ If the child is unconscious, lay the child on her side, supported by a cushion, pillow, rolled-up blanket or something similar.

✱ Send for medical attention.

Treatment for Minor Burns and Scalds

✱ Place the injured part under slowly running water, or soak in cold water for 10 minutes.

✱ Gently remove any constricting articles from the injured area before it begins to swell.

✱ Dress with clean, sterile, non-fluffy material.

DO NOT use adhesive dressings

DO NOT apply lotions, ointments or fat to burn or scald

DO NOT break blisters or otherwise interfere

If in doubt, seek medical aid.

Treatment for Sunburn

✱ Remove the child to the shade and cool the skin by gently sponging the skin with tepid (lukewarm) water.

✱ Give sips of cold water at frequent intervals.

✱ If the burns are mild, gently apply an after-sun cream.

✱ For extensive blistering, seek medical help.

Drowning

If a baby or small child is discovered under water, either in the bath or a pool, follow these guidelines:

✱ Call for emergency medical attention. Dial 999.

✱ Keep the child's neck immobilised as you remove him/her from the water.

✱ Restore breathing and circulation first.

✱ If child is unconscious or you suspect neck injuries, do not bend or turn neck while restoring breathing.

✱ Give rescue breathing if the child is not breathing but has a pulse. Breathe forcefully enough to blow air through water in the airway. Do not try to empty water from child's lungs.

✱ Do not give up. Give CPR (cardiopulmonary resuscitation) if the child does not have a pulse. Continue until child is revived, until medical help arrives or until exhaustion stops you.

Signs and Symptoms

Look for one or more of the following:

✱ unconsciousness;

✱ no pulse;

✱ no visible or audible breath;

✱ bluish-coloured skin;

✱ pale lips, tongue and/or nail bed.

Immediate Treatment

1 Lay child on flat surface or begin first aid in the water.

2 Check ABC (Airway, Breathing, Circulation).

3 If child is not breathing, open airway and start rescue breathing.

4 Check pulse and continue CPR if necessary to restore circulation.

5 When breathing and pulse have been restored, treat for shock.

6 Have child lie down on his/her side to allow water to drain from the mouth.

7 Restore child's body heat by removing wet clothing and covering child with warm blankets.

8 Do not give up if breathing and pulse are not restored. Continue CPR until help arrives.

Cuts and bleeding

Young children often sustain minor cuts and grazes. Most of these occur as a result of falls and only result in a very small amount of bleeding.

NB Always wear disposable gloves in an early years setting to prevent cross-infection.

For Minor Cuts and Grazes

* Sit or lay the child down and reassure them.

* Clean the injured area with cold water, using cotton wool or gauze.

* Apply a dressing if necessary.

* Do not attempt to pick out pieces of gravel or grit from a graze; just clean gently and cover with a light dressing.

Record the injury and treatment in the accident report book and make sure the parents/carers of the child are informed.

For Severe Bleeding

1 Summon medical help – dial 999 or call a doctor.

2 Try to stop the bleeding:

* Apply direct pressure to the wound.

* Wear gloves and use a dressing or a non-fluffy material, such as a clean tea towel.

* Elevate the affected part if possible.

3 Apply a dressing. If the blood soaks through, **DO NOT** remove the dressing; apply another one on top, and so on.

* Keep the child warm and reassure them.

* **DO NOT** give anything to eat or drink.

* Contact the child's parents or carers.

* If the child loses consciousness, follow the ABC procedure for resuscitation.

NB Always record the incident and the treatment given in the accident report book.

REPORTING AND RECORDING ACCIDENTS AND ILLNESSES IN A CHILD CARE SETTING

Any accident, injury or illness that happens to a child in a group setting must be reported to the child's parents or primary carers. If the injury is minor, such as a graze or a bruise, the nursery or school staff will inform parents when the child is collected at the end of the session. If someone other than the child's parent collects the child, a notification slip should be sent home. Parents are notified about:

* the nature of the injury or illness;

* any treatment or action taken;

* the name of the person who carried out the treatment.

In the case of a major accident or illness then the child's parents must be notified as quickly as possible.

EMERGENCY HELP FOR CHILDREN WITH EXISTING MEDICAL CONDITIONS

The following chronic medical conditions are described fully in Unit 11 on CD-ROM. You need to know how to respond and care for a child who has a sudden flare-up while in the group setting.

Asthma

Not all asthma attacks can be prevented. When the child is having an acute attack of wheezing – the difficulty is in breathing *out* rather than in catching one's breath – he needs a reliever drug (a bronchodilator, usually in a blue inhaler case). Most children will have been shown how to deliver the drug by an aerosol inhaler, a spinhaler or a nebuliser.

Guidelines for helping a child who is having an acute asthma attack

* If the attack is the child's *first*, then call a doctor and the parents.

* Stay calm and reassure the child, who may be very frightened.

* Encourage the child to sit up to increase lung capacity.

* If the child has a reliever inhaler or nebuliser, then supervise him while using it.

* Never leave the child alone during an attack.

* Try not to let other children crowd around.

* If these measures do not stop the wheezing and the child is exhausted by the attack, call a doctor. He or she will either give an injection of a bronchodilator drug or arrange admission to hospital.

Epilepsy

Guidelines for meeting the needs of a child with epilepsy in an early years setting

Children with epilepsy should be treated as any other child. Epilepsy is *not* an illness and children should be encouraged to take part in all the activities and daily routine, unless otherwise advised by the child's parents or doctor.

* Teachers and nursery managers should be aware of the child's individual needs and what is best for them should they have a seizure, e.g. What kind of seizure has the child had? Are there any known triggers? How long does the seizure usually last? Does the child need to sleep after a seizure? Do they need to go home? Are they usually confused afterwards? Does the setting have a medical room where the child can recover before going back to class? Is there a school nurse to advise or help if needed?

* Make sure that all contact details are up to date – i.e. home contact numbers, GP and so on.

* Record exactly what happened during a seizure; this will help in an initial diagnosis and also to build up a picture of the child's condition.

* Always contact parents immediately if the child has a seizure, and keep them informed of the child's progress.

* Record any seizure in the appropriate record book.

* Make sure you and all other members of staff know what to do when a child has a seizure.

* Try to minimise embarrassment for the child; if the child has been incontinent during the seizure, deal with it discreetly.

* Always stay with the child during a seizure and until they have recovered completely.

* Supervise activities such as swimming and climbing.

* Try to deal with seizures matter-of-factly. Your attitude will influence the attitude of other children towards the child with epilepsy.

Type of seizure and what might happen

Generalised tonic-clonic (used to be called 'Grand mal')

The child:

* suddenly falls unconscious, often with a cry (caused by a tightening of the voice muscles);

* goes rigid, arching the back (tonic phase);

* may stop breathing and the lips go blue;

* begins convulsive movements (clonic phase); the limbs make rhythmic jerks, the jaw may be clenched and the breathing noisy;

* show saliva at the mouth;

* lose bladder or bowel control.

Then the muscles relax and breathing becomes normal. Usually in just a few minutes the child regains consciousness and may fall into a deep sleep or appear dazed.

The child will not remember anything about the seizure when they come round and will need time to recover. Recovery time varies from minutes for some children to hours for others.

First aid

Do:

✓ protect the child from injury by moving any furniture or other solid objects out of the way during a seizure;

✓ make space around the child and keep other children away;

✓ loosen the clothing around the child's neck and chest and cushion their head;

✓ stay with the child until recovery is complete;

✓ be calmly reassuring.

Don't:

✗ restrain the child in any way;

✗ try to put anything in their mouth;

✗ try to move them unless they are in danger;

✗ give the child anything to eat or drink until they are fully recovered;

✗ attempt to bring them round.

Call an ambulance *only if*:

* it is the child's first seizure and you don't know why it happened;

* it follows a blow to the head;

* the child is injured during the seizure;

* the seizure is continuous and shows no sign of stopping – a rare condition called *status epilepticus*.

Absence (used to be called '*Petit mal*')

The child may:

* appear to be day-dreaming, in a trance or 'switched off';
* have slight twitching movements of the lips, eyelids or head;
* make strange 'automatic' movements such as chewing, fiddling with their clothes or making odd noises.

Do:

✓ sit the child down in a quiet place;
✓ stay with the child until the symptoms go away;
✓ talk calmly and reassuringly to the child;
✓ tell the child what happened while their seizure was happening.

Don't:

✗ try to restrain the child;
✗ try to shake them out of the seizure.

Simple partial

Epileptic activity occurs in just part of the brain; the symptoms depend on the area of the brain affected and the child remains fully conscious.

The child may experience:

* twitching, dizziness and numbness;
* sweating;
* nausea;
* feeling 'strange'.

Do:

✓ stay with the child until the symptoms go away;
✓ talk calmly and reassuringly to them.

Don't:

✗ try to restrain the child.

Complex partial

Epileptic activity occurs in just part of the brain; the symptoms depend on the area of the brain affected. The child might appear to be fully aware of what they are doing – but this is not the case

The child may experience:

* an 'aura' or warning – such as a funny taste in the mouth, flashing lights or a peculiar sound;
* plucking at the clothes;
* smacking of the lips;
* swallowing repeatedly;
* wandering around.

Do:

✓ guide the child from danger;
✓ stay with the child until the symptoms go away;
✓ talk calmly and reassuringly to them;
✓ explain anything they might have missed.

Don't:

✗ try to restrain the child;
✗ assume the child is aware of what is happening or has happened;
✗ attempt to bring them round;
✗ give the child anything to eat or drink until they are fully recovered.

Call an ambulance *only if*:

* it is the child's first seizure and you don't know why it happened;
* the seizure lasts longer than 5 minutes.

Diabetes

Guidelines for meeting the needs of a child with diabetes in an early years setting

Children with diabetes should be treated as any other child. Diabetes is *not* an illness and children should be encouraged to take part in all the activities and daily routine.

*   Make sure that all contact details are up to date – i.e. home contact numbers, GP, diabetic specialist nurse, and so on.

*   Always contact parents immediately if the child becomes unwell, and keep them informed of the child's progress.

*   Ensure that there is always a supply of glucose tablets or sweet drinks in the setting.

*   When on outings, take a supply of sweet drinks or glucose tablets with you.

*   Allow the child to take glucose tablets or snacks when required – most children with diabetes carry glucose tablets with them.

*   Make sure you and all other members of staff know how to recognise and deal promptly with a child who has a hypoglycaemic attack.

*   Always stay with the child if he or she feels unwell, and allow privacy if blood glucose testing is necessary during the day.

*   Observe the child carefully during any vigorous exercise, such as swimming or climbing.

*   Be understanding if the child shows emotional or behaviour problems caused by the necessary restrictions to their routine.

*   Inform the child's parents if you are planning an activity which might involve extra strains and excitement

*   Make sure that the child eats regularly and that cooks are consulted about the child's dietary needs.

Sickle Cell Disorder

Guidelines for working with children who have a sickle cell disorder

*   Know how to recognise a crisis. If the child suddenly becomes unwell or complains of severe abdominal or chest pain, headache, neck stiffness or drowsiness, contact the parents without delay: the child needs urgent hospital treatment.

*   Make sure the child is always warm and dry. Never let a child get chilled after PE or swimming.

*   Make sure the child does not become dehydrated. Allow them to drink more often and much more than normal.

*   Advise parents that the child should be fully immunised against infectious illnesses and ensure that any prescribed medicines (e.g. vitamins and antibiotics) are given.

*   Give support. The child may find it difficult to come to terms with their condition; make allowances when necessary.

*   Talk to the parents to find out how the illness is affecting the child.

*   Help with schoolwork. If badly anaemic, the child may find it difficult to concentrate, and regular visits to the GP or hospital may entail many days off school.

ACCIDENT REPORT BOOK

Every child care setting is required by law to have an accident report book and to maintain a record of accidents. Record the injury and treatment in the accident report book and make sure the parents/carers of the child are informed. Information may be recorded in the format below:

Name of person injured:	Callum Rogers
Date and time of injury:	Tuesday 10th May 2006, 10.43 am
Where the accident happened:	in the outdoor play area
What exactly happened:	Callum fell in the outdoor play area and grazed his right knee
What injuries occurred:	a graze
What treatment was given:	graze was bathed and an adhesive dressing applied
Name and signature of person dealing with the accident:	LUCY COWELL Lucy Cowell
Signature of witness to the report:	Paul Hammond
Signature of parent or guardian:	Maria Rogers

ESTABLISHING HEALTHY AND SAFE ROUTINES

All children benefit from routines in daily care and contribute greatly to the provision of a positive, safe and secure environment. Daily routines include:

*   safety at home times;
*   safety at meal and snack times;
*   safety at sleep and rest times;
*   hygiene routines.

Safety at Home Times

Your setting will have a policy relating to what to do when parents come to collect their child. Many children's settings have door entry phones and a password system for parents and staff to enter the premises. At home time, staff must ensure that the child is collected by the appropriate person. If parents know that they will not be able to collect their child on a particular occasion, they should notify the setting, giving permission for another named person to collect their child. The child's key person should, where possible, be responsible for handover at home times.

Safety at Meal and Snack Times

Meal and snack times should be enjoyable occasions for both staff and children. The following safety guidelines should be followed to ensure health and safety at these times:

*   **Hygiene:** wipe all surfaces where food will be served, before and after meals and snacks. Make sure that children have washed and dried their hands before eating.
*   **Serving food:** check that the food you are giving children is appropriate for them; check they have no allergies, e.g. to milk or wheat. Never give peanuts to children under 4 years old as they can easily choke or inhale them into their

CASE STUDY

Problems at home time

Anna is a 3-year-old child who attends a private nursery group four days a week. Her key person, Jenny, has developed a good professional relationship with Anna's mother and suspects that she and her partner are having problems balancing their home life with their work commitments. Anna's mother, Jane, often arrives late to collect Anna; she is always very flustered and apologetic about it. Anna's father, David, works long hours as a sales rep and is often away from home for weeks at a time. He has only collected Anna on a couple of occasions before – and only when Jane had given prior permission. One Friday afternoon, David arrives at the nursery and explains to Jenny that Jane had rung him to say she was running very late and asked if he could collect Anna on this occasion. When Jenny replies that she must check with the nursery manager before allowing him to take

Anna, David becomes very angry and starts to shout about his rights as a father. As Jenny is trying to calm him down, he suddenly pushes his way past her into the nursery room and scoops Anna up, grabbing her coat from her peg as he rushes out. Five minutes later, Jane arrives and becomes very distressed when she hears what has happened. She tells Jenny that she and David had had a massive row that morning and that he had threatened to leave her.

Discuss this scenario in class and answer the following questions:

1 If you were Jenny, Anna's key person, what should you do?

2 What are the main issues involved in this case study?

3 How can the nursery ensure each child's safety at home time?

4 Find out how your setting deals with issues of safety at home time.

lungs, causing infection and lung damage. Food should be cut up into manageable pieces and should be served at the correct temperature – not too hot or too cold.

* **Seating:** babies should be securely strapped into high chairs, using a five-point harness.

* **Supervision:** supervise children carefully; never leave children unattended with drinks or food in case they choke. Never leave a baby alone, eating finger foods. Babies can choke silently when eating soft foods such as pieces of banana. Never leave babies propped up with a bottle or feeding beaker.

* Make sure you know what to do if a child is choking.

Safety at Sleep and Rest Times

Every setting will have its own routine, providing for the needs of both babies and young children for periods of sleep and rest. You should follow these guidelines:

* Treat each child uniquely – every child has his or her own needs for sleep and rest.

* Be guided by the wishes of the child's parent or carer.

* Keep noise to a minimum and darken the room; make sure that children have been to the toilet.

* Always put babies on their backs to sleep.

* Make sure that the cot or bed is safe and hygienic: no pillows, no small objects

within reach and no ribbon fastenings on garments.

* Find out all you can about the individual child's preferences; some children like to be patted to sleep; others may need to cuddle their favourite comfort object.

* Make sure that someone is always with the child until they fall asleep; reassure them that someone will be there when they wake up.

* Provide quiet, relaxing activities for those children who are unable – or don't want – to sleep, for example, reading a book to them, doing jigsaw puzzles and so on.

Safe Management of Trips and Outings

Any outing away from the children's usual setting – for instance, trips to farms, parks, and theatres – must be planned with safety and security issues as top priority.

Guidelines for safety on trips and outings

* Planning: you may need to visit the place beforehand and to discuss any particular requirements, for example what to do if it rains, or specific lunch arrangements.

* Permission: the manager or head teacher must give permission for the outing, and a letter should be sent to all parents and guardians of the children.

* Transport: if a coach is being hired, check whether it has seat belts for children. The law requires all new minibuses and coaches to have seat belts fitted and minibus drivers to have passed a special driving test.

* Help: usually, help is requested from parents so that adequate supervision is ensured.

* First aid kit and medicines: staff should carry a bag with a simple first aid kit, medication such as inhalers, sun cream, nappies, spare clothes, extra drinks, reins and harnesses.

* Inform parents: about the outing: tell them what the child needs to bring, e.g. packed meal and waterproof coat, emphasise no glass bottles and no sweets. Advise on spending money if necessary – state the maximum amount.

* There should always be trained staff on any outing – however local and low-key the trip may seem.

* The child-to-adult ratio should never exceed 4 to 1. If the children are under 2 years old or have special needs, then you would expect to have fewer children per adult.

* Contact information: you need to have a copy of the children's contact information with you and should regularly check the names of the children against the day's attendance list.

* Swimming trips should only be attempted if the ratio is 1 adult to 1 child for children under 5 years.

* The younger the children, the more adults are required, particularly if the trip involves crossing roads, when an adult *must* be available to hold the children's hands.

ROAD SAFETY

* Road traffic accidents account for 50 per cent of all accidental deaths. Every year, more than 400 children under the age of 15 years are killed, and many more are seriously injured, on the roads of the UK. Educating children about safety on the roads should begin at a very early age, the best method being by example.

* Traffic is the single biggest cause of accidental death for 12- to 16-year-olds.

* Six out of ten teenagers have either been in an accident or had a 'near miss' or know someone at school who has done so.

* Teenagers get distracted when they cross the road by talking and having fun with their friends, chatting on the mobile phone, listening to music, or just thinking about something else.

STRANGERS AND CHILD SAFETY

Many parents worry that their child might be abducted or murdered by a stranger. In fact, this is rare compared with, for example, the risk of a traffic accident. However, it makes sense to teach children the following rules:

* Never go with anyone (even someone they know well) without telling the grown-up who is looking after them.

* If someone they don't know tries to take them away, it's OK to scream and kick.

* Make sure children know always to tell you if they have been approached by someone they don't know.

* Make sure that children know what to do if they become separated from you or are lost.

* If they are in a crowded place, they should stand still and wait to be found.

* They can tell a police officer that they are lost.

* They can go into a shop and tell someone behind the counter.

* They could tell someone who has other children with them.

* As soon as they are old enough, teach a child his or her address and phone number, or the phone number of another responsible person.

> **Guidelines for teaching children about road safety**
>
> * Children need to learn about road safety in the same way as they learn any new skill: the message needs to be repeated over and over again until the child really has learnt it.
>
> * The Green Cross Code is a very good method of teaching road safety (see Fig 10.3).
>
> * Every local authority employs a Road Safety Officer, and the Royal Society for the Prevention of Accidents (RoSPA) runs the Tufty Club for children aged 3 years or over. Invite someone to talk to the children about road safety.
>
> * Children should wear light-coloured clothes or luminous armbands – or both – when out at dusk or when walking on country roads without pavements.
>
> * Children should have lights on their bikes if they cycle in the dark.

ACTIVITY: EVALUATING YOUR HEALTH AND SAFETY POLICY

Ask to see the health and safety policy in your workplace.

1 What aspects of care does it cover?

2 Is it reviewed regularly?

3 Is the policy displayed anywhere?

4 Is there anything you could add to the policy?

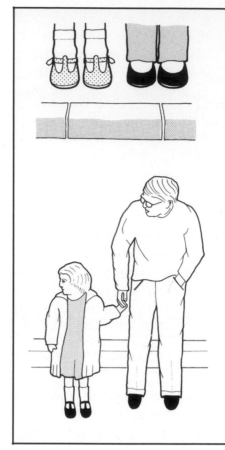

The Green Cross Code

1. **Find a safe place to cross, then stop. Safe places include zebra and pelican crossings.**

2. **Stand on the pavement near the kerb.**

3. **Look all round for traffic and listen.**

4. **If traffic is coming, let it pass. Look all round again.**

5. **When there is no traffic near, walk straight across the road. Never run.**

6. **Keep looking and listening for traffic while you cross. Repeat and use the code every time.**

Fig 10.3 The Green Cross Code

EMERGENCY PROCEDURES IN THE SETTING

Every setting which employs more than five people must have a safety policy. This will cover emergency procedures in the event of a fire, accident or other emergency.

Security Issues and Violence

Early years settings should be secure environments where children cannot wander off without anyone realising. But they also need to be secure so that strangers cannot enter without a good reason for being there. Occasionally you might encounter a problem with violence – or threats of violence – from a child's parents or carers. Your setting will have a policy that deals with this issue.

Fire Safety

In the case of fire or other emergency, you need to know what to do to evacuate the children and yourselves safely. Follow the following rules for fire safety:

* No smoking is allowed in any child care setting.

* Handbags containing matches or lighters must be locked securely away out of children's reach.

* The nursery cooker should not be left unattended when turned on.

* Fire exits must be clearly signed.

* Fire drills should be carried out regularly.

* Registers must be kept up to date throughout the day.

* Fire exits and other doors should be free of obstructions on both sides.

* Instructions about what to do in the event of a fire must be clearly displayed.

* You should know where the fire extinguishers are kept and how to use them.

* Electrical equipment should be regularly checked for any faults.

Missing Children

Strict procedures must be followed to prevent a child from going missing from the setting. However, if a child *does* go missing, a procedure must be followed.

ACTIVITY: POLICIES AND PROCEDURES

Find out what policies and procedures apply to your setting. Make sure you know what your role is in keeping children safe and healthy.

SECTION 3: HOW TO PLAN AND PROVIDE AN ENABLING PHYSICAL ENVIRONMENT FOR CHILDREN

• Current national and international initiatives and philosophies around indoor/outdoor environment • Risk assessment and how to undertake them • Support of curriculum planning • Physical play experiences • The need for a stimulating environment • Risk and challenge in environment • Need for age appropriate activities • Opportunities for learning outdoors

PROVIDING FOR CHILDREN'S DEVELOPMENTAL NEEDS, INDOORS AND OUTDOORS

The early years environment should provide holistic care and education, by addressing the range of children's developmental needs (i.e. their physical needs, intellectual and language needs, emotional and social needs).

Guidelines for addressing children's developmental needs
The early years setting should:

* take account of each child's individual needs and provide for them appropriately;

* be stimulating: it should offer a wide range of activities which encourage experimentation and problem-solving;

* provide opportunities for all types of play;

* provide support for children who may be experiencing strong feelings, e.g. when settling in to a new nursery or when they are angry or jealous;

* encourage children who use them to bring in their comfort objects, e.g. a favourite teddy or a piece of blanket;

* encourage the development of self-reliance and independence;

* ensure that children who have special needs and disabilities are provided with appropriate equipment and support.

A Sense of Belonging

Children and their families need an environment that is reassuring and welcoming; children also need to feel that they belong.

A Comfortable Child and Family-Friendly Environment

'Caring adults count more than resources or equipment.' (*Birth to Three Matters Framework*)

You, the practitioner, are the most important resource in any setting; you can make a real difference to the caring environment by showing that you really care and by developing all the skills of empathy and patience that help to create a welcoming and family-friendly environment. Children who are cared for at home, in a childminder's home or in a rural pre-school group may not have access to special, child-sized equipment or to the range of activities that can be provided in a purpose-built nursery setting. Many pre-school groups have to clear away every item of equipment after each session because the hall or room is used by other groups. In purpose-built early years settings and infant schools, there are child-sized chairs, basins, lavatories and low tables. Such provision makes the environment safer and allows children greater independence.

The Physical Layout of the Environment

Up to a point, certain fixed features will determine how space is used, for example, the siting of doors, sinks, carpeted areas and electric sockets. Within these constraints you will have some flexibility to organise space to suit your needs. Space should be organised in such a way that children – and adults – can move freely between activities and so that children with special needs can have as much independence as possible. The most important factors in designing the layout of any early years setting are that it should:

1 comply with **hygiene and safety** standards:

*   furniture should be well designed to suit its intended purpose; have safe corners (rounded or moulded); be hard-wearing and easily washed or cleaned;

*   electrical equipment, such as computers, televisions and videos and tape recorders, must have electric wires secured neatly and be sited close to a wall socket;

*   fire safety equipment and fire doors should be clearly marked and regularly maintained;

*   a fully equipped first aid box must be kept in a locked cupboard; also, there must be one designated member of staff who is responsible for first aid and for replenishing the box; at least one qualified first aider must be in the setting at all times;

*   equipment and materials should be available for disinfecting and cleaning surfaces and toys;

*   safety devices for doors and windows, and stair-gates, should be in place;

*   safety surfaces should be used in the outdoor area, e.g. under slides and climbing frames;

2 be **child-oriented**:

*   furniture should be child-sized and attractive (perhaps made so by the use of natural wood);

*   toys and activities should be provided which are appropriate to the children's level of development; children need a stimulating environment which encourages experimentation and problem-solving;

*   a quiet area should be available where children can withdraw from peer play and from the gaze of adults;

*   an outdoor space with safe equipment is also important;

3 **provide a safe and pleasant working environment for adults**;

*   allow for **adequate supervision** by adults at all times:

*   furniture should be arranged to allow supervision without excessive walking – and should also be easy to rearrange;

*   materials should be stored conveniently;

*   equipment should be designed to avoid excessive lifting, e.g. nappy-changing units with steps, or cots with drop sides;

*   seating for adults – special glider chairs, settees, and rockers are perfect for bonding with babies. Adult chairs should be low, yet scaled to fit adults, so that staff can interact at child level;

4 **cater for the needs of families**: by providing information for them about their children and their activities and other issues of interest about events and organisations in the local community;

5 **use natural light** where possible; be at the correct temperature and be well ventilated.

Detailed guidelines for organising the physical layout of the setting may be found in Chapter 9.

PROVIDING FOR CHILDREN'S SPECIAL NEEDS

Early years settings may need to adapt their room layout and outdoor areas to improve access, so that all children are included in the opportunities for play and learning; for example, you may need to make changes with children who use wheelchairs or children with visual impairment in mind. You may need to work with parents to find out how children with special needs can be encouraged to participate fully with other children within the nursery. (For more information on working with children with special needs, see Unit 14 on CD-ROM.)

ACTIVITY: ADAPTING THE ENVIRONMENT FOR A CHILD WITH SPECIAL NEEDS

Look at the layout of your own work placement. What physical changes would be necessary to include: (a) a child in a wheelchair; (b) a partially sighted child; (c) a child who uses elbow crutches; (d) a child with a hearing impairment?

DISPLAYING CHILDREN'S WORK – SHARING THE LEARNING

Displays can give a lot of information to children, parents and visitors about the setting's values and ethos, as well as celebrating children's learning. Some displays may be purely for information purposes, for example, a parents' notice board with named photographs of staff members, menus for the week and other useful things. Other displays share the development and learning of children.

Displays of children's work can take different forms:

* **wall display:** boards of varying shapes and sizes are placed on otherwise plain walls so that displays can be created and changed frequently to show recent experiences;

* **window display:** pieces of art or craft work can be attached to windows to create a stained glass effect, but windows should not be covered completely. Children should be able to see out and light should not be restricted;

* **mobile (or hanging) display:** in large rooms, hanging displays can be very useful for learning to be shared. These must be at an appropriate height for the children and also not hinder the movement of adults;

* **table-top display:** these are often called 'interactive' displays as they provide an opportunity for children to handle interesting objects and to use the display as a learning activity;

* Displays are part of your record-keeping process, through which you share the learning as a 'learning community'.

Often, table-top displays are used in conjunction with a wall display.

Guidelines for creating displays

Do:

✓ label individual children's work correctly with their name, preferably in the top left-hand corner or underneath;

✓ let children see you handle their work with respect;

✓ use appropriate language and symbols in any labels that you add;

✓ check that work is trimmed and properly aligned;

✓ make sure that titles and labels are clearly legible;

✓ arrange work at a good viewing height for children;

✓ mount the exhibits – use clean backgrounds and think carefully about colours;

✓ allow space and margins around each piece of work; use appropriate lettering for the age and developmental stage of the children;

✓ talk to the children about the display and encourage them to help when choosing work to put up.

Do not:

✗ use drawing pins (unless instructed to do so by your placement) – they are dangerous and unsightly;

✗ display things where they can be easily damaged, splashed or picked at;

✗ make spelling mistakes;

✗ overcrowd your display space;

✗ waste resources;

✗ leave paper cutters and/or other materials lying around;

✗ cut out parts of the children's drawings or paintings to make them into your own collage. This shows a lack of respect for children's ideas and feelings about their efforts;

When you dismantle the display, put the photos in the child's continuously developing record.

ENCOURAGING CHILDREN TO RELATE TO THE WORLD AROUND THEM

Young children tend to have a genuine curiosity about the natural world around them. If this interest is encouraged it can result in a lifelong awareness and respect for wildlife and the environment. Outdoor time for children in nursery settings is important but limited to a brief period each day in a fenced-in playground with a hard surface, unless there are opportunities for interacting with nature. Most settings can introduce children to a variety of plants and wildlife by taking them outdoors daily, or on trips each day to a park, or sometimes to a children's farm or zoo. Some have an area where children can help with simple gardening activities, such as digging, raking and planting seeds and bulbs. Children may visit a real pond and use nets to examine insects and other pond creatures.

In places where it is not possible to take children outdoors as much as one would wish, you need to find ways to *bring nature indoors*. For example:

* sand, water, pebbles, shells, pinecones, leaves and conkers can be brought in for children's play;

* children can plant seeds and bulbs and watch them grow;

* an aquarium or water table that contains real pond life could be set up in the indoor setting; or children could play with realistic replicas of frogs and fish in the water table;

* prepare an interest table with a variety of natural objects; encourage children to touch them and smell them and to talk about what they are feeling.

ACTIVITY: A NATURAL TREASURE BASKET

Babies learn about their environment using all their senses – touch, smell, taste, sight, hearing and movement. A treasure basket is a collection of everyday objects chosen to stimulate the different senses. Babies have the chance to decide for themselves what they want to play with, choosing in turn whichever object they want to explore.

Choose a sturdy basket or box – one that does not tip over too easily and is not too high for the baby to see in to.

Fill the basket with lots of natural objects – or objects made from natural materials – so that the baby has plenty to choose from:

Examples include:

* fir cones;
* large sea-shells;
* large walnuts;
* pumice stone;
* fruit: e.g. apple, lemon;
* brushes;
* woollen ball;
* wooden pegs;
* small baskets;
* feathers;
* large pebbles;
* gourds.

Make sure that everything you choose for the basket is clean and safe; remember that babies often want to put everything into their mouths – so you need to check that all objects are clean and safe.

Using the treasure basket

Make sure that the baby is seated comfortably and safely, with cushions for support if necessary.

Sit nearby and watch to give the baby confidence. Only talk or intervene if the baby clearly needs attention.

Check the contents of the basket regularly, cleaning objects and removing any damaged items.

Write an observation of the activity, noting the following:

* the length of time the baby plays with each item;
* what he or she does with it;
* any facial expressions or sounds made by the baby.

RISK AND CHALLENGE IN THE ENVIRONMENT

Children are biologically driven to make risk assessments, but only if they are constantly encouraged to use these processes. For example:

* toddlers can be encouraged to come down the stairs (under supervision) sliding on their tummies, feet first. They will pause and check where they are every few steps, making their own risk assessment;

Children who are not supported to make their own risk assessments, by an adult sensitive and helpful to their needs, are more likely to have accidents. In order to set down neural patterns in the brain, children need to develop their sense of balance through spinning, tipping, rolling and tilting. They need rough-and-tumble play, which helps them to have a sense of one part of their body in relation to another. This leads to a sense of identity and embodiment, both central aspects of development and learning. Children who can make risk assessments are more likely to be physically safe. In a predictable environment activities are not controlled by adults all the time, but there is a shape to the day. Children feel safe because they have a sense of what is coming next, such as regular mealtimes and group times for stories, or songs and dances.

Layout of Indoor and Outdoor Learning Environments

In an inclusive early childhood setting, which embraces diversity, the layout and presentation of material provision offer a range of experiences and activities across the birth-to-5-years framework. Increasingly, from the time they can walk, children are integrating with children in the foundation years for parts of the day, which gives a more natural and family-group feeling. Children with special educational needs and disabilities are also included in settings.

Indoor Learning Environment

Given that children from birth to 6 years learn through the senses, the layout needs to support and extend this kind of learning. The layouts from Reggio Emilia and Pistoia in Northern Italy have reminded practitioners in the UK of the importance of:

* an attractive and welcoming entrance area, where children and families are greeted and can find and share information, and feel part of a community;
* natural light;
* the feeling of space without clutter;
* making spaces beautiful using natural materials.

The environment also needs to support and actively encourage and extend the symbolic life of the child, making one thing stand for another (e.g. pretending a leaf is a plate in the outside playhouse). Understanding cause-and-effect relationships is also very important and the learning environment needs to promote this (e.g. kicking the ball hard makes it go a long distance, while tapping it with your toes makes it roll only a little way).

The following should be provided every day:

* wet sand and dry sand (these are two entirely different learning experiences), with equipment nearby in boxes labelled with words and pictures for children to select;
* clean water in a water tray or baby bath, with buckets, guttering, waterwheels, and so on, to make waterfalls, and boxes of equipment labelled with pictures and words;
* found and recycled materials in a workshop area, with glue, scissors, masking tape, and so on;
* small-world toys: doll's house, train set, garage, cars, farms, zoos, dinosaurs;
* paint/graphics materials in a mark-making area, with a variety of paper and different kinds of pencils and pens and chalks (this might be next to the workshop area);
* malleable clay or dough;
* wooden set of free-standing blocks (not plastic, and not bits and pieces from different sets) – unit blocks, hollow blocks and mini hollow blocks (e.g. community playthings);
* construction kit (one or two carefully selected types, such as Duplo® or Brio®);
* book area, which is warm, light and cosy;

* domestic play area;
* dressing-up clothes;
* daily cookery with baking materials and equipment;
* ICT, digital camera, computer – it is preferable to use computer programmes which encourage children to use their imaginations, rather than responding to computer-led tasks;
* nature table, with magnifiers, growing and living things, such as mustard and cress, hyacinths, wormery, fish tank;
* interest table with fascinating objects to handle;
* sewing table;
* woodwork bench;
* a range of dolls and soft toys;
* music and sounds area with home-made and commercially produced instruments;
* story props, poetry and song cards.

Outdoor Learning Environment

Children should be able to learn outside for most of the day if they choose to do so. They need appropriate clothes, and so do adults, so that everyone can be outside in all weathers. The idea that learning can only take place indoors is extraordinary when we stop to think about it.

There should be different surfaces – playground surfaces, grass and an earth patch to dig in, a large, drained sandpit, and planted areas with trees as well as wild areas for butterflies. Settings which do not value the importance of the outdoor learning environment are only offering children half a curriculum.

Children need challenging places to climb and swing, and to be taught how to stay safe and be responsible. Children are biologically driven to make risk assessments, but only if this is encouraged. They need places to run, jump, skip and wheel.

Bikes need to be three-wheeled and two-wheeled, with some needing two or three children cooperating in order to make them work. Scooters and carts to push and pull are also important, as are prams and pushchairs.

Hoses for warmer weather, and a water pump, give children opportunities for learning in many ways, from not splashing others to the science of pumping and spraying. Gardening equipment is needed for the planting areas. Buckets, spades, sieves, and so on, are needed in the sand area.

The outdoor learning environment should echo and mirror the indoor area, but each will offer different experiences. Indoors children will use felt-tip pens and pencils, while outdoors they might chalk on the ground and make marks on a larger scale. Indoors they might use paint and brushes on paper, but outdoors they may have buckets of water and large brushes, and paint on walls and the ground.

Indoors there will be a home corner, and outdoors they will make dens and play in tents; they may wear dressing-up clothes indoors or outdoors.

It is very important that great care is taken of equipment in both environments, so that jigsaw pieces do not end up on a flowerbed, for example. Sets (puzzles, crockery from the home corner, sets of zoo animals, wooden blocks) should not be moved from the area where they belong. If children have made a den and want to have a pretend meal in it, then a picnic box can be taken into the garden, full of bits and bobs. This means that children learn to care for equipment.

Double Provision

Through double provision, the different needs and interests of children from birth to 5 years can be attended to with quality. There might be a workshop area, with carefully selected and presented found materials, such as boxes, tubes, dried flowers, moss, twigs, wool, string, masking tape and glue, scissors and card. Here children could become involved in making models and constructions, and adults can help them to carry out their ideas without losing track of them on the way or becoming frustrated. Children can be helped as they try to join things, and make decisions about whether a string knot would be better than masking tape or glue.

Nearby, on the floor, there might be a beautiful basket full of balls of wool and string, which younger and less experienced children can enjoy unravelling and finding out how these behave. Other children might like to return to this earlier way of using string too.

It is a good idea to try to offer everything at different levels of difficulty, so that there is something for everyone to find absorbing. Engaged children behave better, on the whole.

FEELING VALUED

Children and their families need to feel that they matter and that they are valued for themselves.

Guidelines for helping children to feel valued

* Establish a good relationship with parents; always be welcoming and listen to them.

* Squat down or bend down to the child's level when you are talking with them.
* Praise and encourage children.
* Be responsive to and interested in children's needs.
* Ensure that children experience equality of opportunity and feel included.
* Use positive images in the setting.

SECTION 4: HOW TO DEVELOP AGE-APPROPRIATE ROUTINES WHICH ENCOURAGE CHILDREN TO CARE FOR THEMSELVES

• Basic physical and health needs of children • Caring for children from 1 to 16 years • Older children: caring for the skin • Oral hygiene: caring for children's teeth • The need for rest and sleep • The development of bowel and bladder control • Professional practice in the support of a positive integrated environment

BASIC PHYSICAL AND HEALTH NEEDS OF CHILDREN

From the moment they are born, all children depend completely on an adult to meet all their needs, but the way in which these needs are met will vary considerably according to family circumstances, culture and the personalities of the child and the caring adult.

To achieve and maintain healthy growth and development (that is physical, intellectual, emotional and social development), certain basic needs must be fulfilled:

* food;
* cleanliness;
* sleep, rest and activity;

* protection from infection and injury;
* intellectual stimulation;
* relationships and social contacts;
* shelter, warmth, clothing;
* fresh air and sunlight;
* love, and consistent and continuous affection;
* access to health care;
* appreciation, praise and recognition of effort or achievements;
* security and nurture.

It is difficult to separate these basic needs from practical care, as they all contribute to the holistic development of a healthy child.

Caring for babies from birth to one year is covered in Unit 18 on CD-ROM.

CARING FOR CHILDREN FROM 1 TO 16 YEARS

Care and Protection of the Skin and Hair

As children grow and become involved in more vigorous exercise, especially outside, a daily bath or shower becomes necessary. Most young children love bath time, and adding bubble bath to the water adds to the fun of getting clean.

Guidelines for caring for the skin and hair

* Wash face and hands in the morning.
* Always wash hands after using the toilet and before meals; young children will need supervision.

* Girls should be taught to wipe their bottom from front to back to prevent germs from the anus entering the vagina and urethra.
* Nails should be scrubbed with a soft nailbrush and trimmed regularly by cutting straight across.
* Each child should have his or her own flannel, comb and brush, which must be cleaned regularly.
* Skin should always be thoroughly dried, taking special care with areas such as between the toes and under the armpits; black skin tends to dryness and may need massaging with special oils or moisturisers.
* Observe skin for any defects, such as rashes, dryness or soreness, and act appropriately.
* Hair usually needs washing only twice a week; children with long or curly hair benefit from the use of a conditioning shampoo which helps to reduce tangles. Hair should always be rinsed thoroughly in clean water and not brushed until it is dry (brushing wet hair damages the hair shafts). A wide-toothed comb is useful for combing wet hair.
* Afro-Caribbean hair tends to dryness and may need special oil or moisturisers; if the hair is braided (with or without beads), it may be washed with the braids left intact, unless otherwise advised.
* Rastafarian children with hair styled in dreadlocks may not use either combs or shampoo, preferring to brush the dreadlocks gently and secure them with braid; some will wear scarves or caps in the Rastafarian colours of red, gold, green and black.

> * Devout Sikhs believe that the hair must never be cut or shaved, and young children usually wear a special head covering.

OLDER CHILDREN: CARING FOR THE SKIN

Acne is a common skin condition which usually affects teenagers and young adults. However, it can develop at any age. It is most common on the face, but can also occur on the back, chest, shoulders and neck. Acne consists of blackheads and whiteheads (comedones). *Acne vulgaris* is a more serious condition which consists of larger pimples and pustules or large cysts. Permanent scarring can occur after these spots have gone. Less serious acne can also scar unless proper care is taken.

What Causes Acne?

* The ducts of the sebaceous (oil) glands become blocked with dirt, bacteria and dead skin cells.

* The sebaceous glands produce an oily substance called sebum; they are connected to a hair-containing canal called the follicle. Sebum travels to the surface of the skin through the opening of the follicle. The oil seems to stimulate the lining of the wall of the follicle, causing cells to shed more rapidly and stick together, plugging the opening to the skin's surface. This causes whiteheads and blackheads.

* The mixture of oil and cells also helps bacteria, which is normally present on the skin, to grow in the follicle. The bacteria produce chemicals which can cause the wall of the follicle to break. When this wall is broken the sebum, bacteria and shed skin cells escape, forming skin cysts.

Teenagers are more at risk as the increase of hormone levels during puberty can lead to the sebaceous glands enlarging and producing more sebum. Factors which can lead to acne include stress, diet, or taking hormones or corticosteroids. For women the onset of menstrual periods, pregnancy, and oral contraceptive pills can also affect the skin.

Facts about Acne

* **Acne is *not* caused by dirt:** the blackness of a blackhead is not dirt; it is due mainly to dried oil and shed skin cells in the openings of the follicles. Wash twice a day with mild soap. Always wash in the evening, to remove the dirt from the day. An antibacterial soap product can also be used. Do not wash too often, as excess washing may actually aggravate acne.

* **Greasy hair adds to skin surface oil and can contribute to clogging pores:** ensure that hair is always clean and tied back from the face, to avoid irritation. Do not attempt to hide spots under a fringe, as this will irritate them further.

* **Do not pick, squeeze or scratch the spots:** more redness, swelling, inflammation and scarring may result.

* **Avoid oil-based cosmetics:** use water-based make-up sparingly and ensure that it is removed properly in the evening. Look out for cosmetics which are labelled 'non-comedogenic', as these do not block the pores.

* **Exposure to sun:** some people have found that exposure to the sun can reduce acne.

* **Foods:** there is no evidence that specific foods, such as fried foods or chocolate, can cause acne. However, it could help to avoid fatty or sweet foods. Skin will always benefit from a healthy diet which includes drinking plenty of water. Some people find that their acne seems to become worse when they eat certain foods. If that is the case, then those particular foods should be avoided.

If acne persists, consult medical advice; a doctor will be able to prescribe various treatments depending on the severity and type of acne.

ORAL HYGIENE: CARING FOR CHILDREN'S TEETH

During the first year of life, babies eat their first solid food with the help of their primary teeth (or milk teeth). These 20 teeth start to appear at around the age of 6 months (see Fig 10.5).

There are three types of primary teeth:

* **incisors:** tough, chisel-shaped teeth with a sharp edge to help in biting food;
* **canines:** pointed teeth which help to tear food into manageable chunks;
* **molars:** large, strong teeth which grind against each other to crush food.

Looking after Teeth

Teeth need cleaning as soon as they appear. A substance called **plaque** sticks to the teeth and will cause decay if not removed. Caring for the temporary first teeth – or milk teeth – is important because:

* it develops a good hygiene habit which will continue throughout life;
* if milk teeth decay, they may need to be extracted; this could lead to crowding in the mouth as the natural gaps for the second teeth to fill will be too small;
* painful teeth may prevent chewing and cause eating problems;
* clean, white, shining teeth look good.

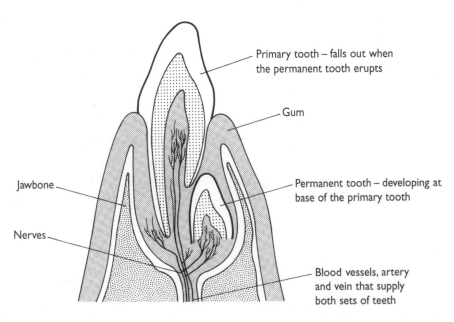

Fig 10.4 Structure of a primary tooth

Primary tooth – falls out when the permanent tooth erupts

Gum

Permanent tooth – developing at base of the primary tooth

Blood vessels, artery and vein that supply both sets of teeth

Jawbone

Nerves

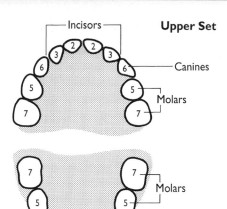

Fig 10.5 The usual order in which primary teeth appear

Use a soft baby toothbrush at first to clean the plaque from the teeth; after their first birthday, children can be taught to brush their own teeth, but will need careful supervision. They should be shown when and how to brush – that is, up and away from the gum when cleaning the lower teeth, and down and away when cleaning the upper teeth. They may need help to clean the back molars.

Rarely, a baby is born with a first tooth and it may have to be removed if it is loose. Most children have 'cut' all 20 primary teeth by the age of 3 years.

There are 32 permanent teeth. These replace the milk teeth, and start to come through at about the age of 6 years. The milk teeth that were first to appear become loose first and fall out as the permanent teeth begin to push through the gums.

Development of Teeth from 6 Years Onwards

* **By 6–7 years:** most children have lost first baby teeth (the first lower incisor teeth). These are replaced by adult teeth. Adult molar teeth erupt, behind the last baby teeth, into space made available by growth of the jaws.

* **By 7–8 years:** the second lower incisors and first upper incisors have replaced baby teeth.

* **During the 9th year:** the second upper incisors erupt followed by lower adult canine teeth. Adult teeth are both larger and more numerous than baby teeth. During this transition the jaws are growing along with the rest of the child. Often, however, the growth of jaws is not enough to make room for all adult teeth. This leads to overcrowding and irregularity of teeth, which may require extractions and orthodontic treatment.

* **By 10–11 years:** by this age, first baby molars have usually been lost and replaced by first adult premolars.

* **By 11–12 years:** by this age, most children have lost all remaining baby teeth and adult second premolars and upper canine teeth erupt;

* **13–21 years:** by this age, children have usually had second molar teeth erupt at the back of the mouth and between 17 and 21 years the final teeth, the third molars or wisdom teeth erupt.

Once all the baby teeth are lost – at around 12–13 years – dentists recommend regular **flossing** to ensure that all the plaque is removed from the teeth. It takes time and practice to master this technique. Children and young people should continue to:

* brush their teeth twice a day;

* try to avoid a daily diet which contains too many sugary foods and drinks;

* try to restrict sugar consumption to three times per day, at meal times. If hungry between meals, they should eat a safe snack containing no sugar.

Fluoride

Some toothpastes contain fluoride, which is a mineral that can help prevent dental decay. Some water boards in the UK add fluoride to the water supply; in areas where the fluoride level is low, dentists recommend giving daily fluoride drops to children from 6 months of age until teething is complete (usually by age 12 years). If water in your area has added fluoride, do not give drops or tablet supplements as an excess of the mineral can cause mottling of the teeth.

Diet

For healthy teeth we need calcium, fluoride, vitamins A, C and D, and foods that need chewing, such as apples, carrots and wholemeal bread. Sugar causes decay and can damage teeth even before they have come through – 'dinky feeders' and baby bottles filled with sweet drinks are very harmful. It is better to save sweets and sugary snacks for special occasions, or to give them only after meals if teeth are cleaned thoroughly afterwards.

Visiting the Dentist

The earlier a child is introduced to the family dentist, the less likely she is to feel nervous about dental inspection and treatment. Regular six-monthly visits to a dentist from about the age of 3 years will ensure that any necessary advice and treatment is given to combat dental caries (tooth decay). Once the child starts primary school, a visiting dentist will check every child's teeth and will refer them for treatment if appropriate.

ACTIVITY: A DENTAL HYGIENE ROUTINE

1   Plan a routine for a toddler that will cover all aspects of dental hygiene:

 * brushing teeth;
 * dietary advice;
 * education about teeth/visits to the dentist.

2   Include examples of books that could be used to help prepare a child for a visit to the dentist.

3   Remember to give a reason for each part of the routine.

THE NEED FOR REST AND SLEEP

Children vary in their need for sleep and in the type of sleep they require. Sleep and rest are needed for:

* relaxation of the central nervous system (CNS): the brain does not rest completely during sleep; electrical activity – which can be measured by an electroencephalogram (EEG) – continues;

* recovery of the muscles and the body's metabolic processes: growth hormone is released during sleep to renew tissues, and produce new bone and red blood cells.

Some children prefer to rest quietly in their cots rather than have a sleep during the day; others will continue to have one or two daytime naps even up to the age of 3 or 4 years.

Older children also need a routine which allows for adequate rest and sleep; young people who are consistently deprived of sleep during puberty are smaller than they should be – this is because the growth hormone is released principally at night, with short bursts every one to two hours during the deep-sleep phase.

Establishing a Bedtime Routine

In the context of modern life in the UK, children benefit from a regular routine at bedtime; it helps to establish healthy habits and makes children feel more secure. A child will only sleep if actually tired, so it is vital that she has had enough exercise and activity. The stress on parents of a child who will not sleep at night can be severe (about 10–20 per cent per cent of very young children have some sort of sleep problem); establishing a routine that caters for the child's *individual needs* may help parents to prevent such problems developing. Principles involved are:

* ensuring that the child has had enough exercise during the day;

* making sure that the environment is conducive to sleep – a soft nightlight and non-stimulating toys might help, with no activity going on around bedtime;

* following the precept 'never let the sun go down on a quarrel' – a child who has been in trouble during the day needs to feel reassured that all is forgiven before bedtime;

* warning the child that bedtime is approaching and then following the set routine – see guidelines below;

* reducing anxiety and stress – it is quite natural for a small child to fear being left alone or abandoned; the parents should let the child know they are still around by, for example, talking quietly or having the radio on, rather than creeping around silently.

Guidelines for a bedtime routine

The following suggestions can be helpful in establishing a bedtime routine.

* Warn the child that bedtime will be at a certain time (e.g. after a bath and story).

* Take a family meal one and a half to two hours before bedtime; this should be a relaxing, social occasion.

* After the meal, the child can play with other members of the family.

* Make bath time a relaxing time to unwind and play gently; this often helps the child to feel drowsy.

* Give a final bedtime drink, followed by teeth cleaning.

* Read or tell a story: looking at books together or telling a story enables the child to feel close to the carer.

* Settle the child in bed, with curtains drawn and nightlight on if desired. Then say goodnight and leave.

Any care must take into account cultural preferences, such as later bedtimes, and family circumstances: a family living in bed and breakfast accommodation may have to share bathroom facilities, or bedtime may be delayed to enable a working parent to be involved in the routine.

ACTIVITY: BEDTIME ROUTINE

1   Arrange to visit a family with a young child (ideally, your family placement) to talk about the child's bedtime routine. Devise a questionnaire to find out the following:

   * any problems settling the child to sleep;
   * any problems with the child waking in the night;
   * strategies used to address the problems.

2   Using the answers from the questionnaire to help you, devise a bedtime routine for a 3-year-old girl who has just started nursery school and whose mother has 3-month-old twin boys.

   Points to include are:

   * how to arrange one-to-one care for the 3-year-old;
   * how to avoid jealousy.

THE DEVELOPMENT OF BOWEL AND BLADDER CONTROL

Newborn babies pass the waste products of digestion automatically; in other words, although they may go red in the face when passing a stool or motion, they have no conscious control over the action. Parents used to boast with pride that all their children were potty trained at 9 months, but the reality is that they were lucky in their timing! Up to the age of 18 months, emptying of the bladder and bowel is still a totally automatic reaction – the child's central nervous system (CNS) is still not sufficiently mature to make the connection between the action and its results.

Toilet Training

There is no point in attempting to start toilet training until the toddler shows that he or she is ready, and this rarely occurs before the age of 18 months. The usual signs are:

   * increased interest when passing urine or a motion – the child may pretend play on the potty with their toys;
   * they may tell the carer when they have passed urine or a bowel motion or look

very uncomfortable when they have done so;

   * they may start to be more regular with bowel motions or wet nappies may become rarer.

Toilet training should be approached in a relaxed, unhurried manner. If the potty is introduced too early or if a child is forced to sit on it for long periods of time, he may rebel and the whole issue of toilet training becomes a battleground. Toilet training can be over in a few days or may take some months. Becoming dry at night takes longer, but most children manage this before the age of 5 years.

Guidelines for toilet training

   * Before attempting to toilet train a child, make sure she has shown that she is ready to be trained. Remember that there is, as with all developmental milestones, a wide variation in the age range at which children achieve bowel and bladder control.
   * Be relaxed about toilet training and be prepared for accidents.
   * Have the potty in the home so that the child becomes familiar

with it and can include it in her play.

* Some children feel insecure when sitting on a potty with no nappy on – try it first still wearing nappy or pants if she shows reluctance.

* It is easier to attempt toilet training in fine weather when the child can run around without a nappy or pants.

* It helps if the child sees other children using the toilet or potty.

* If you start training when there is a new baby due, be prepared for some accidents. Many children react to a new arrival by regressing to baby behaviour.

* Training pants, similar to ordinary pants but with a waterproof covering, are useful in the early stages of training – and having more than one potty in the house makes life easier. Pull-up nappies are a newer version of training pants.

* Always praise the child when she succeeds and do not show anger or disapproval if she doesn't – she may be upset by an accident.

* Offer the potty regularly so that the child becomes used to the idea of a routine, and learn to read the signs that a child needs to use it.

* Don't show any disgust for the child's faeces. She will regard using the potty as an achievement and will be proud of them. Children have no natural shame about their bodily functions (unless adults make them ashamed).

* Some children are frightened when the toilet is flushed; be tactful and sympathetic. You could wait to flush until the child has left the room.

* Cover the potty and flush the contents down the toilet. Always wear disposable gloves.

* Encourage good hygiene right from the start by washing the child's hands after every use of the potty.

* The child may prefer to try the 'big' toilet seat straight away; a toddler seat fixed onto the normal seat makes this easier. Boys need to learn to stand in front of the toilet and aim at the bowl before passing any urine; you could put a piece of toilet paper in the bowl for him to aim at.

Dealing with 'Accidents'

Even once a child has become used to using the potty or toilet, there will be occasions when they have an 'accident'; that is, they wet or soil themselves. This happens more often during the early stages of toilet training, as the child may lack the awareness and the control needed to allow enough time to get to the potty. Older children may become so absorbed in their play that they simply forget to go to the toilet.

You can help children when they have an 'accident' by:

* not appearing bothered; let the child know that it is not a big problem, just something that happens from time to time;

* reassuring the child in a friendly tone of voice and by offering a cuddle if they seem distressed;

* being discreet; deal with the matter swiftly – wash and change them out of view of others and with the minimum of fuss;

* encouraging an older child to manage the incident themselves, if they wish to do so, but always check tactfully afterwards that they have managed;

* following safety procedures in the setting; e.g. wear disposable gloves and deal appropriately with soiled clothing and waste.

ACTIVITY: TOILET TRAINING

* Arrange to interview a parent or carer who has recently toilet trained a child.
* Try to find out the methods used and any problems encountered.
* Write a report of the methods used.
* In class, discuss the problems which can arise in toilet training and compare the strategies used by different families.

* In small groups, make a colourful, eye-catching wall display that provides tips for parents and carers on potty training.

Enuresis (Bedwetting)

Enuresis is a common occurrence; about one in 10 children wets the bed at the age of 6 years, and many of these continue to do so until the age of 8 or 9 years. It is more common in boys than in girls and the problem tends to run in families. In the majority of children, enuresis is due to slow maturation of the nervous system functions concerned with control of the bladder; very rarely, it occurs because of emotional stress or because of a physical problem such as urinary infection.

Managing Bedwetting

* Investigate possible physical causes first, by taking the child to the doctor.

* Protect the mattress with a plastic sheet.

* Do not cut down on the amount a child drinks in a day, although a bedtime drink could be given earlier; never let a child go to bed feeling thirsty.

* Encourage the child to pass urine just before going to bed; it sometimes helps to 'lift' the child just before adults go to bed, taking her to the toilet. It is important, however, that the child is thoroughly awake when passing urine; this is because she will need to recognise the link between passing urine on the toilet and waking up with a dry bed.

* Some parents find that a 'star chart' system of rewards for a dry bed encourages the child to become dry sooner, but there are problems with all reward systems – see Chapter 7. This should be used only if physical problems have been excluded.

* If the child continues to wet the bed after the age of 7 years, a special night-time alarm system can be used: a detector mat is placed under the sheet. This triggers a buzzer as soon as it becomes wet; eventually, the child will wake before he needs to pass urine (this system is said to succeed in over two-thirds of children).

Encopresis (Soiling)

Encopresis is a type of soiling in which children who have no physical problems with their bowel motions deliberately pass them in their pants or on the floor. It occurs after the age at which bowel control is usually achieved and in children who know the difference between the right and wrong place to go. It is fortunately a rare condition but one which needs very sensitive treatment. Encopresis may occur because of emotional problems and stress; if it persists, advice should be sought from the health visitor or doctor.

PROFESSIONAL PRACTICE IN THE SUPPORT OF A POSITIVE INTEGRATED ENVIRONMENT

Early years practitioners need to ensure that all children feel included, secure and valued; this is the cornerstone of a positive, integrated environment. As a professional, your practice should include:

* developing positive relationships with parents in order to work effectively with them and their children;

* understanding the extent of your responsibilities and being answerable to others for your work;

* working effectively as part of a team;

* knowing the lines of reporting and how to get clarification about your role and duties;

* understanding what is meant by confidentiality and your role in the preserving of secret or privileged information that parents or others share with you about their children or themselves.

Dealing with Your Own Feelings

Throughout this chapter the emphasis has been on what *you* can do for the children in your care – how you can promote their development and give them a quality learning environment. It may sometimes feel as if you are less important than they are.

This is far from the truth. Children need you to be strong and positive for them, but you also need to be strong and positive for yourself.

Stress caused by work is the second biggest occupational health problem in the UK (after back problems). Because there's still a stigma attached to mental health problems, employees are often reluctant to seek help in case they're seen as unable to cope.

Many situations can lead to stress at work. These include:

* poor relationships with colleagues;

* work that is too difficult or not demanding enough;

* an unsupportive boss;

* lack of control over the way the work is done;

* lack of consultation and communication;

* poor working conditions;

* too much interference with your private, social or family life;

* being in the wrong job;

* too much or too little to do;

* feeling undervalued;

* too much pressure, with unrealistic deadlines;

* insecurity and the threat of unemployment.

Any one of these situations could leave you feeling low and lacking in confidence. Chapter 11 discusses strategies to use if you are having negative feelings at work or feel under pressure.

Sources of Support for Practitioners

If work-related stress is affecting you, it is important to deal with the problem as soon as possible. One of the most important factors in reducing stress levels is managing time effectively. When you are the 'junior' in a team, the amount you are expected to do can seem overwhelming. Remember, everyone has to go through this at the beginning. Apart from following the guidelines for reducing stress in Chapter 11, you could also:

* discuss the problems with your manager or senior worker; make notes to help

you to focus on what is bothering you and take them with you when you talk to your manager;

* ask your tutor or teacher for advice. Remember that he or she will have seen many students through various practical placements and will have encountered most situations!

CASE STUDY

The stressful situation

Marsha recently obtained a qualification in child care and has been employed as a nursery nurse at Meadlands Day Nursery for 2 weeks. She has just been called in to see her supervisor as her colleagues have reported that she is frequently tearful and unable to contribute to activities in the nursery. Carol, her supervisor, asks why she is unhappy, and Marsha says that she 'doesn't like the atmosphere in the nursery, that there is a lot of bickering between the staff, and she feels that one particular child is constantly being ridiculed by her colleagues'. Carol asks her

to give more information about the complaints, but Marsha bursts into tears and asks if she can go home as she can't cope any more.

1 Identify and write down the stressors (the factors producing stress) which Marsha mentions.

2 How should Carol deal with this situation?

3 Find out about the Type A and Type B personalities from psychology textbooks. Are some personalities more suited to working in early years settings?

CHAPTER 11

The Principles Underpinning the Role of the Practitioner Working with Children

This chapter covers **Unit 5** and is divided into four sections:

Section 1: How to maintain professional relationships with children and adults

Section 2: The skills needed to become a reflective practitioner

Section 3: The differing principles and practices that underpin working with different-age children

Section 4: The current national and local initiatives and issues relevant to the sector

SECTION 1: HOW TO MAINTAIN PROFESSIONAL RELATIONSHIPS WITH CHILDREN AND ADULTS

• Place in multi-disciplinary teams • Employment/employer angle • Working with parents • Communication skills • Responsibilities • Reliability • Accountability • Employment rights and responsibilities

UNDERSTANDING GROUP DYNAMICS AND TEAMWORK

A group is a collection of two or more people who possess a common purpose.

1 **Formal groups** are deliberately created by their managers for particular planned purposes. It is the management who select group members, leaders and methods of doing work.

2 **Informal groups** are formed by people who feel they share a common interest. Members organise themselves and develop a sense of affinity both to each other and to a common cause.

Group Norms

A group norm is a shared perception of how things should be done, or a common attitude, feeling or belief. Norms are closely linked to expectations: as the group norms emerge, individuals start to behave in ways in which they believe other group members expect them to behave.

Group Cohesion

Group cohesion is the extent to which group members are prepared to cooperate and to share common goals. Cohesion encourages compliance to group norms and causes groups to be more stable in their functioning.

Certain factors contribute to the creation of group cohesion. These are discussed in the box below.

Factors which create group cohesion

✱ The frequency and closeness of interactions: the more often people meet and the closer their contact, the more they will perceive themselves as belonging to a distinct group.

✱ Exclusivity of membership: if membership of the group is selective, members feel a sense of achievement in having been chosen.

✱ The nature of the external environment: the environment in which a group operates may offer protection from a hostile external environment, e.g. Neighbourhood Watch groups.

✱ Good interpersonal communication: if communication is easy, then a collective sense of purpose will readily emerge; and the less contact with outsiders, the greater the internal cohesiveness.

✱ The nature of the task: if the individuals are all engaged in similar work, then they will more readily perceive themselves as a group.

✱ Homogeneity of membership: where members are alike in terms of background, education, age, social origin etc., they are likely to share some common attitudes.

✱ Rewards and penalties: a group that can offer rewards or bonuses, or even punish its own members, can exert great pressure on

---

individuals to conform. In such cases, group cohesiveness tends to be very strong.

The Value of Teamwork

In child care settings, a team is a group of people who work together to meet the aims of their establishment – for example, a day nursery with the aim of providing care for an early years group. Most practitioners are required to work alongside colleagues in a team; even someone employed as a nanny in a private home is operating in a team with the family. Some people, furthermore, work in a multidisciplinary team – for example, a team consisting of a doctor, police officer, teacher, social worker and perhaps a parent may attend a case conference on a child at risk.

To function well as a team, the team members must be:

* motivated towards **common goals**;
* provided with the **support** and **encouragement** necessary to achieve these goals;
* able to **communicate** effectively.

LEADERSHIP AND MANAGEMENT

All organisations have to be managed, although the styles of management involved can vary considerably. The managerial team of most organisations must:

* plan;
* establish goals;
* control operations;
* appraise its employees.

A successful team needs good leadership or management. Leadership is the ability to influence the thoughts and behaviour of others. A leader's position may be formal, resulting from designated organisational authority (e.g. a nursery manager) or informal in nature (e.g. depending on the individual's personal ability to exercise power). There is a continuum of possible leadership styles, extending from complete autocracy at one extreme to total democracy at the other.

Autocratic Leadership

Characteristics of the Autocratic Style

* The leader tells the subordinates exactly what to do, without comment or discussion.
* There are rewards for good performance and penalties or threats of sanctions for underperformance.
* There is strict control and a highly formal network of interpersonal relations between the leader and team members.

Advantages of the Autocratic Style

* Everyone knows precisely what is expected of them: tasks, situations and relationships are clearly defined.
* Time management is usually good as the manager sets the standards and coordinates the work.
* Decisions are arrived at speedily as there is no consultation with others.
* Employees receive direct and immediate help towards achieving their goals.

Disadvantages of the Autocratic Style

* It stifles the workers' own initiative.
* It does not make maximum use of the employees' knowledge, skills and experiences.

* Staff cannot reach their true potential.
* If the group leader is absent, e.g. ill or on holiday, important work may not be completed.

Autocratic styles of leadership are not often seen in child care settings.

Democratic Styles

Characteristics of the Democratic Style

* At its extreme, this style uses the 'laissez-faire' (that is, the practice of letting people do as they wish) approach. A group may not even have a leader, but may have someone who acts as a facilitator.
* There is a great deal of communication and consultation between the leader/ facilitator and the group. It is recognised that everyone has a contribution to make.
* Group members actively participate in the leader's/facilitator's decisions. If unanimity is impossible, then a vote is taken.
* Distributive leadership means different members lead on different aspects, reporting to the overall leader/manager.

Advantages of the Democratic Style

* The job satisfaction of group members is greater, through widening their responsibilities and making their work more interesting and varied.
* The morale of group members is improved as they have a key role in planning and decision-taking.
* Specialist knowledge and skills are recognised and used towards achieving goals.
* Targets are more likely to be achieved because they have been formulated by group consensus.

Disadvantages of the Democratic Style

* Some group members may not want to become involved in the decision-making process.
* Time management may be more problematic, because of the extra time necessary for full consultation of the group.
* A lack of positive direction may prevent goals from being attained.
* Employees may feel resentful because they are only involved in minor day-to-day issues and do not have any real say in the major issues.
* Subordinates may require closer supervision.

COMMUNICATION PATTERNS WITHIN CARE ORGANISATIONS

Business Structures

Most business organisations are **hierarchical** in structure. Those at the top of the hierarchy take the most important decisions, and are rewarded by the highest salaries. They communicate their decisions downwards through a chain of command. The number of levels within the hierarchy can vary a great deal, but the fewer there are, generally the greater the efficiency.

Information can flow within the hierarchy in three directions:

1 downwards from top to bottom;
2 upwards from bottom to top;
3 sideways at various levels.

Whatever system of management is used, a large amount of information must flow down the hierarchy from top management to the shop floor (or domestic staff). Research has proved that downward communication can be very inefficient, with only 20 per cent of information reaching the bottom of the pyramid.

Communication from the bottom upwards has two important purposes:

* to feed back information on the action that has been taken in response to messages sent downwards;
* to alert the decision-makers to the feelings and attitudes of those lower down the organisation.

Line Managers

Many large organisations with grouped specialities use line authority. Line managers are directly responsible for achieving the organisation's objectives, and exert direct authority over their subordinates. In line authority:

* authority flows through the chain of command from the apex to the base;
* the chain of command is illustrated by means of an organisation chart;
* each position in the line system involves points of contact between manager and subordinates, and shows clearly both the authority of its occupant and to whom that person is responsible;
* vertical communications proceed only through the line system.

WORKING IN A TEAM

Attending Team Meetings

In most work settings, being part of the staff team means participating in meetings to discuss, and to make decisions about, a wide range of issues. You are expected to attend and you must 'make your apologies'

(to the person holding the meeting) if, for a genuine reason, you are unable to attend.

At any formal meeting, there is usually a set format:

1 An **agenda** (or **programme**): this is a list of items which will be discussed – some items will appear at every meeting. Apologies for absence are usually received and recorded at the start of any meeting.

2 A written record, called the **minutes**. Most meetings begin by looking at the minutes of the last one, to remind everyone what was decided and to find out what has happened since. Someone will be given responsibility for 'taking the minutes'.

3 **Any other business:** most meetings allow time for issues not included in the formal agenda to be brought up and discussed; for example, a problem with discipline that has arisen or equipment that has been damaged since the meeting was arranged.

4 **Date for the next meeting:** this is set and agreed by those attending the meeting.

After the meeting, the person who has taken the minutes will type or write them out neatly and arrange for copies to be sent to all the people who attended or who were invited but were unable to attend.

Some meetings are informal – perhaps arranged to talk about planning next month's topic or theme, or to finalise arrangements for an outing. Others may be more formal, perhaps covering policy matters. There is one person who leads (or chairs) the meeting and makes sure the items on the agenda are being dealt with – it is very easy for people to begin their own conversations or stray from the subject in hand!

Remember that you are there to contribute your ideas and thoughts and to listen to those of others.

At a meeting, try to:

* listen carefully to information being given;

* check that you know what is expected of you at the meeting and afterwards;

* make sure you bring pen and paper and any other things that will be needed (e.g. an observation of a child who is being discussed);

* understand that you may not share the views of others, or agree with all decisions made;

* contribute your ideas and opinions clearly and at the appropriate time – not when everyone has started talking about the next item;

* ask questions about anything you do not understand.

Communication Skills in Team Meetings

In most settings team meetings are held regularly, and are conducted according to an agreed agenda. Ideally, the written agenda should be given to all team members and should include a space for anyone to add their own item for discussion.

Certain factors may detract from the value of team meetings:

* **Distractions:** constant interruptions, from either telephone calls or visitors, will prevent progress from being made.

* **Irrelevant topics:** some meetings become a forum for gossip or other topics that are irrelevant to the task in hand.

* **A dominating member:** one person may be aggressive and outspoken, blocking other people's contributions.

Assertiveness

Assertiveness makes communication at team meetings more effective; this should not be confused with loudness or aggressive behaviour. Assertiveness may be defined, in this context, as standing up for your own basic rights and beliefs, without isolating those of others, and as making your behaviour 'match' your feelings.

Guidelines for being assertive

If you are assertive in your behaviour, you:

* can express your feelings, without being unpleasant;

* are able to state your views and wishes directly, spontaneously and honestly;

* respect the feelings and rights of other people;

* feel good about yourself and others too;

* can evaluate a situation, decide how to act and then act without reservation;

* are true to yourself;

* value self-expression and the freedom to choose;

* may not always achieve your goals, but feel that is not as important as the actual process of asserting yourself;

* are able to say what you have to say, whether it is positive or negative, while also leaving the other person's dignity intact.

Non-verbal Forms of Assertiveness

* good eye contact;
* a confident posture – standing or sitting comfortably;
* talking in a strong, steady voice;
* not clenching one's fist or pointing with a finger.

Verbal Forms of Assertiveness

* avoiding qualifying words (e.g. 'maybe', 'only' or 'just');
* avoiding disqualifying attacking phrases (e.g. 'I'm sure this isn't important, but . . .');
* avoiding attacking phrases (e.g. those that begin with 'you'; use assertive phrases such as 'I feel').

COMMUNICATION SKILLS

The cornerstone of work with children and young people is **communication**. You must be able to interact (or communicate) effectively with a wide range of other people:

* **babies, children and young people**;
* **colleagues** and **managers**;
* different **professionals**, for example health professionals, social workers and teachers.

Each of these professions has its own angle of perception and jargon.

Communicating with Parents

You will find that there are many occasions when you are responsible for passing information clearly to parents. But parents will want to talk, as well as listen, to you. You will need to develop listening skills. Try to set a particular time for parents so that they do not take your attention when you are involved with the children. For some parents this can be very difficult to arrange, especially if they are working.

Guidelines for communicating well with parents

* Maintaining eye contact helps you to give your full attention to a parent.
* Remember that your body language shows how you really feel.
* Try not to interrupt when someone is talking to you. Nod and smile instead.
* Every so often, summarise the main points of a discussion, so that you are both clear about what has been said.
* If you do not know the answer to a parent's question, say so, and that you will find out. Then, do not forget to do this!
* Remember that different cultures have different traditions. Touching and certain gestures might be seen as insulting by some parents, so be careful.
* If the parent speaks a different language from you, use photographs and visual aids. Talk slowly and clearly.
* If the parent has a hearing impairment, use sign language or visual aids.
* When you are talking together, bear in mind whether this is the parent's first child or whether they have had other children already.
* Remember that if the parents have a child with a disability, they may need to see you more often to discuss the child's progress.
* If the parent has a disability, make sure that when you sit together you are at the same level.

* Occasionally, parents might become upset and will shout at you. If this happens, do not shout back. Simply talk quietly and calmly and show that you are listening to them.
* Never gossip.

For more information on working with parents, see Unit 20 on CD-ROM.

RESPONSIBILITY AND ACCOUNTABILITY IN THE WORKPLACE

The supervisor, line manager, teacher or parent will have certain expectations about your role, and your responsibilities should be detailed in the **job contract** – see below. As a professional, you need to carry out all your duties willingly and to be answerable to others for your work. It is vital that all workers know the **lines of reporting** and how to obtain clarification of their own role and responsibility. If you do not feel confident in carrying out a particular task, either because you do not fully understand it or because you have not been adequately trained, then you have a responsibility to state your concerns and ask for guidance.

EMPLOYMENT RIGHTS AND RESPONSIBILITIES

The law in the UK requires that any employee who works for more than 16 hours a week should have a **contract of employment**. This document must contain the following information:

* the name of the employer and employee;
* the title of the job;
* the date when employment commenced;
* the scale of pay;
* the hours of work;
* entitlement to holidays;
* the length of notice required from employer and employee;
* the procedures for disciplinary action or grievances;
* sick-pay provision;
* pensions and pension schemes.

Responsibility for paying income tax and National Insurance contributions will need to be decided; such payments are usually deducted from your gross pay. Those applying for jobs within the private sector may want to consider using a reputable nanny agency; such agencies are used to negotiating contracts designed to suit both employer and employee.

GRIEVANCE AND COMPLAINTS PROCEDURES

If a dispute arises in the workplace, either among employees or between employees and employers, it must be settled. Usually, this is achieved at an early stage through discussion between colleagues or between the aggrieved person and his immediate superior. If the grievance is not easily settled, however, then an official procedure is needed.

Guidelines on complaints and grievances procedures

* All employees have a right to seek redress for grievances relating to their employment, and every employee must be told how to proceed on this matter.

Table 11.1 A specimen contract for a nanny

Date of issue:

....

This is a contract between (employer's names) and (your name). (Your name) is contracted to work as a nanny by (employer's name) at (employer's address), starting on (starting date).

General Information
The employer is solely responsible for accounting for the employer's and employee's National Insurance and Income Tax contributions. Employer should ensure that they have employer's public liability insurance to cover them should the nanny be injured in the course of work.

Remuneration
The salary is .... per *week/month *before/after deduction of Income Tax and National Insurance payable on .... The employer will ensure that the employee is given a payslip on the day of payment, detailing gross payment, National Insurance and Income Tax deductions and net payment. Overtime will be paid at £.......... net per hour or part thereof.

Hours of work
The employee will be required to work (hours) .... (days of the week) .... and may be called upon for baby-sitting up to (nights per week) .... In addition, the employee may be required to work overtime provided that .... days' notice have been given and agreed in advance. Overtime will be paid in accordance with the overtime detailed in the paragraph above. In addition, the employee will

be entitled to .... *days/weeks paid holiday per year. In the first or final year of service, the employee will be entitled to holidays on a pro rata basis. Holidays may only be carried into next year with the express permission of the employer. Paid compensation is not normally given for holidays not actually taken. The employee will be free on all Bank Holidays or will receive a day off in lieu by agreement.

Duties (please specify) ....

....

....

....

....

....

....

The employee shall be entitled to:

a) Accommodation ❑

b) Bathroom *sole use/ shared ❑

c) Meals (please specify) ❑

d) Use of car *on duty/off duty ❑

e) Other benefits: ....

....

....

Sickness
The employer will pay Statutory Sick Pay (SSP) in accordance with current legislation. Any additional sick pay will be at the employer's discretion.

Termination
In the first four weeks of employment, one week's notice is required on either side. After four weeks' continuous service, either the employer or the employee may terminate the contract by giving .... weeks' notice.

Confidentiality
The employee shall keep all affairs and concerns of the employer, their household and business confidential, unless otherwise required by law.

Discipline
Reasons which might give rise to the need for disciplinary action include the following.

a) Causing a disruptive influence in the household.

b) Job incompetence.

c) Unsatisfactory standard of dress or appearance.

d) Conduct during or outside working hours prejudicial to the interest or reputation of the employer.

e) Unreliability in time-keeping or attendance.

f) Failure to comply with instructions and procedures.

g) Breach of confidentiality clause.

In the event of the need for disciplinary action, the procedure will be: firstly, an oral warning; secondly, a written warning, and thirdly, dismissal. Reasons which might give rise to summary dismissal include drunkenness, theft, illegal drug-taking, child abuse.
Signed by the employer

....

Date ....
Signed by the employee

....

Date ....

* Except in very small establishments, there must be a formal procedure for settling grievances.

* The procedure should be in writing and should be simple and rapid in operation.

* The grievance should normally be discussed first between the

employee and their immediate supervisor.

* The employee should be accompanied, at the next stage of the discussion with management, by their employee representative if they so wish.

* There should be a right of appeal.

Managers should always try to settle the grievance 'as near as possible to the point of origin', in the words of the Industrial Relations Code of Practice.

SECTION 2: THE SKILLS NEEDED TO BECOME A REFLECTIVE PRACTITIONER.

• Reflective cycle • Problem solving in child care contexts • Improving your own learning and performance • Evaluate own performance • SMART targets • Giving and receiving feedback with colleagues, children and adults

WHAT IS A REFLECTIVE PRACTITIONER?

A **reflective practitioner** is an individual who has developed the ability to gain self-knowledge – both of him- or herself and of his or her practice. Reflection allows the practitioner to learn about, evaluate, develop and take a position on his or her practice.

Reflective practice is associated with learning from experience; it is an important strategy for all who work in the caring field and is grounded in the individual's range of values, knowledge, theories and practice, which influence the judgements made about a particular situation.

Reflective practice requires a set of skills that the practitioner must use:

* self-awareness;
* the ability to view situations from multiple perspectives;
* the ability to analyse critically and to search for alternative explanations;
* the ability to use evidence in supporting or evaluating a decision or position.

Other skills include the ability to integrate new knowledge into existing knowledge, while making a judgement on the incident or situation. This is because **evaluation** is central to developing any new perspective.

The Reflective Cycle

CASE STUDY

Using the reflective cycle

Description of experience: What happened?

Claire and I were supervising about 12 children aged 3 years who were using the outdoor play equipment, when one of the children, Sasha, climbed to the top of the little slide and pushed Ben very hard so that he fell and bruised his knees. I picked Ben up to examine his knees and to comfort him. Claire – who is my room supervisor – rushed towards Sasha and gave her an angry shove, saying 'You naughty girl – now *you* know what it feels like!' I then told Claire that I was taking Ben indoors to deal with his injury. By the time I came back outside, Sasha was playing happily on the trikes; Ben was no longer crying and he went off to play indoors at the water tray.

Feelings: How did it make you feel?

I was quite shaken. I felt that Claire had reacted instinctively and lashed out without thinking first. She has quite a short fuse, but I have never seen her do anything like that before. I was annoyed that I did not say anything to Claire about it.

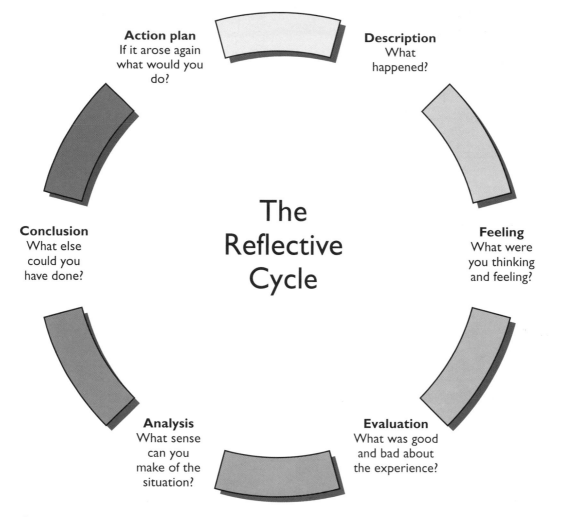

Fig 11.1 The reflective cycle (Gibbs 1988)

Evaluation: What was good and what was bad about the experience?

The good part about the experience was that ultimately neither child was seriously hurt. The bad part was that I had not felt able to talk to Claire about it and felt that the opportunity for telling her how I felt was now lost.

Analysis: What sense can you make of the situation?

I lacked assertiveness. I felt ashamed that I had witnessed bad practice and done nothing about it. I think Claire has been under a lot of stress recently as her mother is in hospital. I think I was hesitant to challenge her because she is senior to me and because normally I would trust her judgement.

Conclusion: what else could you have done?

I could have told Claire that I would like to discuss her behaviour towards Sasha, and could have arranged to see her after work.

STRESS AND CONFLICT IN THE WORKPLACE

There are a number of reasons why conflicts arise in the workplace. The nature of the caring relationship imposes particular stresses that can lead to conflict between team members. There may be:

* **low morale** – individuals may feel unsupported and undervalued in their role;

* confusions over **individual roles** in the hierarchy of the organisation;

* **stresses** associated with the responsibility and accountability for providing care for children who are ill or disadvantaged;

* a **lack of communication** with superiors and colleagues;

* ambiguity over which tasks should take **priority** during the working day;

* an **excessive workload** in both quantitative – i.e. having too much to do – and qualitative – i.e. finding work too difficult – terms;

* feelings of **personal inadequacy and insecurity**, often following destructive criticism of one's work.

Anxiety

Unresolved anxiety will lead to stress. The physical effects of anxiety developed originally as aids to survival and were triggered off by dangerous situations (the 'fight or flight' responses).

There are two types of anxiety:

1 **Objective anxiety:** caused by genuinely stressful events.

2 **Neurotic anxiety:** subjective, often unconscious, feelings which arise within the individual.

Although they have different sources, both types of anxiety are experienced as the same painful emotional state.

Objective anxiety can be addressed by changing the circumstances of the environment in which a person functions, e.g. a social worker who is worried about their own ability to cope with a difficult client can enlist help from their colleagues, or even transfer their responsibilities if necessary.

Neurotic anxiety cannot be removed by controlling external events. Consequently, the ego develops additional ways to protect itself from internal threats. These are called the ego defences.

Ego Defences for 'Coping' with Stress

* **Repression:** unpleasant memories and thoughts are banished from the consciousness and forced into the unconscious mind; this process of repression requires much mental energy, and can quickly lead to abnormal behaviour.

* **Regression:** the individual behaves as they did in an earlier phase of their life; immature behaviour is thus characteristic of those experiencing regression.

* **Displacement:** displacement occurs when an individual diverts their energies away from the area of work which they are finding difficult and instead devotes

themselves completely to other things; for example, a nursery manager whose record-keeping skills are inadequate might channel all their energies into staff training issues, thereby replacing the need to deal with essential administration with an unnecessary concern for trivial matters.

* **Projection:** simple projection occurs when a person unconsciously attributes to another person a characteristic that is, in fact, their own. Personal feelings of dislike, hatred or envy that one person feels towards another and which give rise to internal feelings of neurotic anxiety are projected onto that person. What was originally an internal threat is now experienced as an external threat. Instead of feeling 'I hate you', projection changes this to 'You hate me'. The extreme case is that of the paranoid individual who feels continually threatened by everyone with whom they come into contact.

PROBLEM SOLVING IN CHILD CARE CONTEXTS

A problem occurs when there is a difference between what 'should be' and what 'is' – between the ideal and the actual situation. Problem solving is important in child care contexts, both for the children's learning and for the adult's practice. Problem solving is:

* a **tool**, which helps you to achieve a goal;

* a **skill**, because, once learnt, it stays with you for life, in the same way as being able to read and write; and

* a **process**, because it involves taking a number of steps.

Problem solving is also the foundation of a young child's learning. Opportunities for problem solving occur in the everyday context of a child's life; by observing the child closely, child care practitioners can use the child's social, cognitive, physical and emotional experiences to encourage problem solving and to promote strategies which will be of lasting value.

One of the skills of being a **reflective practitioner** is to learn how to solve problems effectively.

A Problem-solving Cycle

There are various different models of a problem-solving cycle. Some are more suited to engineering problems where scientific investigation is important.

CASE STUDY

A worked example

1   Actual experience: **this is something which is identified as a problem – i.e. there is a difference between what 'should be' and what 'is'.**

Bethany, a 3½-year-old girl, attends a nursery on four days a week. She is a very lively girl and her key person, Emma, has noticed a problem during story time. Bethany wriggles and fidgets throughout the story; she gets up and walks around. She picks toys up and 'whizzes' them through the air. Bethany sometimes copies the other children when they are responding to the adult, but usually whines when fetched back to sit in the group.

2   Analyse the problem: **gather information about the problem, through observation and data from other sources.**

Emma observes Bethany, using an event-sampling observational technique. She discusses the problem with Bethany's mother

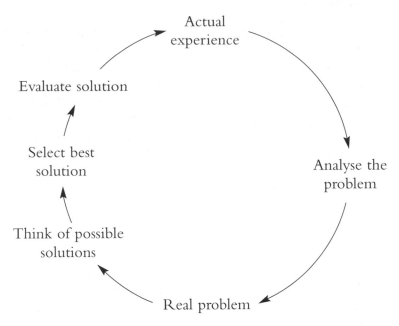

Fig 11.2 A problem-solving cycle

and also tables it to be discussed at the next team meeting. Bethany's mother tells Emma that Bethany is always lively at home and doesn't even sit still at meal times. She has a new baby brother at home who is now 3 months old.

3 Real problem: after analysing the information obtained, the cause of the problem is decided.

Emma decides that the real problem is one of attention-seeking behaviour. Bethany did not have this problem until after the birth of her brother; her mother says that she doesn't even sit still at meal times at home.

4 Think of possible solutions: brainstorm and analyse data; ensure that many possible ideas are explored and as much relevant data as possible is gathered.

After discussion at the team meeting, Emma comes up with a range of possible solutions:

* Encourage Bethany to improve her listening skills by working one to one with her and reading.

* Encourage Bethany to choose a friend with whom to listen to a story read by an adult.

* Plan story times to include more opportunities for active movement.

* Set up a system of rewards – such as a star chart – which would apply to all the children at story time, rewarding wanted behaviour. Bethany's parents would be encouraged to continue this system at home.

* Encourage play with an infant doll – involving Bethany in feeding and caring for the doll.

* Choose books which promote discussion about young babies in the family.

5 Select best solution: make sure the solution is achievable within time and resource constraints.

It is decided to encourage Bethany to play with a doll and to read books about the birth of a new baby in the family, with one-to-one attention. If this does not work, Emma will introduce a reward system, with the parents' cooperation.

6 Evaluate solution: how effective was the solution? If the problem was not solved, you may need to start the whole process again.

Bethany responds well to both strategies. She begins to carry the doll around at home and 'care' for it just like Mummy is caring for her brother. She also enjoys sitting quietly while an adult reads to her. Story time behaviour is greatly improved. Emma plans to work with mothers who are expecting a baby to prepare the older sibling for the event, using books and dolls – both in the nursery and at home.

Observations, discussion and involving the parents were key to solving the problem and also encouraged reflective practice.

CASE STUDY

Problem solving

Helen is a manager in a day nursery in an inner city area. There are six full-time members of staff at the nursery, caring for 34 children. Two newly qualified nursery nurses have recently been employed, and Helen has noticed new tensions within the nursery. One of the new workers, Sarah, has asked for 3 weeks' annual leave at Christmas, so that she can visit her family in Australia. Darren, who has worked there for 8 years, always takes 2 weeks off at that time, to visit Ireland. The other new staff member, Dianne, has suggested a more positive approach to equal opportunities, with more emphasis on multicultural provision, the observance of festivals and more variety in the daily menu etc. One of the more experienced members of staff claims that the nursery already offers equal opportunities and that any changes are both unnecessary and expensive; she also claims that parents are not in agreement with such plans.

In addition, another staff member, Pat, has had a great deal of time off work because her father has recently died; the rest of the staff feel that her absences have gone on for an unreasonable length of time, and they are tired of having to take on extra work.

Divide into groups and discuss the following questions:

1 How should Helen deal with these issues?

2 Do you think they are all equally important, or should any one issue be addressed before the others?

ACTIVITY: PROBLEM SOLVING

Try a similar problem-solving exercise in your workplace, using the problem-solving cycle above. Use structured observations to help monitor the problem you have identified.

3 Which management style works best in this care setting?
Feed back each group's answers into the whole group and summarise the strategies for solving the problems.

IMPROVING YOUR OWN LEARNING AND PERFORMANCE

There are many skills involved in working with and caring for children and young people which all adults need. These include:

*   experience and the support to reflect and learn from experience;

*   confidence and the ability to respond in the best possible ways to individual children;

*   really knowing about the child, trusting that knowledge and the judgements that are based on this;

*   being prepared to learn from the child, for example by listening to what a child tells you and observing what they do.

Working in the field of child care and education can be physically and emotionally exhausting, and professionals will need to consolidate their skills and to develop the ability to be reflective in their practice. You also need to be able to give and receive feedback; this is a skill which needs to be practised in order for it to be effective for both parties.

It is important to keep abreast of all the changes in child care practices by reading the relevant journals such as *Nursery World*, *Early Years Educator* and *Infant Education*, and by being willing to attend training courses when available.

EVALUATING YOUR OWN PERFORMANCE

Self-evaluation is important because it helps you to improve your own practice and to modify plans to meet the learning needs of the children. Using reflective practice will help you to review and evaluate your own practice. Reflective general and specific questions will help to organise this evaluation – for example:

*   Was your contribution to the planning meeting appropriate?

*   Did you achieve your goals? If not, was it because the goals were unrealistic?

*   What other methods could be used?

*   How can I improve my practice?

*   Who can I ask for advice and support?

*   How can I help a child to settle in again after his hospital stay?

*   What is making a child behave inappropriately at meal times?

SMART TARGETS

Each member of a team needs to know exactly what is expected of them. These expectations are called targets or 'objectives'. The targets that are most likely to be achieved are those which are 'SMART'. **SMART** is an acronym for:

*   **Specific:** they must be easy to understand and say exactly what you want to happen.

*   **Measurable:** success can be measured by checking back carefully against the instructions that have been given.

*   **Achievable:** the targets can be reached with reasonable effort in the time you are allowed.

* **Relevant:** the targets must be appropriate, building on previous strengths and skills.
* **Time related:** the targets have clearly set deadlines and are reviewed frequently.

Look at the following scenarios and see how SMART targets can help individuals and teams to plan and to achieve their objectives.

* **Scenario 1:** Paula has been asked if she would organise a display for the nursery room. The only instructions she has been given are: 'Paula, can you put up a nice, colourful display in the nursery room, please?'
* **Scenario 2:** At a different nursery, Mark has also been asked to organise a display. On Wednesday, he was given these instructions: 'Next Monday we need to create an interactive display for the nursery room. It will be on the theme of Autumn. We've already collected some pine cones and autumn leaves, and we also have some good posters, but I'd like you to plan what else we need and let me have a list of resources by tomorrow lunchtime.'

STAFF APPRAISAL AND REVIEW

In any employee, the employer is looking for a range of personal and professional qualities. A system of appraisal and review helps you and your manager or employer to assess how you are performing in your job and whether you are happy. Often, goals may be set and your performance may be measured in relation to these targets.

Guidelines for staff appraisal and review

* An appraisal interview provides an opportunity for both you and your employer to identify any aspects of the job that you are doing really well and any that need to be improved.
* It is on these occasions that you can raise any problems you have – about dealing with particular situations, children, parents or staff.
* When you are carrying out all your duties well, you may be given more responsibility or you may be moved to work in a different area to develop your experience with other age ranges or activities.
* Appraisal should be viewed by staff as a positive action which helps to promote good practice within the setting. This still holds true even when there are criticisms of performance.
* Most appraisals are carried out annually and by interview.
* Appraisals are also useful in identifying staff-development needs; for example, an early childhood practitioner who is lacking in assertiveness may be sent on an assertiveness training course.

GIVING AND RECEIVING FEEDBACK WITH COLLEAGUES, CHILDREN AND ADULTS

Feedback is structured information that one person offers to another, about the impact of their actions or behaviour. It is vital to the success of most workplace tasks, and is an activity we engage in on a daily basis. Feedback should not be confused with *criticism*, which is often an unprepared reaction to people who aren't behaving in the way you want them to; criticism can make the recipient feel undervalued or angry – both unproductive emotions.

Regular, good-quality feedback is one of the most important ingredients in building constructive relationships and in getting jobs done. It can:

* help both parties to have a clear understanding of each other's expectations and responsibilities;

* motivate a good performer to do the job even better;

* support and guide a poor performer as they try new or different ways;

* often be the most realistic measure of how successfully we have completed a task. It is important to our self-esteem;

* help to foster an open climate, where trust and support are mutual expectations.

Giving Feedback

Feedback should be:

* **Balanced:** include a positive message to balance points about less effective behaviour.

* **Focused on performance:** concentrate on things which *can* be changed, and link your feedback to the task or role. Don't direct your comments to personality, character, attitude or things the person can't change, such as their personal circumstances or something in the past.

* **Timely and regular:** talk to the person at an appropriate moment soon after the incident you want to talk about. Offer feedback often – as an everyday habit. Don't wait until the incident has gone stale and don't save your remarks to deliver all at once. Good feedback

needs to be practised regularly to be effective.

* **Clear and direct:** use plain, clear language. Choose phrases the person will understand. Be brief and to the point. Successful feedback is easy to understand.

* **Specific:** give an accurate description of the behaviour you are talking about, and about what you'd like to see instead.

* **Solution-focused:** show that you're willing to give ideas about how the person can tackle the issues you have raised.

Feedback Skills

Skilled people make feedback a positive experience, leaving everyone feeling valued, even if the feedback itself is difficult or negative. If feedback is delivered badly, or not at all, the impact can be demoralising and long-lasting.

Guidelines for giving feedback

* Active listening: listen attentively – be aware of your body language (see p 25 in Chapter 1), in order to understand another person's viewpoint, perspective, needs and feelings;

* Observation: be aware of how people talk, speak, move, react. Try to describe this accurately;

* Clear verbal expression: use direct language and choose words appropriate to the listener;

* Structure your message: introduce the conversation; set the context; explain the issue; summarise the discussion; and end on a positive note;

* Plan and prepare your message: think in advance about the time,

place and content of the conversation;

* Timing: be aware of the other person's needs and priorities. Always choose breaks or quiet moments to talk: this will allow them time to absorb and think;

* Self awareness: be aware of your own feelings; aware of what you find difficult; aware of your limits; and be able to talk about these;

* Resilience: try not to take things personally: learn from the experience;

* Assertiveness: express your needs, feelings, and opinions in an honest, direct and appropriate manner. Show awareness that other people have different perspectives, while explaining your own position.

Receiving Feedback

The information you hear when receiving feedback from others may be new – and even surprising. You may react with strong emotion. Good feedback is an offer of information, not a diagnosis of your character or potential, so you should not react angrily or 'take it too personally'.

Hearing feedback can:

* help you become aware of how you are getting on – the good and the bad, what's working and what isn't;

* give you some ideas to help you plan your own development, in order to reach your full potential;

* give you a 'reality check' – you can compare how you think you are with what other people tell you.

Feedback from a number of different people helps you make a balanced decision about the information you are hearing. Not everyone has good feedback skills; you are likely to get a mixed quality of feedback – some perceptive and supportive, some critical and unspecific.

Guidelines for receiving feedback

* Ask questions: state what you want feedback about. Be specific about what you want to know. Give them time to think about what they want to say.

* Listen: listen attentively. Don't interrupt or digress. Ask for clarification if you're not sure you've understood what you've heard. Try not to be defensive or to reject the information. You need to listen, but not necessarily to agree. Take notes of what is said.

* Check: check what you've heard. Repeat back what they have said and ask for examples of what the speaker means. Give your reactions to the feedback or ask for time to think about it if necessary. Ask for suggestions on what might work better

* Reflect: feedback is information for you to use – it is not a requirement to change. If you are unsure about the soundness of the feedback, check it out with other people. Work out the options open to you and decide what you want to do. It is up to you to evaluate how accurate and how useful the feedback is.

Problems in Receiving Feedback

* You get defensive.

* You try to prove them wrong.

* You feel you have to do something to change yourself.

* You give an answer to justify yourself.

* You dismiss the information.

* You feel helpless to do anything about what you heard.

* You change the focus and attack the speaker.

* You generalise the message and feel bad about everything.

* You generalise the message and think you're perfect at everything.

Barriers to the Feedback Process

Feedback is sometimes difficult to give or receive. The giver and receiver both need to be open to receiving feedback and open to the possibility that the feedback being given may be based on incorrect assumptions. You may find it difficult to **give** feedback because you:

* believe that feedback is negative and unhelpful;

* worry that the other person will not like you;

* believe that the other person cannot handle the feedback;

* have had previous experiences in which the receiver was hostile to feedback.

Receiving corrective feedback may be difficult because you:

* have the urge to rationalise, since the criticism can feel uncomfortable;

* believe that your self-worth is diminished by suggestions for improvement;

* have had previous experiences in which feedback was unhelpful or unjustified.

SECTION 3: THE DIFFERING PRINCIPLES AND PRACTICES THAT UNDERPIN WORKING WITH DIFFERENT-AGE CHILDREN

• Values and principles • Providing the environment for child to develop independence in learning • Child centred v adult led practice • Valuing children's interests and experiences • Schemas

VALUES AND PRINCIPLES

All early childhood practitioners should work within a framework which embodies sound values and principles. The **EYFS** builds on previous developments (Birth to Three Matters, Curriculum Guidance for the Foundation Stage, and the National Standards for Under 8s Daycare and Childminding). The EYFS framework uses the **KEEP** (Key Elements in Effective Practice) principles and the values are threaded throughout the EYFS in the commitment cards (Principles into Practice).

KEEP Principles
Make sure you know, use and act on the KEEP principles.

1   Effective practice in the early years requires committed, enthusiastic and reflective practitioners with a breadth and depth of knowledge, skills and understanding.

2   Effective practitioners use their learning to improve their work

with young children and their families in ways which are sensitive, positive and non-judgemental. Therefore, through initial and on-going training and development, practitioners need to develop, demonstrate and continuously improve their:

* relationships with both children and adults;

* understanding of the individual and diverse ways that children develop and learn;

* knowledge and understanding in order to actively support and extend children's learning in and across all areas and aspects of learning;

* practice in meeting all children's needs, learning styles and interests;

* work with parents and carers and the wider community;

* work with other professionals within and beyond the setting.

The **CACHE Statement of Values** is also a useful tool for checking that you are upholding important child care values.

CACHE statement of values
You must ensure that you:
1 Put the child first by:
   * ensuring the child's welfare and safety;
   * showing compassion and sensitivity;
   * respecting the child as an individual;

* upholding the child's rights and dignity;

* enabling the child to achieve their full learning potential.

2 Never use physical punishment.

3 Respect the parent as the primary carer and educator of the child.

4 Respect the contribution and expertise of staff in the child care and education field, and other professionals with whom they may be involved.

5 Respect the customs, values and spiritual beliefs of the child and their family.

6 Uphold the Council's Equality of Opportunity Policy.

7 Honour the confidentiality of information relating to the child and their family, unless its disclosure is required by law or is in the best interest of the child.

PROVIDING THE ENVIRONMENT FOR CHILDREN TO DEVELOP INDEPENDENCE IN LEARNING

In order for children to develop independence in learning, practitioners need to:

* provide opportunities or challenges for them to be active, to take risks, to make mistakes and to learn from these;

* provide broad and varied experiences which enable them to explore and investigate;

* have a sound knowledge of child development and to be aware of the ways in which they learn;

* provide appropriate levels of assistance for individual children;

* be thoughtful and reflective practitioners who actively encourage them to become independent through giving them responsibility for their learning from a very early stage;

* encourage children to explain key ideas in their own words. Tasks and activities involve them in learning through thinking and doing, rather than by rote;

* help them to be able to show or explain it clearly to others in their own words, orally or in writing or pictures;

* use technology to enable children to work more effectively;

* encourage children and young people to review their own learning strategies, achievements and future learning needs.

High/Scope is a comprehensive educational approach which strives to help children develop in all areas. High/Scope sets out its goals for young children:

* To learn through active involvement with people, materials, events, and ideas.

* To become independent, responsible, and confident—ready for school and ready for life.

* To learn to plan many of their own activities, carry them out, and talk with others about what they have done and what they have learned.

* To gain knowledge and skills in important academic, social, and physical areas.

* The emphasis of the High/Scope philosophy is that children are encouraged to make decisions about their own choice of activities on a 'Plan', 'Do' and 'Review' basis. There will still be some adult-led activities such as PE and other large and small group activities, but mostly the

children will have a choice in planning activities.

(For more information on developing independence in learning, see Chapter 13)

CHILD-CENTRED VERSUS ADULT-LED PRACTICE

What is Child-centred Practice?

A child-centred organisation focuses its practice on improving **outcomes** for children and young people; it also works with others to promote and contribute to better outcomes for all children and their families. Child-centred practice involves more than focusing on the rights and responsibilities of the child or young person. In child-centred practice the intention is to try to keep the interests and the wellbeing of children **central** to the process; to do this, you have to **engage** with children and **involve** them wherever possible in the issues that concern them.

It will also:

* recognise that children are individuals in their own right, 'loaned and not owned' by the significant adults in their lives;

* create opportunities for all children to reach their full potential;

* recognise that educating children together is a truer reflection of the real world;

* recognise the foundation years as being important for learning;

* provide an environment that positively promotes the wellbeing of children;

* be inclusive of all abilities;

* provide for an awareness and direct experience of a diversity of cultures and faiths;

* involve children in decision-making processes in all aspects of their school life.

The Advantages of Child-centred Practice

There are advantages to both children and adults in making your practice child-centred. These include the following points:

* **Services are appropriate for their needs:** insights gained from children can help adults work more effectively; it can also help to ensure that services that are provided are relevant to children's needs.

* **Taking into account the needs of others:** children who learn to express their own needs also learn to consider the needs of others. They may develop skills of cooperation, negotiation and problem solving.

* **Respect and understanding:** children and parents/carers often work together; this can make relationships stronger and promote greater understanding and respect.

* **Promoting self-esteem and self-worth:** when you involve children and you respect their ideas and their capabilities they will grow in confidence and self-esteem.

CASE STUDY

An after-school club for 5- to 6-year-old children

Practitioners wanted to find out how children felt about their after-school clubs. Although parents and carers had important views to contribute, they realised that children also had their own perspectives. When talking with the children, practitioners found that:

* they were unhappy about the lighting – it was too gloomy in some clubs;

* some children said they got hungry and wished there was some food provided;

* some children felt tired and wished there was somewhere for them to have a quiet time, not just the structured activities;

* they were also concerned about their environment – the paint on the walls, the lighting and their access to the garden, and so on.

These were all legitimate and important insights which affected how those children experienced their care and which could have easily been overlooked by adults who may have a different set of concerns. By placing the child at the centre of their practice, the practitioners developed a greater understanding of the sorts of factors that might affect children's lives.

There are many factors which affect children – for example, the local environment, their opportunities for play and social interaction, the impact of traffic and noise pollution on their lives, the quality of the streets and housing for children. On each of these issues children will have a view and a valid contribution to make.

Guidelines for child-centred practice

Practitioners should recognise the importance of:

* being aware of children at all times;

* thinking about how your involvement with their families may affect them and being open to engaging with children, listening to them and realising the potential for them to participate and contribute to your work;

* recognising (when working with very young children) that they may not be able to contribute in any obvious way, but we still need to be aware of them;
* recognising the value of contributions from any older siblings who may have a lot to contribute;
* engaging with children individually, or as little groups. You can talk with them, they can participate in discussions, community meetings, councils;
* encourage children to make scrapbooks, videos, keep diaries, use disposable cameras, make drawings etc.

Adult-led Practice

There will always be aspects of children's care and education which require practitioners to take the lead. This is called adult-led practice. In early years settings, practitioners lead activities which encourage children to use language, to practise skills and to develop thinking. Adult-led and adult-intensive activities may include:

* story and song times;
* activities such as cooking with small groups;
* trips into the local community;
* a new game;
* shared reading and writing;
* scientific investigations;
* new imaginative play settings.

The six areas of learning defined by the Early Years Foundation Stage must be delivered through planned, purposeful play, with a balance of **adult-led** and **child-initiated** activities.

1   **Involvement:** all team members should be involved in planning, but their level of involvement will vary, depending on confidence, professional skills and organisation. (A staff member offering verbal input in a team meeting is involved in planning, but so too is an absent member who later comments on written plans.)

2   **Parents and carers:** planning must involve parents and carers, as they provide vital information about their children's interests, skills and needs that must be taken into account when planning the curriculum. Inform parents and carers also about what is going on in the setting, out of professional respect; doing this will also help them make links between experiences in the setting and at home.

3   **Children:** practitioners should find ways to seek children's opinions and to involve them in their learning. For example:

   * brainstorm with small groups around topic themes and ask the children to suggest stories and activities;
   * ask children to suggest resources for a new imaginative play area;
   * ask children to think about what they would like and intend to do that day, the following day or week.

4   **Child-initiated learning:** this involves planning the learning environment to allow for children to take the initiative. Planning includes:

   * how the environment (outside and inside) is organised;
   * the resources made available;
   * the routines; and
   * the way in which practitioners respond to how children function in the environment.

There should be open-ended opportunities to encourage children to take the initiative. Children need to make use of the environment in different ways; by linking resources, people and play in creative ways, you are promoting child-initiated learning. (See the section on planning for play in Chapter 13.)

5 **Adult-initiated learning:** this involves planning for what you will promote and encourage. Sometimes practitioners will encourage children to use resources that they, rather than the children, have chosen. There are various reasons for choosing to plan in this way:

* practitioners may have identified a learning need from their observations, made it a learning goal and identified specific experiences that will promote this learning;

* children may lack the experience to set up the resources correctly, for example a new game;

* practitioners may want the children to investigate a particular concept, for example forces, using cars in block play;

* in response to their observations, practitioners may think that the resources will interest the children and encourage them to develop their ideas and skills;

* more experienced children may be encouraged to pursue a line of investigation that may not otherwise have occurred to them, or to do independently what previously needed adult help.

VALUING CHILDREN AND YOUNG PEOPLE'S INTERESTS AND EXPERIENCES

Every child needs to be included – and to have full access to the curriculum, irrespective of their ethnic background,

culture, language, gender or economic background. No child should be held back in their learning due to restricted access to learning opportunities. In order to apply curriculum plans, it is important to work closely in partnership with the child's parents/carers. Practitioners sometimes talk about 'my children', but children belong to their parents. When parents and practitioners work well together, respecting what they each bring to the partnership, in a spirit of respect and trust, with a genuine exchange of information and knowledge, the child gains and so do the parents and staff.

SCHEMAS

Schemas are observable patterns of repeat behaviour in children. Children often have a very strong drive to repeat actions, such as moving things from one place to another, covering things up and putting things into containers, or moving in circles or throwing things. These patterns can often be observed running through their play and vary between one child and another. If practitioners build on these interests powerful learning can take place. (See Chapter 13 for more information on schemas.)

SECTION 4: THE CURRENT NATIONAL AND LOCAL INITIATIVES AND ISSUES RELEVANT TO THE SECTOR

• Government initiatives • Local government/regional developments • Community based activities
• Comparing and contrasting different initiatives
• Reviewing current research and implications of practice using professional literature and other sources

GOVERNMENT INITIATIVES

Recent government initiatives include:

* the Children's National Service Framework (2004);

* the Common Assessment Framework for Children and Young People (CAF) (2006);
* the Children's Workforce Strategy (2006).

(The Children's National Service Framework is described in Chapter 1.)

The Common Assessment Framework for Children and Young People (CAF)

The CAF is a shared assessment tool for use across all children's services and all local areas in England. It aims to help early identification of need and promote coordinated service provision.

The purposes of the CAF are:

* to give all practitioners working with children and young people a **holistic** tool for identifying a child's needs before they reach crisis point and a shared language for discussing and addressing them;
* to ensure that important needs are not overlooked and to reduce the scale of assessments that some children and young people undergo;
* to provide a common structure to record information and facilitate information-sharing between practitioners;
* to provide evidence to facilitate requests to involve other agencies, reducing unnecessary referrals and enabling specialist services to focus their resources where they are most needed.

The CAF consists of:

* a simple **pre-assessment checklist** to help practitioners decide who would benefit from a common assessment;
* a **three-step process** (prepare, discuss, deliver) for undertaking a common assessment, to help practitioners gather and understand information about the needs and strengths of the child, based on

discussions with the child, their family and other practitioners as appropriate;
* a **standard form** to help practitioners record and, where appropriate, share with others the findings from the assessment in terms that are helpful in working with the family to find a response to unmet needs.

The assessment process encourages practitioners to consider the needs of the child or young person in three key areas:

Development of Child, Baby or Young Person

* **General health:** physical development; speech, language and communications development; emotional and social development; behavioural development; identity, including self-esteem, self-image and social presentation; family and social relationships; self-care skills and independence.
* **Learning:** understanding, reasoning and problem solving; participation in learning, education and employment; progress and achievement in learning; aspirations.

Parents and Carers

Basic care, ensuring safety and protection; emotional warmth and stability; guidance, boundaries and stimulation.

Family and Environmental Factors

Family history, functioning and wellbeing; wider family; housing, employment and financial considerations; social and community factors and resources, including education.

The Children's Workforce Strategy

The Children's workforce strategy includes the **Common Core of Skills and**

Knowledge for the Children's Workforce. This document sets out the basic skills and knowledge needed by people (including volunteers) whose work brings them into regular contact with children, young people and families. It will enable multidisciplinary teams to work together more effectively in the interests of the child.

The skills and knowledge are described under six main headings:

1 effective communication and engagement with children, young people and families;

2 child and young person development;

3 safeguarding and promoting the welfare of the child;

4 supporting transitions;

5 multi-agency working;

6 sharing information.

Over time, the aim is that everyone working with children, young people and families will be able to demonstrate a basic level of competence in the six areas of the Common Core. In the future, the Common Core will form part of **qualifications** for working with children, young people and families and it will act as a foundation for training and development programmes run by employers and training organisations.

This core area covers the physical, intellectual, linguistic, social and emotional growth and development of babies, children and young people. It is difficult to determine specific times when developmental changes occur, as these will differ from person to person.

The document also requires professionals to know about the **Child Health Promotion Programme** and the **Common Assessment Framework for Children and Young People (CAF)** and, where appropriate, how to use them.

LOCAL GOVERNMENT AND REGIONAL DEVELOPMENTS

Every local authority has certain duties to provide for children and young people in its area. The government sets out the national guidelines for each initiative and the local authority has a duty to implement them. (The main areas relevant to children and young people are described in Chapter 1.)

Sure Start

Under the government's Sure Start programme, **local education authorities** (LEAs) have duties to:

* prepare, submit and publish plans on early years and child care;

* ensure provision of nursery education places for 3- and 4-year-olds;

* convene and work with Early Years Development and Childcare Partnerships (EYDCPs);

* provide information and advice for child care providers;

* prepare an annual review of child care in their area; and

* maintain a children's information service.

Local social services departments have duties to provide child care for children in need.

Children's Trusts

* Children's trusts bring together organisations from across the county in order to achieve better outcomes for children and young people. The new children's trust arrangements enable the different agencies and professionals to work in a more 'joined up' way within a partnership framework.

* Children's trusts all have a strong emphasis on communication, sharing information and working together in

order to achieve the five outcomes; these were identified in the government's *Every Child Matters* strategy as being important to all children and young people, regardless of their background or circumstances.

Provision for Young People at a Local Level

The **Positive Activities for Young People** programme is part of the government's *Every Child Matters: Change for Children* strategy, and is aimed at 8- to 19-year-olds who are at risk of social exclusion and community crime. From 2007, local authorities are required to provide positive activities for young people. They will also be expected to take account of young people's views on activities and facilities currently available to them, as well as any new ones they would like to see in the area. The local authority will then be required to publicise these to young people, and to keep the information up to date.

Youth Matters

In July 2005 the government launched its Green Paper, *Youth Matters*, setting out proposals designed to improve outcomes for 13- to 19-year-olds. It proposed that young people should have:

* more things to do and places to go in their **local area** – and more choice and influence over what is available;

* more opportunities to volunteer and to make a contribution to their local community;

* better information, advice and guidance about issues that matter to them, delivered in the way they want to receive them;

* better support when they need extra help to deal with problems.

The Children and Young People Board

The Children and Young People Board has responsibility for local authority activity in the areas of the wellbeing of children and young people, including education, social care and careers. Its objectives are:

* to articulate and promote a powerful strategic role for local government to achieve better outcomes for children from birth to 19 years;

* to secure maximum support and flexibility for local government to deliver the radical change agenda for children and learning to consolidate the role of local authorities in joining up services (public, private, and voluntary) in localities on behalf of children, young people, their families and the local community and promote an integrated local government offer on youth services (in collaboration with the safer communities board).

COMMUNITY-BASED ACTIVITIES

There are literally hundreds of community-based activities for children and young people in the UK. Most of them are run by concerned individuals who want to make a difference for the children in their area and are **voluntary** organisations (or charities). Some receive funding from national and local government agencies or from the National Lottery. Some belong to a 'parent' organisation. An example of an initiative which works in the community is **Play England**. This is a project of the Children's Play Council of the National Children's Bureau. It is supported by the Big Lottery Fund (BIG). Play England's aim is for all children and young people in England to have regular access to and opportunity for free, inclusive, local play provision and play space. Its objectives are to:

* create, improve and develop children and young people's free local play spaces and opportunities throughout England, according to need;

* research and demonstrate the benefits of play;

* promote equality and diversity in play provision;

* raise awareness and promote standards;

* support innovation and new ways of providing for children's play;

* promote the long-term strategic and sustainable provision for play as a free public service to children;

* ensure that local authorities work with other local stakeholders to develop children's play strategies and plans;

* ensure that good, inclusive and accessible children's play services and facilities are provided locally.

An Example of a Youth Agency: RefugeeYouth, UK

The Barbara Melunsky Refugee Youth Agency, known as **RefugeeYouth**, is a small network of young refugee groups in London and the UK, *run* and *led* by young refugees. Young refugees probably face some of the hardest challenges in life and are often viewed as vulnerable and therefore incapable of helping themselves. RefugeeYouth shows how these young people can be positive leaders and advocates in their field when given the opportunity. RefugeeYouth was originally set up in response to the fact that young refugees found it particularly hard to gain access to work placements. For those involved in running RefugeeYouth, the skills and knowledge acquired enable them to make an active contribution to society now and in the future.

REVIEWING CURRENT RESEARCH AND USING PROFESSIONAL LITERATURE

Using professional literature will help you to inform your practice and in turn promote professional development. Reviewing literature is carrying out an analysis of what others have said or found out about the research area in question.

The first step is to decide which literature is most relevant to you. In other words, what are you hoping to find out? Through the literature, you should be able to confirm your

---

ACTIVITY: RESEARCHING YOUR LOCAL PROVISION FOR CHILDREN AND YOUNG PEOPLE

1 Decide on an area to research, for example:

* the provision of play areas;

* the provision of leisure activities for young people, e.g. youth clubs, arts activities, sports, music and volunteering projects;

* support groups: for lone parents, for disabled children and their families or for young people with mental health problems,

2 Using the library or the internet, investigate the local provision for your chosen topic.

3 Write a short report, detailing the aims of the provider, the service available, and the benefits to the group served.

concerns – discarding, modifying or adding to them as you read. As a result, you will identify a number of **themes** and sub-themes within your original topic which will provide the framework for your enquiry. You then need to **focus** on the themes you have identified.

1 **Be systematic:** keep a careful **record** of all you read, including *exact* bibliographic references. One useful method of keeping track of reading is to use a card index file. Each time you find a book or an article which you think will be useful, note it down on a card, remembering to record a full note of the author, etc. You should include a few notes for each reference to remind you of the main issues raised by the author when you return to it. For example:

   * **Quotes and references:** if you come across a statement which you might wish to quote, or one which you feel summarises the issues well and you might wish to refer to, make sure you write down a full reference, including the page number. This will help you to find it again and, if you use the quotation in writing up the study, you should cite the page number.

   * **Reading in greater depth:** this allows you to identify competing perspectives within each sub-theme, to compare and contrast them and to identify strengths and weaknesses in the views given.

   The search may include books, journals, policy statements, professional journals and other publications, including electronic ones. While books are important, journals tend to be more up to date in their treatment of the issues which you might be researching. Many of the articles available on-line through the internet are highly topical.

2 **Be critical of what you read:** most writers have a particular viewpoint on an issue and you should consider the validity and reliability of statements made, the authority of the author and the professional relevance of the issues raised. Some journals are more authoritative than others.

3 Read **reviews** of books and reports in journals and follow up those which seem promising.

4 **Ask yourself questions** about what you read:

   * **presentation:** is the style appropriate, clear, readable?

   * **authors:** who are they and where are they from?

   * **target audience:** is it aimed at practitioners, academics, researchers?

   * **relevance:** does it raise significant issues?

   * **evidence:** what is the evidence for arguments made? Is it appropriate? Do you have enough information to know if they drew appropriate conclusions?

   * **plausibility:** does it convince you?

   If the focus of your enquiry is the effectiveness of a new policy within your area, for example, on learning and teaching in schools, it will be important to understand and analyse policy documents as well as any other relevant official publications. However, government policy documents will always take a rather one-sided view of the issues, so you need to balance this by reading about aspects of, for example, philosophy (child-centred education), psychology (how children learn) and sociology (poverty and discrimination).

5 Libraries can be very useful in directing you to where to find appropriate information on a particular topic.

CHAPTER 12

Promoting a Healthy Environment for Children

This chapter covers **Unit 6** and is divided into three sections:

Section 1: The principles underpinning the rights of children to a healthy lifestyle and environment

Section 2: The factors that affect the health of children

Section 3: How to plan and implement routines and activities for children

SECTION 1: THE PRINCIPLES UNDERPINNING THE RIGHTS OF CHILDREN TO A HEALTHY LIFESTYLE AND ENVIRONMENT

- Children's rights to a healthy lifestyle
- Legislation relating to the health of children
- Public health environment

THE RIGHTS OF CHILDREN TO A HEALTHY LIFESTYLE

The UN Convention on the Rights of the Child (UNCRC)

These articles of the UNCRC are relevant to *all five* Outcomes in *Every Child Matters*:

✱ **Article 1:** everyone under 18 years of age has all the rights stated in the UN Convention on the Rights of the Child.

✱ **Article 2:** the Convention applies to everyone, whatever their nation, race, colour, sex, religion, abilities, opinion, wealth or social position.

✱ **Article 3:** all organisations concerned with children should work towards what is best for each child.

✱ **Article 4:** governments shall take all necessary steps to make these rights available to all children.

✱ **Article 6:** all children have the right to life. Governments should ensure that children survive and develop healthily.

✱ **Article 12:** governments to ensure that children have the right to express their views freely and to take account of children's views. Children have the right to be heard in any legal or administrative matters that affect them.

✱ **Article 22:** refugee children have the right to protection and assistance and the same rights as other children

wherever they are or whatever their circumstance.

How Human Rights Legislation Relates to the 'Being Healthy' Outcome

In *Every Child Matters*, the 'Being healthy' outcome is 'Enjoying good physical and mental health and living a healthy lifestyle'.

In addition to the UNCRC articles listed above, the following articles relate specifically to the rights of children to enjoy good health:

✱ **Article 23:** special care and support for children with special needs

✱ **Article 24:** right to health care, clean drinking water, nutritious food and a clean environment

✱ **Article 27:** standard of living that meets physical, mental, spiritual, moral and social needs

✱ **Article 31:** right to rest, play and enjoy art and culture

✱ **Article 36:** right to protection from any activities that harm welfare and development

✱ **Article 39:** governments to help restore a child's health, self-respect and dignity after abuse or neglect.

LEGISLATION RELATED TO HEALTH ISSUES

Alcohol and the Law

✱ **Under 5:** it is illegal to give an alcoholic drink to a child under 5 **except** in certain circumstances e.g. under medical supervision.

✱ **Under 14:** a young person under 14 cannot go into the bar of a pub unless the pub has a 'children's certificate'. If

CLEAN WATER = HEALTHY LIVING

WATER WISE
Did you know...? Water covers three-quarters of the world's surface but 99 per cent of it is in the oceans or frozen in polar ice caps. Only 1 per cent is available for humans to use. It evaporates from the seas, rains onto the land and then flows down rivers back to the seas. Clean water is vital for children to survive and be healthy. Save the Children is working to make clean, safe water available to children.

A PRECIOUS RESOURCE
Everyone needs about 30 litres of water a day to stay healthy and clean. We need it to drink, for preparing food, and washing our clothes and ourselves. Three quarters of your body weight is water. You could survive for up to two weeks without food, but without water you would die within three days. In fact, water is vital to all forms of life and without it animals and plants cannot survive. Without water there would be no food.

HEALTH RISKS
Without proper sanitation, water becomes contaminated and carries diseases, like diarrhoea. Malaria, which kills 1 million children every year, is caused by a parasite carried by mosquitoes that breed near water. Save the Children works with communities to combat poor sanitation by building latrines (toilets) and improving hygiene education, Carrying heavy water can also lead to health problems, like backache, inflamed joints or even permanent neck and spinal damage.

Atua district, north western Uganda: children help to collect water to make bricks for an HIV/AIDS training and activity centre

Save the Children

HEAVY WORK
Lack of clean water and poverty go hand in hand. Collecting water from the nearest stream, well or standpipe is a major task. For many children in developing countries, a trip to collect water can take up to six hours, very often in the heat and over difficult terrain. Save the Children helps communities to dig wells and install pumps closer to their homes or schools so that children are able to have both clean water and go to school.

TOO MUCH TOO LITTLE?
Water is something that we all need; yet not everyone gets their fair share. More than 1 billion people (that's one-sixth of the world's population) do not have safe drinking water. Most of these people live in sub-Saharan Africa and South Asia.

In the UK, we turn on the tap and take water for granted. An average family uses about 500 litres of water a day. Could you manage with less and play your part in ensuring that everyone has access to a fair share of clean water?

Fig 12.1 Save the Children poster

ACTIVITY: CLEAN WATER = HEALTHY LIVING

1 Read the information presented on the poster in Figure 12.1 and answer the following questions:

  * What percentage of all the water on earth is available to humans in their environment?

  * What percentage of the world's population does not have safe drinking water?

  * How much water does each person need each day in order to stay healthy and clean?

  * How many litres of water does the average family in the UK use each day?

2 List the main risks to health from contaminated water and a poor water supply.

3 Discuss ways in which you and your peer group could:

  * help to conserve water; and

  * raise awareness about the global health problem of unsafe water supplies.

it does not have one, they can only go into parts of licensed premises where alcohol is *either* sold but not drunk (e.g. an off-licence or a sales point away from the pub) *or* drunk but not sold (e.g. a garden or family room).

* **14- or 15-year-olds:** can go anywhere in a pub, but cannot drink alcohol.

* **16- or 17-year-olds:** can buy (or be bought) beer or cider as an accompaniment to a meal, but not in a bar (i.e. only in an area specifically set aside for meals).

* **Under 18:** except for 16- or 17-year-olds having a meal in a pub (see above), it is against the law for anyone under 18 to buy alcohol in a pub, off-licence, supermarket or other outlet; or for anyone else to buy alcohol in a pub for someone who is under 18.

In Scotland, a person shall not knowingly act as an agent for a person under 18 in the purchase of alcoholic liquor. In Britain, some towns and cities have *local* by-laws banning the drinking of alcohol in public (on public transport, for example).

The Law Concerning Sex and the Age of Consent

The law says that it is legal for young people to consent to have sex from the age of 16. (In Northern Ireland, the age of consent is 17.) However, although a girl under 16 is not committing a criminal offence if she has sex, the boy she's having sex with is breaking the law – even if she has agreed to have sex with him. Gay sex is legal if you are 16 or over in England, Wales and Scotland. In Northern Ireland you must be 17 – and in Jersey 18.

Young people under 16 still have the right to **confidential** help – they can seek advice about sex and relationships however old they are.

Smoking and the Law

From October 2007, under-18s are to be banned from buying cigarettes in England and Wales. In Scotland, the ban came into force in March 2006. Shops that break the new laws could lose their licence to sell tobacco for as long as a year. Lifting the legal age for buying tobacco from 16 to 18 brings the law into line with rules on the sale of alcohol.

Drugs and the Law

Some drugs are legally available in the UK – including alcohol and tobacco. Other drugs, such as cannabis, ecstasy and heroin, are **illegal** and are called **controlled drugs**. The **Misuse of Drugs Act 1971** divides illegal drugs into three classes and provides for maximum penalties as shown on page 365:

The major criminal offences relating to illegal drugs are:

* possession;
* importation and cultivation;
* possession with intent to supply;
* actual supply.

The last two of these (possession with intent to supply and actual supply) are the more serious crimes. However, they do not just apply to 'big-time' drug dealers. You can be convicted of supply for passing a drug to another person. You can be convicted of possession with intent to supply if you plan to pass a drug to another person, or even if you are returning their own drugs to them. Some people have been surprised when, after admitting to the police that they have shared drugs with a friend or bought them on behalf of a friend, they have been charged with supply.

If the police have reasonable grounds to suspect that you are in possession of an illegal drug they can stop and search you in the street.

Class of drug	Drug type	Maximum penalties
Class A	**Amphetamines (speed)** If prepared for injection **Cocaine and crack cocaine** **Ecstasy** (and similar drugs) **Heroin, LSD (acid)** **Magic mushrooms**	**Possession:** 7 years' prison and/or a fine **Possession with intent to supply, or supply:** life imprisonment and/or a fine
Class B	**Amphetamines (speed)**	**Possession:** 5 years' prison and/or a fine **Possession with intent to supply, or supply:** 14 years' prison and/or a fine
Class C	**Anabolic steroids** **Benzodiazepines** (e.g.temazepam, flunitrazepam, valium) **Cannabis**	**Possession:** 2 years' prison and/or a fine **Possession with intent to supply, or supply:** 14 years' prison and/or a fine

PUBLIC HEALTH ENVIRONMENT

In Chapter 1, you can see how the NHS works to maintain and improve health for children and young people. There are other organisations, both statutory and voluntary, which work to maintain a healthy environment – through health education and environmental health departments.

The Primary Health Care Team (PHCT)

The PHCT is a team of professionals which generally includes one or more of the following:

* **General practitioner (GP) or family doctor:** cares for all members of the family and can refer for specialist services.

* **Health visitor:** carries out developmental checks and gives advice on all aspects of child care.

* **Practice nurse:** works with a particular GP; provides services such as immunisation and asthma and diabetes clinics.

* **Community midwife:** delivers antenatal care and cares for the mother and baby until 10 to 28 days after delivery.

* **District nurse:** cares for clients in their own homes.

Some health authorities also employ a **community paediatric nurse:** a district nurse with special training in paediatrics to care for sick children at home.

Services Offered by the Primary Health Care Team

Services will include some or all of the following:

* child health clinics (see below);
* antenatal clinics;
* immunisation clinics;
* specialist clinics e.g. for asthma, diabetes etc.;
* family planning clinics;
* speech and language therapy;
* community dietician;
* community physiotherapists;
* community occupational therapists;
* community paediatrician;
* clinical medical officer (CMO);
* community dental service.

Child Health Clinics

Child health clinics are often held at the health centre or in a purpose-built centre.

In rural areas, the clinic may take turns with other community groups in village halls or community centres. Depending on the population served, clinics may be weekly or fortnightly and are run by health visitors, health care assistants and nursery nurses. A doctor or community paediatrician is usually present at specified times. Services provided at a child health clinic include:

* routine developmental surveillance (or reviews);
* medical examinations;
* immunisations;
* health promotion advice;
* antenatal and parentcraft classes.

The School Health Service

The School Health Service is part of the community child health service and has direct links with those who carry out health checks on children before they start school. The aims of the school health service are to:

* ensure that children are physically and emotionally fit so that they can benefit fully from their education and achieve their potential;
* prepare them for adult life and help them achieve the best possible health during the school years and beyond.

Services Provided by the School Health Service

1 **Routine testing for vision, hearing or speech** – to discover which children may need further tests or treatment. If treatment is thought to be required, the child's parents will be informed and consent requested.

2 The school nurse may work with one or more schools, and provides an important link between the school and health services. School nurses provide the following services:

* **growth measurements** – height and weight;
* advice on management of **health conditions**; for example, if a child has a long-term illness or special need, they will discuss possible strategies with the child's teacher;
* **enuresis** (bedwetting) support and advice, including providing an enuresis alarm;
* **immunisation**;
* advice on **health and hygiene**, sometimes running workshops or similar sessions;
* advice for parents on **specific health issues**, e.g. treating head lice or coping with asthma;
* **eyesight tests** from time to time;
* liaison with the **school doctor**.

3 The attention of the school doctor is drawn to any possible problems, and parents and the GP or family doctor are informed if any further action is considered necessary. The school doctor visits the school regularly and meets with the school nurse (or health visitor) and with teachers to find out whether any pupils need medical attention. In addition, the doctor reviews the medical notes of all children in Year 1 and of all new pupils transferring to the school.

4 Parents are usually requested to complete a **health questionnaire** about their child at certain stages and are asked if they would like their child to have a full medical examination. In addition, the school doctor may ask for parental consent to examine a child if his or her medical records are incomplete or if the doctor particularly wishes to check on

the child's progress. Parents are invited to be present at any medical examination and kept informed if the school doctor wishes to see their child again or thinks that they should be seen by the family doctor or a specialist.

5   The **audiometry team** checks children's hearing on a number of occasions before the age of 13 or 14 years. The school doctor will be told if a child seems to have a hearing problem. The doctor will then examine the child and let the family doctor know the result.

6   The **speech and language therapist** can provide assessment and treatment if the parent, a teacher or the school doctor feels that a child may have a speech or language problem.

Health Education Campaigns

Recent health education campaigns of particular relevance to children and young people include:

*   the **Water is Cool in School Campaign**, aiming to improve the quality of provision of and access to fresh drinking water for children in UK primary and secondary schools;

*   the **School Fruit and Vegetable Scheme (SFV)**: part of the '**5-A-DAY**' programme to increase fruit and vegetable consumption. Under the SFV Scheme, all 4- to 6-year-old children in LEA-maintained infant, primary and special schools are entitled to a free piece of fruit or vegetable each school day;

*   '**Sleep safe, sleep sound, share a room with me**' is the latest campaign from the Foundation for the Study of Infant Deaths; leaflets and posters have been sent to all midwives and health visitors;

*   '**Birth to Five**' is a comprehensive guide to parenthood and the first 5 years

Fig 12.2 Sleep safe poster

of a child's life. It covers child health, nutrition and safety and is given free to all first-time mothers in England.

Health Education by Private Companies

Manufacturers of 'healthy' products such as wholemeal bread or high-protein-balanced foods for babies often promote their products both by advertising and by using educational leaflets. Such leaflets are offered free in health clinics, postnatal wards and supermarkets. Examples of this type of health promotion are:

*   booklets on 'feeding your baby', published by formula milk manufacturers;

*   leaflets on child safety on the roads, produced by manufacturers of child car seats and harnesses;

* the promotion of herbal remedies to encourage a stress-free lifestyle.

There are strict controls over the claims that manufacturers can make about the health-giving properties of their product.

Health Education by the Voluntary Sector

Voluntary organisations are in a strong position to enhance the health of the population. They use a variety of methods:

* **Self-help** – some organisations bring people together to share common problems and to help them to gain more confidence and control over their own health.

* **Direct service provision** – the British Red Cross has a network of shops for the rental of equipment in the home (including walking frames, commodes and chairs).

* **Community health** – voluntary organisations work with local people to identify and solve problems affecting their health. GASP – Group Against Smoking in Public – is a Bristol-based group that campaigns for an increase in the provision of no-smoking areas in bars and restaurants.

* **Health education and promotion** – some organisations undertake fund-raising to provide support for research. The Wellcome Trust is a medical research charity which provides funding for research in the biomedical sciences.

Charities with health promotion agendas also employ advertising methods to get across their message; they often work in conjunction with the Health Development Agency or with private companies, or both. For example, the Child Accident Prevention Trust, with financial support from Start-rite and Volvo, produced a safety leaflet for parents entitled 'First ride, safe ride'. This was aimed at keeping a baby safe in the car.

Health Education Leading to Preventive Action

All **immunisation** programmes are an attempt to prevent disease and, therefore, to promote health – both in the individual and in the general population. The campaign to prevent sudden infant death syndrome is another example of an important health message reaching those who need it.

(See Unit 11 on CD-ROM for information on immunisation and child health surveillance.)

SECTION 2: THE FACTORS THAT AFFECT THE HEALTH OF CHILDREN

• Pre-conception • Parental health and lifestyle
• Families and community • Sociological
• Psychological • Physical • Informed choices
e.g. alcohol, drugs, smoking • Diet and exercise
• Illness and disability

MAINTENANCE OF HEALTH AND SOCIAL WELLBEING

It is now recognised that people's lifestyles and behaviour contribute to their health and wellbeing. Important factors are:

* diet;
* stress;
* smoking;
* sexual behaviour;
* exercise and maintaining mobility;
* recreation and leisure activities;
* alcohol and substance abuse;
* housing and sanitation.

FACTORS AFFECTING HEALTH IN CHILDREN

There are very many factors which affect the healthy growth and development of children. These factors work in combination and so it is often difficult to estimate the impact of any single factor on child health. Factors include:

* nutrition;
* infection;
* poverty and social disadvantage;
* housing;
* accidents;
* environmental factors;
* lifestyle factors;
* emotional and social factors.

Parental Health and Lifestyle

Many of the factors which adversely affect child health are closely interrelated, and make up a **cycle of deprivation**. For example, poorer families tend to live in poorer housing conditions and may also have an inadequate diet. Lack of adequate minerals and vitamins as a result of poor diet leads to an increased susceptibility to infectious diseases, and so on.

Nutrition

Milk, whether human or formula, is the fuel that makes babies grow more rapidly during the first year than at any other time. Both human and formula milk provide the right nutrients for the first months of life, with just the right balance of carbohydrates, proteins, fats, vitamins and minerals (see Unit 12 on CD-ROM).

Eating habits that are developed in childhood are likely to be continued in adult life. This means that children who eat mainly processed, convenience foods will tend to rely on these when they leave home. There are various conditions that may occur in childhood that are directly related to poor or unbalanced nutrition:

* **failure to thrive** (or faltering growth) – poor growth and physical development;
* **dental caries** or tooth decay – associated with a high consumption of sugar in snacks and fizzy drinks;
* **obesity** – children who are overweight are more likely to become obese adults;
* **nutritional anaemia** – due to an insufficient intake of iron, folic acid and vitamin B12;
* **increased susceptibility to infections** – particularly upper respiratory infections, such as colds and bronchitis.

Pre-conception

Life does not begin at birth; an individual is already 9 months old when born. In China a person's age is determined, not by his birth date, but by the date of his conception. A couple who are planning to start a family will certainly hope for a healthy baby; pre-conceptual care means both partners reduce known risks before trying to conceive in order to create the best conditions for an embryo to grow and develop into a healthy baby. The first 12 weeks of life in the womb (or uterus) are the most crucial as this is the period during which all the essential organs are formed.

Poverty and Disadvantage

Poverty is a key determinant of health and wellbeing of children. Health care problems in which the UK prevalence rates are increased by poverty and deprivation include:

* low birth-weight infants;
* injuries;
* hospital admissions.

369

Table 12.1 Guidelines for preconceptual care

Use barrier methods of contraception	Stop smoking
Use a condom or a diaphragm for three months before trying to conceive. It is advisable to discontinue the Pill so that the woman's natural hormonal pattern can be re-established.	Smoking cuts the amount of oxygen supplied to the baby through the placenta and can result in miscarriage or low birth weight. Some men who smoke are less fertile because they produce less sperm.

Eat well	
A balanced diet allows a woman to build up reserves of the nutrients vital to the unborn baby in the first three months: * **eat something from the four main food groups** every day (potato and cereals, fruit and vegetables, milk and milk products and high protein foods); * **cut down on sugary foods** and eat fresh foods where possible; * **avoid prepacked foods** and any foods which carry the risk of salmonella or listeria; * **do not go on a slimming diet;** follow your appetite and do not eat more than you need; * **vegetarian diets** which include milk, fish, cheese and eggs provide the vital protein the baby needs; * **vegans** should eat soya products and nuts and pulses to supply protein, and vitamin B12 may need to be taken as a supplement. * **folic acid tablets and a diet rich in folic acid** taken preconceptually and in pregnancy help the development of the brain and spinal cord.	

Genetic counselling	Avoid hazards at work
If there is a fairly high risk that a child may carry a genetic fault, such as cystic fibrosis or sickle cell disease, genetic counselling is offered. Tests may be done to try to diagnose any problem prenatally but all carry some element of risk in themselves.	Some chemicals and gases may increase the risk of miscarriage or birth defects. Women should be aware of the risks and take precautions after discussion with the environmental health officer.

Substance misuse and abuse	X-rays
Do not take any drugs unless prescribed by a doctor. Existing conditions such as epilepsy or diabetes will need to be controlled before and during pregnancy. Many addictive drugs cross the placental barrier and can damage the unborn baby.	X-rays are best avoided in the first three months of pregnancy although the risks to the foetus are thought to be very small.

Sexually transmitted diseases (STDs)	Cut down on alcohol
STDs should be treated – if either partner thinks there is any risk of syphilis, gonorrhoea, genital herpes or HIV infection, then both partners should attend a 'special clinic' for advice and tests. STDs can cause miscarriage, stillbirth or birth defects.	The best advice is to cut out alcohol completely; moderate drinking (1–2 glasses of wine or beer a day) increases the risk of miscarriage and babies are born smaller and more vulnerable. Heavy drinking, especially in the first few weeks of pregnancy, can cause **foetal alcohol syndrome** in which the baby is seriously damaged.

PARENTAL HEALTH AND LIFESTYLE

Parental substance misuse: Drugs and alcohol

The health of children whose parents misuse substances is affected in a number of ways through physical and emotional neglect, exposure to harm and poor parenting. One of the main difficulties in assessing the harm to children of living with parental substance use is that – in the majority of cases – substance misuse is associated with a range of other factors, for example:

* poverty and deprivation;
* poor physical and mental health;
* poor housing;
* debt;
* offending;
* unemployment.

There are a number of factors which have an impact – directly or indirectly – on the child's health and wellbeing:

* **Parents not available:** the addiction may mean that parents are often absent both physically (because they are out looking for drugs) and emotionally (because they are intoxicated). Either way, they are not available to the child.

* **Poor parenting skills:** substance use is often, but not always, associated with poor or inadequate parenting. This can show itself in a number of ways:

* **Physical neglect:** children are not kept clean, warm, or fed and there is a lack of care for the child's safety.

* **Emotional neglect:** the parent shows little or no affection or nurture.

* **Unpredictable parental behaviour:** for example, lurching between 'too much' or 'not enough' discipline and mood swings – being very affectionate or very remote. This leads to inconsistent parenting which can be confusing and damaging to the child.

* **Living conditions:** the child may be living in an unsafe environment because of the substance use: for example, through the people that come to the house, being left alone for long periods – because the parent is either intoxicated or out – or being taken out late at night to seek drugs or alcohol. Domestic abuse may be a factor in both circumstances although research shows that it is more often associated with **alcohol** misuse.

* **Children aged 0–4 years:** this age range spans a critical stage in a child's life. Physically, the child is vulnerable and totally dependent on others both before birth and for a significant period in the early years. When children experience neglect of their physical needs e.g. through poor nutrition and poor housing, it can lead to failure to thrive and delayed development. The young child also has a need for stimulation and **attachment** in order to develop emotionally. Parents who use drugs are less likely to take advantage of services such as play schemes, trips and parenting groups than other vulnerable families. This may be because of **stigma**. There is then a further impact on the child who will have less opportunity for social experiences of the kind other children enjoy.

* **Children aged 5–11 years:** children in this age range still require physical care but their emotional needs and the development of social skills assume a greater importance. They need routine and consistency in their lives. They also need to have bonds of **attachment**. Children whose home life lacks routine and positive discipline as well as cleanliness, appropriate clothing, adequate food and 'normal' activities may be marked out as different; this leads to the child feeling isolated. They may also have problems with attendance, lateness, concentration and a lack of basic social skills. Over time, they may come to see substance use as the norm and start to engage in risky behaviour themselves, e.g. drug or alcohol use and offending.

* **Older children and young people, aged 12–16 years:** for young people who have taken on the role of carer and are living in a 'role reversal', the loss of childhood may be having a significant impact on them. They may feel that

opportunities which are open to their classmates are closed to them, partly because of their domestic situation, and partly because they may have missed out on many of the earlier opportunities available to them. Their behaviour may deteriorate and lead them into truanting and the risk of exclusion. For some, however, school may be a refuge with opportunities to find supportive adults and participate in 'normal' activities.

* **Young carers:** many children of substance-using parents become carers for them and often for younger siblings too. This is a huge responsibility which affects the child emotionally and inhibits their ability to experience a 'normal' childhood by participating in activities outside the home. It can also affect their behaviour at school, for example, through lateness, tiredness and lack of time for homework.

Passive Smoking

When someone smokes, invisible particles from tobacco smoke mix with the surrounding air. This can be called passive smoke or second-hand smoke. Breathing in this air is called **passive smoking**. Unfortunately it is not just adults who are at risk to the adverse effects of passive smoking. In the UK, surveys in the 1990s found that about half of all children lived in a house where at least one person smokes. Every year in the UK 17,000 children are admitted to hospital with respiratory infections; research has found that many of these children are exposed daily to cigarette smoke. There is also an increased risk of children taking up the smoking habit themselves if one or both of their parents smoke.

Parental smoking is also responsible for a 20–40 per cent increased risk of middle ear disease in children. Young children and toddlers are especially sensitive to the effects of second-hand smoke, due to the fact that their bodies are still growing and developing and they breathe faster then adults and therefore may inhale more smoke.

The Risks to Child Health from Passive Smoking

Children who are exposed to second-hand smoke at home:

* are twice as likely to suffer from **chest infections**, such as bronchitis, pneumonia or bronchiolitis;

* will have **less-developed lungs** which have a reduced ability to function well;

* will suffer **severe asthma attacks** if they are already asthmatic and have them more often;

* have a higher **risk** of developing **asthma** if they were not born with it;

* are more likely to be **hospitalised** before they reach their 2nd birthday;

* will suffer from more **colds, coughs** and **sore throats**;

* are more likely to suffer **ear infections**, fluid in the ears, chronic middle ear disease or 'glue ear', which could lead to some loss of hearing. Many children will need to have the fluid from their ears surgically drained as a result of passive smoking;

* could suffer from possible **heart disorders**;

* will have a higher risk of developing **cancer** as an adult;

* will suffer from some **loss of sense of smell**;

* are more likely to have been born with a **low birth weight**. (See Unit 18 on CD-ROM for problems associated with low birth weight);

* are more likely to die of **cot death**. Infants of mothers who smoke are up to

three times more likely to die from Sudden Infant Death Syndrome compared to those whose mothers do not smoke;

* will be **absent from school** more often due to various illnesses caused from breathing in the tobacco smoke – and will take longer to recover from the above illnesses.

Guidelines for helping to prevent a child from taking up smoking

* Set a healthy example by not smoking – or if you do, talk about how you feel about it.

* Keep your home and car smoke-free. If you choose not to do this, smoke outside or in one room only.

* Talk with them about the dangers of smoking and listen to what they have to say. Be available when they are ready to talk about any health issue.

* Trust your children to make their own decision.

* Support smoking prevention programs and 'No Smoking' policies in schools.

Infection

During childhood there are many infectious illnesses that can affect children's health and development. Some of these infections can be controlled by childhood **immunisations** (see Unit 11 on CD-ROM) – these are diphtheria, tetanus, polio, whooping cough, measles, meningitis, mumps and rubella. Other infections can also have long-lasting effects on children's health.

The Prevention of Infection

An infection starts when certain disease-causing micro-organisms enter the body and start to multiply. These are called **pathogens**

(or germs). Infections may be localised to one part of the body; for example, **conjunctivitis** is limited to the eye. Or they may be more widespread, affecting many of the body systems (e.g. **measles**). Not all micro-organisms are **pathogenic** (disease-causing in humans).

Germs can only be seen with the aid of a powerful microscope and may be subdivided into these categories:

* bacteria;
* viruses;
* protozoa;
* fungi;
* animal parasites.

Bacteria

Bacteria are abundant almost everywhere – in the air, soil and water – and most are harmless to humans. Indeed some bacteria are beneficial, e.g. those that live in the intestines and help to break down food for digestion.

Bacteria need warmth, moisture, and food to survive.

Examples of diseases caused by bacteria include:

* food poisoning, or salmonella;
* cholera;
* typhoid;
* whooping cough (pertussis);
* tuberculosis;
* tetanus;
* gonorrhoea (a sexually transmitted disease);
* tonsillitis.

Viruses

Viruses are the smallest known type of pathogenic micro-organism and cannot be seen under an ordinary microscope. They can only replicate *inside* host cells; this makes them difficult to treat because killing the virus also puts the host cell at risk. The best defence against viruses therefore is to stop them getting into the cells in the first place.

Examples of diseases caused by viruses include:

* flu;
* colds;
* measles;
* mumps;
* rubella;
* chicken pox;
* shingles (herpes zoster);
* tetanus;
* HIV/AIDS;
* rabies.

Protozoa

All types of protozoa are simple one-celled animals and are of microscopic size. About 30 different types of protozoa are troublesome parasites of humans.

Examples of diseases caused by protozoa include:

* diarrhoeal infections;
* trichomoniasis – a sexually transmitted infection;
* malaria;
* toxoplasmosis – a disease acquired from cats.

Fungi

Fungi are simple, parasitic life forms, including moulds, mildews, mushrooms and yeasts. Some fungi are harmlessly present all the time in areas of the body such as the mouth, skin, intestines and vagina but are prevented from multiplying through competition from

bacteria. Other fungi are dealt with by the body's immune system.

Examples of fungal infection include:

* thrush (candidiasis);
* athlete's foot;
* ringworm.

Animal Parasites

Parasites are organisms which live *in* or *on* any other living creature. They obtain their food from the host's blood or tissues and are thus able to reproduce. Parasites may remain permanently with their host or may spend only part of their life cycle in association.

Examples of infection by parasites include:

* head lice;
* scabies mites;
* fleas;
* threadworms.

How Infection is Spread

Infection enters the body in several ways; by:

* **droplet infection:** this occurs by breathing in air containing tiny droplets of infected mucus from an infected person's sneeze or cough. Colds, flu, pneumonia and whooping cough are spread by coughs and sneezes;
* **touching infected people:** germs can be spread by touching someone who is infected or the things they have used, e.g. towels, combs and cups. Chickenpox and measles can be caught by touching infected people, and athlete's foot can be caught by walking on wet floors or mats used by infected people;
* **infected food or drink:** food and drink can be infected with germs by coughs and sneezes, dirty hands, flies,

mice and pet animals. Infected food and drink cause food poisoning and dysentery.

Natural Defences Against Infection

We are all born with natural immunity – which is the ability of the body to resist infection. The body has a complex immune system which works in partnership with other protective body systems:

* **The skin** forms a physical barrier against germs entering your body. Skin is tough and generally impermeable to bacteria and viruses. The epidermis contains special cells called Langerhans cells that are an important early-warning feature of the immune system. The skin also secretes anti-bacterial substances – most bacteria and spores that land on the skin die quickly.

* **Nose, mouth and eyes** are also obvious entry points for germs. Tears and mucus contain an enzyme (lysozyme) that breaks down the cell wall of many bacteria. Saliva is also anti-bacterial. Since the nasal passage and lungs are coated in mucus, many germs not killed immediately are trapped in the mucus and soon swallowed.

* **The respiratory system** uses cilia, mucus and coughing to rid the body of inhaled microbes and pollutants.

* **Acid** in the stomach and **enzymes** in the intestines destroy many pathogens.

If foreign materials enter the body in spite of these protective mechanisms, then the immune and defence mechanisms come into play.

How the Immune System Works

The natural barriers of the immune system are the skin and the mucosal membranes which line the digestive, the respiratory and the genito-urinary systems, which can be accessed from outside the body. If this physical and chemical barrier is broken down by trauma or as a result of infection on the surface, the invading pathogens can enter the body, the bloodstream and the lymphatic system and potentially find a niche elsewhere in the body tissue to multiply and form a colony. The immune system works by using a collection of specialised cells:

1   **White blood cells**

* All white blood cells are known as **leucocytes.** White blood cells are not like normal cells in the body – they actually act like independent, living single-cell organisms able to move and capture things on their own. The two most important white blood cells in our immune system are phagocytes and lymphocytes:

* **Phagocytes**: These cells fight infection by surrounding and engulfing the pathogens – or germs – and then attacking them with a range of chemicals and enzymes. They are *not* effective against viruses.

* **Lymphocytes**: Once the phagocytes have attacked the invaders, the resultant parts would then be processed by other white blood cells, including the lymphocytes. If there have been similar invaders before, the lymphocytes may have a 'memory' of this and rapidly produce antibodies to set an early attack before the invading germs get a chance to multiply.

2   **Antibodies**

Once the lymphocytes have made a particular kind of antibody they can make it much faster next time; also it may stay in your blood for a while.

This makes you **immune** to the disease. You may never catch it again, or if you do, you will only have it mildly. You can also get vaccinated against certain diseases. Specially treated germs are injected into you, to give you a mild attack of the disease. Your body responds by making antibodies, so you become immune for the future.

The Lymphatic System

The lymphatic system plays an important part in our defence against infection. Lymph is a clearish liquid that contains some white blood cells and some chemicals that are also found in blood. Lymph helps fight infections and drains fluid from body tissues back into the bloodstream. The lymph permeates the body just as blood does, but it circulates through muscle movements rather than being pumped around the body like blood. Any random bacteria that enter the body also find their way into the lymphatic system. One job of the lymph system is to drain and filter these fluids to detect and remove the bacteria. Small lymph vessels collect the liquid and move it towards larger vessels so that the fluid finally arrives at the lymph nodes for processing.

Lymph nodes contain filtering tissue and a large number of lymph cells. When fighting certain bacterial infections, the lymph nodes swell with bacteria and the cells fighting the bacteria, to the point where you can actually feel them. Swollen lymph nodes – often called swollen glands – are therefore a good indication that you have an infection of some sort. These swollen glands may be felt in the neck, in the armpits and in the groin area.

How Antibiotics Work

Normally, our bodies are fit enough to fight an infection with all the parts of our immune system. Antibiotics are chemicals developed to help us in the fight. They reduce the risk of tissue damage while the immune system fights off the infection, and reduce the risk of death if it is unsuccessful. There is an argument that antibiotics are used too much; for minor infections with low risks we should wait for the body's own defences. One problem of giving a course of antibiotics for an infection is that as well as killing off the harmful bacteria causing the infection, some of your 'commensal flora' will die too, leaving an opportunity for others to grow. A good example is 'thrush' or candida infection. This yeast-like fungus normally lives on the skin and in the gut and vagina in small, well-controlled numbers but after a dose of antibiotics it gets a chance to multiply and cause further harm.

There is also a danger that people will develop **resistance** to antibiotics.

The Immune System in Children

A baby is born with some natural immunity and can be further protected by:

*   infection-fighting cells;
*   antibodies and other substances found in breast milk.

A child's own experiences of infection boost his or her immunity. For some infections, immunity is lifelong while for others it is shortlived. Some illnesses, such as the common cold, are caused by one of several strains of virus, which is why having one cold doesn't automatically prevent another one later. Immunisation makes a child immune without having the illness itself. Sometimes the immune system doesn't work properly, as with AIDS and some rare conditions; sometimes it overworks and causes allergy. It can also be affected by emotional distress and physical exhaustion.

ACTIVITY

* What are the natural defences to infection?

* Which part of the blood protects you against infection?

* What is the role of the lymphatic system in preventing infection?

* Describe two ways in which your body can become immune to a disease.

(For information on childhood immunisation, see Unit 11 on CD-ROM.)

THE EFFECTS OF POVERTY ON CHILD HEALTH

Poverty is the single greatest threat to the health and wellbeing of children in the UK. Growing up in poverty can affect every area of a child's development: physical, intellectual, emotional, social and spiritual.

Poverty and Social Disadvantage – the Facts

* **Accident and illness**: children from the bottom social class are four times more likely to die in an accident than those living in households with high incomes and have nearly twice the rate of long-standing illness.

* **Quality of life**: a third of children in poverty go without the meals, or toys, or the clothes that they need.

* **Poor nutrition**: living on a low income means that children's diet and health can suffer.

* **Space to live and play**: poorer children are more likely to live in sub-standard housing and in areas with few shops or amenities, where children have little or no space to play safely.

* **Growth**: they are also more likely to be smaller at birth and shorter in height.

* **Education**: children who grow up in poverty are less likely to do well at school and have poorer school attendance records.

* **Long-term effects**: as adults they are more likely to suffer ill health, be unemployed or homeless. They are more likely to become involved in offending, drug and alcohol abuse. They are more likely to become involved in abusive relationships.

Poverty is linked with the health of children because:

* **Healthy eating costs more**: it costs more to provide a nutritionally balanced diet than one that is based on foods that tend to be high in sugar and fats.

* **Poor housing conditions**: low-income families tend to live in poorer housing, which may also be overcrowded, compared with those who are better off.

* **Unemployment**: parents who are unemployed have a higher incidence of mental health problems, long-term physical illness, disability and also higher mortality rates.

All these factors can have a lasting impact on the physical, emotional and social wellbeing of the child and family. Poverty is closely linked with **social disadvantage**; this means that families who have low incomes are likely to have fewer physical and personal resources to cope with illness. They will be at a disadvantage socially. They are also less likely to attend health clinics and, therefore, to receive adequate medical care, both preventative and in response to illness.

Housing

Poor housing is another factor which puts people at a social disadvantage. Low-income families are more likely to live in:

* homes which are damp and/or unheated – this increases the risk of infection, particularly respiratory illnesses;

* neighbourhoods which are unattractive and densely populated, with few communal areas and amenities – children without access to a safe garden or play area may suffer emotional and social problems;

* overcrowded conditions – homeless families who are housed in 'hotels' or bed and breakfast accommodation often have poor access to cooking facilities and have to share bathrooms with several other families; often children's education is badly disrupted when families are moved from one place to another.

Homelessness

It is estimated that about 180,000 children become homeless in England each year. Most of them will be living in temporary hostel accommodation or 'bed and breakfast' housing. The vast majority of these children are in lone parent families, with very little financial or extended family support. Most of these families become homeless to escape from violence from a male partner or ex-partner, or from neighbours. The experience of homelessness causes many health problems for the children of such families:

* mental health problems, including delays in social or language development;

* behavioural problems;

* disruption of social relationships and difficulty in forming new friendships;

* experience of marital conflict and domestic violence.

Accidents

Some childhood accidents have lasting effects on a child's healthy growth and development, and many are preventable (see Chapter 10).

Emotional and Social Factors

A child who is miserable and unhappy is not healthy, although he or she may appear *physically* healthy. Children need to feel secure and to receive unconditional love from their primary carers. Child abuse, although not common, is bound to affect a child's health and wellbeing, and can have long-lasting health implications. See Chapter 9 for information about child abuse.

Environmental Factors

Pollution of the environment can have a marked effect on children's health and development. The three main threats to health are water pollution, air pollution and noise pollution.

Water Pollution

We all need clean, non-polluted water to prevent the spread of infectious diseases and poisoning. Many harmful germs are carried in water, including cholera, typhoid and the polio virus. In developing countries, over 4 million children die each year from drinking unclean water, mainly because it is contaminated with harmful organisms. Toxic chemicals in industrial, agricultural and domestic waste are common pollutants of water. In the UK water is purified before we use it. Although water treatment can remove bacterial contamination, it does not remove heavy chemical pollution. Examples of chemical pollutants in water that can affect children include:

* **Lead:** this can enter into our bodies via air, food and water. It concentrates in the liver, kidney and bones and can cause mental retardation.
* **Nitrates:** these enter water from fertilisers that leach out of the soil; too much nitrate in drinking water has been found to cause a serious blood disorder in babies under 3 months, called 'blue baby syndrome'.

Air Pollution

Children are particularly vulnerable to air pollution. This is partly because they have a large lung surface area in relation to their small body size; this means that they absorb toxic substances quicker than adults do and are slower to get rid of them. The effects of air pollution from factory chimneys, the use of chemical insecticides and car exhausts include:

* **Lead poisoning:** children are particularly susceptible to lead poisoning, mostly caused by vehicle exhaust fumes. Even very low levels of lead in the blood can affect children's ability to learn. Higher levels are associated with damage to the kidneys, liver and reproductive system.
* **Asthma:** air pollution can act as a trigger for asthma and can make an existing condition worse. The incidence of asthma is much higher in traffic-polluted areas.
* **Cancer:** the use of insecticides and fertilisers by farmers has been linked with various childhood cancers. Radio-

activity from nuclear power stations has also been found to cause cancer.

Noise Pollution

Noise pollution can also be a hazard to child health. There is evidence to suggest that high levels of noise, mostly caused by heavy traffic, are responsible for medical and social problems. For example, it has been found that children living on noisy main roads had far fewer friends than those in quiet suburbs, and that traffic noise adversely affects children's progress at school.

THE INVERSE CARE LAW

The families who are most in need of child health surveillance are often those who are least likely to make use of the services provided. Although children in the UK today enjoy better health than at any other time, the provisions of a National Health Service have not led to equality of health experience. The following box outlines people who might be seen as priority groups by health visitors and the primary health-care team when organising caseloads and targeting resources. The health care of such priority groups is difficult and often involves a working partnership with other community services, such as social service departments or housing departments.

PRIORITY GROUPS FOR HEALTH SURVEILLANCE

* Very young or unsupported parents, particularly those with their first baby.
* Parents thought to be at particular risk of abusing their children.
* Parents who are socially isolated, due to mental-health problems or linguistic or cultural barriers.

* Families living in poor housing, including bed and breakfast accommodation or housing where there is overcrowding.

* Parents with low self-esteem or a lack of confidence.

* Parents with unrealistic expectations about the child, or with a poor understanding of the child's needs.

* Parents and/or children suffering significant bereavement (or separation as a result of a recent divorce).

* Parents who have experienced previous SIDS (sudden infant death syndrome) in the family.

LIFESTYLE FACTORS

Substance Misuse: Smoking, Alcohol and Drugs

* One in five secondary school children have tried drugs.

* One in four say they drink alcohol.

* One in ten smoke regularly.

* Boys admit to drinking more alcohol than girls, an average of 11.5 units in a week compared with 9.5 units for girls.

* 1,000 young people under the age of 15 are admitted to hospital each year with alcohol poisoning. All need emergency treatment.

* Girls are more likely to be regular smokers (10 per cent of girls compared with 7 per cent of boys). Again, there is a steep increase in the prevalence of smoking with age (1 per cent of 11-year-olds compared with 20% per cent of 15-year-olds).

[Information taken from: *Drug Use, Smoking and Drinking Among Young People in England in 2005*.]

Smoking

Smoking is dangerous at any age, but the younger people start, the more likely they are to become lifelong smokers and to die early. There are also the risks associated with **passive smoking** (see page 372, this chapter). Non-smokers who breathe in **second-hand smoke** are at risk of the same diseases as smokers, including cancer and heart disease.

How Smoking Affects the Body

Why do People Start Smoking?

Smoking usually begins in adolescence. Various factors combine to make it more likely that a young person will smoke; these include:

* Availability: if cigarettes are readily available at home.

* Role models: if role models, e.g. parents, teachers and friends smoke.

* Peer pressure: there is a strong need to conform to the norms of one's peer group.

* Confidence: smoking is a social habit which gives confidence.

* Rebellion: as a gesture of defiance against authority.

Studies have shown that a teenager who smokes just two or three cigarettes has a 70% per cent chance of becoming addicted.

Children are three times more likely to smoke if their parents smoke.

Two-thirds of teenage smokers say they would find it hard to go without cigarettes for a week.

Half of smokers under the age of 16 who try to buy cigarettes from shops succeed in doing so.

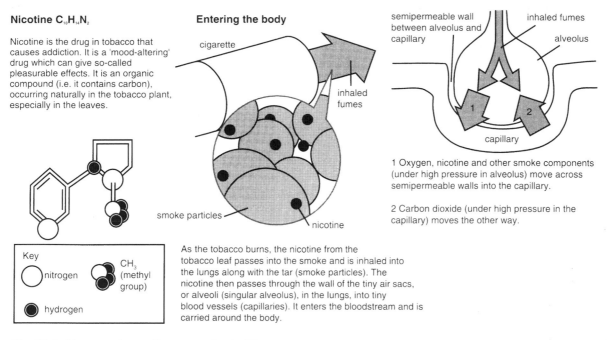

Nicotine C₁₀H₁₄N₂

Nicotine is the drug in tobacco that causes addiction. It is a 'mood-altering' drug which can give so-called pleasurable effects. It is an organic compound (i.e. it contains carbon), occurring naturally in the tobacco plant, especially in the leaves.

Entering the body

cigarette

inhaled fumes

smoke particles

nicotine

Key
○ nitrogen
◐ CH₃ (methyl group)
● hydrogen

semipermeable wall between alveolus and capillary

inhaled fumes

alveolus

capillary

1 Oxygen, nicotine and other smoke components (under high pressure in alveolus) move across semipermeable walls into the capillary.

2 Carbon dioxide (under high pressure in the capillary) moves the other way.

As the tobacco burns, the nicotine from the tobacco leaf passes into the smoke and is inhaled into the lungs along with the tar (smoke particles). The nicotine then passes through the wall of the tiny air sacs, or alveoli (singular alveolus), in the lungs, into tiny blood vessels (capillaries). It enters the bloodstream and is carried around the body.

Fig 12.3 How smoking affects your body (1)

(**NB** The Government is raising the legal minimum age at which tobacco can be bought in England and Wales from 16 to 18 years, from October 2007.)

Alcohol

Young people see alcohol on sale all around them, in supermarkets, off-licences, pubs and restaurants. They might also see their parents drinking alcohol. This can make it harder to understand that *misusing* alcohol is dangerous. It is important for young people to be aware of the following risks:

* **Bingeing**: this is drinking large amounts of alcohol over a short period to get drunk quickly. It is especially risky for young people because their bodies are not mature and so alcohol will have more of an effect on them.

* **Types of drinks and mixing drinks**: certain types of drink preferred by young people are much stronger than average, for example strong beers and ciders. There can be as much alcohol in a 330ml bottle of 'alco-pop' as a generous shot of whisky.

* **Combining alcohol with drugs**: drinking alcohol and taking some drugs is very dangerous; for example, alcohol increases the risk of a serious drug overdose.

* **Accidents and aggression**: after drinking alcohol young people are far more likely to have an accident, and some are more likely to become involved in a fight.

* **Long-term heavy use of alcohol**: this can lead to many problems including liver, heart and stomach conditions.

Drugs

Most teenagers come into contact with drugs and know where they can be obtained. Research shows that almost a third of 15-year-olds have tried an illegal

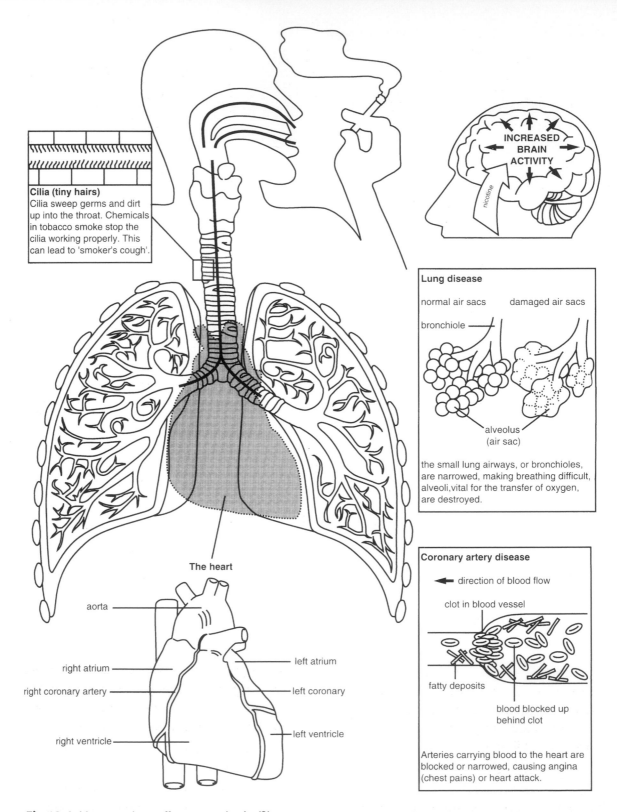

Cilia (tiny hairs)
Cilia sweep germs and dirt up into the throat. Chemicals in tobacco smoke stop the cilia working properly. This can lead to 'smoker's cough'.

INCREASED BRAIN ACTIVITY

nicotine

Lung disease

normal air sacs   damaged air sacs

bronchiole

alveolus (air sac)

the small lung airways, or bronchioles, are narrowed, making breathing difficult, alveoli,vital for the transfer of oxygen, are destroyed.

The heart

aorta

right atrium

right coronary artery

right ventricle

left atrium

left coronary

left ventricle

Coronary artery disease

← direction of blood flow

clot in blood vessel

fatty deposits

blood blocked up behind clot

Arteries carrying blood to the heart are blocked or narrowed, causing angina (chest pains) or heart attack.

Fig 12.4 How smoking affects your body (2)

Fig 12.5 Why do people take drugs?

drug at some point, usually cannabis. Most teenagers who experiment with 'soft' drugs (such as cannabis) do not move onto hard drugs (such as heroin) or become addicted.

DIET AND EXERCISE

The National Diet and Nutrition Surveys (2004) of young people showed that all age groups showed:

* a preference for high-fat-content diets, shown by the high consumption of chips, snack foods, biscuits, chocolate confectionery and soft drinks;

* low consumption of fruits and vegetables;

* that the prevalence of eating disorders such as anorexia nervosa and bulimia nervosa, which predominantly affect females, has increased in recent years.

Table 12.2 A Guide to Illegal Drugs

Drug name	**Alkyl Nitrates**
Other names	• Poppers • Amyl nitrate, butyl nitrate, isobutyl nitrate • Product names include: Ram, Thrust, Rock Hard, Kix, TNT, Liquid Gold
What it looks like	• Clear or straw-coloured liquid in a small bottle • Vapour which is breathed in through the mouth or nose from a small bottle or tube
Effects	• Brief but intense 'head rush' • Flushed face and neck • Effects fade after 2 to 5 minutes
Health risks	• Headache, feeling faint and sick • Regular use can cause skin problems around the mouth and nose • Dangerous for people with anaemia, glaucoma, and breathing or heart problems • If spilled can burn the skin • May be fatal if swallowed • Mixing Viagra with alkyl nitrates may increase risk of heart problems
Legal status	• Amyl nitrate is a prescription-only medicine • Possession is not illegal, but supply can be an offence
Drug name	**Amphetamines**
Other names	• Speed, whizz, uppers, amph, billy, sulphate
What it looks like	• Grey or white powder that is snorted, swallowed, smoked, injected, or dissolved in drink • Tablets which are swallowed
Effects	• Excitement – the mind races and users feel confident and energetic • While on the drug, some users become tense and anxious • Leaves users feeling tired and depressed for one or two days and sometimes longer
Health risks	• High doses repeated over a few days may cause panic and hallucinations • Long-term use can lead to mental illness • Mixing Viagra with amphetamines may increase the risk of heart problems
Legal status	• Class B (but Class A if prepared for injection)
Drug name	**Cannabis**
Other names	• Marijuana, draw, blow, weed, puff, shit, hash, ganja, spliff, wacky backy **Cannabis is the most commonly used drug among 11 to 25 year olds**
What it looks like	• A solid, dark lump known as 'resin' • Leaves, stalks ands seeds called 'grass' • A sticky, dark oil • Can be rolled (usually with tobacco) in a spliff or joint, smoked on its own in a special pipe, or cooked and eaten in food
Effects	• Users feel relaxed and talkative • Cooking the drug then eating it makes the effects more intense and harder to control • May bring on a craving for food (this is often referred to as having the 'munchies')
Health risks	• Smoking it with tobacco may lead to users becoming hooked on cigarettes • Impairs the ability to learn and concentrate • Can leave people tired and lacking energy • Users may lack motivation and feel apathetic • Can make users paranoid and anxious, depending upon their mood and situation • Smoking joints over a long period of time can lead to respiratory disorders, including lung cancer
Legal status	• Class C
Drug name	**Ecstasy**
Other names	• E, doves, XTC, disco biscuits, hug drugs, burgers, fantasy • Chemical name: MDMA (currently many tablets contain MDEA, MDA, MBDB) **4% of 16 to 25s have used ecstasy in the last 3 months.**
What it looks like	• Tablets of different shapes, size and colour (but often white) which are swallowed
Effects	• Users feel alert and in tune with their surroundings • Sound, colour and emotions seem much more intense • Users may dance for hours • The effects last from 3 to 6 hours

Table 12.2 (continued)

Health risks	• Can leave users feeling tired and depressed for days • Risk of overheating and dehydration if users dance energetically without taking breaks or drinking enough fluids (users should sip about a pint of non-alcoholic fluid such as fruit juice, sports drinks or water every hour) • Use has been linked to liver and kidney problems • Some experts are concerned that use of ecstasy can lead to brain damage causing depression in later life • Mixing Viagra with ecstasy may increase the risk of heart problems
Legal status	• Class A • Other drugs similar to ecstasy are also illegal and Class A
Drug name	**Gases, Glues, and Aerosols**
Other names	• Products such as lighter gas refills, aerosols containing products such as hairspray, deodorants and air fresheners, tins or tubes of glue, some paints, thinners and correcting fluids
What it looks like	• Sniffed or breathed into the lungs from a cloth or sleeve • Gas products are sometimes squirted directly into the back of the throat
Effects	• Effects feel similar to being very drunk • Users feel thick-headed, dizzy, giggly and dreamy • Users may hallucinate • Effects don't last very long, but users can remain intoxicated all day by repeating the dose
Health risks	• Nausea, vomiting, black-outs and heart problems that can be fatal • Squirting gas products down the throat may cause body to produce fluid that floods the lungs and this can cause instant death • Risk of suffocation if the substance is inhaled from a plastic bag over the head • Accidents can happen when the user is high because their senses are affected • Long-term abuse of glue can damage the brain, liver and kidneys
Legal status	• It is illegal for shopkeepers to sell to under 18s, or to people acting for them, if they suspect the product is intended for abuse
Drug name	**Heroin**
Other names	• Smack, brown, horse, gear, junk, H, jack, scag
What it looks like	• Brownish-white powder which is smoked, snorted or dissolved and injected
Effects	• Small doses give the user a sense of warmth and well-being • Larger doses can make them drowsy and relaxed
Health risks	• Heroin is addictive (even when smoked) • Users who form a habit may end up taking the drug just to feel normal • Excessive amounts can result in overdose, coma, and in some cases death • Injecting can damage veins • Sharing injecting equipment puts users at risk of dangerous infections like hepatitis B or C and HIV/AIDS
Legal status	• Class A
Drug name	**LSD**
Other names	• Acid, trips, tabs, blotters, microdots, dots
What it looks like	• ¼ inch squares of paper, often with a picture on one side, which are swallowed. Microdots and dots are tiny tablets
Effects	• Effects are known as a 'trip' • Users will experience their surroundings in a very different way • Sense of movement and time may speed up or slow down • Objects, colours and sounds maybe distorted
Health risks	• Once a trip starts, it cannot be stopped • Users can have a 'bad trip' which can be terrifying • 'Flashbacks' may be experienced when parts of a trip are relived some time after the event • Can complicate mental health problems
Legal status	• Class A

Bulimia nervosa was greatly increased among 10- to 19-year-old females.

Overweight and obesity in children and adolescents of secondary school age are on the increase. Factors that may be contributing to this trend are the high intake of high-fat-content foods and an inactive lifestyle where more time is spent on sedentary activities outside school such as watching television or videos. Another factor that should be taken into consideration is that fewer children walk to school.

The researchers concluded that the combination of an unhealthy diet and non-active lifestyle could have a significant impact on children's health and wellbeing. A well-balanced diet during childhood that ensures sufficient intakes of vitamins and minerals are being consumed and non-sedentary behaviour will help to reduce the risk of developing diseases in adulthood.

Some children take no regular physical exercise, apart from at school, and this is often because of the family's attitude and habits. Taking regular exercise allows children to develop their motor skills and to 'run off' any pent-up feelings of frustration and aggression.

* Coronary heart disease is the greatest single risk to health in the UK.
* Adults who are physically inactive have about double the chance of suffering from coronary heart disease.
* Children who do not take much exercise tend to become inactive adults.
* Obesity is more common in children who take little exercise

Eating Disorders in Childhood and Adolescence

The most common eating disorders affecting children and adolescents are obesity, anorexia nervosa and bulimia nervosa. All three have profound implications for the successful development of the individual's self-concept and resulting self-esteem.

1 **Obesity**: obesity or fatness results from taking in more energy from the diet than is used up by the body. Some children appear to inherit a tendency to put on weight very easily, and some parents and carers offer more high-calorie food than children need. Obesity can lead to emotional and social problems as well as the physical problem of being more prone to infections. An obese child is often the target for bullying, and if severely obese, the child will be unable to participate in the same vigorous play as their peers. (See Unit 12 on CD-ROM for more information on obesity.)

2 **Anorexia nervosa**: People with anorexia nervosa have an extreme fear of gaining weight; they feel fat, even when they have lost so much weight that it becomes obvious to others. Those affected are predominantly adolescent girls from the higher social classes in the developed world, but recent evidence points to problems in children as young as 7 years old, with a slight increase in the number of boys affected.

Features of the disorder are:

* regularly skipping meals and obsessively counting calories;
* disappearing from the table directly after meals (in order to make themselves vomit);
* eating only low-calorie food;
* showing a keen interest in buying or cooking food for others;
* wearing very loose clothes to hide the body;
* an obsession with exercise;

* dramatic weight loss or gain;
* saying they are unhappy with their body;
* lanugo (baby-like hair on the body; thinning of hair on the head).

There are various theories on the causes of anorexia, including the following:

* Affected individuals do not wish to grow up and are trying to keep their childhood shapes. In part, this may be influenced by the media obsession with achieving the 'perfect' (i.e. slim) body, and also by the desire to defer the 'storm and stress' of adolescence.

* Those affected see anorexia as a way of taking control over their lives.

* Some specialists see it as a true phobia about putting on weight.

* It may be due to an attempt to avoid adult sexual feelings and behaviours.

* The affected individual is over-involved in their own family, so that when they enter adolescence there is a confrontation between the peer group and the family.

* It may be a physical illness caused in part by **hormonal** changes or a disorder of the hypothalamus (the part of the brain concerned with hunger, thirst and sexual development).

* It is caused by depression, a personality disorder or, rarely, schizophrenia.

3 **Bulimia nervosa**: People with bulimia nervosa eat large amounts of food in '**binges**' and then make themselves sick to get rid of the food. They may also:

* take large amounts of laxatives;

* not look overweight or underweight, and because of this their eating problems are often difficult to detect;

* eventually do serious harm to their bodies; in severe cases, repeated vomiting leads to dehydration and loss of the body's vital salts, especially potassium – this may result in weakness and cramps. The acid present in stomach juices may damage tooth enamel;

* become clinically depressed or even suicidal.

As with anorexia, there is no *single* cause to account for the disorder. Many of the theories about bulimia are closely linked to those above, and include a morbid fear of fatness and a constant craving for food, developed after months or years of fasting.

Without help, eating disorders can take over young people's lives, leaving them feeling guilty and bad about themselves. Life can become lonely and depressing and young people often become isolated from their friends. There is a small but definite risk of suicide. The future health of young people is also affected; for example, anorexia nervosa in the teenage years can cause, amongst other problems, permanent infertility and osteoporosis (brittle bones) in adult life.

ILLNESS AND DISABILITY

Children with a chronic physical illness are twice as likely to suffer from emotional problems or disturbed behaviour as those without. This is especially true of physical disorders which involve the brain, for example, epilepsy and cerebral palsy. Serious illness or disability can cause a lot of work and stress for everyone in the family, especially the parents. Children who are ill – and frequently in hospital – experience more stressful situations than children without an illness.

Long-term Effects on Health

The affected child might:

* have fewer opportunities to learn everyday skills, and to develop their interests and hobbies;

* have to miss a lot of school and have particular difficulties with learning;

* see themselves as different from other children, when what they really want is to be just the same as their friends;

* become depressed;

* be vulnerable to bullying.

Children with a disability will experience similar effects on their health and wellbeing. (See Chapter 14 for further information.)

SECTION 3: HOW TO PLAN AND IMPLEMENT ROUTINES AND ACTIVITIES FOR CHILDREN

BEING A GOOD ROLE MODEL

There are many ways in which you can contribute to the promotion of health in child care settings. The most important part of your role is to be a **good role model** for children. Opportunities for teaching children about health and safety are covered in the box below.

Guidelines for teaching children about health and safety

* Provide healthy meals and snacks.

* Practise good hygiene routines, such as hand-washing and teeth-brushing.

* Choose books and displays which reinforce healthy lifestyles.

* Use drama and music sessions to encourage children to express their feelings in a safe environment.

* Create interesting board games with a healthy theme, e.g. how to avoid accidents when playing outside.

* Welcome visitors to talk about their work in health care, e.g. invite a health visitor or dentist to explain the importance of good hygiene routines.

* Demonstrate safety and hygiene routines, e.g. a road safety officer or police officer could visit the setting to teach children how to cross the road safely.

ACTIVITY: EATING DISORDERS IN CHILDHOOD AND ADOLESCENCE

* Discuss the prevalence of ultra-slim models in the media – on film, in television and in magazines. Try to collect articles and advertisements in which photos of very slim models are used and analyse their appeal.

* Teenage dolls – such as Barbie and Bratz – promote an idealised role model which is unhealthy and can damage the self-concept of the child. Discuss this statement.

* Make the home area into a hospital ward and encourage role-play as patients, nurses and doctors.

PROMOTING CHILD HEALTH USING OBSERVATION

Throughout your training, you will have learnt about child development and about the importance of knowing what to expect from children at each developmental stage. When working with children, you can use this knowledge and your powers of **skilled observation** to detect any developmental or health problems. Increasingly, trained early childhood practitioners are being employed in child health clinics to assist doctors and health visitors in carrying out routine screening tests and to offer parents advice on all aspects of child health and development.

ROUTINES AND ACTIVITIES FOR CHILDREN AND YOUNG PEOPLE

ACTIVITY: A HEALTHY EATING ACTIVITY FOR YOUNG CHILDREN

* You will need: paper and felt tip pens; food magazines; scissors; a chart or poster showing the healthy eating food pyramid or circle; paper plates – one for each child; paper glue.

* Ask the children to sit in a circle on the floor and close their eyes.

* Ask them to imagine that it is lunchtime and they are quite hungry.

* Ask the children what they would like to eat. What are their favourite foods? Then ask them to open their eyes.

* Write their favourite foods down on a chart. Ask them to describe what their favourite foods look like.

* Draw a picture of their favourite foods. (Many young children will choose junk food as their favourites, depending on their previous nutrition experiences.)

* Next, show the children a picture of the food pyramid. Ask them to find their favourite foods on this food pyramid. Point out the different foods recommended on the food pyramid.

* Pass out one paper plate to each child. Instruct them to cut out pictures of their favourite foods from the magazines. Then ask them to glue these pictures onto their paper plate to make a food collage. Encourage the children to pick nutritious food choices as well as their not-so-nutritious favourites.

ACTIVITY: HEALTH AWARENESS

1 In groups, plan an activity to use with a group of nursery or school-age children. Choose from the following topics:

* accident prevention;
* care of the teeth;
* the importance of hand-washing.

2 Follow these guidelines when planning your activity:

* decide how many children will be involved – their ages and stages of development;
* choose an appropriate activity: e.g. a story-telling session, a puppet show, a board game, role-play session or creative activity;
* think about your aims and be specific: e.g. 'My activity aims to help children understand the importance of cleaning your teeth';
* design the activity and arrange to carry it out with a group of children in your setting(s).

3 After the activity, evaluate its success and suggest ways you could improve it in future.

CHAPTER 13

Play and Learning in Children's Education

This chapter covers **Unit 7** and is divided into four sections:

Section 1: The relevant theoretical approaches in the field of play and education

Section 2: How to use appropriate tools to assess the learning needs of individual children

Section 3: How to plan and provide learning opportunities in consultation with others

Section 4: How to record and evaluate the planning and assessment cycle

SECTION 1: THE RELEVANT THEORETICAL APPROACHES IN THE FIELD OF PLAY AND EDUCATION

• Pioneers in play and education • International perspectives • Creating a rich learning environment • Play and early learning

PIONEERS IN QUALITY, INTEGRATED, EARLY YEARS PROVISION

Throughout history there have always been people who have been prepared to stand up and fight for what young children need. They are the pioneers who help everyone working with young children, past and present, to move forward. Not all of us have the kind of personality which makes us a pioneer but we can all do our bit for the children in our care.

The pioneers in this chapter are often called educational pioneers, but each one of them cared for children as much as they educated them. Each one of them believed in integrated early years provision. This has a long and respected heritage and the greatest influence in the UK in the last century has been that of Friedrich Froebel. Other pioneers include Maria Montessori, Rudolf Steiner, Margaret McMillan and Susan Isaacs.

Friedrich Froebel (1782–1852)

Froebel, who founded the first kindergarten in 1840, studied for a time with Pestalozzi in his school in Switzerland. Through his observations of children, Froebel learned how important it was for children to have real experiences which involved them in being physically active. Froebel's ideas are now very much part of everyday thinking about the integration of early years services.

But most people have never heard of the man himself – only his ideas remain. Froebel believed that everything links and connects with everything else: he called this the **Principle of Unity**. But he also believed in what he called the **Principle of Opposition**. For example, the first Gift is a soft ball, but the second Gift is a hard wooden ball. He thought that these kinds of contrasts were important in helping children to think.

A summary of Froebel's ideas

* Froebel thought schools should be communities in which the parents are welcome to join their children.

* He believed that parents were the first educators of their child.

* Froebel thought that children learned outdoors in the garden, as well as indoors. He encouraged movement, games and the study of natural science in the garden.

* He invented finger play, songs and rhymes.

* He encouraged the arts and crafts and a love of literature, as well as mathematical understanding.

* He thought that children should have freedom of movement, clothes which were easy to move about in, and sensible food which was not too rich.

* Froebel deeply valued symbolic behaviour, and he encouraged this even in very young children. He realised how important it is for children to understand that they can make one thing stand for another, for example: a daisy can stand for a fried egg, a twig can stand for a knife, a leaf can stand for a plate, a written word can stand for a name.

* He thought that the best way for children to try out symbolic behaviour was in their play. He thought that, as they pretend and imagine things, children show their highest levels of learning. He thought that children's best thinking is done when they are playing.

* He also designed various items and activities to help symbolic behaviour. He encouraged children to draw, make collages and model with clay.

* He encouraged play with special shaped wooden blocks, which he called the Gifts.

* He made up songs, movements and dancing, and the crafts, which he called his Occupations.

* He allowed children to use the Gifts and Occupations as they wished, without having to do set tasks of the kind that adults usually asked of them. Thus he introduced what is now called free-flow play.

* He emphasised the expressive arts, mathematics, literature, the atural sciences, creativity and aesthetic (beautiful) things. He believed that each brought important but different kinds of knowledge and understanding.

* He also placed great emphasis on ideas, feelings and relationships. Relationships with other children, he believed, were as important as relationships with adults.

Maria Montessori (1870–1952)

Maria Montessori began her work as a doctor in the poorest areas of Rome, at the beginning of the 1900s. She worked with children with learning difficulties. She spent many hours **observing** children and this is one of the great strengths of her work. She came to the conclusion, now supported by modern research, that children pass through sensitive periods of development when they are particularly receptive to particular areas of learning. Like Piaget (and others), she saw children as active learners.

A summary of Montessori's ideas

* Montessori devised a structured teaching programme which she based on her observations of children who were mentally challenged, and she believed she was making Froebel's work more scientifically rigorous in doing this.

* She also used the work of an educator called Seguin who had given manual dexterity exercises to children who were handicapped. This he did because he believed that, if they could learn to use their hands, they would be able to find work later.

* Montessori designed a set of what she called didactic materials which encouraged children to use their hands. Her approach moved children through simple to complex exercises.

* Whereas Froebel stressed the importance of relationships, feelings and being part of a community, Montessori stressed that children should work alone. She thought that this helped children to become independent learners.

* For her, the highest moment in a child's learning was what she called the polarisation of the attention. This means that the

child is completely silent and absorbed in what they are doing.

* Unlike Froebel, Montessori did not see the point in play. She did not encourage children to have their own ideas until they had worked through all her graded learning sequences: she did not believe that they were able to do free drawing or creative work of any kind until they had done this. Montessori has had less influence on the maintained sector of education than she has on private schools.

Rudolf Steiner (1861–1925)

Steiner believed in three phases of childhood. These involved:

1   The **will**, 0–7 years: he believed the spirit fuses with the body at this stage.

2   The **heart**, 7–14 years: he believed that the rhythmic system of the beating heart, the chest and the respiratory system meant that feelings were especially important during this time.

3   The **head**, 14 years onwards: this is the period of thinking.

There are a few schools in the UK which use Steiner's methods. These **Waldorf Schools** are all in the private sector. Like Montessori, Steiner has had less influence on the statutory public sector than on the private sector.

A summary of Steiner's ideas

* Steiner believed in reincarnation. To him, this meant that, during the first 7 years of life, the child is like a newcomer finding their way, and the child's reincarnated soul needs protection.

* The child needs a carefully planned environment to develop in a rounded way.

* What the child eats is very important (Steiner was a vegetarian). The child also needs proper rest (rest and activity need to be balanced).

* The child's temperament is also considered to be very important. A child might be calm (sanguine), easily angered (choleric), sluggish (phlegmatic), or peevish (melancholic). Often, children are a combination of types.

* The golden rule for the adult is never to go against the temperament of the child, and always to go with it.

* Steiner was like Froebel in that he believed in the importance of the community. He believed that maintaining relationships with other people is very important, and for this reason children would keep the same teacher for a number of years.

* When children are about to sing and act out a circle game, everyone waits for the last child to join the group. The song is sung many times so that quicker children learn to help and support slower children.

* Steiner's curriculum is very powerful for children with special educational needs who can integrate because other children are actively helped to care about them.

* Steiner thought the symbolic behaviour of the child was important, but in a different way from Froebel. In the first 7 years of life, he told special Steinerian fairy

tales. He believed children 'drink' these in and absorb them. He gave them dolls without faces, wooden blocks with irregular shapes, silk scarves as dressing-up clothes and particular colour schemes in rooms (pink at first). Baking, gardening, modelling, painting and singing would all take place in a carefully designed community.

Margaret McMillan (1860–1931)

Margaret McMillan, like Montessori, began her work using the influence of Seguin. This meant that she emphasised manual dexterity exercises long before Montessori's ideas reached the UK. However, as time went on, she used Froebel's ideas more and more (she became a member of the Froebel Society in 1903).

A summary of McMillan's ideas

* McMillan believed first-hand experience and active learning to be important.

  She emphasised relationships, feelings and ideas, as much as the physical aspects of moving and learning.

* She believed that children become whole people through play. She thought play helps them to apply what they know and understand.

* McMillan pioneered nursery schools, which she saw as an extension of, not a substitute for, home.

* She believed in very close partnership with parents: she encouraged parents to develop alongside their children, with adult classes in hobbies and languages made available to them.

* The British nursery school, as envisaged by McMillan, has been admired and emulated across the world. Nursery schools have gardens, and are communities which welcome both parents and children. Such nursery schools stood out as beacons of light in the poverty-stricken areas of inner cities like Deptford and Bradford in the 1920s.

* McMillan said that in a nursery school families could experience 'fresh air, trees, rock gardens, herbs, vegetables, fruit trees, bushes, opportunities to climb on walls, sand pits, lawns, flowers and flower beds and wildernesses'. In her book, *The Nursery School*, she wrote, 'most of the best opportunities for achievement lie in the domain of free play, with access to various materials'. This was published in 1930.

* Perhaps her most important achievement of all is to have been described as the 'godmother' of school meals and the school medical services. She believed that children cannot learn if they are undernourished, poorly clothed, sick or ill with poor teeth, poor eyesight, ear infections, rickets etc. Recent reports emphasise that poor health and poverty are challenges still facing those who work with families in the UK today.

* McMillan placed enormous importance on the training of adults working with children, and on the need for them to be inventive and imaginative in their work.

Susan Isaacs (1885–1948)

Susan Isaacs, like Margaret McMillan, was influenced by Froebel. She was also influenced by the theories of Melanie Klein, the psychoanalyst. Isaacs made **detailed observations** of children in her Malting House School in Cambridge during the 1930s.

A summary of Isaacs' ideas

* Isaacs valued play because she believed that it gave children freedom to think, feel and relate to others.

* She looked at children's fears, their aggression and their anger. She believed that, through their play, children can move in and out of reality. This enables them to balance their ideas, feelings and relationships.

* She said of classrooms where young children have to sit at tables and write that they cannot learn in such places because they need to move just as they need to eat and sleep.

* Isaacs valued parents as the most important educators in a child's life. She spoke to them on the radio, and she wrote for parents in magazines. In her book *The Nursery Years*, she wrote:

If the child has ample opportunity for free play and bodily exercise, if this love of making and doing with his hands is met, if his interest in the world around him is encouraged by sympathy and understanding, if he is left free to make believe or think as his impulses take him, then his advances in skill and interest are but the welcome signs of mental health and vigour.

* Isaacs encouraged people to look at the inner feelings of children. She encouraged children to express their feelings. She thought it would be very damaging to bottle up feelings inside.

* She supported both Froebel's and Margaret McMillan's view that nurseries are an extension of the home and not a substitute for it, and she believed that children should remain in nursery-type education until they are 7 years of age.

* She kept careful records of children, both for the period they spent in her nursery and for the period after they had left. She found that many of them regressed when they left her nursery and went on to formal infant schools. Modern researchers have found the same.

ACTIVITY: REMEMBERING OUR LEARNING

Think back to your own schooldays. Were any of the lessons based on a transmission model of learning? Evaluate your learning experience.

ACTIVITY: INVESTIGATING FROEBEL'S WORK

* Research a set of wooden hollow blocks and wooden unit blocks (examples of these are made by Community Playthings). Can you find any mathematical relationships between the different blocks? Plan how you could help children to learn about shape using wooden blocks. Implement your plan, and evaluate your observations with children aged 3–7 years.

* Try to find 12 examples of finger rhymes. These are songs or rhymes using the fingers for actions. Make a book of them for children to enjoy. Make sure you include a multicultural range of action songs and think also about children with disabilities. Share the book with a child aged 2–7 years. Evaluate your observations.

* Research what children did in kindergartens in the last century. For example, each child had their own little garden.

* Plan how you will organise a garden activity. What equipment will you need? Where will you do this? How will you clear up?

* Plant some flowers or vegetables with children, and watch them grow.

* Observe a child aged 2–7 years, and evaluate your garden activity in relation to that particular child's cognitive and language development.

* Imagine that you are Friedrich Froebel today. What do you think he might like or dislike about your early years setting?

ACTIVITY: INVESTIGATING MARGARET MCMILLAN'S WORK

Plan an outdoor area for an early years setting. Emphasise the child's need for movement, and curiosity about nature, and provide an area for digging and playing in mud. Evaluate your plan.

ACTIVITY: INVESTIGATING EDUCATION AND CARE

1 Research the age at which children start compulsory schooling in six countries, including one country in Africa, Asia, Europe and Australia/New Zealand. You can use the internet or telephone the relevant embassies, who will help you track down this information.

2 Research the different ways in which Froebel, Montessori and Steiner would (a) introduce children to a set of wooden blocks and (b) help children to use the blocks. Implement each approach with a group of children in three separate sessions. Evaluate your observations, noting the way your role as an early years worker changed according to which approach you used. Note the differences in the way the children

responded, especially in relation to creativity (see Chapter 3), language and communication (see Chapter 4) and play (this chapter). Which approaches encouraged the child to be a symbol-user? Evaluate your observations.

3   With the emergence of psychology as a discipline of study in the 1920s, theories suggested that play helps children:

*   rehearse adult roles and prepare for their future lives (Groos, 1920s);

*   deepen their thinking, keep their bodies functioning well through movement play, and engage in flexible and adaptable thinking (play helps adults to do these things too) (Huizinga, 1940s);

*   experience a natural childhood, which helps them, supported by sensitive adults, to self-heal after emotional trauma (Anna Freud, 1940s and 1950s);

*   find out what is important to them and resolve dilemmas – childhood play reveals the fears and fascinations of children (Erikson, 1950s);

*   develop transitional objects and imaginary friends, which are used by the child to deal with separations from those they love (e.g. sleeping with teddy or needing teddy when parting from mother), and develop imaginative play (so that teddy becomes a character with a full life); they try things out as they are, as they were, as they might be and as they want them to be; they gain control of their lives (Winnicott, 1960s);

*   make the most of learning through the senses and movement, and using first-hand experiences, such as going shopping when learning about pretending (playing shops), gradually developing games with rules, such as snakes and ladders, snooker or football (Piaget, 1930s to 1980s);

*   operate on a higher, more abstract plane than they can manage in ordinary life – Vygotsky emphasised that other people, especially adults, are important to children as they play; he believed that play helps children to do things in advance of what they can manage in real life, such as drive a car or pour the tea from a teapot (Vygotsky's influence reached the West in the 1980s).

DIFFERENT EDUCATIONAL AND PHILOSOPHICAL APPROACHES TO THE CURRICULUM FOR BABIES

Every culture decides what the children should learn, and there are variations across the world. In India, spirituality is emphasised, while in Laos and Hong Kong, literacy and numeracy are the focus.

The Reggio Emilia Approach

The approach in Reggio Emilia in Northern Italy emerged after World War II and, by 1976, governed the schools in that region for young children (from birth to 6 years). It took away the monopoly the Roman Catholic Church held over education, despite a campaign suggesting that this model of education was corrupting for children. Loris Malaguzzi, the pioneer, realised that **pedagogy** (understanding the relationship between developing, learning and teaching) must not be 'the prisoner of certainty'. He thought Piaget was right in warning us that we need a balance by informing our practice through theory and research. In the 1840s the educational pioneer Friedrich Froebel had similarly experienced the resistance of the German churches to his kindergartens, and placed emphasis on linking theory with practice. This is a recurring theme in the history of education that is centred on the child's development and learning rather than on the transmission of knowledge identified as important by those who hold power.

Malaguzzi coined the phrase '**the hundred languages of the child**' to refer to all the different ways in which children express themselves, through talking, singing, dancing, painting, making models, role play, and so on. He considered each of these to be a language.

The Te Whariki Curriculum Framework

In New Zealand the Maori people and the Pakeha (white people) have worked together to make a major contribution to the early childhood curriculum (birth to 6 years) in the Te Whariki curriculum framework, which is based on four principles:

∗ empowerment – Whakamana;

∗ holistic development – Kotahitanga;

∗ family and community – Whanau Tangata;

∗ relationships – Nga Hononga.

There are five strands, each with goals:

1 Wellbeing – Mana Atua
   Goals: health is promoted; emotional wellbeing is nurtured; kept from harm.

2 Belonging – Mana Whenua
   Goals: connecting links with the family and wider world are affirmed and extended; children know they have a place; they feel comfortable with the routines, customs and regular events; they know the limits and boundaries of acceptable behaviour.

3 Contribution – Mana Tangat
   Goals: there are equitable opportunities for learning, irrespective of gender, ability, age, ethnicity or background; children are affirmed as individuals; they are encouraged to learn with and alongside others.

4 Communication – Mana Reo
   Goals: children develop non-verbal communication skills for a range of purposes; they develop verbal communication skills for a range of purposes; they experience the stories and symbols of their own and other cultures; they discover and develop different ways to be creative and expressive.

5 Exploration – Mana Aoturoa
   Goals: Children's play is valued as meaningful learning and the importance of spontaneous play is recognised; children gain confidence in and control of their bodies; they learn strategies for active exploration, thinking and reasoning; they develop working theories for making sense of the natural, social, physical and material worlds.

The Centres of Innovation (COIs), a ministerial initiative led by Anne Meade, are further building on the good practice emerging from Te Whariki:

∗ through encouraging action research in settings which are innovating practice;

∗ supporting them in sharing their practice, knowledge and understanding.

CREATING A RICH LEARNING ENVIRONMENT

In Chapter 9 you will find many examples of what makes a rich learning environment, so that you select equipment and materials which provide a non-biased and positive world view. You will find that there are many links between Chapter 9, which looks at working with children, and this chapter, which focuses on how adults can plan for rich play, learning environments indoors and outdoors, and developing learning.

How to Provide an 'Enabling Environment' that Supports and Encourages Learning

Children gain access to a quality curriculum through **people** and **provision**.

Every child needs full access to the curriculum regardless of their ethnic background, culture, language, gender, special educational needs or disability, or economic background. No child should be held back in their learning because of restricted access to the curriculum.

The role of the adult in supporting children's development and learning through developmentally appropriate materials, equipment and resources is of huge importance.

EFFECTIVE COMMUNICATION WITH BABIES AND YOUNG CHILDREN

Adults who tune in to children are affectionate and sensitive to non-verbal ways in which babies, toddlers and young children communicate. Research shows that personal rhythms and patterns as children move and learn to speak make a contribution to their later language and reading development. Children with poor timing and rhythm do less well. The rhythm, tone and way babies and toddlers are talked to help them to develop verbal/signed language with confidence and understanding. Throughout our lives, 85 per cent of communication is non-verbal.

The Basic Skills Agency has reported a decline in basic language development in young children in recent years. This fits with a survey of findings by the National Association of Head Teachers, who also found children less developed in basic language skills. Children need direct eye contact with adults in order to develop shared sustained conversations and communications. The National Literacy Trust is responding to the findings of health visitors through the 'Talk to your Baby Campaign' (managed by Liz Attenborough). The Trust found that only two types of less expensive buggy have reversible seats. More are now on the market, according to companies who manufacture buggies.

It is important to remember that babies do not communicate verbally or use signs. The communications we have with them are non-verbal. Their skin is very sensitive to touch. They turn their head if we stroke their cheek. They love to be cuddled and held and spoken to gently. They enjoy eye contact and looking at faces, and if you give them time to reply when you gently say 'Coo' to them at about 3 months, they might reply, after a pause. The tone of voice you use is important as babies quickly become startled and frightened by shouting or sudden movements.

It is fascinating to observe a sleeping baby, too. Their facial expression constantly changes from smile, to pout, to frown, to relaxed.

Babies are helped by those who:

* observe the baby's unique way of telling us they are distressed;

* learn the signals that indicate a baby is about to become very upset, such as squirming, arching the back, yawning and turning away, possetting that is not linked to feeding;

* act on the signals the baby is giving before becoming very distressed;

* avoid undressing a baby who finds this difficult, by wrapping their upper body, including their arms, in a towel during changing. This stops the arms shooting out and causing 'startle' movements which further upset the baby;

* cradle a baby in their arms and rock them gently, with the baby's head on their shoulder and gently stroking the baby's back;

* respond to a baby becoming tired during a proto-conversation (conversation with no words), when the baby signals this by yawning or turning away; the adult responds and stops the 'conversation' and simply cuddles the baby to allow them to relax and rest after such an exhausting 'chat';

* know that being in a quiet, dimly lit place can help babies to sleep when they need to;

* share a book with a baby, which can calm them (they love to look at patterns of grids and circles);

* help babies to find what self-calms them, such as sucking a fist, and place the baby so that they easily find their fist to suck;

* know how important pushchair design is for communication and language; chairs which face the adult encourage communication and shared experience, while those which face the child forward do not; given that many children spend long periods in pushchairs (which is constraining development and learning), both language development and learning to 'read' centrally important non-verbal signals, such as eye contact, pointing/ looking at a shared focus, reading facial expression, are at risk of underdevelopment.

CREATING POSITIVE RELATIONSHIPS IN AN ENABLING ENVIRONMENT FOR BABIES AND YOUNG CHILDREN

A good learning atmosphere (**ethos**) is one in which the adults support and extend the development and learning of the children.

Guidelines for effective communication with babies and young children

* Sing to, talk to and hold the baby. Carry the baby and show him things as they happen, objects and people.

* Play games with babies – stick your tongue out, and after a delay the baby does the same; peek-a-boo games are greatly enjoyed by older babies.

* Allow the child personal space – let the baby quietly lie or sit and watch a mobile. Babies like to lie under a tree, watching the leaves rustling. Babies need to listen to sounds around them, for example the sound of someone opening a door or dropping something in the next room. Having a radio on all the time stops them from doing this.

* Babies need places where they can be propped up safely (e.g. with

cushions on a mat on the floor so they can watch people).

* Babies like to explore objects – find out about Elinor Goldschmied's treasure baskets, which are suitable for sitting babies. A video is available from the National Children's Bureau.

* Make available a bag with various low-cost odds and ends in it, such as a bath sponge and a cotton reel. Choose objects that can be changed or thrown away regularly, and check them for safety.

* Use home-made or commercial toys, such as a baby safety mirror (really worth buying), a pop-up toy, a wobbling toy, bath toys that float and sink, a teddy bear or soft doll, rattles (which are good for hands to hold and make interesting sounds) and baby books which can be chewed and sucked.

* Provide comfortable flooring to crawl over, a mixture of carpets and other surfaces to explore, and grass to crawl on. Soft surfaces are great for beginner-walkers, who fall over a lot!

* Provide stable furniture for babies to pull themselves up on and to cruise between.

* The book *Play It My Way* by the RNIB has a wealth of activities suitable for children from birth to 3 years and children with complex needs.

The adults create a warm, affectionate atmosphere, have high aspirations, observe and tune in to the child's learning, and make individual plans to help the child to learn with a high sense of wellbeing in ways which are appropriate for them. In a quality learning environment, adults value the uniqueness of each child. It is essential to create a learning environment in which children feel appreciated, valued and where those close to them (usually their families) are also valued.

It is through other people that children learn to feel valued, or not. When children feel their efforts are appreciated and celebrated, they develop a positive self-image with high wellbeing. This helps learning more than almost anything else.

On the other hand, if children spend time with adults who only praise and recognise results, most are bound to fail. We learn from our mistakes and errors and things that do not go as planned only if we feel that our efforts have been valued. This keeps children (and adults) highly motivated and interested in learning more. It is important that early childhood practitioners work in a close partnership with parents/carers, in a spirit of trust, with a genuine exchange of information and knowledge. When this happens, everyone gains, especially the child.

Children need adults who provide a safe learning environment indoors and outdoors, which is predictable. This means that staff work together as a team to create consistent boundaries and ways of doing things, so that children feel secure and safe. This enables children to become explorers and problem solvers, and encourages reasoning and enquiring minds.

Some babies are more sensitive to others in dealing with transitions:

* from day to night sleep cycle;
* the stress of being undressed for a nappy change;
* sudden noises;
* being handed over to someone new to hold them.

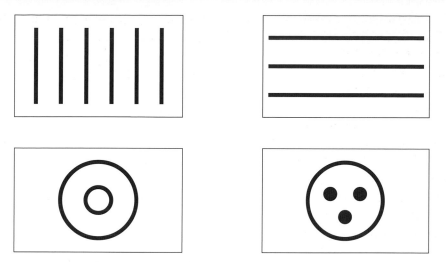

Fig 13.1 Babies love books (based on *The Social Baby*, Murray and Andrews 2003)

If, during the first months, babies are not helped to return to their comfort zone at these times, they might become increasingly unsettled or very passive. This will constrain their development and learning.

For Children Who are Mobile – Crawlers and Toddlers Who are Beginner-walkers

1   Make room for vigorous movement and provide places to run and jump. Offer a soft ball or a larger bouncy ball to kick and throw outside.

2   Wooden and natural-material objects to feel, mouth and hold, and make simple towers to knock down.

3   Finger painting.

4   Non-toxic crayons and paper.

5   Wet and dry silver sand (not builder's sand).

6   Find some good recipes for play dough. Some involve cooking, which makes the dough last longer. Check the dough is safe to put in the mouth and even to eat, as some children might do so.

7   Provide opportunities for water play, carefully supervised, at bath-time, in paddling pools or with bowls of water. Remember, children can drown in very shallow water, so always supervise this.

8   Babies who sit enjoy treasure baskets, developed by Elinor Goldschmied; and toddlers enjoy heuristic play, which she also devised.

9   A tea set, toy cars and other play props will encourage pretend symbolic play with an interdependent adult to connect with.

10 The learning environment indoors and outdoors should facilitate schemas and their development, as part of brain development. For example:

  * small trucks on wheels to transport objects about;

  * soft toys to throw (trajectories);

  * boxes, baskets and bags to put things in (inside and outside);

  * blankets to cover teddies, dolls, and so on (enveloping).

Fig 13.2 Supporting and extending a grid schema using open-ended materials (dough)

11 Picture books and simple texts, such as *Spot the Dog.*

12 Dressing-up clothes – hats, shoes and belts are best for toddlers.

13 Flowers are for picking, as far as toddlers are concerned. Encourage children to pick daisies and dandelions rather than flowers from the flowerbed. They enjoy putting flowers in a vase of water to place on the meal table.

14 Sing action songs and rhymes.

Outdoors

A variety of resources is needed:

* bats, balls, hoops, beanbags (called small apparatus);
* climbing frame (large apparatus);
* wheeled trucks, pushchairs for dolls and teddies;
* plants and growing area, with a wild area to encourage butterflies; perhaps a pond with a safety fence;
* grassy area and other soft surfaces;
* hard surface to make contrasting surfaces;
* well-drained sandpit.

CASE STUDY

Using everyday events for learning 1

When Joey (10 months) is changed, he dislikes the plastic changing mat. He tries to move off it. His key worker respects his feelings and puts a towel on the mat. She talks about what she is doing and why, and she sings 'Ten little toes' to help him relax. He giggles in anticipation of each toe being gently touched.

This everyday event has helped Joey learn about:

* himself and where he ends;
* affectionate and sensitive communication between people;
* making sense of what someone says;
* music, with its melody (tune) and pitch (loudness);
* eye contact when people talk to each other, and facial expressions;
* having fun together.

Babies and toddlers learn better if they are not anxious. Laughing releases chemicals into the brain which open it up to learning. Anxiety closes the brain off to the possibility of learning.

CASE STUDY

Using everyday events for learning 2

At lunchtime, a group of sitting babies and toddlers were encouraged to choose their pudding. A plate of freshly prepared fruit was placed on the table. A tiny portion was given to the babies to try out. Several showed they wanted more through their movements. The key person passed the plate to the babies, who were allowed to take more for themselves.

This encouraged:

* learning that one portion of fruit is the same as the next;
* physical coordination;
* a feeling of control over what happens;
* decision-making.

CASE STUDY

Playing with an adult: interdependent relationships

The key person sat on the floor, facing Rebecca, and sang 'Row, row, row the boat' with her. She sang the song and did the actions twice through, and then stopped. Rebecca touched her on the thigh and the key person responded 'Again? You want to sing again?' The singing and moving were repeated, and Rebecca smiled with pleasure.

In this play:

* Rebecca is helped to be imaginative;
* her idea to repeat the song is taken up;
* she is encouraged to use initiative and not be passive;
* she is learning the basis of drama, music and dance.

These case studies were given by Ruth Forbes, author of 'Beginning to Play'.

Children Aged 3–6 Years: Indoors and Outdoors

Children should be offered a full range of provision, whether they choose to be indoors or outdoors.

* There should be pictures with word labels on shelves and boxes.
* There should be a warm, light and cosy book corner, with cushions and chairs, and a book den outdoors, preferably under a shady tree.

* There should be progression in what is offered; for example, the water tray would have elaborate waterfall, pipes and guttering, canals, and challenges and problem-solving opportunities, in an atmosphere where children's reasoning is valued.
* Small-world equipment should be separated into clearly labelled boxes with pictures, with zoo, prehistoric and farm animals separated, and transport separate from space travel, hospital, domestic play, and so on.
* A well-planned home corner is essential, and basic. Shops, cafes, garages, and so

on, can be offered as well, but never *instead* of a home corner for this age group. Many children need this play for their wellbeing. Dressing-up clothes need to be offered alongside this.

* Children need opportunities for weighing balances, and calibrated equipment such as measuring jugs, sieves, colanders and egg whisks to encourage scientific and mathematical exploration, such as reasoning, problem solving and hypothesising – developing a theory, such as when the water gets to the top of this jug, it spills over all the outside edges; if I do this, then that happens every time. *If* and *then* are important aspects of making a hypothesis.

* There needs to be an interactive interest table and display at child height, with fascinating objects to handle, beautifully and accessibly presented. More is written about display elsewhere in this book.

* There should be a mark-making area, with a variety of paper and different kinds of pencils and pens. This is usually placed next to the workshop area, which will contain materials and glue, scissors, masking tape, and so on.

* There should be an area for wooden blocks which are free-standing and mathematically related shapes and sizes. Community Playthings unit blocks are basic. Hollow blocks are additional. Again, so that the mathematical relationships can be developed fully, it is best to add more of the same brand, rather than having a huge number of incompatible sets of blocks.

* There will need to be a construction area (e.g. Duplo® or Brio®). It is best not to have a huge number of different kinds of construction kit, as each one will be expensive and there will not be enough

of any set for children to use them with satisfaction. It is worth spending time deciding which to buy in bulk, with perhaps two types which offer children a rich range of experiences and endless possibilities. There will need to be simple ways of using the kit, but ways of using it with greater sophistication and elaboration too.

* The workshop should offer paint and clay every day. One of the reasons why clay is not always provided is that practitioners do not know how to care for it. It is a valuable natural material, which children use with pleasure and great skill if they have access to it daily. It is best kept in a thick polythene bag, placed in a covered plastic bucket. It can be cut into manageable chunks with a wire cheese-cutter. A hole can be made using the thumb, and a tiny amount of water can be poured into the hole. This is then covered with a clay lid, smoothed over it. If the clay seems rather sticky when taken from the bucket, it can be thrown on to a porous surface to dry it out. Children love to help with this. They quickly learn how to make thumb pots and coil pots, especially if shown examples on a display table. Showing children how people made pots in the past is a good way of introducing history in a meaningful way.

* There should be an area for movement. This should have sufficient clean floor space on which children can roll and crawl. Having a floor mat can help, although it does indicate that the learning environment is not of a high standard of cleanliness.

* There should be a computer, and ideally a word-processor, as well as digital cameras for children to use.

* There will be a cookery area with baking materials and equipment. This requires a shelf with easy-to-handle containers of basic ingredients, aprons, wooden spoons and easy-to-hold pans to cook in, and metal spoons to measure ingredients. A child-friendly cookery book is essential, so that children learn the sequences and how to find their way through a recipe.

* There should be growing things, such as mustard and cress, hyacinths, a fish aquarium or a wormery. Having magnifying lenses, and pots to put objects and creatures in for nature study without damaging them is important. Teaching children to return live spiders and other mini-beasts to their natural habitat safely and gently is essential.

* The outdoor area needs to be available for most of the day. In some settings children remain indoors until it is safe to let them in the garden, as it is difficult to supervise families arriving and leaving, and a child could slip out of the building unnoticed. Ideally the garden is separate from the main entrance to the setting.

* The outdoor area should complement the indoor area, so that, for example, there are opportunities for mark making, but indoors there may be pencils and felt-tip pens, while outdoors there may be buckets of water and paint brushes to make water markings on the ground.

There is no one way to set out the areas indoors and outdoors, but the layout should not be constantly changed. When you go to the supermarket and find the layout changed, how do you feel? Is it difficult to find things?

* The layout of the room should reflect the multicultural society of the UK.

* There should be appropriate attention to the layout for children with SEN and disabilities.

* The environment should be safe and easy to explore, with easy access to the materials, encouraging autonomy.

Learning through Landscapes (LTL)

This is the national school grounds charity, campaigning for positive outdoor learning and play experiences for all children in education and child care. Since 1990, LTL has been undertaking research and evaluation, developing innovative projects and programmes, and providing training and support to raise awareness of the importance and special nature of the outdoors. Today, both school and early years communities, and those working on their behalf, turn to LTL for guidance in developing and implementing improvements to their outdoor environment for the benefit of children. LTL has been involved in the production of more than 100 high-quality publications, including books, videos and teaching resources. All are designed to help schools and early years settings realise the full potential of the outdoors – for all aspects of play and learning. For further details on the work of Learning through Landscapes and information about the early years and primary membership schemes, Early Years Outdoors and Schoolgrounds UK, you can visit the website at www.ltl.org.uk or write to: Learning through Landscapes, Third Floor, Southside Offices, The Law Courts, Winchester SO23 9DL.

Fig 13.3 Outdoor space is an important part of the provision

Children Aged 5–8 Years

The provision should be the same, but there will be elaboration of the writing and reading areas; and the nature of the decision-making, child choices and freedom of movement will need to show progression.

Guidelines for timetabling the curriculum

* Children learn best when they are in a predictable environment. This means that although their activities should not be controlled by adults all the time, there should be a shape to the day. Children feel safe if they have some sense of what is coming next, for example if there are regular mealtimes.

* The way that the day is organised should fit with children's natural rhythms. Adults need to keep in mind that it is important not to work to a tight, inflexible routine for their convenience. There are times when children go at a fast pace, and times when they tire, times when they want to be alone or to have a quiet cuddle, and times when they enjoy working with other children or adults.

Children benefit from having their own dictionary, in which they are helped to put words that are important for them. They find word banks helpful, for example words about shopping in a box placed near the 'shop', or words about plants and flowers in a box next to the nature table. 'Doing' words (verbs) such as 'go' and 'jump', are well situated near the movement area. There will need to be reference books carefully placed to help children find out more.

Children with Disabilities

There should be a tray on the table to stop objects falling off the edge for children with disabilities such as visual impairment or movement restriction, and ramps for children who are wheelchair users.

It is important to avoid clutter, so that everything provided is there for a reason. Clutter is confusing and distracting. If children know where to put things they use the learning environment more effectively, and they develop awareness of participating positively in the community.

It is important not to underestimate what any child can do, while offering the support and encouragement they need. This is especially important if a child has special educational needs or disabilities.

Learning with and through Other Children

Children learn with and through other children as well as with and through adults they trust and like. They identify children they wish to be friends with. However, this is only possible if they are free to choose what they do for large parts of the day. Even babies who crawl and sit, who are not yet walking, like to choose their friends.

Learning with and through Adults

Children need adults to provide a safe and predictable environment, and a warm, affectionate atmosphere. They learn only if adults are sensitive to their needs and interests, providing stimulating things to experience, and encouraging them to have a go at things, explore and be autonomous.

Adults need to be consistent, so that different messages are not given by different people. For example, if one adult allows children to sit on tables and another does not, children will push the boundaries until they find out whether or not this is allowed!

Adults need to be sensitive to when children need help so that children receive:

* the right help;
* at the right time;
* in the right way.

Adults need to observe children carefully, to see if the child:

* is struggling;
* is avoiding doing something;
* is interested but does not know what to do.

Direct teaching can help to avoid temper tantrums, frustration, anxiety and sadness.

A child may pick up a cloak in the dressing-up area, but find he cannot tie a bow. He puts it down and instead chooses a jacket which fastens with Velcro. But really he wanted the cloak, and if an adult had helped him to tie the strings, he would have carried out his plan.

Children usually need direct teaching when they try to cut with scissors.

The **Effective Early Learning** project at CREC in Birmingham emphasises the need for the adult to:

* show sensitivity to children;
* encourage the child's autonomy;
* offer stimulating experiences which are challenging and interesting.

SELF-RELIANCE, SELF-CONFIDENCE, INDEPENDENCE AND AUTONOMY – WHAT IS THE DIFFERENCE?

It is important to know the difference between a child being self-reliant, self-confident, independent and autonomous.

* **Self-reliant** children do not expect help from others. This is not always a good thing, as they can be left to themselves, but may actually appreciate an offer of help. It can mean that they only attempt to do what they know they can manage unaided, and are not very adventurous about trying new things.

* **Self-confident** children will have a go at things and ask for help when they need it. They trust their ability to learn.

* **Independent** children can carry out certain tasks of life without help, such as getting dressed or managing a Sellotape dispenser. They are confident that they can manage themselves and have developed the dispositions which will help them to learn, such as problem solving, knowing the sequence for toileting and washing, or finding what they need to model with clay.

* **Autonomous** children can be independent, but they also enjoy the company of those who know more than they do, and from whom they can learn

and find out more. For example, they might not be able to read stories of Beatrix Potter when they are 4 years old, because they are not yet fluent readers (and nor should they be), but they do enjoy being read to and sharing the pictures in the book. They enjoy acting out the story of Miss Moppet, the cat trying to catch the mouse, while the adult reads the story out loud. According to Vygotsky, what we can do with help today, we can do alone tomorrow.

WHY SHOULD CHILDREN PLAY?

Play is one of the most difficult aspects of a child's development to understand and support. It is also one of the most important for development and learning. Play lays down neural patterns in the brain which are important foundations for future learning, such as being a flexible, imaginative thinker, understanding other points of view, and appreciating the feelings and lives of others.

Childhood Memories of Play

Before you read this section, think back to your own childhood. Talk about your childhood memories of play with your friends. It is one of the best ways to find out what is important to children as they grow up.

✳ Did you make dens in the garden, under a table or with your bedclothes?

✳ Did you pretend you were in outer space, on a boat, on a desert island, going shopping or keeping house?

✳ Did you feel you had hours and hours to play?

✳ Did you enjoy using inexpensive play props, or were your favourite toys expensive, commercially produced toys?

Fig 13.4 Children read books to enjoy from babyhood. This is the beginning of learning to read.

Fig 13.5 Children benefit when adults enjoy sharing stories with them in a relaxed unhurried way

Children Who do not Play

It is a myth to say that all children play – they do not. In different parts of the world and according to the culture in which children grow up, play may or may not be encouraged. It is often seen as something children grow out of, possibly the quicker the better, rather than part of deep learning.

There are various reasons why children might not play:

* A sick, unhappy or overoccupied child will not play.

* Children who are abused verbally, sexually or physically, or who have experienced upheaval in their close relationships with people, may have difficulty playing.

* The culture or family does not encourage play.

* Children are biologically driven to play, but they need people to develop their play fully. Play takes great energy and commitment on the part of the child.

Play Therapy

In some cases, children who do not play can be helped by play therapy. Play therapists undertake specialist training, and help children who are emotionally vulnerable to heal. They are often based in hospitals and special schools. Most children will begin to play if given sensitive adult help in any early years setting or at home. Once children know how to play, there is usually no stopping them. Most children therefore do not need the specialist help of a play therapist. Their natural childhood play helps them to self-heal.

Play in Children with Special Educational Needs

Children with special educational needs have often been underestimated in their ability to play. Even children with severe learning difficulties can play – if play is seen as a combination of being allowed to wallow deeply in feelings, ideas and relationships and exploring the physical self, together with the application of skills and competencies. This gives us a very positive view of play and makes it a possibility for most children.

Too Busy to Play

Some children lead overoccupied lives, which leave them little time, energy or

CASE STUDY

Jo

Jo, who is 4 years old, has autism, and is fascinated by strips of material, which he loves to wave in front of his face and brush across his nose. The practitioner does not label this an obsession, but instead builds on his interest. She provides a variety of ribbon-like strips, and over several weeks he begins to experiment with a wider range. After a few months he is interested in eye contact with her, provided the ribbons are swaying in front of his face. One day, he parts the ribbons and looks her directly in the eye. He says 'Boo'.

Children with special educational needs and disabilities often dance the developmental ladder. They may do some things at the same time as most children their age, or they may have a different timescale for different aspects of their development. One of the helpful things about the EYFS framework is that it supports practitioners in developing the learning (including play) of a diverse range of children, in ways which are inclusive.

personal space for play. They are mainly involved in adult-dictated activities, being encouraged to read and write early, do number work, perhaps learn a musical instrument, ballet dancing, take part in drama sessions, join woodwork and PE clubs and play computer games, so that they almost never have any time for themselves. Researchers suggest it is likely that many children in the UK could be described as experiencing overoccupied childhoods. These children often become very dependent on adults. They will say things like 'I don't know what to do' or 'I need you to help me'. Such children are very easily bored. This is because they are not developing their inner resources and do not know how to harness the energy that is needed in order to play.

Recent research suggests that children, especially boys, who do not play are more likely to bring personal and social tragedy on themselves and their communities, for example by becoming persistently drunken drivers. Lack of early childhood play is also becoming linked by some researchers with attention deficit hyperactivity disorder (ADHD). Some researchers believe that play and laughter actually 'fertilise' the brain.

CASE STUDY

Children with English as a second language

Noor (3 years) is a new arrival in England. She has been separated from most of her family, but her mother is reunited with three of her children after fleeing from a war zone. She is in the home corner. She finds a sheet from the doll's bed and wraps it round her. She puts the doll into the sling she has made. She finds the broom and sweeps the floor. She finds the saucepan and puts it on the stove, pretending to prepare a meal. The practitioner smiles when she catches her eye, and sits near her, but does not invade her focused play.

It is difficult to do two new things at once. Adjusting to a new country is dealt with by playing out familiar everyday things, such as caring for the baby and meal preparation. It would be very difficult to talk in a new language too. This will come later. Now she needs the sensitive encouragement of the practitioner.

Second-hand Experiences in Play

The themes of television programmes and computer games are very often taken up by children in their play. When children pretend to be fantasy characters – such as those appearing in cartoon programmes and computer games – whose activities they have not experienced in their own lives, their play is usually at a very low level. Only when children can link their own real experiences with the second-hand experiences they see on television can their play be rich. It is therefore best to limit the time that children spend on second-hand experiences, unless these link directly to first-hand experiences that the child has had.

CASE STUDY

Work and play

In Sweden, researchers found that 6-year-olds, when asked the difference between work and play, explained that work needs adults to help, but that children cannot do this for very long. Play is much more difficult because children have to have their own ideas. One girl said that in order to play she needed acres of time.

THE CHILD'S RIGHT TO PLAY

The Charter of Children's Rights (1989) states that every child in the world should have the right to play. Play is not the same as recreation or relaxation. Play is about high levels of learning, while recreation is about relaxing and not thinking very hard.

So why should children have the right to play? Play is central to a child's learning. It makes a very big contribution to development and to learning about:

* ideas and imagination;
* feelings;
* relationships;
* flexible and abstract ways of thinking;
* the moral and spiritual self;
* the physical self.

Sometimes people say that play is the only way a child learns. In fact, it is not. However, play is a major part in a network of learning, and it is important because it enables the child to bring together, coordinate and make whole everything they learn.

WHAT IS PLAY?

Through play, children bring together and organise their ideas, feelings, relationships and their physical life. It helps them to use what they know and to make sense of the world and people they meet. When they play, children can:

* rearrange their lives;
* rehearse the future;
* reflect on the past;
* be creative and imaginative;
* organise their learning for themselves;
* get their thoughts, feelings, relationships and physical bodies under their own control.

Fig 13.6 Through play, children try out their skills and competencies

The act of playing gives children a sense of mastery and competence that helps them to face the world and cope with it. This is crucial for the development of good self-esteem and for becoming a rounded personality.

Learning to Play

Some people believe that children are born knowing how to play naturally. In fact, children learn to play, although they are also predisposed towards it. So it is both nature and nurture. Often it is older children who teach younger children how to play. In situations where children play in mixed age groups, younger children easily learn about quality play from those who are experienced and good at it. For example, Maori children traditionally learn in this way.

However, in modern life, in places where parents often feel that it is dangerous to play out in the streets, where families are smaller, and where children are at school in classes of children of the same age, there are not many opportunities for younger children (2–5 years)

Fig 13.7 A child will sometimes enjoy playing alone

to learn about play from older children (5–8 years or older). This means that many modern children increasingly depend on adults to help them into quality play. The prior (childhood) experience of adults who play with children is therefore very important. Research suggests that it is especially important that adults working professionally with young children know and understand what play is. They need to be trained to understand its central contribution to the learning that children experience. Adults need to support and extend children's play with sensitivity and skill.

Defining Play

Play is one of the most complicated concepts to study and understand, and there is a mass of literature written about it. People are often afraid of things they do not know much about and do not understand. In addition, play has become a political issue. There are those who think it has no place in a child's education and there are those who believe it must have a central place. This debate has gone on for 200 years. On the whole, it is those who work with children on a daily basis, and experts in child

development who have contact with young children all over the world, who argue that play is central to a child's learning.

Play from the Inside Out

Play comes from within children. Bruce argues that the way children develop in their play should not be seen as progress through a prescribed sequence or hierarchy. This is because any child can be helped to play – babies, toddlers and older children including those who have disabilities. Early years workers will form a positive view of play if they approach its development as a learning web that the child weaves (see Figure 13.8).

Bruce has elaborated and enhanced this definition with her 12 features of play (see page 415).

Assessing Quality Play

Bruce's 12 features are often used to assess and evaluate the quality of play. If most of these 12 features are present (7 or more) when children are observed in their play, then probably they are involved in quality play. If only a few features are present, it does not necessarily mean that the child is not doing anything of quality. It may mean that the child is doing something other than play – the child might be representing things, be involved in a game with rules or be enjoying a first-hand experience. It is very useful for staff working with young children in a whole variety of early years settings to become skilled at knowing what is play and what is not, even though this is not always easy. It is certainly not helpful to call everything that children do 'play'.

There is a biological reason for children's play – it stops the brain from getting too set in its ways. It allows ideas, feelings and relationships to flow and it opens up a child's thinking. It helps reasoning, problem solving and creativity.

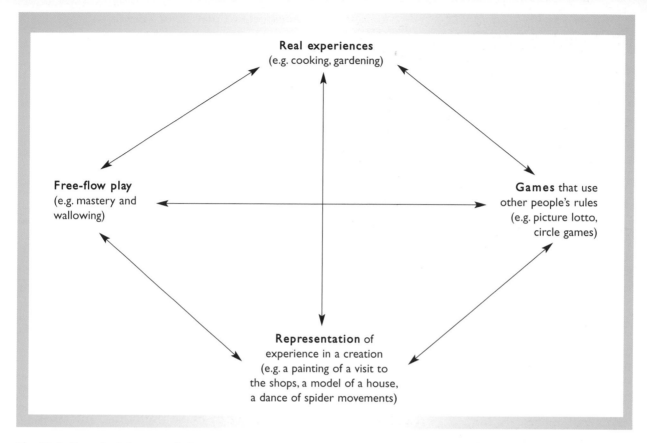

Real experiences
(e.g. cooking, gardening)

Free-flow play
(e.g. mastery and
wallowing)

Games that use
other people's rules
(e.g. picture lotto,
circle games)

Representation of
experience in a creation
(e.g. a painting of a visit to
the shops, a model of a house,
a dance of spider movements)

Fig 13.8 Bruce's definition of play

The 12 features of play – to recognise, monitor and cultivate free-flow play

1 Using first-hand experiences.
2 Making up rules.
3 Making props.
4 Choosing to play.
5 Rehearsing the future.
6 Pretending.
7 Playing alone.
8 Playing together.
9 Having a personal agenda.
10 Being deeply involved.
11 Trying out recent learning.
12 Coordinating ideas, feelings and relationships for free-flow play.

Creative, imaginative adults

Play continues to be important for adults who are creative and imaginative, and innovative thinkers (Bruce, *Cultivating Creativity* 2004). There is also participation in leisure pursuits, as in the previous stage of development. People who play are less likely to become stressed, depressed, bored or narrow. They are more interested in life, more interesting to be with and tend to be more sensitive to other people (Bruce 1991).

The Development of Free-Flow Play

Early Stages

Babies and toddlers are beginning to find out through their senses, movements and

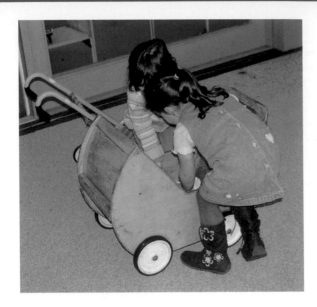

Fig 13.9 Free-flow play

relationships with other people what play is, for example by playing with their own hands.

Emergent Pretend Play

Children begin to pretend and develop spontaneous, creative and imaginative play, known as free-flow play. This means they are beginning to use symbolic behaviour. This is one of the most important stages of development for human beings.

More Elaborate Play

Play elaborates pretend themes, includes more people, involves props and ideas, sustained characters and stories or narratives, leads to expression of feeling and requires more skill. Creative free-flow play is often left out of the school curriculum at this stage in the UK, but in countries like Denmark, Germany and Japan, children still play in school at this age. Unfortunately for us in the UK, this means that just at the stage when play is beginning to flow well, it is often cut off in its prime. Without

safe streets to play in or friends to play with at home, children cannot compensate for the play they miss out on at school. Free-flow play is very important for a child's development and learning at this stage.

Childhood Play Turns to Creative Pursuits

Play consolidates and becomes very sophisticated (if it survives). At this stage, play divides into hobbies, games and leisure pursuits, and into creative pursuits, for example drama, sculpture, making computer programmes, dancing, singing and playing music. The play spiral, devised by Janet Moyles, suggests that children first play freely with materials, such as play dough, and are then directed through play tutoring, for example to play shops, being shown how to make the dough into play props for the shop. They are then encouraged to engage in free play about shops.

Piaget and Vygotsky both thought that play led to the enjoyment of games. They proposed that play turns into games in middle childhood (from about 8 years), unlike Erikson, Winnicott or Bruce, who see play as turning into adult creativity.

Time to Play

Children need a free choice of activity in order to play. They also need *time* to play. A rigid timetable makes it very difficult for them to develop quality, free-flowing play. Play cannot flow under these circumstances, and so learning will be held back. If adults truly believe that play is central to learning, play – including free-flow play – needs to be encouraged by flexible timetabling of the day.

Table 13.1 Moyles's forms of play

Basic form	Detailed form	Type of play	Examples
1 Physical Play	Gross Motor Fine motor Psychomotor	Construction Deconstruction Manipulation Coordination Adventurous play Creative movement Sensory exploration Object play	Building blocks Clay, sand and wood Interlocking blocks Musical instruments Climbing apparatus Dance Junk modelling Finding-out table
2 Intellectual play	Linguistic Scientific Symbolic and mathematical	Communication and explanation Acquisition Exploration Investigation Problem solving Representation and pretend mini-worlds	Hearing and telling stories Water play Doll's house Homes and drama Number games
3 Social and emotional play	Therapeutic Linguistic Repetitious Empathetic Gaming	Aggression and regression Relaxation/solitude/parallel play Communication, interaction and cooperation Mastery and control Sympathy and sensitivity Emulation of roles Morality Competition and rules	Wood, clay and music Puppets and telephone Anything Pets and other children Home corner and shop Discussion Word and number games

Piaget's stages of play

* Babyhood (0–18 months): play involves sensori-motor behaviour (the senses and movement).

* The early years of symbolic play (18 months–5 years): play involves making something stand for (represent) something else.

* The school years (5–8 years): children move from play to taking part in games. Children are able to play more cooperatively. The rules of games are quite different from the rules of play. In games the rules are given; in play children make up the rules as they go along.

THE DEVELOPMENTAL ASPECTS OF PLAY

Babies

* Natural materials give a wider range of possibilities for learning through the senses and movement.

* Lying under a tree and watching the leaves through dappled sunlight.

* Crawling on grass in the garden.

* Sitting and manipulating fir cones in a heap on the floor.

These encourage creative, imaginative, manipulative and physical play.

Toddlers

* Sliding down a small slide on the tummy, feet first.
* Rolling down a grassy slope.
* Pushing a cart along, with a doll in it.

These encourage creative, imaginative, manipulative and physical play.

Young Children

* Making a den and gathering play props (child-initiated).
* Picking daisies, dandelions, twigs and pebbles to make a play scenario, with a house, garden and shops.
* Making a cake with a face decorated on it from raisins and cherries (child-initiated).

These encourage creative, imaginative, manipulative and physical play.

Older Children

Older children need play, just as much as do the under-5s. In later childhood and early adolescence, free-flow play turns into creative arts, sciences and humanities ('Cultivating Creativity' – Bruce, 2004). They compose songs, create dances, drawings, paintings, models and scientific hypotheses. Their enthusiasm for orderly thinking shows itself through games with rules and in organised sports. Winning becomes important as they begin to understand that winning means following the rules. This is the age when team sports become important. However, even when teenagers are just 'hanging out' together, they are learning – sharing information and knowledge and understanding social relationships.

Teenagers would probably not refer to their social activities as 'play', but surveys of the views of children and young people show that they want:

* opportunities to be physically active – indoors and outdoors;
* the chance to meet with their friends;
* the chance to be somewhere quiet;
* choice and variety.

They also identified the following barriers to their play:

* fears for their safety, especially from bullying;
* traffic;
* dirty and/or run-down play areas and parks;
* lack of choice;
* play provision that is too far away;
* lack of youth clubs, drama groups, music clubs and outward bound groups.

MAKING PROVISION FOR PLAY

Space for Play – Indoors and Outdoors

Play does not happen to adult order. Both the indoor and outdoor areas need to be made into spaces which encourage children to develop their own play. For example, both the environment and the equipment must be safely maintained. There should be appropriate materials to encourage play, such as dressing-up clothes, den-making materials and small-world objects. There must be space to run and jump and corners to hide away in.

Material Provision

Children need things to play with – play props. Sometimes children will make their own props, or they may select play clothes and objects from the material that you provide. Staff will be continually making plans for new activities based on their observations of how children play. As part of these plans they will provide play props which encourage the children to play more deeply.

Choosing Play Materials

Children do not need expensive equipment in order to play. For example, they may find and play with twigs and pebbles. In the park they will be running and using the space. In the garden they might climb or dig. On the seashore they will collect pebbles, seaweed and shells. They might splash in rock pools and build castles out of sand. In a setting they will use the material provisions that adults put there. So it is very important that adults choose materials carefully and plan the physical environment to support play. Then children can get the most out of opportunities for free-flow play. Children can use scissors, for example, to develop fine motor skills, and they can learn to put straws in cartons of fruit juice, rather than doing fine motor exercises that are not connected to real life. Performing exercises which do not relate to the day-to-day context of a child's life can actually stop them from learning well. When life becomes a drudge, full of boring, repetitive tasks, children quickly lose the excitement of learning. So it is better to avoid prestructured toys and to provide open-ended and more traditional toys, such as dolls, cars, wooden blocks and play dough.

Adult Support for Play

There may have to be a visit to a real shop before a play shop scenario can develop. Children need interdependent relationships with other children and often an adult in order to develop their play agenda. When adults 'teach' play this can constrain children. When children are left without support, the play is low-level. Interdependent relationships mean adults take up and help children to develop their ideas, supported as they do so, so that the 12 features of play emerge. Children really appreciate adults who help them to keep their play flowing, provided the adult is sensitive to their play ideas.

Guidelines for selecting play materials

1   Prestructured materials, such as a miniature post box, more often hold back rather than encourage free-flow play. If there is only one way of doing things, children cannot develop in their imaginative play and they will probably carry out a very narrow range of physical actions. So-called educational toys, made by commercial manufacturers and usually very expensive, are often prestructured in this way.

2   Open-ended materials encourage children to think, feel, imagine, socialise and concentrate deeply. They will tend to use a range of fine and gross motor skills. Examples of open-ended materials are:

*   found materials, such as those used in junk modelling;
*   transforming raw materials, like clay and dough;
*   self-service areas in the provision;
*   wooden blocks;
*   dressing-up clothes and cookery items in the home area.

Guidelines for encouraging free-flow play

*   Use adult-led sessions to introduce children to the materials first through real experience (part of the learning web: see Fig 13.8, page 415). For example, do some cooking and then use the experience in a play scenario in the home area. Children will still see how to use their experiences

in their own free-flow play, both safely and creatively.

* Do not make children complete adult-led tasks, that is, 'work', before being allowed to play, as this undermines play. But play is also undervalued when adults leave children without any help when they play. In these situations the play quickly becomes repetitive and superficial. If adults are only found in those areas where children are doing 'work', while children are being sent off to 'play' without any help, children will receive unfortunate messages about how adults value their play.

* Free-flow play literally occurs when the play begins to flow with quality according to the 12 features described earlier in this chapter (see page 415). Free-flow play can fade and vanish in a moment, but adults can be a great help to children in keeping going.

PLANNING FOR PLAY

Remember that you are planning for play, and not planning the play. The difference is that planning for play means you plan the environment so that children can initiate their own spontaneous play, whereas planning the play means that you direct the children in what to do in their play.

Well-Planned Play

Some of the children have visited the market and shown great interest. You set up a market in the garden, with stalls and play props. Children begin to play markets, and you support them, sensitively tuning in to their play ideas.

The same approach is important when working with babies and toddlers.

Planning for play – the baby likes to sit and reach for objects and put them in her mouth. The practitioner makes a selection of objects, some easy to put in the mouth, some less so, and presents these on the floor. The baby spends nearly half an hour trying these out.

This is very different from a situation where the practitioner decides to introduce sphere-shaped objects to all the babies. She holds a ball and presents it to the baby, who takes it and tries to put it in her mouth. The baby drops the ball. The practitioner tries a different ball and the same thing happens again. The baby loses interest when a third ball is presented. This would not be well-planned play.

TYPES OF PLAY

Different types of play have been linked to particular kinds of material provision and to different aspects of a child's development:

* **Particular kinds of material provision**: the home area, construction kits, the outdoor area, natural materials, a messy area, a computer, wooden blocks, climbing frames, bats and balls, hoops, clay, paint.

* **Different aspects of a child's development**: manipulative play, practice play and repetitive play, symbolic play, superhero play, exploratory play, discovery play, investigative play, pretend play, ludic play, heuristic play, role play, therapeutic play, solitary play, parallel play, cooperative play, epistemic play, imaginative play, physical play, manipulative play, creative play, rough-and-tumble play, boisterous play, fantasy play, phantasy play and socio-dramatic play. (Some of these forms are defined below.)

Considering play in terms of the different definitions has become increasingly unwieldy, with more and more categories being added all the time. It is probably better to focus on:

* Setting up the basic areas of provision to live quality play opportunities.

* How adults can help children to play both alone and together, through interdependent relationships.

All the types of play listed in the box below can be catered for if the setting is arranged with great care. This is why it is very important for staff to plan the curriculum that they intend to provide for young children.

Types of play

* Symbolic play: usually occurs from 1 year and includes pretend play, role play, socio-dramatic play and imaginative play. A symbol is when one thing stands for another.

* Creative play: this label is often given to describe play with natural materials, such as sand, water, clay, dough, musical instruments and sensory materials. It is also used to describe the creation (making) of an idea that the child has, and may not need any play props. The child might 'create' the idea of being a dog or an engine. The links between the processes of creativity, the imagination and play are strong. (You can read more about cultivating scientific, artistic and humanitarian creativity in 'Cultivating Creativity' by Bruce, 2004.)

* Pretend play or ludic play: when an action or object is given a symbolic meaning which is different from real life – a clothes peg becomes a door key.

* Role play: this occurs when pretend symbols are used together – the child pretends to drive to the shops and unlocks the car door with a pretend clothes-peg key, sits on a box (a car seat) and turns the steering wheel (a dinner plate).

* Socio-dramatic play: when children role-play and pretend-play together.

* Imaginative play or creative play: children use their own real-life experiences and rearrange them – they might make a pretend swimming pool out of wooden blocks. One of them pretends to be a lifeguard and rescues someone who cannot swim. The children already know about learning to swim and rescue. Imaginative play links with creative play, role play, domestic play, fantasy play, phantasy play and play with dolls and small world.

* Fantasy play: here, children role-play situations they do not know about, but which might happen to them one day – the experience of getting married, going to the moon in a space rocket or going to hospital.

* Phantasy play: here, children role-play unreal events, using characters from cartoons on TV – Power Rangers, Superman. The theme of war tends to dominate this kind of play. Because it is not rooted in real experience, it is difficult to help children to use this kind of play for their benefit.

* Manipulative play: this occurs when children use and celebrate physical prowess – playing on a skateboard with great competence or riding a two-wheeled bicycle. It is about what they can do, not about what they are struggling to do (which would

not be play). This kind of play helps children to develop their motor skills. It links with physical play with large equipment indoors and outdoors.

*   Physical play: this also helps children to develop their gross and fine motor skills.

*   Play using props: sometimes children make their own props and use them to pretend-play – they might make a telephone out of boxes and then pretend to book a doctor's appointment. This is sometimes called constructive play, but it is really a representation.

*   Rough-and-tumble play: this often involves chasing, catching, pretend fights and pillow fights. Unless children are sufficiently coordinated to manage their play safely, it often ends in tears; it requires great sensitivity to other people in order not to hurt them physically. This form of play often occurs before going to sleep and it bonds those playing emotionally and socially. It is difficult to cater for in the early years setting, as it tends to frighten those not taking part.

*   Therapeutic play: this kind of play helps children who are in emotional pain to find out more about how they feel, to face their feelings and to deal with them, so that they gain some control over their lives. Helping children through play therapy requires professional training, but every child can improve their mental health through the feeling of control that play gives. Some children need more help than early years workers can give, and specialists may be called in.

Helping babies, toddlers and young children to play – a summary

*   Think back to your own childhood memories of play. What did you enjoy doing? Remembering will help you to help children to play.

*   Take time to observe babies, toddlers and young children as they play. This will help you to tune into the children's play agendas and help you play along.

*   Think about equality, diversity and inclusion. Some children might be left out of the play when they want to join in. Use what you know about access strategies.

*   Both boys and girls need to experience a broad range of play. Pay attention to gender issues.

*   Babies and children with special educational needs might require extra help to develop their play; all children can play at some level.

*   When babies, toddlers and young children play, they learn at a very high level.

*   You cannot make children play, because play only happens when conditions are right. Work at getting conditions right for play in your setting.

*   People matter. Adults who help babies, toddlers and children to play are adults who help children to learn.

*   Give play a high priority – it is a central form of learning.

*   The provision of play props is important. These should be open-ended and flexible. Do not prestructure props and equipment so that there is only one way to use them.

* Children need places for play, indoors and outdoors.
* Babies and children need uninterrupted time for play.
* Allow children freedom of movement indoors and outdoors.
* Give children freedom of choice for activities. Some children like doll play, while others prefer to play on climbing frames.
* Mixed age groups encourage play because older children will help toddlers and younger children and teach them how to play.
* Adults can help play – by play tutoring. This is not *actually* play: it is a way that adults can help children take a step towards their own play.
* Adults can also help children by entering into the spirit of play. You can play with children as long as you do not try to take over their play and control it.
* Know about and provide for each aspect in the network of learning.
* Encourage quality first-hand experiences through carefully chosen provision both indoors and outdoors.
* Help children to represent and keep hold of their experience by using a range of materials and activities.
* Organise games.
* Observe children at play, and add provision to support and extend their play. For example, add shoes to the dressing-up box if children are playing 'shoe shops'.
* Do not invade, dominate or change the direction of the children's play. Join the free-flow play and try to catch what it is about so that you can help it along.
* Make a safe and healthy environment.
* Maintain the environment. For example, if the block area has become very messy, ask a group of children to help you tidy it. No one can play well in a chaotic area.
* Watch out for the 12 features of play (see page 415) so that you know what a child is doing. Then you can help out if necessary by joining in or by extending the provision.
* Help the children to stay in character when they are making a play story. Help children to keep in mind the storyline of their play scenario.
* Remember, babies, toddlers and young children use what they already know to learn more, and they need other people to help them (Gopnik, Melzoff and Kuhl 1999).

Fig 13.10 Sharing a story in a group

ACTIVITY: MAKING TIME FOR PLAY

1 Plan ways of giving children sufficient time to develop rich, free-flow play. Include a flexible routine for children, with a balance between leaving children to get on with it (a leave-it-to-nature approach) and adult-led activities (a transmission model). Implement your plan and observe a child of 3–4 years. Evaluate your observations.

2 Research how the day is timetabled for children in a reception class compared to children in Key Stage 1, Years 1 and 2. Observe a child of 4–7 years for a day: remember to include the mid-morning, afternoon and lunchtime play periods.

3 Plan an outdoor area suitable for children aged 3–7 years. Remember, it should be possible for a child to do everything that is on offer indoors in the outdoor play area also. How will you organise outdoor experiences of paint, water, sand, drawing, home area, clay? In one school there was a clay table indoors and a mud patch to dig in outdoors. In this way, the outdoor provision complemented the indoor provision. Observe a child of 3–7 years in the outdoor area. Evaluate their experiences and compare these with your plan of an outdoor area.

ACTIVITY: INVESTIGATING PLAY

1 Plan how you could assess what kind of learning a child is involved in – is it play or is the child benefiting from a quality first-hand experience, for example cooking?

2 Observe children aged 1 year (if possible), 2–3 years, 3–5 years and 5–7 years. Use the 12 features of play (see page 415) as observation tools. Evaluate your findings.

3 Observe children aged 1–3 years, 3–5 years and 5–7 years playing in the home area or the small-world area (doll's house, farm, road). Again, use the 12 features to understand (assess) the learning. Plan how you could add to the provision in the light of your observations. Evaluate your activity.

4 Observe a child with special educational needs. Is the child playing according to the 12 features of free-flow play? Evaluate your observations.

5 Observe a child who is sick but able to play – at home in bed or in a hospital. Identify which of the 12 features of free-flow play the child exhibits. Plan how to help the child. Implement your plan and evaluate the activity.

6 Describe how you could encourage play opportunities through the structured telling of a story.

7 Make a miniature garden using twigs and spontaneously with the garden, observe the play. Write down what the child says and does. Evaluate your activity.

8 Make a den. Who lives in it? Imagine the characters and make up a story. You might act it out for a group of children at story-time.

SECTION 2: HOW TO USE APPROPRIATE TOOLS TO ASSESS THE LEARNING NEEDS OF INDIVIDUAL CHILDREN

• Planning cycle • Observation informs planning • Observation informs practice • Observation informs assessment • IEP (individual education plan) based on observations • Information from other services/professionals • Awareness of differentiation/learning styles

YOUR ROLE IN PLANNING FOR CHILDREN'S LEARNING

Practitioners working directly with young children have an important role. Children remember and look back with pleasure and affection to those who supported and extended their learning in their earliest years. It is important to be an active member of staff, participating in the planning cycle:

* Take your carefully gathered observations of children to meetings.

* Be an advocate for the child's developing learning.

* Make sure you are aware of lines of accountability and reporting.

The Planning Cycle: Planning the Curriculum

It is important to note that there is a shift from making curriculum plans (which are too rigid to meet the needs or develop the interests of individual children) to curriculum planning, which is flexible and ever-changing. The principles set out in the box below have a long tradition and have informed the curriculum frameworks of the four UK countries as they exist today. The principles inform the planning alongside observations of individual children. This means that the emphasis is on planning within an effective curriculum framework,

rather than making a plan using a rigid and prescribed curriculum syllabus.

The curriculum framework has three parts, which involve:

1   **child**: processes in the child's development and learning, such as movement, communication, play and symbolic behaviour, and emotional wellbeing;

2   **context**: the access the practitioners create so that the child is helped to learn, and how learning builds on the child's social relationships, and family and cultural experiences;

3   **content**: what the child learns and understands – the content of the curriculum framework for each of the four UK countries is different.

These three aspects of a quality learning environment need to be balanced, or the curriculum framework offered will be of poor quality. In England, Wales, Scotland and Northern Ireland this is about helping children from birth to 6 years develop and learn.

The 'three Cs' of a quality learning environment (often called the curriculum framework) are based on principles which have long and respected traditions, mainly in the Western world.

Principles supporting the early childhood curriculum frameworks in the UK

1   The best way to prepare children for their adult life is to give them what they need as children.

2   Children are whole people who have feelings, ideas, relationships with others, a sense of self and wellbeing, and who need to be physically, morally and spiritually healthy.

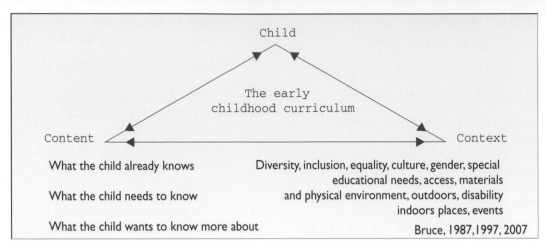

Fig 13.11 Diagram of the three Cs

3 Children do not learn in neat and tidy compartments. Everything new they learn links with everything they have already learnt.

4 Children learn best when they are respected and helped to be autonomous, active learners.

5 Self-discipline is emphasised as the only kind of discipline worth having. Children need their efforts to be valued in their own right.

6 There are times when children are especially able to learn particular things.

7 What children can do (rather than what they cannot do) is the starting point for a child's learning.

8 There are many different kinds of symbolic behaviour. These show the inner thoughts, feelings and ideas of the child, through the way they draw, paint, make things, dance, sing, talk/sign, enjoy making stories, mark-make or pretend-play. The Italian educator Malaguzzi calls this the 'one hundred languages of children'.

9 Relationships with other people are central to a child's emotional and social wellbeing.

10 Quality education is about the child, the context in which learning takes place, and the knowledge and understanding which the child develops and learns.

(Bruce 1987, updated 2006)

OBSERVATION INFORMS PLANNING

Curriculum Planning Begins with the Child

In order to plan a quality curriculum framework, the first step is to observe children as individuals. Observation helps adults to tune in to what interests a child, and to see how to support and extend their interest. Building on the interests and prior knowledge of a child is central in planning a quality curriculum. When children are interested in the experiences and activities they are offered, they learn more effectively, and adults can add to this and provide children with what they need. Building on the interests and needs of a child are important, and the two go together.

Giving children what they need means linking the child's interests with what is needed in the official curriculum framework documents of the country. The role of the practitioner is to **observe, support and extend** the child's learning.

Children are biologically driven to seek out what they need for their development in movement, communication, symbolic development and ability to problem-solve; and to do this they learn through their senses (visual, auditory, tactile, olfactory, taste), through movement and through relationships with people and their cultural context.

Very important pioneer work is being undertaken in England by the charity JABADAO (the National Centre for Movement, Learning and Health) in relation to planning a curriculum framework which is effective in giving young children developmental movement play (DMP) central to later learning, such as reading and writing. JABADAO helps practitioners working with children from birth to 6 years to develop an understanding of balance (vestibular learning) and proprioception (a sense of how one part of the body relates to another). These are essential for laying down patterns in the brain which form the basis of future learning, such as the kinds of eye tracking needed for reading.

OBSERVATION INFORMS PRACTICE

Throughout, this book stresses the importance of observation and how it informs the way practitioners can become involved in:

* creating learning environments indoors and outdoors, based on what they have observed that children are interested in;

* supporting the individual and group interests of children;

* extending the interests of individual children, when appropriate;

* meeting the needs of children as unique individuals;

* sharing and exchanging through rich dialogue and observations with parents/carers.

The new English Early Years Foundation Stage (from birth to 5 years of age) covers the year leading into Key Stage 1 with the Foundation Profile. This helps practitioners to assess the development, learning and well-being of children across the year, using observations which make formative assessments to plot progress. It is a holistic approach, covering the six areas of learning set out in the **EYFS** theme called 'Learning and Development'.

The early learning goals are not expectations, but **aspirations**. For example, more than half the children in England achieve the goals for personal, social and emotional development, but only about one third reach the goals for communication, language and literacy because, against advice of early childhood experts, they were set too high. Children in other countries are not expected to reach this level as they turn 5 years of age, and yet they do better in the long term, despite being taught to read and write later (typically at 6–7 years of age). Looking at the progress of children across the six areas of learning has proved important. For example, it has been shown that children who achieve well on the goals for physical development are achieving better in pencil control in the literacy goals. There are important messages here:

* Early is not best.
* Narrow approaches constrain rather than help development and learning.
* Learning with quality takes time to embed.
* Children learn through a variety of richly deserved experiences, and so it is often difficult to track down their exact learning journey. Indirect teaching is powerful.
* Adult-led teaching needs to be very sensitive and be based on observation, tuning in to the child at the right time in the right way.

OBSERVATION INFORMS ASSESSMENT

Throughout this chapter and Chapter 8, we have seen how important observation is.

* **Baseline assessment**: when we first meet a child we need to get to know them and their family/carers. We use our first observations as a way of doing this, along with what parents/carers know and understand.
* **Formative assessment**: as our observations build, we are able to gain a fuller picture of the child, and we quite literally form assessments as we accompany the child on their learning journey.
* **Summative assessment**: at regular points (depending on whether a child has special needs) or when the child is leaving the setting and moving on, we take stock and pause to reflect on an aspect of development and learning, or on the whole child's learning.

End of EYFS Assessment

The EYFS profile is the way a child's development and learning is summarised at the end of the Early Years Foundation Stage.

The Early Years Foundation Stage Profile makes both formative and summative assessments, but only in the final year of the Early Years Foundation Stage. However, many local authorities – in conjunction with different schools, settings and childminders – have developed books (profiles) with younger children using the same principles. For example, Peterborough Local Authority has developed a book called *A Celebration of My Achievement* for every child from birth to the end of reception, which includes the Foundation Profile.

The Early Years Foundation Stage Profile brings together six interrelated areas:

1 planning and implementing the *Curriculum Guidance for the Foundation Stage* (play and a broad curriculum embracing diversity and inclusion – special educational needs, disability and English as an additional language);
2 observing children's learning;
3 assessment over time and across areas of learning;
4 evidence and recording;
5 supporting learning;
6 assessment as a shared process between children, parents and practitioners.

The Profile captures the early learning goals as a set of 13 assessment scales, each having 9 points:

* Points 1–3 describe progress towards the goals, using the stepping stones.
* Points 4–8 are drawn from the goals themselves and are in approximate order of difficulty (but in points 1–8 it is not

unusual for a child to achieve later points before earlier ones as they are not designed to be in a fixed order).

* Point 9 is where a child is deepening their understanding of a goal achieved, such as 'knowing right from wrong', which is a difficult concept for adults too, as can be seen when nations go to war.

EVALUATING ACTIVITIES AND EXPERIENCES WE PROVIDE TO PROMOTE CHILDREN'S DEVELOPMENT AND LEARNING

We need to link our assessments of the child's individual progress with the way we evaluate what we provide for children. This means that observations need to inform planning, and how we evaluate our planning to see how it worked. Then we can change, modify, consolidate, support and extend each child's personal learning. This will help us to see if what we are providing is appropriate, and whether it is helping or constraining a child's development and learning.

THE EARLY YEARS FOUNDATION STAGE

From September 2008, this document will come into statutory force. Training in the new framework has begun in Local Authorities. The EYFS (from birth to five years) replaces the 'Birth to Three Matters' framework, the 'Curriculum Guidance for the Foundation Stage' and the 'National Standards for Under 8s Daycare and Childminding'. The EYFS is a principled framework with four complementary themes:

* A Unique Child;
* Positive Relationships;
* Enabling Environments;
* Learning and Development.

Each theme is broken down into four **commitments** which describe how the principles can be put into practice. The **Principles into Practice cards**, the CD-ROM and the DVD show how practitioners can use the principles in everyday practice.

The planning cycle: summary of steps in planning

1 Observe the child

The child should be observed at different times; engaged in different experiences and activities; with different people (adults and children) and alone.

* What does the child choose to do?
* What interests this child?
* What is the child biologically driven to do (e.g. jump or wriggle if sitting down for more than 5 minutes)?

2 Support the learning

* How often are the child's favourite experiences available?
* Does the child need some help from an adult?
* Is the child choosing to learn outdoors more than indoors?
* Are there plenty of opportunities to repeat the experiences chosen?
* Children need enough time for experiences and activities, and sensitive supportive conversations and companionship with adults as they are engaged in them.

3 Extend the learning

We use what we know as a base from which to learn new things. The child who knows how to make roti easily

---

extends this and learns how to make bread. Adults can help children by giving them vocabulary, explaining and engaging with children in shared and sustained conversations during activities and experiences. Extending learning is about helping children to take the next steps in their learning. Next steps can be in a broadening direction or an upward direction.

4 Next steps in planning

* Broadening – doing more of the same, but with a slight difference. Bread is made in every culture across the world, so helping children to understand what it always contains is helpful in developing a concept of 'bread' (e.g. making roti and then making a type of bread typical in the UK, and seeing that both use flour and water as the base, which is then cooked in an oven or on a hot surface).

* Onwards and upwards – introducing something new, to show a contrast with what went before, but which definitely builds on what went before. Making a carrot cake is a bit like making bread, but eggs are also needed, and the mixture is stirred and beaten rather than rolled and pummelled.

PLANNING THE GENERAL LEARNING ENVIRONMENT

Planning begins with the observation of the child as a unique, valued, and respected individual, with their own interests and needs. We could say this is all about getting to know the child. But further general planning is also necessary, because there is only so much that children can learn on their own. They need an environment that has been carefully thought through, along with the right help in using that environment. This aspect of planning ensures that the learning environment indoors and outdoors is balanced in what it offers, so that it helps all children in general, but also caters for individual children.

In this way the curriculum:

* is differentiated for individual children;

* is inclusive and embraces diversity (where there are particular concerns the Common Assessment Framework helps to make a needs analysis);

* offers experiences and activities which are appropriate for most children of the age range, because it considers the social and cultural context, and the biological aspects of children developing in a community of learning;

* links with the requirements of legally framed curriculum documents (which include the first three points).

AWARENESS OF DIFFERENTIATION/LEARNING STYLES: INCLUSION AND DIVERSITY

Most children learn in a rather uneven way. They have bursts of learning and then they have plateaux when their learning does not seem to move forward (but really they are consolidating their learning during this time). This is why careful observation and assessment for learning of individual children plus a general knowledge of child development are all very important. Catching the right point for a particular bit of learning during development is a skill. So is recognising the child's pace of learning. Children have their own personalities and moods. They are affected by the weather, the time of day, whether they need food, sleep or the lavatory, the experiences they have, their sense of wellbeing and their social relationships with children and adults.

Gifted and Talented Children

People who are talented in music, dance and mathematics tend to show promise early in their lives. The most important thing is that adults provide a rich and stimulating learning environment, indoors and outdoors, which encourages children to develop and extend their thinking, understand and talk about their feelings, and understand themselves and others. It is frustrating for gifted children when they are constrained and held back in their learning. It is also important to remember that however gifted or talented a child may be in a particular respect, he or she is still a child. They need all the things that any child needs, and should not be put under pressure to behave and learn in advance of their general development.

Children with Special Educational Needs (SEN) and Disabilities

Some children will be challenged in their learning, and those working with children with special educational needs and disabilities will need to be particularly resourceful, imaginative and determined in helping them to learn. Many children with SEN and disabilities are underestimated by the adults working with them. For example, most 6-year-old children can run confidently across a field. In general, visually impaired children in mainstream settings are not expected to try to do this, and so they don't. No one suggests it to them or offers them help to do it. With the right help, the child might manage it, becoming physically

more confident and mobile as a result. The experience of running across a field depends on the child's development, personality and mood. Walking hand-in-hand first might be important. Talking as you go helps. The child may need tips about picking up their feet, and eventually perhaps running towards your voice. If the child tumbles he will need reassurance, and not an anxious adult. Saying 'Can I help you up?' is more helpful than rushing over and asking 'Are you hurt?'

USING INFORMATION FROM OTHER PROFESSIONALS TO PLAN THE LEARNING ENVIRONMENT

Any setting which provides a curriculum for children relies on team work and on information gained from a wide variety of professionals as well as from the child's parents, and of course, the children themselves. These include:

1   The early years team or school team – your supervisor or line manager will ensure that:

    *   all the curriculum areas are provided for;

    *   team members understand their own roles; and

    *   planning is regularly discussed (reviewed) and adapted where necessary.

2   A special educational needs coordinator (SENCO) will be asked to create individual education plans (IEPs) for children with special needs (see Unit 14 on CD-ROM for more information on IEPs and the role of special educational needs professionals).

3   Advisers from the local education authority or early years partnership.

Planning a Predictable Environment which Encourages Learning

Children need to feel there is some kind of predictable shape to their day; otherwise they feel confused and insecure. This does not mean keeping to strict and rigid routines – that would constrain learning – but the following points are important:

∗ **Greetings**: every child and the adult accompanying them should be greeted as they arrive. Otherwise they will not feel welcome, or feel that they matter. Staff need to plan how to bring this about.

∗ **Anchor activities**: some children need to be with a member of staff when they part from their parent/carer. They benefit from a familiar and comforting activity, with the adult close to them, talking with them and helping them to make the transition from home into the early childhood setting. A rocking-horse, sand-play or play with dough are often used in this way in the planning of the day.

∗ **Children need to know that they will be nurtured**: this is especially important if they are upset or take a tumble and hurt themselves. Many settings plan for this through a key person system. This means that a member of staff is assigned to each child as their advocate and comforter. The child goes to them for group time, and the adult links with their family/carer, and ensures that at curriculum planning meetings the child's interest and needs are planned for.

Planning for the Child's Learning Journey (the Processes of Learning) and not just Focusing on the Results (Products of Learning)

It is through other people that children feel valued or not. When children feel their efforts are appreciated and celebrated, they learn more effectively. If adults only praise and recognise results, children are more likely to lose heart and become less motivated to learn. Planning should therefore emphasise experiences and activities which focus on process rather than product. Examples would be finger-painting rather than handprints, so that children can freely make their own patterns in the paint. At the end, the paint is cleared away, with no pressure on children to produce a product. However, staff might photograph the processes involved in finger-painting and display these on the wall, to remind children of what they did. Children love to reflect on their learning journeys, and talk about them later with interested adults, other children and their parents/carers.

Process of finger-painting

∗ Mix the powder paint with the water, and perhaps add a little flour to thicken it.

∗ Tip the paint onto the tabletop.

∗ Make different patterns with the paint.

∗ Wash your hands.

∗ Help to clear up (if appropriate – not babies and toddlers), usually showing children each step of the process, helping them to learn about sequences, which will be important in learning science, mathematics, as well as how to read and write.

Planning a Safe and Predictable Environment

Children need a safe and predictable environment. It is important for staff to work as a team so that different messages are not given by different people. For example, if one adult allows children to sit on tables and another does not, children will push the boundaries to find out what they are. They will push the boundaries because they are confused. They do this because they are trying to work out what they are and are not allowed to do. When children feel safe, they explore and enjoy stimulating provision that has been planned for them.

Making Risk Assessments

Children are biologically driven to make risk assessments, but only if they are constantly encouraged to use these processes. For example, toddlers can be encouraged to come down the stairs (under supervision) sliding on their tummies, feet first. They will pause and check where they are every few steps, making their own risk assessment. Children who are not supported to make their own risk assessments, by an adult sensitive and helpful to their needs, are more likely to have accidents.

In order to set down neural patterns in the brain, children need to develop their sense of balance (vestibular learning) through spinning, tipping, rolling and tilting. They need rough-and-tumble play, which helps them to have a sense of one part of their body in relation to another. This leads to a sense of identity and embodiment, both central aspects of development and learning. Children who can make risk assessments are more likely to be physically safe. In a predictable environment activities are not controlled by adults all the time, but there is a shape to the day. Children feel safe because they have a sense of what is coming next, such as regular mealtimes and group times for stories, or songs and dances.

SECTION 3: HOW TO PLAN AND PROVIDE LEARNING OPPORTUNITIES IN CONSULTATION WITH OTHERS

• Understanding of curriculum frameworks in the UK
• Activities linked to curriculum framework • Group planning • Approaches to planning

THE EARLY CHILDHOOD CURRICULUM IN UK COUNTRIES

England

The Early Years Foundation Stage emphasises the way **observation** informs **planning**. It builds on the approach of 'Birth to Three Matters':

'When we plan for children we base our ideas for activities and experiences on our knowledge of the children in our care. We notice one child's interest in water, another's curiosity about snails or the pleasure at listening to a story. This is where our planning begins.'

The Early Years Foundation Stage (EYFS) will achieve the five 'Every Child Matters' outcomes, which are:

* Staying safe;
* Being healthy;
* Enjoying and achieving;
* Making a positive contribution;
* Achieving economic well-being.

The EYFS sets standards for the development, learning and care of young children at birth to five years when they attend a home learning environment (HLE) or group setting. It provides for equality of opportunity and anti-discriminatory practice. It creates a framework in which parents and professionals can work in partnership. It improves the quality and consistency of provision across all settings and supports development and learning around the individual child's interests and needs, informed by ongoing observational assessment. The Principles guide the EYFS through four **themes**:

* A Unique Child;
* Positive Relationships;
* Enabling Environments;
* Learning and Development.

Each theme is broken down into four **commitments** which describe how the principles are put into practice. There is

a set of cards, **Principles into Practice**, which explains how the principles are put into practice in day-to-day work with children. There is a poster summarising this and a CD-ROM. A DVD has been developed by Manchester Metropolitan University on Birth to Three.

Scotland

The key documents are *Birth to Three: Supporting Relationships, Responsive Care and Respect* and the newly developing generic framework for the curriculum, known as the '3–18 framework', 'Excellence for All'.

Table 13.2 EYFS themes

Theme	Principle	Commitments
A Unique Child	Every child is a competent learner from birth who can be resilient, capable, confident and self-assured	1 Child development 2 Inclusion 3 Safety 4 Health and well-being
Positive Relationships	Children learn to be strong and independent from a base of loving and secure relationships with parents and/or a key person	1 Respect from each other 2 Partnership with parents 3 Supporting learning 4 The role of the key person
Enabling Environments	The environment plays a key role in supporting and extending children's development and learning	1 Observation, assessment and Planning 2 Supporting every child 3 The learning environment 4 The wider context (transitions, continuity, multi-agency working; Every Child Matters)
Learning and Development	Children develop and learn in different ways and at different rates and all areas of learning and development are equally important and inter-connected	1 Play and exploration 2 Active learning 3 Creativity and critical thinking 4 Areas of learning and development: * Personal, social and emotional development * Communication, language and literacy * Problem-solving, reasoning and numeracy * Knowledge and understanding of the world * Creative development * Physical development

Birth to Three

The document is based on principles summarised as:

* the best interests of children;

* the central importance of relationships;

* the need for all children to feel included;

* an understanding of the ways in which children learn.

The document shares the belief (stated in the *National Care Standards: Early Education and Care up to the Age of 16*) that children have a right to:

* dignity;

* privacy;

* choice;

* safety;

* realising potential;

* equality and diversity.

There is a strong emphasis on recognising and valuing the important role of parents. (This is so in all four countries of the UK.) Parents constantly ask for more information about their child's development and learning. Talking together with other parents and practitioners, including health visitors, empowers parents, along with television programmes and magazines aimed at supporting parents positively. This helps to ease anxieties which parents experience, for example about their child's behaviour, or eating and sleeping patterns.

A Curriculum Framework for Children 3 to 5 (moving towards the new framework 'Excellence for All')

This is also a document based on principles.

There are five key aspects of children's development and learning:

1   Emotional, personal and social development;

2   Communication and language;

3   Knowledge and understanding of the world;

4   Expressive and aesthetic development;

5   Physical development and movement.

The framework:

* **promotes effective learning**: looking at the roles and responsibilities of adults in organising for children's learning; looking at the assessment and planning process; valuing observations that inform these; recording, reporting and evaluating;

* **sees each child as a unique individual**: working together with homes and families, children with special educational needs, fostering equal opportunities, collaborating with other agencies and supporting transitions.

Wales

The Foundation Stage (3–7)

Between 2004 and 2008, 41 settings in Wales (The Learning Country) are being trialled as part of a pilot project integrating:

* desirable outcomes for children's learning before compulsory school age;

* the programmes of study and focus statements in the current Key Stage 1 national curriculum in Wales.

This is described as the draft **Framework for Children's Learning**.

There are seven areas of learning in the Foundation Phase, with an emphasis on experiential learning, learning by doing and by solving real-life problems both inside and outdoors:

1   Personal and social development and wellbeing;

2   Language, literacy and communication skills;

3 Mathematical development;

4 Bilingualism and multicultural understanding;

5 Knowledge and understanding of the world;

6 Physical development;

7 Creative development.

Northern Ireland

Curricular Guidance for Pre-School Education

The document emphasises the importance of valuing the diverse experiences children bring to preschool, and building on this through providing a rich play environment. Children need to learn without experiencing a sense of failure. This requires:

✱ a stimulating environment, with adequate supervision, in which children are safe, secure and healthy;

✱ an environment inside and outside the playroom with opportunities to investigate, satisfy curiosity, explore and extend their sense of wonder, experience success and develop a positive attitude towards learning;

✱ appropriate periods of time for learning through sustained involvement in play;

✱ adults who are sensitive and encouraging, with whom children feel secure in their relationships, knowing that adults are there to support them;

✱ adults who treat children as individuals and participate in their play sensitively.

The curriculum framework needs to include opportunities, through play and other experiences, to develop the learning associated with:

1 Personal, social and emotional development;

2 Physical development;

3 Creative/aesthetic development;

4 Language development;

5 Early mathematical experiences;

6 Early experiences in science and technology;

7 Knowledge and appreciation of the environment.

EXPERIENCES AND ACTIVITIES LINKED TO CURRICULUM FRAMEWORKS: PROVIDING LEARNING OPPORTUNITIES

Personal, Social and Emotional Development

In every country in the UK there is great emphasis in the curriculum frameworks from birth to 6 years on the emotional wellbeing of the child. These are basic emotions: anger, pride, shame, humiliation, disgust, surprise, love, enjoyment, fear, sadness.

Emotional development requires:

✱ emotional self-awareness;

✱ self-managing your emotions;

✱ empathy with how others feel and think;

✱ handling relationships.

Adults can help children to develop emotionally (and become **emotionally literate**) if they encourage children to:

✱ stop and calm down before they act;

✱ say, or show the adult, what the problem is;

✱ be clear what it is they want or hope for;

✱ think of different ways to solve the problem;

✱ work out the consequences;

✱ try out what seems to be the best plan.

Adults also help children to develop emotionally if they encourage participation

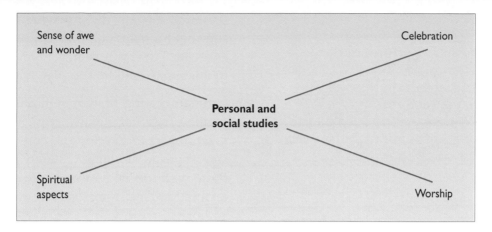

Fig 13.12 Personal, emotional and social development

in nature (awe and wonder and spirituality) and in the arts (dance, music, visual arts, drama, pottery, and so on).

Sue Gerhardt, in her book *Why Love Matters*, stresses the importance of children developing warm, affectionate relationships with those who care for them, to whom they become attached. Early friendships are also important. (Look again at Chapter 6 to remind yourself about this.)

Celebration

It is important to realise that celebrations such as Diwali, Ramadan and Christmas can only be *celebrated* by Hindus, Muslims or Christians. It is therefore easy to introduce these to children in ways which

are tokenist and superficial. We can learn about the celebrations of others, but we cannot actually celebrate with them unless we are of that faith. This may be why events such as New Year's Eve and New Year's Day are gaining in popularity. They are ways in which everyone can celebrate together in the UK, because they are not faith-based.

COMMUNICATION, LANGUAGE AND LITERACY

Again and again in this book (and particularly in Chapter 4), the importance of tuning in to the body language and early efforts to talk of babies and young children has been emphasised.

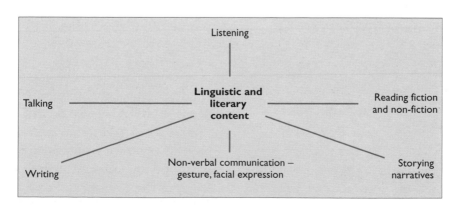

Fig 13.13 Elements of communication, language and literacy

Non-verbal communication
Facial expression, gesture, body movement/language, hand movements, pauses, rhythms of speech, eye contact, moving in synchrony with someone speaking to you, blushing, intonation of the voice, narrowed or wide-open eyes.

Parent/carer-facing prams and buggies are important, and getting down to the child's level is too. Talking with babies and children at their height, face-to-face, helps language to develop.

Conversations develop with quality when adults and children are:

* talking about the same things;
* looking at things together (shared focus);
* sharing an experience they both find interesting.

Having a conversation is different from making children reply to questions that have definite answers (**closed questions**). In a real conversation, people take it in turns to say things that they are thinking or feeling. One speaker does not decide what the other speaker has to reply.

When questions are asked, they should be **open-ended, and asked for a real reason**. Children quickly realise when adults are asking questions just for the sake of it.

Turn-taking

Young children find it difficult to wait for their turn.

Singing songs or saying rhymes *together* means that no one has to wait and everyone can join in. This is very important at large-group time.

Research suggests that knowing about rhyme and rhythm helps children to learn to *read and write*. For this reason, it is very important to encourage children to play with words.

Communicating Matters (DfES 2005) is a multiprofessional initiative which helps practitioners to develop the communication and language of young children, including those with special educational needs and disabilities. This is now part of every local authority's training.

Reading

Why do we want children to read?

The aim is to produce children who are bookworms, who want to read for pleasure and understanding, information and knowledge, and not children who only look at books when directed to do so, who are just dutiful readers.

Reading, across the world, begins by listening to stories and rhymes.

Musical Development and Learning to Read and Write

The areas of the brain which are for movement, gestures, sound and language are close to each other and form interactive networks. Ring games and traditional songs and dances help the brain along in a natural way, and this helps children learn to read – and later to write.

If you sing 'Dinner-time, it's dinner-time' to children, especially children with special needs, complex needs, or who are learning English as an additional language, you will probably find they understand more easily what you are saying. It helps children to segment the sounds, and to identify and pronounce them.

Of course, the sound of words is important in learning to read, but we have to remember that saying or singing 'duck' in the north of England is different from the south. The context is very important too, especially when words are spelt differently, such as 'When you have **read** this book, you might like to **read** another one'.

Singing helps children because many of the words rhyme, and this makes the text predictable; it is also more manageable because the poetry is in a verse or small chunk.

Clapping the rhythm or dancing to the song while singing also helps the brain to sort things out.

Listening to Stories

It is important to remember that stories are not always in written form:

* stories can be told (the Gaelic, Celtic and Maori traditions use storytelling powerfully);

* stories can be told in pictures, which are subtle.

Stories have a special way of using language called **book language**, such as 'Once upon a time . . .'. Children need a wealth of experience of book language before they can read well and become enthusiastic readers.

Children need many different forms (genres) of stories; they need core texts, favourite stories and new stories.

Criteria for selecting appropriate books

* **Everyday events**: these help children to recognise common events and feelings. They help children to heighten their awareness of words which describe everyday situations.

* **Poems**: these help rhyming and rhythm, and the chorus often gives a predictable element; the repetition helps children. This is also true of many stories, but poems are an enjoyable experience for young children, who may not be able to concentrate on a whole story in the early stages.

* **Folk stories**: these introduce children to different cultures. However, avoid stories in which animals behave as if they were humans or in which animals behave in a way which is out of character (e.g. a spider who saves the life of a fly in an act of bravery). These are called anthropomorphic stories. They can confuse young children who are trying to sort out what is and is not true.

* **True stories**: these lead to an understanding of non-fiction books, which are full of information on different topics and subjects.

* **Make-believe stories**: these lead to an understanding of fiction. Avoid stories of witches and fairies for very young children (under 4 years); children need to be clear about the distinction between reality and imagination, otherwise they may be fearful and have nightmares. Bear in mind that it is one thing for a 4-year-old to make up their own stories about monsters, witches or ghosts (the child has control), but if an adult introduces these characters the child may be scared.

* **Action rhymes and finger rhymes**: these help children to predict what is in a text. Predicting is a

very large part of learning to read; knowing what comes next is important.

* Repeating stories: knowing a story well helps children begin to read. Sometimes adults say 'Oh, but he is not reading, he just knows it off by heart'. Knowing what comes next is probably one of the most important parts of learning to read.

* Think about issues of gender, ethnicity, culture and disability, and be sure that all children see positive images of themselves in the stories you tell and in the books that you offer.

Children Need Adults to Tell and Read them Stories

* Children need one-to-one stories. These are called bedtime-type stories. The child can interact with the reader and get deeply involved. The adult and child can pause, chat, go back and revisit, and read at their own pace.

* Small-group stories, with two to four children, are more difficult for children because the adult needs to keep the story going, and so cannot allow constant interruptions. Skilled adults are able to welcome many of the children's contributions, but the larger the group, the more important it becomes for children to be able to listen. Large groups, with four to eight children, are less sensitive to the individual needs of children, so these need to be more of a theatre show or performance by the adult in order to keep the attention of the children. They cannot be so interactive. It is better not to use poetry cards and action songs with very large groups (eight or more children). This

Fig 13.14 One-to-one stories are like bedtime stories and they are an important part of learning to read

gives children the rhythm, intonation and pace and small manageable chunks of text in a song. This makes for a good community experience of reading together.

Poetry cards are of great benefit. They can be made out of cardboard boxes, and can be large and rather like theatre props. Children enjoy playing with them afterwards if they are left near the book corner. Children are often to be seen pointing at the print, in word approximation, landing at the end, and starting at the beginning. They are often joined by a friend. Encouraging children to share stories together, whether or not they can read fluently, is very helpful. This encourages emergent readers to **approximate-read**, and to pick out the words they know with confidence. Being able to have a go and to do so with confidence and pleasure are crucial.

Helping Children to Read

You can help children to read by enjoying a book or poetry card together, without any pressure. Children can see how a book is used, where to begin, how to turn a page and the direction of print, using pictures as clues, finding familiar words and guessing. Being able to guess and predict what the print says is important. Children are usually fascinated by guesses that go wrong, realising this as they learn to link what they read with meaning, and to work out the words using their increasing ability to segment and blend the graphemes and phonemes. It is important to say 'What do you think he says next?' Show the child any patterns, for example a phrase that is repeated, and talk about the letters, words and sentences as you go. Picture cues are very important when learning to read, so talk about these and the clues they give.

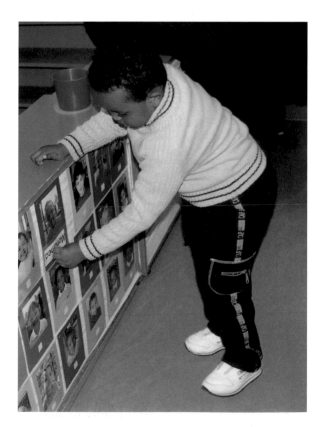

Fig 13.15 Photographs and names: picture cues help children to read

Alphabet books and friezes are important as they help children to segment words, and to focus on the initial grapheme and phoneme in a word, while offering a meaningful picture to help the child along. Regularly singing the alphabet is helpful too. Pointing out children with the same letter at the beginning of their name helps, and there can be fascinating discussions about why George is pronounced with a 'J' sound, while Gary is with a 'G' sound. English speakers need to learn early to spot exceptions with detective joy!

Children often know favourite stories by heart. This gives children a sense of control and ability to feel they can predict what the text says. It gives them a can-do feeling, crucial in learning. Decide as a team which books you will introduce as core texts, to help children become familiar with them. Note which books are favourites of particular children, and use these with the child in the same way.

Above all, remember that learning to read should be fun, and it should hold meaning for the child.

Aspects of Print which are Important when Learning to Read

✱ The meaning of the words (**semantic** aspect).

✱ The flow of the words (the **syntax** or grammar).

✱ The look and sound of the print (**grapho-phonic** aspects).

✱ Discriminating between a sentence, a word and the smallest aspects (**graphemes** and **phonemes**).

✱ Segmenting words into phonemes (**decoding**) and blending phonemes into words (**encoding**), using onset and rime to help this along in rhymes and songs, poetry cards, dance and actions.

✱ Book language (**vocabulary**).

ACTIVITY: STAGES OF READING

Observe children aged 3–7 years. Identify which children are emergent, beginner or fluent readers. What are the factors that you use to decide? Evaluate the advantages and disadvantages of shared stories.

Remember that the child's own name is the best starting point for learning letters, because children are emotionally attached to their name.

Onset and Rime – a Type of Phonics Particularly Useful for English Speakers

Because English is an irregular language, it is particularly hard to learn to read and write. Some argue that we should get children off to an early start for just this reason. Most early childhood experts take the view that the human brain needs to be sufficiently matured to tackle the fine detail of discriminating the sounds and look of English print. Even in countries where the language is very regular, such as Finland and Sweden, this is the approach. However, the brain does function easily and without stress in relation to learning about communication (both non-verbal and spoken/signed language) and music, gesture and movement. This means that singing and dancing, and talking with and listening to children, all have a huge contribution to make in helping children towards reading and writing by 6 or 7 years of age. This age is generally regarded, throughout the world, as the best time to learn to read and write, because the structures dealing with this level of symbolic functioning are there.

These words are nearly the same: 'pot', 'dot', 'got'; 'mess', 'cress', 'dress'; 'mum', 'chum', 'drum'.

The last chunk rhymes, but the first chunk is different in each case. This is a type of **analytic phonics** called **onset and rime**.

Many early childhood reading and writing experts consider that learning about onset and rime through poems, songs and action rhymes, poetry cards and books are more powerful ways of helping young children to read in English than teaching isolated sounds using flashcards (**synthetic phonics**) as the main strategy. A fierce debate about this seems to arise roughly every 10 years. Most experts argue that the more strategies we have to offer children as they learn to read, the more we can find the ones that suit them best. One size does not fit all children.

The Rose Review on Reading (2006), commissioned by the Secretary of State for Education, emphasises the importance of a rich language environment, encouraging children to enjoy being read to from fiction and non-fiction books from babyhood; it sees reading and writing as inextricably intertwined and emphasises the importance of a broad range of experiences, as advocated by the EYFS (Early Years Foundation Stage). It focuses on the importance of song, rhythm and rhyme for young children in encouraging them to make the important connections needed between the letter and sound relationships.

There is great opposition by early childhood experts to the suggestion that young children should be directly taught synthetic phonics through daily drill in large groups. However, daily group time (remember, large groups are four to eight children), with song, dance and rhyme, and encouragement to make children phonologically aware and able to discriminate sounds with more and more ease, and to link these with the print in the rhymes using poetry cards, would be welcomed. Practitioners doing this need to be aware that onset and rime is a type of phonics which also encourages synthetic phonics in a meaningful context.

Children need to learn to **segment** (break down) sounds and print. They also need to learn to **blend** (join) sounds and print. The smallest sounds are phonemes and the smallest print is a grapheme. Children need to make **grapho-phonic** relationships. They need to begin to see that what they have segmented can be blended back into a word. The ideal age to do this, experts in most countries say, is between 6 and 7 years of age.

Songs like 'Humpty Dumpty' are simple examples of this:

Humpty Dumpty sat on a wall,

Humpty Dumpty had a great fall.

Children quickly begin to see the last chunk is the same (-umpty), while the beginnings are different ('H' and 'D').

Studies of the brain suggest that the brain loves complexity, and that singing, dancing, moving, doing action songs and seeing print in meaningful patterns is part of the inter-connectedness of different parts of the brain.

The brain develops important interconnecting networks, which include those in the chart below. Movement, communication, play, symbol use, problem solving and understanding why things happen (cause and effect), become more complex, coordinated and sophisticated as the networks for learning in the brain develop.

Many experts believe that removing the meaningful context and teaching letter–sound relationships in isolation and separately, although systematic to those adult readers devising the system, actually make

reading and writing more difficult for many children. This is particularly so for children who have low-incidence disabilities, such as visual or hearing impairments, or children with English as an additional language.

Pioneers of education such as Froebel and Steiner used song and dance with action songs to great effect in helping children towards reading and writing. In most countries of the world this is the approach, particularly in countries like Finland and Sweden, where children start to learn to read late (6–7 years), yet within weeks become the best readers in the world. These languages are regular compared with the many exceptions in English. This is another reason why using a single strategy of synthetic phonics is not likely to be as effective in English literacy development as a broader approach, which includes both synthetic and analytic phonics (especially onset and rime). The brain works in an interconnected way to make sense of the sounds and relationships with print. This is the opposite of the accretion model, which builds from the simple to the more complex, using isolation and removing context as part of the simplification. This approach was widely used at the beginning of the 1900s.

The big debate is really about whether, as with other aspects of development, children begin with the whole, gross aspects of movement, sound and visual discriminations before picking out the fine detail, or whether they begin with the detail and piece together the whole out of all the parts. For children with little language experience, or with English as an additional language, this is a challenge, many experts believe. Most adults report that when learning a new language they understand the finer parts of the sounds and look of the words more easily if they learn songs and rhythms. This is because it is easier to pick out the detail of the patterns. Adam Ockelford is a musician who is also an educator (RNIB). He has pointed out that when children with complex needs are sung to, for example, 'Dinner is ready', they react when they might not do so if the words are simply said.

Writing

Writing has two aspects:

* what it says – the construction of meaning;
* the look of it – the handwriting and letter shapes (transcription).

When children begin to write, they are constructing a **code**. Most languages have a written code. Writing develops when children begin to use symbols. Often they begin by putting letter-type shapes into their drawings. These gradually get pushed out to the edges of the drawing, to look more like words and sentences. Practitioners need to observe the shapes, sizes and numbers children experiment with. Children need to be free to experiment without criticism or pressure. Left-handed children must never be encouraged to write with the right hand.

Young children find capital letters, which are more linear, easier to write than lower-case letters, which have more curves, and so they tend to experiment with capitals first. It is when children begin to experiment with curves that they are indicating they have more pencil control, and so can begin to form letters more easily.

Children need:

* to manipulate and try out different ways of 'writing' using their own personal code – tracing or copying

Fig 13.16 Children's writing

letters as adult-led tasks undermines this because their own movement patterns and laying down of neural pathways are an important part of the process;

✳ to explore what writing is;

✳ adults who point out print in books and in the environment, on notices and street signs, for example.

It is important to value writing from different cultures, for example Urdu, Arabic (which is read from right to left) and Chinese (which is read up and down on the page).

The pace and sequence of events which leads to writing and the age at which it occurs will vary greatly from child to child, depending on the child's interest, mood and personality, aptitude and, very importantly, prior experience and understanding of what writing is about. Compared with other countries, children in England are expected to begin formal writing and reading exceptionally young.

There is a high illiteracy rate in England, and many experts are concerned that this is because, by starting too soon, many children lose heart and are put off by the end of their primary school years. Young children are more likely to enjoy and see the point of reading and writing for the rest of their lives if they are introduced to reading and writing carefully and without feeling pressured. The first words that children write are full of their own feelings. These words need to be valued and respected. A child's own name is important to them, and they often write the names of people they love, plus the words 'love from'.

It is important to talk with children about environmental print, and to pick out their favourite letters (often those in their name).

Guidelines for encouraging later creative writing

✳ Learning about different roles, characters and themes is essential if children are going to learn to write stories.

✳ Having dressing-up clothes to act out stories helps children to create narratives, a skill needed for later writing.

✳ Ask children to act out a story you have told.

✳ Encourage children to act out stories that *they* have made up, and which you have written down for them. Vivian Gussin-Paley, in her school in Chicago, did this as a daily part of the curriculum.

✳ Act out stories in an atmosphere of *sharing*. This should not involve a *performance* of the story. The idea is to help children to understand how stories are made. This will help them later when they want to write their own stories.

✳ Young children should not be expected to perform stories in school assemblies, or in situations with audiences full of strangers (e.g. for the summer or Christmas show). It is not good practice to encourage children to perform before they have gone through the sequence: make – share – show. They need to be able to make their own stories, and to share these with friends and adults whom they know well before they perform.

✳ To perform becomes appropriate only in junior school. Any earlier, and some children begin over-acting and playing to the audience rather than becoming involved in the story; other children are put off forever because of the stress of being made to perform. Waving at people in the audience during a performance may be very sweet for adults to see, but it is a clear sign that the child is not involved in what they are doing and so is not ready to perform. The exercise is a failure in terms of involving a child in a story.

* Research suggests that, if children are encouraged to play in the early years, they will be better at creative writing at 7 years of age.

REASONING, PROBLEM-SOLVNG AND NUMERACY

Mathematics involves problem solving and reasoning in particular ways. Of course, these aspects of thinking are part of every area of learning, creative and physical development, emotional, social and personal development, learning to use language, to communicate with or without words or signs, and to read and write, as well as in developing scientific thinking and other aspects of knowledge and understanding of the world.

In mathematics, finding an elegant, logical and beautiful answer to a problem is deeply satisfying to a child, providing the problem is one generated by the child. Then it will have meaning.

Children learn about **topological** space (on/off, over/under, in/out, surrounding, across, near/far) before they learn about **Euclidian** space (circles, squares, etc.).

Learning the words for these in everyday situations helps children to develop reasoning and the ability to solve problems. 'Put the chair under the table' uses a topological term. These topological words link with **schemas**, which are patterns in the brain that help learning. They also feature in the 250 most used words in the English language. They are, researchers at Warwick University have shown, very important in learning to read because they are used so frequently. Children quickly recognise them, and so do not need to segment and blend as they read them. Instead they just recognise them from sight.

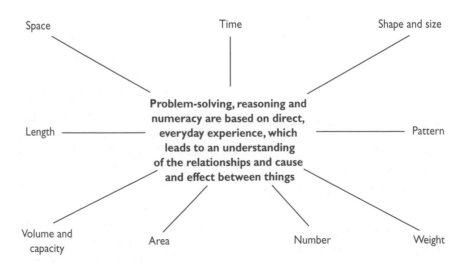

Fig 13.17 Elements of mathematics

Fig 13.18 Talking together about reflections in the mirror

Number

Number has several different aspects:

* **Matching**: this looks like this – two identical cups in the home corner.

* **Sorting**: this looks different from this – the cup and the saucer.

* **One-to-one correspondence**: one biscuit for you, one biscuit for me.

* **Cardinal numbers**: the two cups remain two cups however they are arranged (this means that the child understands the number, e.g. two).

* **Ordinal numbers**: this is first, second, third (e.g. the sequence in cooking: first I wash my hands, second I put on my apron . . .).

Children learn about number in these ways:

* reciting – number songs;

* nominal understanding – they pick out numbers on house doors, buses, in shops, on shoe sizes;

* subitising – remembering number patterns to recognise how many, for example, four dots, one on each corner of

a square, or on a domino (chimpanzees can do this with numbers up to seven);

* counting backwards – 5, 4, 3, 2, 1, lift-off!

There are three counting principles:

1 A number word is needed for every object that is counted. This is the one-to-one correspondence principle.

2 The numbers always have the same order, 1, 2, 3 (not 1, 3, 2). This is called the stable order principle.

3 When children count, they have grasped the cardinal number principle if they understand both points 1 and 2, because they know that a number is an outcome. This means that when you count, 1, 2, 3, the answer is 3.

Time

Time has two aspects:

1 Personal time: it feels a long time before a car journey ends – it might be an hour, but it feels like a day.

2 Universal time, including:

* succession: Monday, Tuesday, Wednesday . . .

* duration: day, night, an hour, a minute . . .

Guidelines for learning number

* Do not do exercises or tasks with young children which are isolated from their experience.

* Remember that children learn mathematics through cooking, tidy-up time, playing in the home area, painting and being in the garden. Mathematics is everywhere.

* Numbers are found on rulers, calibrated cooking jugs, the doors of houses, and so on.

✳ Counting is only one part of exploring numbers. It is one thing for children to be curious about numbers on calibrated jugs, weights and measures, but they need to be free to experiment and explore. This is very different from formally teaching them numbers through adult-led tasks, unrelated to real life.

Do not be too specific with young children. Begin by teaching the time with '1 o'clock', 'half past ten', and so on. Introduce more exact time-telling later. When children look at a watch and enjoy finding the numbers they are learning in an informal way.

Shape and Size

Use general terms to help children learn about these aspects of mathematics. Talk about shape and size when you do things together. Children need experience of action and language. This means plenty of talking while they do things. Children need adults to describe things that are 'bigger than' and 'smaller than' to learn that these things are **relative**, not **absolute**, sizes. Something is 'big' only in relation to something else. Always use relative terms with children. Children are very three-dimensional in their perception, so introduce words like cube and cylinder before oblong and circle. Use everyday things, like tins of food or a football to explain that this is a cylinder and a sphere.

Length

Again, it is helpful to children if relative words are used, such as 'longer than' or 'shorter than'. Young children do not yet understand the absolute nature of 1 metre, although it is helpful to show them that there is a metre behind the car in the parking space. Children need to be surrounded by rulers and tapes so that they become aware that things can be measured. Which is the tallest plant? Who has the longest foot? Gradually they develop an understanding of the exactness of absolute measurements.

Volume and Capacity

'This glass is full.' 'This bucket is nearly empty.' Listen to yourself speak and you will be surprised at how often you use mathematical language in everyday situations. This informal approach encourages children's dispositions towards learning in an enjoyable and relaxed way.

Area

Area is about ideas such as the blanket that covers the area of the mattress on the bed. Another example would be a pancake covered with lemon and sugar – the lemon and sugar cover the area of the pancake. Children often explore area in their block play.

Weight

Again, it is best to introduce the concept of weight using relative ideas. 'This tin of soup is heavier than that apple.' Rather than using a weighing machine, use a balance, so that children see this. Remember that young children need to experience weight physically. They love to carry heavy things.

CASE STUDY

Exploring weight

Kit, 3 years, carried a huge piece of ice about one freezing winter. He enjoyed throwing it and watching it skim across an icy stream. He kept saying, 'This is heavy.' His parents helped him to make comparisons: 'Is it heavier than this stone?' 'Is it heavier than this twig?'

They love to lift each other up, and often carry bags around.

Computers

There is an urgent need for better computer programs to be developed for the use of young children. Many current examples are nothing more than technological forms of template-type activities. This does not encourage children to think at a deep level. It might be fun, but it is certainly not educational. The most appropriate computer programs invite children to be interactive.

Children benefit from using a word-processor and printer, as well as using digital cameras. They enjoy picking out letters and punctuation marks, and through this kind of play they learn about important aspects of reading, writing and numbers, which will be used in a more elaborate way later.

CREATIVE DEVELOPMENT

Creative development is often seen as linked only with the arts. In fact, it is a very important part of human development which applies to the:

✱ arts (dance, music, drama, the visual arts, including sculpture, ceramics and pottery, painting and drawing, collage);

✱ sciences (biology, chemistry, physics, applied engineering, environmental studies, industry);

✱ humanities (history, geography, cultural aspects).

You can read more about creative development in *Cultivating Creativity: Babies, Toddlers and Young Children* (Bruce 2004).

Creativity in the Arts and Crafts

Children need experiences which are real, direct and first-hand, such as using clay and paint regularly. Some children choose solid media, such as dough, clay and wood. Others choose to draw and paint on paper. Representing a dog is quite different when using clay, wood at the woodwork bench, paint or pretending to be a dog in the home corner. It is important that adults directly teach children skills with the woodwork bench, or in using clay or scissors, as and when the need arises. Teaching skills in context is important. Often when children stand and watch other children use scissors, they are indicating that they are interested to learn. Adults need to be good observers and tune in to these situations.

Guidelines for promoting children's creativity

Remember, the idea is for the child to become involved in these activities. Adults often use children's art lessons as a chance to do art for themselves! Resist the temptation.

✱ **Do not** draw for children.

✱ **Do not** use templates.

✱ **Do not** ask children to trace.

✱ **Do not** ask children to colour in.

✱ **Do not** ask children to copy your model step by step.

✱ **Do** give children real, first-hand experiences, such as looking at plants or mini-beasts in the pond.

✱ **Do** give children opportunities to represent things, and to keep hold of their experiences (e.g. by making a model of the plant out of clay).

✱ **Do** encourage lots of different ideas. It is best when every child in a group has made a different model. This means that children are doing their own thinking and are not dependent on adults for ideas.

> **＊ Do** remember that children are creative in lots of different ways. Arts and crafts are only one area in which children are creative. Children can be creative scientists, creative mathematicians, creative writers, and so on.

Sculpture and Pottery

Children need to have opportunities to make three-dimensional models, with clay, wet sand, wax, soap carving, wood, dough, junk and recycled materials. This will involve them in using Sellotape, scissors, rolling pins, string, wire and other materials. Most of the time these materials can be offered as general areas of provision, available all the time. Clearly, the woodwork can only be used when an adult joins the children, in order to maintain a safe environment. However, sometimes, each of these areas can become a focused group, where an adult is anchored to teach directly. For example, a group of children might be taught how to make coil pots with clay in the clay area. If a child has been enjoying making paper spirals, the adult would make a point of inviting them to do this. Children should be able to decline such an invitation, however.

Drawing and Painting

For drawing it is best to use plain white paper of varied sizes, plus pencils, wax crayons, felt-tip pens, chalks and slates, and charcoal.

For painting there should be powder paints and different thicknesses of brushes. Materials should be stored carefully so that children can take and access what they need when they need it. Children should be offered pots of basic coloured paints, but they should also be able to mix paints, provided they are taught to do so. They simply need the basic colours – red, yellow, blue, and white and black for light and dark shades of colour.

Book Making

Children love to make books, but need help to do so initially. If they see that you have made recipe books, books of stories and poems, and books for display with information, they will want to do the same. They need to learn how to fold and cut the paper. An adult may need to be with them so that they do not give up.

Collage and Workshop Area

This requires glue, found materials, junk and recycled materials and scissors. Materials can

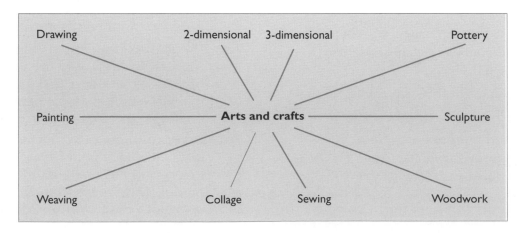

Fig 13.19 Elements of arts and crafts

be set out in attractive baskets or boxes covered in wallpaper. Glue should always be non-toxic.

Creativity in Dance, Music and Drama

Dance

Use what children do naturally – spinning, running, jumping, stamping, to make into a dance. A 'Singing in the Rain' dance was made by a group of 5-year-olds in Year 1 Key Stage 1, helped by their teacher, Dee De Wet. The children watched a video extract from the film, 'Singing in the Rain', and then they experimented with moving about:

* with fancy feet;
* by jumping in puddles;
* by swishing through puddles;
* by dashing about under an umbrella.

They made a dance sequence. Each child had an umbrella and raincoat, and used the above sequences in line with the traditional music from the film. Every child made their own dance, and yet they all danced at the same time, and were sensitive to each other's movement and ideas.

Guidelines for helping children to make dances

* Use an action phrase, for example 'shiver and freeze'. Ask the children to move like the words in the phrase.

* Show different objects, perhaps something spiky. Ask the children to move in a spiky way and make a dance.

* Take an idea from nature or everyday life: rush and roar like the wind; be a machine or a clock; dance like shadows moving or fish in the aquarium.

* For inspiration, use only experiences which the children have had very recently.

The book by Mollie Davies, *Movement and Dance in Early Childhood* (2003), gives more ideas on how to help young children dance, both boys and girls.

Music

Recent studies in neuroscience show that music is important in helping language and memory to develop. Adults naturally sing 'Up we go' when they lift a baby or toddler out

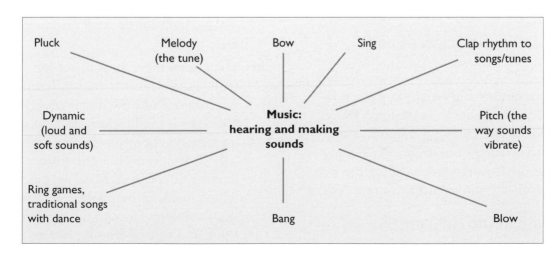

Fig 13.20 Music: hearing and making sounds

of a pram. Music helps children to remember words. But music is important in its own right. Everyday sounds have rhythm, such as the tick-tock of an alarm clock. Tearing paper, shaking the salt box, jangling a bunch of keys, fire engines . . . Children love to go on listening walks, and to make the sounds they have heard using home-made musical instruments you help them to make. The importance of singing and listening to a wide range of music from different cultures cannot be overemphasised.

Drama

Some people argue that drama began in ancient times when people tried to explore the forces of good versus evil. In their play, children experiment with goodies and baddies, friendship and foes, kindness and unkindness. Penny Holland's work shows how adults can help children to explore these major themes of what it is to be human. Telling children stories and sharing poetry cards with them also helps. Retelling stories with props is beneficial. The adult might help children to act out the story of Pegasus using 'My Little Pony', with paper wings attached with sticky tape. Children might wear dressing-up clothes to retell the story of *Where the Wild Things Are* by Maurice Sendak, including the rumpus dance.

Creativity in the Sciences and Technologies

Creative scientists and technicians see new connections and new ways of doing things. They look at the same old things in a new way, which changes things for ever. Seeing the barbs on a teasel when walking the dog by the river led one scientist to invent Velcro.

Creativity in the Humanities

Thinking in new ways about what has gone before can have a huge impact on history,

geography and culture. Nelson Mandela changed the world when, instead of following tradition and having trials to condemn the atrocities which had taken place during apartheid in South Africa, he developed a council of truth and reconciliation, so that people admitted and faced publicly the full horror of their actions, but without fear of reprisal in doing so. He was given the Nobel Prize for Peace.

SCIENTIFIC KNOWLEDGE AND UNDERSTANDING OF THE ENVIRONMENT

Just as mathematics is everywhere, so science is everywhere. Einstein, the famous scientist, said that science is really just the refinement of everyday life.

Use all the provision, indoors and outdoors, sand, water, wood, clay, paint. Use the nature around you. Look at animals, insects, birds, amphibians. Do not just look at these in books. Find ways to show children real-life examples. Use books only to follow up and remember real experiences.

The Physical Sciences

* **Electricity**: electrical circuits are easy to make with children and can be used to make a light for the doll's house or the train tracks.

* **Heat**: remember, heat is not just about temperature. Heat is energy. Temperature is a measure of how much energy. Cookery is the best way to help children understand about temperature. Making a jelly or ice cream is a good way of looking at coldness. Making something which needs to be cooked in the oven shows children about high temperatures. Look at a central-heating system and the radiators. Think about the sun and how it makes the tarmac on the playground

feel warm on a sunny day in the summer. Look at the fridge. Play with ice cubes in the water tray. Again, talk about relative heat. Is this hotter than that? Describe what is happening, think about the cause and effect, why things happen as they do. Metal feels colder than wood, but why? They are both at room temperature. Does the metal conduct the heat out of your hand?

* **Sound**: listen to the sounds around you. Help children to be aware of them. Children love to tape-record sounds and find ways to imitate sounds they hear. Some sounds are quieter and some are noisier than others. Children are not very concerned about how many decibels a sound is, but they are interested that a shout is louder than a whisper.

* **Light**: use torches and lanterns. Make rainbows with prisms. Put on puppet shows and have lighting effects. Use cellophane to make different colours of light. Children in Key Stage 1 enthusiastically make light effects for stories they have made up or enjoyed from books. Experiment with shadows and shadow puppets.

* **Gravity**: use parachutes, or drop objects from heights.

* **Floating and sinking**: this is a difficult concept. Young children benefit from a waterwheel and different experiments with boats, but true understanding takes time.

The Natural Sciences

Use **mixtures** to demonstrate how materials can be changed and recovered (salt and water, sugar and water, earth and water, flour and water, mud pies, and mud and straw to make bricks). All these mixtures have properties which children can explore:

* Salt dissolves in water. So does sugar. When the water evaporates, the salt or sugar can be seen again.

* Flour and mud do not dissolve. They become suspended in water.

* You can look at transformations using water, ice and steam. You can reverse these, and turn steam into water again.

* Study what happens when you cook an egg. You cannot reverse this transformation.

Early technology can be explored by looking at activities such as weaving. If you have a frame with string going up and down and from side to side, near the entrance, then children and families will enjoy the in-and-out movement of threading pieces of material, wool, ribbon, and so on. These weavings often become attractive wall hangings in the office or entrance hall of the setting.

It is important to use technology which is easy for children to understand. Examples would be a tin opener, an egg whisk or scissors. Encourage children to use wooden blocks and construction kits.

Look at both types of technology:

* low technology, such as an egg whisk, waterwheels;

* high technology, such as digital cameras, tape recorders for music and stories, computers, word processors and printers, telephones for conversations.

Guidelines for looking at animals

* Where do animals live? You can find ants, spiders and birds and look at their habitats. Remember, never kill animals, and always return them to their habitat; make a point of explaining this to the

children. There are now pots with magnifying glasses in them, which make it easier to look at these creatures without squashing them accidentally.

* **What do animals eat?** Study cats, birds, fish and talk about their diets.

* **How do animals eat?** Talk about claws, type of feet, mouths, beaks, types of teeth, jaws which chew (cows), jaws which gnash. Study dogs, cats, humans. A bird that eats nuts needs a beak that is a good nutcracker! A bird that catches fish needs a long beak.

* **How do animals protect themselves?** Look at camouflage, claws, tusks, fur for warmth, oil on ducks' feathers to make them waterproof.

There are reasons why animals, birds and insects have developed as they have done. The points above will give children an introduction to the evolution of the animal world in ways they can understand.

Guidelines for looking at plants

* Why do plants have leaves? Do all plants have leaves?

* Why is a tree trunk like it is? Do all trees have exactly the same sort of trunk? Make some bark rubbings. Hug trees to see if you can reach all the way round them with your arms.

* Why do flowers have colours? Insects are important for plant life.

* Why do some flowers have scent and nectar? Again, plants might need to attract insects and birds to visit them.

GEOGRAPHY, HISTORY AND CULTURE

Young children are interested in people, families and homes. They like to learn about what people in the community do. They show this in their role-play. Through role-play and visits to offices, shops, clinics, the vet, the station, they learn about different communities. They develop a sense of geography.

They are also interested in old objects, in what things were like when they were babies or when their parents were babies, and what sort of childhood their grandparents had. Collecting artefacts of bygone days and inviting older people to share and talk about their lives, often with the aid of photographs, help children to develop a sense of history. Having a timeline helps too, again using photos to show the order and sequence of events.

PHYSICAL DEVELOPMENT

Remember:

* Children need to move as much as they need to eat and sleep.

* They learn through action and language that gives it meaning.

* They need to be skilled in a range of movements, using both fine and gross motor skills.

* They need repetition to consolidate.

* Movement needs to be appropriate – stroke a dog gently, but throw hard to make a splash with a pebble in a puddle.

Large Apparatus

This can include:

* climbing frame;

* ropes to swing on;

* planks to walk on with ladders;

* things to jump off.

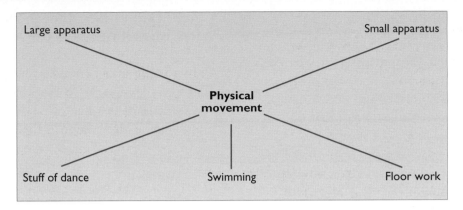

Fig 13.21 Elements of movement

Children need to be encouraged to become generally skilled in movement.

Small Apparatus

This includes bats, balls, hoops, beanbags and ropes. It is very important to encourage turn-taking and cooperation.

Floor Work

This enables children to explore:

* weight transfer from one part of the body to another;

* travel from one spot to another;

* flight: jumps – the five basic jumps are: on two legs, from one leg to the other, on the left leg, on the right leg, from two legs to one leg.

Give children a general theme to investigate through floor work, for example starting low and getting higher. Do not make children do just one thing, such as a handstand. There are lots of ways of changing your balance – a handstand is only one. To help children enjoy creating and solving problems about weight transfer, you can say, 'Can you start on your feet and stop with another bit of you touching the floor?' In this way you are helping children with **reasoning** and **problem-solving** as they think about their own

movements. Being aware of your own body and comfortable in it is called embodiment. This increases **wellbeing** and self-confidence.

KEY STAGE 1 IN ENGLAND – CONTINUING THE LEARNING JOURNEY

This is a DfES initiative designed to help schools give children a positive experience as they move into Key Stage 1 in England, so that there is an effective building upon the Early Years Foundation Stage. The EYFS is from birth to 5 years. This means that children in Year 1 might be within its remit.

The principles of the Early Years Foundation Stage should be used to promote continuity in learning, so that teachers are aware of children's achievements and can implement the next steps in their learning. Information from the Early Years Foundation Stage Profile supports this process. The curriculum in year 1 of the primary school should be responsive to children's needs.

If this is achieved, an effective transition is brought about, and children undertake the programme of Key Stage 1 positively building on the 6 areas of the Foundation Stage. The EYFS has statutory force from September 2008.

The English National Curriculum

The English National Curriculum was established by the **Education Reform Act 1988 (ERA)**. It provides a minimum requirement for a curriculum and it has recently been reviewed. It states that the curriculum of each school should be 'balanced and broadly based' to promote the 'spiritual, moral, cultural, mental and physical development of pupils . . . and of society' and to prepare pupils for 'the opportunities, responsibilities and experiences of adult life'.

In England, there are **programmes of study** for each subject, plus **attainment targets** in each subject, through which teachers can make rounded assessments of children using **levels of description**. Teachers are encouraged to make plans of work and to keep observation-based records. Checklists for record-keeping are not encouraged.

The subjects in the English National Curriculum are:

* Three core subjects – English, maths and science (soon to be four, including citizenship);

* foundation subjects – design and technology, information technology, history, geography, art, music, physical education and a modern language (from 11 years old).

The teaching of religious education must be provided under the heading cultural, moral and spiritual and sex education.

The National Strategies for the EYFS primary and secondary phases have renewed the literacy and numeracy aspects. The four **Key Stages** in the English National Curriculum are:

Key Stage 1 (Years 1 and 2: 5–7 years)

Key Stage 2 (7–11 years)

Key Stage 3 (11–14 years)

Key Stage 4 (14–16 years).

Children are assessed through **Standard Assessment Tasks** (SATs) at the end of each Key Stage (the Early Years Foundation Profile is the end-of-stage assessment for the EYFS). Staff in early years settings are able to use the end of the Early Years Foundation Stage Profile assessment in the last year to:

* support and encourage a multilingual classroom;

* identify children with special educational needs;

* encourage a dialogue between home and school, perhaps building on a home visit which is made just before the child starts school.

However, research shows that summer-born children, especially if they are boys, have lower SAT scores than older children. Many early years experts interpret this as evidence suggesting an early start to formal education carries long-term disadvantages for a large proportion of children.

The Welsh National Curriculum

There are three or four core subjects, depending on whether Welsh is the first language of the child and on whether the child is being educated in a Welsh-medium school: English, maths, science and Welsh. Welsh is tested at the end of each Key Stage if it is a core subject, as are the other core subjects. Welsh is studied by all children up to Key Stage 3, but tests are optional if it is the child's second language. The other subjects are the same as for the English National Curriculum, except:

* at Key Stage 4, when modern language and technology are optional;

* in art and music, where there is still a requirement to make and perform dances, music and art.

There will no longer be SATs at the end of Key Stage 1 and children will follow an extension of the curriculum for 3- to 5-year-olds.

The Scottish Curriculum

Scottand is developing a 3–18 curriculum, 'Excellence for All': teachers decide when a child is ready to move to the next level. A sample of teacher assessments are monitored as a moderation exercise. This checks that all teachers are using the same criteria correctly. The results of the teacher assessments are shared with parents. 79 per cent of parents voted against SATs being introduced into the Scottish system. The words on the Scottish Parliament's mace are influencing the principles informing the developing Scottish curriculum framework. They are:

* justice;
* integrity;
* wisdom;
* passion.

Subjects covered are:

* English;
* mathematics;
* science;
* design and technology;
* creative and expressive studies;
* language studies.

The Northern Ireland Curriculum

The Northern Ireland Curriculum places religious education outside the areas of study. In other ways, it is like the English National Curriculum in that it follows similar testing procedures: children are tested at the end of each Key Stage.

The areas of study are:

* English – at Key Stage 1 – this includes drama and media studies;
* mathematics;
* science;

* design and technology – which may soon be combined with science;
* environment and society – which includes geography and history, and may soon include home economics;
* creative and expressive studies – which includes PE and dance; art and design; music;
* language studies – only at secondary level. When the Irish language is offered, another modern language must also be offered by the school.

GROUP PLANNING

Planning the Indoor and Outdoor Learning Environment

It is important to build on the traditions of the UK, which have emerged out of nursery schools and which have been tried and tested for excellence in the EPPE (Effective Provision of Preschool Education) research directed by Kathy Sylva at the University of Oxford.

Remember:

* to make the areas of the building flexible and easy to transform for different uses;
* that the way light shines in a building changes the atmosphere;
* that temperature is important;
* that areas should be uncluttered and beautifully arranged.

There should be nothing in a learning environment, either indoors or outdoors, that has not been carefully thought through and well organised. Many areas are full of clutter, which confuses children, so that they do not know what they are allowed to do, or how to look after the equipment and resources. When children feel insecure, they behave badly. They keep testing the boundaries to find out if there are any, and what they are. Children without boundaries are unhappy.

Children from birth to 3 years enjoy the companionship and stimulation of being with older children, but they also become exhausted if they do not have a safe nest to retreat into, where they can be quiet and calm. The environment indoors and outdoors is planned with this in mind at the Kate Greenaway Maintained Nursery School and Children's Centre, where the children range from 1 to 5 years.

ACTIVITY: KATE GREENAWAY: A SUCCESSFUL PLAN

Please look at Figure 13.22 and explore the following features:

* Sleeping area: beginning at the left-hand side of the page, you will see that there is an area for children between the ages of 1 and 3 years to sleep. Children sleep here only if they need to, and their sleep patterns are discussed with parents/carers. The colours are neutral and there is a chair for an adult to sit in, should a child need to be cuddled as they fall asleep. It is important to find out about home sleep patterns. The room is quiet and calm, but the door is left open, so that staff can observe, and children feel near their important adult (key person) and therefore secure.

* Quiet area: this is next to the sleeping area, and is also for the children aged 1–3 years. It is fenced-off from the rest of the room. There is a sofa where the practitioner or parents can sit and cuddle a child, and there is a carefully selected range of books next to it. Hanging above the bookcase are several story/song sacks, which are used regularly at group times. Parents and practitioners often sit with children and share these. Sometimes they sit on the sofa together with children beside them and on their laps. Sometimes they sit on the floor, with their back supported against the sofa. A sofa is probably one of the most important pieces of equipment in a room for children aged 1–3 years. There are beanbags in soft neutral colours, with soft toys. There are a few jigsaw-type toys on the floor.

* Boundaries: children can see through the fence, and they quickly learn to open the gate, so that they can go into the quiet area or leave it, according to how they feel. There is a clear boundary about the use of this space. It is for quiet and calm, and if children want or need to be more boisterous, they are encouraged to move to the next area or into the garden, with the explanation that there are more things they will enjoy there. Sometimes a practitioner will take a child into the area if they feel the toddler is becoming tired and needs some quieter, calmer time. Obviously it is important that the practitioner stays with the child and helps them, perhaps looking at a book together, or hugging a soft toy while sitting on the practitioner's lap.

* Natural materials: in the main area for the 1- to 3-year-olds there is a set of wooden blocks, beautifully presented on shelves. Nearby there are shelves with a wooden Brio® train set. As many materials as possible are of natural materials, although plastic is not banned. There is a basket with stones and natural sponges in it for children to hold and manipulate, or make patterns with. Toddlers are often seen quietly lining these up and

concentrating deeply. There is a cupboard with musical instruments in it for group sessions with an adult leading. Near the sink is an area for dough and an area for mark-making.

* Home area: there is also a domestic play/home corner area. For children of this age group there should always be an area where they can become involved in the beginnings of role-play and pretend play. We have seen in Section 1 that even the youngest children are beginning to understand that they can imitate what adults do in their role-play, and pretend to eat food. Food preparation play is one of the earliest forms of role-play and pretend play in young children throughout the world.

* The indoor climbing frame is very popular when children arrive. The changing area is off this room, and there is a lavatory for children to use as they become toilet trained. Children from the Foundation Stage are welcome to use this area, providing they do not overwhelm the younger children. Often children who are vulnerable, experiencing trauma, developmentally young for their age or who have special needs enjoy this area, as it is appropriate for their needs. However, the staff whose work is with the 1–3-year-olds focus on those children, and treat the older children as visitors. If they begin to take too much of their attention, they are directed, gently and positively, out of this space.

* Sharing spaces: next door, there is a truly shared space, where children of all ages (1–5 years) can dance and move. A kitchen off this area also provides opportunities for staff to make snacks for children, which can be served to children at a table in this area. It is next to another shared space, which is the messy area. Here, there is double provision. Whatever is available at a more advanced level is also available at a simpler level. This double provision means there is progression and differentiation. Children can become involved in the way that is appropriate for them. For example, there is the opportunity for children to mix their own paint colours at a table, but on the floor there are trays of ready-mixed paint which children can use in a large builder's tray on the floor. Toddlers can be dressed appropriately to experience this, and so can older children if they wish. But the children who want to paint a picture, and choose their colours carefully, can also do so at the table. There is something for everyone. The children aged 1–3 years are only allowed to use this area if their key person goes with them. This is because they need a great deal of support, and so the mess does not get out of hand, thereby maintaining a safely structured experience which everyone enjoys together. Parents and grandparents also enjoy joining their children here.

* There is another reason why it is important to offer young children experiences down on the floor, rather than on the table. This is because (as JABADAO shows) belly-crawling, crawling on knees and floor-based movements lay down essential patterns in the brain for future effective learning, influencing reading, writing, mathematics and wellbeing, for example.

* Controlling messy play activities: only one very messy experience/activity is

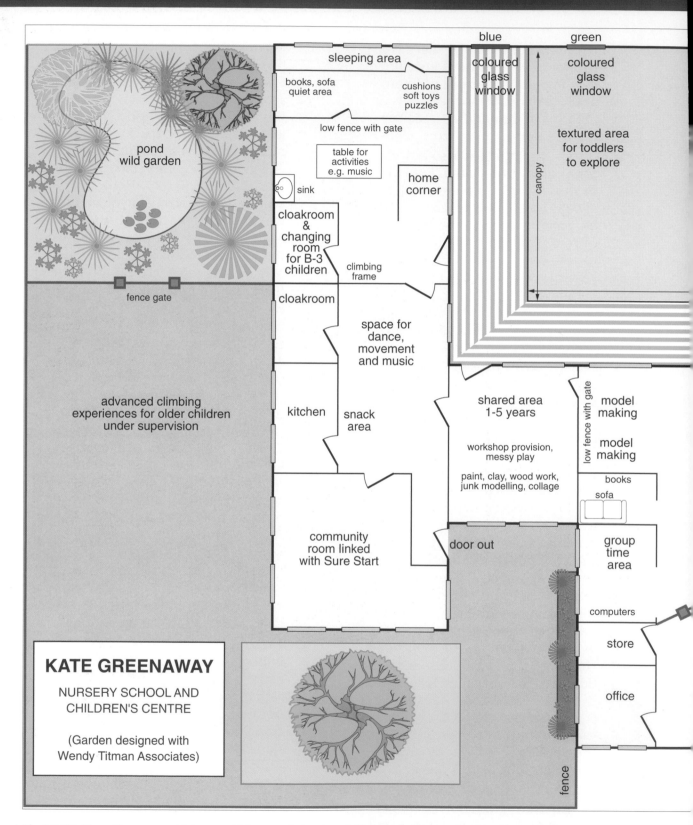

Fig 13.22 Kate Greenaway Maintained Nursery School and Children's Centre (garden designed with Wendy Titman Associates)

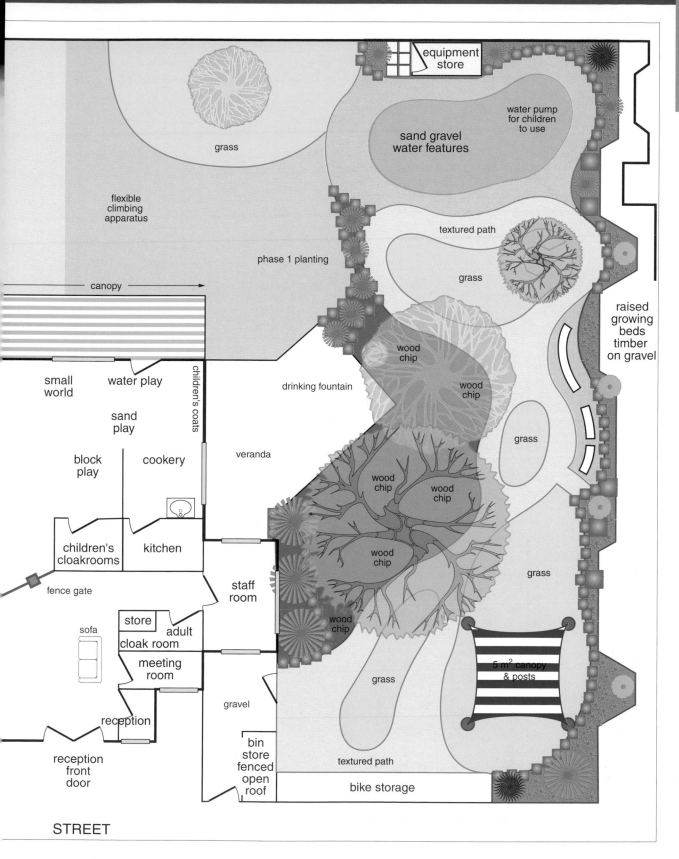

equipment store

water pump for children to use

sand gravel water features

grass

flexible climbing apparatus

phase 1 planting

textured path

grass

raised growing beds timber on gravel

canopy

small world

water play

children's coats

drinking fountain

wood chip

wood chip

grass

sand play

veranda

wood chip

wood chip

block play

cookery

wood chip

grass

children's cloakrooms

kitchen

wood chip

staff room

wood chip

grass

fence gate

sofa

store

adult cloak room

meeting room

5 m² canopy & posts

grass

reception

gravel

reception front door

bin store fenced open roof

textured path

bike storage

STREET

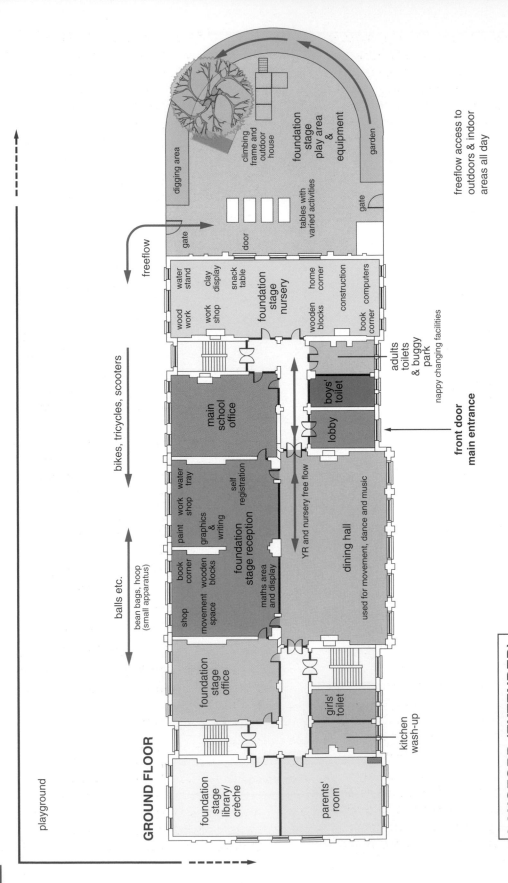

playground

GROUND FLOOR

foundation stage library/crèche

parents' room

kitchen wash-up

girls' toilet

foundation stage office

shop

movement space

book corner

wooden blocks

paint

work shop

graphics & writing

water tray

foundation stage reception

maths area and display

self registration

dining hall

used for movement, dance and music

main school office

lobby

boys' toilet

adults toilets & buggy park

nappy changing facilities

front door main entrance

YR and nursery free flow

bean bags, hoop (small apparatus)

balls etc.

bikes, tricycles, scooters

freeflow

foundation stage nursery

wood work

work shop

water stand

clay display

snack table

wooden blocks

construction

home corner

book corner

computers

gate

door

tables with varied activities

digging area

climbing frame and outdoor house

foundation stage play area & equipment

garden

gate

freeflow access to outdoors & indoor areas all day

LANGFORD (EXTENDED) PRIMARY SCHOOL

Fig 13.23 Langford (extended) primary school has a Foundation Stage layout with the nursery class and reception class working together. The school received positive feedback from Ofsted inspections.

offered per day, so that the mess is controlled carefully and children do not feel insecure and without boundaries. The practitioners in the 1–3 years area and the Foundation Stage plan this space together. What is provided is the result of their observations of children, linked to the two frameworks, *Birth to Three Matters* and *Curriculum Guidance for the Foundation Stage*. There is always paint, clay and modelling with found/junk materials, involving a workshop area with glue, sticky tape, scissors and string, For example, while the older children might sit or stand at a table and make a model of a car, a house or a puppet, a young child might prefer to sit at a basket on the floor and manipulate different balls of string and simply find out about string and its properties. The older children often return to these simpler activities when they have finished making a model, and they need the comfort of doing something less challenging after all their effort.

* More boundaries: there is a gate in a fenced-off area between the shared messy space and the Foundation Stage area. The children can use this easily once they have been shown how to, or they enjoy working it out themselves from the earliest age. However, the youngest children only go though this gate as they arrive and leave the setting with their parent/carer. They do not use the Foundation Stage area because it is set up with activities and experiences which are for children from 3 years upwards.

* Graphics area: this has carefully structured pencils, felt-tip pens and paper, scissors, masking tape and Sellotape. Everything is labelled with a picture and the word in

boxes of wood or baskets. Having natural materials in which to keep equipment, such as wood and baskets, and wooden units, makes the colours neutral and gives the area a feeling of calm and focus.

* Planning should fit in with children's natural rhythms. Adults need to bear in mind that it is important not to work to a tight, inflexible routine, which is really for their own convenience rather than serving the needs of the children. There are times when children go at a fast pace, and times when they tire; times when they want to be alone, or have a cuddle and be nurtured; and times when they enjoy working with other children and adults. Different children will need different things at different times of the day. All the children will not need to sleep at the same time. One 2-year-old might need a sleep before lunch and enjoy it once rested, while another will sleep after lunch, relaxed with a comfortable, full stomach.

Kate Greenaway achieved an outstanding Ofsted report in 2006 for work with children from birth to 3.

Now answer the following questions:

* Why is it so important to have a quiet area for children?

* Which part of the building is planned to encourage role-play?

* What does double provision mean – and what are its benefits for the children?

* Compare this layout with that of 'your setting' – which may not have been specifically planned for its purpose. Using the list above, consider each area in your setting and discuss ways in which it could be improved to benefit both children and staff.

A Sense of Belonging to the Group

A well-planned environment allows children to learn in their own individual way while giving them a sense of belonging to the community. Eating together needs careful planning, but helps to bring this about. Planning where children should sit and how the group will be arranged enhances the curriculum through everyday activities of daily living. These are powerful learning opportunities. As adults talk with children, and help them, encouraging them to help each other and be as independent as possible, the children benefit if planning is thorough.

* Do children know how to help themselves to vegetables?

* Do they clear away their own plates after eating?

Using Everyday Experiences

Some of the richest learning comes from experiences of everyday living. Examples would be getting dressed, choosing what to do, going shopping, using what you have bought in cooking, using a recipe book, washing up, sharing a story or photographs of shared events

Fig 13.24 Helping children to become involved

(visiting the park), laying the table, eating together, sorting the washing, washing clothes. It is a challenge to find ways of making this manageable for children to take part in with independence, but careful planning makes this both possible and enjoyable, and the learning goes deep. For further information, see the case studies on page 439.

APPROACHES TO PLANNING

Planning from Birth to 5 Years

Children in a group setting need a carefully planned learning environment. It is important, however, that practitioners engage with assessing where a child is in their learning, using observation informed by knowledge of child development, and then planning using the appropriate document.

In England the planning would be linked to the Early Years Foundation Stage. In each country of the UK planning will link into the official curriculum framework (see Section 1), but planning is always informed by observation of individual children, especially if the child has special educational needs or disabilities. Even babies 'tell' us things and can be involved in what we plan for them if we observe what interests them.

As we have already seen, if we become skilled observers we can identify what interests babies, toddlers on the cusp of language or children with special needs and disabilities. In this way every child can participate and can influence what we are planning. This is an important part of the government's 'Every Child Matters' agenda. The award-winning 'Listening to Children' project developed by Penny Lancaster is helpful.

Long-term Planning

This focuses on what is known about the general development and learning needs of most children between birth and 5 years of age, and makes general provision for these in what is planned indoors and outdoors. As we have seen throughout this chapter, what a baby of 1 year old is interested in or needs is different from that of a child aged 3, 4 or 5 years. However, we have also seen that children are very diverse, and there are huge differences between what each child does at a particular age. The long-term plan gives a general sense of direction and makes everyone aware of the principles, values and philosophy that support the curriculum. The long-term plan may also take a particular emphasis for a time (perhaps for several months), such as the way children and adults communicate non-verbally and use spoken language/sign; how to get the most from the outdoor environment; the settling in of children; creativity; or play.

Medium-term Planning

This is the way in which the principles and general framework set by the long-term planning are applied.

The medium-term planning will need to be **adjusted constantly** because it will be influenced by the observations made of individual children. This is why, for children from birth to 3 years, it needs to include reviews of care routines, key person relationships and the way the day is organised to offer play and experiences, including the materials and physical resources. The 'Listening to Children' initiative is helping us to involve children more in what we plan for them. In a broad way, it will plan for experiences and activities staff will offer across several weeks. EYFS is helping staff to plan in this way in England. New training materials are supporting Scottish practitioners developing the Birth to Three Framework. Planning is informed by observations throughout the EYFS, from birth to five years.

Short-term Planning

This is usually based on observation sheets of individual children's interests and needs. These observations inform the medium-term planning; it is constantly modified so that it is relevant and useful for each child's learning.

Using the observations, practitioners and parents can make assessments for learning and plan what the child needs next. This will not necessarily mean giving the child something new. More often than not it means deepening what the child has found interesting. For example, planning may arise out of several observations of a baby crawling to grab spherical objects, such as a soft ball or a wooden ball. Rather than deciding that now the baby has experienced spheres, the next shape is a cube, and providing cubes, a more appropriate plan would be to deepen the opportunities for sphere play by providing a range of spheres and placing them everywhere within crawling possibilities for the baby to find and enjoy. You could also introduce spherical fruit and vegetables (e.g. apples, oranges and tomatoes) and cut them up for snacks, at the same time talking/signing so that children are offered the names and descriptions and what they are for (function).

Planning to extend learning is often of the deepening kind, rather than introducing new things all the time.

The same is true with children aged 3–5 years. The child might still be exploring spheres! Finding a dandelion clock and comparing its shape with a clover flower found in the garden is exciting, and can lead to a deepening understanding of flowers and why the petals are on the flower in a particular shape, or an exploration of seed dispersal. This sort of deepening of understanding more often than not involves the practitioners in deepening their knowledge too. Just enjoying the plants in

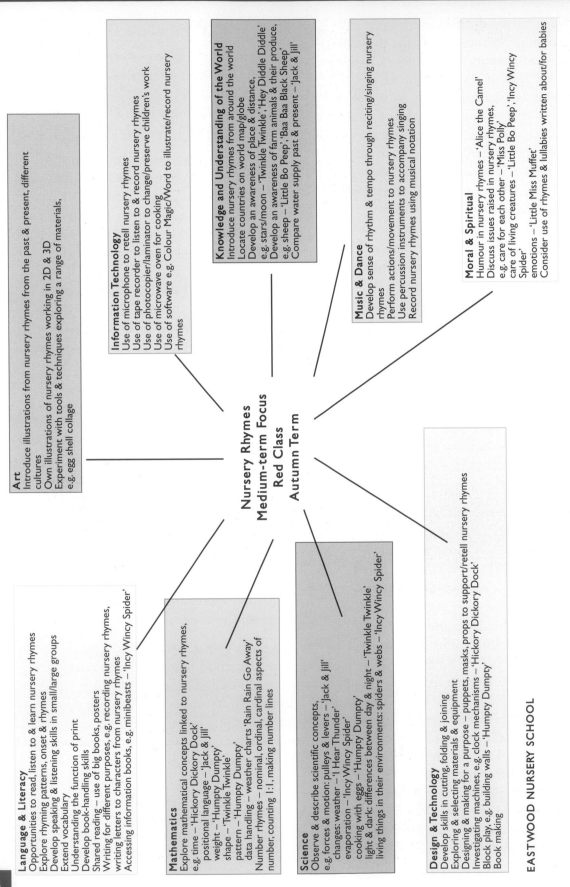

Language & Literacy
Opportunities to read, listen to & learn nursery rhymes
Explore rhyming patterns, onset & rhymes
Develop speaking & listening skills in small/large groups
Extend vocabulary
Understanding the function of print
Develop book-handling skills
Shared reading — use of big books, posters
Writing for different purposes, e.g. recording nursery rhymes,
writing letters to characters from nursery rhymes
Accessing information books, e.g. minibeasts — 'Incy Wincy Spider'

Mathematics
Explore mathematical concepts linked to nursery rhymes,
e.g. time — 'Hickory Dickory Dock'
positional language — 'Jack & Jill'
weight — 'Humpty Dumpty'
shape — 'Twinkle Twinkle'
pattern — 'Humpty Dumpty'
data handling — weather charts 'Rain Rain Go Away'
Number rhymes — nominal, ordinal, cardinal aspects of
number, counting 1:1, making number lines

Science
Observe & describe scientific concepts,
e.g. forces & motion: pulleys & levers — 'Jack & Jill'
changes: weather — 'I Hear Thunder'
evaporation — 'Incy Wincy Spider'
cooking with eggs — 'Humpty Dumpty'
light & dark: differences between day & night — 'Twinkle Twinkle'
living things in their environments: spiders & webs — 'Incy Wincy Spider'

Design & Technology
Develop skills in cutting, folding & joining
Exploring & selecting materials & equipment
Designing & making for a purpose — puppets, masks, props to support/retell nursery rhymes
Investigating machines, e.g. clock mechanisms — 'Hickory Dickory Dock'
Block play, e.g. building walls — 'Humpty Dumpty'
Book making

Art
Introduce illustrations from nursery rhymes from the past & present, different cultures
Own illustrations of nursery rhymes working in 2D & 3D
Experiment with tools & techniques exploring a range of materials,
e.g. egg shell collage

Information Technology
Use of microphone to retell nursery rhymes
Use of tape recorder to listen to & record nursery rhymes
Use of photocopier/laminator to change/preserve children's work
Use of microwave oven for cooking
Use of software e.g. Colour Magic/Word to illustrate/record nursery rhymes

Knowledge and Understanding of the World
Introduce nursery rhymes from around the world
Locate countries on world map/globe
Develop an awareness of place & distance,
e.g. stars/moon — 'Twinkle Twinkle', 'Hey Diddle Diddle'
Develop an awareness of farm animals & their produce,
e.g. sheep — 'Little Bo Peep', 'Baa Baa Black Sheep'
Compare water supply past & present — 'Jack & Jill'

Music & Dance
Develop sense of rhythm & tempo through reciting/singing nursery rhymes
Perform actions/movement to nursery rhymes
Use percussion instruments to accompany singing
Record nursery rhymes using musical notation

Moral & Spiritual
Humour in nursery rhymes — 'Alice the Camel'
Discuss issues raised in nursery rhymes,
e.g. care for each other — 'Miss Polly',
care of living creatures — 'Little Bo Peep', 'Incy Wincy Spider'
emotions — 'Little Miss Muffet'
Consider use of rhymes & lullabies written about/for babies

**Nursery Rhymes
Medium-term Focus
Red Class
Autumn Term**

EASTWOOD NURSERY SCHOOL

Fig 13.25 Example of a medium-term plan

PERSONAL, SOCIAL AND EMOTIONAL

Using pulleys to turn-take (see also construction and woodwork). Printing and woodwork to help William hit and stab in acceptable ways without putting him under pressure to cooperate with others before he is ready to do so. Valuing his creative constructions, which raises his self-confidence and contributes to his wellbeing.

KNOWLEDGE AND UNDERSTANDING OF THE WORLD

Splash painting (see mathematical development).
A pulley over the sand tray, using his trajectory schema, helps him to encounter light/heavy and forces in physics.
Collaborating with others helps him to appreciate other cultures and diversity amongst human beings.
Gardening and digging ready for vegetable planting and in particular for William to transport earth to fill the garden tubs.

COMMUNICATION, LANGUAGE AND LITERACY

The post office satisfies William in that he can stamp letters and deliver them. Stories offered include 'The Hungry Giant' (about a giant who hits), 'Mr. Gumpy's Outing' and poetry, 'Noisy Poems'. Whilst involved in these experiences, genuine conversations take place around things which are of great interest to him. His language has developed dramatically. This is a combination of improved hearing since the adjustment of his grommets and being supported and extended through dialogue with adults whilst involved in activities that fascinate him.

CREATIVE DEVELOPMENT

Constructions and blockplay, or rockets using Sellotape and recycled materials (up and down, side to side trajectories).

WILLIAM'S TRANSPORTING AND TRAJECTORY CLUSTER OF SCHEMAS (JAN/FEB)

SPIRITUAL

Gardening encourages him in a sense of awe and wonder. Having his constructions valued leads to love and respect.

MATHEMATICAL DEVELOPMENT

Splash painting involves mathematics and distance. Post-office play with different-sized bags and baskets and all the problems associated with getting big boxes into small containers before being able to transport them, offer different experiences (volume, capacity, problem solving).

PHYSICAL DEVELOPMENT

Everything William does indoors and outdoors offers him opportunities for gross and fine motor coordination. Grommets in his ears help him to experience fully the physical environment.

Fig 13.26 William's transporting and trajectory cluster of schemas

the garden and talking about them while doing so would be a good plan. The medium–term plan could be adjusted to include a pretend flower shop, which might support and extend the interests and needs of other children. One type of plan which is widely used as a medium–term plan, or as a plan for an individual child, is called a PLOD (possible line of direction). This was first conceptualised with staff at Redford House Workplace Nursery at Froebel College in Roehampton, and later developed with staff at Pen Green Children's Centre.

Guidelines for medium-term planning

* You will be observing children, getting to know them and their characters. You need to match your observations to your medium-term plans.

* The staff, planning together, should look at how they can create a rich learning environment which links the long-term plans to each child as an

Example of a medium-term plan
Developed from observations of children into a water theme
(about 3/4 weeks duration usually, depending on the interest in it from the children).

In a medium-term plan, the focus is on creating a learning enviroment:

- which is well-resourced and well-organised
- where adults are clear about how they will work on specific areas at particular times, and make a bridge between long-term plans for the group as a whole, and short-term immediate action plans for particular children.

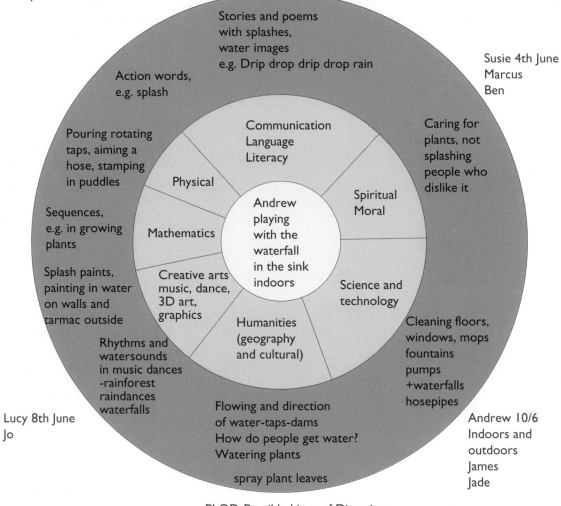

PLOD-Possible Lines of Direction

Fig 13.27 Example of a medium-term plan, in which personal, emotional and social learning occurs throughout

individual. The medium-term plan must grow gradually and must be flexible, open to changes and moderations.

* You will need to look at the observation profiles of all the children.

* Many early years settings now target particular children on particular days. This means each child is observed regularly, and the curriculum is planned in a differentiated way to cater for the interests and needs of individual children.

CASE STUDY

Observation and planning

In one setting, observations of the target child over a week showed that the waterfall was greatly used. The waterfall consisted of three beakers of graded sizes. When the tap was turned on, a waterfall was created, which led to much glee and discussion. The nursery school's development plan identified science as a major area, with money set aside to buy more equipment. The staff planned to support and extend the learning by introducing cascades of water in many different ways. They developed a project (or medium-term plan) on water, to last for as long as the interest continued.

Guidelines for short-term planning

* A short-term plan focuses on target children for one week. In this way each child is observed regularly.

* Short-term planning is more specific, but should not be rigid.

* Staff will use weekly and daily planning sessions to build particular learning intentions for particular children.

* Some activities will be planned to provide opportunities for children to explore and experiment (indirect teaching). Some will be adult-led (direct teaching).

* The staff will prepare by deciding what resources are needed, at what time in the day and who will be there at particular points.

CASE STUDY

Andrew

An early years practitioner has observed Andrew (3 years), who spends 20 minutes with the waterfall beakers. He lines them up next to the tap so that the water falls exactly as he wants. He has a bowl of corks under the waterfall. He aims the water at them one by one to make them bob about.

The nursery nurse feeds back this observation of Andrew, who is the target child that day, to a group of staff. They decide to put the waterfall out again. In addition they will provide a bigger version in the outside area, using buckets and old water trays. They plan who will be in which areas and they hope Andrew will learn:

* that water flows;

* that it splashes;

* that it cascades in the outdoor waterfall more than the indoor waterfall;

* that it flows downwards if it can;

* that it makes a trajectory (which is a moving line);

* that it has force to move things in its way.

To extend Andrew's interest, they plan a visit to the local shopping mall where there is a fountain. They also link the short-term plans made for Andrew with the medium-term plan described above.

Quality learning takes place when you are able to match what is offered in the curriculum to the interests and needs of individual children. Good teaching means helping children to learn, so that they make connections with what they already know, and at times are helped to extend this.

PLANNING A QUALITY CURRICULUM

Although it can seem a daunting task to provide a quality learning environment for children from birth to the age of 8 years, remember that the things which matter most are:

✱ your relationship with the children, their families and the other staff;

✱ the provision that you offer;

✱ the conversations that you have with children as they experience the materials – the learning context is crucial.

Bear these factors in mind when you plan – quality is more likely to result. If you can help children to enjoy learning, you will have given them a good start, which they will take with them through their lives. The shaded area in Figure 13.28 shows the importance of operating the curriculum in such a way that both the teacher and the child contribute actively as much as possible.

Staying Anchored and Available to Children at their Height or at Floor Level

It is very difficult for children when adults flit about and do not stay in one place for long enough for children to engage with them in focused ways. It does not encourage children to focus either.

It is a good idea, as part of planning the curriculum framework in the learning environments, indoors and outdoors, to see where there might need to be anchored adults working in depth with children. The following points are important:

✱ The anchored adult needs to sit at the child's height or on the floor so as to give full attention to a child or children in one area while retaining an overview of the rest of the room.

✱ The practitioner must be free to focus on what the children in a particular area are doing (e.g. playing with wooden blocks or in the movement

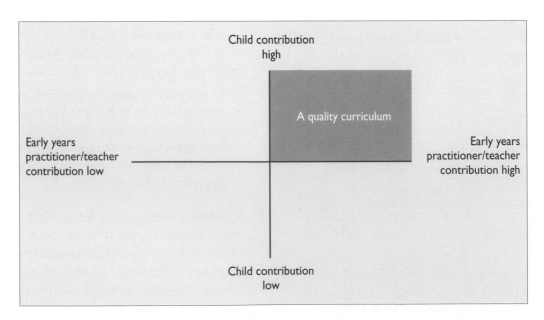

Fig 13.28 Children and adults learning together

corner) and be able to have engaging conversations, listening to what children say and being sensitive to what they do, allowing them plenty of time (e.g. cooking together or planting bulbs in the garden).

✱ Another adult must be free to help children generally, for example to deal with children's toilet needs, to hang up a painting or comfort a tearful child, or simply respond to children who ask for help.

✱ If each adult has a clear understanding of their role in the team, it helps each practitioner to focus on children and reduces the temptation to chat with other adults instead of engaging with the children.

It is always useful to move around the environment on your knees in order to see it from a child's-eye view (or crawl to gain a toddler or mobile baby's view). Lying on your back helps to understand a baby's view from a cot. In other words, what would a child see as they move about the learning environment?

SECTION 4: HOW TO RECORD AND EVALUATE THE PLANNING AND ASSESSMENT CYCLE

THE ASSESSMENT PROCESS

The purpose of assessment is to provide useful information about children's learning and development which can be shared with other staff, with parents and the child, and which will be helpful in informing future planning. Each child will develop and make progress at his or her own pace, and as we have seen, observations are vital to the planning and assessment cycle. Effective

assessment is important because it helps adults to match learning activities and experiences to the needs of the child.

Assessment should be an integral part of the daily routine in an early years setting. It occurs when adults listen, watch and interact with a child or group of children.

✱ **observational** assessment, in everyday situations, informs the planning process – this is sometimes called 'assessment for learning'.

✱ **planning** – or setting targets – for learning will draw attention to aspects for observation and assessment during play;

✱ **recording** – record keeping: will draw together the bits of information needed for effective reporting;

✱ **evaluation** of learning and teaching will influence future planning.

Reflection

Reflecting on our practice is at the heart of the assessment process. Taking time to step back and to reflect on what has been successful in children's learning and what might have been planned in a different way enables staff to make changes which promote more effective learning. Reflection should be an integral part of observation, planning, recording, reporting and evaluating, and will be most effective when staff take time to share and modify their observations with other colleagues.

Planning

Effective planning establishes clear goals for learning which are designed to match the needs and the achievements of children. Planning, whether long or short term, should leave staff feeling enabled and also well prepared in their contributions to children's learning. Sharing this information with children and parents will support the learning partnership.

Although staff in early years settings should plan a broad set of learning opportunities throughout the year, there may be times when there is particular emphasis on certain aspects of the curriculum, for example on music making and dance, or exploration of living things. Alternatively, a set of learning experiences may be grouped around seasonal or other themes, or local events, festivals or outings.

* **Long-term** planning gives a picture of how these activities are providing children with a broad and balanced range of learning experiences over a period.

* **Short-term** planning allows observations and assessments of children's development and learning to inform the weekly or daily programme. In setting out a range of learning opportunities, plans therefore need to take account of what individual children and small groups of children have recently learned and of their current needs and interests.

Planning should also be **flexible** so that it can take account of children's ideas and responses to learning experiences and allow learning to develop. When there has been a need to alter a plan, future plans should be reviewed and adjusted to ensure that a broad and balanced range of learning continues to be provided or that goals for learning are revised. In this way the learning opportunities provided should be influenced by and responsive to children's interests within an overall long-term plan.

Staff Interaction

It is from observation and assessment of children at play that we learn how and what they learn. Of course, it is not possible to observe everything where large numbers of children are involved in a range of play. This means that observation and assessment should be focused and selective. It should have purpose.

Observation and assessment must influence the learning situation, to be of true value. For example:

* staff may recognise where additional support or challenge is required for individuals or groups of children. In this case observation and assessment should lead to prompt action as a result of the observation;

* to use the evaluation of observations to inform planning, for example, to practise a skill or offer a new learning experience;

* to direct staff support for the following day or week.

Observation is also useful in helping staff to evaluate the effectiveness of their provision and of their interactions during learning.

Recording

Day-to-day records of observations and assessments help staff to plan learning experiences which take account of children's needs and development. Records should also provide a profile of each child's progress in different aspects of their development and learning. Profiles will provide the information necessary to report to parents, colleagues and other professionals.

Record-keeping should be kept manageable; if it is too detailed it takes valuable time away from interacting with children. It should concentrate on what is significant in children's learning rather than attempt to record everything that happens. Staff in some settings use notebooks, diaries or post-its to record observations which are then used in making plans to develop children's learning.

This recognises a link between planning and recording. Planning helps to focus what is recorded and the observations made during learning influence future planning, setting out the next steps in learning.

Such records can be used to build up a full picture of each child's progress in learning. Alternatively, from time to time during the year, staff may complete parts of a record as a way of taking stock of children's progress.

The record should:

* cover each of the key aspects of children's development and learning;

* include brief comments on significant strengths and development needs observed during a child's learning.

They can also include photographs and examples of children's work.

Reporting

Reporting is a means of:

* promoting partnership with parents;

* sharing information with children, colleagues and other professionals, and

* shaping the next steps in learning.

Records begin when a child is preparing to start the early years setting. Parents and children complete statements such as 'I can . . .' and 'I enjoy . . .', with pictures or photographs and statements. This helps to involve children in recognising their capabilities and also values the learning which they have already achieved.

Reporting to parents informally: There are many opportunities for informal reporting to parents during day-to-day contacts; sending home examples of children's work will continue this process. Children can be involved in self-assessment, for example by discussing photographs or examples of work which might be included in profiles.

Information from parents about learning at home can also be included. Records (see above) may provide evidence for making oral and written reports to parents.

This information will also be shared with primary schools and other professionals.

Evaluating

Reflecting on observations and assessment is an important part of staff development. It involves:

* thinking about what has worked well in providing learning experiences and in interacting with children;

* thinking about improvements that could have been made to help learning take place more effectively, for example by asking a question in a different way, providing a different resource, or challenging children more during an interaction.

Evaluating aspects of children's learning over time will help in judging whether the learning experiences and interactions are helping them to make good progress. Discussing all of this with other staff will help in promoting children's learning effectively.

Guidelines for evaluating plans

* A medium-term plan can be used to check the balance of the long-term plan. Is science being developed so that it reaches every child? Not all children will learn exactly the same science, but they should all have appropriate opportunities.

* How does science link with the official documents? What science are children supposed to have

learned about at this stage in their education?

* Are the medium-term planning resources working well for this group of children in their learning? Most experts agree that if there are good plans for individual children, the whole group tends to benefit.

* Are the adults using observation of children to inform their planning?

* Are the adults giving support to individual children's learning as well as to the group?

* Are adults able to extend the learning to add knowledge that children did not previously have (e.g. Andrew might be interested in water pumps)? (See page 468.)

* Are children learning about areas other than science? Is there a good balance in this curriculum?

EVALUATING THE PLANNING AND ASSESSMENT CYCLE

As you discuss your work with colleagues, you will be able to make realistic, honest and forward-looking self-evaluations, which will empower you in your professional development.

Margaret Carr, a Professor of Early Childhood Studies in New Zealand, has developed 'Teaching Stories' to help practitioners assess and evaluate their work with children and families. You can use these to help you evaluate your practice through thinking about how it feels to be a child in your setting.

A child's questions:

BELONGING: DO YOU KNOW ME?

How do you appreciate and understand my interests and abilities and those of my family?

WELLBEING: CAN I TRUST YOU?

How do you meet my daily needs with care and consideration?

EXPLORATION: DO YOU LET ME FLY?

How do you engage my mind, offer challenges and extend my world?

COMMUNICATION: DO YOU HEAR ME?

How do you invite me to listen and communicate, and respond to my own particular efforts?

CONTRIBUTION: IS THIS THE PLACE FOR US?

How do you encourage and facilitate my endeavours to be part of the group?

(Margaret Carr, 'Teaching Stories')

CHAPTER 14

Caring for Children

This chapter covers **Unit 8** and is divided into three sections:

Section 1: The range of settings which provide care for children

Section 2: The diverse care needs of children

Section 3: How to work effectively in multi-professional teams to support the care of children

SECTION 1: THE RANGE OF SETTINGS WHICH PROVIDE CARE FOR CHILDREN

• Children, family and the outside world • Diverse caring groups • Statutory, private, voluntary and independent settings • Links between regulations and settings

The Children Act 1989 states that: 'Children are best looked after within the family, with support if necessary.' Parents want the best for their children and have hopes and aspirations for them. They want them to feel safe and loved, have people around them who are constant and show they care about them, and they want them to achieve and enjoy life. The same principles apply when children are 'looked after' by social services. Because of these children's experiences, they may have a lot of needs and hopes that are more difficult for professionals to help them with.

Attachment is important: a key objective for the Department for Education and Skills (DfES) is to ensure that children are securely attached to carers capable of providing safe and effective care for the duration of childhood.

Local authorities work together with families who need help and support to promote the welfare and safety of their children. To do this they work closely with other services such as health, education, housing, police and probation, as well as with voluntary organisations.

CHILDREN'S SOCIAL SERVICES

Children's social services seek to promote the wellbeing of children in need and looked-after children. They work in partnership with key agencies, service users and the community, to pursue continuous improvements in quality, efficiency and cost through best value. The duties of social services are prescribed in statute. Until recently, children's social services have usually been provided jointly with services for adults, via social services departments within local authorities. However, structural changes in response to the **Children Act 2004** mean that **education** and **social care** services for children are now brought together under a **director of children's services** in each local authority.

Social workers with responsibilities for children and families may work in the following areas:

Safeguarding and Promoting the Welfare of Children

✱ **Lead responsibility**: the social worker has lead responsibility, on behalf of social services, for undertaking an assessment of the child's needs and the parents' capacity to respond appropriately to the child's identified needs within their wider family and environment. In the great majority of cases, children are safeguarded while remaining at home by social services working with their parents, family members and other significant adults in the child's life to make the child safe, and to promote his or her development within the family setting.

✱ **Child protection**: for a small minority of children, where it is agreed at a child protection conference that a child is at continuing risk of '*significant harm*', the child's name will be placed on a **child protection register**. Social services are then responsible for coordinating an inter-agency plan to safeguard the child, which sets out and draws upon the contribution of family members, professionals and other agencies.

* **Care order**: in a few cases, social services, in consultation with other agencies and professionals, may judge that a child's welfare cannot be adequately safeguarded if he or she remains at home. In these circumstances, they may apply to the court for a **care order**, which commits the child to the care of the local authority.

* **Protection**: Where the child is thought to be in immediate danger, social services may apply to the court for an emergency protection order, which enables the child to be placed under the protection of the local authority for a maximum of 8 days.

Supporting Disabled Children

As part of its wider role to promote the welfare of children in need, children's social services have specific duties in respect of disabled children and their families. They have to provide a range of services to families with disabled children to minimise the impact of any disabilities and enable them to live as normal a life as possible. Typically, they provide **short-term breaks** in foster families or residential units, **support services** in the home and, increasingly, assistance for disabled children to participate in out of school and leisure activities in the community alongside their non-disabled peers. (See also Unit 14 on CD-ROM.)

Supporting Looked-after Children

Where the local authority looks after a child following the imposition of a care order, or accommodates a child with the agreement of their parents, it is the role of the social worker to ensure that adequate arrangements are made for the child's care and that a plan is made, in partnership with the child, their parents and other agencies, so that the child's future is secure.

Foster care: children are generally looked after in foster care. A minority will be cared for in children's homes and some by prospective adoptive parents. Irrespective of the setting in which children are accommodated, all looked-after children will have a social worker and carers (e.g. foster carers, residential care staff) responsible for their day-to-day care, who should be involved in making plans or decisions about the young person.

Looked-after Children

Children who are in the care of local authorities are described as 'looked-after children'. They are one of the most vulnerable groups in society. The majority of children who remain in care are there because they have suffered some sort of abuse or neglect.

There are two main reasons for children being in local authority care:

1 **Care order**: children who are subject to a care order made by the courts under s 31 of the Children Act 1989 (about 65 per cent of all looked-after children); for the courts to grant a care order they have to be satisfied that a child is suffering or would suffer 'significant harm' without one.

2 **Voluntary agreement**: children who are accommodated by the local authority on a voluntary basis under s 20 of the Children Act 1989 (about a third of all looked-after children).

At any one time, around 60,000 children are looked after in England, although some 90,000 pass through the care system in any year. 42 per cent of looked-after children return home within 6 months. The system aims to support rehabilitation back into families where that is possible.

Early Intervention

What happens *before* children become looked after has a major influence on what happens during their period in care. Most children become looked after because of adverse experiences in their families. A key aim of *Every Child Matters* is to enable local authority children's services to act earlier and more decisively when children are experiencing unacceptable and damaging family situations.

The government has two sets of targets:

1   improving the stability of placements for looked-after children, and

2   improving their educational achievement.

They are delivered by working closely with local authorities to ensure that their policies and practices support placement stability.

Special Guardianship

Special guardianship is a new legal option intended to provide permanence for children for whom adoption is not appropriate. A special guardianship order (SGO) gives the special guardian parental responsibility for the child. Unlike adoption, under an SGO the parents remain the child's parents and retain parental responsibility, though their ability to exercise their parental responsibility is extremely limited. The intention is that the special guardian will have clear responsibility for all the day-to-day decisions about caring for the child or young person and for taking any other decisions about their upbringing, for example their education. A special guardian may exercise parental responsibility to the exclusion of others with parental responsibility, such as the birth parents, and without needing to consult them in all but a few circumstances.

A special guardianship order will:

* give the carer clear responsibility for all aspects of caring for the child or young person, and for taking decisions to do with their upbringing;

* provide a firm foundation on which to build a lifelong permanent relationship between the carer and the child or young person;

* preserve the basic legal link between the child or young person and their birth family;

* be accompanied by proper access to a full range of support services, including, where appropriate, financial support.

A special guardianship order is flexible and can work in a variety of situations:

* for older children who do not wish to be legally separated from their birth family, but could benefit from greater legal security and permanence;

* for children in long-term foster care or those who are cared for on a permanent basis by members of their wider family;

* for children and carers who have cultural and religious difficulties with adoption as set out in law.

CHILD CARE SETTINGS

Statutory Child Care Settings

Sure Start Children's Centres

Sure Start children's centres are a focal point within each community for parents and carers of children up to age 5 years. They pull together everything families need – from midwives, health visitors and early years provision (integrated day care and early learning) to parenting support, skills training and help to find employment. They perform outreach work to those in the community who are most isolated. They also offer a base for childminder networks and links to other daycare provision, out-of-school clubs and extended schools. (For more information, see Chapter 1.)

Residential Children's Homes

Children's homes exist to ensure that the needs of children are met when they cannot live with their own family. They offer a safe place for children to develop and grow, as well as providing food, shelter, and space for play and leisure in a caring environment. Generally, when children and young people need to live away from their families, they will stay with foster carers. It is only when foster care is either not possible or not desirable that residential care is chosen.

Children and young people have to live away from their own families for all sorts of reasons. These include:

* their parents are unwell;
* they have problems with their family and need to spend some time away from home (e.g. behaviour problems or educational difficulties);

* they may have a disability and need a break from living with their families;
* they are in the care of local authority, subject to a court order or voluntary agreement.

All children and young people who come to live in a children's home must have a care plan which states:

* why a child is living in a home;
* what is supposed to happen while they are living there; and
* what is supposed to happen at the end of their stay.

Most children *will* go home, but a few go to live with other families and a few go to live in other homes. Older children who are not planning to return home are given help to prepare them for living on their own; this is called the 16+ Careleavers Service (formerly Aftercare).

Children go to their own school if they have a school place, or social workers help to get them back into school.

Some young people still attend resources in the community (e.g. school, college, etc.).

It is considered very important that children and young people stay in touch with their family and friends. It is only when they might be hurt, or a court order says that contact is not allowed, that some children will not be able to have visits from their family or will not be able to visit them.

Foster Care

Foster care is arranged through local social services departments or through independent fostering agencies. There are different types of foster care, depending on the needs of both the child and their family. These include short-term care for just a few days or weeks, long-term placements, as well as care for disabled children or children with behavioural problems.

The main categories of foster care are:

* **Emergency**: when children need somewhere safe to stay for a few nights.

* **Short-term**: when carers look after children for a few weeks or months, while plans are made for the child's future.

* **Short breaks**: when disabled children, children with special needs or children with behavioural difficulties regularly stay for a short time with a family, so that their parents or usual foster carers can have a break.

* **Remand**: when young people are remanded by a court to the care of a specially trained foster carer.

* **Long-term**: not all children who need to permanently live away from their birth family want to be adopted, so instead they go into long-term foster care until they are adults.

* **'Family and friends' or 'kinship'**: a child who is the responsibility of the local authority goes to live with someone they already know, which usually means family members such as grandparents, aunts and uncles or their brother or sister.

* **Specialist therapeutic**: for children and young people with very complex needs and/or challenging behaviour.

Anyone can apply to be a foster carer, so long as they have the qualities needed to look after children who cannot live with their parents. There is no maximum age limit for being a foster carer.

Adoption

Adoption is a way of providing a new family for children who cannot be brought up by their own parents. It is a legal procedure in which all the parental responsibility is transferred to the adopters. Once an adoption order has been granted it can't be reversed except in extremely rare circumstances. An adopted child loses all legal ties with their first mother and father (the 'birth parents') and becomes a full member of the new family, usually taking the family's name.

The majority of adoption agencies are part of the local authority social services (in England and Wales) or social work (in Scotland) department. Some are voluntary societies – for example, Barnardo's.

Adoption differs from fostering in that foster carers *share the responsibility* for the child with a local authority and the child's parents. Also, fostering is usually a temporary arrangement, though sometimes foster care may be the plan until the child grows up.

* Up to 4,000 children in the UK are currently waiting for permanent new families. These children are from a great variety of ethnic and religious backgrounds.

* Many of the children waiting for new families are of school age, and over half of them are in groups of brothers and sisters who need to be placed together.

* There are disabled children and children whose future development is uncertain; some children will have been abused and/or neglected and all will have experienced moves and uncertainty; their resulting behaviour may be challenging.

In order to adopt a child, individuals must be:

* over 21;
* happy to make space in their life and home for a child;
* patient, flexible and energetic, and
* determined to make a real difference to a child's life, for a lifetime.

It usually takes at least 6 months for social workers from an adoption agency to get to know prospective adopters, assess them and help prepare them for the task ahead.

Confidential enquiries will be made of the local social services or social work department and the police.

Applicants will be examined by their GP and will be asked to provide personal references from at least two friends.

The agency's independent adoption panel will consider a report on the application and recommend whether or not applicants should be approved as adopters. In Scotland, prospective adopters must be given the opportunity to meet the panel.

Adoption UK was established in 1971 and is the only national self-help group run by and for adoptive parents and foster carers, offering support before, during and after adoption. It provides independent support, information and advice on good practice to all concerned with adoption. In particular, it offers a wealth of relevant experience from generations of adoptive families to prospective and established adopters and to all those who work with them.

Private, Independent and Voluntary Child Care Settings

Some private and voluntary settings provide child care in children's centres, neighbourhood nurseries and extended schools. These programmes are founded on partnerships between local authorities, schools and providers. Others provide care within their own privately managed settings: nurseries, crèches, day nurseries and playgroups.

Childminding

Childminders are often the child care of choice for working parents. Childminders can:

* provide consistent one-to-one care, tailored to the individual needs of a child;
* form a stable ongoing relationship with the child, continuing from infancy through to when they need care around schooling;
* provide care for siblings together;
* be very flexible over the hours of care provided and deliver or pick up children to and from other forms of care;
* provide care in a home that can include involvement in activities such as cooking, shopping, gardening and family mealtimes.

A registered childminder works in their own home and is registered and inspected by Ofsted, demonstrating the quality and standards of their care. Ofsted ensures that every registered childminder meets the national standards, such as:

* ensuring that they are suitable to be with children;
* checking that they provide a safe, stimulating and caring environment, giving children opportunities for learning and play;
* making sure they work in partnership with parents and carers.

In addition, in order to become registered, a childminder must undertake police and health checks, have a regular inspection of their home and take an introductory childminding course and first aid training. Registered childminders can only look after a certain number of children at any one time, which allows them to focus more on each child. Many childminders are part of a childminding network.

(For more information on private and voluntary care provision, see Chapter 1.)

LINKS BETWEEN REGULATIONS AND SETTINGS

The main pieces of legislation underpinning social services for children and young people are the Children Act 1989, the Children (Leaving Care) Act 2000 and the Adoption and Children Act 2002.

Children Act 1989

Local authorities have specific legal duties in respect of children under the Children Act 1989, including:

* to safeguard and promote the welfare of children in their area who are in need;

* provided that this is consistent with the child's safety and welfare, to promote the upbringing of such children by their families, by providing services appropriate to the child's needs;

* to make enquiries if they have reasonable cause to suspect that a child in their area is suffering, or likely to suffer significant harm, to enable them to decide whether they should take any action to safeguard or promote the child's welfare.

Children (Leaving Care) Act 2000

This places responsibilities on local authorities to provide greater support to young people living in and leaving care. These include:

* a duty to assess and meet the needs of young people aged 16 and 17 who qualify for the new arrangements;

* the provision of a personal adviser and pathway plan for all young people aged 16–21 (or beyond, for those who qualify for the new arrangements);

* a duty to assist those leaving care, including with employment, education and training (the duty to assist with education and training and to provide a personal adviser and pathway plan continues for as long as a young person remains in an agreed programme, even beyond the age of 21).

Adoption and Children Act 2002

This act aligns adoption law with the Children Act 1989 to make the child's welfare the paramount consideration in all decisions to do with adoption. It includes:

* provisions to encourage more people to adopt looked-after children, by helping to ensure that the support they need is available;

* a new, clear duty on local authorities to provide an adoption support service and a new right for people affected by adoption to request and receive an assessment of their needs for adoption support services;

* provisions to enable unmarried couples to apply to adopt jointly, thereby widening the pool of potential adoptive parents;

* stronger safeguards for adoption by improving the legal controls on inter-country adoption, arranging adoptions and advertising children for adoption;

* a new special guardianship order (see above) to provide security and permanence for children who cannot return to their birth families, but for whom adoption is not the most suitable option;

* a duty on local authorities to arrange advocacy services for looked-after children and young people leaving care, in the context of complaints.

The Children Act 2004 requires all local areas to produce a single, strategic, comprehensive plan for all services affecting children and young people in their area. A Children and Young People's Plan has the five wellbeing outcomes set out in the Children Act at its heart. These are to:

1 Be Healthy;

2 Stay Safe;

3 Enjoy and Achieve;

4 Make a Positive Contribution;

5 Achieve Economic Wellbeing.

Local authorities work together with families who need help and support to promote the welfare and safety of their children. To do this they work closely with other services such as health, education, housing, police and probation, as well as with voluntary organisations.

Services are planned and provided to support:

* children and families 'in need' – this is a broad definition and can include a wide section of the population;

* children who may need looking after (coming into care) by the local authority;

* children at risk of suffering 'significant harm';

* children who have suffered abuse and who need protection;

* children seeking asylum without their parents;

* disabled children and their families;

* young people.

CARE PLANS

As part of each local authority's duty to provide care, they must produce care plans for all looked-after children.

The Children Act 1989 defines the purpose of the care plan in care proceedings:

1 It influences the decision of whether to make a care order or not.

2 It should set the framework for the case management following the care order being made, specifying the goals to be achieved and the desired outcomes for the child.

3 These purposes are also applicable to the care plans for children accommodated under s 20 of the Children Act. For these children the plan should:

* determine why it is in the child's best interests to become looked after or whether other support services would be able to meet their needs;

* identify the child's assessed needs and the services which will be provided to meet those needs;

* set the framework for the services provided to the child and family to enable the desired goals and outcomes to be achieved for the child.

The government's 10-year strategy for child care: *Choice for parents: the best start for children* was launched in 2004 and sets out a vision for a child care system that meets parents' requirements for choice, availability, quality and affordability. The strategy sets out a clear role for childminders and childminding:

* for more robust childminder networks, based on children's centres and extended schools;

* for childminders and home-based child-carers to be able to access professional support and continuous professional development through children's centres and other child care providers;

* to put in place training opportunities for childminders and other home-based carers, with the aim of enabling more to achieve level 3 qualifications, work in partnership with other providers, and develop long-term careers as part of the children's workforce;

* for local authorities (LAs) to monitor the supply of childminders in local neighbourhoods, taking action to increase provision where necessary.

THE CYCLE OF DISADVANTAGE

'Children in care are written off by the education system, with nearly eight out of 10 gaining no qualifications', children's charity Barnardo's says. In 2006, Barnardo's *Failed by the System* report assessed the experiences of the 80,000 children looked after by councils. The report claimed that multiple care home and foster care placements, repeated school changes, exclusion and insufficient support all contributed to a cycle of disadvantage.

Findings of the report into children in care included the facts that of children in care:

* more than half reported being bullied at school as a direct result of being in care;

* four out of 10 said no one had attended their school parents' evenings;

* nearly half said no one went to sports days or other school events;

* the number of care placements young people had lived in varied between one and 30 – half had been in more than four placements;

* more than half were not currently in employment, training or education;

* almost half the group had attended six or more schools and 11 per cent had attended more than 10.

THE INTEGRATED CHILDREN'S SYSTEM (ICS)

The ICS has been developed to improve outcomes for children defined as being in need, under the Children Act 1989. It provides a conceptual framework, a method of practice and a business process to support practitioners and managers in undertaking the key tasks of assessment, planning, intervention and review.

It is based on an understanding of children's developmental needs in the context of parental capacity and wider family and environmental factors.

THE PARENTS' INFORMATION SERVICE (PIS)

This is a free, confidential, independent national telephone helpline. The service provides information and professional advice to any adult concerned about the mental health or emotional wellbeing of a child or young person up to the age of 25.

THE HOME CHILDCARERS SCHEME

The scheme was set up in 2003 to help widen the availability of tax credit support by ensuring that parents can access approved forms of child care to use within their own homes. A home child carer:

* is a person who looks after children within the parents' home;

* is a professional child carer, offering children safe, good-quality care and providing them with play and learning opportunities that contribute to their development;

* has to meet criteria set out in a code of practice that is monitored by Ofsted. At present, only registered childminders can apply to be approved by Ofsted as home child carers. Since the government has announced an extension to this scheme, the Sure Start Unit in the Department for Education and Skills are preparing a consultation on who should carry out the work and how the approval and registration process should operate in future.

SECTION 2: THE DIVERSE CARE NEEDS OF CHILDREN

• Review care needs in view of child development • Activities for daily living • Promoting and supporting children's independence and self-care

REVIEWING CARE NEEDS IN VIEW OF CHILD DEVELOPMENT

As children grow and develop, different care needs come into focus; this is particularly true when a child differs from the developmental norm. Maslow's hierarchy of needs is a useful tool for considering these needs in a developmental framework:

Maslow's theory of human needs has relevance to child development and care. For

Fig 14.1 Maslow's hierarchy of needs

example, at the basic level of physiological needs, a child who is cold or hungry will be unable to respond to planned activities. Mia Kellmer Pringle (1920–1983) has suggested that there are four significant developmental needs which have to be met from birth. These are: the need for love and security; the need for new experiences; the need for praise and recognition; and the need for responsibility.

The Need for Love and Security

This is probably the most important need as it provides the basis for all later relationships. The young child instinctively wants to move away and become more independent, but separating from the parent figure may be difficult. Each child deals with this challenge in his or her own way.

✳ **Security**: in their first year, their need for security may be met by having a comfort blanket or a favourite toy – Winnicott called this a **transitional object**. (See Chapter 6.)

✳ **Routine**: another aspect of the child's need for love and security is the need for routine and predictability. This is why having daily routines is so important in child care. By meeting children's need for routine, carers are helping the child to feel acknowledged and independent and this increases their self esteem.

✳ **Attachment**: Pringle, like Bowlby, recognised the child's need to have a steady, durable and caring relationship with empathetic adults. A continuous, reliable, loving relationship, first within the family unit, then with a growing number of others, can meet this need. It can give the child a sense of

self-worth and identity. In child care settings, the key person system helps to meet this need.

The Need for New Experiences

New experiences are a fundamental requirement for cognitive development. Children learn from their experiences. In early life it is largely through play and language that the child explores the world and learns to cope with it. As children pass through each stage of development they often return and work on a previous level in a new way. For experiences to be meaningful, they must extend what children have already learned; they should present children with social, intellectual and physical challenges.

In adolescence, another form of play is important – the young person experiments with different kinds of role, for example, girlfriend, boyfriend, worker or leader. Language remains a crucial factor in intellectual growth – it helps in learning to reason, to think and in making relationships.

The Need for Praise and Recognition

Growing up requires an enormous amount of learning – emotional, social and intellectual. Consequently strong incentives are necessary for children to continue through the difficulties and conflicts that they will inevitably encounter. The most effective incentives are praise and recognition sustained over time.

✳ **Self-fulfilling prophecy**: children feel like failures when they cannot live up to the unrealistic hopes of their parents and are less likely to repeat their efforts. The lower the expectation of the carer, the lower the level of effort and achievement of the child – sometimes called the self-fulfilling prophecy.

* **Intrinsic motivation**: if you make children feel anxious when they have not succeeded they will avoid activities likely to lead to failure. It is important to praise children appropriately when they try hard or have achieved something new, however small it might seem. This will motivate children to greater effort and lead to the desire to achieve something for its own sake; this is called intrinsic motivation.

The Need for Responsibility

Being responsible involves knowing what is to be done and how to do it. Children have different levels of understanding at different ages. Your role is to structure the environment to provide challenging tasks according to their different interests and ability levels. The need for responsibility is met by allowing children to gain personal independence, first through learning to look after themselves in matters of everyday care; then through a gradual extension of responsibility over other areas until they have the freedom and ability to decide on their

ACTIVITY: ASSESSING NEEDS

CASE STUDY

Jack, a 3-year-old boy

Jack is an only child who lives with his young mother, Samantha, in a small flat in an inner-city area. Jack's mother is at her wit's end with the daily effort of coping with Jack's behaviour. Every weekday, Samantha drops Jack off at his childminder's house at 8.15 am and goes to a department store where she works as a catering assistant. She picks him up again at 5.45 pm and rushes home to prepare the evening meal. Jack always watches television while she cooks and then they eat their meal together. As soon as he has finished, Jack starts demanding attention. First he wants a story,

then he wants to play a space adventure game that his grandma gave him; and then he starts throwing his toys around. Samantha usually reacts to his demands by shutting him in his room and telling him that he can only come out again when he has learned how to behave. At other times she threatens to cancel the Sunday outings with his father. Weekends are usually taken up with household chores. Jack's father takes him to the park or to his grandparents' house on Sundays. Jack loves these visits, but Samantha finds that he demands even more of her attention when he comes home.

Look at the four needs described on page 486. For each need, list the possible consequences of failure to meet that need – in terms of the effects on the child.

Identify any needs which are not being met for Jack's healthy development. Try to think of ways in which all the needs could be met, both for Jack and for his mother, Samantha.

own actions. Cooperation rather than competition allows children more freedom to accept and exercise responsibility. You can help by building group work into your planning activities.

WHAT ARE ACTIVITIES FOR DAILY LIVING (ADL)?

There are various interpretations of Activities for Daily Living, which were originally designed as a tool for assessing patients' needs in order to provide the best possible care. One useful model for Activities for Daily Living was drawn up by Nancy Roper in the 1970s. Drawing on studies in psychology and sociology, she identified 12 activities of living which make up a person's daily life, regardless of a person's age, sex or whether or not that person is healthy. (Dying is seen as the final activity of living.) Each activity can be related to two ranges or continua: lifespan and dependence/independence.

Lifespan

* Infancy: from birth throughout the first year of life.
* Childhood: from 1 to about 10/11 years.
* Adolescence: teenage years.
* Adulthood: young adulthood, middle years, late.
* Old age: more and more people are living well into their eighties, nineties and beyond.

Dependence/Independence

The dependence/independence continuum ranges between two extreme poles: total dependence to total independence. In the early stages of life, there is full dependence, which develops into independence with age into adulthood and then, to at least some degree, lessening independence with old age.

There are also some people for whom total independence is unachievable and maintenance of a safe environment must be an *assisted* ADL. Others can lose their independence throughout life, in either a temporary or a permanent situation following accidents or illness. Each ADL is performed at a level of dependence which relies on two factors:

* **Stage of life or lifespan**: for example, a newborn baby cannot perform all ADLs independently.
* **Loss of previous independence**: for example, through accident or illness.

The 12 Activities of Daily Living

1 Maintaining a safe environment.
2 Communicating.
3 Breathing.
4 Eating and drinking.
5 Eliminating.
6 Personal cleansing and dressing.
7 Controlling body temperature.
8 Mobilising.
9 Working and playing.
10 Expressing sexuality.
11 Sleeping.
12 Dying.

Maintaining a Safe Environment
Lifespan Factors

Maintaining a safe environment during childhood and adolescence includes assessing for the following hazards:

* choking and suffocation (especially in young children and babies);
* accidents: falls, burns, scalds, poisoning;
* infection;

Factors influencing Activities of Daily Living

Biological	Promoting and maintaining health; preventing disease; and physical disease.
Psychological	Cognitive or intellectual development; emotional development and coping mechanisms.
Sociocultural	Social; cultural; spiritual; religious and ethical components.
Environmental	Pollutants; light rays and sound waves; clothing; cross-infection; buildings relevant to the individual's life (e.g. personal home, nursing homes, clinics, health centres and hospitals).
Politico-economic	Health and economic status; health and political activity; health in industrialised and developing countries; politico-economic influences affecting an individual's health.

* excessive heat or cold;

* road accidents;

* sporting injuries.

Dependence/Independence Factors

* Children with sensory impairments – particularly blindness and deafness – may need the environment adapted to allow them independence.

* Those with learning difficulties may not be able to learn about maintaining a safe environment and it is often a carer's duty to provide assistance in this ADL.

Communicating

The ADL of communicating is an integral part of human behaviour. Four skills are classified for effective communication: speaking, listening, reading and writing. Communication can be classed as **verbal** (such as a conversation) or **non-verbal** (gestures, body language, facial expressions, etc.).

Lifespan Factors

* A baby can communicate, to a certain extent, his needs and emotions: for example, crying to be fed or for a drink; laughing or sleeping when content.

* Children can get frustrated at their lack of vocabulary when trying to express themselves.

* During adolescence, a unique vocabulary is often built up within peer groups, which has no meaning to adults or others outside these groups.

Dependence/Independence Factors

* Communication and communication techniques are learnt throughout life.

* Often, a child's parent can understand her child's vocabulary when to anyone else the words make no sense at all.

* Some people communicate with sign language, and this can be difficult when dealing with practitioners who do not have this ability.

* Verbal communication can be affected by hearing; visual communication, including reading, needs at least some sight, and writing skills require an adequately functioning hand (although some people have adapted to use their mouths or feet when necessary).

* Learning ability affects communication skills.

* Within our multicultural society, different dialects and accents can all add strain to communication.

* Non-verbal communication, or body language, can also be affected by cultural differences; for example, different types of clothes, the acceptance of touch and gesticulations.

* Physical conditions can affect communication; for example, not enough lighting can inhibit some normal non-verbal signals; extremes of temperature can reduce concentration; and surrounding noise can interrupt the flow of a conversation.

Breathing

Lifespan Factors

From the moment of birth and our very first breath, our lives are dependent on breathing. Our lifespan ends when breathing does, whether it is unaided or assisted.

Dependence/Independence Factors

* Breathing is the only ADL where independence, in normal circumstances, is there from the time of birth through to the time of death.

* There are, however, certain dependencies regarding breathing (e.g. some people are 'dependent' on smoking; others are 'dependent' on avoiding exposure to high pollen counts (if they have asthma)).

* Exercise will normally raise even a healthy person's respiration rate.

* Shock can induce respiratory and/or cardiac failure.

* The effects of anxiety can be helped by deep breathing and other breathing exercises.

* Pollution is a global issue, and legislation exists in most countries on smoking, work regulations and safety guidelines, especially regarding hazardous substances.

Eating and Drinking

This ADL varies depending on where in the lifespan a person is.

Lifespan Factors

* Babies cannot choose, so their choice is made by their mothers, either to breast-feed or to bottle-feed.

* Children can be fussy eaters but even the fussiest can be fed the necessary nutrients and vitamins without even knowing it.

* Adolescents tend to be quite active and have big appetites to feed their growing bodies, while adults balance out, taking more control over the amount they eat and drink.

* By old age, the appetite has declined again, partly due to diminished physical activity.

Dependence/Independence Factors

* This is determined by the stage a person is in the lifespan and the level of any physical and mental disabilities, either from birth or acquired through accident or illness.

* For a healthy diet, we should consume satisfactory levels of protein, carbohydrates, fats and fibre.

* A certain level of intelligence is required to eat a well-balanced diet and to prepare and cook food to a healthy level.

* There is also an emotional aspect to eating, with disorders such as obesity, bulimia and anorexia on the increase.

* There is a religious element to eating and drinking. For example, devout Catholics will eat only fish on Fridays, orthodox Jews eat kosher food and Muslims are forbidden to touch pork.

* Even in the UK, some people are too poor to eat a healthy diet.

Eliminating

As with most of the other ADLs, eliminating – passing urine and faeces – varies with where a person is on the lifespan.

Lifespan Factors

* Newborn babies have no control over their elimination processes.

* Young children may have the occasional 'accident'; this normally no longer occurs in adolescence and throughout adulthood.

* Control sometimes deteriorates again with old age.

Dependence/Independence Factors

* Dependence in this ADL changes throughout the lifespan, with the two very much interlinked. As well as this, at any stage through the life process a person's dependence can change, especially following surgery, illness or accident.

* Though perfectly natural, there is a lot of taboo surrounding elimination. Some people cannot use public toilets, for example, or will flush first, to drown out the noise they might make.

* The risk of disease is higher for those who do not have a sanitary water and sewage system. Diseases such as cholera, typhoid, paratyphoid and dysentery are still a cause of high mortality in many areas of the world.

Personal Cleansing and Dressing

Lifespan Factors

* Babies usually have all their hygiene needs tended to by a parent or other adult. Bath water should be at body temperature; nappies should be changed when necessary and the area cleaned to prevent soreness of the skin. Tooth-brushing is introduced as early as possible.

* During childhood, skills in self-care and feelings of modesty begin to develop and children can attend to most of their hygiene needs, usually under supervision. They will also start choosing what they want to wear, although they can often be persuaded to wear more appropriate clothing.

* At adolescence, puberty causes changes in the skin and sweat glands – and consequently the need for hygiene. It is also a time when experimentation occurs with clothes, hair and make-up.

* In adulthood, bathing takes on different aspects, for example a cold shower to wake up or a warm bath to relax.

* In old age, physical problems may make personal hygiene harder to maintain. As well as this, problems associated with incontinence make the need for hygiene all the more important.

Dependence/Independence Factors

As with most of the ADLs, dependence is closely linked with the lifespan in personal cleansing and dressing. In old age especially, a decline in physical health and abilities makes impossible things which younger adults take for granted, for example washing feet or cutting toenails. Not all societies place the same emphasis on hygiene and cleanliness. Recent research in the UK found that exceptionally clean children had a higher incidence of eczema and asthma than their not-so-clean counterparts. This suggests that coming into contact with common dirt and grime is actually good for you.

Controlling Body Temperature

Lifespan Factors

* Babies, especially newborns, lose heat very quickly, especially through the head, and this can quickly become a life-threatening situation. Over the first few months of life, a baby's temperature can fluctuate wildly, with very little stimuli.

* In adulthood, a woman's temperature increases slightly at the time of ovulation, during a period and during pregnancy. The menopause can cause hot flushes.

* In older age, the control of body temperature is less effective and older people can quickly succumb to the ill effects of colder weather.

Dependence/Independence Factors

* Relevant throughout the lifespan, dependence can also come during times of infection or fever when antipyretic drugs are needed to reduce a high body temperature.

* Extremes of environmental temperature or changes in environmental temperature can all affect the regulation of body temperature.

* The availability of hot and cold water and central heating in homes all play a part in this ADL.

* Money is needed for heating, warm clothes, food and bedding, all necessary for maintaining body temperature. Those most at risk of hypothermia in the UK are children and the elderly. (The government now gives each elderly person a winter fuel allowance to help them pay their winter fuel bills.)

Mobilising

Lifespan Factors

* Even before birth, movement is an important aspect of human development.

* Progress after birth goes from moving arms and legs to crawling, standing, walking, jumping and running. As the body systems develop with age, mobility skills improve.

* In adolescence, activity increases and continues normally throughout adulthood.

* Pregnant women may find that their mobility becomes somewhat restricted due to extra weight and postural compensation.

* With old age, movements again become restricted, with weaker bones and joints, less energy and less height.

Dependence/Independence Factors

* Dependence is closely related to lifespan, although, for some people, total independence is not achievable.

* Aids for living may help some people, such as walking sticks, wheelchairs etc.

* Many forms of employment, despite modern technology, are still extremely *manual* and hold a risk to a person's mobilisation. Even in nursing and other caring occupations, back problems are still common.

Working and Playing

Lifespan Factors

* Playing is a universal activity for children, absent in only the most deprived conditions.

* In adulthood, the choice of occupation is an essential task.

* The link between work and play remains strong, indicated by some occupations, such as that of sportsmen and women, where 'play' becomes 'work'.

* With retirement there is more opportunity for play again.

Dependence/Independence Factors

* Children tend to be dependent on adults for the development of play and the provision of playthings.

* In adulthood, independent control comes as financial independence from working and is maintained throughout adulthood and into old age and retirement.

* In some poorer countries, children never have the luxury of play, being sent to work at a very early age.

Expressing Sexuality

Lifespan Factors

* In infancy and childhood, cuddling, rocking and stroking are pleasurable experiences and children quickly discover how to recreate them by touching themselves, although there is no sense of sexuality at this stage. They also mimic the concept of sexuality in everyday play, for example dressing up and playing 'mummies and daddies'.

* At the onset of puberty in adolescence, the menarche occurs for girls usually at the age of around 12. Puberty is an emotional as well as physical time for both boys and girls. The UK has one of the highest incidences of teenage pregnancy in the world – in spite of sex education programmes in schools.

* In adulthood, expressing sexuality in explicit ways, especially in long-term relationships, is the norm, although attitudes have changed with the emergence of AIDS and HIV.

* In old age, there is a tendency to dismiss this ADL even though people enjoy sex and sensuality well into later life.

Dependence/Independence Factors

* A child's dependence is on education and guidance, and this follows throughout life.

* Disabled people can be slower to learn, but their basic rights are the same as everyone's, as are their needs and their right not to be abused.

* Sexual abuse *does* happen; many adults who suffer sexual problems, though by no means all, have suffered some form of sexual abuse as a child. Rape is much better recognised now and as such, a continuing improvement in the medical and police investigations and after-care. Male rape is much less often reported and consequently less understood.

* Society is also affected by the threat of AIDS and HIV.

Sleeping

Lifespan Factors

* Children require more sleep than adults and they also have more stages of sleep when growth hormones are secreted.

* By 15 years old, most people have a sleep duration of 7–8 hours, although during the adolescent growth spurt more sleep is needed by the body.

* By old age, sleep tends to occur for shorter periods and sleep tends to be more easily disturbed. The use of sleeping tablets is much higher among this age group.

Dependence/Independence factors

* The actual activity of sleep is performed by individuals independently, directly linked with the lifespan.

* A child is dependent on others for safe sleeping conditions.

* Adults may be dependent on others for good sleep, for example needing quiet when working on shifts in antisocial hours.

* Anxiety is the most common cause of disturbance of sleep

Dying

Lifespan Factors

* The lifespan starts with birth and ends with death. It does not rely on age to determine its length.

* Death can occur at any time, before the birth, just after the birth, during childhood, adulthood or old age.

Dependence/Independence Factors

* Death is inevitable for everyone and, apart from suicide, there is little independence, although some people are said to have 'hung on' for a particular event or 'given up' for some reason.

* In old age it is accepted that the systems of the body will gradually slow down and eventually die.

* In terminal illness it is almost impossible to diagnose or predict a person's exact time of death, even when that death is clearly inevitable.

* Death is treated differently throughout the world and society. Each culture has its own beliefs. In modern society, death and grief have become almost taboo and people tend to grieve quickly and quietly, as if trying to 'get it over with'.

HOW TO PROMOTE AND SUPPORT CHILDREN'S INDEPENDENCE AND SELF-CARE

At each developmental stage, children and young people will have different skills and abilities. Although children do not make significant progress in self-care until the toddler years, there are signs of growing independence much earlier.

1 At about **8 months**, babies begin to understand how objects relate to one another and may begin using them for their intended function (e.g. brushing their hair, 'chatting' on the play phone, etc).

2 At around **10–11 months**, babies start learning how to drink out of a cup, and will also begin to hold out their arms or legs to help when getting dressed.

3 By around **12–15 months**, babies are able to hold a cup in both hands and drink from it, and will recognise themselves in the mirror.

4 By **18 months** most children go through a period of saying 'no'; it's their way of asserting their new feelings of self–identity.

5 Between **1 and 4 years**, children can:

   * **use a fork and spoon**: they may start wanting to use utensils as early as 13 months; most children have mastered this skill by 17 or 18 months;

   * **take off their own clothes**: children usually learn to do it between 13 and 20 months;

   * **brush their teeth**: they may start wanting to help with this task as

early as 16 months, but probably won't be able to do it on their own until sometime between the third and fourth birthday;

* **wash and dry their hands**: this skill develops between 19 and 30 months and is something children should learn before or at the same time as using the toilet;

* **get dressed**: they may be able to put on loose clothing as early as 20 months, but will need a few more months before they can manage a T-shirt and another year or 2 months after that before they are able to get dressed all by themselves. By 27 months, they will probably be able to pull off their shoes;

* **use the toilet**: most children are not physically ready to start toilet training until they are at least 18–24 months old, and some won't be ready to begin for as much as a year after that. Two key signs of readiness include being able to pull their own pants up and down and knowing when they have to go before it happens;

* **prepare their own breakfast**: children as young as 3 years may be able to get themselves a bowl of cereal when they are hungry, and most can do it by the time they are 4½ years.

5 **Children aged 4–8**: children aged 4 and 5 can eat skilfully with a knife and fork and can undress and dress themselves, except for laces, ties and back buttons. By 6–7 years old, children are completely independent in washing, dressing and toileting skills.

6 **Children aged 8–12**: children are competent at most self-caring tasks,

although they may need reminding about washing regularly. The level of independence shown, for example when crossing roads alone, will depend on the individual child's past experiences and level of maturity.

7 **Young people aged 12–16**: young people tend to identify more with friends and begin to separate from their parents. They are less dependent on family for emotional support and are becoming skilled at making decisions. Again, the level of independence will vary according to the young person's level of maturity and temperament. It will also depend on how much responsibility the young person has been given by his or her parents.

Your Role in Promoting Independence and Self-care in Children and Young People

* **Encouragement** is the most important factor in helping children towards independence.

* **Praise**: whenever children attempt a new skill, *whether they succeed or not*, praise them and urge them to try again.

* **Don't interfere**: try not to step in too quickly to help; it is essential that they have enough time to manage these things on their own, at their own pace. Never pressure children to try something before they are ready.

* **Be flexible**: put up with the experimentation, even if it means a lot of mess and you could obviously do it a lot quicker yourself. The more they practise, the better they will be.

* **Set limits**: keep a watchful eye on children as they begin to experiment with doing things on their own. Set

limits and explain them: tell them why it is dangerous to turn on the oven or use the bread knife yet.

* **Promoting independence at meal times**: as soon as the child can pick up tiny objects with finger and opposing thumb (at around 6–9 months) encourage self-feeding with tiny sandwiches, little bits of banana, cooked carrot or grated apple. NB Always supervise, because of the dangers of choking.

* Let babies **hold their cup** even though you control it: gradually pass the control over to them.

* Encourage **fine motor skills** by giving the child a fat crayon and a piece of card to scribble on.

* **Promoting independence when dressing**: zips, buttons and hooks are difficult for small children: choose clothing with elastic waistbands, velcro, or ones which slip on with zips and buttons partly closed. Lay out clothing so that children can lift it the right way round: trousers front up, jumpers and dresses front down; this is so that they can sit down and put them on. Help them to put their shoes on, but let them fasten them themselves whenever possible. (Children sit with their knees turned out and naturally put shoes on with the fastenings on the inside where they can see them; that's why they are always on the wrong feet.)

* Promoting independence in **older children and young people**: as with all children, praise them for their efforts as well as their abilities. Encourage them to communicate – to voice their own opinions. Listen to their ideas and show respect for them.

SECTION 3: HOW TO WORK EFFECTIVELY IN MULTI-PROFESSIONAL TEAMS TO SUPPORT THE CARE OF CHILDREN

• Professionalism • Valuing and respecting colleagues (other professionals) • Procedures and working methods • Communication in a multi-professional team • Confidentiality in a multi-professional team • Understanding roles and respect of other professionals

PROFESSIONALISM

What is a Profession?

The terms 'profession' and 'professional' are used in a variety of ways. Professions are usually described as having:

* a philosophy of public service and altruism;

* skills based on theoretical knowledge derived from research, for example the medical and legal professions;

* members who are tested for their competence before being allowed to practise;

* members who receive an extensive period of education and training;

* an explicit code of conduct for practice;

* a system of self-regulation.

The job title of 'nursery worker' or 'early years practitioner' often invokes an image of a well-meaning amateur who has learned many of the skills on the job. For years, the work has been undervalued, underpaid and of low status. The government's recent *Ten year strategy for childcare: Choice for parents* hopes to change public perceptions of the child care profession. The strategy draws on two models:

1   the social pedagogue model;

2   the specialist teacher model.

1   The **social pedagogue** model draws on Danish experience, where a holistic approach is taken to care and education by the social pedagogues. The title 'social pedagogues' means that the professional embraces a concept of upbringing involving social and emotional development. Across Denmark, social pedagogues are the main workers in nurseries and other child care settings and their training typically involves a 3- or 4-year degree, with courses covering behavioural sciences, working with conflict, promoting teamwork and subjects aimed at building self-esteem.

2   The **specialist teacher** model means that the professional is trained to work with children up to 4 years, in nurseries and other care settings. (Babies and toddlers in day care and nurseries in New Zealand and Spain are overseen by teachers who specialise in the development of the very young.)

The strategy, which concentrates on the early years, is aimed at strengthening the children's workforce and making it easier for people of different professions to move within it.

(For more information on professionalism and professional practice, see Chapter 11.)

VALUING AND RESPECTING COLLEAGUES

We all have different views about how we conduct our lives. It is inevitable that each practitioner will encounter colleagues with different backgrounds, beliefs and outlooks on life. Regardless of your own view, you should always respect the views of others. This involves:

*   not passing judgement on the way other people live;

*   avoiding stereotyping people on the basis of age, sex or ethnicity (or colour) (see Chapter 9);

*   not trying to impose your views on others.

Only if people feel that their individual values and beliefs are respected will they develop the confidence to express themselves freely and to make choices.

PROCEDURES AND WORKING METHODS

Practitioners need to be able to work independently, as well as in a team. Positive feedback about their role and contribution to the setting is important in order to develop an effective team approach and for each individual to be seen as a valued member of the school or nursery team. Clear communication and expectations, particularly about behaviour management, are necessary in order to provide a consistent approach. Open communication within a climate of trust will facilitate the building of an effective relationship between teachers and early years practitioners. In working with other multidisciplinary professionals, it is important to define your role and responsibilities, together with those of others within the team and other agencies.

COMMUNICATION IN A MULTIPROFESSIONAL TEAM

In working with other professionals, practitioners must:

*   understand what information other organisations can offer and share with

individuals, families, carers, groups and communities;

* work effectively with others to improve services offered to individuals, families, carers, groups and communities.

Practitioners working in child care and education settings liaise with members of different teams. These include professionals from:

* **health**: health visitors, speech therapists, physiotherapists, school nurses etc.

* **education**: teachers, specialist teachers, educational psychologists, educational welfare officers, governors etc.

* **social services**: social workers, youth workers, outreach workers, probation officers, etc.

Children's trusts comprise multiprofessional teams of social workers, early years workers, learning mentors, education welfare officers, and nurses.

The **Sure Start** projects for children under 5 years and their parents are organised on a multiprofessional basis, with social workers, health visitors, outreach workers, and early years workers sharing their perceptions and skills.

Supportive and effective relationships need to be developed with all these professionals and with parents too. The need for each practitioner to have effective communication and teamwork skills is therefore important. (See Chapter 1 for information on developing effective communication skills.)

CONFIDENTIALITY IN A MULTIPROFESSIONAL TEAM

Confidentiality is an important principle in child care and education because it serves to impose a boundary on the amount of personal information and data which can be disclosed without consent. Confidentiality arises where a person disclosing personal information reasonably expects his or her privacy to be protected, such as in a relationship of trust. It is useful to understand the meaning of the following terms:

* **consent**: agreement to an action based on knowledge of what the action involves and its likely consequences;

* **disclosure**: the giving-out of information which might commonly be kept secret, usually voluntarily or to be in compliance with legal regulations or workplace rules;

* **privacy**: the right of an individual or group to stop information about themselves from becoming known to people other than those they choose to give the information to.

The client's right to confidentiality is not absolute. Also, the client's secret may often be shared with other professional persons within the agency and also in other agencies; the obligation then binds all equally.

Breach of confidentiality has been likened to theft of property, but it is more serious. The invasion of privacy resulting from a failure in confidentiality often leads to a greater and more fundamental loss than does theft. Confidentiality relates directly to the principle of respect for other people. A client wants to be reassured about confidentiality.

How far this information should be communicated outside the agency is often problematic. The client should be assured of the following rights:

* Other agencies and individuals should only be consulted with the client's consent (this may be overridden in extreme cases such as that of a child at risk).

* Records should only show information that is essential to provide the service, and

in many instances should be available to the scrutiny of the client. (For example, for some time now, patients have had the right to see their medical records.)

Your Role and Confidentiality

Anyone working with young children, whether in a nursery setting, a school or in the family home, will need to practise confidentiality. Confidentiality is respect for the privacy of any information about a child and his or her family. Children and their parents and carers need to feel confident that:

* you will not interfere in their private lives and that any information you are privileged to hold will not become a source of gossip. Breaches of confidentiality can occur when you are travelling on public transport, for example, and discussing the events of your day; always remember that using the names of children in your care can cause a serious breach of confidentiality if overheard by a friend or relative of the family;

* you will ensure that any child or family's personal information is restricted to those who have a real *need to know*, for example when a child's family or health circumstances are affecting their development;

* you will not write anything down about a child that you would feel concerned about showing their parents or carers;

* you understand when the safety or health needs of the child override the need for confidentiality; parents need to be reassured that you will always put the safety and wellbeing of each child before any other considerations.

A Sample Confidentiality Policy for a Nursery
The nursery's work with children and families will sometimes bring us into

contact with confidential information. To ensure that those using and working in the nursery can do so with confidence, we will respect confidentiality in the following ways:

* Parents will only have access to any records of their own children and will not be given any information about any other children.

* Information given by parents/carers to the nursery leader will not be passed on to other adults without permission.

* Details requested on the registration form, including address and telephone number, are also deemed confidential and will only be used for nursery management purposes.

* The nursery is registered under the Data Protection Act and will not pass any information on to other organisations.

* Any discussions with parents about their children will take place privately and, if appropriate, may be arranged outside of nursery hours at a time suitable to parents.

* Staff will not discuss individual children, other than for purposes of curriculum planning/group management, with people other than the parents/carers of that child. All staff and voluntary helpers will be made aware of our confidentiality policy and required to respect it.

* Any issues relating to nursery children and their families or members of staff should not be discussed outside the nursery setting.

* The undertakings above may be overridden if information is requested as evidence in cases of suspected child abuse.

Glossary

Adult-led activities: the adult decides what the child should do

Ageism: discriminatory behaviour relating to someone's age

Allergy: a hypersensitivity to certain antigens called allergens

Ambience: the general atmosphere of a place

Amenorrhoea: the absence of menstrual periods

Anaemia: a condition in which the concentration of the oxygen-carrying pigment, haemoglobin, in the blood is below normal

Analyse: to examine closely, or consider, information looking at all the various components (parts)

Anencephaly: a condition in which most of the brain and skull are absent. Stillbirth or death shortly after delivery is inevitable

Anorexia nervosa: a recognised eating disorder, characterised by severe weight loss, wilful avoidance of food, and intense fear of being fat

Anterior fontanelle: a diamond-shaped soft area at the front of the head, just above the brow. It is covered by a tough membrane; you can often see the baby's pulse beating there under the skin. The fontanelle closes between 12 and 18 months of age

Articulation: the ability to speak clearly

Attention deficit disorder: a disorder of childhood characterised by marked failure of attention, impulsiveness and increased motor activity

Bias: prejudice or pre-conceived notion.

Bibliography: detailed list of written source material – usually now to include other media such as videos, TV programmes and website information

Bilingual: speaking two languages

Biological path of development: brain, physical and genetic aspects of development

Blood pressure: the pressure exerted by the flow of blood through the main arteries

Blood transfusion: the infusion of large volumes of blood or blood components directly into the bloodstream

Book language: the formal language that is found in books – 'And they lived happily ever after'

Brochure: a book giving information about the aims and philosophy in action of the early childhood work setting

Care orders: these are issued when intervention is necessary if there is a situation where 'significant harm' to the child could result

Central nervous system: the brain and spinal cord – the control centres of the body

Children in need: children whose health or development is likely to be significantly impaired without the provision of services, and children with disabilities

Children's Centres: there will be an Integrated Children's Centre (ICC) in every community, beginning with those in the areas of highest poverty and disadvantage. They will play an important role in integrated working, community building and supporting parents to have aspirations and confidence

Chromosome: a threadlike structure in the cell nucleus that carries genetic information in the form of genes

Chromosome analysis: the study of the chromosomal material in an adult's, child's or unborn baby's cells to discover whether a chromosomal abnormality is present, or to establish its nature

Cochlear implant: a device for treating severe deafness that consists of one or more electrodes surgically implanted inside or outside the cochlea in the inner ear

Code of practice for equal opportunities: document stating how the equal opportunities policy is to be put into practice

Communication: facial expressions, body language, gestures and verbal or sign languages – language involves reception (understanding) and expression. Talking about feelings, ideas and relationships through signs or words

Comprehensible input: using actions and gestures to make what is said understandable

Concept: being able to link past, present and future ideas which share some properties or attributes. A child may sit on a variety of chairs, but a concept of a chair is an idea the child has in the mind

Conservation: linking past, present and future ideas (concepts) but being able to hold in mind several aspects of an idea at the same time (decentrating)

Content: what the child knows and understands, wants to know more about and needs to know according to the culture and society in which the child grows up

Context: this is made up of people and provision. It creates both the access to learning and the ethos in which the child learns

Contextual sensitivities: the child is not seen in isolation from the people, culture and experiences which influence development and learning

Creativity: making something of the idea you imagined, for example a dance, model, poem, mathematical equation – i.e. making something through an act of creativity

Cultural artefacts: the objects which are familiar to the child because they relate to the child's culture

Cultural identity: feeling part of a culture

Cultural path of development: social, cultural, intellectual, linguistics, representational and play aspects of development

Curriculum: this is a balance between the knowledge and understanding of the child's development, contextual sensitivities and what the child learns and understands

Development: the general sequence in the way that the child functions in terms of movement, language, thinking, feelings, etc. Development continues from birth to death and can be linked to a web or network

Developmentally appropriate curriculum: this is a curriculum appropriate for most children at the particular age and stage of development for which the curriculum is designed. The term was developed in the USA by the National Association for the Education of Young Children (NAEYC)

Diabetes mellitus: a disorder caused by insufficient production of the hormone insulin by the pancreas

Differentiated curriculum: this helps individual children to learn in ways which are suitable for their stage of development, personality, linguistic needs, cultural background, interests and needs

Diphtheria: an acute bacterial illness that causes a sore throat and fever; it was responsible for many childhood deaths until mass immunisation against the bacillus was introduced

Dyslexia: a specific reading disability characterised by difficulty in coping with written symbols

Empowerment: helping people to believe in themselves, so that they feel able to attempt something they might not previously have thought they could do

Encopresis: incontinence of faeces (soiling) not due to any physical defect or illness

Enuresis: the medical term for bed-wetting

EPPE: the Effective Provision of Pre-School Education (EPPE) Project and the Effective Pre-School and Primary Education 3-11 (EPPE 3-11) Project. The longitudinal EPPE study (1996–2008) has studied 2,500 children to find the impact of pre-school provision and followed them through until year 5 so far. The findings are that the children who attended settings of high quality, which employed trained early years teachers, continue to show higher reading and mathematics scores when 10 years old, compared with the children who attended low quality settings or stayed at home. The level of qualifications of the parents (especially the mother) was significant for the children who stayed at home (see Chapter 13 and Unit 16)

Equal opportunities policy: a statement of non-discriminatory aims and values

Ethnic group: a traditional way to describe a group of people who share the same culture, language, physical features or religion

Ethos: the characteristic spirit of a group of people or community, e.g. a happy ethos or a caring ethos.

Evaluation: an appraisal or assessment based on available information which is analysed

EYFS: Early Years Foundation Stage (see Appendix)

Family: a group of people living together or apart who have strong emotional relationships and who are significant to each other through blood or other links

Fatherese: when men (often fathers) talk to babies in a high-pitched tone about what is happening

Gastro-enteritis: inflammation of the stomach and intestines, often causing sudden and violent upsets – diarrhoea, cramps, nausea and vomiting are common symptoms

Gender role: the way that boys learn to be male and girls learn to be female in the culture they grow up in. The gender role might be narrow or broad according to the culture.

Genetic counselling: guidance given (usually by a doctor with experience in genetics) to individuals who are considering having a child but who are concerned because there is a blood relative with an inherited disorder

Goodness of fit: the match between a child's temperament and a parent's way of bringing up the child. This influences the child's social development

Graphic representation: making marks on paper which relate to prior or future experiences

Haemophilia: an inherited bleeding disorder caused by a deficiency of a particular blood protein

Hepatitis B: inflammation of the liver, caused by a virus. A mother can unknowingly pass the infection to the child she carries in her womb

Heritage, myths and legends: stories, poems, dances, songs which have been handed down across time; many contain a shred of original truth which has since been embroidered out of recognition

Holistic: seeing a child in the round as a whole person, emotionally, intellectually, socially, physically, morally, healthily, culturally and spiritually

Home Learning Environments: these are created by registered childminders in their homes, and are inspected by Ofsted. These are different from Nannies who work with children in their own homes

Homophobia: fear of gay or lesbian homosexual people

Human immuno-deficiency virus (HIV): A virus which causes AIDS

Hydrocephalus: an excessive accumulation of cerebrospinal fluid under increased pressure within the skull. Commonly known as 'water on the brain', hydrocephalus occurs in more than 80% of babies born with spina bifida

Hyperactivity: abnormally increased activity

Hypoglycaemia: an abnormally low level of glucose (sugar) in the blood

Hypothesis: making a prediction that if you do one thing, something else will happen as a result

Illiteracy: when someone cannot write or read

Imagination: having a new idea which has emerged from your first-hand experiences of life

Immunisation: the process of inducing immunity as a preventative measure against certain infectious diseases

Intellectual/cognitive: these words both refer to the ideas and thinking of the child. Cognition emphasises that children are aware, active learners, and that understanding is an important part of intellectual life. Intelligence is about the ability to profit from experience

IQ: a measurement of some aspects of intelligence, through an intelligence quotient which gives a score. An IQ of 100 is the average

Jaundice: yellowing of the skin and the whites of the eyes caused by an accumulation of the pigment bilirubin in the blood

KEEP: Key Elements of Effective Practice illustrates the key elements of early-years' expertise required to implement the Principles for Early-Years' Education. It provides a way of evaluating and then strengthening the impact of initial training and practice with children, parents and other professionals within and beyond settings. KEEP relates to the common core of skills and knowledge for the children's and young people's workforce. Effective practitioners are committed, enthusiastic and reflective and have breadth and depth in their knowledge, understanding and skills. Effective practitioners use their own learning to develop and improve their practice with young children and their families in ways which are sensitive, positive and non-judgemental; they engage actively in their initial training and on-going training; and they continuously improve. In effective practice, the following aspects are continuously developing and improving: relationships with children and adults; understanding the diverse ways that children develop and learn; knowledge and understanding so that the practitioner can actively support and extend a child's learning in the areas of development and learning in ways which connect them to each other; work with other professionals within the setting and beyond it.

Laissez-faire: leaving learning to nature. The idea is that if the environment and relationships are good, the child will learn naturally (nature)

Learning skills in context: children learn to master things and become competent when they are doing something that really needs doing, rather than an exercise that is removed from meaningful situations

Lines of reporting: procedures for ensuring child protection

Listeria: a bacterial infection resulting from eating chilled foods, particularly soft cheeses, meat pâté. It causes a 'flu-like' illness, can also cause miscarriages, and is sometimes fatal in babies and elderly people

Literacy: when spoken language is put into code, it is written. When written codes are decoded, they are read

Longitudinal: over a length of time

Material provisions: play dough, paint, paper, pencils, home area, etc

Meninges: the covering of the brain and spinal cord. In meningitis, they become inflamed because of infection by bacteria or a virus

Micturition: a term for passing urine

Motherese: when adults (often mothers) talk to babies in a high-pitched tone about what is happening

Multicultural: drawing on the rich variety of cultural influences

Multilingual: speaking many languages

Muscular dystrophy: an inherited muscle disorder of unknown cause in which there is slow but progressive degeneration of muscle fibres

Neonate: a newly born infant (under the age of one month)

The network for learning: this involves children in first-hand experiences, games, representation and play

Neuroscience: studies of the brain which are providing evidence which helps early childhood specialists to work with young children.

Nutrient: essential dietary factors, such as carbohydrates, proteins, certain fats, vitamins and minerals

Objectivity: impartiality, detachment

Open-ended materials: there are many possible ways to use the material, for example clay, wooden blocks

Operations: linking past, present and future ideas (concepts) but concentrating on one aspect of an idea at a time (centrating)

Ophthalmologist: a doctor who specialises in care of the eyes

Optimum period: the best time for the child to learn something

Optometry: the practice of assessing vision and deciding whether glasses are needed to correct any visual defect

Parental responsibility: parents should have responsibility to bring up their own children but may need support in order to do so

Perception: making sense, understanding and getting feedback through the senses and movements of your own body

Peripatetic: travelling about

Personality: the experiences children have of life and of other people influence this, as well as the child's own natural temperament. It thus involves both nature and nurture

Placenta: the organ that develops in the uterus during pregnancy and links the blood supplies of mother and baby; often referred to as the 'afterbirth'

Plaque: a rough, sticky coating on the teeth that consists of saliva, bacteria and food debris

Play-tutoring: the adult teaches the child what is involved in play

Possetting: the regurgitation (or bringing back) of small amounts of milk by infants after they have been fed

Posterior fontanelle: a small triangular-shaped soft area near the crown of the head; it is much smaller and less noticeable than the anterior fontanelle

Pre-eclampsia: a serious condition in which hypertension, oedema and protein in the urine develop in the latter part of the pregnancy

Prescription drugs: medicines that are only available on the authorization of a doctor because they may be dangerous, habit-forming, or used to treat a disease that needs to be monitored

Pre-structured materials: where there are only a few narrow ways to use the material 'correctly', for example stacking toys

Principle of paramountcy: the welfare of the child is paramount

Private sector: profit-making services – e.g. a private nursery

Prognosis: a medical assessment of the probable course and outcome of a disease

Provision: the way in which time, space and materials are structured in the curriculum

Racism: discriminatory behaviour relating to someone's race

Rationale: reasoned explanation/statement of reasons

Representation: ways of keeping hold of first-hand experiences – drawing or models, dances, music, etc.

Schemas: patterns of linked actions and behaviours which the child can generalise and use in a whole variety of different situations, for example up and down, in and out, round and round

Self-esteem: the way you feel about yourself – good or bad – leads to high or low self-esteem

Self-identification or self-labelling: choosing how you would like to be described

Self-identity: a sense of who you are; liking yourself, respecting yourself and developing the skills and care to look after yourself

Self-image/self-concept: how you see yourself and how you think others see you

Sensation: being aware that you are having an experience through seeing, smelling, hearing, touching, tasting, moving (kinaesthetic)

Sensori-motor: using the senses and your own movement/actions

Sexual orientation: whether someone is heterosexual, bisexual, transsexual or homosexual

Social constructivist: using nature and nurture to help the child learn through people and provision offered

Social referencing: babies and young children look at adults to see how they react, as a guide to how they should react to a situation themselves

Special educational needs: it has been estimated that, nationally, twenty per cent of children will have special educational needs at some point during their time at school. These range from a temporary need to a more permanent need. Special educational needs is covered in more detail in Unit 14

Spina bifida: this occurs when the spinal canal in the vertebral columns is not closed (although it may be covered with skin). Individuals with spina bifida can have a wide range of physical disabilities. In the more severe forms the spinal cord bulges out of the back, the legs and bladder may be paralysed, and obstruction to the fluid surrounding the brain causes hydrocephalus

Statutory service: any service provided and managed by the state or government – e.g. the NHS or a local authority day nursery

Stereotype: a limited image of someone and what they can do or be

Structured/guided play: the adult decides what the play is to be about and helps the child to carry this out, for example stacking toys, building a tower of wooden blocks, acting out a scene such as going shopping

Sudden Infant Death Syndrome (SIDS): often termed 'cot death', Sudden Infant Death Syndrome is the sudden and unexpected death of a baby for no obvious reason

Summarise: review or recap the main points

Symbolic behaviour: making something stand for something else

Temperament: this is the style of behaviour which comes naturally to you, for example relaxed

Tetanus (lockjaw): a bacterial infection in which the muscles of the jaw and neck go into spasm. Rarely seen in the UK now because of the effective immunisation campaign

Theory: a prediction about how something will be. This can then be tested out

Tokenist: a stereotyped symbol which is like a short-hand code for a culture. It gives a superficial and often inaccurate introduction to a culture, people with disabilities or of different genders

Transitional bilingualism: using the first language in order to learn English (or the main language)

Transmission: shaping the child's behaviour so that the child has the knowledge the adult wants to transmit (or send) to him or her (nurture)

Tuberculosis (TB): an infectious disease, caused by the tubercle bacillus, which commonly affects the lungs. It used to be a major killer in childhood and early adult life

Uterus: another name for the womb

Vaccination: a type of immunisation in which killed or weakened micro-organisms are introduced into the body, usually by injection

Visualisation technique: thinking positive images about how you would like things to be

Voluntary organisation: an association or society which has been created by its members rather than being created by the state, for example a charity

Appendix

THE EARLY YEARS FOUNDATION STAGE

The Early Years Foundation Stage (EYFS) will achieve the five 'Every Child Matters' outcomes, which are:

* Staying safe;
* Being healthy;
* Enjoying and achieving;
* Making a positive contribution;
* Achieving economic well-being.

The EYFS sets standards for the development, learning and care of young children at birth to five years when they attend a home learning environment (HLE) or group setting. It provides for equality of opportunity and anti-discriminatory practice. It creates a framework in which parents and professionals can work in partnership. It improves the quality and consistency of provision across all settings and supports development and learning around the individual child's interests and needs, informed by ongoing observational assessment. The Principles guide the EYFS through four **themes**:

* A Unique Child;
* Positive Relationships;
* Enabling Environments;
* Learning and Development.

Each theme is broken down into four **commitments** which describe how the principles are put into practice. There is a set of cards, **Principles into Practice**, which explains how the principles are put into practice in day-to-day work with children. There is a poster summarising this and a CD-ROM. A DVD has been developed by Manchester Metropolitan University on Birth to Three.

It will only Need a Tweak if the Practice is Already Good

It is important to bear in mind that with the introduction in England of the *Early Years Foundation Stage* (*DfES*) from 2008, the new framework will have statutory force. The *Early Years Foundation Stage* (EYFS) (launched March 2007) is a single framework for care, learning and development for children in all kinds of early childhood settings from birth until the August following their fifth birthday. This includes home learning environments (HLE) such as those provided by childminders and nannies as well as integrated care, development and learning in the maintained and private, voluntary and independent sectors.

Theme	Principle	Commitments
A Unique Child	Every child is a competent learner from birth who can be resilient, capable, confident and self-assured	1. Child development 2. Inclusion 3. Safety 4. Health and well-being
Positive Relationships	Children learn to be strong and independent from a base of loving and secure relationships with parents and/or a key person	1. Respect from each other 2. Partnership with parents 3. Supporting learning 4. The role of the key person
Enabling Environments	The environment plays a key role in supporting and extending children's development and learning	1. Observation, assessment and planning 2. Supporting every child 3. The learning environment 4. The wider context (transitions, continuity, multi-agency working; Every Child Matters)
Learning and Development	Children develop and learn in different ways and at different rates and all areas of learning and development are equally important and inter-connected	1. Play and exploration 2. Active learning 3. Creativity and critical thinking 4. Areas of learning and development: • Personal, social and emotional development • Communication, language and literacy • Problem-solving, reasoning and numeracy • Knowledge and understanding of the world • Creative development • Physical development

Index